WORLD WAR II

MORE WILDSIDE CLASSICS

Please see www.wildsidepress.com for a complete list!

WORLD WAR II

A Cataloging Reference Guide

by
Buckley Barry Barrett

WILDSIDE PRESS

WORLD WAR II

This edition published in 2006 by Wildside Press, LLC.
www.wildsidepress.com

CONTENTS

ACKNOWLEDGMENTS

Thanks to Nannette, Ross, and Elizabeth, for their patience and support during the six years needed to complete both the World War I and World War II phases of this project. Also, my appreciation goes to Ross and Rita Barrett for the encouragement and lodging given by them during my many visits to the Graduate Research Library at the University of California, Los Angeles, where I gathered much useful information for both titles.

INTRODUCTION

This guide seeks to improve the subject access to World War II information stored in most academic and public libraries in the United States. By describing and listing the classification or shelving schemes and controlled descriptors used by these libraries for cataloging the literature, I would hope to provide researchers with enough specific examples and overriding principles to find more materials than otherwise possible.

The scope of the work includes the Second World War as well as the preceding decades leading up to and pointing toward the conflict. Full cataloging coverage of World War I, its precedents, and related matters can be found in my volume on that conflict. Since this is mostly an historical tool, I have also included many of the countries involved and have rounded out the coverage with pertinent engineering, military, and naval concepts and facts.

Two main divisions make up the work: 1. Subject classification systems used for shelving and; 2. Controlled subject, biographical, and corporate headings used in electronic, card, or microform catalogs.

The first division contains two sections listing and describing Library of Congress and Dewey Decimal call numbers, with each section providing selected cross-references to the other system. Most academic or research libraries catalog by L.C., whereas public libraries tend toward the Dewey system. Numbers given in this guide concentrate heavily on the world war; but overall outlines of both schemes are given as well, for the sake of context and because the global war under study influenced or was influenced by matters of society, politics, economics, literature, and science in addition to history and other areas.

With a better comprehension of the major classification arrays utilized in the United States, researchers can look in a greater number of shelf locations and can find similar materials located in proximity. Certain library electronic or card catalogs may also allow for a type of remote subject browsing by call number or classification, which can prove a valuable complement to subject-term searching in the catalog.

The second primary section of the book contains Library of Congress subject headings along with proper biographical and corporate agency names. These are all placed in alphabetical order as might occur in libraries' separate subject or unified dictionary catalogs.

Most public and academic libraries in the United States look to the Library of Congress for authorized subject words and phrases; so, the search vocabulary need not change from library to library. The subject headings of this division of the book represent events, places, people, government departments, armies, navies, air forces, weapons, strategies, and other objective and subjective matters related to the war, its historical period, and the process of studying this era. Researchers may find that some of the biographical entries listed herein can be found in particular libraries as authors or topics. In a similar fashion one may find some of the government or other agency headings utilized as corporate authors or subjects.

I have given L.C. and/or Dewey call numbers or class ranges for a large sample of main and peripheral headings in order to assist with intelligent browsing of the stacks or shelf inventory records. The principal purpose here, however, is to improve catalog search results through the listing of a large volume of pertinent subject and corporate quasi-subject terms and types.

To summarize, this work attempts to provide readers with a library subject-control system for use in World War II research in both academic, public, and special libraries. With greater knowledge of both classified storage patterns and controlled indexing terminology, one can find a greater number of materials and can also pinpoint more specific items that might otherwise remain lost or buried.

I. LIBRARY OF CONGRESS CLASSIFICATION SYSTEM (LC)

The Library of Congress classification system divides knowledge and history into groups of alphanumeric symbols. Single, double, or triple letters are followed by numbers from 1 through 9999. These numbers are sometimes broken down into more specialized topics by decimilization and/or letter-number symbols. Libraries finish LC call numbers with alphanumeric combinations generally derived from author's last names and sometimes from titles.

Each class letter section or schedule devised, published, and employed by LC represents a different discipline or area of information, and LC has developed each section more or less independently from the other sections through the years from around the early 20th Century.

As a result of this somewhat autonomous growth, patterns of usage vary from schedule to schedule. For example, the 'D' class covering Old World, Eastern, and Oceanic history featues double and even triple letters for certain areas. Great Britain is represented by 'DA' and Eastern Europe by 'DJK'. On the other hand, the 'E' and 'F' schedules cover North and South America without any multiple letters. Number spans also vary from class to class and even within. For instance, the 'VK' section of Naval Science ('V') goes up to around VK1660 or so in covering navigation and merchant marine, whereas 'VM' only reaches about VM990 in classifying naval architecture.

The LC system differs from the Dewey classification in a number of ways. The most obvious, of course, is the use of letters rather than numerals as the primary means of division. As will be seen in more detail in the next segment of this book, Dewey divides knowledge up into ten basic sets of 100 numbers each. For instance, history may often be found in the 900-999 section. Subdivisions are handled by the use of tens, digits, or decimals. Thus, much of the specific World War Two material may be in the 940.53-940.5499 area, while LC places equivalent items in the D731-D838 range in using letters followed by numbers in combination in order to separate different subjects or historical periods.

Call numbers built from either system can prove involved and lengthy, although complex DDC numbers may appear longer due to their general lack of breaks or pauses. LC schedules present more specific and more required choices, whereas DDC (Dewey Decimal Classification) specifies less and allows libraries to tack on one or more standardized decimal additions if desired for a more thorough description.

The Library of Congress array does not appear as essentially logical as the Dewey method because LC has neither the consistency nor the mnemonic hierarchy of its rival. LC's variable use of one, two, or three letters to begin different topical areas (e.g. 'D', 'DA-DX', and 'DJK' versus 'E' and 'F') does not stem from any pattern, and neither does its sometimes application of alphabetic subdivisions for greater subject detail (e.g. V858 for U.S. submarines as opposed to V859.G3 for German subs.).

In practice, LC brings similar titles together in useful groups just as well as Dewey, while usually allowing for more range expansion room and shorter, less crowded numbers. In some subject sections, LC has indeed left space for the future addition of entirely new and unused number sets out to 9999. For Dewey, however, new topics more often lead to longer, more awkward call numbers or to continued employment of the same old numbers but with new and unrelated meanings in mixed company.

Because of some of the reasons stated herein, most academic and some (generally larger) public libraries in the United States have chosen the Library of Congress system to catalog their resources. In summary, LC appears preferable for larger collections as well as for special ones due to its provision of more detail with less clutter.

This section of the guide first outlines the overall LC scheme and then gives a specific listing of the divisions most pertinent to world war and military research. LC alphanumerics are accompanied by descriptions and Dewey equivalents where feasible. Be aware of continuing changes and additions made to LC and Dewey in order to keep them as dynamic methods of classification. Some of these changes are noted as possible.

Both of the class systems allow for a certain amount of choice in matching topics with numbers, and yet each method also takes a somewhat different view of the universe and its knowledge. Hence, as in comparing and contrasting two languages, we see that each offers its own variety of internal synonyms and that these do not always exactly equal particular words in the other language.

A unified alphabetic index follows the conclusion of the Dewey class listing and contains both LC and Dewey numbers. Some topics do not have exact possibilities for call-number assignment and may seem to belong in more than one area, and sometimes perfectly equated LC/Dewey translations do not appear to exist. Accordingly, researchers should use the LC/Dewey index plus LC headings sections in order to determine the most classification numbers.

4

LC CLASS NUMBERS: DESCRIPTIONS: POSSIBLE DEWEY NUMBERS

A	General works (gen. almanacs, encyclopediae, etc.)	000-099
B	Philosophy, psychology, religion	100-299
C	History (auxiliary: civilization, gen. archaeology, heraldry, gen. biography)	900-909, 920-929, 930-939+
D	History (general, Eastern Hemisphere, Oceania)	909, 930-969, 990, 996
D-DX	World history, Europe, Africa, Asia, Oceania	900-949, 990's
DA-DR	Europe and Turkey 940's, 956.1	
D25	Military history (world) 355.48, 904.7, 909	
D501-680	WORLD WAR I 940.3-940.499	
D731-838	WORLD WAR II 940.53-940.5499	
E	America & North America (gen.), United States 970, 973	
F	United States (local history), Canada, Latin America 971-972, 974-989	
G	Geography, anthropology, sports, & recreation 910-919, 301, 790's	
H	Social sciences (economics, commerce, sociology, communism) 300-319, 330-389	
J	Political science, international law 320-329, 341	
K	Law 340, 342-349	
L	Education 370-379	
M	Music 780-789	
N	Arts & architecture (visual, decorative & applied) 700-709, 720-769	
P	Languages & literatures 400-499, 800-899	
PN	Literature (gen. & gen. collections) 800-809	
PR	English literature 820-829	
PS	American literature in English 810-819	
Q	Sciences (pure), math, & computer science 500-599, 611-612	
R	Medicine, psychiatry, & nursing 610-619, 649	
S	Agriculture, forestry, hunting 630-639, 574, 581, 799	
T	Technology, photography, manufacturing, handicrafts, home, economics 600-609, 620-629, 640-650, 660-699, 770-779	
U	Military science & engineering 355-358, 623	
V	Naval science, navigation, & naval architecture 359, 623, 629	
Z	Bibliography & library science (bibliog's. sometimes classed with A-Z subject #s) 010-028+	

D	History (general, Eastern Hemisphere, Oceania)	909, 930-969, 990-996
D25	World military history 355.48, 904.7, 909	
D51-838, D901+	Europe (gen.) 940-949	
D731-838	WORLD WAR II 940.53-940.5499	
DA	Great Britain 941-942	
DB	Austria, Czechoslovakia, Hungary 943.6-943.9	
DC	France 944	
DD	Germany 943	
DG	Italy 945	
DJK	Eastern Europe (after about 1977-78) 943.7-943.9, 947, 947.8, 949.6-949.84	
DK	Russia, Finland, Poland	
DL	Scandinavia	
DP	Iberian Peninsula	
DQ	Switzerland 949.4	
DR	Balkan Peninsula, Eastern Europe (prior to about 1978-79) 949.6-949.8, 943.7-943.9, 947, 947.8, 956	

5

DS	Asia	950-959
DT	Africa	960-969
DU	Oceania, Australia, New Zealand	990-996
D1-1075+	HISTORY (gen., world wars, Eur. overall, etc.)	909, 940, 950
D25	Military history (world)	355.48, 904.7, 909
D25.A2	Dictionaries, chronologies, etc. (military history: world)	
D27	Naval history (world)	359, 904.7
D208	Modern history (1453-)	901.93, 909.8+, 940
D215	Naval history (1453-)	
D299	Modern history (1789-)	909.8+
D358	Modern history (1801-1914/20)	909.81
D359	Europe (1801-1914)	940.28
D361	Military history (1801-1914/20)	355.033003+
D362	Naval history (1801-1914/20)	
D371-379	Eastern question (1801-1914/20)	949, 320.956, 327.41-42
D410-460+	WORLD HISTORY (20th c.: overall)	
D410	Periodicals, associations, yearbooks (20th c.)	
D410.5	Current events yrbks. (20th c.: nonserial: includes pictorial titles: by time then author)	
D411	Primary sources (20th c.: collections)	
D412-412.8	Biography (20th c.: memoirs and collective)	
D412	Biography (20th c.: collective: gen.)	920.02
D412.5	Women (20th c.: collective biography)	
D412.6	Public figures (20th c.: collective biog.: men)	920.02, 909.82, 940.50922
D412.7	Rulers, kings, etc. (20th c.: collective biography)	929.7
D412.8	Queens, princesses, etc. (20th c.: collective biography)	
D413.A-Z	Biography (20th c.: individual or memoir by name)	
D414-415	World history (20th c.: collected)	
D414	World history (20th c.: several authors)	
D415	World history (20th c.: single-author collections)	
D416	Pamphlets, minor works (20th c.)	
D419	Dictionaries (20th c. history)	909.8203, 320.03, 320.904
D421-425	World history (20th c.: general titles)	
D421	World history (20th c.: gen.)	909.82
D422	Popular histories (20th c.)	
D424	Europe (20th c.)	940.288-5
D425	Popular histories (20th c.: Europe)	
D426	Pictorial and graphic histories (20th c.)	779.990194, 909.82
D427	Chronologies, outlines, syllabi, tables, etc. (20th c.)	909.82, 940.28
D429	Civilization, customs, social life (20th c.: SEE ALSO CB415, GT146)	940.5, 320.904, 327.09
D431	Military history (20th c.)	355.020904, 355.009, 355,033+
D436	Naval history (20th c.)	359.409, 904.7, 359.47
D437	Air warfare	358.41409, 358.41447
D440-460	Politics and diplomacy (20th c.)	
D440	Annual registers (20th c.: politics and diplomacy)	
D441	Primary sources (20th c.: politics and diplomacy)	
D442	Politics and diplomacy (20th c.: collected works)	
D443	Politics and diplomacy (20th c.: gen.: world pol., Triple Alliance & Entente, etc.)	940.5, 320.904, 327.09
D445	Politics and diplomacy (20th c.: gen. special: projected, possible wars, other polit. events)	

D446	Anglo-Saxon supremacy
D447	Pangermanism
D448	Panlatinism
D448.5	Panceltism
D449	Panslavism
D450	Pamphlets, minor works (20th c.: politics and diplomacy)
D451-457	Diplomacy (20th c.)
D451	Primary sources (20th c.: diplomacy)
D453	Diplomacy (20th c.: gen.) 909.82, 327.3-9, 320.9
D455	Diplomacy (20th c.: gen. special)
D457	Pamphlets, minor works (20th c.: diplomacy)
D458	Triple Alliance (1882: SEE ALSO D397, D443, D511)
D459	Triple Entente (1907: SEE ALSO D443, D511)
D460	Little Entente (1919)
D461-475	Eastern question (20th c.) 320.95, 956.03, 325.342
D463	Eastern question (20th c.: gen.)
D469.A-Z	Eastern question (20th c.: by country)
D471-72	Central Asian question (20th c.)
D471	Central Asian question (1914-)
D472.A-Z	Central Asian question (20th c.: by country)
D475	Moroccan question (20th c.: PREFER DT317)
D501-680	WORLD WAR I (1914-1918) 940.3-940.499
D503	Museums, exhibitions, etc. (WWI)
D505	Primary sources, documents (WWI)
D510	Dictionaries & encyclopedias (WWI: includes 'Times' index and chronology)
D511-520	CAUSES, AIMS, RESULTS (WWI) 940.31-2
D511	Causes, aims, results (WWI: gen.) 940.311, .314
D514	Russia (WWI: causes, aims, results: includes Panslavism)
D515	Germany (WWI: causes, aims, results)
D516	France (WWI: causes, aims, results)
D517	Great Britain (WWI: causes, aims, results)
D519	Japan (WWI: causes, aims, results)
D520.I7	Italy (WWI: causes, aims, results: includes Treaty of London, 1915)
D520.U6-7	United States (WWI: causes, aims, results)
D521	WORLD WAR I (GEN.) 940.3, 940.4
D522	Pictorials (WWI: SEE ALSO D527)
D522.23	Movies (WWI)
D522.3	Maps & atlases (WWI: PREFER G1037)
D522.42	Historiography (WWI)
D522.7	Juvenile works (WWI)
D526-526.7	Poetry, satire, etc. (WWI: PREFER PQ-PT)
D526.2	English poetry, satire, etc. (WWI: PREFER PR, PS)
D526.3	French poetry, satire, etc. (WWI)
D526.5	German poetry, satire, etc. (WWI)
D528	Battlefield guides (WWI: gen.: SEE ALSO specific battles)
D528.5	Mobilization and beginnings (WWI)
D529	Reports, Official (WWI: military)

D530-549	WESTERN FRONT (WWI)	
D530	MilLITARY OPS. (WWI: West: gen.)	940.41+, .421, .424, .4272, .431, .434
D531-538	GERMAN MILITARY OPS. (WWI: West & overall)	
D531	German military ops. (WWI: West & gen.: includes Hindenburg, Ludendorff memoirs)	940.343, .40943, .413+, 943.084-085
D538.5.A-Z	Local history (WWI: Ger.: by place)	
D544-549+	Anglo-French & Allied military ops. (WWI)	
D544	Allies & Allied military ops. (WWI: gen.)	940.412+, .414, .42-3, 944.0814
D546-547.8+	BRITISH M ILITARY OPS., British Empire, & England (WWI)	
D546	British military ops. (WWI: gen.)	354.42066, 940.48341, .412+, 941.083
D547.A-Z	British Empire & Britain (WWI: by place or name)	
D547.A1	Colonies (WWI: G.B.: gen.)	
D547.A8	Australia & Anzacs (WWI)	
D547.C2	Canada (WWI)	
D547.I5	India (WWI)	
D547.I6	Ireland (WWI)	
D547.N5	New Zealand (WWI)	
D547.8.A-Z	Local history (WWI: England: by place)	
D547.8.L7	London, Eng. (WWI)	
D548-549	French military ops. & France (WWI)	
D550-569	EASTERN FRONT (WWI)	
D550	Russian military ops. and Eastern Front (WWI: gen.)	940.4147, .40947
D551	Russo-German conflict (WWI: gen.)	
D556	Russo-Austrian conflict (WWI: gen.)	
D560-565	Balkan conflict (WWI)	
D566-569	Near East, Turkey, Italy, Greece (WWI)	
D568.2	Egypt (WWI)	
D568.3	Gallipoli & the Dardanelles (WWI)	
D568.7	Palestine (WWI)	
D569	Italy (WWI) 940.4145	
D570-570.9+	UNITED STATES MILITARY OPS. & U.S. (WWI)	940.373, 41273, .40973, 327.73
D570	United States (WWI: gen.) 940.373	
D570.A3	Legislative compendia (WWI: U.S.)	
D570.A4	Histories, Official (WWI: U.S.)	
D570.A5-Z	American military ops. & U.S. (WWI: gen. unofficial)	940.373, 41273, .40973, 327.73
D570.15	Pamphlets, minor works (WWI: U.S.)	
D570.2-.79	United States military ops. (WWI: organiz. units: land, sea, air: SEE D570.A4-Z, D545 etc. for overall participation, battles, etc.)	
D570.25-.358	Armies etc. (WWI: U.S.)	940.412+, .44973, .45
D570.25.A-Z	General staff & headquarters (WWI: U.S.)	
D570.33	Infantry (WWI: U.S.: newer bks. may use A1 or #'s as in D570.27)	
D570.348	Marines (WWI: U.S.: inland ops.)	
D570.4-.5	United States naval ops. (WWI: SEE ALSO D589.U5-8)	940.45+, .41273
D570.6	United States aerial ops. (WWI: PREFER D606 for general works)	940.44973

D570.8.A-Z	United States (WWI: special topics: SEE D639 for outside U.S.)	
D570.8.P7	Political prisoners (WWI: U.S.)	
D570.8.S5	Service flags (WWI: U.S.)	
D570.85.A-W	States of the U.S. (WWI)	974-979
D570.85.C21.A-Z	Local history (WWI: Calif.)	
D570.85.N4-5	New York (WWI)	
D570.88.A-Z	Nationalities (WWI: U.S.)	
D571	Japanese military ops. (WWI: gen.)	
D573-578	Colonies (WWI)	
D577	Pacific, Asiatic, & other colonies (WWI: Ger.: gen.)	
D578.N4	New Guinea (WWI)	
D580-595	NAVAL OPS. (WWI)	940.45
D580	Freedom of the seas & naval ops. (gen.: WWI)	
D582.A-Z	British naval ops. & Anglo-German naval conflict (WWI: by battle, ship, etc.)	
D589.U5-8	United States naval ops. (WWI: SEE ALSO D570.4-5)	
D590-595	Submarine ops. & submarine chasers (WWI)	940.451+
D591	German submarine ops. (WWI: gen.)	940.4512
D600-607	AIR FORCE OPS. (WWI)	940.44
D602	British aerial ops. (WWI)	940.44941
D603	French aerial ops. (WWI)	940.44944
D604	German aerial ops. (WWI)	940.44943
D605	Russian aerial ops. (WWI)	
D606	United States aerial ops. (WWI)	940.44973
D607.5	Gas warfare (WWI: PREFER UG447)	
D608	Tank warfare (WWI)	358.18, 940.4+
D609.A3-Z	Registers & lists (WWI: decorated, dead, wounded: by country)	
D610-621	DIPLOMACY (WWI)	940.32
D610	Diplomacy (WWI: gen.)	
D611	Neutrality, other special diplomatic history (WWI)	
D614.A-Z	Treaties (WWI: misc. separate)	
D614.A2	Treaties (WWI: misc. separate: collections)	
D614.B5	Brest-Litovsk, Ukraine (WWI: treaty: 9 Feb. 1918)	
D614.B6	Brest-Litovsk, Russia (WWI: treaty: 3 Mar. 1918)	
D617	Italy & Italian neutrality (WWI: dipl. history)	
D619	United States (WWI: neutrality & dipl. history)	940.32273, .373
D621.S3	Scandinavia (WWI: dipl. hist.)	
D621.S45	Norway (WWI: dipl. hist.)	
D621.S5	Sweden (WWI: dipl. hist.)	
D622-639	WORLD WAR I (SPECIAL TOPICS)	
D622	Catholic Church (WWI)	
D623.A2	Occupied territories (WWI: gen.: includes laws)	
D623.A3-Z	Occupied territories (WWI: by country)	
D625-626	Atrocities, war crimes, trials (WWI)	
D626.G3	Atrocities, war crimes, trials (WWI: Ger. & Central Powers)	
D627.A1	Periodicals & associations (WWI: prisons)	940.472+
D627.A2	Prisons & prisoners (WWI: gen.)	
D627.A3-Z	Prisons & prisoners (WWI: by country)	
D628-630	MEDICAL SERVICES, HOSPITALS, RED CROSS (WWI)	940.475+, .477+
D629.A-Z	Red Cross & medical services (WWI: by country)	
D629.G7	Medical services & Red Cross (WWI: G.B.)	
D629.U6	Medical services & Red Cross (WWI: U.S.: gen.)	

D631	Censorship, press, publicity (WWI: gen.: SEE ALSO D639.P6-7 for propaganda) 940.315097
D632	Press, publicity, censorship (WWI: U.S.)
D635	Economic matters (WWI: commerce, finance, mail: SEE ALSO HC56, HF3030, HJ236,HJ8011)
D636	Alien enemies (WWI)
D637	Charities, refugees, relief work (WWI: gen.) 940.477+
D638.A-Z	Refugees, relief work, charities (WWI: by country or area)
D638.U5	Relief work, refugees, etc. (WWI: U.S.)
D639.A-Z	WORLD WAR I (MISC. SPECIAL: SEE D570.8 for U.S.)
D639.A65	Animals (WWI: use of)
D639.D4	Dead (WWI: burial, cemeteries, etc.)
D639.N4	Blacks (WWI: Negroes)
D639.P6	Propaganda (WWI: gen.: SEE ALSO D631-633 for press) 940.488+
D639.P7.A-Z	Propaganda (WWI: by country)
D639.P77	Protest movements (WWI)
D639.P87	Public opinion (WWI: gen.)
D639.P88.A-Z	Public opinion (WWI: by place)
D639.R4	Religion, Christianity (WWI) 940.478
D639.S2	Science & technology (WWI)
D639.S7-8	Espionage, secret service, spies (WWI)
D639.T8	Transportation (WWI)
D639.W7	Women & women's work (WWI) 940.315042
D640	Personal accounts (WWI: SEE ALSO D570.9 for U.S. soldiers) 940.481+
D642-651	PEACE (WWI) 940.312, .3141
D642	Primary sources, documents (WWI: peace: collections)
D643	TREATIES (WWI: Allies-Central powers) 940.3141
D643.A2-A7	Treaties (WWI: Ger.: 28 June 1919)
D643.A2	Treaty of Versailles (WWI: 28 June 1919: collected texts)
D643.A5.1919+	Treaty of Versailles (WWI: texts by date)
D643.A67	Resolution of peace (WWI: U.S. Congress by date)
D643.A68	Treaties (WWI: U.S.-Ger.)
D643.A8-Z	Treaties (WWI: countries other than Ger.)
D643.A8-A9	Treaties (WWI: Austria: 10 Sept. 1919)
D643.A8	Treaty of St. Germain (WWI: texts by date)
D643.A83	Treaties (WWI: U.S.-Austria)
D643.B5	Treaties (WWI: Bulg.: 27 Nov. 1919)
D643.B6	Treaty of Neuilly-sur-Seine (WWI: texts)
D643.H7-9	Treaties (WWI: Hungary: 4 June 1920)
D643.H7	Treaty of Trianon (WWI: non-U.S. texts)
D643.H8	Treaties (WWI: U.S.-Hung.)
D643.T8	Treaties (WWI: Turkey: S`evres: 10 Aug. 1920)
D644	Peace (WWI: gen.) 940.312
D646	Pamphlets, minor works (WWI: peace)
D647.A2	Peace commissions (WWI: gen.)
D648	Indemnity & reparations (WWI: gen.) 940.31422
D649.A-Z	Reparations & indemnity (WWI: by country)
D649.G3	Reparations (WWI: Ger.)
D649.G3.A4-5	Dawes Plan (WWI)
D649.G3.A6-7	Young Plan (WWI)

D650.A-Z	Peace (WWI: other special topics)
D650.D5	Disarmament (WWI: Ger.)
D650.I6	Inter-allied Military Commission of Control in Germany (WWI)
D650.J4	Jews (WWI: peace topic)
D650.M5	Occupation, Military (WWI: Rhineland)
D650.T4	Territorial questions (post-WWI: gen.: SEE D651 for specific places) 940.31424
D651.A-Z	TERRITORIAL QUESTIONS (post-WWI: by place)
D651.A4	Africa (post-WWI territorial ?s)
D651.A41	German East Africa (post-WWI territorial ?s)
D651.A42	German Southwest Africa (post-WWI territorial ?s)
D651.A5	Albania (post-WWI territorial ?s)
D651.A95	Austria (post-WWI territorial ?s)
D651.B2	Baltic provinces (post-WWI territorial ?s)
D651.B3	Belgium (post-WWI territorial ?s)
D651.B8	Bulgaria (post-WWI territorial ?s)
D651.C4-7	China (post-WWI territorial ?s)
D651.C5	China (post-WWI relns.: U.S.)
D651.C6	China (post-WWI relns.: Japan)
D651.C78	Croatia (post-WWI territorial ?s)
D651.C8	Cuba (post-WWI territorial ?s)
D651.C9	Czechoslovakia (post-WWI territorial ?s)
D651.F5-7	France (post-WWI territorial ?s)
D651.F5	France (post-WWI territorial ?s: gen.)
D651.F6.A2-Z	France (post-WWI relns.: U.S.: inclu. defensive alliance bet. Fr., U.S., G.B.)
D651.G2	Georgia, Transcaucasia (post-WWI territorial ?s)
D651.G3	Germany (post-WWI territorial ?s)
D651.G5-7	Great Britain (post-WWI territorial ?s)
D651.G5	Great Britain (post-WWI territorial ?s: gen.)
D651.G6	Great Britain (post-WWI relns.: U.S.: inclu. defensive alliance w. Fr., U.S.)
D651.G7	Great Britain (post-WWI relns.: countries other than U.S.)
D651.G8	Greece & unredeemed Greeks (post-WWI territorial ?s)
D651.H7	Hungary (post-WWI territorial ?s)
D651.I6-8	Italy (post-WWI territorial ?s: inclu. Fiume)
D651.I7	Italy (post-WWI relns.: U.S.)
D651.J3-5	Japan (post-WWI territorial ?s)
D651.J4	Japan (post-WWI relns.: U.S.)
D651.N5	Nicaragua (post-WWI territorial ?s)
D651.P2	Pacific Islands, German (post-WWI territorial ?s)
D651.P3	Palestine (post-WWI territorial ?s)
D651.P4	Persia (post-WWI territorial ?s)
D651.P7	Poland (post-WWI territorial ?s)
D651.P75	Portugal (post-WWI territorial ?s)
D651.P89-9	Prussia, East & West (post-WWI territorial ?s)
D651.R6	Rumania (post-WWI territorial ?s)
D651.R8	Russia (post-WWI territorial ?s)
D651.S13	Saar Valley (post-WWI territorial ?s)
D651.S3	Samoa, Western (post-WWI territorial ?s)
D651.S53	Slovenia (post-WWI territorial ?s)
D651.S9	Syria (post-WWI territorial ?s)

D651.T8	Transylvania (post-WWI territorial ?s)	
D651.T85	Trieste (post-WWI territorial ?s)	
D651.T9	Turkey (post-WWI territorial ?s)	
D651.T95	Tyrol (post-WWI territorial ?s)	
D651.U6	Ukraine (post-WWI territorial ?s)	
D651.Y8-9	Yugoslavia (post-WWI territorial ?s)	
D652-659	POST-WAR ERA & RECONSTRUCTION (WWI)	940.3144, .34-39
D653	Reconstruction & post-war era (WWI: gen.)	
D659.A-Z	Reconstruction (WWI: countries outside U.S.)	
D659.F8	France (WWI: Reconstruction)	
D663-680	Monuments, memorials, celebrations (WWI)	940.46+
D675.A-Z	Monuments, memorials, celebrations (WWI: U.S.: by city)	
D680.G7	Monuments, memorials, celebrations (WWI: G.B.)	

D720-728	World history (1919-39)	
D720	Inter-war period (1919-39: gen.)	940.5-.52
D723	Inter-war period (1919-39: special)	
D725	Inter-war period (1919-39: essays, minor works)	
D726	Civilization, customs, social life (1919-39: sometimes Europe alone)	
D726.5	Fascism (1919-39: SEE ALSO JC481 and 'D' numbers for Italy, Ger.)	
		320.533, 321.94094
D727	Politics & diplomacy (1919-39)	327.0904, .4, 909.822-23, 940.51-52
D728	Axis (Ger.-Italy: 1919-39)	940.51-52

D731-838	WORLD WAR II (1939-1945)	940.53-940.5499
D731	Periodicals, serials, collections (WWII)	
D731.S73	'Stars and Stripes' (WWII: periodical)	
D732	Associations, societies (WWII)	
D733	Museums, exhibitions, etc. (WWII)	
D733.A1	Museums, exhibitions, etc. (WWII: gen.)	
D733.A2-Z	Museums, exhibitions, etc. (WWII: by country)	
D733.5	Collectibles, relics, trophies (WWII)	
D734	CONFERENCES (WWII)	
D734.A1.A-Z	Conferences (WWII: gen. & multi.)	
D734.A2-Z999	Conferences (WWII: single)	
D734.A7-8	Atlantic Charter (Newfoundland: 14 Aug. 1941)	
D734.B4	Conferences (1941: Berlin: Potsdam, Ger.)	
D734.C2	Conferences (1943: Cairo, Eg.)	
D734.C25	Conferences (1943: Casablanca, Mor.)	
D734.C7	Conferences (1945: Crimea: Yalta, Rus.)	
D734.T4	Conferences (1943: Tehran, Iran)	
D735	Primary sources, documents (WWII: sometimes by gov. agency, A-Z)	
D735.A1	Primary sources, documents (WWII: collection, preservation)	
D735.A7	Atlantic Declaration (Charter': 14 Aug. 1941)	
D736	Biography (collective: WWII: for individuals SEE DA-F class numbers for person's country: SEE ALSO D811 for personal narratives) 940.5481-5482 (ALSO country numbers ended sometimes by 0922-0924)	
D739	World War II (collected works)	
D740	Dictionaries & encyclopedias (WWII)	940.5303

D741	CAUSES, AIMS, RESULTS (WWII: gen.)	940.5311, 327+
D742.A-Z	Causes, aims, results (WWII: by country)	940.534-539
D742.C5	China (WWII: causes, aims, results)	
D742.F8	France (WWII: causes, aims, results)	
D742.G3	Germany (WWII: causes, aims, results)	
D742.G7	Great Britain (WWII: causes, aims, results)	
D742.J3	Japan (WWII: causes, aims, results)	
D742.R9	Russia (WWII: causes, aims, results)	
D742.U5-6	United States (WWII: causes, aims, results)	
D743	WORLD WAR II (GEN.)	940.53, .54
D743.2	Pictorials (WWII: SEE ALSO D746)	
D743.22	Documentary films, slides, etc. (WWII: catalogs: SEE ALSO D746.3 for older titles)	
D743.23	Movies & movie propaganda (WWII)	791.43+, 940.53+
D743.25	Posters (WWII: SEE D746.5 for older titles)	769.4994+
D743.27	Collectibles (WWII)	
D743.3	Maps & atlases (WWII: PREFER G1038)	
D743.4	Instruction (WWII)	
D743.42	Historiography (WWII)	
D743.5	Chronologies, tables, outlines (WWII)	940.530202
D743.6	Examinations, questions, etc. (WWII)	
D743.7	Juvenile works (WWII)	
D743.9	Pamphlets, minor works, sermons (WWII)	
D744	World War II (gen. special: deception, strategy, psychological aspects, world politics, misc.)	
D744.4	Ethics, religious questions (WWII)	
D744.5.A-Z	Religious & ethical questions (WWII: by country)	
D744.5.I8	Italy (WWII: religious & ethical ?'s)	
D744.5.J3	Japan (WWII: religious & ethical ?'s)	
D744.5.R9	Russia (WWII: religious & ethical ?'s)	
D744.6	Social aspects (WWII)	
D744.7.A-Z	Social aspects (WWII: by country)	
D745-745.7	Poetry, satire, etc. (WWII: PREFER PQ-PT)	
D745	Satire, poetry, etc. (WWII: gen.)	940.5481, .5483, misc. 800
	literature #'s	
D745.2	English poetry, satire, etc. (WWII: PREFER PR, PS)	
D745.3	French poetry, satire, etc. (WWII)	
D745.5	German poetry, satire, etc. (WWII)	
D745.7.A-Z	Poetry, satire, etc. (WWII: languages besides Eng., Fr., Ger.)	
D745.7.I8	Italian poetry, satire, etc. (WWII)	
D745.7.R9	Russian poetry, satire, etc. (WWII)	
D746	Views (WWII: SEE ALSO D743.2+)	
D746.3	Documentary films, slides, etc. (WWII: catalogs: SEE ALSO D743.22 for media catalogs of newer titles)	
D746.5	Posters (WWII: SEE D743.25 for newer titles)	
D747	Battlefield guides (WWII: gen.: particular battles at D756.5 etc.)	

D748-754	DIPLOMACY (WWII)	940.532+, 327.+
D748	Diplomacy (WWII: gen.)	
D749	Neutrality, small states, other special diplomatic history (WWII)	
D749.5.A-Z	Treaties (WWII: separate: by name)	
D749.5.A5	Anglo-Soviet Treaty (26 May 1942)	
D750-754	Diplomacy (WWII: by place)	940.5322-5325
D750	Great Britain (WWII: dipl. history)	940.532241
D751	Germany (WWII: dipl. history)	940.532443
D752	France (WWII: dipl. history)	940.532244
D752.8	America & American neutrality (WWII: dipl. history)	
D753-753.8	United States (WWII: dipl. hist., inclu. neutral years)	940.532573, .532273, 973.917
D753.2.A-Z	Mutual-aid agreements (WWII: U.S.: by country)	
D753.2.G7	Lend-lease, mutual aid (WWII: U.S.-G.B.)	
D753.2.R9	Lend-lease, mutual aid (WWII: U.S.-Rus.)	
D753.3	Espionage, conspiracy, propaganda in U.S. (WWII)	
D753.8	Japanese-Americans (WWII: SEE ALSO D769.8.A6)	
D754.A-Z	Diplomacy (WWII: misc. countries or areas)	
D754.A34	Africa (WWII: dipl. history)	
D754.C95	Czechoslovakia (WWII: dipl. history)	
D754.I5	Ireland (WWII: dipl. history: gen.)	
D754.I6	Irish Free State (WWII: dipl. history)	
D754.I7	Northern Ireland (WWII: dipl. history)	
D754.I8	Italy (WWII: dipl. history)	
D754.J3	Japan (WWII: dipl. history)	940.532452
D754.L4	Levant (WWII: dipl. history)	
D754.N34	Near East (WWII: dipl. history)	
D754.S29	Scandinavia (WWII: dipl. history)	
D754.S8	Sweden (WWII: dipl. history)	
D754.T8	Turkey (WWII: dipl. history)	
D754.Y9	Yugoslavia (WWII: dipl. history)	
D755-755.9	TIME PERIODS (WWII)	
D755	World War II (Sept. 1939-Dec. 1941)	
D755.1	World War II (Sept. 1939-May 1940)	
D755.2	World War II (1940)	
D755.3	World War II (1941)	
D755.4	World War II (1942)	
D755.5	World War II (1943)	
D755.6	World War II (1944)	
D755.7	World War II (1945)	
D755.8	World War II (VE Day to VJ Day)	
D756-763	WESTERN FRONT & Western Europe (WWII)	940.5421
D756	MILITARY OPS. (WWII: WEST: gen.)	
D756.3	Military ops. (WWII: West: gen. special)	
D756.5.A-Z	BATTLES, campaigns, sieges (WWII: WEST: by place)	
D756.5.A7	Bulge, Battle of the (Ardennes: 1944-45)	
D756.5.A78	Arras, Battle of (1940)	
D756.5.B7	Britain, Battle of (1940)	
D756.5.C2	Calais, Battle of (1940)	
D756.5.D5	Dieppe Raid (1942)	
D756.5.D8	Dunkirk, Battle of (1940)	
D756.5.M4	Meuse, Battle of the (Monthermé: 1940)	
D756.5.V3	Verdun, Battle of (WWII: 1940)	

```
D757-757.9  GERMANY & GERMAN MILITARY OPS. (WWII)
D757        German military ops. (WWII: gen.)        940.5343, .54013, .5413,
                                                      .5421, 943.086
D757.1      Armies (WWII: Ger.)       940.541343
D757.2      Army corps (WWII: Ger.)
D757.3      Infantry (WWII: Ger.)
D757.32.A-Z Infantry (WWII: Ger.: by author, division, name, etc.)
D757.39     Mountain troops (WWII: Ger.)
D757.4.A-5  Artillery (WWII: Ger.)
D757.4.A-53 Anti-aircraft artillery (WWII: Ger.)
D757.4.A-Z  Mountain troops (WWII: Ger.: by author, division, name, etc.)
D757.54-57  Panzer troops (WWII: Ger.)
D757.54     Panzer troops (WWII: Ger.: gen.)
D757.55.A-Z Panzer troops (by author, division, name, etc.)
D757.55.R6  Roten teufel, Die (WWII: Panzer troops)
D757.56.1st- Panzer divisions (by #)
D757.57.1st- Panzer regiments (by #)
D757.6      Airborne troops (WWII: Ger.)
D757.63     Parachute troops (WWII: Ger.)
D757.65     Signal Corps (WWII: Ger.: Nachrichten truppen)
D757.8      Engineers (WWII: Ger.)
D757.83     Nebeltruppe (WWII: Ger.)
D757.85     Waffen SS (WWII: Ger.: Waffenschutzstaffel)
D757.855    Technische Truppen (WWII: Ger.)
D757.9.A-Z  Local history (WWII: Ger.: by place)       940.5343+, 943.1-9+
D757.9.B4   Berlin, Ger. (WWII)       943.155086
D757.9.H3   Hamburg, Ger. (WWII)
D757.9.M9   Munich, Ger. (WWII)
D759-760    GREAT BRITAIN & BRITISH MILITARY OPS. (WWII)
D759        British military ops. & Great Britain (WWII: gen.)       940.54091,
                                                      .5341-5342, 942.084
D759.5.1st- Armies etc. (WWII: G.B.: by #)       940.541241-541242
D759.5.51st Highland Division (WWII: G.B.: 51st)
D759.52     Artillery (WWII: G.B.)
D759.523    Anti-aircraft Command (WWII: G.B.)
D759.527    Anti-aircraft, Light Artillery regiments (WWII: G.B.)
D759.528    Armored divisions etc. (WWII: G.B..)
D759.53     Infantry (WWII: G.B.)
D759.54     Cavalry (WWII: G.B.)
D759.55     Engineers (WWII: G.B.)
D759.6      Airborne troops (WWII: G.B.)
D759.63     Parachute troops (WWII: Brit.)
D760.8.A-Z  LOCAL HISTORY (WWII: G.B.: by place)       941.084, 942.084,
                                                      942.1-9+, 940.5341-5342+
D760.8.B3   Bath, Eng. (WWII)
D760.8.B4   Belfast, N. Ire. (WWII)
D760.8.B7   Bristol, Eng. (WWII)
D760.8.C6   Coventry, Eng. (WWII)
D760.8.D6   Dover, Eng. (WWII)
D760.8.E3   East Downing, Eng. (WWII)
D760.8.E7   Essex, Eng. (WWII)
D760.8.E88  Exeter, Eng. (WWII)
D760.8.K4   Kent, Eng. (WWII)
```

```
D760.8.L6    Liverpool, Eng. (WWII)
D760.8.L7    London, Eng. (WWII)           942.1084, 940.534421
D760.8.M3    Manchester, Eng. (WWII)
D760.8.S75   Stepney, Eng. (WWII: Middlesex)
D760.A-Z     British military ops. (WWII: special by group or region)    940.5412
D760.A1          Colonies (WWII: G.B.: gen.)
D760.A8          Auxiliary Territorial Service (WWII: G.B.)
D760.D4          Devonshire Regiment (WWII: G.B.)
D760.I7          Irish Guards (WWII: G.B.)
D760.P5          Pioneer Corps (WWII: G.B.)
D760.R7          Royal Armored Corps (WWII: G.B.)
D761-762     FRANCE & FRENCH MILITARY OPS. (WWII)
D761         French military ops. & France (WWII: gen.)    940.5344, .540944,
                                                           944.0815-0816
D761.1           Armies (WWII: Fr.)        940.541244
D761.15              Army corps (WWII: Fr.)
D761.2           Divisions (WWII: Fr.)
D761.3           Infantry (WWII: Fr.)
D761.38             Zouaves (WWII: Fr.: infantry)
D761.5           Chasseurs & Chasseurs Alpine (WWII: Fr.)
D761.6           Artillery (WWII: Fr.)
D761.7           Parachute troops (WWII: Fr.)
D761.9.A-Z   French military ops. (WWII: misc.)
D761.9.A1        Colonies (WWII: Fr.: gen.)
D761.9.F7        Free French, France Combattante, French Volunteer Force (WWII)
D761.9.P6        Polish troops (WWII: French Army)
D762.A-Z     Local history (WWII: Fr.: by place)    944.1-9+
D762.P3          Paris, Fr. (WWII)         944.360816
D763.A-Z     WESTERN EUROPE (WWII: EXCEPT Ger., G.B., Fr.)
D763.B4-42   Belgium & Belgian military ops. (WWII)    940.3493, 949.3
D763.B4      Belgian military ops. (WWII: gen.)
D763.B41     Divisions etc. (WWII: Bel.)
D763.B42     Local history (WWII: Bel.)
D763.D4          Denmark (WWII: gen.)
D763.D42.A-Z     Local history (WWII: Den.: by place)
D763.I8-82       Italy & Italian military ops. (WWII)    940.40945, .41345, 945.091
D763.I8          ITALIAN military ops. (WWII: gen.)
D763.I81.1st-    Divisions etc. (WWII: Ital.: by #)
D763.I813.A-Z    Divisions etc. (WWII: Ital.: by name or author)
D763.I815-817    Corpo Volontari Della Libert`a (WWII: Ital.)
D763.I815        Corpo Volontari Della Libert`a (WWII: Ital.: gen.)
D763.I817.A-Z    Corpo Volontari Della Libert`a (WWII: Ital.: by name)
D763.I82.A-Z         Local history (WWII: It.: by place)
D763.L9              Luxembourg (WWII: Grand Duchy)
D763.M3          Malta (WWII)
D763.N4-42       Netherlands & Dutch military ops. (WWII)    940.3492071,
                                                            949.207
D763.N4          Dutch military ops. (WWII: gen.)
D763.N41.1st-    Divisions etc. (WWII: Dutch: by #)
D763.N42.A-Z     Local history (WWII: Neth.: by place)
```

D763.N6-62	Norway & Norwegian military ops. (WWII)	940.3481, 948.1041
D763.N6	Norwegian military ops. (WWII)	
D763.N61.1st-	Divisions etc. (WWII: Nor.: by #)	
D763.N613.A-Z	Divisions etc. (WWII: Nor.: by name or author)	
D763.N62.A-Z	Local history (WWII: Nor.: by place)	
D763.S5	Sicily (WWII)	
D763.5	Arctic areas (WWII: Greenland etc.)	
D764-766.7	EASTERN FRONT (WWII)	
D764	RUSSIA & Eastern Front (WWII: gen.)	940.540947, .532247, .5347, .541247, 947.0842
D764.3.A-Z	Battles, campaigns, sieges (WWII: Rus., Eastern front: by place)	
D764.3.L4	Leningrad, Siege of (WWII)	
D764.3.S7	Stalingrad, Battle of (1942-43)	
D764.5.1st-	Divisions etc. (WWII: Rus.: by #)	940.541247
D764.52	Artillery (WWII: Rus.)	
D764.53	Infantry (WWII: Rus.)	
D764.54	Cavalry (WWII: Rus.)	
D764.6.A-Z	Russian military ops. (WWII: special: by region, name, author)	
D764.6.G7	Gvardia (WWII: Rus.: gen.)	
D764.6.G8.1st-	Gvardia (WWII: Rus.: by #)	
D764.6.U82	Ural Mts. (WWII)	
D764.7.A-Z	Local history (WWII: Rus.: by place)	
D764.7.K5	Klintsy, Rus. (WWII)	
D764.7.M58	Moscow, Rus. (WWII)	
D765-765.2+	Poland & Polish military ops. (WWII)	
D765	Polish military ops. (WWII: gen.)	940.53438, .5409438, 943.8053
D765.13	Divisions etc. (WWII: Pol.)	
D765.2.A-Z	Local history (WWII: Pol.)	
D765.2.W3	Warsaw, Pol. (WWII)	
D765.2.W7	Wroclaw, Breslau, Pol. (WWII)	
D765.3-35	Finland & Finnish military ops. (WWII)	940.53471, 534897, .54094897, 948.97032
D765.3	Finnish military ops. (WWII: gen.)	
D765.32	Divisions etc. (WWII: Fin.)	
D765.35.A-Z	Local history (WWII: Fin.)	
D765.4	Austria (WWII: gen.) 940.53436, 943.6052	
D765.45.A-Z	Local history (WWII: Austria)	
D765.45.V45	Vienna, Austria (WWII)	
D765.45.V6	Vorarlberg, Austria (WWII)	
D765.5-55	Czechoslovakia & Czech military ops. (WWII)	940.53437, 943.703
D765.5	Czech military ops. (WWII: gen.)	
D765.53	Divisions etc. (WWII: Czech.)	
D765.55.A-Z	Local history (WWII: Czech.)	
D765.55.P7	Prague, Cz. (WWII)	
D765.56	Hungary (WWII: gen.) 940.53439, 943.905	
D765.562.A-Z	Local history (WWII: Hung.)	
D765.562.B8	Budapest, Hun. (WWII)	

```
D766-766.79    Balkans, Near East, Eastern Mediterranean (WWII)
D766           NEAR EAST, BALKANS, E. MEDITERRANEAN (WWII: gen.)
                                    940.53495+, 949.5+, 956.03, 962.052
D766.3         Greece (WWII: gen.)        940.53495, 949.5074
D766.32.A-Z    Local history (WWII: Greece)
D766.32.A8     Athens, Gr. (WWII)
D766.32.C4     Cephalonia, Gr. (WWII)
D766.4-42      Rumania & Rumanian military ops. (WWII)    940.53498, 949.802
D766.4         Rumanian military ops. (WWII)
D766.413       Divisions etc. (WWII: Rum.)
D766.42.A-Z    Local history (WWII: Rum.)
D766.6-62      YUGOSLAVIA & Yugoslavian military ops. (WWII)      940.53497,
                                                                  949.7022
D766.6         Yugoslavian military ops. (WWII)
D766.6.A1-5    Associations, societies (WWII: Yug.)
D766.6.A2      Yugoslavia (WWII: collections)
D766.61.1st-   Divisions etc. (WWII: Yug.: by #)
D766.613.A-Z   Divisions etc. (WWII: Yug.: by name)
D766.62.A-Z    Local history (WWII: Yug.)
D766.62.B4     Belgrade, Yug. (WWII)
D766.62.Z3     Zagreb, Yug. (WWII)
D766.7.A-Z  Balkans & Near East (WWII: misc. countries: by name)
D766.7.A4      Albania (WWII)
D766.7.B8      Bulgaria (WWII)
D766.7.C7      Crete (WWII)
D766.7.I55     Iran (WWII)
D766.7.I57     Iraq (WWII)
D766.7.I7      Palestine (WWII: Israel)
D766.7.S9-95   Syria (WWII)
D766.7.T8      Turkey (WWII)
D766.8-99   AFRICA(WWII)
D766.8         Africa (WWII: gen.)        940.536, .5423, 960.31
D766.82           North Africa (WWII)    940.5361, .5423, 961.03
D766.84           East Africa (WWII)        940.53676, 967.6
D766.9-99   Africa (WWII: by country)
D766.9            Egypt (WWII)        940.5423, .5362, 962.052
D766.92           Ethiopia & Ethiopian military ops. (WWII)        940.5423
D766.93           Libya (WWII)        940.5423, 961.203
D766.95           Belgian Congo (WWII)
D766.96     French Equatorial Africa (WWII)
D766.97           South Africa & South African military ops. (WWII)    940.5368, 540968,
                                                                       968.055
D766.99.A-Z    Africa (WWII: misc. countries: by name)
D766.99.A6     Algeria (WWII)
D766.99.M3     Madagascar (WWII)
D766.99.M8     Morocco (WWII)        940.5364, 964.04
D766.99.T7-8   Tunisia (WWII)        940.53611, 961.104
```

D767-767.99	ASIA & THE PACIFIC THEATRE	
D767	Pacific Theatre & Asia (WWII: gen.)	940.5425-5426
D767.2-25	JAPAN & JAPANESE MILITARY OPS. (WWII)	
D767.2	Japanese military ops. & Japan (WWII: gen.)	940.5352, .540952, .541352, 952.033
D767.23	Divisions etc. (WWII: Japan)	
D767.25.A-Z	Local history (WWII: Japan: by place)	
D767.25.H6	Hiroshima, Japan (WWII)	
D767.25.N3	Nagasaki, Japan (WWII)	
D767.25.T5-6	Tokyo, Japan (WWII) 952.135	
D767.255	Korea (WWII) 940.53519	
D767.3	CHINA & CHINESE MILITARY OPS. (WWII)	940.5351, .540951, .5425, 951.042
D767.35-352	Cochin China (Vietnam: WWII)	
D767.35	Vietnam (WWII: gen.) 940.53597, 959.703	
D767.352.A-Z	Local history (WWII: Cochin China: by place)	
D767.352.S3	Saigon, Viet. (WWII)	
D767.4	Philippine Islands (WWII) 940.53599, .5409599, .5425-5426, 959.03	
D767.45	French Indochina (WWII) 940.53597, 959.703	
D767.47	Thailand (WWII)	
D767.5	Malay Peninsula (WWII) 959.503	
D767.55	Singapore (WWII) 959.5203	
D767.6-63	India & Burma (WWII) 940.5425, .5354, 954.0359	
D767.6	Burma & India (WWII)	
D767.63	Free India (Azad Hind: WWII: 1943-45: includes Indian National Army)	
D767.7	Dutch East Indies & Indonesia (WWII) 940.53598, .5425, 959.8022	
D767.8-82	AUSTRALIA & AUSTRALIAN MILITARY OPS. (WWII)	
D767.8	Australian military ops. & Australia (WWII: gen.) 940.532294, .5394, .540994, .541294, .5426, 994.042	
D767.813	Divisions etc. (WWII: Australia) 940.541294	
D767.82.A-Z	Local history (WWII: Australia: by place) 994.1-8	
D767.82.M44	Melbourne, Australia (WWII) 994.51	
D767.85-852	New Zealand (WWII) 940.53931, .5409931, .5426, 993.1032	
D767.85	New Zealand military ops. (WWII)	
D767.851	Divisions etc. (WWII: New Z.) 940.5412931	
D767.852.A-Z	Local history (WWII: New Z.)	
D767.852.W44	Wellington, N.Z. (WWII) 993.127	
D767.9-99	OCEANIA OR PACIFIC ISLANDS (WWII)	
D767.9	Pacific Islands (WWII: gen.) 940.5426, .54439, .544952, .54539, .545952, .5352	
D767.913	Aleutian Islands (WWII: PREFER D769.87.A4)	
D767.917	Gilbert Islands (WWII)	
D767.92	Hawaiian Islands (WWII) 940.539969, 996.903	
D767.94	Midway Islands (WWII)	
D767.95	New Guinea (WWII) 940.5426, .5395	
D767.98	Solomon Islands (WWII: gen.) 940.53935, .5426	
D767.982.A-Z	Solomon Islands (WWII: by specific is.: SEE ALSO D767.99.A-Z for alternative #'s)	
D767.982.B5	Bougainville (WWII)	
D767.982.C4	Choiseul (WWII)	
D767.982.G92	Guadalcanal (WWII)	
D767.982.N34	New Georgia (WWII)	

D767.99.A-Z	PACIFIC ISLANDS (WWII: misc. by name)
D767.99.B46	Bismarck Islands (WWII)
D767.99.B54	Bougainville (WWII)
D767.99.C3	Caroline Islands (WWII)
D767.99.E55	Ellice Islands (WWII)
D767.99.G38	Gilbert Islands (WWII)
D767.99.G88	Guadalcanal (WWII)
D767.99.G9	Guam (WWII)
D767.99.I9	Iwo Jima (WWII)
D767.99.M27	Mariana Islands (WWII: gen.)
D767.99.M272.A-Z	Mariana Islands (WWII: by specific is.: SEE ALSO D767.99.A-Z for direct alternatives, e.g. D767.99.G9 for Guam)
D767.99.M272.G9	Guam (WWII)
D767.99.M3	Marshall Islands (WWII)
D767.99.N4	New Britain (WWII)
D767.99.N415.A-Z	Local history (WWII: New Britain)
D767.99.N415.R32	Rabaul, New Brit. (WWII)
D767.99.N42	New Caledonia (WWII)
D767.99.N44	New Georgia (WWII)
D767.99.N46	New Hebrides (WWII)
D767.99.N47	New Ireland (WWII)
D767.99.O45	Okinawa (WWII)
D767.99.P4	Palau Islands (Pelew Is.: WWII)
D767.99.R9	Ryukyu Islands (WWII)
D767.99.S3	Saipan (WWII)
D767.99.T3	Tarawa (WWII)
D767.99.T45	Tinian (WWII)
D767.99.T89	Truk (WWII)
D767.99.W35	Wake Is. (WWII)
D768-769	Americas (WWII)
D768	North & South America (WWII: gen.)
D768.15	Canada (WWII) 940.5371, .532271, .540971, .541271, 971.063
D768.18	Latin America (WWII) 940.538, .53228, .53248, .53258, 980.033
D768.2	Mexico (WWII) 940.5372
D768.3	Brazil (WWII) 940.5381, .544381, 981.061
D769-769.99	UNITED STATES MILITARY OPS. & U.S. (WWII) 940.532273, .5373, .540973, .541273, .5428
D769	United States (WWII: gen.) 940.532273, .5373, .540973, .541273, .5428
D769.A1-15	Associations, societies (WWII: U.S.)
D769.A2	United States (WWII: collections)
D769.A3	Legislative compendia (WWII: U.S.)
D769.A5-Z	United States & U.S. military ops. (WWII: gen.: SEE ALSO E806 for internal, general U.S. history, 1939-45) 940.5373, .540973, .532273, 973.917
D769.1	United States (WWII: gen. special)
D769.15	Pamphlets, minor works (WWII: U.S.)

D769.2-799   United States military ops. (WWII: land,air, & sea: SEE D769.A5-Z for
                  gen. works)   940.541273,.544373,.544973
D769.2-779   United States military ops. (WWII: organiz. units: land, sea: D769.A5-Z,
                  D756.5, D767 etc. for overall efforts, area campaigns, & battles)⁴
D769.2   United States military ops. (WWII: gen. special)
D769.25-4   ARMIES ETC. (WWII: U.S.)
D769.25   General staff & headquarters (WWII: U.S.)
D769.26   Armies (WWII: U.S.: by # or author)
D769.27   Army corps (WWII: U.S.)
D769.29-309   Divisions etc. (WWII: U.S.)
D769.29   Divisions etc. (WWII: U.S.: gen.)
D769.295.A-Z Divisions etc. (WWII: U.S.: by name)
D769.295.A5   Americal Division (WWII: U.S.)
D769.3.1st-   Divisions etc. (WWII: U.S.: by #)
D769.305-307 Armored divisions (WWII: U.S.)
D769.305   Armored divisions (WWII: U.S.: gen.)
D769.3053   Armored divisions (WWII: U.S.: by #)
D769.3055.1st- Armored regiments (WWII: U.S.: by #)
D769.3058   Reconnaisance battalions (WWII: U.S.)
D769.306.1st-   Tank battalions (WWII: U.S.: by #)
D769.307.1st-   Tank destroyer battalions (WWII: U.S.: by #)
D769.308   Cavalry divisions (WWII: U.S.: 1st)
D769.309   Civil Affairs Division (WWII: U.S. Army)
D769.31.1st- Infantry (WWII: U.S.: regiments, combat teams, etc.: by #)
D769.32   Cavalry (WWII: U.S.: gen.)
D769.325.1st- Cavalry groups etc. (WWII: U.S.: by #)
D769.33   Combat engineers (WWII: U.S.: gen.)
D769.335.1st- Engineer battalions etc. (WWII: U.S.: by #)
D769.337.A-Z Engineer battalions etc. (WWII: U.S.: by name)
D769.34.1st-   Field artillery groups etc. (WWII: U.S.: by #)
D769.342   Anti-aircraft artillery (WWII: U.S.: gen.)
D769.343.1st- Anti-aircraft artillery battalions (WWII: U.S.: by #)
D769.345   Airborne troops (WWII: U.S.: gen.)
D769.346.1st- Airborne troop battalions etc. (WWII: U.S.: by #)
D769.347   Parachute troops (WWII: U.S.)
D769.35   Chemical Corps (WWII: U.S.: gen.)
D769.353.A-Z Chemical Corps battalions etc. (WWII: U.S.: by type, sub-arranged
                  by # if applic.)
D769.36   Signal Corps (WWII: U.S.: gen.)
D769.363.1st- Signal Corps battalions etc. (WWII: U.S.: by #)
D769.369-372 Marines (WWII: U.S.: land ops. only: SEE D767, D769.45, D774,
                  D790, U-V for naval or aerial ops.)
D769.369   Marine Corps (WWII: U.S.: gen.)
D769.37.1st- Marine Corps divisions (WWII: U.S.: by #)
D769.372.1st- Marine Corps regiments (WWII: U.S.: by #)
D769.375   Chaplain Corps (WWII: U.S. Army)
D769.39   WACS (Women's Army Corps: WWII: U.S.)
D769.4   Armies etc. (WWII: U.S.: misc.)

21

D769.45-599	UNITED STATES NAVAL OPS. & Coast Guard ops. (WWII: fleets, squadrons, bases, etc.: SEE D773-4, D783 for overall works, specific ships & engagements, submarines) 940.545973
D769.45	United States naval ops. (WWII: special topics: land batteries, defensive areas, Marine Corps except land, etc.)
D769.5-539	Fleets, squadrons, etc. (WWII: U.S. Navy)
D769.5.1st-	Fleets (WWII: U.S. Navy: by #)
D769.52.A-Z	Naval forces & divisions (WWII: U.S.: by name)
D769.52.E7	Escort carriers (WWII: U.S.) 940.545
D769.53.1st-	Task forces (WWII: U.S.: by #)
D769.535	Service squadrons (WWII: U.S.: gen.)
D769.537	Service squadrons (WWII: U.S.: by #)
D769.54	Naval bases (WWII: U.S.: gen.) 940.545373
D769.542.A-Z	Naval bases (WWII: U.S.: by location)
D769.542.G9	Guam (WWII: U.S. naval base)
D769.542.H38	Hawaii (WWII: U.S. naval base)
D769.542.S345	San Diego, Calif. (WWII: U.S. naval base)
D769.55-555	Naval construction battalions (WWII: U.S.)
D769.55	Seabees or naval construction battalions (WWII: U.S.: gen.)
D769.552.1st-	Seabees (WWII: U.S.: by battalion #)
D769.554	Naval construction maintenance (WWII: U.S.: gen.)
D769.555.1st-	Naval construction maintenance units (WWII: U.S.:by#)
D769.585	Coast Guard Reserve (WWII: U.S.: temporary inclu. U.S. Volunteer Port Security Force)
D769.59	Naval Chaplain Corps (WWII: U.S.)
D769.597	Naval Reserve & Women's Reserve (WAVES: WWII: U.S.)
D769.598	Coast Guard Reserve & Women's Reserve (SPARS: WWII: U.S.)
D769.64	Sino-American Cooperative Organization (WWII: for aerial ops. such as Flying Tigers SEE D790)
D769.72	Transportation service (WWII: U.S.: gen.: PREFER D810.T8)
D769.73	Transportation Corps (WWII: U.S.)
D769.73.1st-	Quartermaster depots (WWII: U.S.: by #)
D769.733.1st-	Transportation Corps battalions etc. (WWII: U.S.: by #)
D769.74	Ordnance battalions etc. (WWII: U.S.: gen.)
D769.743.1st-	Ordnance battalions etc. (WWII: U.S.: by #)
D769.75	Supply forces & army service forces (WWII: U.S.: gen.)
D769.76	Technical intelligence service (WWII: U.S.)
D769.77	Provost-Marshall-General's Bureau (WWII: U.S.: gen.)
D769.775	Military Police (MP's: WWII: U.S.)
D769.8.A-Z	United States (WWII: special topics: SEE D810.A-Z for outside U.S.)
D769.8.A6	Alien enemies (WWII: U.S.: inclu. Japanese relocation centers: SEE ALSO D753.8. For alien property custody SEE JX5313.U6) 940.5315+, .547273, .53163
D769.8.C4	Civil liberties & freedom of speech (WWII: U.S.: SEE UB342.U5 for conscientious objectors)
D769.8.F6	Foreign population war effort (WWII: U.S.)
D769.8.F7.A-Z	Nationalities & the war (WWII: U.S.: by name: for Indians SEE D810.I5)
D769.8.L6	Local government (WWII: U.S.)
D769.8.P7	Political prisoners (WWII: U.S.: SEE ALSO D805.U5 for prisons & prisoners)
D769.8.S5	Service flags (WWII: U.S.)
D769.8.T8	Trophies, Military (WWII: U.S.)

D769.85-87	World War II (gen. particip.: U.S.: by area or state)
D769.85.A-W	LOCAL HISTORY (WWII: U.S.: by state: SEE ALSO F1-951+)
D769.85.C2	California (WWII: gen.) 979.4052
D769.85.C21.A-Z	Local history (WWII: Calif.: by place)
D769.85.D6	Washington, D.C. (District of Columbia: WWII)
D769.85.F5-51	Florida (WWII)
D769.85.M7	Mississippi (WWII)
D769.85.N33-34	New Mexico (WWII)
D769.85.N4-5	New York (WWII) 979.7042
D769.85.W8-81	Wyoming (WWII)
D769.87.A-Z	Territories (WWII: U.S.: by place)
D769.87.A4	Aleutian Islands (WWII)
D769.87.H3	Hawaiian Islands (WWII: SEE ALSO D767.92)
D769.87.P7	Puerto Rico (WWII)
D769.88.A-Z	Nationalities (WWII: U.S.) 940.5315+
D769.88.A7	Armenians (WWII: U.S.)
D769.88.M4	Mexican-Americans (WWII: as troops) 940.5404
D769.9	Personal accounts (WWII: U.S.: PREFER D811)
D770-784	NAVAL & SUBMARINE OPS. (WWII) 940.545
D770	Battle of the Atlantic, freedom of the seas, general naval ops. (WWII) 940.545
D771	Anglo-German naval conflict & blockade (WWII: gen.) 940.545, .5452
D772.3	Russo-German naval conflict (WWII: Arctic areas & Baltic) 940.545947, .545943
D772.A-Z	German-Anglo naval conflict & blockade (WWII: by battle, ship, etc.) 940.545941-43
D772.A66	Ark Royal (WWII: aircraft carrier)
D772.A7	Athenia (WWII: steamship)
D772.B5	Bismarck (WWII: battleship)
D772.F5	Firedrake (WWII: destroyer)
D772.G7	Graf Spee, Admiral (WWII: battleship)
D772.H6	Hood (WWII: battle cruiser)
D772.P4	Penelope (WWII: cruiser)
D772.S25	San Demetrio (WWII: tanker)
D773-774	UNITED STATES NAVAL OPS. (WWII: SEE ALSO D769.45-599 for specific fleets, squadrons, bases, units) 940.545973
D773	United States naval ops. (WWII: gen.: inclu. blockade, patrol) 940.545973
D774.A-Z	United States naval ops. (WWII: by battle, ship, etc.)
D774.A7	Arkansas (WWII: battleship)
D774.B48	Bismarck Sea, Battle of (1943-44)
D774.B6	Boise (WWII: cruiser)
D774.C57	Coral Sea, Battle of (1942)
D774.E5	Enterprise (WWII: aircraft carrier)
D774.E7	Essex (WWII: aircraft carrier)
D774.H3	Hancock (WWII: aircraft carrier)
D774.H4	Helena (WWII: cruiser)
D774.H6	Hornet (WWII: aircraft carrier)
D774.L4	Lexington (WWII: aircraft carrier: 1st with name)
D774.M3	Marblehead (WWII: cruiser)
D774.M35	Maryland (WWII: battleship)
D774.M5	Midway, Battle of (1942)
D774.N4	New Orleans (WWII: cruiser)
D774.O3	O'Bannon (WWII: destroyer)

D774.P55	Philippine Sea, Battle of (1944)	
D774.P7	Princess (WWII: aircraft carrier)	
D774.S3	Saratoga (WWII: aircraft carrier)	
D774.S318	Savo Island, Battle of (1942)	
D774.S32	Savo Island (WWII: aircraft carrier)	
D774.S45	Solomons, Battle of the (1942-44)	
D774.S6	South Dakota (WWII: battleship)	
D775	Anglo-Italian naval conflict (WWII: gen.)	940.545941, .545945
D775.5.A-Z	Italian-Anglo naval conflict (WWII: by battle, ship, etc.)	
D775.5.S8	Sydney (WWII: cruiser)	
D777	JAPANESE NAVAL OPS. (WWII: gen.)	940.545952, .5426
D777.5.A-Z	Japanese naval ops. (WWII: by battle, ship, etc.)	
D779.A-Z	Naval ops. (WWII: misc. countries: by place)	
D779.A8	Australian naval ops. (WWII)	940.545994
D779.C2-29	Canadian naval ops. (WWII)	
D780-784	SUBMARINE & ANTI-SUBMARINE OPS. (WWII)	940.5451
D780	Antisubmarine & submarine ops. (WWII: gen.)	940.54516
D781	German submarine ops. (WWII: gen.)	
D782.A-Z	German submarine ops. (WWII: by battle, ship, etc.)	
D782.M6	Montevideo (WWII: steamship)	
D782.R6	Robin Moor (WWII: steamship)	
D783	United States submarine ops. (WWII: gen.)	
D783.5.A-Z	United States submarine ops. (WWII: by battle, ship, etc.)	
D783.5.C6	Coast Guard Reserve Boat 3070 (WWII)	
D783.5.S4	Seawolf (WWII: submarine)	
D783.5.S6	Silversides (WWII: submarine)	
D783.5.S8	Sturgeon (WWII: submarine)	
D783.6	Japanese submarine ops. (WWII: gen.: SEE ALSO D784.J3)	
D783.7.A-Z	Japanese submarine ops. (WWII: by battle, ship, author, etc.)	
D784.A-Z	Submarine ops. (WWII: misc. countries: by place)	
D784.G7	British submarine ops. (WWII: GB)	
D784.J3	Japanese submarine ops. (WWII: SEE ALSO D783.6)	
D785-792	AIR FORCE OPS. (WWII)	940.544
D785	Aerial ops. (WWII: gen.)	940.544
D785.U57-63	U.S. Strategic Bombing Survey reports (WWII)	
D785.U57	Strategic Bombing Survey (WWII: U.S.: gen.)	
D785.U58.A-Z	Strategic Bombing Survey (WWII: U.S.: by industry attacked)	
D785.U6	European aerial ops. (WWII: U.S. bombing survey)	
D785.U63	Pacific aerial ops. (WWII: U.S. bombing survey)	
D786	British aerial ops. (WWII)	940.544941
D787	German aerial ops. (WWII)	940.544943
D788	French aerial ops. (WWII)	940.544944
D790	United States aerial ops. (WWII)	940.544973
D792.A-Z	Aerial ops. (WWII: misc. countries)	
D792.A8	Australian aerial ops. (WWII)	940.544994
D792.C2-29	Canadian aerial ops. (WWII)	
D792.I8	Italian aerial ops. (WWII)	
D792.J3-39	Japanese aerial ops. (WWII)	940.544952
D792.R9	Russian aerial ops. (WWII)	
D793	Tank warfare (WWII)	
D794	Cavalry (WWII)	
D794.5	Commando ops. (WWII)	

D795	ENGINEERING OPS. (WWII)
D795.A2	Engineering ops. (WWII: gen.)
D795.A3-Z	Engineering ops. (WWII: by country)
D795.G3	German engineering ops. (WWII)
D795.G7	British engineering ops. (WWII)
D795.J3	Japanese engineering ops. (WWII)
D795.U6	United States engineering ops. (WWII)
D796	Medals, badges, decorations (WWII: inclu. individual s & lists: SEE ALSO D797 for older works)
D796.5.A-Z	Medals, badges, decorations (WWII: by country)
D797	LISTS & REGISTERS (WWII: decorated, dead, wounded: SEE ALSO D796 for newer titles) 940.5467
D797.A2	Registers & lists (WWII: dead, wounded, decorated: gen.)
D797.A3-Z	Registers & lists (WWII: dead, wounded, decorated: by country)
D797.A8	Dead, wounded, decorated (WWII: Australia)
D797.A83	Dead, wounded, decorated (WWII: South Australia)
D797.U6	Dead, wounded, decorated (WWII: U.S.: gen.) 940.546773
D797.U62.C2	Dead, wounded, decorated (WWII: U.S.: Calif.)
D797.U7	Dead, wounded, decorated (WWII: U.S.: special)
D798-810	WORLD WAR II (SPECIAL TOPICS)
D798-799	PRESS, radio, censorship, propaganda & publicity (WWII: SEE ALSO D746.5 for posters, D753.3 for enemy propaganda in U.S., D810.P6-7 for propaganda elsewhere)
D798	News media (WWII: gen.)
D799.A-Z	Censorship, news media, etc. (WWII: by country)
D799.G3	News media, censorship, etc. (WWII: Ger.)
D799.G7	News media, censorship, etc. (WWII: G.B.)
D799.U6	News media, censorship, etc. (WWII: U.S.)
D800	Economic matters (WWII: commerce, mail, finance, monetary & fiscal planning, etc. in gen.: SEE ALSO HC, HF, HJ for specific places)
D801	Alien enemies (WWII) 940.5315, .53163
D801.A2	Alien enemies (WWII: gen.) 940.5315, .53163
D801.A3-Z	Alien enemies (WWII: by country)
D801.F8	Alien enemies (WWII: Fr.)
D802	OCCUPIED TERRITORIES (WWII: events, laws, etc.)
D802.A2	Occupied territories (WWII: gen.)
D802.A3-Z	Occupied territories (WWII: by country, area, etc.)
D802.A45	Alsace-Lorraine (WWII: occupied terr.)
D802.B3	Baltic States (WWII: occupied terr.)
D802.J3	Japanese territories (WWII)
D802.L3	Latvia (WWII: occupied terr.)
D802.M15	Macedonia (WWII: occupied terr.)
D802.M2	Malaya (WWII: occupied terr.)
D802.M25	Manchuria (WWII: occupied terr.)
D802.M3	Marshall Islands (WWII: occupied terr.)
D802.R8	Russia (WWII: occupied terr.)
D802.R95	Ruthenia (WWII: occupied terr.)
D802.S55	Sicily (WWII: occupied terr.)
D802.S67	Slovenia (WWII: occupied terr.)
D802.T7	Tripolitania (WWII: occupied terr.)

D803-805	CONCENTRATION CAMPS (WWII)
D803-804	ATROCITIES, war crimes, trials (WWII)
D803	War crimes, atrocities, concentration camps, trials (WWII: gen.)
D804.A-Z	Trials & concentration camps (WWII: atrocities, war crimes: by country accused)
D804.G3	Concentration camps (WWII: Ger.)
D804.G4	Atrocities, war crimes, trials (WWII: Ger.)
D804.G42	Nuremberg Trial of Major German War Criminals (1945-46)
D804.G425.A-Z	Trials (WWII: atrocities, war crimes: Germ.: post-Nuremberg before American Military Tribunals, 1946-49: by main defendant)
D804.G43.A-Z	Trials (WWII: atrocities, war crimes: Germ.: post-Nuremberg: misc. by defendant)
D804.J3	Trials (WWII: atrocities, war crimes: Jp.)
D804.J3	Concentration camps (WWII: Jpn.)
D804.J32	Tokyo Trials (1946-48)
D804.J33.A-Z	Trials (WWII: atrocities, war crimes: Jp. except Tokyo: by place or defendant)
D805	PRISONS & PRISONERS (WWII: inclu. internment, extermination, & concentration camps) 940.5472+
D805.A1	Periodicals & associations (WWII: prison)
D805.A2	Prisons & prisoners (WWII: gen.)
D805.A3-Z	Prisons & prisoners (WWII: by country)
D805.A3-Z.A1-19	Periodicals (WWII: by country)
D805.F8	French prisons & prisoners (WWII)
D805.G3	German prisons & prisoners (WWII)
D805.G7	British prisons & prisoners (WWII)
D805.R9	Russian prisons & prisoners (WWII: SEE ALSO D805.S65 for Soviet) 940.547247
D805.S65	Soviet prisons & prisoners (WWII: SEE ALSO D805.R9)
D806-807	MEDICAL SERVICES, HOSPITALS, RED CROSS (WWII)
D806	Hospitals, medical services, etc. (WWII: gen.) 940.5475
D807.A-Z	Red Cross & medical services (WWII: by country) 940.54764-69
D807.A8	Medical services & Red Cross (WWII: Australia)
D807.G7	Medical services & Red Cross (WWII: G.B.)
D807.H3	Medical services & Red Cross (WWII: Hawaiian Islands)
D807.U6	Medical services & Red Cross (WWII: U.S.: gen.) 940.547673
D807.U6-89	Medical services & Red Cross (WWII: U.S.)
D807.U62.A-W	United States medical services (WWII: by state)
D807.U62.C3	United States medical services (WWII: Calif.)
D807.U72.1st-	Army hospitals (WWII: U.S.: general: by #)
D807.U722.1st-	Army hospitals (WWII: U.S.: evacuation: by #)
D807.U73.1st-	Field hospitals (WWII: U.S.: by #)
D807.U74.A-Z	Hospital ships (WWII: U.S.: by name)
D807.U85.1st-	Navy base hospitals (WWII: U.S.: by #)
D807.U87.1st-	Navy mobile base hospitals (WWII: U.S.: by #)
D808-809	RELIEF WORK, REFUGEES, DISPLACED PERSONS, CHARITIES (WWII)
D808	Refugees, relief work, charities (WWII: gen.) 940.5477
D809.A-Z	Charities, refugees, relief work (WWII: by country) 940.54778+
D809.B4	Relief work, refugees, displaced persons, charities (WWII: Belgium)
D809.G7	Relief work, refugees, displaced persons, charities (WWII: G.B.)
D809.U5	Relief work, refugees, displaced persons, charities (WWII: U.S.: domestic & abroad)

D810.A-Z	WORLD WAR II (MISC. SPECIAL: SEE D769.8.A-Z for U.S.)
D810.A53	Aleuts (WWII)
D810.A6	Anarchism & anarchists (WWII)
D810.A65	Animals (WWII: inclu. use of dogs, horses, etc.)
D810.A7	Art (WWII)
D810.A75	Astrology (WWII)
D810.B3	Germ warfare (WWII: bacterial)
D810.B66	Bomb reconnaissance (WWII)
D810.B7	Boy Scouts (WWII)
D810.C2	Camouflage (WWII)
D810.C26	Cartography (WWII)
D810.C35	Chaplains (WWII: gen.) 940.5478
D810.C36.A-Z	Chaplains (WWII: by country)
D810.C36.U6	Chaplains (WWII: U.S.: SEE ALSO D769.375 & D769.59)
D810.C4	Children & orphans (WWII)
D810.C5-68	RELIGION (WWII: churches)
D810.C5	Churches (WWII: gen.)
D810.C53	Adventists (WWII)
D810.C56	Baptists (WWII)
D810.C6	Catholic Church (WWII)
D810.C62	Christian Scientists (WWII)
D810.C63	Church of the Brethren (WWII)
D810.C64	Evangelical and Reformed Church (WWII)
D810.C65	Quakers (WWII: Society of Friends)
D810.C66	Lutheran Church (WWII)
D810.C665	Mennonites (WWII)
D810.C67	Methodist Church (WWII)
D810.C674	Nihon Kirisuto Kyodan (WWII: churches)
D810.C6745	Eastern Orthodox Church (WWII)
D810.C68	Presbyterian Church (WWII)
D810.C69	Civil defense (WWII: SEE UA926-929 for more technical works)
D810.C7	Communications (WWII)
D810.C8	Confiscation (WWII)
D810.C82	Conscientious objectors (WWII)
D810.C83	Cossacks (WWII)
D810.C88	Cryptography (WWII)
D810.D4	Dead (WWII: treatment, cemeteries, etc.)
D810.D5	Deportation (WWII)
D810.D6	Destruction & pillage (WWII: SEE ALSO D785.U58-63 for U.S. Strategic Bombing Survey)
D810.E2-5	EDUCATION (WWII)
D810.E2	Education (WWII: gen.)
D810.E3-46	Education (WWII: U.S.)
D810.E3	Education (WWII: U.S.: gen.)
D810.E4.A-W	Education (WWII: U.S.: by state)
D810.E4.M8-81	Education (WWII: Missouri)
D810.E4.W6-61	Education (WWII: Wisconsin)
D810.E45.A-Z	College, school, etc. (WWII: U.S.: by name)
D810.E45.H38	Harvard Univ. (WWII)
D810.E46.A-Z	Fraternities (WWII: U.S. educ.: by name)
D810.E6	Elks, Benevolent...Order of (WWII)
D810.E8	Entertainment, recreation, hospitality (WWII: civilian services for military)
D810.F83	Fuel supplies (WWII)

```
D810.G57    Girl Scouts (WWII)
D810.G9     Gypsies (WWII)
D810.I5     Indians (WWII)
D810.J4     Jews & the Holocaust (WWII)
D810.L4     Lawyers (WWII)
D810.M6 or .M8  Moslems or Muslims (WWII)
D810.N2     Naturalized subjects (WWII: in belligerent countries: gen.)
D810.N3.A-Z Naturalized subjects (WWII: in belligerent countries: by place: SEE
               D753.8 for Japanese-Am's. in U.S., D769.8.A6 for alien
               enemies in the U.S.)
D810.N4     Blacks (WWII: Negroes)
D810.P4     Photography (WWII)
D810.P53    Pigeons (WWII)
D810.P6     Propaganda (WWII: gen.: SEE ALSO D798-799 for press)
D810.P7.A-Z Propaganda (WWII: by country)        940.54886-54889+
D810.P7.G3  Propaganda, German (WWII)
D810.P7.U6  United States propaganda (WWII)
D810.P75    Prophecies (WWII)
D810.P76    Protest movements (WWII)
D810.P8     Public opinion (WWII: gen.)
D810.P85.A-Z Public opinion (WWII: by country)
D810.P85.G7     British public opinion (WWII)
D810.R3     Race problems (WWII)
D810.R33    Radar, radio, etc. (WWII)
D810.R6     Rotary International (WWII)
D810.S2     Science & technology (WWII)
D810.S42    Search & rescue ops. (WWII: gen.)
D810.S45.A-Z Rescue & search ops. (WWII: by country)
D810.S46    Sex (WWII)
D810.S47    Shinto (WWII)
D810.S5     Slavs (WWII)
D810.S6     Socialism (WWII)
D810.S7-8   SECRET SERVICE, espionage, military intelligence (WWII: spies)
                                                940.5485-5487+
D810.S7     Espionage, secret service, intelligence (WWII: gen.: spies)
D810.S8.A-Z Spies (WWII: by name)
D810.S8.D55     Donovan, William, 1883-1959 (WWII: spy)
D810.S8.S85     Stephenson, William, Sir (WWII: spy)
D810.S8.T65     Trepper, Leopold (WWII: spy)
D810.T4     Temperance (WWII)
D810.T8     Transportation (WWII: inclu. merchant marine)
D810.V45    Veterinary service (WWII)
D810.W7     Women & women's work (WWII)
D810.Y7     Y.M.C.A., Y.W.C.A. (WWII)
D810.Y74    Youth (WWII)
D811        Personal accounts (WWII: SEE ALSO DA-F country #'s for biographies
               & memoirs)                       940.5481-5482+
D811.A2     Personal accounts (WWII: collections)
D811.A3-Z   Personal accounts (WWII: individual: by name)
D811.5.A-Z  Personal accounts (WWII: noncombatants: by name)
D812        Armistice (WWII: gen.)              940.5314, .532+
D813.A-Z    Armistice (WWII: by country)        940.5314, .532+
D813.F7     Armistice (WWII: Fr.)
D813.G3     Armistice (WWII: Germ.)
```

D814-821	Peace (WWII) 940.5314, .532+
D814	PRIMARY SOURCES, documents (WWII: PEACE: collections: gen.)
D814.1	Surrender documents (WWII: Ger.)
D814.2	Surrender documents (WWII: It.)
D814.3	Surrender documents (WWII: Jp.)
D814.4-47	Council of Foreign Ministers (WWII)
D814.4	Council of Foreign Ministers (WWII: gen.)
D814.413	MEETINGS (Cncl. For. Min.: London: 1945: 11 Sept.-2 Oct.)
D814.415	Meetings (Cncl. For. Min.: Moscow: 1945: 16-26 Dec.)
D814.42	Meetings (Cncl. For. Min.: Paris: 1946: Apr.)
D814.425	Meetings (Cncl. For. Min.: Paris: 1946: 15 June-July)
D814.43	Meetings (Cncl. For. Min.: New York: 1946: Nov.-Dec.)
D814.44	Meetings (Cncl. For. Min.: Moscow: 1947: 10 Mar.-24 Apr.)
D814.45	Meetings (Cncl. For. Min.: London: 1947: 25 Nov.-16 Dec.)
D814.46	Meetings (Cncl. For. Min.: Paris: 1949: 23 May-20 June)
D814.47	Meetings (Cncl. For. Min.: Berlin: 1954: 25Jan.-18 Feb.)
D814.55-9	TREATIES (WWII: with Axis powers)
D814.55	Treaties (WWII: Axis powers: collections)
D814.56	Peace conferences (WWII: gen.)
D814.565	Conferences (Paris: 29 July-15 Oct. 1946)
D814.6	Treaties (WWII: Allies-Ger.)
D814.7	Treaties (WWII: Allies-It.)
D814.8	Treaties (WWII: Allies-Japan)
D814.9.A-Z	Treaties (WWII: Allies-misc. Axis powers: by country)
D814.9.B9	Treaties (WWII: Allies-Bulg.)
D815	Peace (WWII: gen.)
D816	Peace (WWII: gen. spec.)
D816.5	Pamphlets, minor works (WWII: peace)
D818	Indemnity & reparations (WWII: gen.)
D819.A-Z	Reparations & indemnity (WWII: by country)
D819.G3	Reparations (WWII: Ger.)
D819.J3	Reparations (WWII: Jp.)
D820.A-Z	Peace (WWII: special topics)
D820.D5	Disarmament (WWII)
D820.P7	Nationalities (WWII: population transfers: gen.)
D820.P7-72	Population transfers (WWII)
D820.P72.A-Z	Population transfers (WWII: by nationality)
D820.P72.J	Population transfers (WWII: Jews)
D820.T4	TERRITORIAL QUESTIONS (post-WWII: gen.: SEE D821 for specific places)
D821.A-Z	Territorial questions (post-WWII: by place)
D821.L4	Levant (post-WWII territorial ?s)
D821.L5	Lithuania (post-WWII territorial ?s)
D821.P3	Palestine (post-WWII territorial ?s)
D821.R95	Ruthenia (post-WWII territorial ?s)
D821.T8	Transylvania (post-WWII territorial ?s)
D821.Y8	Yugoslavia (post-WWII territorial ?s: inclu. Trieste)

D824-829	RECONSTRUCTION (WWII)
D824	Primary sources, documents, collections (WWII: Reconstruction)
D825	Reconstruction (WWII: gen.) 940.53144
D826	Pamphlets, minor works (WWII: Reconstruction)
D827	United States (WWII: Reconstruction: gen.)
D828.A-W	United States (WWII: Reconstruction: by state)
D828.A8-81	Arkansas (WWII: Reconstruction)
D828.C6-61	Colorado (WWII: Reconstruction)
D828.N9-91	North Dakota (WWII: Reconstruction)
D828.T4-41	Texas (WWII: Reconstruction)
D828.V8-81	Washington, D.C. (WWII: Reconstruction: Virginia)
D829.A-Z	Reconstruction (WWII: outside U.S.: by country, nationality, etc.)
D829.A33	South Africa (WWII: Reconstruction)
D829.D8	Dutch East Indies (WWII: Reconstruction)
D829.E2	Far East (WWII: Reconstruction)
D829.J4	Jews (WWII: Reconstruction)
D829.L5	Lithuania (WWII: Reconstruction)
D829.P3	Palestine (WWII: Reconstruction)
D830-838	MONUMENTS, MEMORIALS, CELEBRATIONS (WWII: memorials dedicated to special divisions classed with them)
D830	Memorials, monuments, celebrations (WWII: gen.) 940.5465
D831	Memorials, monuments, celebrations (WWII: misc.)
D833-836	Memorials, monuments, celebrations (WWII: U.S.) 940.546573
D833	Celebrations, memorials, monuments (WWII: U.S.: gen.) 940.546573
D835.A-Z	Monuments, memorials, celebrations (WWII: U.S.: by state) 940.546574-54679+
D835.C2-21	Monuments, memorials, celebrations (WWII: U.S.: Calif.) 940.5465794
D835.D6	Monuments, memorials, celebrations (WWII: U.S.: District of Columbia)
D835.I3-31	Monuments, memorials, celebrations (WWII: U.S.: Ill.)
D835.N4-5	Monuments, memorials, celebrations (WWII: U.S.: N.Y.)
D836.A-Z	Monuments, memorials, celebrations (WWII: U.S.: by city)
D836.L62	Monuments, memorials, celebrations (WWII: U.S.: Los Angeles)
D836.N49	Monuments, memorials, celebrations (WWII: U.S.: New York City)
D838.A-Z	Monuments, memorials, celebrations (WWII: outside U.S.: by place)
D838.A8	Monuments, memorials, celebrations (WWII: Australia)
D838.F8	Monuments, memorials, celebrations (WWII: Fr.: gen.)
D838.F8.P3	Monuments, memorials, celebrations (WWII: Fr.: Paris)
D838.G3	Monuments, memorials, celebrations (WWII: Ger.)
D838.G6	Monuments, memorials, celebrations (WWII: G.B.: gen.)
D838.G7.A-Z	Memorials, monuments, celebrations (WWII: G.B.: local: by place)
D838.G7.L5	Monuments, memorials, celebrations (WWII: G.B.: London)
D838.N45	Monuments, memorials, celebrations (WWII: N.Z.)
D838.R9	Monuments, memorials, celebrations (WWII: Rus.)
D839-845+	HISTORY (1945-)
D839.5	Biography (1945-: collective)
D839.7.A-Z	Biography (1945-: individual by name: SEE ALSO DA-F country & era #s)
D840	Modern history (1945-) 909.824-825+
D843	Foreign relns. & politics (1945-)
D847	Soviet Bloc (1945-)
D921	Description & travel (Europe: 1901-1950) 914.045
D1051+	Europe (1945-) 940.55+

DA	GREAT BRITAIN 941-942
DA10-18	British Empire & colonies (SEE ALSO JV1000-1099 for other collective works & D-F for specific colonies)
DA11	Description & travel (Brit. Empire)
DA16	British Empire (gen.) 909.824+
DA20-690	England
DA25	Primary sources, documents (Eng.)
DA30	England (gen.) 941, 942
DA34	Dictionaries, chronologies, etc. (G.B.)
DA40	Politics (Eng.: gen.)
DA42	Politics (Eng.: modern)
DA45	Diplomacy (G.B.: gen.) 327.41+
DA47	Foreign relns. (G.B.-other countries) 327.410+
DA47.1	Foreign relns. (G.B.-Fr.) 327.41044
DA47.2	Foreign relns. (G.B.-Ger.) 327.41043
DA47.65	Foreign relns. (G.B.-Rus.) 327.41047
DA47.9.A-Z	Foreign relns. (G.B.-misc. countries: SEE E183.8 for U.S.)
DA50-69.3	Military history (G.B.)
DA50	British military history (gen.) 355.00941
DA52	Dictionaries, Military (G.B.)
DA54	Biography, Military (G.B.: collective)
DA69	Military history (G.B.: 20th. c.: gen.) 355.00941, .033041, .033241, .033541
DA69.3.A-Z	Biography, Military (G.B.: 20th c.: inclu. memoirs) 355.3310922-24
DA69.3.A1	Biography, Military (G.B.: 20th c.: collective)
DA69.3.A57	Alexander, Harold Rupert (G.B.: 20th c. mil. biog.)
DA69.3.M56	Montgomery, Bernard Law Montgomery, 1st Viscount (G.B.: 20th c. mil. biog.)
DA69.3.W37	Wavell, Archibald Percival Wavell, 1st Earl of (G.B.: 20th c. mil. biog.)
DA70-89	Naval history (G.B.)
DA70	British naval history (gen.) 359.00941
DA72	Dictionaries, Naval (G.B.)
DA74	Biography, Naval (G.B.: collective)
DA89	Naval history (G.B.: 20th c.) 359.00941, .4741
DA89.1.A-Z	Biography, Naval (G.B.: 20th c.: by name)
DA89.1.A1	Biography, Naval (G.B.: 20th c.: collective)
DA89.5-6	Air force history (G.B.)
DA89.5	British air force history (gen.) 358.400941
DA89.6.A-Z	Biography, Air force (G.B.: inclu. memoirs)
DA89.6.A1	Biography, Air force (G.B.: collective)
DA89.6.J6	Joubert de la Ferté, Philip Bennet, Sir (G.B.: air force biog.)
DA300	England (1485-)
DA470	England (1702-)

DA566-566.9   England (20th c.: misc. overall)
DA566   Great Britain (20th c.: gen.)   941.082
DA566.4   Civilization, customs, social life (G.B.: 20th c.)
DA566.5   Military & naval history (G.B.: 20th c.)
DA566.7   Foreign relns. & politics (G.B.: 20th c.)
DA566.8   Satire, caricature (G.B.: 20th c.)
DA566.9.A-Z   Biography (G.B.: 20th c.: inclu. memoirs)   941.0820922-24
DA566.9.A1   Biography (G.B.: 20th c.: collective)
DA566.9.B15   Baldwin, Stanley, 1st Earl (G.B.: 20th c.)
DA566.9.B2   Balfour, Arthur James Balfour, 1st Earl of (G.B.: 20th c.)
DA566.9.B37   Beaverbrook, William Maxwell Aitken, Baron (G.B.: 20th c.)
DA566.9.B5   Birkenhead, Frederick E. S., 1st Earl of (G.B.: 20th c.)
DA566.9.C43   Chamberlain, Austen, Sir (G.B.: 20th c.)
DA566.9.C5   Churchill, Winston Leonard Spencer, Sir (G.B.: 20th c.)
DA566.9.E28   Eden, Anthony (G.B.: 20th c.)
DA566.9.G8   Grey, Edward (G.B.: 20th c.)
DA566.9.L5   Lloyd George, David (G.B.: 20th c.)
DA566.9.M25   MacDonald, James Ramsay (G.B.: 20th c.)
DA566.9.N7   Northcliffe, Alfred C. W. Harmsworth, 1st Viscount (G.B.: 20th c.)
DA566.9.O7   Oxford and Asquith, Herbert Henry Asquith, 1st Earl of (G.B.:
                   20th c.)
DA567-570   England (1901-10: King Edward VII)   941.082
DA570   Great Britain (1901-10: gen.)
DA573-578   England (1910-36: King George V)   941.083
DA573   George V (G.B.: King: 1910-36)
DA574.A-Z   Biography (G.B.: 1910-36: inclu. memoirs)
DA574.A1   Biography (G.B.: 1910-36: collective)
DA574.A2-45   Biography (G.B.: 1910-36: various royalty)
DA574.A8   Astor, Nancy W. Langhorne, Viscountess (G.B.: 1910-36 era)
DA574.M6   Mosley, Oswald, Sir, Baronet (G.B.: 1910-36 biog.)
DA576   Great Britain (1910-36)
DA577   Great Britain (1914-19: WWI era)
DA578   Great Britain (1920-39)
DA580-583   England (1936: King Edward VIII)   941.084
DA580   Edward VIII (G.B.: King: 1936)
DA583   Great Britain (1936)
DA584-589   England (1937-52: King George VI)   941.084
DA584   George VI (G.B.: King: 1937-52)
DA585.A-Z   Biography (G.B.: 1937-52: inclu. memoirs)
DA585.A1   Biography (G.B.: 1937-52: collective)
DA585.A2   Elizabeth (G.B.:1937-52 royal biog.: Consort of George VI)
DA585.A5.A-Z   Biography (G.B.: 1937-52: misc. royalty)
DA586   Great Britain (1937-52)
DA587   Great Britain (1939-45: WWII era)
DA630   Description & travel (G.B.: 1901-45)   914.1-2, 914.10482
DA650   Guidebooks (G.B.)

DA670.A-Z	Local history (G.B.: counties, regions, etc.: by name)	942+
DA670.C4	Channel Islands (G.B.) 942.34	
DA675-689	Local history (London, Eng.) 942.1	
DA677	London, Eng. (gen.) 942.1	
DA679	Guidebooks (London, Eng.) 914.21	
DA684	London, Eng. (1901-50) 942.1082	
DA685.A-Z	London, Eng. (boroughs, streets, etc.)	
DA686-687	Buildings (London, Eng.)	
DA687.A-Z	Buildings (London, Eng.: by name)	
DA687.D7	Downing St. (London, Eng.: No. 10)	
DA688	Social life, culture, customs (London, Eng.)	
DA689.A-Z	Scenic places (London, Eng.: bridges, parks, etc.)	
DA689.B8	Bridges (London, Eng.: inclu. London Bridge)	
DA689.M7	Monuments, statues, memorials (London, Eng.)	
DA689.P17	Palaces (London, Eng.)	
DA689.P6	Port of London (Eng.)	
DA690.A-Z	Local history (Eng.: towns besides London) 942.2+	
DA690.C75	Coventry, Eng.	
DA722	WALES (19th & 20th c.) 942.908+	
DA821	SCOTLAND (20th c.) 941.1082	
DA880.A-Z	Local history (Scotland: counties, regions, etc.)	
DA880.O5-6	Orkney Islands (Scot.)	
DA880.S5	Shetland Islands (Scot.)	
DA959	IRELAND (20th c.) 941.5082	
DA962	Ireland (1914-21)	
DA963	Ireland (1922-: Irish Free State, Eire, etc.)	
DA964.A-Z	Diplomacy (Ire.: 20th c.)	
DA964.A2	Foreign relns. (Ire.: 20th c.: gen.)	
DA964.G3	Foreign relns. (Ire.-Ger.: 20th c.)	
DA964.G7	Foreign relns. (Ire.-G.B.: 20th c.)	
DB	AUSTRIA, HUNGARY, CZECHOSLOVAKIA	943.6-9
DB1-860	AUSTRIA 943.6	
DB17	Austria & Austro-Hungarian Empire (gen.)	
DB26	Description & travel (Austria: 1901-45)	
DB38	Austria (1801-) 943.604	
DB46-49	Politics & diplomacy (Austria)	
DB48	Austrian question (20th c.)	
DB49.A-Z	Foreign relns. (Austria: by other country)	
DB86.7	Austria (1914-18: WWI era)	
DB91	Austria (20th c.: gen.)	
DB91-99+	Austria (20th c.) 943.605	
DB96	Austria (1918-: Republic) 943.6051	
DB98.A-Z	Biography (Austria: 20th c.: by name: inclu. memoirs)	
DB98.D6	Dollfuss, Englebert (Austria)	
DB98.S3	Schuschnigg, Kurt (Austria)	
DB99	Austria (1938-1945: Ger. annex.) 943.6052	

DB191-217	CZECHOSLOVAKIA (PREFER DB2000-3150 for titles cataloged after 1979)	943.7
DB215	Czechoslovakia (20th c.)	943.7024-703+
DB215.3	Czechoslovakia (1939-1945: Ger. occup.)	943.703
DB250	Bosnia & Bosnia-Herzegovina (20th c.)	
DB280	Bukowina (20th c.)	
DB379	Slavonia & Croatia (1918-)	
DB420	Dalmatia (20th c.)	
DB500	Galicia (20th c.)	
DB540	Herzegovina (20th c.)	
DB540.5	Liechtenstein (SEE ALSO DB881-898 for newer books)	
DB660	Silesia (20th c.)	
DB679-679.3	Slovakia (1918-45: PREFER DB2000+)	
DB780	Tyrol & Vorarlberg (20th c.)	
DB847	Vienna, Austria (gen. hist. & descr.)	
DB855	Vienna (20th c.)	
DB861-975+	HUNGARY, Liechtenstein	
DB872	Budapest (20th c.)	
DB881-898	LIECHTENSTEIN (SEE ALSO DB540.5 for older titles)	
DB886, 891	Liechtenstein (gen. hist. & descr.)	
DB893	Diplomacy (Liech.: gen.)	
DB894.A-Z	Foreign relns. (Liech.: by country)	
DB894.G3	Foreign relns. (Liech.-Ger.)	
DB906	HUNGARY (gen.)	943.9
DB925	Hungary (gen.: pubn. dates 1801+)	
DB926	Diplomacy (Hung.: gen.)	
DB926.3.A-Z	Foreign relns. (Hung.-other lands)	
DB926.3.G3	Foreign relns. (Hung.-Ger.)	
DB926.3.S65	Foreign relns. (Hung.-Sov. Un.)	
DB947-957+	Hungary (20th c.)	943.9043+
DB947	Hungary (20th c.: gen.)	
DB950.A-Z	Biography (Hung.: 20th c.: by name, inclu. memoirs)	
DB950.H6	Horthy, Miklós (Hung.: 20th c.)	
DB953	Hungary (1914-1918: WWI era)	943.9043
DB955	Hungary (1918-1945)	943.9051-2
DB2000-3150+	CZECHOSLOVAKIA (inclu. Bohemia, Moravia, Slovakia: SEE ALSO DB191-217 for earlier titles)	
DB2000-2299	Czechoslovakia	943.7+
DB2011	Czechoslovakia (gen.)	
DB2020	Description & travel (Czech.: 1901-45)	
DB2062	Czechoslovakia (1801-1976 pubns.)	
DB2078.A-Z	Foreign relns. (Czech.: by country)	
DB2185-2232+	Czechoslovakia (1918-)	
DB2185	Primary sources, documents (Czech.: 1918-)	
DB2186	Czechoslovakia (1918-: gen.)	
DB2189	Foreign relns. (Czech.: 1918-: gen.)	
DB2191.A-Z	Biography (Czech.: 1918-)	
DB2191.B45	Benes, Edward (Czech.: era of 1918-)	
DB2191.M37	Masaryk, Jan (Czech.: era of 1918-)	
DB2191.M38	Masaryk, Tomas G. (Czech.: era of 1918-)	
DB2195-2202	Czechoslovakia (1918-39)	943.703
DB2196	Czechoslovakia (1918-39: gen.)	
DB2199	Foreign relns. (Czech: 1918-39)	
DB2200-2201.A-Z	Biography (Czech.: 1918-39)	
DB2202	Munich Four-power Agreement	

DB2205-2211	Czechoslovakia (1939-45: Ger. occup.)	943.703
DB2206	Czechoslovakia (1939-45: Ger. occup.: gen.)	
DB2208.7	Politics (Czech.: 1939-45)	
DB2209	Foreign relns. (Czech.: 1939-45)	
DB2211.A-Z	Biography (Czech.: 1939-45: inclu. memoirs)	
DB2211.H33	Hácha, Emil (Czech.: 1939-45 period)	
DB2415-2421	Moravia (20th c.)	
DB2416	Moravia (20th c.: gen.)	
DB2629	Prague, Cz. (20th c.)	
DB2795-2822+	Slovakia (1800-1945)	
DB2805-2822+	Slovakia (1918-: in Czech Republic)	
DB2806	Slovakia (1918-)	
DB2809	Foreign relns. (Slovakia: 1918-)	
DB2813	Slovakia (1918-39)	
DB2815-2822	Slovakia (1939-45)	
DB2816	Slovakia (1939-45: gen.)	
DB2819	Foreign relns. (Slovakia: 1939-45)	
DB2821.A-Z	Biography (Czech.: 1939-45: by name)	
DB2821.T57	Tiso, Jozef (Czech.: 1939-45 era)	
DB2822	Slovakia (1944: uprising)	
DB2826	Slovakia (1945-68)	
DC	FRANCE 944	
DC3	Primary sources, documents (Fr.)	
DC17	France (gen. hist., culture)	
DC28	Description & travel (Fr.: 1871-1945)	
DC33.7	Civilization, customs, social life (Fr.: 1901-)	
DC38	France (gen. hist.: pubn. 1815-)	
DC44-47	Military history (Fr.)	
DC45	French military history (gen.)	355.00944, .033044
DC47	Military history (Fr.: 19th-20th c.)	
DC49-53	Naval history (Fr.)	
DC50	French naval history (gen.)	
DC53	Naval history (Fr.: 19th-20th c.)	
DC55-59	Politics & diplomacy (Fr.)	
DC55	Diplomacy (Fr.: gen.)	
DC58	Foreign relns. (Fr.: 19th-20th c.)	
DC59.8.A-Z	Foreign relns. (Fr.: by country)	327.440+
DC59.8.G3	Foreign relns. (Fr.-Ger.)	327.44043
DC59.8.G7	Foreign relns. (Fr.-G.B.)	327.44041
DC59.8.R9	Foreign relns. (Fr.-Rus.)	
DC59.8.S65	Foreign relns. (Fr.-Sov.Un.)	
DC110	France (1515-)	
DC334-354+	France (1871-1940: 3rd Repub.)	
DC334	Primary sources, documents (Fr.: 1871-1940)	
DC335	Third Republic (Fr.: 1871-1940)	
DC339	Military history (Fr.: 1871-1940)	
DC342	Biography (Fr.: 1871-1940: collective)	
DC342.8.A-Z	Biography (Fr.: 1871-1940: by name: inclu. memoirs & autobiog.)	
DC342.8.J6	Joffre, Joseph J. (Fr.: 1871-1940 era)	
DC342.8.P4	Pétain, Henri Philippe (Fr.: 1871-1940 era)	

DC361-373	France (20th c.: overall)
DC361	France (20th c.: gen.)　　944.081
DC365	Civilization, customs, social life (Fr.: 20th c.)
DC367	Military history (Fr.: 20th c.)
DC368	Naval history (Fr.: 20th c.)
DC369	Foreign relns. & politics (Fr.: 20th c.)　　944.08
DC371	Biography (Fr.: 20th c.: collective)
DC373.A-Z	Biography (Fr.: 20th c.: by name)
DC373.B5	Blum, Léon (Fr.: 20th c.)
DC373.B7	Briand, Aristide (Fr.: 20th c.)
DC373.D3	Daladier, Édouard (Fr.: 20th c.)
DC373.G3	De Gaulle, Charles (Fr.: 20th c.)
DC373.L33	Lattre de Tassigny, Jean Joseph (Fr.: 20th c.)
DC373.L35	Laval, Pierre (Fr.: 20th c.)
DC373.M3	Maurras, Charles M. (Fr.: 20th c.)
DC373.R45	Reynaud, Paul (Fr.: 20th c.)
DC387	France (1914-18: WWI era)　　944.0814
DC389-396	France (1919-40: Reconstruc.)
DC389	Reconstruction (Fr.: 1919-40)　　944.0815
DC394	France (1924-31: Gaston Doumergue)
DC396	France (1932-40: Albert F. Lebrun)
DC397	France (1939-45: WWII period: inclu. Pétain collab.)　　944.0816
DC601-609+	Local history (Fr.: north, east, Riviera, etc.)
DC611.A-Z	Local history (Fr.: regions, prov.'s, depts., etc.: by name)
DC611.B841-915	Brittany (Fr.)
DC611.C8-839	CORSICA (Fr.)
DC611.N841-899	Normandy (Fr.)
DC611.N899	Normandy (Fr.: 20th c.)
DC611.P981-992	PYRENEES (Fr.)
DC701-790+	Local history (Paris, Fr.)　　944.36
DC707	Description & travel (Paris, Fr.: ALSO gen. hist.)
DC708	Guidebooks (Paris, Fr.)
DC715	Social life, culture, customs (Paris, Fr.)
DC736	Paris, Fr. (1914-21)
DC737+	Paris, Fr. (1922-)　　944.360816
DC801.A-Z	Local history (Fr.: towns besides Paris)
DC801.B83	Brest, Fr.
DC801.C11	Caen, Fr.
DC801.D56	Dieppe, Fr.
DC801.L96-988	Lyons, Fr.
DC801.M34-38	Marseilles, Fr.
DC801.V45	Verdun, Fr.
DC801.V55-57	Versailles, Fr. (ALSO Trianon)
DC890	Colonies, French (PREFER D-F for individual colonies or JV1800-1899 for collective works)
DC928	ANDORRA (modern hist.)
DC945	MONACO
DC989	Nice, Fr. (1860-)

DD	GERMANY & Prussia	943	
DD16	Guidebooks (Ger.)		
DD17	Germany (gen. hist., culture, etc.)		
DD42	Description & travel (Ger.: 1919-45)	914.3009042	
DD67	Civilization, customs, social life (Ger.)		
DD68	German culture (in other lands: gen.)		
DD74	Races & ethnography (Ger.)		
DD76	National characteristics (Ger.)		
DD89	Germany (gen.: pubn. 1801-)		
DD99-105	Military history (Ger.)		
DD100.A2	Biography, Military (Ger.: collective: gen.)		
DD100.A3-Z	Biography, Military (Ger.: collective: officers)		
DD101	German military history (gen.)	355.00943	
DD104	Military history (Ger.: 20th c.)	355.00943, .033043, .033242, .033543	
DD106	Naval history (Ger.)	359.00943, .4743	
DD110-120	Politics & diplomacy (Ger.)		
DD110	Primary sources, documents (Ger.: for. relns. & politics)		
DD112	Diplomacy & politics (Ger.: gen.)	320.943, 327.43+	
DD117	Foreign relns. (Ger.: 19th-20th c.)	327.43+	
DD119.3	Germans (in other lands: gen.)		
DD119.5	Propaganda, German		
DD120.A-Z	Foreign relns. (Ger.: by country)	327.430+	
DD120.F8	Foreign relns. (Ger.-Fr.)	327.43044	
DD120.G7	Foreign relns. (Ger.-G.B.)	327.43041	
DD120.I6	Foreign relns. (Ger.-Ire.)		
DD120.I8	Foreign relns. (Ger.-It.)		
DD120.J3	Foreign relns. (Ger.-Japan)	327.43052	
DD120.R9	Foreign relns. (Ger.-Rus.)	327.43047	
DD120.S65	Foreign relns. (Ger.-Sov. Un.)		
DD120.U6-7	Foreign relns. (Ger.-U.S.)		
DD175	Germany (1519-)		
DD228-231	Germany (1888-1918: Kaiser Wilhelm II era)	943.084	
DD228.6	Diplomacy (Ger.: 1888-1918: gen.)	327.43+	
DD228.7.A-Z	Foreign relns. (Ger.:1888-1918: by country)		
DD228.8	Germany (1914-1918: WWI period)	943.08	
DD231.A-Z	Biography (Ger.: 1888-1918+: by name)		
DD231.H5	Hindenburg, Paul von (Ger.: 1888-1918+ period)		
DD232	Germany (20th c.: gen.)		
DD233-251+	Germany (1918-: revolution & Republic)	943.085	
DD233	Periodicals & associations (Ger.: 1918-)		
DD234	Primary sources, documents (Ger.: 1918-)		
DD237	Germany (1918-: revolution & Republic: gen.)		
DD239	Civilization, customs, social life (Ger.: 1918-)		
DD240-241	Diplomacy & politics (Ger.: 1918-)		
DD240	Politics & diplomacy (Ger.: 1918-)		
DD241.A-Z	Foreign relns. (Ger.: 1918-: by country)		
DD241.A5	Foreign relns. (Ger.-Albania: 1918-)		
DD241.A7	Foreign relns. (Ger.-Argen.: 1918-)		
DD241.A9	Foreign relns. (Ger.-Austria: 1918-)		
DD241.B4	Foreign relns. (Ger.-Bel.: 1918-)		
DD241.B7	Foreign relns. (Ger.-Brazil: 1918-)		
DD241.B8	Foreign relns. (Ger.-Bulg.: 1918-)		
DD241.C2-29	Foreign relns. (Ger.-Can.: 1918-)		
DD241.C95	Foreign relns. (Ger.-Czech.: 1918-)		
DD241.D3	Foreign relns. (Ger.-Den.: 1918-)		

DD241.E3   Foreign relns. (Ger.-Egypt: 1918-)
DD241.F5   Foreign relns. (Ger.-Fin.: 1918-)
DD241.F8   Foreign relns. (Ger.-Fr.: 1918-)
DD241.G7   Foreign relns. (Ger.-G.B.: 1918-)
DD241.G8   Foreign relns. (Ger.-Greece: 1918-)
DD241.H9   Foreign relns. (Ger.-Hung.: 1918-)
DD241.I4   Foreign relns. (Ger.-India: 1918-)
DD241.I6   Foreign relns. (Ger.-Ire.: 1918-)
DD241.I8   Foreign relns. (Ger.-It.: 1918-)
DD241.J3   Foreign relns. (Ger.-Japan: 1918-)
DD241.N4   Foreign relns. (Ger.-Neth.: 1918-)
DD241.N8   Foreign relns. (Ger.-Nor.: 1918-)
DD241.P7   Foreign relns. (Ger.-Pol.: 1918-)
DD241.P8   Foreign relns. (Ger.-Port.: 1918-)
DD241.R8   Foreign relns. (Ger.-Rum.: 1918-)
DD241.R9   Foreign relns. (Ger.-Rus.: 1918-)
DD241.S7   Foreign relns. (Ger.-Sp.: 1918-)
DD241.S8   Foreign relns. (Ger.-Swe.: 1918-)
DD241.S9   Foreign relns. (Ger.-Swit.: 1918-)
DD241.S95   Foreign relns. (Ger.-Syria: 1918-)
DD241.T8   Foreign relns. (Ger.-Tur.: 1918-)
DD241.U6-69+   Foreign relns. (Ger.-U.S.: 1918-)
DD241.U7+   Foreign relns. (Ger.-Uruguay: 1918-)
DD241.Y8   Foreign relns. (Ger.-Yug.: 1918-)
DD243   Biography (Ger.: 1918-48: group)
DD244   Public figures (Ger.: 1918-48: men)
DD245   Women (Ger.: 1918-48)
DD247.A-Z   Biography (Ger.: 1918-48: inclu. memoirs: by name)
DD247.B7   Brüning, Heinrich (Ger.: 1918-48 era)
DD247.E2   Ebert, Friedrich (Ger.: 1918-48 era)
DD247.G6   Goebbels, Joseph (Ger.: 1918-48 era)
DD247.G67   Göring, Hermann (Ger.: 1918-48 era)
DD247.H37   Hess, Rudolf (Ger.: 1918-48 era)
DD247.H5   Hitler, Adolf (Ger.: 1918-48 era)
DD247.P5   Papen, Franz von (Ger.: 1918-48 era)
DD247.R47   Ribbentrop, Joachim von (Ger.: 1918-48 era)
DD247.R58   Rosenberg, Alfred (Ger.: 1918-48 era)
DD247.S335   Schacht, Hjalmar Horace Greeley (Ger.: 1918-48 era)
DD247.S6-7   Speer, Albert (Ger.: 1918-48 era)
DD247.S8   Strasser, Otto (Ger.: 1918-48 era)
DD248   Germany (1918: Revolution)
DD249   Germany (1919-25: Ebert period)
DD251   Germany (1925-34: Hindenburg era)   943.085
DD252-256   Germany (1930-45, 1933-45: eras of Hitler & National Socialism)
                                                                            943.086
DD253   Third Reich (Ger.: 1930+-45: contemporary works)
DD253.A1   Periodicals, associations, collections (Ger.: 1930-45)
DD253.1st-   SS (Nazi Party: Ger.: by local #)

DD253.2-8   Nazi Party (Ger.: 1930-45)   329.43, 324.243+, 943.086
DD253.2   Periodicals & documents (Ger.: Nazi Party)
DD253.25   Nationalsozialistische Deutsche Arbeiter-Partei (Ger.: 1930-45: gen.)
DD253.27   Meetings (Nazi Party: Ger.: gen.)
DD253.28.Date   Nazi Party meetings (Ger.: specific by date)
DD253.28.1923   Meetings (Nazi Party: Ger.: 1923)
DD253.28.1926   Meetings (Nazi Party: Ger.: 1926)
DD253.28.1927   Meetings (Nazi Party: Ger.: 1927)
DD253.28.1929   Meetings (Nazi Party: Ger.: 1929)
DD253.28.1933-38   Meetings (Nazi Party: Ger.: 1933-38)
DD253.29-3   Nazi Party (Ger.: admin. offices)
DD253.39-45 Nazi Party (Ger.: geog. divisions)
DD253.46-73 Nazi Party (Ger.: branches or gliederungen)
DD253.49   Deutsches Jungvolk (Nazi Party)
DD253.5   Hitler Youth (Hitlerjugend)
DD253.58   Nationalsozialistische Frauenschaft
DD253.6-65   SS (Nazi Party: Ger.)
DD253.6   Schutzstaffel (SS: Nazi Party: gen.)
DD253.62.A-Z   SS (Nazi Party: by Ger. locality)
DD254   German propaganda (1933-45: in other countries: gen.)
DD255.A-Z   Propaganda, German (1933-45: by place)
DD255.F8   Propaganda, German (1933-45: France)
DD255.G7   Propaganda, German (1933-45: Gt. Brit.)
DD255.R9   Propaganda, German (1933-45: Rus.: SEE ALSO DK272.7.G3)
DD255.U6-7   Propaganda, German (1933-45: United States)
DD256   Germany (1939-45: WWII period)
DD256.3   Resistance (Ger. vs. Nazis)
DD256.5   Germany (1930-45: postwar titles)
DD257   Germany (1945-: Allied occupation)
DD257.25   Germany (1945-: Reunification ?)
DD448   Prussia (1871-1918: gen.)
DD452-454   Prussia (1918-45)
DD452   Prussia (1918-45: gen.)
DD453   Prussia (1918-33)
DD454   Prussia (1933-45)
DD491.A-Z   Local history (Prus.: provinces, regions, etc.)
DD491.R4-52   Rhine Province (Prus.)
DD491.S3-39   Saxony (Prus.)
DD491.W4-52   Westphalia (Prus.)
DD701-800   Local history (Ger.: large areas)
DD791-800   German Austria & Bavaria
DD801.A-Z   Local history (Ger.: provinces, regions, states, etc.)
DD801.A31-69   Alsace-Lorraine (Ger.)
DD801.B31-55   Bavaria   943.3
DD801.B422   Bavaria (1939-45)
DD801.R7-76   Rhine River (Ger.)   943.4
DD851-900   Berlin, Ger.
DD859   Guidebooks (Berlin, Ger.)
DD860   Berlin, Ger. (gen.)   943.155
DD866   Social life, culture, customs (Berlin, Ger.)
DD879   Berlin, Ger. (1914-21)
DD880   Berlin, Ger. (1922-45)   943.155086
DD883   Berlin, Ger. (districts, sections)
DD887   Streets, bridges, etc. (Berlin, Ger.)
DD896   Buildings, Public (Berlin, Ger.)

DD901.A-Z	Local history (Ger.: areas, towns except Berlin)
DD901.A25-28	Aachen, Ger. (Aix-la-Chapelle)
DD901.B4	Bayreuth, Ger.
DD901.B443	Berchtesgaden, Ger.
DD901.B65	Brandenburg, Ger.
DD901.B71-79	Bremen, Ger.
DD901.D2-29	Danzig
DD901.D28	Danzig (19th-20th c.)
DD901.D71-79	Dresden, Ger.
DD901.D95	Düsseldorf, Ger.
DD901.E75	Essen, Ger.
DD901.F71-79	Frankfurt, Ger.
DD901.H55-59	Heidelberg, Ger.
DD901.M71-95	Munich, Ger.
DD901.M77	Munich, Ger. (gen.)
DD901.M9	Munich, Ger. (1871-1950)
DD901.N91-97	Nuremberg, Ger.
DD901.S81-89	Strassburg, Ger.
DD901.S95-97	Stuttgart, Ger.
DD905	Colonies, German (PREFER D-F #s for specific colonies or JV2000-2099 for collective titles)

DF	Greece	949.5
DF701-951+	GREECE (Modern)	
DF751	Greece (gen.)	949.5
DF765	Military history (Greece)	
DF775	Naval history (Greece)	
DF785	Diplomacy (Greece: gen.)	
DF787.A-Z	Foreign relns. (Greece: by country)	
DF787.G3	Foreign relns. (Greece-Ger.)	
DF787.G7	Foreign relns. (Greece-G.B.)	
DF787.I8	Foreign relns. (Greece-It.)	
DF833	Greece (20th c.: gen.)	949.507
DF836.A-Z	Biography (Greece: 20th c.)	
DF838	Greece (1914-18: WWI)	949.506
DF848	Greece (1924-35: Republic)	
DF849	Greece (1935-47: George II era)	949.5074
DF901.A-Z	Local history (Greece: regions, islands, provinces, etc.)	
DF901.C78-89	Crete	
DF915-936	Athens, Gr.	
DF925	Athens, Gr. (1910-)	

DG	ITALY, Sicily, Sardinia, Malta	945
DG48-84	Military history (It.)	
DG401-579	Italy (476-)	
DG403	Primary sources, documents (It.)	
DG417	Italy (gen. hist., culture, etc.)	
DG429	Description & travel (It.: 1919-44)	
DG450	Civilization, customs, social life (It.: 1816-1945)	
DG467	Italy (gen.: titles dated after 1800)	
DG481	Biography, Military (It.: collective)	
DG482	Italian military history (gen.)	355.00945
DG484	Military history (It.: 1792-20th c.)	
DG486	Naval history (It.: gen.)	359.00945

DG491-499	Diplomacy & politics (It.)	
DG491	Politics & diplomacy (It.: gen.)	320.945, 327.45+
DG498	Foreign relns. (It.: 1861-1945)	
DG499.A-Z	Foreign relns. (It.: by country)	327.450+
DG499.A5	Foreign relns. (It.-Alb.)	
DG499.E7	Foreign relns. (It.-Eth.)	
DG499.F8	Foreign relns. (It.-Fr.)	
DG499.G3	Foreign relns. (It.-Ger.)	
DG499.G7	Foreign relns. (It.-G.B.)	
DG499.J3	Foreign relns. (It.-Japan)	
DG499.R9	Foreign relns. (It.-Rus.)	
DG499.S65	Foreign relns. (It.-Sov.Un.)	
DG499.S9	Foreign relns. (It.-Swit.)	
DG499.U6-7	Foreign relns. (It.-U.S.)	
DG499.Y8	Foreign relns. (It.-Yug.)	
DG555-575	Italy (1871-1947: United Italy: Monarchy)	
DG555	Italy (1871-1947: gen.)	945.09
DG556.A-Z	Biography (It.: 1871-1941)	
DG556.S6	Spaventa, Silvio (It.: 1871-1945 era)	
DG566-575	Italy (1900-46: times of Vittorio Emanuele III, Umberto II)	
DG566	Vittorio Emanuele III (It.: King, 1900-46: gen. inclu. times)	
DG570	Italy (1914-18: WWI)	945.0814
DG571	Italy (1919-45: Fascism)	945.0815-0816
DG571.A1	Periodicals, associations, yearbooks (It.: 1919-45)	
DG572	Italy (1939-45: WWII era)	945.0816
DG574	Biography (It.: 1871-1947: collec.)	
DG575.A-Z	Biography (It.: 1900-46: by name, inclu. memoirs)	
DG575.B2	Badoglio, Pietro (It.: 1900-46 period)	
DG575.B3	Balbo, Italo (It. 1900-46 period)	
DG575.C51	Ciano, Galeazzo, Conte (It.: 1900-46 period)	
DG575.M8	Mussolini, Benito (It.: 1900-46 period)	
DG575.N5	Nitti, Francesco (It. 1900-46 period)	
DG600-980	Local history (It.: large areas, cities)	
DG651-662	Lombardy & Milan, It.	
DG660-662	Milan, It.	
DG670-679	Venice, It. (city state & modern)	
DG731-760	Tuscany & Florence, It.	
DG760	Florence, It.	
DG791-800+	PAPAL STATES	
DG796	Papal States (modern)	
DG799	Holy SEE (1870-)	
DG800	Vatican City (1929-)	
DG803-818	Rome, It. (modern era)	
DG806	Description (Rome, It.: 1861-1950)	
DG808	Rome, It. (476-: gen.)	
DG812	Rome, It. (1527-)	
DG813	Rome, It. (1871-)	
DG840-855	Naples, It. (kingdom & later)	

```
DG869          SICILY (20th c.)
DG869.2        Sicily (1900-45)
DG975.A-Z          Local history (It.: non-metro. towns, provinces, etc.)
DG975.S2           San Marino (Republic)
DG975.S29-33   SARDINIA
DG987-999          MALTA & Maltese Islands
DG990          Malta (gen.)
DG990.5        Military history (Malta)
DG990.7            Naval history (Malta)
DG991-991.6        Foreign relns. & politics (Malta)
DG992.7        Malta (1798-1964: Brit. era)
DG993          Malta (1802-1947)
DG994          Malta (20th c.)


DH-DJ          Low Countries
DH39           Description & travel (Bel. & Holl.: 1901-50)
DH401-925          Belgium & Luxembourg
DH418-811+         BELGIUM         949.3
DH433              Description & travel (Bel.: 1831-1945)
DH540          Military history (Bel.: gen.)
DH545          Military history (Bel.: 1815-)
DH566          Diplomacy & politics (Bel.: gen.)
DH569.A-Z          Foreign relns. (Bel.: by country)
DH569.F8           Foreign relns. (Bel.-Fr.)
DH569.G3           Foreign relns. (Bel.-Ger.)
DH677          Belgium (20th c.)              949.304
DH681          Belgium (1909-34: King Albert)        949.3041
DH682          Belgium (1914-18: WWI)
DH683          Belgium (1920-)
DH685.A-Z      Biography (Bel.: 1909-34)
DH687          Belgium (1934-51: reign of Leopold III)      949.3042
DH689.A-Z      Biography (Bel.: 1934-51)
DH801.A-Z      Local history (Bel.: provinces, regions, etc.)
DH801.A6-69        Antwerp area (Bel.)
DH801.F4-49        Flanders area (Bel.)
DH801.N2-29        Namur area (Bel.)
DH801.S6           Soignes Forest (Bel.)
DH802-809      Brussels, Bel.
DH807.5        Brussels, Bel. (20th c.)
DH811.A-Z          Local history (Bel.: towns except Brussels)
DH811.A55-68       Antwerp, Bel.
DH811.L5           Li`ege, Bel.
DH901-925      LUXEMBURG
DH905          Luxemburg (gen. hist., culture, etc.)
DH906          Description & travel (Lux.: to 1945)
DH908          Luxemburg (gen.)              949.35
DH908.5            Diplomacy & politics (Lux.)
DH908.6.A-Z        Foreign relns. (Lux.: by country)
DH908.6.G3         Foreign relns. (Lux.-Ger.)
DH916          Luxemburg (1815-)
```

DJ	NETHERLANDS (HOLLAND)	949.2
DJ39	Description & travel (Neth.: 1901-45)	
DJ124	Military history (Neth.)	
DJ142	Politics & diplomacy (Neth.: gen.)	
DJ147	Diplomacy & politics (Neth.: 1795-20th c.)	
DJ149.A-Z	Foreign relns. (Neth.: by country)	
DJ149.G3	Foreign relns. (Neth.-Ger.)	
DJ281-287	Holland (1890-1948: Queen Wilhelmina)	
DJ281	Netherlands (1890-1948: gen. & biogs. of Queen Wilhelmina)	
		949.2071
DJ283.A-Z	Biography (Neth.: by name)	
DJ285	Netherlands (1914-18: WWI)	949.2071
DJ287	Netherlands (1939-48: inclu. WWII period)	
DJ401.A-Z	Local history (Neth.: islands, provinces, regions, etc.)	
DJ411.A-Z	Local history (Neth.: towns, cities, etc.)	
DJ411.A5-59	Amsterdam, Neth.	
DJ411.A8	Arnhem, Neth.	
DJ500	Colonies, Dutch (PREFER D-F #s for indiv. colonies or JV2500-2599 for collective)	

DJK	EASTERN EUROPE (gen.: pubns. after about 1977-78: SEE DR for earlier & for specific countries)
DJK17	Description & travel (Eastern Europe: 1901-50)
DJK38	Europe, Eastern (gen.)
DJK41	Primary sources, documents (Eastern Europe: politics)
DJK42	Politics (Eastern Europe: gen.)
DJK43-44	Foreign relns. (Eastern Europe)
DJK49	Eastern Europe (1918-45)
DJK61-66	Black Sea region
DJK71-75	Carpathian Mts. region
DJK76	Danube River Valley (gen.)
DJK77	Pannonia

DK	Russia, Poland, Finland, Soviet Asia	
DK1-275+	RUSSIA	947
DK3	Primary sources, documents (Rus.)	
DK17	Russia (gen.)	
DK27	Description & travel (Rus.: 1901-44)	914.70904
DK32	Civilization, customs, social life (Rus.: gen.)	
DK33	Races & ethnography (Rus.)	
DK36	Dictionaries, chronologies, etc. (Rus.)	
DK50-54	Russian military history	
DK50.5-8	Biography, Military (Rus.: collective)	
DK54	Military history (Rus.: 1917-)	355.00947, .033+
DK59	Naval history (Rus.: 1917-)	359.00947

DK60-63	Politics & diplomacy (Rus.)	
DK60	Primary sources, documents (Rus.: politics & diplomacy)	
DK61	Politics & diplomacy (Rus.: gen.)	320.947
DK63	Politics & diplomacy (Rus.: 1894-1939)	
DK63.3	Politics & diplomacy (Rus.: 1939-)	
DK65-69	Diplomacy (Rus.)	
DK65	Primary sources, documents (Rus.: for. relns.)	
DK66	Foreign relns. (Rus.: gen.)	327.47
DK67-69	Foreign relns. (Rus.: particular areas)	327.470+
DK67	Foreign relns. (Rus.-Europe)	
DK67.3	Foreign relns. (Rus.-Cath. Church)	
DK67.4	Foreign relns. (Rus.-Balkan Penin.)	
DK67.5.A-Z	Foreign relns. (Rus.-specific Eur. countries)	
DK67.5.B8	Foreign relns. (Rus.-Bulg.)	
DK67.5.C95	Foreign relns. (Rus.-Czech.)	
DK67.5.F5	Foreign relns. (Rus.-Fin.)	
DK67.5.F8	Foreign relns. (Rus.-Fr.)	
DK67.5.G3	Foreign relns. (Rus.-Ger.)	
DK67.5.G7	Foreign relns. (Rus.-G.B.)	
DK67.5.G8	Foreign relns. (Rus.-Greece)	
DK67.5.H9	Foreign relns. (Rus.-Hung.)	
DK67.5.I8	Foreign relns. (Rus.-It.)	
DK67.5.P7	Foreign relns. (Rus.-Pol.)	
DK67.5.R8	Foreign relns. (Rus.-Rum.)	
DK67.5.S8	Foreign relns. (Rus.-Swe.)	
DK67.5.Y8	Foreign relns. (Rus.-Yug.)	
DK68.A3-Z	Foreign relns. (Rus.-Asia: gen.: pubns. 1801-)	
DK68.7.A-Z	Foreign relns. (Rus.-particular Asian countries)	
DK68.7.C5	Foreign relns. (Rus.-China)	327.47051
DK68.7.I4	Foreign relns. (Rus.-India)	
DK68.7.I55	Foreign relns. (Rus.-Iran)	
DK68.7.J3	Foreign relns. (Rus.-Japan)	327.47052
DK68.7.T8	Foreign relns. (Rus.-Tur.)	
DK69	Foreign relns. (Rus.-U.S.: PREFER E183.8.R9)	327.47073
DK69.3.A-Z	Foreign relns. (Rus. & non-U.S. Am. countries)	
DK69.3.C2-29	Foreign relns. (Rus.-Can.)	
DK69.3.M6	Foreign relns. (Rus.-Mex.)	
DK246	Russia (20th c.: gen.)	947.084
DK251-264	Russia (1894-1917: Czar Nicholas II)	
DK254.A-Z	Biography (Rus.: 1894-1917: by name, inclu. memoirs)	
DK254.L3-46	Lenin, Vladimir Ilich (Rus.: 1894-1917: biog. & works)	
DK254.L3.A2-219	Lenin, Vladimir Ilich (Rus.: collected works by)	
DK254.L4-46	Lenin, Vladimir Ilich (Rus.: biogs.)	
DK258-260	Russia (1894-1917)	947.083
DK258	Nicholas II (Rus.: Czar, 1894-1917)	
DK262	Russia (1904-17: empire status)	
DK263-264.3	Russian Revolution (1905-6)	
DK264.8	Russia (1914-18: WWI era)	947.083
DK265-265.9+	Russian Revolution (1917-21)	
DK265.A56-Z	Russian Revolution (1917-21: gen.)	
DK265.15	Pictorials, satires, etc. (Rus. Rev., 1917-21)	
DK265.17	Pamphlets, minor works, sermons (Rus. Rev., 1917-21)	

DK265.2	Russian military ops. (Rev., 1917-21)
DK265.3	Russian naval ops. (Rev., 1917-21)
DK265.4	Russian Revolution (1917-21: Allied interventon, 1918-20)
DK265.42.A-Z	Allied intervention (Rus. Rev.: by country)
DK265.8.A-Z	Local history (Rus. Rev., 1917-21: by place)
DK265.8.L195	Leningrad, Rus. (Rev., 1917-21)
DK265.8.M6	Moscow, Rus. (Rev., 1917-21)
DK265.8.S5	Siberia (Rev., 1917-21)
DK265.8.S63	Central Asia (Rus, Rev., 1917-21)
DK265.8.U4	Ukraine (Rev., 1917-21)
DK265.9.A-Z	Russian Revolution (1917-21: special topics)
DK265.9.A5	Anarchists (Rus. Rev., 1917-21)
DK265.9.A6	Politics (Rus. armed forces, 1917-21)
DK265.9.C62	Cossacks (Rus. Rev., 1917-21)
DK265.9.E2	Economic aspects (Rus. Rev., 1917-21)
DK265.9.F5	Russian Revolution (1917-21: foreign particip.: gen.)
DK265.9.F52.A-Z	Foreign participation (Rus. Rev., 1917-21: by country)
DK265.9.K73	Red Guard (Rus. Rev., 1917-21: Krasnaia Gvardiia)
DK265.9.S4	Spies, secret service, etc. (Rus. Rev., 1917-21)
DK265.9.S6	Soviets (Rus. Rev., 1917-21: councils)
DK265.9.W57	Women (Rus. Rev., 1917-21)
DK266	Soviet Union (1918-) 947.084
DK266.A3	Primary sources, documents (Rus.: 1918-)
DK266.A4-Z	Russia (1918-: gen.)
DK266.3	Soviet Union (1918-: special inclu. espionage, sabotage)
DK266.5	Soviet Union (1918-24: Lenin era) 947.0841
DK267-273	Soviet Union (1925-53: Stalin regime)
DK267	Russia (1925-53: Stalin era: gen.) 947.0842
DK267.3.1925-1953	Pamphlets, minor works, addresses (Rus.: 1925-53)
DK268.A1	Biography (Rus.: 1925-53: collective)
DK268.A2-Z	Biography (Rus.: 1925-53: inclu. memoirs: by name)
DK268.D9	Dzerzhinsky, Feliks (Rus.: 1925-53 era)
DK268.L5	Litvinov, Maksim M. (Rus.: 1925-53 era)
DK268.M64	Molotov, Viacheslav M. (Rus.: 1925-53 era)
DK268.S75	Stalin, Joseph (Rus.: works by)
DK268.S8	Stalin, Joseph (Rus.: biogs.)
DK268.T75	Trotsky, Leon (Rus.: 1925-53 era)
DK268.3	Civilization, customs, social life (Rus.: 1925-53)
DK269	Emigrés, Russian (1925-53)
DK269.5	Propaganda, Russian (1925-53: internal)
DK270	Soviet propaganda (1925-53: foreign: gen.)
DK272.A-Z	Propaganda, Soviet (1925-53: foreign: by country)
DK272.F8	Propaganda, Soviet (1925-53: France)
DK272.G3	Propaganda, Soviet (1925-53: Ger.)
DK272.G7	Propaganda, Soviet (1925-53: G.B.)
DK272.J3	Propaganda, Soviet (1925-53: Japan)
DK272.U6-7	Propaganda, Soviet (1925-53: U.S.)
DK272.5	Anti-Soviet propaganda (1925-53: gen.)
DK272.7.A-Z	Propaganda, Anti-Soviet (1925-53: by partic. country)
DK272.7.G3	Propaganda, Anti-Soviet (1925-53: by Ger.: SEE ALSO DD255.R9)
DK272.7.J3	Propaganda, Anti-Soviet (1925-53: by Japan)
DK273	Soviet Union (1939-45: WWII period) 947.0842

DK401-441+	POLAND (SEE ALSO DK4010-4800 for newer titles from perhaps 1976 on)	943.8
DK402	Primary sources, documents (Pol.)	
DK404	Poland (gen. history, culture, etc.)	
DK407	Description & travel (Pol.: 1867-1945)	
DK411	Civilization, customs, social life (Pol.)	
DK414.A3-Z	Poland (gen.: pubns. 1801+)	
DK417	Military history (Pol.: SEE ALSO DK4170+ for newer titles)	
DK417.7	Naval history (Pol.)	
DK418	Diplomacy & politics (Pol.)	
DK418.5.A-Z	Foreign relns. (Pol.: by country)	
DK418.5.F8	Foreign relns. (Pol.-Fr.)	
DK418.5.G3	Foreign relns. (Pol.-Ger.)	
DK418.5.G7	Foreign relns. (Pol.-G.B.)	
DK418.5.R9	Foreign relns. (Pol.-Rus.)	
DK418.5.A-Z	Foreign relns. (Pol.: by country)	
DK418.5.F8	Foreign relns. (Pol.-Fr.)	
DK418.5.G3	Foreign relns. (Pol.-Ger.)	
DK418.5.G7	Foreign relns. (Pol.-G.B.)	
DK418.5.R9	Foreign relns. (Pol.-Rus.)	
DK434.9	Poland (1795-1918) 943.803	
DK439	Poland (1914-18: WWI) 943.803	
DK440	Poland (1918-: Republic: inclu. wars of 1918-21)	943.804
DK440.3	Treaties (Pol., 1921: Riga)	
DK440.5.A-Z	Biography (Pol.: 1918-: inclu. memoirs)	
DK440.5.A1	Biography (Pol.: 1918-: collective)	
DK440.5.B4	Beck, Joseph (Pol.: 1918+ biog.)	
DK440.5.P5	Pilsudski, Joseph (Pol.: 1918+ biog.)	
DK440.5.S55	Sikorski, Wladyslaw (Pol.: 1918+ biog.)	
DK441	Poland (1939-45: WWII era) 943.8053	
DK443	Poland (1945-)	
DK445-465	FINLAND (PREFER DL1002-1180+ for pubns. from around 1970 on)	948.97
DK459	Finland (20th c.: inclu. Revolution, 1917-18)	948.9703
DK459.3	Treaties (Fin.: 1918)	
DK459.4	Treaties (Fin.-Rus.: 1920)	
DK459.45	Finland (1939-) 948.97032	
DK459.5	Russo-Finnish War (1939-40: SEE ALSO DL1095-1105)	947.0842, 948.97032
DK461.A-Z	Biography (Fin.: 20th c.)	
DK461.M32	Mannerheim, Carl (Fin.: 20th c.)	
DK501-973+	Local history (Russia)	
DK501	Russia, Northern	
DK502.3-505	Baltic States	
DK502.7	Baltic States (gen.)	
DK503	Russia, Eastern & Estonia (SEE DK511.E4 for earlier pubns. on Estonia)	947.41
DK503.73	ESTONIA (1800-1918) 947.41	
DK503.74-746	Estonia (1918-40)	
DK503.75-77	Estonia (1940+)	
DK504	LATVIA (SEE DK511.L15 for earlier pubns.)	947.43
DK504.73	Latvia (1800-1918)	
DK504.74-76	Latvia (1918-40)	
DK504.77-79	Latvia (1940+)	

DK505	LITHUANIA (SEE DK511.L2 for earlier pubns.)	947.5
DK505.73	Lithuania (1800-1918)	
DK505.74-76	Lithuania (1918-40)	
DK505.77-79	Lithuania (1940+)	
DK507	White Russia (Western Russia)	
DK508-508.9+	UKRAINE	
DK508.54	Military history (Ukr.)	
DK508.55	Cossacks (Ukr.)	
DK508.554	Politics (Ukr.: gen.)	
DK508.56	Diplomacy (Ukr.: gen.)	
DK508.57	Foreign relns. (Ukr.: by country)	
DK508.79-835	Ukraine (1917-44)	
DK508.8	Ukraine (1917+: earlier pubns.)	
DK508.812	Ukraine (1917-44: gen.)	
DK508.833-835	Ukraine (1921-44)	
DK508.9.A-Z	Local history (Ukraine: regions, oblasts, etc.)	
DK508.9.C37	Carpathian Mts. (Uk.)	
DK508.9.D64	Dnepropetrovsk (Uk.)	
DK508.92-939	Kiev (Uk.)	
DK508.95.A-Z	Local history (Ukraine: towns etc.)	
DK508.95.I24	Yalta, Uk. (Jalta)	
DK508.95.K54	Kiev, Uk. (Kyiv)	
DK508.95.O33	Odessa, Uk.	
DK508.95.S49	Sevastopol, Uk.	
DK509	Russia, Southern (Black Sea, Caucasus, Armenia, etc.)	
DK510	Russian S.F.S.R. (Russia)	
DK510.7-72	Russian S.F.S.R. (1917-45)	
DK511.A-Z	Local history (Eur. Russia, Poland: provinces, governments, regions, etc.)	
DK511.A5	Archangel (Rus.)	
DK511.B2	Baku (Rus.)	
DK511.C1-35	Caucasus area (Rus.)	
DK511.C7	Crimea (Rus.)	947.717
DK511.D7	Don River Valley (Rus.)	
DK511.E4-8	ESTONIA (SEE DK503 for later pubns.)	947.41
DK511.E6	Estonia (gen.)	
DK511.G3-47	Georgia (Rus.: SEE DK670 for later pubns.)	
DK511.L15-18	LATVIA (SEE DK504 for later pubns.)	947.43
DK511.L178	Latvia (1914-18: WWI)	
DK511.L18	Latvia (1918-)	
DK511.L195	Leningrad area (Rus.)	
DK511.L2-28	LITHUANIA (SEE DK505 for later pubns.)	947.5
DK511.L26	Lithuania (1914-19)	
DK511.L27	Lithuania (1919-)	
DK511.M6	Moscow area (Rus.)	
DK511.U7	Ural Mts. (Rus.)	947.87
DK511.V65	Volga River Valley (Rus.)	
DK511.W5	White Russia (Belorussia)	947.65
DK541-579	Leningrad, U.S.S.R.	947.45
DK561	St. Petersburg, Rus. (gen.)	
DK568	Petrograd, Rus. (1801-)	
DK591-609	Moscow, Rus.	947.31
DK600	Social life, culture, customs (Moscow, Rus.)	
DK601	Moscow, Rus. (to 1950)	

DK651.A-Z	Local history (Rus.: towns other than Moscow in Eur., Pol. areas)
DK651.K37	Kiev, Rus.
DK651.M5	Minsk, Rus.
DK651.O2	Odessa, Rus.
DK651.R5	Riga, Rus.
DK651.R7	Rostov, Rus.
DK651.S45	Sevastopol, Rus.
DK651.S65	Smolensk, Rus.
DK651.S7	Stalingrad, Rus. 947.4785
DK651.T28	Tallinn, Rus. (Reval)
DK651.W2	Warsaw, Pol.
DK651.Y25	Yalta, Rus.
DK670-679	GEORGIA (Rus.: SEE DK511.G3 for earlier pubns.)
DK676.5-6	Politics (Georgian S. S. R.: gen.)
DK677.4-6	Georgian S. S. R. (1801-1921)
DK677.7-9+	Georgian S. S. R. (1921+)
DK680-689	ARMENIA (SEE ALSO DK509 for some gen. works, DS161-199 for earlier titles)
DK687+	Armenian S. S. R. (1920+)
DK689	Local history (Armenian S. S. R.)
DK690-699	Azerbaijan S. S. R.
DK697.3-5	Azerbaijan S. S. R. (1917+)
DK699.2-39	Baku, Rus.
DK750-973+	Russian Asia 957-958
DK750	Asia, Russian
DK751-781	Siberia 957
DK753	Siberia (gen. hist., exploration, culture, etc.) 957
DK755	Description & travel (Siberia: 1801-1945)
DK761	Siberia (gen.)
DK766	Siberia (19th-20th c.) 957.08
DK771.A-Z	Local history (Siberia: provinces, regions, etc.)
DK771.B3	Lake Baikal (Sib.)
DK771.K2	Kamchatka (Sib.)
DK771.S2	Sakhalin (Siberia)
DK771.T8	Transbaikalia (Sib.)
DK781.A-Z	Local history (Siberia: towns etc.)
DK781.V5	Vladivostok, Rus.
DK845-973	Asia, Soviet Central 958
DK858	Russian Central Asia (to 1920)
DK859	Soviet Central Asia (1920+)
DK4010-4800	POLAND (SEE ALSO DK401-441 for older titles prior to 1976-77) 943.8
DK4040	Poland (gen.)
DK4070	Description & travel (Pol.: 1867-1944)
DK4110	Social life, culture, customs (Pol.)
DK4120	Races & ethnography (Pol.: gen.)
DK4121.5.A-Z	Races & ethnography (Pol.: by specific element)
DK4121.5.C9	Czechs (in Pol.)
DK4121.5.G4	Germans (in Pol.)
DK4121.5.T3	Tatars (in Pol.)
DK4121.5.U4	Ukrainians (in Pol.)
DK4121.5.W5	White Russians (in Pol.)
DK4122	Poles (in other lands)
DK4140	Poland (gen.: pubn. dates 1801+)

DK4170-4178	Military history (Pol.)
DK4170	Polish military history (gen.: SEE ALSO DK417 for older works)
DK4173	Military history (Pol.: 1795-1918)
DK4174	Military history (Pol.: 1919-)
DK4177-4178	Naval history (Pol.)
DK4178.5-4185	Diplomacy & politics (Pol.)
DK4179	Politics (Pol.)
DK4180	Foreign relns. (Pol.: gen.)
DK4182	Polish question
DK4185.A-Z	Foreign relns. (Pol.: with particular countries)
DK4185.F8	Foreign relns. (Pol.-Fr.)
DK4185.G3	Foreign relns. (Pol.-Ger.)
DK4185.R9	Foreign relns. (Pol.-Rus.)
DK4380	Poland (1864-1918) 943.803
DK4382	Poland (20th c.)
DK4390	Poland (1914-18: WWI) 943.803
DK4392	Poland (1915-18: Austrian occupation)
DK4397	Primary sources, documents (Pol.: 1918-45)
DK4397-4420	Poland (1918-45) 943.804
DK4400	Poland (1918-45: gen.)
DK4402	Politics & diplomacy (Pol.: 1918-45)
DK4402.5	Foreign relns. (Pol.: 1918-45)
DK4403.5	Poland (1918-26)
DK4404-4409	Poland (1918-21: wars, inclu. Russo-Polish of 1919-20)
DK4405	Russo-Polish War (1919-20: plus other Polish conflicts of the time)
DK4406	Polish military ops. (1918-21, inclu. Russo-Polish conflict)
DK4406.5	Personal accounts (Russo-Polish War, other Polish conflicts of 1918-21)
DK4407.3	Treaties (Russo-Polish, other Polish conflicts: Riga: 1921)
DK4407.A-Z	Battles, campaigns, sieges (Russo-Polish, other Polish conflicts, 1918-21: by name)
DK4407.G3	Galicia, Pol. (Polish wars, 1918-21)
DK4407.L9	Lvov, Siege of (Polish wars, 1918-21)
DK4409.4	Poland (1926: Coup)
DK4409.5	Poland (1926-39)
DK4410-4420	Poland (1939-45: WWII era) 943.8053
DK4410	Poland (1939-45: WWII era: gen., inclu. Ger. occup.)
DK4415	Poland (1939-41: Russ. occup.)
DK4419	Biography (Pol.: 1918-45: collec.)
DK4420.A-Z	Biography (Pol.: 1918-45: by name, inclu. memoirs)
DK4420.B4	Beck, Josef (Pol.: 1918-45 era)
DK4420.P3	Paderewski, Ignacy Jan (Pol.: 1918-45 era)
DK4420.P5	Pilsudski, Jozef (Pol.: 1918-45 time)
DK4420.S5	Sikorski, Wladyslaw (Pol.: 1918-45 period)
DK4600-4800	Local history (Pol.)
DK4600.A-Z	Local history (Pol.: provinces)
DK4600.G34	Galicia (Pol.)
DK4600.L63	Lodz Voivodeship (Pol.)
DK4600.P67	Pomerania (Pol.)
DK4600.P77	Prussia, East (Pol.)
DK4600.S48	Silesia Voivodeship (Pol.)
DK4600.V5	Vistula River & Valley (Pol.: Wisla)
DK4610-4645	Warsaw, Pol.
DK4630	Warsaw, Pol. (gen.)
DK4633	Warsaw, Pol. (1918-)

DK4650-4685	Danzig, Pol. (Gdansk)	
DK4670	Gdansk, Pol. (Danzig: gen.)	
DK4673	Danzig, Pol. (1919-45: time of free city)	
DK4700-4735	Krakow, Pol. (Cracow)	
DL	SCANDINAVIA, Northern Europe, Finland	
DL1-87+	Europe, Northern (plus Scandinavia and Finland)	
DL10	Description & travel (Scan., N. Eur., Fin.: 1901-50)	
DL52	Military history (Scan., N. Eur., Fin.)	
DL53	Naval history (Scan., N. Eur., Fin.)	
DL55	Foreign relns. & politics (Scan., N. Eur., Fin.: gen.)	
DL83	Northern Europe, Scandinavia, Finland (1901-45)	948.08
DL101-291+	DENMARK	
DL103	Primary sources, documents (Den.)	
DL109	Denmark (gen.) 948.9	
DL118	Description & travel (Den.: 1901-50)	
DL154	Military history (Den.)	
DL154.7	Naval history (Den.: 19th-20th c.)	
DL159	Diplomacy (Den.: gen.)	
DL159.5.A-Z	Foreign relns. (Den.-other lands)	
DL159.5.G3	Foreign relns. (Den.-Ger.)	
DL159.5.G7	Foreign relns. (Den.-G.B.)	
DL250	Denmark (20th c.) 948.905	
DL255-257	Denmark (1912-47: time of Christian X) 948.9051	
DL255	Christian X (Den.: 1912-47 period: ALSO gen. histories of time)	
DL256	Denmark (1914-18: WWI)	
DL256.5	Denmark (1919+)	
DL257.A-Z	Biography (Den.: 1912-47)	
DL271.A-Z	Local history (Den.: counties, islands, regions)	
DL276	Copenhagen, Den.	
DL291	Local history (Den.: towns etc.)	
DL301-398+	ICELAND 949.12	
DL365	Iceland (1801-1918)	
DL375	Iceland (1918-) 949.1204	
DL396-398	Local history (Ice.)	
DL398.A-Z	Local history (Ice.: towns etc.)	
DL398.R5	Reykjavik, Ice.	
DL401-596+	NORWAY 948.1	
DL403	Primary sources, documents (Nor.)	
DL418	Description & travel (Nor.)	
DL454	Military history (Nor.) 355.009481	
DL456	Naval history (Nor.)	
DL458	Diplomacy & politics (Nor.: gen.)	
DL459.A-Z	Foreign relns. (Nor.-other specific countries) 327.4810+	
DL459.G3	Foreign relns. (Nor.-Ger.)	
DL459.G7	Foreign relns. (Nor.-G.B.)	
DL459.S8	Foreign relns. (Nor.-Swe.)	
DL527	Norway (20th c.) 948.104	
DL529.A-Z	Biography (Nor.: 20th c.)	
DL529.A1	Biography (Nor.: 20th c.: collective)	
DL529.Q5	Quisling, Vidkun (Nor.: 20th c.)	
DL530-533	Norway (1905-57: Haakon VII era) 948.1041-1045	
DL530	Haakon VII (Nor.: King, 1905-57)	
DL531	Norway (1914-18)	
DL532	Norway (1939-45)	

```
DL576.A-Z    Local history (Nor.: counties, regions, etc.)
DL576.B4     Bergen (Nor.)
DL576.S8     Stavanger (Nor.)
DL576.T4        Telemark (Nor.)
DL576.T9        Trondheim (Nor.)
DL581           Oslo, Nor. (Christiana)        948.2
DL596.A-Z    Local history (Nor.: towns, villages, etc.)
DL596.B4     Bergen, Nor.
DL596.M7     Moss, Nor.
DL596.S8     Stavanger, Nor.
DL596.T8     Trondheim, Nor.
DL596.V6     Voss, Nor.
DL601-991+      SWEDEN        948.5
DL618        Description & travel (Swe.: 1901-50)
DL654        Military history (Swe.)
DL656        Naval history (Swe.)
DL658-659       Diplomacy & politics (Swe.)
DL658.A2        Primary sources, documents (Swe.)
DL658.A3-Z      Politics & diplomacy (Swe.: gen.)        320.9485, 327.485
DL658.8         Foreign relns. (Swe.: 1818-20th c.)
DL659.A-Z    Foreign relns. (Swe.-other lands: by name)   327.485+
DL659.F5     Foreign relns. (Swe.-Fin.)
DL659.G3     Foreign relns. (Swe.-Ger.)
DL659.G7     Foreign relns. (Swe.-G.B.)
DL659.N8     Foreign relns. (Swe.-Nor.)
DL659.R9        Foreign relns. (Swe.-Rus.)
DL659.S65       Foreign relns. (Swe.-Sov. Un.)
DL659.U6-7      Foreign relns. (Swe.-U.S.)
DL860        Sweden (20th c.)        948.505
DL867        Gustav V (Swe.: King, 1907-50)
DL867-870    Sweden (1907-50: Gustav V)
DL867.5      Diplomacy & politics (Swe.: 1907-50)        948.5051-2
DL868           Sweden (1914-18: WWI era)
DL868.5         Sweden (1919-)
DL869        Biography (Swe.: 1907-50: collec.)
DL870.A-Z       Biography (Swe.: 1907-50: by name)
DL870.B47       Bernadotte af Wisborg, Folke, greve (Swe.: 1907-50 period)
DL971-991    Local history (Swe.)
DL976        Stockholm, Swe.
DL1002-1180+    FINLAND (PREFER this but ALSO SEE DK445-465 for pre-1970
                        pubns. in some libs.)        948.97
DL1005       Primary sources, documents (Fin.)
DL1015.2     Description & travel (Fin.: 1901-44)
DL1015.3     Description & travel (Fin.: 1945-80)
DL1032          Finland (gen.)        948.97
DL1036-1037     Military history (Fin.)        355.0094897
DL1040-1042     Naval history (Fin.)
DL1046          Diplomacy (Fin.: gen.)        327.4897
DL1048.A-Z      Foreign relns. (Fin. & other partic. lands)
DL1048.G3       Foreign relns. (Fin.-Ger.)
DL1048.R9       Foreign relns. (Fin.-Rus.)
DL1048.S65      Foreign relns. (Fin.-Sov. Un.)
```

```
DL1065        Finland (1809-1917: Russian control)    948.9702
DL1066        Primary sources, documents (Fin.: 20th c.)
DL1066.5      Finland (20th c.)            948.9703
DL1084            Finland (1918-39)            948.97031
DL1088-1088.5 Biography (Fin.: 1918-39)
DL1090-1105+  Finland (1939-45)            948.97032
DL1090            Primary sources, documents (Fin.: 1939-45)
DL1092            Finland (1939-45: gen.)
DL1093-1093.5 Biography (Fin.: 1939-45)
DL1095-1105+  Russo-Finnish War (1939-40: might ALSO try DK459.5)
                                   948.97032, 947.0842
DL1095        Associations, periodicals, conferences (Russo-Fin. War, 1939-40)
DL1096        Primary sources, documents (Russo-Fin. War, 1939-40)
DL1097        Russo-Finnish War (1939-40: gen.)
DL1099            Military ops. (Russo-Fin. War, 1939-40)
DL1102            Personal accounts (Russo-Fin. War, 1939-40: collective)
DL1102.5          Personal accounts (Russo-Fin. War, 1939-40: individual)
DL1103.A-Z        Battles & local history (Russo-Fin. War, 1939-40)
DL1105.A-Z        Russo-Finnish War (1939-40: special topics)
DL1125        Finland (1945-)
DL1170.A-Z    Local history (Fin.: regions, provinces, etc.)
DL1175        Helsinki, Fin.              948.971
DL1175.42         Helsinki, Fin. (gen.)
DL1175.48         Helsinki, Fin. (1917-)
DL1180.A-Z        Local history (Fin.: towns except Helsinki)


DP            Iberian Peninsula      946
DP1-402+      SPAIN          946
DP42          Description & travel (Sp.: 1901-50)
DP78.5        Military history (Sp.: 1808-20th c.)       355.00946
DP83-86       Diplomacy & politics (Sp.)
DP83          Primary sources, documents (Sp.: dipl. & polit. hist.)
DP84          Politics & diplomacy (Sp.)
DP85.8        Diplomacy (Sp.: 1814-20th c.)
DP86.A-Z      Foreign relns. (Sp.: with partic. countries)    327.460+
DP86.G3           Foreign relns. (Sp.-Ger.)        327.46043
DP86.I8           Foreign relns. (Sp.-It.)
DP86.R9           Foreign relns. (Sp.-Rus.)        327.46047
DP86.S65          Foreign relns. (Sp.-Sov. Un.)
DP233         Spain (1886-20th c.: gen.)        946.08
DP234-247     Spain (1886-1931: period of Alfonso XIII)
DP235-236     Biography (Sp.: 1886-1931)
DP238         Alfonso XIII (Sp.: King, 1886-1931)
DP240         Spain (1886-1931: gen.)
DP246         Spain (1914-18: WWI)
DP247         Spain (1918-31)          946.08
DP250-269     Spain (1931-39: 2d Repub.)              946.081
DP251         Primary sources, documents (Sp.: 1931-39)
DP254             Second Republic (Sp.: 1931-39: gen.)
DP257-258         Diplomacy & politics (Sp.: 1931-39)
DP257             Politics & diplomacy (Sp.: 1931-39: gen.)
DP258.A-Z     Foreign relns. (Sp.-specific lands: 1931-39)
DP258.F8      Foreign relns. (Sp.-Fr.: 1931-39)
DP258.G3      Foreign relns. (Sp.-Ger.: 1931-39)
DP258.I8          Foreign relns. (Sp.-It.: 1931-39)
```

DP258.P8   Foreign relns. (Sp.-Port.: 1931-39)
DP258.R9   Foreign relns. (Sp.-Rus.: 1931-39)
DP258.S65   Foreign relns. (Sp.-Sov. Un.: 1931-39)
DP258.U6-7   Foreign relns. (Sp.-U.S.: 1931-39)
DP260   Biography (Sp.: 1931-39: collective)
DP264.A-Z Biography (Sp.: 1931-39: by name: inclu. memoirs)
DP264.F7   Franco Bahamonde, Francisco (Sp.: 1931-39 period)
DP267   Spain (1931-36: Alcalá Zamora y Torres era)
DP268   Spain (1936-39: Azaña period)
DP269-269.9+ Spain (1936-39: Civil War)   946.081
DP269   Spanish Civil War (1936-39)   946.081
DP269.A2-55   Primary sources, documents (Sp.: 1936-39: Civil War)
DP269.A56-Z   Military operations (Sp. Civil War, 1936-39: gen. titles on the war)
DP269.15   Pictorials, satires, etc. (Sp. Civil War, 1936-39)
DP269.17   Pamphlets, minor works, sermons (Sp. Civil War, 1936-39)
DP269.2.A-Z   Battles, campaigns, sieges (Sp. Civil War, 1936-39: by name)
DP269.2.A4   Toledo, Siege of (Sp. Civil War: 1936: Alcazar)
DP269.2.G8   Guadalajara, Battle of (Sp. Civil War: 1937)
DP269.23   Spanish military ops. (Civil War, 1936-39: Loyalists)
DP269.25   Spanish military ops. (Civil War, 1936-39: Insurgents)
DP269.27.A-Z Local history (Sp. Civil War, 1936-39: by place name)
DP269.27.C3   Catalonia (Sp. Civil War, 1936-39)
DP269.27.M3   Madrid, Sp. (Civil War, 1936-39)
DP269.3-35   Naval ops. (Sp. Civil War, 1936-39)
DP269.4   Aerial ops. (Sp. Civil War, 1936-39)
DP269.45   Spanish Civil War (1936-39: foreign particip.: gen.)
DP269.47.A-Z Foreign participation (Sp. Civil War, 1936-39: by country)
DP269.47.G3   Foreign participation (Sp. Civil War, 1936-39: Ger.)
DP269.47.I8   Foreign participation (Sp. Civil War, 1936-39: It.)
DP269.47.R8-9 Foreign participation (Sp. Civil War, 1936-39: Rus.)
DP269.47.U6-7 Foreign participation (Sp. Civil War, 1936-39: U.S.)
DP269.5-55   Atrocities (Sp. Civil War, 1936-39)
DP269.63-65   Prisons & prisoners (Sp. Civil War, 1936-39)
DP269.67   Concentration camps (Sp. Civil War, 1936-39: outside Sp.)
DP269.8.A-Z   Spanish Civil War (1936-39: special topics)
DP269.8.E2   Economic matters (Sp. Civil War, 1936-39)
DP269.8.R4   Religion (Sp. Civil War, 1936-39)
DP269.8.S4   Espionage, spies (Sp. Civil War, 1936-39)
DP269.9   Personal accounts (Sp. Civil War, 1936-39)
DP270   Spain (1939-)   946.0824
DP271.A-Z Biography (Sp.: 1939-)
DP302.A-Z Local history (Sp.: provinces, regions, etc.)
DP302.A41-55 Andalusia (Sp.)
DP302.C36-51 Canary Islands   964.9
DP302.C57-69 Catalonia (Sp.)
DP302.G31-41 GIBRALTAR
DP302.G51-65 Granada (Sp.)
DP302.T51   Toledo (Sp.)
DP302.V11-25 Valencia (Sp.)
DP350-374 Madrid, Sp.   946.41
DP361   Madrid, Sp. (1801-1950)
DP402.A-Z Local history (Sp.: towns except Madrid)
DP402.B2-3   Barcelona, Sp.
DP402.C2-3   Cadiz, Sp.
DP402.S3-32   Saragossa, Sp.

```
DP402.S36-48     Seville, Sp.
DP402.T7-74           Toledo, Sp.
DP402.V15-25          Valencia, Sp.
DP501-900+       PORTUGAL      946.9
DP525            Description & travel (Port.: 1816-1950)
DP547            Military history (Port.)
DP551            Naval history (Port.)
DP555-557        Diplomacy & politics (Port.)      320.9469, 327.469+
DP555            Primary sources, documents (Port.: dipl. & polit. hist.)
DP556            Politics & diplomacy (Port.: gen.)
DP557.A-Z        Foreign relns. (Port.-other countries: by name)
DP557.G3             Foreign relns. (Port.-Ger.)
DP557.G7             Foreign relns. (Port.-G.B.)
DP557.S7             Foreign relns. (Port.-Sp.)
DP557.U6-7           Foreign relns. (Port.-U.S.)
DP670            Primary sources, documents (Port.: 20th c.)
DP672            Portugal (20th c.: gen.)      946.904
DP675            Portugal (1910-: Republic)    946.904
DP676.A-Z        Biography (Port.: 1910-)
DP677            Portugal (1914-18: WWI)       946.9041
DP678            Portugal (1919: Revolution)
DP680            Portugal (1919-)      946.9041-9042
DP702.A-Z        Local history (Port.: regions, provinces, areas)
DP702.A81-99         AZORES           946.99
DP702.A9             Azores (19th & 20th c.)    946.99
DP702.M11-23         Madeira Is.
DP752-776        Lisbon, Port.             946.942
DP764            Lisbon, Port. (1840-1950)
DP802.A-Z        Colonies, Portuguese (SEE ALSO D-F for indiv. places & JV4200-4299
                     for collective)

DQ               SWITZERLAND       949.4
DQ3              Primary sources, documents (Swit.)
DQ24             Description & travel (Swit.: 1901-50)
DQ36             Civilization, customs, social life (Swit.)
DQ59                 Military history (Swit.)
DQ68-76              Diplomacy & politics (Swit.)      320.9494, 327.4940+
DQ68                 Primary sources, documents (Swit.)
DQ69             Politics & diplomacy (Swit.: gen.)
DQ75             Diplomacy & politics (Swit.: 1798-20th c.)
DQ76.A-Z         Foreign relns. (Swit.-specific countries)      327.4940+
DQ76.F8          Foreign relns. (Swit.-Fr.)
DQ76.G3              Foreign relns. (Swit.-Ger.)       327.494043
DQ76.G7              Foreign relns. (Swit.-G.B.)
DQ76.I8              Foreign relns. (Swit.-It.)        327.494045
DQ76.R9          Foreign relns. (Swit.-Rus.)
DQ76.U6-7        Foreign relns. (Swit.-U.S.)       327.494073
DQ201            Switzerland (20th c.)      949.407
DQ206-207        Biography (Swit.: 20th c.)
DQ301-800        Local history (Swit.: cantons, cantonal capitals)
DQ401-420            Bern, Swit.       949.45
DQ441-460            Geneva, Swit.     949.45
DQ501-520            Lucerne, Swit.    949.45
DQ781-800            Zurich, Swit.     949.45
```

DQ820-829	ALPS	949.47
DQ841.A-Z	Local history (Swit.: lakes, peaks, regions other than those in DQ820+ Alps #s) DQ841.L8 Lucerne, Lake (Swit.)
DQ851.A-Z	Local history (Swit.: towns except cantonal capitals in DQ301-800)

DR	EASTERN EUROPE & Balkan Peninsula (SEE DJK for gen. bks. on E. Eur. after about 1977-78) 949.6-8
DR15	Description & travel (E. Eur. & Balkan Penin.: 1901-50)
DR45	BALKAN PENINSULA & Eastern Europe (1901-: gen.)
DR46	Balkan War (1912-13) 949.6
DR47	Balkan Peninsula (1913-19)
DR48	Balkan Peninsula (1919-45)
DR51-98	BULGARIA 949.77
DR52	Primary sources, documents (Bulg.)
DR60	Description & travel (Bulg.: 1879-1950)
DR70	Military history (Bulg.)
DR72	Diplomacy & politics (Bulg.)
DR73.A-Z	Foreign relns. (Bulg.-specific countries)
DR73.G3	Foreign relns. (Bulg.-Ger.) 327.4977043
DR73.R9	Foreign relns. (Bulg.-Rus.)
DR85	Bulgaria (1879-1943) 949.7702
DR85.5.A-Z	Biography (Bulg.: 1879-1943: inclu. memoirs)
DR87.7	Bulgaria (1912-13: Balkan War period)
DR87.8	Bulgaria (1914-18: WWI)
DR89	Bulgaria (1918-43: Boris III era)
DR90	Bulgaria (1943-: inclu. regency of Simeon II, 1943-46)
DR95-98	Local history (Bulg.)
DR97	Sofia, Bulg.
DR101-196+	MONTENEGRO 949.76
DR109	Description & travel (Montenegro: 1860-1950)
DR117	Montenegro (gen.)
DR158	Montenegro (1914-18: WWI)
DR159	Montenegro (1918-: part of Yug.)
DR201-296	RUMANIA 949.8
DR203	Primary sources, documents (Rum.)
DR209	Description & travel (Rum.: 1866-1950)
DR219	Military history (Rum.)
DR225	Naval history (Rum.)
DR226	Diplomacy & politics (Rum.)
DR229.A-Z	Foreign relns. (Rum. & partic. countries)
DR229.G3	Foreign relns. (Rum.-Ger.) 327.498043
DR229.R9	Foreign relns. (Rum.-Rus.)
DR250-266	Rumania (1866-1944)
DR250	Rumania (1866-1944: gen.)
DR258	Rumania (1912-13: Balkan War era)
DR260-263	Rumania (1914-27: Ferdinand) 949.802
DR260	Primary sources, documents (Rum.: 1914-27)
DR261	Ferdinand (Rum.: King, 1914-27: ALSO works on era)
DR262.A-Z	Biography (Rum.: 1914-27)
DR263	Rumania (1914-18: WWI)
DR264-266	Rumania (1918-44) 949.802
DR265	Michael (Rum.: regent period, 1927-3; King, 1940-47)
DR266	Carol II (Rum.: King, 1930-40)
DR267	Romania (1944-)

DR281-296   Local history (Rum.)
DR286   Bucharest, Rum.   949.82
DR301-396   YUGOSLAVIA (Serbia: SEE ALSO DR1202+ for later pubns.)   949.7-71
DR309   Description & travel (Yug.: 1860-1944)
DR317   Yugoslavia (gen.)
DR319   Military history (Yug.)
DR326   Diplomacy & politics (Yug.)
DR327.A-Z   Foreign relns. (Yug.-specific countries)
DR357   Yugoslavia (20th c.)   949.702, .7102
DR359.A-Z   Biography (Yug.: 20th c.)
DR359.A2   Biography (Yug.: 20th c.: collective)
DR359.M5   Mihailovi´c, Draza (Yug.: 20th c.)
DR359.T5   Tito, Josip Broz (Yug.: 20th c.)
DR360-363   Yugoslavia (1903-21: Peter I)   949.701-702
DR360   Peter I (Yug.: King, 1903-21: ALSO covers era)
DR363   Yugoslavia (1914-18: WWI)
DR364-369   Yugoslavia (1918-45: inclu. Croatia, Serbia, Slovenia)   949.7021-
                                                        7022, 949.7102 (Serbia)
DR364   Primary sources, documents (Yug.: 1918-45)
DR366   Yugoslavia (1918-45: gen.)
DR367.A-Z   Diplomacy & politics (Yug.: 1918-45)
DR367.A1   Politics & diplomacy (Yug.: 1918-45: gen.)
DR367.G3   Foreign relns. (Yug.-Ger.: 1918-45)
DR367.G7   Foreign relns. (Yug.-G.B.: 1918-45)
DR367.I8   Foreign relns. (Yug.-It.: 1918-45)
DR367.R9   Foreign relns. (Yug.-Rus.: 1918-45)
DR367.U6-7   Foreign relns. (Yug.-U.S.: 1918-45)
DR368   Yugoslavia (1921-34: Alexander)
DR369   Yugoslavia (1934-45: Peter II)   949.7022
DR370   Yugoslavia (1945-)
DR381-396   Local history (Yug.)
DR381.A-Z   Local history (Yug.: provinces, regions, etc.)
DR386   Belgrade, Yug.
DR401-741   TURKEY & Albania (primarily Tur.)
DR403   Primary sources, documents (Tur.)
DR428   Description & travel (Tur.: 1901-50)
DR448   Military history (Tur.)   355.009561
DR451   Naval history (Tur.)
DR476   Politics & diplomacy (Tur.: 1876-1918: inclu. Panislamism)
DR477   Diplomacy & politics (Tur.: 1918-)   327.5610+, 320.9561
DR479.A-Z   Foreign relns. (Tur.-particular countries)
DR479.G3   Foreign relns. (Tur.-Ger.)
DR479.G7   Foreign relns. (Tur.-G.B.)
DR479.R9   Foreign relns. (Tur.-Rus.)
DR577   Turkey (20th c.)   956.102
DR588   Turkey (1914-18: WWI era)
DR589   Turkey (1918-22: Mohammed VI)
DR590   Turkey (1923-60: Republic)   956.1024
DR592.A-Z   Biography (Tur.: 1909-: inclu. memoirs)
DR592.K4   Kemal, Mustafa (Tur.: 'Atatürk': 1909- era)
DR701.A-Z   Local history (Tur.: Eur. regions: by name)
DR701.A5   Aegean Sea
DR701.D2   Dardanelles (Tur.)
DR701.G3   Gallipoli (Tur.)

DR701.S49-86	ALBANIA (Scutari: SEE ALSO DR941-979 for later titles)	949.65
DR701.S5	Scutari (Albania: gen.)	
DR701.S6	Albania (1914-17: Kingdom)	949.6502
DR701.S7	Albania (1917-25)	949.6502
DR701.S8	Albania (1925-39: Zog I)	949.6502
DR701.S85	Albania (1939-43: Ital. rule)	949.6502
DR701.S86	Albania (1946-: Republic)	
DR716-739	Istanbul, Tur. (Constantinople)	956.3
DR941-979+	ALBANIA (SEE ALSO DR701.S49-86 for earlier works)	949.65
DR941	Albania (gen.)	
DR970-975	Albania (1912-44)	
DR971	Albania (1912-44: gen.)	
DR972	Albania (1912-18: SEE ALSO DR46+ for Balkan War etc.)	
DR974	Albania (1925-39)	949.6501-6502
DR975	Albania (1939-44)	
DR977	Albania (1944-)	949.6502-6503
DR1214-1307+	YUGOSLAVIA (SEE ALSO DR301+ for earlier pubns.)	949.7
DR1214	Yugoslavia (gen., descrip., culture, hist.)	949.7
DR1221	Description & travel (Yug.: 1901-44)	914.971+
DR1245-1246	Yugoslavia (gen. hist.)	949.7
DR1251	Military history (Yug.: gen.)	
DR1257-1258	Foreign relns. (Yug.: gen.)	
DR1280	Yugoslavia (1914-18: WWI era: SEE ALSO DR301+ for earlier pubns.)	949.7, .701
DR1288-1298	Yugoslavia (1918-45)	949.702
DR1288	Primary sources, documents (Yug.)	
DR1289	Yugoslavia (1918-45: gen.)	949.702-7022
DR1291	Politics & diplomacy (Yug.: 1918-45)	
DR1292	Foreign relns. (Yug.: 1918-45)	
DR1293-1294	Biography (Yug.: 1918-45)	
DR1294.A-Z	Biography (Yug.: 1918-45: by name, inclu. memoirs)	
DR1294.M54	Mihailovic, Draza (Yug.: 1918-45 era)	
DR1295	Yugoslavia (1918-21: reign of Peter I)	
DR1296	Yugoslavia (1921-34: Alexander I)	
DR1297-1298	Yugoslavia (1934-45: time of Peter II)	
DR1297	Peter II (Yug.: monarch, 1934-45)	
DR1298	Yugoslavia (1941-45: Axis occup.)	949.7022
DR1300-1305	Biography (Yug.: 1934-45+)	
DR1350.A-Z	Local history (Yug.: regions not limited to partic. sections or old republics)	
DR1350.A35	Adriatic coast (Yug.)	
DR1350.D35	Danube River Valley (Yug.)	
DR1350.D55	Dinaric Alps (Yug.)	
DR1352-2285+	Local history (Yug.: sections & old republics: Slovenia, Bosnia, Montenegro, etc.)	
DR1352-1485+	SLOVENIA	949.73
DR1370, 1376	Slovenia (gen.)	
DR1434	Slovenia (1914-18: WWI)	
DR1435-1443	Slovenia (1918-45)	
DR1436	Slovenia (1918-45: gen.)	
DR1443	Slovenia (1941-45: occupation)	

DR1502-1645	CROATIA 949.72
DR1510, 1535	Croatia (gen.)
DR1582	Croatia (1914-18: WWI)
DR1583-1591	Croatia (1918-45)
DR1584	Croatia (1918-45: gen.)
DR1591	Croatia (1941-45: WWII)
DR1620-1630	Dalmatia (Yug.: local Croatia) 949.72
DR1620-1636+	Local history (Croatia)
DR1633-1636	Slavonia (Yug.: local Croatia) 949.72
DR1652-1785	BOSNIA & Hercegovina (Herzegovina: SEE ALSO DR357 etc.)
	949.742
DR1660, 1685	HERZEGOVINA (Hercegovina) & Bosnia (gen.)
DR1732	Bosnia & Hercegovina (1914-18: WWI)
DR1733-1741	Bosnia & Hercegovina (1918-45)
DR1734	Hercegovina & Bosnia (1918-45: gen.)
DR1741	Bosnia & Hercegovina (1941-45: Axis occup.)
DR1801-1928	Montenegro (SEE ALSO DR357+, DR1214) 949.745
DR1810, 1835	Montenegro (gen.)
DR1878-1883	Montenegro (1878-1918: Nicholas I)
DR1883	Montenegro (1912-18: Balkan wars & WWI)
DR1884-1893	Montenegro (1918-45)
DR1885	Montenegro (1918-45: gen.)
DR1887	Politics & diplomacy (Montenegro: 1918-45)
DR1890-1891	Biography (Montenegro: 1918-45)
DR1893	Montenegro (1941-45)
DR1932-2125+	SERBIA (SEE ALSO DR301+ & DR1202 areas) 949.71-71022
DR1940	Serbia (gen., descrip., culture, history)
DR1965	Serbia (gen. histories)
DR1970	Military history (Serbia)
DR1972	Politics (Serbia: gen.)
DR1975	Diplomacy & politics (Serbia: gen.)
DR1976.A-Z	Foreign relns. (Serbia-other specific places)
DR2030-2032	Serbia (1903-18: Peter I Karadordevic)
DR2030	Peter I Karadordevic (Serbia: ruler, 1903-18: ALSO gen. works on period)
DR2031	Biography (Serbia: 1903-18)
DR2032	Serbia (1914-18: WWI)
DR2033-2040	Serbia (1918-45: part of Yug.)
DR2033	Primary sources, documents (Serbia: 1918-45)
DR2034	Serbia (1918-45: gen.)
DR2035	Civilization, customs, social life (Serbia: 1918-45)
DR2036	Politics (Serbia: 1918-45)
DR2038	Biography (Serbia: 1918-45)
DR2040	Serbia (1941-45: WWII era)
DR2075-2125	Local history (Serbia)
DR2106-2124	Belgrade, Serbia (Yug.)
DR2152-2285+	MACEDONIA 949.76
DR2160, 2185	Macedonia (gen., descrip., culture, hist.)
DR2230	Macedonia (1912-45)
DR2237	Macedonia (1912-19)
DR2240	Macedonia (1919-45)
DR2242	Macedonia (1941-45: WWII)

```
DS              ASIA        950-959
DS9             Description & travel (Asia: 1901-50)      915.044
DS19-23.1       Mongols (SEE ALSO DS793.M7 for Mongolia)
DS31            Dictionaries, chronologies, etc. (Asia)
DS33.3          Politics & diplomacy (Asia: gen.)         320.95, 327.5+
DS33.4.A-Z      Foreign relns. (Asia-particular other areas or countries)
DS35            Asia (20th c.)        950.4

DS41-329        MIDDLE EAST & Southwestern Asia        953, 955, 956
DS49            Description & travel (Mid. East, SW. Asia: 1901-50)      915.6044
DS52-53         Aegean islands        949.9
DS54            Cyprus       956.45
DS62            SOUTHWESTERN ASIA & Middle East (gen. histories)
DS62.4          NEAR EAST & Southwestern Asia (modern)
DS63            Politics & diplomacy (Middle East, SW. Asia)        320.956, 327.56+
DS63.2.A-Z      Foreign relns. (Mid. East, SW. Asia: by specific country)      327.560+
DS67-79           IRAQ        956.7
DS70.95           Diplomacy & politics (Iraq: gen.)
DS70.96.A-Z       Foreign relns. (Iraq-other specific places)
DS70.96.G3        Foreign relns. (Iraq-Ger.)
DS70.96.G7        Foreign relns. (Iraq-G.B.)
DS77            Iraq (1517-1918: Turkish period)      956.703
DS79            Iraq (1919-)          956.704
DS79.5          Iraq (1921-33: Faisal I)
DS79.52         Iraq (1933-39: Ghazi I)
DS79.53           Iraq (1939-58: Faisal II)       956.7042
DS79.8.A-Z        Biography (Iraq: 1919-: by name)
DS80-90         LEBANON          956.92
DS85            Lebanon (1861-1918: close of Turkish era)
DS86            Lebanon (1919-)          956.92034+
DS92-99         SYRIA        956.91
DS95            Syria (gen.)
DS95.5          Diplomacy & politics (Syria: gen.)
DS95.6.A-Z        Foreign relns. (Syria-other countries)        327.56910+
DS95.6.F8         Foreign relns. (Syria-Fr.)
DS95.6.G3         Foreign relns. (Syria-Ger.)
DS95.6.G7         Foreign relns. (Syria-G.B.)
DS97.5          Syria (1517-1918: Turkish period)      956.9103
DS98            Syria (1918-45: French mandate)       956.9104-91041
DS101-151       PALESTINE, Israel, & the Jews       956.94, 909.04924
DS102             Primary sources, documents (Palestine & the Jews)
DS107.3           Description & travel (Palestine: 1901-50)
DS109           Jerusalem, Pal.
DS109.93        Jerusalem, Pal. (1917-)
DS110.A-Z         Local history (Palestine: regions, towns, etc.)
DS110.J6          Jordan River (Pal.)
DS112-113         Civilization, customs, social life (Palestine & the Jews)
DS114             Dictionaries, chronologies, etc. (Palestine, the Jews)
DS117             Jews, Palestine, & Israel (gen. histories)
DS119-119.8       Politics & diplomacy (Palestine, Jews)
```

DS123   Israel (70 A.D.+)
DS125   Palestine (19th-20th c.)   956.9403-9404
DS125.3.A-Z   Biography (Palestine: 19th-20th c.)
DS125.3.A2   Biography (Palestine: 19th-20th c.: collective)
DS125.3.B37   Ben-Gurion, David (Palestine: 19th-20th c.)
DS125.3.W45   Weizmann, Chaim (Palestine: 19th-20th c.)
DS125.5   Palestine (1914-18: WWI)   956.9403-9404
DS126   Palestine (1919-48: Brit. control)   956.9404
DS126.3   Israel & the Jews (1939-45: WWII era: PREFER D810.J4 to cover
                titles on ethnic group)
DS133-151   Jews (outside Palestine)
DS134   Jews (outside Israel: gen.)   909.04924
DS135.A-Z   Jews (by country or area) Usually 004924 after Dewey place #s
DS135.E5-6   Jews (Eng. and G.B.)
DS135.E8-9   Jews (Eur.)   940.04924 (single '0' after decimal in this case)
DS135.F8-9   Jews (Fr.)   944.004924
DS135.G3-5   Jews (Ger.)   943.004924
DS135.G3.A5-Z Jews (Ger.: gen.)
DS135.G33   Jews (Ger.: 19th-20th c.)
DS135.I8-9   Jews (It.)   945.004924
DS135.R9-95   Jews (Rus.)   947.004924
DS135.S8   Jews (S. Am.: PREFER E #s in most cases)
DS135.U6-7   Jews (U.S: PREFER E184.J5 in most cases)   973.004924
DS140-140.5 Jews (outside Israel: economic, political, social conditions)
DS141   Jewish question
DS143   Jews, Modern
DS145   Anti-Semitism
DS145.P49-7   Protocols of the Wise Men of Zion (WWI: anti-Semitism)
DS149-151   Zionism, Restoration, Judenstaat
DS153-154   JORDAN   956.95
DS154.4   Jordan (1517-1918: Turkish rule)   956.9503
DS154.5   Jordan (1919-)   956.9504
DS161-199   ARMENIA (SEE ALSO DK509 for some gen. titles, DK680-689 for later
                works)   956.62
DS195   Armenia (1901-)   956.6202
DS201-248   SAUDI ARABIA & Arabian Peninsula   953
DS207   Description & travel (Arabian Penin.: 1801-1950)
DS223   Arabian Peninsula (gen.)
DS227   Diplomacy & politics (Saudi Arabia: gen.)
DS228.A-Z   Foreign relns. (Saudi Arabia-specific countries)
DS228.G3   Foreign relns. (Saudi Arab. Penin.: Ger.)
DS228.G7   Foreign relns. (Saudi Arab. Penin.: G.B.)
DS244   Saudi Arabia (1914-: gen.)   953.04-05
DS244.53   Saudi Arabia (1932-: Ibn Saud)   953.052
DS247.A-Z   Local history (Arabian Penin.: regions, sultanates, etc.: by place)
DS247.A2   Aden
DS247.B2-28   Bahrein
DS247.K8-88   Kuwait
DS247.O6-68   Oman
DS247.Y4-48   Yemen
DS248.A-Z   Local history (Arabian Penin.: cities)
DS248.M4   Mecca, Saudi Arabia

```
DS251-325    IRAN (Persia)          955
DS251        Description & travel (Iran: 1801-1950)
DS274        Diplomacy & politics (Iran)
DS274.2.A-Z     Foreign relns. (Iran-other countries)      327.550+
DS274.2.G3      Foreign relns. (Iran-Ger.)       327.55043
DS274.2.G7      Foreign relns. (Iran-G.B.)       327.55042
DS274.2.R9      Foreign relns. (Iran-Rus.)       327.55047
DS274.2.U6-7    Foreign relns. (Iran-U.S.)       327.55073
DS298-316    Persia (1794-1925: Kajar dynasty)       955.04-051
DS298        Iran (1794-1925: Kajar dynasty: gen.)
DS315        Iran (1909-25: Ahmed era)        955.05-051
DS317        Iran (1925-41: Pahlavi family: Riza Shah)      955.052
DS318        Iran (1941-78?: Pahlavi: Mohammed Riza)      955.053
DS335-498       SOUTHERN ASIA & Indian Ocean Region     954, 958.1, 959.1
DS335           INDIAN OCEAN REGION & Southern Asia (gen.)
DS350-375       AFGHANISTAN        958.1
DS356        Afghanistan (gen.)        958.1
DS361        Afghanistan (19th-20th c.: gen.)        958.103-104
DS368        Afghanistan (1901-19: Habibullah)       958.103-104
DS369.4      Afghanistan (1933-: Muhammad Zahir Shah & others)      958.1043
DS376-498       INDIA, Pakistan, Ceylon, Burma, etc.      954, 959.1
DS401-498       PAKISTAN (pre-1947), India, Ceylon, Burma, etc.     954
DS401-481       India (overall) & pre-1947 Pakistan     954
DS403        Primary sources, documents (India, pre-1947 Pak.)
DS413        Description & travel (India, pre-1947 Pak.)
DS442.6      Military history (India: 1901-)
DS443        Naval history (India)
DS448        Diplomacy & politics (India, pre-1947 Pak.: 20th c.)
DS450.A-Z    Foreign relns. (India-other specific places)      327.540+
DS450.G3     Foreign relns. (India-Ger.)       327.54043
DS450.J3     Foreign relns. (India-Japan)       327.54052
DS463-480.83 India (1761-1947: Brit. rule)       954.03
DS463        India (1761-1947: Brit. rule: gen.)
DS480.4      India (1914-19)       954.0356-0357
DS480.45     India (1919-47)       954.035+
DS480.5      India (1916-21: Viscount of Chelmsford)
DS480.8      India (1931-36: Marquis of Willingdon)
DS480.82     India (1936-43: Marquis of Linlithgow)      954.0359
DS480.83     India (1943-47: Earl of Wavell)      954.0359
DS481.A-Z    Biography (India: 1901-: inclu. memoirs)
DS481.A1        Biography (India: 1901-: collective)
DS481.B6        Bose, Subhas Chandra (India: 1901+ era)
DS481.G3        Gandhi, Mohandas (India: 1901+ era)
DS481.N35       Nehru, Jawaharlal (India: 1901+ era)
DS481.S8        Sultan Muhammad Shah, Sir, Agha Khan (India: 1901+ era)
```

DS485-498   Local history (India, Pak., Burma, Ceylon, Indian Ocean islands, etc.)
DS485.A-Z   Local history (Indian region kingdom, states, etc.)
DS485.B39-492 Bengal (E. Pak.)
DS485.B39-493 Pakistan (Bengal: East & West)   954.14
DS485.B493   Bengal (W. Pak.)   954.14
DS485.B79-892 BURMA (SEE DS527-530 for later items)   959.1
DS485.B89   Burma (1851-1947)   959.104
DS486.A-Z   Local history (India, Burma, etc.)
DS486.B7   Bombay, India
DS486.C2   Calcutta, India
DS486.R25   Rangoon, Burma
DS488-490   CEYLON   954.93
DS489.5   Sri Lanka (Ceylon: gen.)
DS491.A-Z   INDIAN OCEAN ISLANDS
DS491.A5-6   Andaman & Nicobar Islands
DS491.M3   Maldive Islands

DS501-935+   FAR EAST, Eastern & Southeastern Asia   950-952, 958-959
DS503   Primary sources, documents (Far East, E. & SE.Asia)
DS504   Dictionaries, guidebooks, etc. (Far East, E. & SE.Asia)
DS508   Description & travel (Far East, E. & SE.Asia: 1901-50)   915.0441
DS516-517   Russo-Japanese War (1904-5)   952.031, 947.083
DS518-518.9   EASTERN ASIA (history & foreign relns.: inclu. SE. Asia)
DS518   Far East (1904-45: inclu. Far Eastern question: SEE ALSO DU29)
                                                            327.5, 950.41
DS518.2   Far Eastern question (France)
DS518.3   Far Eastern question (Ger.)
DS518.4   Far Eastern question (G.B.)
DS518.5   Far Eastern question (Netherlands)
DS518.6   Far Eastern question (Port.)
DS518.7   Far Eastern question (Russia)
DS518.8   Far Eastern question (U.S.)
DS518.9.A-Z   Far Eastern question (misc. countries: SEE DS845 for Japan,
                     DS740.63 for China)
DS519   Yellow Peril
DS521-689   SOUTHEAST ASIA, Dutch East Indies, Philippines   959
DS521-605   Southeast Asia   959
DS521-560   INDOCHINA   959-959.7
DS521-526+   Asia, Southeast (newer titles)
DS521   Southeast Asia (newer titles: gen.)   959
DS522.4   Description & travel (SE. Asia: 1901-50: for earlier books SEE
                     DS525)   915.9045+
DS525   Southeast Asia (gen. histories: older titles have descrip. & travel)
DS526.6   Southeast Asia (1900-45)
DS527-530   BURMA (SEE DS485.B89 for earlier titles)
DS527.4   Burma (gen.)
DS527.6   Description & travel (Burma: 1824-1945)
DS530   Burma (1885-1945)

DS531-560	FRENCH INDOCHINA	959.4, 959.6-7
DS532	Primary sources, documents (Fr. Indoch.)	
DS534	Description & travel (Fr. Indoch.: 1788-1950)	915.97043
DS541	French Indochina (gen.)	
DS544	Military history (Fr. Indoch.)	
DS545	Naval history (Fr. Indoch.)	
DS549	French Indochina (1884-1945)	959.703
DS554	CAMBODIA (SEE ALSO DS557.C2 for older works)	959.6
DS554.5-58	Foreign relns. (Cambodia: plus gen. hist.)	
DS554.7-73	Cambodia (1863-1954)	959.603
DS555	LAOS (SEE ALSO DS557.L2 for earlier titles)	959.4
DS555.5-58	Foreign relns. (Laos: ALSO gen. hist.)	
DS555.7-73	Laos (1893-1954)	959.403+
DS556	VIETNAM (Annam)	959.7
DS556.2	Primary sources, documents (Viet.)	
DS556.36	Description & travel (Viet.: 1801-1954)	915.97043
DS556.5	Annam (Vietnam: gen.)	
DS556.57	Diplomacy (Viet.: gen.)	
DS556.58.A-Z	Foreign relns. (Viet.-other countries: by place)	
DS556.58.F8	Foreign relns. (Viet.-Fr.)	
DS556.58.J3	Foreign relns. (Viet.-Japan)	
DS557.A-Z	Local history (Fr. Indoch.: regions: earlier titles: by place)	
DS557.C2	CAMBODIA (SEE DS554 for later works)	
DS557.L2	LAOS (SEE DS555 for later titles)	
DS558.8	Vietnam (1802-1954)	
DS558.82	Biography (Viet.: collective)	
DS558.83.A-Z	Biography (Viet.: by name: inclu. memoirs: Ho Chi Minh at DS560.72.H6)	
DS558.A-Z	Local history (Fr. Indoch.: towns: earlier works)	
DS558.A6	Angkor, Cam.	
DS558.H3	Hanoi, Viet. (for later titles use DS560.92.H3)	
DS558.S3	Saigon, Viet. (SEE DS559.93.S2 for later titles)	
DS559.92.A-Z	Local history (Viet.: regions, protectorates, etc.)	
DS559.92.A5	Annam (Fr. protectorate only)	
DS559.93.A-Z	Local history (Viet.: cities, towns, etc.)	
DS559.93.S2	Saigon, Viet. (for earlier works use DS558.S3)	959.7
DS560	NORTH VIETNAM (1945-75)	959.7
DS560.6	North Vietnam (gen.)	
DS560.68	Diplomacy (N. Viet.)	
DS560.69.A-Z	Foreign relns. (N. Viet.-other countries)	
DS560.72.A-Z	Biography (N. Viet.: 1945-: inclu. memoirs)	
DS560.72.H6	Ho Chi Minh (N. Viet.)	
DS560.9.A-Z	Local history (N. Viet.: regions etc.)	
DS560.92.A-Z	Local history (N. Viet.: cities etc.)	
DS560.92.H3	Hanoi, N. Viet. (SEE DS558.H3 for earlier titles)	
DS561-589	THAILAND (Siam)	959.3
DS565	Description & travel (Thai.: 1801-1950)	
DS573	Military history (Thai.)	
DS574	Naval history (Thai.)	
DS575	Politics & diplomacy (Thai.)	
DS575.5.A-Z	Foreign relns. (Thai.-other places)	
DS575.5.J3	Foreign relns. (Thai.-Japan)	
DS578	Thailand (19th-20th c.)	959.303-304
DS585	Thailand (1935-46: time of Ananda Mahidol, or Rama VIII)	959.3043

```
DS588-589    Local history (Thai.)
DS589.B2     Bangkok, Thai.
DS591-599    MALAY PENINSULA, Malaya, & the Straits      959.5
DS596        MALAYA & Malay Peninsula (gen.)
DS596.5          Malay Peninsula (to 1946)        959.503
DS598.A-Z        Local history (Malay Penin.: protectorates, regions, settlements)
DS598.S7     Singapore       959.52
DS599.A-Z    Local history (Malay Penin.: towns etc.)
DS599.M3     Malacca, Malay Penin.
DS600-605    MALAY ARCHIPELAGO & Indonesia       959.8
DS603        Malay Archipelago (gen.)
DS611-649    DUTCH EAST INDIES & Indonesia
DS613            Primary sources, documents (Dutch E. Ind.)
DS619            Description & travel (Dutch E. Ind. & Indon.: 1801-1945)
DS636            Military history (Dutch E. Ind.)
DS637            Naval history (Dutch E. Ind.)
DS638                Politics & diplomacy (Indon.: gen.)
DS640.A-Z            Foreign relns. (Indon.-other countries)
DS640.J3            Foreign relns. (Indon.-Japan)
DS643            INDONESIA (1798-1942: colonial era)        959.8022
DS643.5            Indonesia (1942-45: Japanese occupation)        959.8022
DS646.1            Sumatra (Indon.: gen.)        959.81
DS646.15.A-Z    Local history (Sumatra, Indon.)
DS646.15.P3     Palembang, Sumatra
DS646.17-29     Java (Indon.)        959.82
DS646.2            Description & travel (Java, Indon.: 1801-1945)
DS646.27          Java (Indon.: gen. hist.)
DS646.29.A-Z        Local history (Java, Indon.)
DS646.29.B23        Bandung, Java
DS646.29.B3         Batavia, Java (Djakarta)
DS646.3-38         BORNEO & the Dyaks        959.53-55, .83
DS646.3            Dyak Islands & Borneo (gen.)        959.53, .83
DS646.33-34     British North Borneo        959.53
DS646.335.A-Z   Local history (Br. N. Borneo)
DS646.335.B24   Balikpapan, Br. N. Borneo
DS646.35          Brunei        959.55
DS646.36-38     Sarawak        959.54
DS646.4            Celebes        959.84
DS646.5            Timor        959.86
DS646.6            Moluccas        959.85
DS647.A-Z    Local history (Dutch E. Ind.: islands, regions, etc.)
DS647.B2     Bali (Indon.)        959.86
DS648        British East Indies (SEE DS646.3 for Borneo)
DS649        German East Indies
DS651-689    PHILIPPINE ISLANDS        959.9
DS653        Primary sources, documents (Philip.)
DS659        Description & travel (Philip.: 1898-1945)        915.99043
DS663-664        Civilization, customs, social life (Philip.)
DS665-666        Races & ethnography (Philip.)
DS668.A3-Z       Philippine Islands (gen.: pubn. 1801+)        959.9
DS671        Military history (Philip.)        355.009599
DS672        Naval history (Philip.)
```

```
DS672.8      Politics & diplomacy (Philip.: gen.)        320.9599, 327.599
DS673.A-Z    Foreign relns. (Philip.: by country)        327.5990+
DS673.J3     Foreign relns. (Philip.-Japan)       327.599052
DS673.U6-7   Foreign relns. (Philip.-U.S.)        327.599073
DS682-684    Military & naval history (Philip.: inclu. battles vs. Sp. & U.S.: PREFER
             E717.7 for Battle of Manila Bay [1898] & U.S.-Sp. naval
confront.)
DS685        Philippine Islands (1901+)    959.903
DS686        Philippine Islands (1935-46: Commonwealth)     959.9035
DS686.2.A-Z  Biography (Philip.: 1935-46: inclu. memoirs)
DS686.2.A2   Biography (Philip.: 1935-46: collective)
DS686.2.L3   Laurel, José P. (Philip.: 1935-46 period)
DS686.2.R6   Romulo, Carlos P. (Philip.: 1935-46 era)
DS686.3      Philippine Islands (1935-44: Manuel Quezon era)     959.9035
DS686.4      Philippine Islands (1942-46: Japanese occup. [1942-45] & Osmeña
             rule [44-46])
DS688.A-Z    Local history (Philip.: islands, provinces, regions)
DS688.B2     Bataan (Luzon, Philip.)       959.91
DS688.B6     Bisayas (Visayan Islands, Philip.)     959.95
DS688.C4     Cebu (Philip.)        959.95
DS688.C67    Corregidor (Philip.)      959.91
DS688.D3     Davao (Philip.)
DS688.L9     Luzon (Philip.)       959.91
DS688.M2     Mindanao (Philip.)       959.97
DS688.M28    Mindoro (Philip.)        959.93
DS688.M5     Mountain Province (Philip.)
DS688.N5     Negros Islands (Philip.)     959.95
DS688.P15    Palawan (Philip.)        959.94
DS688.P2     Panay (Philip.)       959.95
DS688.S9     Sulu Archipelago (Philip.)    959.99
DS689.A-Z    Local history (Philip.: towns & cities)
DS689.B2     Baguio, Philip.
DS689.C5     Cebu, Philip. (town)
DS689.M2     Manila, Philip.       959.91

DS701-796+   CHINA        951
DS710        Description & travel (China: 1901-48)       915.1043-1044
DS721        Civilization, customs, social life (China: gen.)
DS730-731    Races & ethnography (China)
DS732        Chinese (in other lands: gen.)
DS733        Dictionaries, chronologies, etc. (China)
DS735.A3-Z   China (gen.: pubn. 1801+)      951
DS740.4      Diplomacy (China: gen.)       327.51
DS740.5.A-Z  Foreign relns. (China & other lands: by name)     327.510+
DS740.5.G2-3 Foreign relns. (China-Ger.)     327.51043
DS740.5.G5-6 Foreign relns. (China-G.B.)
DS740.5.G6.H6    Foreign relns. (China-Hong Kong)
DS740.5.G6.J3    Foreign relns. (China-Japan)      327.51052
DS740.5.S65  Foreign relns. (China-Sov. Un.)     327.51047
DS740.5.U6-7 Foreign relns. (China-U.S.)  [PREFER E183.8.C5]     327.51073
DS740.63     Far Eastern question (China: 1861-1945)
```

DS761	China (1861-1912)	
DS764.4-767.7	Chinese-Japanese War (1894-5)	951.03, 952.031
DS765	Sino-Japanese War (1894-5: gen.)	
DS770-772	Boxer Rebellion (China: 1899-1901)	951.03
DS773.32-6	Chinese Revolution (1911-12)	951.03
DS773.83-776	China (1912-49 [Republic] & 20th c. overall)	951.03-04
DS773.83	Primary sources, documents (China: 20th c. & 1912-49)	
DS774	China (1912-49 [Republic] & 20th c. overall: gen.)	951.04
DS775.2	Civilization, customs, social life (China: 20th c. & 1912-49)	
DS775.4	Military history (China: 20th c. & 1912-49)	
DS775.5	Naval history (China: 20th c. & 1912-49)	
DS775.7	Politics (China: 20th c. & 1912-49)	
DS775.8	Foreign relns. (China: 20th c. & 1912-49)	
DS776	Biography (China: 20th c. & 1912-49: collective: SEE partic. era for indiv.)	
DS776.4	China (1912-28: gen.)	951.041
DS777.A2-567	Sun Yat Sen (China: 1912-49 era: writings of)	
DS777.A3	Sun Yat Sen (China: 1912-49 era: autobiography)	
DS777.A597.A-Z89	Sun Yat Sen (China: 1912-49 era: biograpy & criticism)	
DS777.15.A-Z	Biography (China: 1912-49 period: except Sun Yat Sen)	
DS777.2	China (1913: 2d Rev.)	
DS777.43	May 4th Movement (China: 20th c.)	
DS777.46	Northern Expedition (China: 1926-28)	
DS777.462	Tsinan, Ch. (N. Exped., 1926-28: incident)	
DS777.47-514	China (1928-37: Nationalist rule)	951.042
DS777.47	China (1928-37: gen.)	
DS777.487	Biography (China: 1928-37 era: collective)	
DS777.488.A-Z	Biography (China: 1928-37 era: indiv. inclu. memoirs)	
DS777.488.C5	Chiang Kai Shek (China: 1887-1975: SEE DS778.M3 for Mao Tse Tung)	
DS777.5	Chinese-Japanese Conflict (1931-33)	951.042, 952.033
DS777.51	Shanghai, Ch. (Ch.-Jpn. Confl.: 1932: invasion)	
DS777.5132-5139	Long March (China: 1934-35: Communists)	
DS777.5134	Long March (China: 1934-35: Communists: gen.)	
DS777.514	Sian, Ch. (1936: incident)	
DS777.518	China (1937-45)	951.042
DS777.5194-5	Biography (China: 1937-45)	
DS777.52-533	Sino-Japanese Conflict (1937-45)	940.53, 951.042, 952.033
DS777.52	Primary sources, documents (Sino-Jpn. Confl., 1937-45)	
DS777.53	Chinese-Japanese Conflict (1937-45: gen.)	940.53, 951.042, 952.033
DS777.5314	Personal accounts (Sino-Jpn. Confl., 1937-45: collections)	
DS777.5315.A-Z	Personal accounts (Sino-Jpn. Confl., 1937-45: indiv. by name)	
DS777.5316.A-Z	Battles, campaigns, etc. (Sino-Jpn. Confl., 1937-45: by name)	
DS777.533.A-Z	Sino-Japanese Conflict (1937-45: misc. topics)	
DS777.533.I53	Indemnity (Sino-Jpn. Confl., 1937-45)	
DS777.533.M3	Marco Polo Bridge Incident (Sino-Jpn. Confl.: 1937)	
DS777.533.S65	Spies, intelligence (Sino-Jpn. Confl., 1937-45)	
DS777.533.U53	Underground movements (Sino-Jpn. Confl., 1937-45)	
DS777.534	Southern Anhui (China: Sino-Jpn. Confl.: 1941: incident)	
DS777.535	China (1945-49: Republic: gen.)	951.042
DS777.54	Chinese Civil War (1945-49: gen.)	
DS778.A-Z	Biography (China: 1949+)	
DS778.M3	Mao Tse Tung (China: 1893-1976: SEE DS777.488.C5 for Chiang Kai Shek)	

DS781-784.2+	MANCHURIA	951.803-804
DS783.7	Manchuria (19th-20th c.)	
DS783.7.L4-45	League of Nations Commission of Enquiry (Manchuria: Lytton Commission)	
DS783.7.L45	Lytton Commission (Manchuria: League of Nations Commission of Enquiry: summary & var. reports)	
DS783.8	Mukden, Manch. (Ch.-Jpn. Confl.:1931: incident)	
DS784	Manchoukuo (1932-45: P'u-i era)	
DS785.A5-Z	CENTRAL ASIA & Tibet (pubns. to 1950: gen.) 951.5, 958 (C. Asia)	
DS786	TIBET & Central Asia (1951+ pubns.: gen.)	
DS793.A-Z	Local history (China: dependencies, provinces, areas, etc.)	
DS793.G6	Gobi (China)	
DS793.H5	Honan (China)	
DS793.H7	Hunan (China)	
DS793.K4	Kiangsi (China)	
DS793.K6	Kwangsi (China)	
DS793.K7	Kwangtung (China)	
DS793.K8	Kweichow (China)	
DS793.L6	Lop-nor (China: lake)	
DS793.M7	MONGOLIA (SEE ALSO DS19-23.1 for Mongols) 951.7	
DS793.S8	Szechwan (China)	
DS793.Y25	Yangtze River (China) 951.2	
DS793.Y8	Yunnan (China)	
DS795	Peiping, China (Peking) 951.156	
DS796.A-Z	Local history (China: cities & towns)	
DS796.C2	Canton, China	
DS796.H3	Hankow, China	
DS796.H7	HONG KONG	951.25
DS796.M2	MACAO	951.26
DS796.M8	Mukden, China	
DS796.N2	Nanking, China	
DS796.S2	Shanghai, China	951.132
DS796.T5	Tientsin, China	
DS796.T7	Tsingtao, China	
DS798.92-799.99+	FORMOSA (Taiwan: SEE ALSO DS895.F7-77 for many pre-1970 pubns.) 951.249	
DS799	TAIWAN (Formosa: gen. hist., culture, descrip.)	
DS799.15	Description & travel (Formosa: to 1945) 915.1249044	
DS799.5	Formosa (gen.) 951.249	
DS799.625	Diplomacy (Formosa: gen.)	
DS799.63.A-Z	Foreign relns. (Formosa-other places)	
DS799.63.J3	Foreign relns. (Formosa-Japan)	
DS799.69-72	Formosa (1895-1945) 951.24904	
DS799.693	Primary sources, documents (Formosa: 1895-1945)	
DS799.7	Taiwan (1895-1945: gen.)	
DS799.714	Military history (Formosa: 1895-1945)	
DS799.716	Politics (Formosa: 1895-1945)	
DS799.718	Foreign relns. (Formosa: 1895-1945)	
DS799.72.A-Z	Biography (Formosa: 1895-1945)	
DS801-897+	JAPAN 952	
DS803	Primary sources, documents (Japan)	
DS805	Dictionaries, gazeteers, guidebooks (Japan)	
DS806	Japan (gen. & cultural)	
DS810	Description & travel (Japan: 1901-45) 915.2043	

DS821	Civilization, customs, social life (Japan: gen.)
DS822.25	Civilization, customs, social life (Japan: 1868+)
DS822.4	Civilization, customs, social life (Japan: 1912-45)
DS827.A-Z	Civilization, customs, social life (Japan: by special topic)
DS827.B98	Bushido (Jpn. custom)
DS827.D4	Death (Jpn. custom)
DS827.S3	Samurai (Jpn. custom)
DS833	Dictionaries, chronologies, etc. (Japan)
DS834	Biography (Japan: collective)
DS834.1	Biography (Japan: Imperial family & rulers)
DS835	Japan (gen. history, descrip., culture)
DS838	Military history (Japan: overall) 355.00952
DS838.7	Military history (Japan: 1868+) 355.00952, .033052, .033252, .033552
DS839	Naval history (Japan: gen.) 359.00952
DS839.7	Naval history (Japan: 1868+) 359.00952, .4752
DS840-849	Diplomacy & politics (Japan) 320.952, 327.52
DS840	Primary sources, documents (Japan)
DS841	Politics & diplomacy (Japan: gen.)
DS844	Pamphlets & minor works (Jpn. polit. & dipl. hist.)
DS845	Diplomacy (Japan: gen.) 327.52
DS847	Pamphlets & minor works (Jpn. for. relns.)
DS849.A-Z	Foreign relns. (Japan-other places) 327.520+
DS849.A75	Foreign relns. (Japan-Asia) 327.5205
DS849.A8	Foreign relns. (Japan-Australia) 327.52094
DS849.B9	Foreign relns. (Japan-Burma)
DS849.C15	Foreign relns. (Japan-Cambodia)
DS849.C5	Foreign relns. (Japan-China) 327.52051
DS849.G3	Foreign relns. (Japan-Ger.) 327.52043
DS849.G7	Foreign relns. (Japan-G.B.) 327.52041
DS849.I4	Foreign relns. (Japan-India)
DS849.I45	Foreign relns. (Japan-Indoch.)
DS849.I5	Foreign relns. (Japan-Indonesia)
DS849.I8	Foreign relns. (Japan-It.)
DS849.K5	Foreign relns. (Japan-Korea)
DS849.M3	Foreign relns. (Japan-Malayas)
DS849.N45	Foreign relns. (Japan-New Zea.)
DS849.P5	Foreign relns. (Japan-Philip.) 327.520599
DS849.R9	Foreign relns. (Japan-Rus.) 327.52047
DS849.S65	Foreign relns. (Japan-Sov. Un.) 327.52047
DS849.T4	Foreign relns. (Japan-Thai.)
DS849.U6-7	Foreign relns. (Japan-U.S.) 327.52073
DS849.V5	Foreign relns. (Japan-Viet.)
DS881.85+	Japan (1868+: modern era) 952.03
DS885	Japan (20th c.) 952.03-04
DS885.5.A-Z	Biography (Japan: 20th c.: inclu. memoirs: SEE ALSO DS890)
DS885.5.A1	Biography (Japan: 20th c.: collective)
DS885.5.K6	Konoye, Fumimaro, Prince (Japan: 20th. c.)
DS886	Japan (1912-26: Taisho time: Yoshihito) 952.032
DS887	Japan (1914-18: WWI era) 952.032
DS888	Japan (1912-26: special topics: inclu. large earthquakes like 1923)
DS888.15-DS890	Japan (1926-1989: Showa period: Hirohito rule) 952.033
DS888.15	Japan (1926-1989: Hirohito rule: collected, non-serial works)
DS888.2	Japan (1926-1989: Hirohito rule: gen.)
DS888.5	Japan (1926-45) 952.033
DS889	Japan (1945+: may ALSO cover 1926+) 952.04

DS889.2	Japanese propaganda (1926-89: in other lands: gen.)	
DS889.3.A-Z	Propaganda, Japanese (1926-89: abroad: by place)	
DS889.3.C5	Propaganda, Japanese (1926-89: China)	
DS889.3.G7	Propaganda, Japanese (1926-89: G.B.)	
DS889.3.I5	Propaganda, Japanese (1926-89: Indonesia)	
DS889.3.P5	Propaganda, Japanese (1926-89: Philip.)	
DS889.3.U6	Propaganda, Japanese (1926-89: U.S.)	
DS889.7-9	Biography (Japan: 1926-89: royal family)	
DS889.8	Hirohito (Japan: Emperor, 1926-89)	
DS890.A-Z	Biography (Japan: 1926-89: inclu. memoirs: SEE ALSO DS885.5)	
DS890.A1	Biography (Japan: 1926-89: collective)	
DS890.N23	Nagumo, Chuichi, Vice Adm. (Japan: 1926-89 period)	
DS890.T64	Tojo, Hideki, Gen., 1884-1948 (Japan: 1926-89 era)	
DS890.Y25	Yamamoto, Isoroku, Adm., 1884-1943 (Japan: 1926-89 era)	
DS895.A-Z	Local history (Japan: islands, provinces, regions)	
DS895.B6	Bonin Islands (Japan)	952.85
DS895.F7-77	FORMOSA (Taiwan: SEE ALSO DS799 for many post-1969 pubns.)	
		951.249
DS895.F72	Taiwan (Formosa: gen.)	
DS895.F75	Formosa (19th-20th c.)	951.24903-24904
DS895.H6	Hokkaido (Japan)	952.4
DS895.K9	Kurile Islands (Japan)	957.7
DS895.O4	Okinawa (Japan)	952.81
DS895.R9	Ryukyu Islands (Japan)	952.81
DS896	Tokyo, Japan (SEE DS897.T6 for earlier works)	952.135
DS896.6	Tokyo, Japan (gen.)	
DS896.64	Tokyo, Japan (1867-1945)	952.13503
DS897.A-Z	Local history (Japan: towns & cities)	
DS897.H48	Hiroshima, Japan	952.19
DS897.K8	Kyoto, Japan	952.191
DS897.N285	Nagasaki, Japan	952.2
DS897.O8	Osaka, Japan	952.183
DS897.T6	Tokyo, Japan (SEE DS896 for later pubns.)	952.135
DS901-935+	KOREA	951.9
DS901	Primary sources, documents (Korea)	
DS907	Korea (gen.)	
DS910	Politics & diplomacy (Korea)	
DS910.2.A-Z	Foreign relns. (Korea-other lands)	327.5190+
DS910.2.C5	Foreign relns. (Korea-China)	327.519051
DS910.2.J3	Foreign relns. (Korea-Japan)	327.519052
DS910.2.R9	Foreign relns. (Korea-Rus.)	
DS916	Korea (20th c.)	951.903-904
DS916.5.A-Z	Biography (Korea: 20th c.: inclu. memoirs)	
DS916.5.R5	Rhee, Syngman (Korea: 20th c.)	
DS917	Korea (1945+)	

DT	AFRICA 960-969	
DT1-38	Africa (overall) 960	
DT12	Description & travel (Africa: 1901-50)	916.0431-0432
DT29	Africa (1884-1945: gen.)	960.23-31
DT31-38	Politics & diplomacy (Africa: inclu. colonialism)	320.96, 327.6
DT31.5	Diplomacy & politics (Africa: 19th-20th c.: gen.)	
DT32.5	Foreign relns. (Africa-G.B.: 19th-20th c.)	960.23-3, 325.3+
DT33.5	Foreign relns. (Africa-Fr.: 19th-20th c.)	
DT34.5	Foreign relns. (Africa-Ger.: 19th-20th c.)	
DT35.5	Foreign relns. (Africa-It.: 19th-20th c.)	
DT43-154	EGYPT & the Egyptian Sudan 962	
DT43	Primary sources, documents (Egypt)	
DT55	Description & travel (Egypt & Egyp. Sudan: 1901-50)	916.2044-2045
DT77	Egypt (gen.)	
DT81	Military history (Egypt)	
DT82	Politics & diplomacy (Egypt: gen.)	
DT82.5.A-Z	Foreign relns. (Egypt & various countries)	327.620+
DT82.5.G3	Foreign relns. (Egypt-Ger.) 327.62043	
DT82.5.G7	Foreign relns. (Egypt-G.B.) 327.62041	
DT107	Egypt (1879-1952)	962.03-052
DT107.2.A-Z	Biography (Egypt: 1879-1952)	
DT107.7	Egypt (1914-17: Hussein Kamil) 962.04	
DT107.8	Egypt (1917-36: Fuad I) 962.04-051	
DT107.82	Egypt (1936-52: Faruk I) 962.052	
DT108	EGYPTIAN SUDAN (inclu. Anglo-Egyptian: for newer titles SEE	
	DT154.1-159) 962.4	
DT108.6	Anglo-Egyptian Sudan (1899-1955) 962.403	
DT124	Nile River (20th c.: descrip. & travel) 962.044-045	
DT137.A-Z	Local history (Egypt: provinces, regions, etc.)	
DT137.A7	Arabian Desert (Egypt)	
DT139-152	Cairo, Egypt 962.16	
DT143	Cairo, Egypt (gen. hist. & descrip.)	
DT154.1-159	SUDAN & Anglo-Egyptian Sudan (SEE DT108 for older works)	
DT154.A-Z	Local history (Egypt: cities, towns, other)	
DT154.A4	Alexandria, Egypt	
DT154.K63	Khartoum, Egypt	
DT154.S9	Suez Canal (Egypt: inclu. Isthmus) 962.15	
DT155.6	Sudan (gen.)	
DT156.7	Sudan (1900-1955)	
DT160-177	NORTH AFRICA (Egypt & Barbary States) 961-962	
DT165	Description & travel (N. Africa: 1901-50) 916.2043	
DT176	North Africa (19th-20th c.) 961.023-03+	
DT181-346	BARBARY STATES 961.1-2, 964-965, 966	
DT190	Description & travel (Barbary States: 1901-50)	
DT204	Barbary States (19th-20th c.) 961.023-03+	
DT211-239	LIBYA 961.2	
DT220	Description & travel (Libya: 1901-50)	
DT227	Politics & diplomacy (Libya: gen.)	
DT227.5.A-Z	Foreign relns. (Libya & other particular places)	
DT227.5.G3	Foreign relns. (Libya-Ger.)	
DT227.5.I8	Foreign relns. (Libya-It.)	
DT235	Libya (1912-45) 961.203	

```
DT238-239    Local history (Libya)
DT239.A-Z    Local history (Libya: towns etc.)
DT239.T7     Tripoli, Libya
DT241-269    TUNISIA            961.1
DT250        Description & travel (Tunisia: 1901-50)
DT257        Politics & diplomacy (Tunisia: gen.)
DT257.5.A-Z      Foreign relns. (Tunisia-other lands: by name)
DT257.5.I8       Foreign relns. (Tunisia-It.)
DT264            Tunisia (1881-1957: Fr. Protectorate)        961.104
DT271-299    ALGERIA           965
DT280        Description & travel (Algeria: 1901-50)
DT294.5-295.3    Algeria (1901-62: for older titles use DT295)
DT294.5-7        Algeria (1901-45)           965.04 (1900-62)
DT295        Algeria (1901+: for newer works SEE DT294.5-295.3)        965.04+
DT299.A-Z    Local history (Algeria: towns etc.)
DT299.A5     Algiers, Alg.          965.3
DT299.O7     Oran, Alg.
DT301-330    MOROCCO           964
DT310        Description & travel (Morocco: 1901-50)
DT317        Politics & diplomacy (Morocco: gen.)
DT317.5.A-Z      Foreign relns. (Morocco-other specific places)
DT317.5.F8       Foreign relns. (Morocco-Fr.)
DT317.5.G3       Foreign relns. (Morocco-Ger.)
DT324        Morocco (19th-20th c.)          964.03-04
DT329.A-Z    Local history (Morocco: cities, towns, etc.)
DT329.C3     Casablanca, Mor.           964.3
DT329.T16    Tangier Zone, Mor.         964.2
DT330        SPANISH MOROCCO           964.2
DT331-346    SAHARA DESERT          966
DT333        Sahara Desert (gen. hist., descrip. etc.)
DT351-364        CENTRAL AFRICA          967
DT365-469        EAST AFRICA             967.6, 963
DT365.7      East Africa (1884-1960: gen.)  967.6
DT367        ITALIAN EAST AFRICA & Northeast Africa        963
DT367.75     NORTHEAST AFRICA (1900-74)        963.05+
DT371-390    ETHIOPIA (Abyssinia)            963
DT378        Description & travel (Ethiopia: 1901-50)
DT386        ABYSSINIA (19th -20th c.)        963.03-05+
DT387-387.6      Ethiopia (1889-1928: inclu. 1895-6 conflict w. Italy)     963.043-054
DT387.7          Ethiopia (1928-74: Haile Selassie)  963.055-06
DT387.8          Italo-Ethiopian War (1935-6)        963.056
DT387.8.A1-7     Primary sources, documents (Italo-Eth. War, 1935-6)
DT387.8.A8-Z     Italo-Ethiopian War (1935-6: gen.)  963.056
DT390.A-Z        Local history (Ethiopia: kingdoms, regions, towns, etc.)  963.056
DT390.A3             Addis Ababa, Eth.
DT391-398    ERITREA        963.5
DT401-420    SOMALILAND          967.7
DT406        BRITISH SOMALILAND        967.73-7305+
DT411        FRENCH SOMALILAND (Djibouti or Afars & Issas)        967.71-7104+
DT416        ITALIAN SOMALILAND           967.73-7305+
```

DT421-435 BRITISH EAST AFRICA & East Africa   967.6
DT431   EAST AFRICA (to 1960)
DT433.5-434   KENYA (newer books)
DT433.57-433.577   Kenya (1895-1963: Brit. era)
DT433.575   Kenya (1920-63)
DT434.E2   Kenya (older books)
DT434.Z3   ZANZIBAR (Brit. colony: SEE DT449.Z2+ for newer)
DT435   Zanzibar (island & coast)
DT436-449   TANGANYIKA (German East Africa)   967.82
DT444   German East Africa (gen.: later Tanganyika)
DT447   Tanganyika (to 1960: newer titles)
DT449.Z2-Z29 ZANZIBAR (SEE DT434.Z3 & DT435 for older titles)
DT449.Z28   Zanzibar (1890-1963)
DT451-465   MOZAMBIQUE (Portuguese East Africa)   967.9
DT469.A-Z   East African islands
DT469.M21-38 MADAGASCAR   969.1
DT471-720   WEST AFRICA   966-967, 968.8
DT491-518   BRITISH WEST AFRICA   966, 966.4-51, .7, .81, .9
DT521-553   FRENCH WEST AFRICA   966, 966.1-3, .52, .68, .81
DT561-584   CAMEROONS (German West Africa) & Togoland 966.6695, .81, 967.1
DT591-617   ANGOLA (Portuguese West Africa)   967.3
DT641-665   BELGIAN CONGO   967.5
DT671.A-Z   West African islands
DT671.C2   CAPE VERDE ISLANDS   966.58
DT701-720   SOUTHWEST AFRICA (German Southwest Africa)   967.1, 968.8
DT730-995   SOUTHERN AFRICA   968
DT751-848   BRITISH SOUTH AFRICA 968-968.7
DT769   Military history (S. Afr.)   355.00968
DT779   SOUTH AFRICA (1909-: Union)   968.05+
DT779.5   South Africa (1914-18: WWI period)
DT779.6   South Africa (1919-39)   968.05-054
DT779.7   South Africa (1939-45: WWII era)   968.055
DT855   BRITISH CENTRAL AFRICA (1901-52)   968.97
DT858-865   NYASALAND (Malawi, Brit. Cent. Afr. Protec.)
DT946-965   RHODESIA

DU   OCEANIA (Pacific Ocean)   990-996, 909.0964
DU22   Description & travel (Pacific: 1898-1950)
DU28   Civilization, customs, social life, races (Pacific)
DU28.3   PACIFIC OCEAN (Oceania: gen.)   990, 990.09, 909.0964
DU29   Diplomacy & politics (Pacific: gen.: inclu. colonial rule)
DU30   Foreign relns. (Pacific-U.S.)
DU40   Foreign relns. (Pacific-G.B.)
DU50   Foreign relns. (Pacific-Fr.)
DU60   Foreign relns. (Pacific-Ger.)
DU65   Foreign relns. (Pacific-Sp.)

DU80-480   AUSTRALIA, New Zealand, Tasmania
DU80-398   AUSTRALIA   994
DU80   Primary sources, documents (Australia)
DU104   Description & travel (Australia: 1901-50)   919.4044
DU107   Civilization, customs, social life (Australia)
DU110   Australia (gen.)   994
DU112.3   Military history (Australia)   355.00994, .033094
DU112.4   Naval history (Australia)   359.00994

DU113   Diplomacy (Australia: gen.)   327.94
DU113.5.A-Z   Foreign relns. (Australia-other specific lands)   327.940+
DU113.5.G7   Foreign relns. (Australia-G.B.)   327.94041
DU113.5.J3   Foreign relns. (Australia-Japan)   327.94052
DU113.5.U6-7   Foreign relns. (Australia-U.S.)   327.94073
DU114.A2   Biography (Australia: collective)
DU114.A3-Z   Biography (Australia: by name: SEE ALSO DU116.2 for later works)
DU114.B52   Blamey, Thomas, Sir (Australia)
DU116   Australia (1901-45: Commonwealth)   994.04
DU116.2   Biography (Australia: 1901-45: SEE DU114 for earlier pubns.)
DU120-122 Races & ethnography (Australia)
DU145-398 Local history (Australia)
DU145   Canberra, Australia (inclu. Capital Territory)
DU150-180   New South Wales (Australia)   994.4
DU161   New South Wales (Australia: 1837-1950: gen.)
DU178   Sydney, Australia   994.41
DU180.A-Z Local history (New S. Wales, Aust.: towns, regions, etc. except
                   Sydney)
DU200-230 Victoria (Australia)   994.5
DU212   Victoria (Australia: 1851-1950: inclu. descrip.)
DU228   Melbourne, Australia   994.51
DU230.A-Z   Local history (Victoria, Aust.: all except Melbourne)
DU250-280   Queensland (Australia)   994.3
DU260-270   Queensland (Australia: gen.: inclu. descrip.)
DU278   Brisbane, Australia   994.31
DU280.A-Z Local history (Queens., Aust.: all except Brisbane)
DU280.C3   Cape York Peninsula (Queens., Aust.)
DU280.M7   Moreton Bay (Queens., Aust.)
DU280.T7   Torres Strait (Queens., Aust.)
DU300-330   South Australia   994.23
DU310-320   South Australia (gen. & descrip.)
DU328   Adelaide, Australia   994.231
DU330.A-Z Local history (S. Australia except Adelaide)
DU350-380   Western Australia   994.1
DU360-370   Western Australia (gen. & descrip.)
DU378   Perth, Australia   994.11
DU380.A-Z   Local history (W. Australia except Perth)
DU380.F8   Fremantle. Australia
DU390   Central Australia   994.2
DU392-398 Northern Australia   994.29
DU395-396 Northern Australia (gen. & descrip.)
DU398.A-Z   Local history (N. Australia: regions, towns, etc.)
DU398.D3   Darwin, Australia   994.295
DU400-430 NEW ZEALAND   993.1
DU411   Description & travel (N. Zea.: 1840-1950)   919.31042-310435
DU420   New Zealand (gen.)   993.1-1037+
DU420.5   Military history (N. Zea.)   355.009931
DU421   Politics & diplomacy (N. Zea.: gen.)
DU421.5.A-Z   Foreign relns. (N. Zea.-other specific places)   327.9310+
DU421.5.J3   Foreign relns. (N. Zea.-Japan)   327.931052
DU421.5.U6-7   Foreign relns. (N. Zea.-U.S.)   327.931073
DU422.A-Z Biography (N. Zea.: inclu. memoirs: by name)
DU423   Races & ethnography (N. Zea.)
DU428   Wellington, N.Z.   993.127

DU430.A-Z	Local history (N. Zea.: regions, towns, dependencies, etc. except Wellington)	
DU430.A8	Auckland, N.Zea.	993.122
DU430.C5	Christchurch, N. Zea.	993.155
DU430.C6	COOK ISLANDS	996.23-24
DU450-480	TASMANIA (Van Diemen's Land)	994.6
DU460-470	Van Diemen's Land (Tasmania: gen. & descrip.)	
DU480.A-Z	Local history (Tasmania: regions, towns, etc.)	
DU480.H6	Hobart, Australia (Tasmania)	994.61

DU490   MELANESIA (gen.: SEE DU520-950 for specific islands, groups, atolls, etc.)   993, 993.2-7, 996.1

DU500   MICRONESIA (gen.: SEE DU520-950 for particular islands, island groups, atolls, etc.)   996.5-68

DU510   POLYNESIA (gen.: SEE DU520-950 for specific island groups, individual islands, atolls, etc.)   996, 996.1-4, .9

DU520-950	SOUTH SEAS (Oceanica: islands, chains, groups, etc.)	
DU520	ADMIRALTY ISLANDS	993.7
DU550	BISMARCK ARCHIPELAGO (gen.)	993.6
DU553.A-Z	Local history (Bismarck Arch.: islands, groups, etc. by name)	
DU553.N35	New Britain (Bismarck Arch.: inclu. Rabaul)	
DU553.N4	New Ireland (Bismarck Arch.)	
DU560-568	CAROLINE ISLANDS	996.6
DU563	Description & travel (Caroline Islands)	
DU565	Caroline Islands (gen.)	
DU567	Caroline Islands (modern hist.)	
DU568.A-Z	Local history (Caroline Islands: islands, groups, towns, etc.)	
DU568.P7	Ponape (Carolines)	
DU568.T7	Truk Islands (Carolines)	
DU568.U5	Ulithi (Carolines)	
DU568.Y3	Yap (Carolines)	
DU590	ELLICE ISLANDS	996.81
DU600	FIJI ISLANDS	996.11
DU615	GILBERT ISLANDS (inclu. Tarawa & Makin Atolls)	996.81
DU620-629	HAWAIIAN ISLANDS	996.9
DU623	Description & travel (Hawaiian Is.: to 1950)	919.69043
DU625	Hawaiian Islands (gen.)	996.9
DU627.4	Hawaiian Islands (annex. to U.S.)	
DU627.5.A1-5	Primary sources, documents (Hawaiian Is.: 1900-59)	
DU627.5.A6-Z	Hawaii (1900-59: U.S. Territory)	996.903
DU627.7.A-Z	Biography (Hawaii: 1891-1959: inclu. memoirs)	
DU628.A-Z	Local history (Hawaii: islands, counties, etc.)	
DU628.H25	Hawaii (island)	996.91
DU628.K3	Kauai (Haw. Is.)	996.94
DU628.L3	Lanai (Haw. Is.)	996.923
DU628.M3	Maui (Haw. Is.)	996.921
DU628.M5	Midway Islands (Haw. Is.)	996.99
DU628.M7	Molokai (Haw. Is.)	996.924
DU628.O3	Oahu (Haw. Is.)	996.93
DU629.A-Z	Local history (Hawaii: towns, volcanoes, etc.)	
DU629.H5	Hilo, Haw.	
DU629.H7	Honolulu, Haw.	996.931

DU640-648	MARIANA ISLANDS (Ladrones)	996.7
DU645	Ladrone Islands (Marianas: gen.)	
DU647	Guam (Mariana Is.)	996.7
DU648.A-Z	Local history (Mariana Is.: islands, towns, etc.)	
DU648.S35	Saipan (Mariana Is.)	
DU648.ST4	Tinian (Mariana Is.)	
DU700	MARQUESAS ISLANDS	996.31
DU710	MARSHALL ISLANDS (inclu. Kwajalein Atoll)	996.83
DU720	NEW CALEDONIA	993.2, .97
DU740-746	NEW GUINEA	995
DU740	Papua & New Guinea (gen.: inclu. Brit. terr. & Port Moresby, Owen Stanley Mts., Lae, Salamaua, etc.)	995, 995.3
DU742	German New Guinea (N.E.: SEE ALSO DU550+ for Bismarck Arch.)	993.6, 995
DU744-744.5	DUTCH NEW GUINEA (West)	995.1
DU760	NEW HEBRIDES	993.4
DU810-819	SAMOAN ISLANDS	996.13-14
DU817.A6-Z	Samoa (modern hist.)	
DU819.A1	American Samoa	996.13
DU819.A2	Western Samoa (was Ger. Samoa)	996.14
DU819.A3-Z	Local history (Samoan Is.: partic. islands, towns, etc.)	
DU819.P3	Pago Pago, Samoa	
DU840	SANTA CRUZ ISLANDS	993.5
DU850	SOLOMON ISLANDS (inclu. Guadalcanal, New Georgia, Choiseul, Savo, Florida, Bougainville, etc.)	993.5
DU870	SOCIETY ISLANDS (inclu. Tahiti, Bora Bora, etc.)	996.21
DU880	TONGA ISLANDS	996.12
DU950.A-Z	Pacific Islands (smaller misc.: by name)	
DU950.W28	WAKE ISLAND	996.5
DX1-301	GYPSIES	
DX145	Gypsies in Europe (gen. & elsewhere)	
DX211-275	European Gypsies (by place)	
DX222	Gypsies in Czechoslovakia	
DX229	Gypsies in Germany	
DX241	Gypsies in Russia (inclu. Poland & Lith.)	
E	WESTERN HEMISPHERE (gen.) & United States	970
E1-143	AMERICA (gen.)	970
E18.185	America (1901-)	970.05
E31-45	NORTH AMERICA	970
E45	North America (gen.)	
E77-99	Indians (N. Am.)	970.00497, .1-5, 973.0497
E98.M5	Military skill (Indians of N. Am.)	
E151-860+	UNITED STATES	973-979.9+
E151	United States (gen. & cultural, serials, societies, etc.)	
E161	Civilization, customs, social life (U.S.: gen.)	
E169	Description, travel, civilization, customs (U.S.: 1914-45)	917.3049
E169.1	Americanization, civilization, etc. (U.S.)	
E171	Periodicals & yearbooks (U.S.)	
E172	Associations, societies (U.S.)	
E173	Primary sources, documents (U.S.)	
E174	Dictionaries & encyclopedias (U.S.)	973.03
E174.5	Chronologies (U.S.)	

| E178 | United States (gen. hist.) | 973 |

E178   United States (gen. hist.)   973
E181   Military history (U.S.)   355.00973, .033073
E182   Naval history (U.S.)   359.00973, .4773
E183   Politics (U.S.: gen.)   320.973
E183.7   Diplomacy (U.S.: gen.)   327.73
E183.8.A-Z   Foreign relns. (U.S.-other places)   327.730+
E183.8.C5   Foreign relns. (U.S.-China)   327.73051
E183.8.F8   Foreign relns. (U.S.-Fr.)   327.73044
E183.8.G3   Foreign relns. (U.S.-Ger.)   327.73043
E183.8.G7   Foreign relns. (U.S.-G.B.)   327.73041
E183.8.I8   Foreign relns. (U.S.-It.)   327.73045
E183.8.J3   Foreign relns. (U.S.-Japan)   327.73052
E183.8.R9   Foreign relns. (U.S.-Russia)   327.73047
E183.8.S65   Foreign relns. (U.S.-Sov.Un.)   327.73047
E184.A-Z   Races, ethnography, religious groups (U.S.)   973.04+
E184.A1   Races, ethnography, religious groups (U.S.: gen.)
E184.B7   British (in U.S.)
E184.F8   French (in U.S.)
E184.G3   Germans (in U.S.)
E184.I8   Italians (in U.S.)
E184.J3   Japanese (in U.S.)
E184.J5   Jews (in U.S.)
E184.O6   Orientals (in U.S.)
E184.R9   Russians (in U.S.)
E185   Blacks (in U.S.)   973.0496
E185.63   Blacks as soldiers & seamen (U.S.)
E660-738   United States (1865-1900+)   973.8-89
E660.A-Z   Statesmen (U.S.: collected works: inclu. some working through 1921:
            SEE E742.5 for rest of 20th c.)
E660.W7-75   Wilson, Woodrow (U.S.: 1865-1900 era: works)
E664.A-Z   Biography (U.S.: 1865-1900: by name)
E664.L7   Lodge, Henry Cabot (U.S.: 1865-1900 era)
E714-735   Spanish-American War (1898)   973.89-898
E717.7   Philippine Islands (Sp.-Am. War, 1898: ALSO Battle of Manila Bay)
            973.8937
E740-749   United States (20th c.: overall)   973.9
E740   Associations, periodicals, societies (U.S.: 20th c.)
E740.5   Primary sources, documents (U.S.: 20th c.)
E741   United States (20th c.: gen.)   973.9
E742.5.A-Z   Statesmen (U.S.: collected works: 20th c.: SEE E660 for up to 1921)
E742.5.I25   Ickes, Harold (U.S.: 20th c.: works)
E742.5.R5-7   Roosevelt, Franklin Delano (U.S.: 20th c.: works)
E742.5.W3   Wallace, Henry A. (U.S.: 20th c.: works)
E743   Politics (U.S.: 20th c.)   320.973, .904
E743.5   Subversive activities (in U.S.: propaganda, espionage, 5th column,
            etc.)
E744   Foreign relns. (U.S.: 20th c.: gen.)   327.73
E745   Military history (U.S.: 20th c.: inclu. biog.: more than 1 war)
            355.00973, .033073, .033273, .033573
E746   Naval history (U.S.: 20th c.)   359.00973, .4773

E747	Biography (U.S.: 20th c.: collective)
E748.A-Z	Biography (U.S.: 20th c.: by name)
E748.B32	Baruch, Bernard (U.S.: 20th c.)
E748.D48	Dewey, Thomas (U.S.: 20th c.)
E748.F24	Farley, James (U.S.: 20th c.)
E748.G23	Garner, John Nance (U.S.: 20th c.)
E748.H67	Hopkins, Harry (U.S.: 20th c.)
E748.H93	Hull, Cordell (U.S.: 20th c.)
E748.I28	Ickes, Harold (U.S.: 20th c.)
E748.K55	Knox, W. Frank (U.S.: 20th c.)
E748.S895	Stimson, Henry (U.S.: 20th c.)
E748.W23	Wallace, Henry A. (U.S.: 20th c.)
E748.W7	Willkie, Wendell (U.S.: 20th c.)
E765-783	United States (1913-21: Woodrow Wilson period) 973.913
E766	United States (1913-21: gen.)
E767	Wilson, Woodrow (U.S.: Pres., 1913-21)
E768	Foreign relns. (U.S.: 1913-21)
E772	Woodrow Wilson Foundation
E780	United States (1914-18: WWI era: internal) 973.913
E783	Politics (U.S.: 1920 Pres. campaign)
E784	United States (1919-33: inclu. Roaring Twenties) 973.913-916
E785	United States (1921-3: Warren G. Harding era: gen.: SEE JX235 ALSO for arms limitation conference, Pacific possessions treaty, etc.) 973.914
E791	United States (1923-9: Calvin Coolidge period: gen.: SEE ALSO JX1952 & JX1987 for Kellogg-Briand Pact of 1928) 973.915
E801	United States (1929-33: Pres. Herbert Hoover: inclu. London & 3-Power naval conferences & treaties: SEE ALSO JX1974) 973.916
E802	Hoover, Herbert (U.S.: Pres., 1929-33)
E805-812	United States (1933-45: Pres. Franklin D. Roosevelt) 973.917
E805	Politics (U.S.: Pres. campaign, 1932)
E806	United States (1933-45: gen.)
E807	Roosevelt, Franklin D. (U.S.: Pres., 1933-45)
E807.1	Roosevelt, Franklin D. (U.S.: Pres., 1933-45: family, inclu. Eleanor)
E810	Politics (U.S.: Pres. race, 1936)
E811	Politics (U.S.: Pres. race, 1940)
E812	Politics (U.S.: Pres. race, 1944)
E813-815	United States (1945-53: Pres. Harry S Truman) 973.918
E813	United States (1945-53: gen.)
E814	Truman, Harry S (U.S.: Pres., 1945-53)
E836	Eisenhower, Dwight D. (U.S.: 1953-61) 973.9210924, 940.540973, 355.0024
F	UNITED STATES (local), Canada, Newfoundland, Mexico, Central & South America 974-79+, 971-2, 980-89
F1-975+	United States (local: regions, states, towns, etc.) 974-79
F1-15	New England (overall) 974
F4	New England (gen. hist.) 974
F6-105	New England states 974.1-6
F9	New England (1865-1950) 974.04-042
F16-30	Maine 974.1
F19	Maine (gen.)
F25	Maine (1865-1950)

F61-75	Massachusetts	974.4
F70	Massachusetts (1865-1950: SEE D570.85.M4-41 for war years, 1914- 18 & D769.85.M4-41 for 1939-45)	974.404-043
F73.5	Boston, Mass. (1865-1950)	
F106	Atlantic Coast (U.S.: Maine to Flor.)	974-975
F116-205	Middle Atlantic states & District of Columbia	
F116-130	New York	974.7
F119	New York (gen.)	
F124	New York (1865-1950: SEE D570.85.N4-5 for 1914-18 war years & D769.85.N4-5 for 1939-45)	974.704
F127.A-Z	Local history (New York: regions, counties, etc.)	
F127.H8	Hudson River (N.Y.)	
F127.L8	Long Island (N.Y.)	
F128	New York City, N.Y.	974.71
F128.3	New York City, N.Y. (gen.)	
F128.5	New York City area (N.Y.: 1901-50)	974.7104-043
F128.67.A-Z	New York City, N.Y. (streets, bridges, railroads)	
F128.68.A-Z	New York City, N.Y. (sections, suburbs, rivers)	
F129.A-Z	Local history (N.Y.: cities, towns, etc. except N.Y.C.)	
F129.A3	Albany, N.Y.	
F129.B8	Buffalo, N.Y.	
F130.A-Z	Races, ethnography, religious groups (N.Y.)	
F130.G3	Germans (in N.Y.)	
F130.I8	Italians (in N.Y.)	
F130.J5	Jews (in N.Y.)	
F131-145	New Jersey	974.9
F139	New Jersey (1865-1950: SEE D570.85.N3-31 for 1914-18 war years & D769.85.N3-31 for 1039-45)	
F146-160	Pennsylvania	974.8
F154	Pennsylvania (1865-1950)	
F158	Philadelphia, Penn.	974.811
F191-205	District of Columbia	975.3
F194	Washington, D.C. (gen.)	
F196	Social life & politics (Washington, D.C.)	
F199	Washington, D.C. area (1878-1950)	975.303-304
F203	Local history (Washington, D.C.: cemeteries, churches, hotels, statues, parks, circles, streets, etc.)	
F203.4.A-Z	Monuments, statues, memorials (Washington, D.C.)	
F203.7.A-Z	Washington, D.C. (streets, bridges, railroads)	
F203.7.P4	Pennsylvania Ave. (Washington, D.C.)	
F204.A-Z	Buildings (Washington, D.C.)	
F204.W5	White House (Washington, D.C.)	
F206-220	South Atlantic states & the South (U.S.: covers south of Mason-Dixon Line)	975-976
F215	South & South Atlantic states (1865-1950)	975.04, 976.04
F221-235	Virginia	975.5
F232.A-Z	Local history (Virginia: regions, counties, etc.)	
F232.C43	Chesapeake Bay region (Va.)	
F234.A-Z	Local history (Virginia: towns etc.)	
F234.A7	Arlington National Cemetery (Arlington, Va.)	
F234.N8	Norfolk, Va.	
F251-265	North Carolina	975.6
F259	North Carolina (1865-1950)	
F281-295	Georgia	975.8

F296-395	Gulf states, Mississippi Valley, Middle West, & Texas	975.9-976.4, 976.7-9
F296	Gulf states (U.S.: gen.) 976	
F306-320	Florida 975.9	
F316	Florida (1865-1950) 975.906	
F317.A-Z	Local history (Florida: regions, counties, etc.)	
F317.G8	Gulf Coast (Florida)	
F317.M7	Florida Keys (Monroe County, Fl.)	
F319.A-Z	Local history (Florida: towns etc.)	
F319.P4	Pensacola, Florida	
F321-335	Alabama 976.1	
F326	Alabama (to 1950)	
F336-350	Mississippi 976.2	
F351-355	Mississippi Valley & the Midwest 976-977	
F354	Middle West & Mississippi River Valley (1865-1950) 977.03	
F366-380	Louisiana 976.3	
F381-395	Texas 976.4	
F391	Texas (1846+: SEE D570.85.T4-41 for 1914-18 war years & D769.85.T4-41 for 1939-45) 976.405-406	
F392.A-Z	Local history (Texas: regions, counties, etc.)	
F392.G9	Gulf Coast (Texas)	
F394.A-Z	Local history (Texas: towns etc.)	
F394.D2	Dallas, Texas	
F394.E4	El Paso, Texas	
F394.H8	Houston, Texas 976.41411	
F396-475	Southwest (Old) & lower Mississippi Valley (Ark., Tenn., Ken., Missouri) 976.7-9, 977, 977.8	
F461-475	Missouri 977.8	
F474.S2	St. Louis, Mo. 977.866	
F476-590	Northwest (U.S.: Old) 977	
F484.5	Old Northwest (U.S.: 1865-1950) 977.03	
F486-500	Ohio 977.1	
F536-550	Illinois 977.3	
F546	Illinois (1865-1950) 977.303	
F548	Chicago, Ill. 977.311	
F548.5	Chicago, Ill. (1892-1950) 977.31103-033	
F551-556	Great Lakes (U.S.) 977	
F561-575	Michigan 977.4	
F591-705	West (U.S.) & Trans-Mississippi 978	
F595	Trans-Mississippi & the West (1880-1950) 978.02-033	
F601-615	Minnesota 977.6	
F631-645	North Dakota 978.4	
F676-690	Kansas 978.1	
F691-705	Oklahoma 976.6	
F721-785	Rocky Mts. area (Mont., Idaho, Wyo., Colo.) 978	
F726-740	Montana 978.6	
F771-785	Colorado 978.8	
F786-850	Southwest (New: New Mex., Ariz., Utah, Nev.) 978.9-979.3, 979	
F791-805	New Mexico 978.9	
F801	New Mexico (1848-1950)	
F804.A-Z	Local history (New Mex.: towns etc.)	
F804.L6	Los Alamos, New Mex.	

F851-915+	Pacific States & Alaska	979
F852	Pacific Northwest (1859-1950)	979.5
F856-870	California	979.4
F861	California (gen.)	979.4
F866	California (1869-1950: SEE D570.85.C2-21 for 1914-18 war years & D769.85.C2-21 for 1939-45)	979.404-4053
F867	Southern California	979.49
F868.A-Z	Local history (Calif.: regions, counties, etc.)	
F868.L8	Los Angeles County (Calif.)	979.493
F868.S156	San Francisco Bay area (Calif.)	979.46
F868.S23	Santa Barbara County (Calif.)	979.491
F869.A-Z	Local history (Calif.: towns etc.)	
F869.L8	Los Angeles, Calif.	979.494
F869.S22	San Diego, Calif.	979.498
F869.S3	San Francisco, Calif.	979.461
F870.A-Z	Races, ethnography, religious groups (Calif.)	
F870.A1	Races, ethnography, religious groups (Calif.: gen.)	
F870.G3	Germans (in Calif.)	
F870.J3	Japanese (in Calif.)	
F870.J5	Jews (in Calif.)	
F870.O6	Orientals (in Calif.)	
F886-900	Washington (state)	979.7
F891	Washington (state: to 1950)	
F897.A-Z	Local history (Wash. state: regions, counties, etc.)	
F897.P9	Puget Sound (Wash.)	
F899.A-Z	Local history (Wash. state: towns etc.)	
F899.S4	Seattle, Wash.	979.777
F901-951	Alaska area	979.8
F909	Alaska (1894-1959)	979.803-804
F951	Aleutian Islands & Bering Sea (SEE D769.87.A4 for 1939-45 & Jpn. occupation)	979.84, 940.096451, 909.096451824
F965	Territories (U.S.: inclu. Alaska & Hawaii: SEE ALSO DU620-629 for Haw.)	
F970	Territories (U.S.: island types in gen.: SEE ALSO DU647 for Guam & DU620-629 for Haw.)	
F1001-1140+	CANADA	971
F1015	Description & travel (Can.: 1867-1950)	917.1045-1063
F1026	Canada (gen.)	
F1027	French Canadians	
F1028	Military history (Can.)	355.00971
F1028.5	Naval history (Can.)	359.00971
F1029	Diplomacy (Can.: gen.)	327.71
F1029.5.A-Z	Foreign relns. (Can.-other places)	327.710+
F1029.5.F8	Foreign relns. (Can.-Fr.)	327.71044
F1029.5.G3	Foreign relns. (Can.-Ger.)	327.71043
F1029.5.G7	Foreign relns. (Can.-G.B.)	327.71041
F1029.5.I8	Foreign relns. (Can.-It.)	
F1029.5.J3	Foreign relns. (Can.-Japan)	
F1029.5.R9	Foreign relns. (Can.-Rus.)	327.71047
F1029.5.U6-7	Foreign relns. (Can.-U.S.)	327.71073
F1033	Canada (1867+)	971.05+
F1034	Canada (1914+: SEE ALSO D768.15 for 1939-45 war years)	971.061+

F1035.A-Z	Races, ethnography, religious groups (Can.)	
F1035.G3	Germans (in Can.)	
F1035.J3	Japanese (in Can.)	
F1035.8	Maritime Provinces (Can.: Atlantic coast)	971.5-8
F1036-1040	Nova Scotia	971.6
F1041-1045	New Brunswick	971.5
F1056-1059.7	Ontario (Can.)	971.3
F1075-1080	Alberta	971.23
F1086-1089.7	British Columbia	971.1
F1088	British Columbia (gen. hist.)	
F1089.5.A-Z	Local history (Br. Colum.: towns, cities, etc.)	
F1089.5.V22	Vancouver, B.C.	971.134
F1121-1139	Newfoundland	971.8, .803 (1934-49)
F1135-1139	Labrador	
F1170	Saint Pierre & Miquelon	971.88

F1201-3799+	LATIN AMERICA & the West Indies	972, 980-989
F1201-1392	MEXICO	972-972.7
F1215	Description & travel (Mex.: 1867-1950)	917.2048+
F1227.5	Military & naval history (Mex.)	
F1228	Diplomacy (Mex.: gen.)	
F1228.5.A-Z	Foreign relns. (Mex.-other places)	327.720+
F1228.5.G3	Foreign relns. (Mex.-Ger.)	327.72043
F1228.5.J3	Foreign relns. (Mex.-Japan)	327.72052
F1228.5.R9	Foreign relns. (Mex.-Rus.)	327.72047
F1228.5.S65	Foreign relns. (Mex.-Sov.Un.)	327.72047
F1228.5.U6-7	Foreign relns. (Mex.-U.S.)	327.72073
F1234	Mexico (1910-46)	972.081-082
F1386	Mexico City area (Mex.)	972.53
F1391.A-Z	Local history (Mex.: cities, towns, etc. except for Mex. City)	
F1392.A-Z	Races, ethnography, religious groups (Mex.)	
F1392.G4	Germans (in Mex.)	
F1392.J4	Jews (in Mex.)	
F1401-1419	Latin America (gen.)	980
F1409	Description & travel (Latin Am.: 1811-1950)	918.042-043
F1414	Latin America (1898-)	980.032+
F1415	Diplomacy (Latin Am.: gen.)	327.8
F1416.A-Z	Foreign relns. (Latin Am. & other places except U.S.) 327.80+	
F1416.F8	Foreign relns. (Latin Am.-Fr.)	
F1416.G3	Foreign relns. (Latin Am.-Ger.)	327.8043
F1416.G7	Foreign relns. (Latin Am.-G.B.)	
F1416.I8	Foreign relns. (Latin Am.-It.)	
F1416.J3	Foreign relns. (Latin Am.-Japan)	327.8052
F1416.R9	Foreign relns. (Latin Am.-Rus.)	
F1418	Foreign relns. (Latin Am.-U.S.)	327.8073
F1421-1577	CENTRAL AMERICA	972, 972.8+
F1438	Central America (1821-1950)	972.804-805
F1440.A-Z	Races, ethnography, religious groups (C.Am.)	
F1440.G3	Germans (in C.Am.)	
F1561-1577	PANAMA	972.87
F1566.5	Panama (1903-52)	972.8705-052
F1569.A-Z	Local history (Pan.: provinces, regions, etc.)	
F1569.C2	CANAL ZONE & Panama Canal	972.875

```
F1601-2175+   WEST INDIES    972.9
F1611             Description & travel (W.Ind.: 1810-1950)        917.29044-045
F1621         West Indies (gen. hist.)
F1621.5       Diplomacy (W.Ind.: gen.)
F1622             Foreign relns. (W.Ind.-U.S.)
F1622.5.A-Z       Foreign relns. (W.Ind.-partic. places)
F1622.5.G3        Foreign relns. (W.Ind.-Ger.)
F1622.5.G7        Foreign relns. (W.Ind.-G.B.)
F1623         West Indies (1898-)         972.904-905
F1629.A-Z         Races, ethnography, religious groups (W.Ind.)
F1630-1640        BERMUDA ISLANDS          972.99
F1636-1637        Bermuda (gen. hist.)
F1650-1660        BAHAMA ISLANDS           972.96
F1656-1657        Bahamas (gen. hist.)
F1741-1991  GREATER ANTILLES (Cuba, Haiti, Puerto Rico, Jamaica, etc.)
                                                         972.9, .91-95
F1741         Antilles (Greater: gen. hist. of the chain)        972.9
F1751-1849        CUBA          972.91
F1765             Description & travel (Cuba: 1898-)        917.291046
F1776         Cuba (gen.)
F1776.1       Military & naval history (Cuba)
F1776.2       Diplomacy (Cuba: gen.)
F1776.3.A-Z       Foreign relns. (Cuba-other places)
F1776.3.G3        Foreign relns. (Cuba-Ger.)
F1776.3.G7        Foreign relns. (Cuba-G.B.)
F1776.3.U6-7      Foreign relns. (Cuba-U.S.)
F1788         Cuba (1933-)            972.91063
F1789.A-Z     Races. ethnography, religious groups (Cuba)
F1789.J4      Jews (in Cuba)
F1791-1799        Havana Province (Cuba)
F1799.A-Z         Havana, Cuba    972.9123
F1861-1896        JAMAICA         972.92
F1871         Description & travel (Jam.: 1811-1950)
F1881         Jamaica (gen.)
F1886         Jamaica (1810-1953)        972.92034-9205
F1891.A-Z     Local history (Jam.: regions, islands, etc.)
F1895.A-Z     Local history (Jam.: towns etc.)
F1895.K5          Kingston, Jam.
F1895.M6          Montego Bay, Jam.
F1895.P6          Port Royal, Jam.
F1896.A-Z         Races, ethnography, religious groups (Jam.)
F1900-1940        HAITI          972.94
F1927         Haiti (1915-50)          972.9405-9406
F1931-1941        DOMINICAN REPUBLIC          972.93
F1951-1983        PUERTO RICO          972.95
F1965         Description & travel (Puerto R.: 1898-)
F1971         Puerto Rico (gen.)
F1975         Puerto Rico (1898-1952)          972.9504-9505
F1981.A-Z         Local history (Puerto R.: regions, towns, etc.)
F1981.S2          San Juan, P.R.
```

```
F2001-2151  LESSER ANTILLES & Caribbes        972.9, .97-98
F2001       Antilles (Lesser: gen.)        972.9
F2006       LEEWARD ISLANDS (inclu. St. Thomas, Virgin Islands, etc.)   972.97
F2011       WINDWARD ISLANDS (inclu. Barbados, St. Lucia. etc.)         972.98
F2016       Venezuelan coast islands (Aruba, Curaçao, Tobago, Trinidad, etc.)
                                                                        972.98
F2033-2129      Lesser Antilles (indiv. islands in alphab. order)
F2131-2151      Lesser Antilles (by political group)
F2131-2133      BRITISH WEST INDIES        972.9, .973
F2136       VIRGIN ISLANDS (U.S.)     972.9722
F2141       DUTCH WEST INDIES         972.986
F2151       FRENCH WEST INDIES        972.976
F2161-2175      CARIBBEAN SEA AREA         972.9, 909.096365
F2171       Description & travel (Carib. Sea: 1811-)
F2175       Caribbean Sea area (1811-)        972.904-905


F2201-3799+     SOUTH AMERICA          980-989
F2212-2217      Local history (S.Am.: regions)
F2212       ANDES
F2213       Pacific Coast (S.Am.)
F2214       Atlantic Coast (S.Am.)         980.009821, .009636
F2216       South America (northern: Brazil, Ven., Peru, etc.)
F2217       South America (southern: Arg., Chile, Uru., etc.)
F2223       Description & travel (S.Am.: 1811-1950)
F2231       South America (gen.)        980
F2236           South America (1830-)        980.03
F2237           South America (1939-)        980.033+
F2239.A-Z   Races, ethnography, religious groups (S.Am.)
F2239.B8    British (in S.Am.)
F2239.F8    French (in S.Am.)
F2239.G3    Germans (in S.Am.)
F2239.I8    Italians (in S.Am.)
F2239.J5    Jews (in S.Am.)
F2251-2299      COLOMBIA       986.1+
F2277           Colombia (1904-46)     986.1062-10631
F2301-2349      VENEZUELA       987
F2321           Venezuela (gen.)
F2321.2         Diplomacy (Venez.: gen.)
F2321.3.A-Z     Foreign relns. (Venez. & other places)
F2321.3.G3      Foreign relns. (Venez.-Ger.)
F2326           Venezuela (1935-)        987.0632
F2351-2471      GUIANA (Brit., Dutch, & Fr.)        988
F2501-2659  BRAZIL     981
F2515       Description & travel (Brazil: 1890-1950)       918.1045-1061
F2521       Brazil (gen.)
F2522       Military & naval history (Brazil)
F2523       Diplomacy (Brazil: gen.)        327.81
F2523.A-Z       Foreign relns. (Brazil-other lands)
F2523.G3        Foreign relns. (Brazil-Ger.)
F2523.G7        Foreign relns. (Brazil-G.B.)
F2535       Brazil (1822-)        981.04+
F2537       Brazil (1889-)        981.05+
F2538       Brazil (1930-54)   981.06-061
```

```
F2541-2636+    Local history (Brazil: regions, states, etc.)
F2611          Rio de Janeiro (Brazil: state)
F2646          Rio de Janeiro, Br.          981.53
F2659.A-Z      Races, ethnography, religious groups (Brazil)
F2659.A5       Americans (in Brazil)
F2659.F8       French (in Brazil)
F2659.G3       Germans (in Brazil)
F2659.J3          Japanese (in Brazil)
F2659.J5          Jews (in Brazil)
F2659.P8          Portuguese (in Brazil)
F2661-2699 PARAGUAY        989.2
F2681          Paraguay (gen.)
F2682             Diplomacy (Paraguay)
F2682.A-Z         Foreign relns. (Paraguay-other places)
F2682.G3          Foreign relns. (Paraguay-Ger.)        327.892043
F2689          Paraguay (1938-)        989.2071-2072
F2699.A-Z      Races, ethnography, religious groups (Paraguay)
F2699.G3          Germans (in Paraguay)
F2699.I8          Italians (in Paraguay)
F2701-2799 URUGUAY         989.5
F2721          Uruguay (gen.)
F2722             Diplomacy (Urug.: gen.)
F2722.5.A-Z       Foreign relns. (Urug. & other partic. places: by name)
F2722.5.G3        Foreign relns. (Urug.-Ger.)        327.895043
F2722.5.I8        Foreign relns. (Urug.-It.)
F2728          Uruguay (1904-)        989.5061-5063
F2781          Montevideo, Urug.        989.513
F2799.A-Z      Races, ethnography, religious groups (Urug.)
F2799.F7          French (in Urug.)
F2799.G3          Germans (in Urug.)
F2799.J4          Jews (in Urug.)
F2801-3021 ARGENTINA       982
F2815          Description & travel (Arg.: 1806-1950)        918.2043-2062
F2831          Argentina (gen.)
F2832          Military & naval history (Arg.)
F2833          Diplomacy (Arg.: gen.)
F2833.5.A-Z       Foreign relns. (Arg.-partic. lands)   327.820+
F2833.5.F8        Foreign relns. (Arg.-Fr.)
F2833.5.G3        Foreign relns. (Arg.-Ger.)        327.82043
F2833.5.G7        Foreign relns. (Arg.-G.B.)
F2833.5.I8        Foreign relns. (Arg.-It.)
F2833.5.J3        Foreign relns. (Arg.-Japan)
F2833.5.U6-7      Foreign relns. (Arg.-U.S.)
F2846          Argentina (1810-)        982.03+
F2848          Argentina (1910-43)        982.06
F2849          Argentina (1943-: Inclu. Perón regime & biog.)        982.061-062
F2850-2991        Local history (Arg.: provinces, regions, etc.: alphab. order)
F2861             Buenos Aires (Arg.: province)
F3001             Buenos Aires, Arg.        982.11
F3011.A-Z      Local history (Arg.: towns etc.)
```

```
F3021.A-Z     Races, ethnography, religious groups (Arg.)
F3021.A1      Races, ethnography, religious groups (Arg.: gen.)
F3021.A5      Americans (in Arg.)
F3021.B86     British (in Arg.)
F3021.F8      French (in Arg.)
F3021.G3      Germans (in Arg.)
F3021.I8      Italians (in Arg.)
F3021.J5      Jews (in Arg.)
F3021.U5      Ukrainians (in Arg.)
F3031             FALKLAND ISLANDS          997.11
F3051-3285        CHILE          983
F3063             Description & travel (Chile: 1810-1950)        918.3044-30643
F3081         Chile (gen.)
F3083         Diplomacy (Chile: gen.)
F3083.5.A-Z       Foreign relns. (Chile-other places)
F3083.5.G3        Foreign relns. (Chile-Ger.)
F3083.5.J3        Foreign relns. (Chile-Japan)
F3083.5.U6-7      Foreign relns. (Chile-U.S.)
F3099         Chile (1921-)               983.063-064+
F3285.A-Z     Races, ethnography, religious groups (Chile)
F3285.G3      Germans (in Chile)
F3285.J4      Jews (in Chile)
F3301-3359        BOLIVIA          984
F3326         Bolivia (1938-)     984.051
F3359.A-Z     Races, ethnography, religious groups (Bolivia)
F3359.G3      Germans (in Bolivia)
F3401-3619        PERU          985
F3423         Description & travel (Peru: 1820-1950)
F3431         Peru (gen.)
F3433         Diplomacy (Peru: gen.)
F3434.A-Z     Foreign relns. (Peru-other places)
F3434.G3          Foreign relns. (Peru-Ger.)
F3434.J3          Foreign relns. (Peru-Japan)
F3434.U6-7        Foreign relns. (Peru-U.S.)
F3448         Peru (1919-)              985.0631-0632
F3619.A-Z     Races, ethnography, religious groups (Peru)
F3619.A5          Americans (in Peru)
F3619.G3          Germans (in Peru)
F3619.J3          Japanese (in Peru)
F3701-3799        ECUADOR          986.6
F3737             Ecuador (1895-1944)        986.607-6072
```

U	Military science (gen.)	355
U-UH	MILITARY SCIENCE, MILITARY ENGINEERING, & AIR FORCES	355-359, 623
UA	Armies (organization, descrip., status)	
UB	Administration, Military	
UC	Maintenance & transportation, Military	
UD	Infantry	
UE	Cavalry (armored & mechanized)	
UF	Artillery	
UG	Military engineering & air forces	
UH	Military science (misc. services: medical etc.)	

U1-900+	MILITARY SCIENCE (GEN.)	355
U1	Periodicals & associations (military: in English) 355.005-006	
U9	Almanacs, annuals, etc., Military (U.S.)	
U10.A-Z	Almanacs, annuals, etc., Military (countries besides U.S.)	
U10.G7	Almanacs, annuals, etc., Military (G.B.)	
U13.A-Z	Museums, Military (inclu. exhibitions)	355.0074
U13.A1	Military museums & exhibitions (gen.)	
U13.A2-Z	Exhibitions & museums, Military (by country)	355.00740+
U13.F8	Museums, Military (Fr.)	
U13.G7	Museums, Military (G.B.)	
U13.G72.L69	Imperial War Museum (London, G.B.)	
U13.S65	Museums, Military (Sov.Un.)	
U13.U6-7	Museums, Military (U.S.)	355.0074073
U21.75	Women & the military (sociology)	
U24-25	Dictionaries & encyclopedias (mil. sci.)	355.003
U27-45	Military science (history)	
U27	Military science (history: gen.)	355.009
U39	Military science (modern: 1800-)	
U41	Military science (19th c.)	
U42	Military science (20th c.)	355.00904
U43.A-Z	Military science (history: by country or area)	
U51-55	Biography, Military (SEE ALSO D-F war & country #s) 355.3310922-0924, .00922-00924	
U52	Military biography (U.S.: collective)	
U53.A-Z	Biography, Military (U.S.: individual)	355.330973
U54.A-Z	Biography, Military (except U.S.: group by place)	
U55.A-Z	Biography, Military (except U.S.: individual)	
U56	Military clubs (U.S.)	
U58	Clubs, Military (G.B.)	
U59.A-Z	Clubs, Military (by place, except U.S. & G.B.)	
U102	Military science (gen. titles: pubn. date 1789-)	355, .43
U110-145	Handbooks & manuals, Soldiers'	355.00202
U110	Soldiers' handbooks & manuals (gen.)	
U113	Manuals & handbooks, Soldiers' (U.S.)	
U115.A-Z	Handbooks & manuals, Soldiers' (by place except U.S.)	
U130-135	Handbooks, Officers'	
U150-155	Military planning	
U153	Planning, Military (U.S.)	
U162	Strategy (mil. sci.: pubn. 1789-)	355.43
U162.6	Deterrence	
U165	Tactics, Military (pubn. 1811-)	355.42

U167.5.A-Z	Military tactics (special topics: by name)	
U167.5.A35	Advanced guard	
U167.5.D4	Desert warfare	
U167.5.E57	Envelopment (mil. sci.)	
U167.5.F6	Forest fighting	
U167.5.H3	Hand-to-hand fighting	
U167.5.J8	Jungle warfare	
U167.5.L5	Blitzkrieg (lightning war)	
U167.5.M3	Machine-gun warfare	
U167.5.M6	Motorized units (mil. sci.)	
U167.5.N5	Night fighting	
U167.5.R34	Raids (mil. sci.)	
U167.5.S7	Street fighting	
U167.5.W5	Winter warfare	
U168	Logistics (mil. sci.) 355.411	
U170-175	Field service (mil. sci.)	
U180-185	Encampments 355.412	
U200	Landing maneuvers & debarkation	
U215	Rearguard action	
U220	Reconnaisance & patrols 355.413, 358.45	
U225	Survival (combat: escape & evasion)	
U240	Guerrilla warfare & small wars 355.02184, 356.15	
U241	Anti-guerrilla warfare	
U250-255	Maneuvers (mil. sci.)	
U250	Maneuvers (mil. sci.: gen.) 355.52	
U253	Maneuvers (mil. sci.: U.S.)	
U255.A-Z	Maneuvers (mil. sci.: places besides U.S.)	
U260	Combined ops. (joint: air, army, navy)	
U261	Amphibious ops. 359.83, .96	
U262	Commando tactics 355.425	
U264	Atomic weapons (SEE ALSO UG1282.A8)	
U265	Military expeditions	
U290	Drill camps, instruction bases, maneuver grounds (gen.)	
U293	Instruction camps, maneuver grounds, etc. (U.S.)	
U294.5.A-Z	Drill camps, maneuver grounds, etc. (U.S.: by name)	
U300-305	Artillery & rifle ranges	
U303	Rifle & artillery ranges (U.S.)	
U310	War games 355.5	
U311	Models, Military	
U312	Map maneuvers & problems	
U320-325	Physical training (mil. sci.) 355.54+	
U323	Training, Physical (mil. sci.: U.S.)	
U327	Sports, Military (gen.)	
U328.A-Z	Military sports (by place)	
U390-395	Research, Military 355.07	
U393	Military research (U.S.)	

U400-714	EDUCATION, MILITARY 355.07
U400	Military education & training (gen.) 355.07
U403	Training & education, Military (modern hist.)
U405	Education, Military (gen.: pubns. 1801+)
U407-439	Education, Military (U.S.)
U408	Military education (U.S.: gen.) 355.0071073
U408.3	U.S. military education (gen. special)
U410.A-R3+	U.S. Military Academy (West Point) 355.0071173
U410.C3-H8	U.S. Military Academy (admin.)
U410.E1	Reports, Official (U.S. Mil. Acad. Superinten.: annual)
U410.E5	Reports, Congressional (U.S. Military Academy: by date)
U410.H2	Rosters, Officers' (U.S. Mil. Acad.)
U410.H3-4	Registers, Official (U.S. Mil. Acad.)
U410.H5	Cullum's Register (U.S. Mil. Acad.)
U410.H5-8	U.S. Military Academy (registers, unoff.)
U410.L1	U.S. Military Academy (gen. hist.)
U410.L1.A1-5	West Point (U.S. Mil. Acad.: official hist's.)
U410.L3	Pictorials (U.S. Mil. Acad.)
U410.M1.A1-Z	Biography (U.S. Mil. Acad.: by name)
U410.M1.P1	West Point (descrip. & life)
U412	National War College (U.S.: Wash., D.C.)
U413	Army War College (U.S.)
U415	Military education (U.S.: Command & Gen. Staff Coll.)
U428.5	Reserve Officers' Training Corps (U.S.: R.O.T.C.)
U440-444	Military education (Can.)
U505-630	Education, Military (Eur.) 355.007104+
U505	Military education (Eur.: gen.)
U510-549.3	Education, Military (G.B.)
U510	Military education (G.B.: gen.)
U511	British military education (special time periods)
U518.A-Z	Royal Military Academy (Woolwich: div'd like U410.A-Z)
U518.L1	Royal Military Academy (Woolwich: gen. hist's.)
U520.A-Z	Royal Military College (Sandhurst)
U520.L1	Sandhurst (Royal Mil. Coll.: descrip. & life)
U565-569	Education, Military (Fr.)
U570-574	Education, Military (Ger.) 355.0071043
U570	Military education (Ger.: gen.)
U571	German military education (special times)
U572.A-Z	Military education (Ger.: special topics)
U574.A-Z	Training, Military (Ger.: by school location)
U585-589	Education, Military (It.)
U590-594	Education, Military (Nor.)
U600-604	Education, Military (Rus.) 355.0071047
U625	Education, Military (Balkan States)
U635-660	Education, Military (Asia)
U635	Military education (Asia: gen.)
U640-644	Education, Military (China) 355.0071051
U640	Military education (China: gen.)
U650-654	Education, Military (Japan) 355.0071052
U650	Military education (Japan: gen.)
U651	Japanese military education (special periods)
U700-704	Education, Military (Australia) 355.0071094
U705-709	Education, Military (New Z.)

U719-740+	Observations, Military	
U719	Military observations (collected: 2 or more wars)	
U735	Observations, Military (Russo-Jpn. War, 1904-5)	
U738	Observations, Military (WWI)	
U739.5	Observations, Military (Sp. Civil War, 1936-9)	
U739.8	Observations, Military (Sino-Jpn. War, 1937-45)	
U740	Observations, Military (WWII)	
U750-773	MILITARY LIFE & CUSTOMS	355.1
U750	Customs, Military (gen.)	
U765	Life & customs, Military (modern: gen.)	355.1
U766	Military life & customs (modern: U.S.)	355.10973
U767	Military life & customs (modern: G.B.)	355.10941
U768	Military life & customs (modern: Fr.)	
U769	Military life & customs (modern: Ger.)	355.10943
U770	Military life & customs (modern: It.)	
U771	Military life & customs (modern: Rus.)	355.10947
U773	Military life & customs (modern: misc. countries besides U766-771)	
U790	Curiosities, Military (inclu. collector's hdbks.)	
U799-897	ARMS & ARMOR (Hist.)	
U799	Periodicals & associations (arms & armor: hist.)	
U800.A3-Z	Arms (gen.: pubn. dates 1801+)	355.8, 623.4
U804	Museums, exhibitions, etc. (arms)	
U804.A2-Z	Museums, exhibitions, etc. (arms: by country)	
U815	Armament (modern: gen.)	
U818	Armament (modern: U.S.)	
U820.A-Z	Armament (modern: Eur.: by place)	
U820.G3	British armament (modern)	
U820.G7	German armament (modern)	
U821.A-Z	Armament (modern: Asia: by country)	
U821.J3	Japanese armament (modern)	
U880	Guns (gen.)	623.4
U884	Small arms (gen.)	
U889	Small arms (19th-20th c.)	
U897.A-Z	Small arms (by region or country)	
UA	ARMIES (organiz. & world status)	355
UA10	Military status (world: gen.)	355.03
UA10.5	National security (gen.)	
UA11	Policy, Military (gen.)	
UA14	Colonial troops	
UA15	Armies & navies (of the world)	
UA16	Military missions	
UA17	Costs, Military	355.622
UA17.5.A2	Manpower (gen.)	355.22, .61
UA17.5.A3-Z	Manpower (by country)	
UA18.A2	Mobilization, Industrial (gen.)	355.28
UA18.A3-Z	Industrial mobilization (by country: SEE ALSO D-F for specific wars)	

UA21-876+	MILITARY STATUS (worldwide: place by place)	355.0330+
UA21-645	MILITARY STATUS (W. Hemis.)	
UA21	America (mil. status: gen.) 355.03301812	
UA22-602	MILITARY STATUS (N. Am.)	
UA22	North America (mil. status: gen.) 355.03307	
UA23-585	MILITARY STATUS (U.S.) 355.033273	
UA23.A1.A-Z	Periodicals & associations (military: U.S.)	
UA23.A2-Z	United States (mil. status: gen.)	
UA23.2-6	U.S. Dept. of Defense 353.6-7	
UA23.2	Reports, Official (U.S. Dept. Defense: formerly War Dept.)	
UA23.6	U.S. Dept. of Defense (gen. hist.)	
UA24-39	U.S. Army	
UA24.A1-7	Reports, Official (U.S. Army: War Dept., Dept. o/t Army, Adj. Gen.,	
	Inspec. Gen., etc.: annual)	
UA24.A1-149	U.S. War Dept. (ann. reports)	
UA25	U.S. Army (gen.) 355.00973, .30973, .310973	
UA26.A1-6	Army posts (U.S.: gen.)	
UA26.A7-Z	Army posts (U.S.: by place)	
UA27.3.1st-	Armies (U.S.: by #/author)	
UA27.5.1st-	Divisions (U.S.: by #/author)	
UA27.A-Z	Divisions (U.S. Army: by place)	
UA27.P5	Division of the Philippines (U.S. Army)	
UA28	Infantry (U.S.: gen.) 356.10973	
UA29.1st-	Infantry regiments (U.S.: by #/author)	
UA30	Armored units & cavalry (U.S.: inclu. mechanized: gen.) 357.10973	
UA31.1st-	Cavalry & armored regiments (U.S.: by #/author)	
UA32	Artillery (U.S.: gen.) 358.10973, .120973	
UA33.1st-	Artillery batteries (U.S.: by #/author)	
UA34.A-Z	U.S. Army (special troops: by name)	
UA37	Lists & registers (U.S. Army: vets.)	
UA42-560	RESERVES, ARMY (U.S.: Nat. Guard, militia, volunteers, etc.)	
UA42.A1-59	Reports, Official (army reserves: U.S.)	
UA42.A6.A-Z	Associations, periodicals, societies (U.S.: army reserves)	E740
UA42.A7-Z	U.S. National Guard (gen.)	
UA45	Women's reserves (U.S.)	
UA50-549	MILITIA (U.S.: inclu. Nat. Guard etc.: state by state)	
UA90-99	Reserves, Army (U.S.: Calif.)	
UA90	California National Guard (gen.)	
UA91	Primary sources, documents (Calif. army reserves)	
UA92	Lists & registers (Calif. Nat. Guard)	
UA93-94	Infantry (U.S.: Calif. reserves)	
UA96	Artillery (U.S.: Calif. reserves: gen., inclu. field)	
UA97-97.5	Coast artillery (U.S.: Calif. reserves)	
UA97.7-75	Antiaircraft artillery (U.S.: Calif. army reserves)	
UA159.1-9	Reserves, Army (U.S.: Hawaii)	
UA170-179	Volunteers (Nat. Guard, militia, etc.: Illinois)	
UA290-299	Reserves, Army (U.S.: Missouri)	

UA360-369   Reserves, Army (U.S.: N.Y.: militia, volunteers, Nat. Guard, etc.)
UA360   New York National Guard (gen.)
UA361   Primary sources, documents (N.Y. army reserves)
UA362   Lists & registers (N.Y. Nat. Guard)
UA363-364   Infantry (U.S.: N.Y. reserves)
UA366-367.75   Artillery (U.S.: N.Y. reserves)
UA366   Field artillery (U.S.: N.Y. reserves: ALSO gen. artil.)
UA367-367.5   Coast artillery (U.S.: N.Y. reserves)
UA367.7-75   Antiaircraft (U.S.: N.Y. army reserves)
UA420-429   Reserves, Army (U.S.: Penn.)
UA470-479   Reserves, Army (U.S.: Texas)
UA565.A-Z   Auxiliaries, Army (U.S.)
UA565.W6   WACS (Women's Army Corps: U.S.)
UA600-602   Military status (Can.)
UA600   Canada (mil. status: gen.)   355.033271, .033571, .033071
UA602.3   Latin America (mil. status: gen.)   355.03328, .03308
UA603-605   Mexico (mil. status)
UA606-608   Military status (Central Am.)
UA607.A-Z   Central America (mil. status: by country)
UA607.P3   Panama (mil. status)
UA609-611   West Indies (mil. status)
UA612-645   Military status (S.Am.)
UA612   South America (mil. status: gen.)   355.03308, .03328
UA613-615   Argentina (mil. status)   355.033082
UA619-621   Brazil (mil. status)
UA622-624   Chile (mil. status)
UA634-636   Paraguay (mil. status)   355.0330892
UA637-639   Peru (mil. status)
UA640-642   Uruguay (mil. status)   355.0330895
UA643-645   Venezuela (mil. status)
UA646-829   MILITARY STATUS (Eur.)
UA646   Europe (mil. status)   355.03304, .03324, .03354
UA646.53   Baltic Sea (mil. status)   355.033016334, .4716334, 359.4716334
UA646.55   Mediterranean Sea (mil. status)   355.03301638, 359.471638
UA646.6   North Sea (mil. status)   355.033016336
UA646.7   Scandinavia (mil. status)   355.033048, .033248, .033548
UA646.85   Northern Europe (mil. status)   355.033048
UA647-668   Military status (G.B.)   355.033041-033042, .033241, .033541
UA647   Great Britain (mil. status)   355.033041
UA648   Primary sources, documents (G.B.: War Dept., Parliament, other
                 re military)
UA649-668   G.B. Army
UA649   G.B. Army (gen.)   355.00941, .310941
UA650-653   Infantry (G.B.)
UA650   Infantry (G.B.: gen.)   356.10941
UA651.A-Z   Infantry regiments (G.B.: by name)
UA651.C6   Coldstream Guards (G.B.)
UA654-657   Cavalry (G.B.)   357.10941
UA658   Artillery (G.B.)   358.10941, .120941
UA663   Welsh troops (G.B.)
UA664   Scottish troops (G.B.)
UA665   Irish troops (G.B.)
UA668   Colonial troops (G.B.: inclu. natives: gen.)

UA670-679   Military status (Austria & Austria-Hung.)
UA670   Austria & Austria-Hungary (mil. status) 355.0330436
UA672   Austria-Hungary. Army (gen.) 355.309436
UA673   Infantry (Austria & Austria-Hung.)
UA674   Cavalry (Austria & Austria-Hung.)
UA680-689   Belgium (mil. status)   355.0330493
UA690-699   Denmark (mil. status)   355.0330489
UA700-709   Military status (Fr.)
UA700   France (mil. status: gen.) 355.033044
UA702   France. Army (gen.)   355.00944, .30944
UA702.3   Army posts (Fr.: gen.)
UA702.32.A-Z   Army posts (Fr.: by place)
UA703-705   France. Army (infantry, cavalry, armor, artillery)
UA709   Colonial troops (Fr.)
UA710-719   Military status (Ger.)
UA710   Germany (mil. status: gen.)   355.033043, .033243, .033543
UA712   Germany. Army (gen.)   355.00943, .30943, .310943
UA713.A1-Z9.A-Z   Infantry (Ger.)   356.10943
UA713.A1-5   Primary sources, documents (Ger. infantry)
UA713.A6-Z4   Infantry (Ger.: gen.)
UA713.Z6.1st-   Infantry (Ger.: by regiment #)
UA713.Z9.A-Z   Infantry (Ger.: by group name)
UA714   Armored units & cavalry (Ger.)   357.10943, .50943, 358.180943
UA715   Artillery (Ger.)
UA716.A-Z   Germany. Army (special units: by name)
UA717   Militia (Ger.)
UA718.A-Z   Germany. Army (local)
UA719   Colonial troops (Ger.)
UA720-729   Greece (mil. status)   355.0330495
UA730-739   Netherlands (mil. status)   355.0330492
UA740-749   Military status (It.)
UA740   Italy (mil. status)   355.033045
UA742   Italy. Army (gen.)   355.30945
UA743   Infantry (It.)
UA744   Armored units & cavalry (It.)
UA745   Artillery (It.)
UA745.5   Swiss Guards (Papal Guards)
UA750-759   Military status (Norway)
UA750   Norway (mil. status)   355.0330481
UA760-769   Portugal (mil. status)
UA770-779   Military status (Rus. or Sov.Un.)
UA770   Russia (mil. status)   355.033047, .033247, .033547
UA771   Primary sources, documents (Rus. military)
UA772   Russia. Army (gen.) 355.30947, .00947
UA773.A1-Z9.A-Z   Infantry (Rus.)
UA773.A1-5   Primary sources, documents (Rus.)
UA773.A6-Z4   Infantry (Rus.: gen.)
UA773.Z6.1st-   Infantry (Rus.: by regiment #)
UA773.Z9.A-Z   Infantry (Rus.: by group name)
UA774   Armored units & cavalry (Rus.)
UA775   Artillery (Rus.)
UA780-789   Spain (mil. status)   355.033046
UA790-799   Sweden (mil. status)   355.0330485
UA800-809   Switzerland (mil. status)   355.0330494

```
UA810-819   Military status (Tur.)
UA810       Turkey (mil. status)        355.0330561
UA820-827   Military status (Balkan States)
    UA820       Balkan States (mil. status: gen.)   355.0330496
    UA822       Balkan States (mil. status: descrip. & hist.)
    UA824       Bulgaria (mil. status)      355.03304977
    UA826       Rumania (mil. status)       355.0330498
    UA827       Yugoslavia (mil. status)    355.0330497
UA829.A-Z   Military status (misc. Eur. countries)
UA829.C95   Czechoslovakia (mil. status)        355.0330437
UA829.H9    Hungary (mil. status)       355.0330439
UA829.P7    Poland (mil. status)        355.0330438
UA830-853   MILITARY STATUS (Asia)
UA830           Asia (mil. status: gen.)        355.03305, .03325, .03355
UA835-839       Military status (China)
UA835           China (mil. status)         355.033051, .033251, .033551
UA837           China. Army (gen.)          355.30951, .00951
UA840-844       India (mil. status)             355.033054
UA845-849       Military status (Japan)
UA845       Japan (mil. status: gen.)   355.033052, .033252, .033552
UA846       Primary sources, documents (Jpn. military)
UA847       Japan. Army (gen.)          355.00952, .30952, .310952
UA848.A-Z       Japan. Army (service branches by name)
UA849.A-Z       Japan (mil. status: states, provinces, etc.)
UA853.A-Z   Military status (Asia: by country except India, China, Japan)
UA853.B9    Burma (mil. status)
UA853.I5    Indonesia (mil. status)
UA853.M3    Malaya (mil. status)
UA853.P5        Philippines (mil. status)   355.0330599
UA853.V5        Vietnam (mil. status)
UA855-868   Military status (Africa)
UA855           Africa (mil. status: gen.)  355.03306
UA856           South Africa (mil. status)      355.00968, .033068
UA858           Algeria (mil. status)   355.033065
UA859           Cameroon (mil. status)
UA860       Ethiopia (mil. status)      355.033063
UA860.5     Kenya (mil. status)         355.03306762
UA865       Egypt       355.033062
UA867           Morocco (mil. status)       355.033064
UA867.5         Tunisia (mil. status)       355.0330611
UA868           Libya (mil. status)         355.0330612
UA870-874   Military status (Australia)
UA870       Australia (mil. status)     355.033094, .033294, .033594
UA871       Primary sources, documents (Australia: military status)
UA872       Australia. Army (descrip. & hist.)      355.00994, .30994, .310994
UA873.A-Z       Australia. Army (special branches by name)
UA874.A-Z       Australia (mil. status: states, territories, localities)
UA874.3-7   Military status (New Z.)
UA874.3         New Zealand (mil. status: gen.)         355.0330931
UA874.5         New Zealand. Army (descrip. & hist.)    355.309931
UA874.6.A-Z     New Zealand. Army (special sections)
UA875-876   Military status (Pacific islands)
UA875           Oceania (mil. status)       355.03309
UA876.A-Z       Pacific Islands (mil. status: by island or group name)
```

UA910-915	Mobilization	
UA910	Mobilization (gen.)	355.28
UA913	Mobilization (U.S.)	355.280973
UA915.A-Z	Mobilization (except U.S.: by name of place)	
UA915.G7	Mobilization (G.B.)	355.280941
UA917.A2	Demobilization (gen.)	355.29
UA917.A3-Z	Demobilization (by country)	
UA920	Attack & defense plans (gen.)	355.0330+, .0332+, .0335+, .4+
UA923	Defense & attack plans (U.S.)	355.033073, .4773
UA925.A-Z	Plans, Attack & defense (countries except U.S.)	
UA926.A3-Z	Civil defense (gen.: SEE ALSO numbers within wars, such as D810.C69 for WWII)	
UA926.5	Bomb shelters (plus other special civil defense topics like psych. aspects)	
UA927	Civil defense (U.S.: gen.)	
UA928-928.5.A-Z	Defense, Civil (U.S. states, cities, etc.)	
UA929.A-Z	Civil defense (countries besides U.S.)	
UA929.G7	Civil defense (G.B.)	
UA929.S65	Civil defense (Sov.Un.)	
UA929.5	Industrial defense (gen.)	355.28, .26
UA929.6-8	Defense, Industrial (U.S.)	
UA929.9.A-Z	Industrial defense (places besides U.S.)	
UA929.95.A-Z	Industrial defense (by specific industry: SEE ALSO H industry #s)	
UA929.95.A35	Agriculture (defense)	
UA929.95.C5	Chemical industry (defense)	
UA929.95.E4	Electric plants (defense)	
UA929.95.G7	Grain industry (defense)	
UA929.95.P4	Petroleum industry (defense)	
UA929.95.P93	Public utilities (defense)	
UA929.95.R3	Railroads (defense)	
UA929.95.T4	Telecommunication (defense)	
UA929.95.T7	Transportation (defense)	
UA929.95.W3	Waterworks (defense)	
UA930	Strategic lines, bases, etc.	355.43
UA940	Military communications (gen.)	355.27, .41, .6
UA943-944	Communications, Military (U.S.)	
UA945.A-Z	Military communications (except U.S.: by country)	
UA950-979	Communication routes (mil. sci.)	
UA950	Travel routes (mil. sci.: gen.)	
UA953-954	Communication routes (U.S.)	
UA955.A-Z	Communication routes (except U.S.)	
UA960	Roads & highways (gen.)	
UA963-964	Highways (U.S.)	
UA965.A-Z	Roads (places outside U.S.)	
UA970-975	Waterways	
UA975.A-Z	Waterways (outside U.S.)	
UA975.G3	Waterways (Ger.)	
UA979	Travel routes (misc.)	
UA985-997	Military geography	355.47+, .0330+, 359.47+
UA990	Geography, Military (gen. inclu. Eur.)	355.47
UA993	Military geography (U.S.)	355.4773, 359.4773
UA995.A-Z	Military geography (except U.S.)	
UA997	Preservation of maps & charts	

UB	ADMINISTRATION, MILITARY (command, intelligence, law, etc.)
	355, .6
UB1	Periodicals (mil. admin.)
UB15	Administration, Military (gen. hist.)
UB21-124	MILITARY ADMINISTRATION (by country)
UB23-25	Military administration (U.S.) 353.6, 355.60973
UB23	Administration, Military (U.S.: gen.)
UB24.A-W	Military administration (U.S.: by state)
UB26-27	Military administration (Can.)
UB27.5-54	Military administration (Lat.Am.)
UB55-95	Military administration (Eur.)
UB55	Administration, Military (Eur.: gen.)
UB57-64	Military administration (G.B.)
UB57	Administration, Military (G.B.: gen.) 355.60941, 354.41066
UB58.1900+	Military administration (G.B.: by time period)
UB59	Military administration (G.B.: Eng. & Wales)
UB61	Military administration (G.B.: Scot.)
UB67-68	Military administration (Belg.)
UB69-70	Military administration (Den.)
UB71-72	Military administration (Fr.) 354.44066
UB73-74	Military administration (Ger.) 354.43066, 355.60943
UB75-76	Military administration (Greece)
UB79-80	Military administration (It.)
UB81-82	Military administration (Norway)
UB85-86	Military administration (Rus.: Eur.) 354.47066
UB86.5	Military administration (Scan.: gen.)
UB87-88	Military administration (Sp.)
UB95.A-Z	Military administration (misc. Eur. lands)
UB95.P7	Military administration (Pol.)
UB99-113	Military administration (Asia)
UB99	Administration, Military (Asia: gen.)
UB101-102	Military administration (China) 354.51066
UB103-104	Military administration (India
UB105-106	Military administration (Japan) 354.52066, 355.60952
UB109-110	Military administration (Rus.: Asia & Sib.)
UB113.A-Z	Military administration (misc. Asian lands)
UB115-119	Military administration (Africa)
UB121-122	Military administration (Australia) 354.94066
UB122.5	Military administration (New Z.)
UB123-124	Military administration (Pac. islands)
UB145	Military administration (gen.: pubn. 1801-1970) 355.6
UB146	Military administration (gen.: pubn. 1971+) 355.6
UB147	Military service as a profession
UB160-165	Accounting & accounts, Military (inclu. records, muster rolls, etc.)
UB160	Muster rolls & accounts, Military (gen.: inclu. gen. corresp.: admin.)
UB170-175	Adjutant generals' offices
UB180-197	Military administration (civil sections)
UB180	Civilian personnel (mil. admin.: gen.) 355.23
UB193	Personnel, Civilian (mil. admin.: U.S.)

UB200-245	Command control	355.41, .33, .6
UB200	Generals, marshals, commanders (admin.: duties etc.)	355.331
UB210	Leadership, Military	
UB212	Command & control systems	
UB220-225	Staffs, Army	
UB220	Staffs, Military (gen.)	
UB223	Army staffs (U.S.)	
UB225.A-Z	Military staffs (countries besides U.S.)	
UB230-235	Headquarters, Military	
UB230	Military headquarters ops. (gen.: inclu. aides, adjutants, etc.)	
UB240-245	Inspection, Military	
UB246-249	Security (defense info.)	
UB246	Information security (mil. data: gen.)	
UB247	Military information (security: U.S.)	
UB248.A-Z	Military information (security: besides U.S.)	
UB249	Security, Industrial (defense purposes)	
UB250-271	Intelligence, Military	
UB250	Military intelligence (gen.)	355.3432
UB251.A-Z	Intelligence, Military (by country)	
UB251.G3	Military intelligence (Ger.)	355.34320943
UB251.G7	Military intelligence (G.B.)	
UB260	Attachés, Military	
UB270-271	Espionage & spies (mil. admin.)	
UB270	Spies (mil. admin.)	327.12
UB271.A-Z	Espionage (by country responsible: SEE D-F #s for other cases in particular countries or particular wars)	
UB271.G3	German espionage (gen.)	327.120943
UB271.G32.A-Z	Spies, German (by name)	
UB271.G7	British espionage (gen.)	327.120941
UB271.R9	Russian espionage (gen.)	327.120947
UB271.R92.A-Z	Spies, Russian (by name)	
UB271.U6	Espionage (U.S.: gen.)	327.120973
UB271.U62.A-Z	Spies, United States (by name)	
UB273	Sabotage (mil. sci.: gen.)	355.3437
UB274	Sabotage equipment (mil. sci.)	
UB275	Propaganda & psych. warfare (mil. sci.: gen.: SEE ALSO BF1045.M55 & HM263 for indiv. & social aspects)	355.3434
UB276	Propaganda & psych. warfare (U.S.)	355.34340973
UB277.A-Z	Psychological warfare & propaganda (countries except U.S.)	
UB277.G3	Propaganda & psych. warfare (Ger.)	355.34340943
UB277.J3	Propaganda & psych. warfare (Japan)	355.34340952
UB277.R9	Propaganda & psych. warfare (Rus.)	355.34340947
UB277.S65	Propaganda & psych. warfare (Sov.Un.)	355.34340947
UB280-285	Orders, passes, field correspondence (mil. sci.)	
UB280	Passes, orders, field correspondence (mil. sci.: gen.)	
UB290	Cryptography & ciphers	358.24
UB320-325	Recruitment, enlistment, promotion, discharge (mil. sci.)	
UB320	Promotion, discharge, recruitment, enlistment (mil. sci.: gen.)	355.2, .61
UB323	Enlistment, recruitment, promotion, discharge (mil. sci.: U.S)	355.20973
UB325.A-Z	Discharge, promotion, recruitment, enlistment (mil. sci.: countries besides U.S.)	
UB330-336	Medical & mental examinations (mil. recruits)	
UB330	Mental & medical examinations (mil. recruits: gen.)	355.2236

UB337	Classification, Military
UB340-345	Conscription & exemption (mil. service)
UB340	Induction & exemption (mil.) 355.22363, .225
UB341	Conscientious objectors (gen.) 355.224
UB342.A-Z	Conscientious objectors (by country)
UB343-344	Draft & exemption (mil.: U.S.) 355.2236306073
UB345.A-Z	Compulsory service & exemption (mil.: besides U.S.)
UB345.G3	Exemption & draft (mil.: Ger.)
UB345.J3	Draft & exemption (mil.: Japan)
UB350-355	Universal service
UB356-405	Veterans' benefits & services 355.115
UB356	Veterans' education, employment, etc. (gen.) 355.1152, .1154
UB357-358	Education & employment of veterans (U.S.) 355.1150973
UB359.A-Z	Employment & education of veterans (countries except U.S.)
UB360	Rehabilitation of disabled veterans (gen.) 355.1156, .1154
UB363-364	Disabled veterans (U.S.: rehab.)
UB365.A-Z	Veterans' rehabilitation (places besides U.S.)
UB366.A-Z	Occupational rehabilitation of veterans (by occup.)
UB368-369	Medical care of veterans 355.115
UB370-375	Pensions, Veterans' 355.64, .1151
UB380-385	Veterans' homes & hospitals
UB380	Soldiers' & sailors' homes
UB382-384	U.S. Veterans' Administration
UB383	National Home & Vets' Admin. (U.S.: gen.)
UB384.A-W	Soldiers' & sailors' homes (U.S.: state)
UB385.A-Z	Veterans' homes & hospitals (besides U.S.)
UB390-397	Cemeteries & graves, Military
UB400-405	Pensions, Survivors' (mil.)
UB407-409	Warrant officers (mil.)
UB407	Officers, Warrant (mil.: gen.)
UB410-415	Officers, Military (inclu. appt., promo., retire.)
UB410	Rank, appointment, promotion, retirement, etc. (mil. officers: gen.) 355.332
UB412-414	Officers, Military (U.S.) 355.3320973
UB415.A-Z	Military officers (except U.S.: by country)
UB415.G3	Officers, Military (Ger.) 355.3320943
UB415.G7	Officers, Military (G.B.) 355.3320941
UB416	Minorities & women in the armed forces (gen.) 355.22 (women), .3
UB417	Women & minorities in the armed forces (U.S.: gen.)
UB418.A-Z	Minorities & women in the armed forces (U.S.: by group name)
UB418.A47	Afro-Americans (armed forces)
UB418.B69	Boys (armed forces)
UB418.H57	Hispanic-Americans (armed forces)
UB418.W65	Women (armed forces: U.S.)
UB419	Minorities & women in the armed forces (places besides U.S.)
UB420-425	Furloughs
UB430-435	Military decorations, medals, rewards, etc. 355.1342
UB430	Decorations, Military (gen.)
UB433	Medals, decorations, etc. (mil.: U.S.)
UB440-445	Retired military 355.1342
UB448-449	Medical care for retired military

UB461-736	MILITARY LAW
UB465	Law, Military (gen.: pubn. 1801+) 343.01
UB481	International military law (PREFER JX areas) 341.6
UB485	Customs & laws of war (inclu. treatment of prisoners: SEE ALSO JX)
UB500-504	Military law (U.S.: PREFER KF7201-7755) 343.010973, .0106073
UB505-509	Military law (Can.)
UB590-684	European military law
UB590	Military law (Eur.: gen.)
UB600-604	Military law (Austria)
UB615-619	Military law (Fr.)
UB620-624	Military law (Ger.) 343.010943
UB625-629	Military law (G.B.: PREFER KD6000-6355) 343.010941
UB655	Military law (Rus.: gen.) 343.010947
UB655.A2	Military law (Rus.: statutes & compil's.)
UB655.A7-Z	Law, Military (Rus.: commentaries, digests, etc.)
UB655.9-656.5	Regulations, Army (Rus.)
UB657	General orders (Rus. military: collections)
UB657.A5	Orders, General (Rus. military: offic. compil's.)
UB657.A6-7	Orders, Special (Rus. military: collec's. & compil's.)
UB680-683	Military law (Balkan states)
UB685-710	Asian military law
UB685	Military law (Asia)
UB690-694	Military law (China)
UB700-704	Military law (Japan) 343.010952
UB705-709	Military law (Phil. Islands)
UB730-734	Military law (Australia)
UB734.5	Military law (New Z.)
UB780-789	Offenses & crimes, Military
UB780	Crimes, Military (gen.) 355.1334
UB783	Military crimes (U.S.: SEE ALSO KF7615-7618)
UB785.A-Z	Military crimes (countries outside U.S.)
UB787	Mutiny (mil.)
UB788	Desertion (mil.)
UB789	Looting & other mil. crimes
UB790-795	Military discipline 343.014, .13325
UB793	Discipline, Military (U.S.: SEE ALSO KF7590)
UB800	Military prisons & prisoners (gen.) 365.48, 355.13325, 344.03548
UB803	Prisons, Military (U.S.: SEE ALSO KF7675)
UB805.A-Z	Military prisons (outside U.S.)
UB810	Corporal punishment & flogging (mil. sci.: gen.)
UB813	Punishment, Corporal (U.S.)
UB815.A-Z	Flogging & corp. punish. (countries besides U.S.)
UB820	Military police (gen.) 355.13323
UB825.A-Z	Police, Military (by country)
UB840	Military justice (admin.: gen.) 343.0143, .133
UB845.A-Z	Judiciary, Military (by country except U.S., for which SEE KF7601-7679)
UB850	Courts-martial, Military (gen.) 343.0146, 355.13325
UB855.A-Z	Courts-martial, Military (besides U.S., for which SEE KF7625-7659)
UB857.A-Z	Cases (courts-martial, mil.: by place: for U.S. SEE KF7642, 7652, etc.)
UB860	Courts of inquiry, Military (gen.)
UB865.A-Z	Inquiry, Courts of (mil.: by country)
UB867.A-Z	Cases (courts of inquiry: by place: SEE KF7642 etc. for U.S.)
UB870	Commissions, Military (gen.)
UB875.A-Z	Military commissions (by country except U.S., for which SEE KF7661)

UC	MAINTENANCE & TRANSPORT, MILITARY
UC10	Military maintenance & transport (gen.) 355.6-8
UC12	Transport & maintenance (mil. sci.: gen. spec.)
UC15	Requisitions, Military
UC20-258	ORGANIZATION (mil. maint. & transport: by country)
UC20-88	Maintenance & transport (mil.: U.S.)
UC20	Military maintenance & transport (U.S.: gen.)
UC23	Maintenance & transport (mil.: U.S.: by time period)
UC23.1917-1918	Military maintenance & transport (U.S.: WWI era)
UC23.1941-1945	Military maintenance & transport (U.S.: WWII era)
UC30-34	Quartermaster's Dept. (U.S.) 355.8
UC40-44	Subsistence Dept. (U.S. Army)
UC45	Construction Div. (U.S. Army)
UC46	Military construction (U.S.: gen.: SEE ALSO UG for engineer., VC420+ & VG590+ for naval) 358.22
UC70-75	Paymaster's Dept. (U.S. Army)
UC90-93	Maintenance & transport (mil.: Can.)
UC158-233	Maintenance & transport (mil.: Eur.)
UC158	Military maintenance & transport (Eur.: gen.)
UC180-183	Maintenance & transport (mil.: Ger.)
UC184-187	Maintenance & transport (mil.: G.B.)
UC184	Supply & transport depts. (mil.: G.B.)
UC185	Pay & allowances (mil.: G.B.)
UC208-211	Maintenance & transport (mil.: Rus.)
UC234-245	Maintenance & transport (mil.: Asia)
UC234	Military maintenance & transport (Asia: gen.)
UC241	Maintenance & transport (mil.: Japan)
UC255	Maintenance & transport (mil.: Australia)
UC256.5	Maintenance & transport (mil.: New Z.)
UC257-258	Maintenance & transport (mil.: Pac. islands)
UC260-267	Supplies & stores, Military (inclu. procure., storage, specs., surplus, etc.)
UC260	Military supplies & stores (gen.)
UC263-264	Stores & supplies, Military (U.S.)
UC265.A-Z	Procurement (mil. supplies: countries besides U.S.)
UC267	Contracts, Military (supplies)
UC270-360	Transport, Military 358.25, .44, 355.27
UC270	Transportation, Military (gen.) 358.25
UC273-274	Military transport (U.S.)
UC275.A-Z	Transport, Military (besides U.S.: by place)
UC277	Packing & shipment (mil. supplies)
UC310	Railroads (mil. transp.: gen.) 623.63, 355.83
UC313	Military railroads (U.S.: gen.) 355.830973
UC314.A-Z	Railroads (mil. transp.: U.S. regions or states)
UC315.A-Z	Transport, Railroad (mil.: places besides U.S.)
UC320-325	Waterways & troopships (mil. transp.) 359.3264
UC320	Troopships & waterways (mil. transp.: gen.)
UC330-335	Air transport, Military 358.44
UC333-334	Military air transport (U.S.) 358.440973
UC340-345	Motor transport (mil. sci.) 355.83
UC343	Transport, Motor (mil. sci.: U.S.)
UC347	Motorcycles (mil. transp.) 623.7472
UC349	Coolies (mil. transp.)
UC350	Camels, elephants, etc. (mil. transp.)
UC355	Dogs (mil. transp.: SEE ALSO UH100) 355.424

UC360	Snowshoes, skis, skates, etc. (mil. transp.)	
UC400-440	Camps & barracks, Military	
UC400	Barracks & camps, Military (gen.)	355.412, .7
UC403-404	Military barracks & camps (U.S.)	355.70973
UC405.A-Z	Military quarters & camps (besides U.S.)	
UC410	Billeting	
UC415	Furnishings (mil. qtrs.)	
UC420	Fuel & light (mil. qtrs.)	
UC425	Fires (mil. qtrs.)	
UC430	Latrines & sewers (mil. qtrs.)	
UC440	Laundries, Military	
UC460-535	Clothing & equipment, Military	
UC460	Equipment & clothing, Military (gen.)	
UC463-464	Military clothing & equipment (U.S.)	
UC465.A-Z	Clothing & equipment, Military (places besides U.S.)	
UC480	Uniforms, Military (gen.)	355.14
UC483-484	Military uniforms (U.S.)	355.140973
UC485.A-Z	Uniforms, Military (besides U.S.)	
UC490-495	Shoes, footwear, gloves (mil.)	
UC493	Military footwear (U.S.)	
UC500-505	Helmets, hats, etc. (mil.)	
UC500	Military headgear	
UC520	Equipment, Military (gen.)	355.8
UC523-524	Military equipment (U.S.)	355.80973
UC525.A-Z	Equipment, Military (countries except U.S.)	
UC529.A-Z	Equipment, Military (special: by name)	
UC529.C2	Canteens (mil. equip.)	
UC529.K6	Knapsacks (mil. equip.)	
UC530-535	Badges, insignia, etc. (mil.: SEE ALSO UB430+ for decorations)	
UC533	Insignia, badges, etc. (mil.: U.S.)	
UC540-585	Field kits & equip. (mil.)	
UC540	Military kits & field equip. (gen.)	355.81
UC543-544	Field kits & equip. (mil.: U.S.)	
UC550-555	Bunks & bedding (mil.)	
UC570-585	Tents, Military	
UC590-595	Flags, colors, standards (mil.)	
UC590	Military flags, colors, standards (gen.)	355.15
UC593-594	Colors, flags, standards (mil.: U.S.)	
UC595.A-Z	Standards, colors, flags (mil.: places besides U.S.)	
UC600-695	Horses & mules, Military	
UC700-780	Food, cooking, water, etc.	355.65-66, .81
UC700	Subsistence (mil.: gen.)	
UC703-704	Subsistence (mil.: U.S.)	
UC705.A-Z	Subsistence (mil.: countries besides U.S.)	
UC710-715	Rations (mil.)	
UC720	Cooking (mil.: gen.)	
UC723	Messing (mil.: cooking: U.S.)	
UC730-735	Bakeries (mil.)	
UC730	Field ovens (mil.)	
UC740-745	Clubs, Officers' (mil.)	
UC743	Officers' clubs & messes, Military (U.S.)	
UC750-755	Post exchanges & canteens, Military	
UC753	Canteens & post exchanges, Military (U.S.)	

UC760	Refrigerators, Military
UC770	Slaughterhouses, Military
UC780	Water supplies, Military
UD	INFANTRY (tactics, use, gen. hist's.: SEE ALSO UA for specific armies) 356
UD1	Periodicals & associations (infantry)
UD7	Infantry (collections)
UD10	Organization (infantry: gen.)
UD15	Infantry (gen. hist.) 356.09, 109, 355.009
UD21-124	INFANTRY (hist.: by area or country regardless of specific unit: SEE ALSO UA)
UD23	Infantry (U.S.) 356.10973
UD26	Infantry (Can.)
UD55-95	Infantry (Eur.)
UD55	European infantry (gen.) 356.1094
UD57-64	Infantry (G.B.)
UD57	British infantry (gen.) 356.10941
UD58	Infantry (G.B.: by date)
UD71	Infantry (Fr.) 356.10944
UD73	Infantry (Ger.) 356.10943
UD79	Infantry (It.) 356.10945
UD85	Infantry (Rus.: Eur.) 356.10947
UD99-113	Infantry (Asia)
UD99	Asian infantry (gen.) 356.1095
UD101	Infantry (China) 356.10951
UD105	Infantry (Japan) 356.10952
UD109	Infantry (Rus.: Asian)
UD121	Infantry (Australia) 356.10994
UD122.5	Infantry (New Z.)
UD145	Infantry (gen.: pubn. 1801+) 356.1
UD150-155	Manuals, Infantry
UD150	Infantry manuals (gen.) 356.10202
UD153	Handbooks, Infantry (U.S.)
UD155.A-Z	Manuals, Infantry (places besides U.S.)
UD157-302	TACTICS, MANEUVERS, & DRILLS (infantry)
UD157	Maneuvers, drills, & tactics (infantry: gen.) 356.18, 355.42
UD160-162	Drills, tactics, & maneuvers (infantry: U.S.)
UD160	Infantry tactics & maneuvers (U.S.: gen.)
UD161	Drill regulations (infantry: U.S. reserves)
UD215-269	Tactics, maneuvers, & drills (infantry: Eur.)
UD215	Infantry tactics & maneuvers (Eur.: gen.)
UD219-221	Tactics, maneuvers, & drills (infantry: Australia)
UD228-230	Tactics, maneuvers, & drills (infantry: Fr.)
UD231-233	Tactics, maneuvers, & drills (infantry: Ger.)
UD234-236	Tactics, maneuvers, & drills (infantry: G.B.)
UD243-245	Tactics, maneuvers, & drills (infantry: It.)
UD252-254	Tactics, maneuvers, & drills (infantry: Rus.)
UD270-280	Tactics, maneuvers, & drills (infantry: Asia)
UD270	Infantry tactics & maneuvers (Asia: gen.)
UD271-273	Tactics, maneuvers, & drills (infantry: China)
UD277-279	Tactics, maneuvers, & drills (infantry: Japan)
UD295-298	Tactics, maneuvers, & drills (infantry: Australia & New Z.)

UD310	Marching & guides (mil.: gen.)	
UD313-314	Guides & marching (mil.)	
UD315.A-Z	Marching & guides (countries except U.S.)	
UD315.G3	German marching (mil.)	
UD317	River & stream crossing (infantry)	
UD320-325	Arms manuals (infantry)	
UD323-324	Manual of arms (infantry: U.S.)	
UD330	Firing or sharpshooting (infantry: gen.)	
UD333-334	Sharpshooting (infantry: U.S.)	
UD340-345	Bayonet drill	
UD370-375	Equipment, Infantry	
UD380-425	Small arms (infantry)	355.824+, 623.44
UD380	Arms, Small (infantry: gen.)	
UD382	Inspection (small arms: infantry)	
UD383-384	Infantry arms (small: U.S.)	
UD385.A-Z	Small arms (infantry: countries besides U.S.)	
UD390-395	Rifles, carbines, etc. (infantry)	355.82425, 623.4425
UD390	Carbines, rifles, etc.	
UD395.A-Z	Rifles (infantry: by type)	
UD395.G4	Garand rifle	
UD395.M17	M1 rifle	
UD395.M3	Mauser rifle	
UD395.S8	Springfield rifle	
UD395.U6	United States magazine rifle	
UD396	Shotguns	
UD400	Bayonets	
UD410	Pistols & revolvers (gen.)	355.8243, 623.443
UD413-414	Revolvers & pistols, Infantry (U.S. models)	
UD420-425	Swords	
UD430	Reserves & militia, Infantry	
UD440-445	Field service, Infantry	
UD450	Mounted infantry (gen.)	
UD453-454	Infantry, Mounted (U.S.)	
UD460-465	Mountain warfare & troops	356.164
UD470-475	Ski troops	356.164
UD475.A-Z	Ski troops (by country)	356.16409+
UD475.G3	German ski troops	356.1640943
UD480-485	Airborne & parachute troops	356.166
UD480	Parachute & airborne troops (gen.)	
UD483-484	Troops, Airborne (U.S.)	356.1660973
UE	ARMOR & CAVALRY (SEE ALSO UA for specific armies) 357-358.1	
UE1	Periodicals & associations (armor & cavalry)	
UE7	Cavalry & armor (collections)	
UE10	Organization (armor & cavalry: gen.)	
UE15	Armor & cavalry (gen. hist.: inclu. several countries)	357.09, .109, 358.1809
UE21-124	CAVALRY & ARMOR (by place: SEE ALSO UA for specific units)	
UE23	Armor & cavalry (U.S.)	357.0973
UE55-95	Armor & cavalry (Eur.)	
UE55	Cavalry & armor (Eur.: gen.)	357.094
UE57-64	Armor & cavalry (G.B.)	
UE57	Cavalry & armor (G.B.: gen.)	357.0941
UE58	Armor & cavalry (G.B.: by date)	
UE71	Armor & cavalry (Fr.)	357.0944

UE73	Armor & cavalry (Ger.)	357.0943
UE79	Armor & cavalry (It.)	
UE85	Armor & cavalry (Rus.: Eur.)	357.0947
UE99-113	Armor & cavalry (Asia)	
UE99	Cavalry & armor (Asia: gen.)	357.095
UE101	Armor & cavalry (China)	
UE105	Armor & cavalry (Japan)	357.0952
UE109	Armor & cavalry (Rus.: Asia)	
UE121-122.5	Armor & cavalry (Australia & New Z.)	357.099+
UE145	Horse cavalry (pubn. 1801+)	357.1
UE147	Mechanized & armored cavalry	357.5, 358.18
UE149	Armor & cavalry (essays & speeches)	
UE150-155	Manuals, Armor & Cavalry	
UE153-154	Armor & Cavalry manuals (U.S.)	
UE157-302	TACTICS, MANEUVERS, & DRILLS (armor & cavalry)	
UE159	Tactics, maneuvers, & drills (armored & mechanized cavalry)	
UE160-302	MANEUVERS & TACTICS (armor & cavalry: by place)	
UE160	Tactics, maneuvers, & drills (armor & cavalry: U.S.: gen.)	
UE161	Drill regulations (armor & cavalry: U.S. reserves)	
UE215-269	Drills, tactics, & maneuvers (armor & cavalry: Eur.)	
UE215	Tactics, maneuvers, & drills (armor & cavalry: Eur.: gen.)	
UE228	Tactics, maneuvers, & drills (armor & cavalry: Fr.)	
UE231	Tactics, maneuvers, & drills (armor & cavalry: Ger.)	
UE252	Tactics, maneuvers, & drills (armor & cavalry: Rus.)	
UE270-280	Maneuvers & tactics (armor & cavalry: Asia)	
UE270	Tactics, maneuvers, & drills (armor & cavalry: Asia: gen.)	
UE271	Tactics, maneuvers, & drills (armor & cavalry: China)	
UE277	Tactics, maneuvers, & drills (armor & cavalry: Japan)	
UE295	Tactics, maneuvers, & drills (armor & cavalry: Australia)	
UE360	Reconnaisance, Cavalry	355.413, 358.45
UE400-405	Firing (armor & cavalry)	
UE420-425	Sword exercises (cavalry)	
UE430	Training camps (armor & cavalry: gen.)	
UE433-434	Camps, Training (armor & cavalry: U.S.)	
UE435.A-Z	Training camps (armor & cavalry: places besides U.S.)	
UE460-475	Horses, Cavalry	
UE460	Cavalry horses (gen.)	
UE500	Camel troops & camelry	
UF	ARTILLERY (SEE ALSO UA for specific armies & units)	358.1+,
		355.82+
UF1	Periodicals & associations (artillery)	
UF6	Museums, Artillery (inclu. exhibitions)	
UF6.A1.A-Z	Artillery museums & exhibitons (gen.)	358.12
UF6.A2-Z	Museums, Artillery (by country or region)	
UF6.x2.A-Z	Museums, Artillery (by city within area, whose 1st letter & shelf # are shown by 'x' in 'x2')	
UF7	Artillery (titles in collections)	
UF9	Dictionaries & encyclopedias (artillery)	358.1203
UF10	Organization (artillery forces)	
UF15	Artillery (gen. hist.)	358.109, .1209, 355.82, .821

UF21-121	ARTILLERY (by place: SEE ALSO UA for particular armies)
UF23	Artillery (U.S.) 358.120973, .10973, 355.820973
UF57	Artillery (G.B.: gen.) 358.120941
UF58	Artillery (G.B.: by date periods)
UF58.1939-45	Artillery (G.B.: WWII)
UF71	Artillery (Fr.) 358.120944
UF73	Artillery (Ger.) 358.120943
UF79	Artillery (It.)
UF81	Artillery (Norway)
UF85	Artillery (Rus.: Eur.)
UF99-113	Artillery (Asia)
UF99	Artillery (Asia: gen.)
UF101	Artillery (China)
UF105	Artillery (Japan) 358.120952
UF121-122.5	Artillery (Australia & New Z.)
UF130-135	Laws, Ordnance
UF133	Ordnance laws (U.S.: PREFER KF7335
UF145	Artillery (pubn. 1801+) 358.12
UF148	Exercises, problems, etc. (artillery)
UF150-155	Manuals (artillery) 358.120202
UF153-154	Artillery manuals (U.S.)
UF157-302	TACTICS, MANEUVERS, & DRILLS (artillery)
UF157	Maneuvers, drills, & tactics (artillery: gen.)
UF160-302	DRILLS, MANEUVERS, & TACTICS (artillery: by place)
UF160	Tactics, maneuvers, & drills (artillery: U.S.: gen.)
UF162.A-W	Drill regulations (artillery: U.S. reserves: by state)
UF163	Tactics, maneuvers, & drills (artillery: Can.)
UF215-269	Maneuvers & tactics (artillery: Eur.)
UF215	Tactics, maneuvers, & drills (artillery: Eur.: gen.)
UF228	Tactics, maneuvers, & drills (artillery: Fr.)
UF231	Tactics, maneuvers, & drills (artillery: Ger.)
UF234	Tactics, maneuvers, & drills (artillery: G.B.)
UF243	Tactics, maneuvers, & drills (artillery: It.)
UF252	Tactics, maneuvers, & drills (artillery: Rus.)
UF270-280	Maneuvers & tactics (artillery: Asia)
UF270	Tactics, maneuvers, & drills (artillery: Asia: gen.)
UF271	Tactics, maneuvers, & drills (artillery: China)
UF277	Tactics, maneuvers, & drills (artillery: Japan)
UF295-298	Tactics, maneuvers, & drills (artillery: Australia & New Z.)
UF320	Stream & river crossing (artillery)
UF340-345	Target practice
UF356	Reserves, Artillery
UF370	Horses, Artillery
UF380-385	Wagons & carts, Artillery
UF390	Motor transport, Artillery
UF400	Field artillery (gen.) 358.12
UF403-404	Artillery, Field (U.S.)
UF405.A-Z	Field artillery (places besides U.S.)
UF405.G3	German field artillery
UF410	Horse artillery
UF420	Camel batteries
UF430	Elephant batteries

UF440-445	Mountain artillery	
UF443-444	Artillery, Mountain (U.S.)	
UF450-455	Seacoast artillery	
UF450	Coast artillery (gen.)	
UF453-454	Artillery, Seacoast (U.S.)	
UF460-465	Siege artillery	
UF460	Artillery, Siege (gen.)	
UF470-475	Howitzers & mortars	
UF473	Mortars & howitzers (U.S.: gen.)	
UF475.A-Z	Artillery, Howitzer & mortar (places besides U.S.)	
UF475.F8	Howitzers & mortars (Fr.)	
UF475.G7	Howitzers & mortars (G.B.)	
UF475.J3	Howitzers & mortars (Japan)	
UF480	Garrison & fortress artillery (gen.)	
UF483	Fortress & garrison artillery (U.S.: gen.)	
UF490	Railroad artillery (gen.)	
UF493	Artillery, Railway (U.S.: gen.)	
UF495.A-Z	Railway artillery (countries besides U.S.)	
UF495.F8	Railway artillery (Fr.)	
UF495.G3	Railway artillery (Ger.)	
UF500-505	Weapons systems (artillery)	
UF520-537	Ordnance & small arms	355.82, 623.4+, .44
UF520	Small arms & ordnance (gen.)	355.82
UF523	Ordnance & small arms (U.S.)	355.820973
UF525.A-Z	Small arms & ordnance (besides U.S.: by place)	
UF526	Research, Ordnance & small-arms	
UF526.3	Ordnance & small-arms research (U.S.)	
UF526.5.A-Z	Small-arms & ordnance research (places besides U.S.)	
UF527	Instruction (ordnance & small arms)	
UF530	Manufacture (ordnance & small arms: gen.)	623.4+, 338.476234
UF533	Small arms & ordnance (manufacture: U.S.: gen.)	338.4762340973
UF534.A-W	Manufacture (small arms & ordnance: U.S.: by state)	
UF537.A-Z	Manufacturers (small arms & ordnance)	
UF540	Armories, arsenals, magazines (gen.)	
UF543	Arsenals, armories, etc. (U.S.: gen.)	
UF545.A-Z	Magazines, armories, etc. (countries except U.S.)	
UF550	Ordnance stores, accounts, etc. (gen.)	
UF553	Stores, Ordnance (U.S.: gen.)	
UF560-780	ORDNANCE PROPER	
UF560-565.A-Z.A-Z(II-IV) etc.	Ordnance material (by type, mark #, ed. date, etc.)	
UF560-565... .B.L	Breech-loading ordnance	
UF560-565... .H	Hotchkiss ordnance	
UF560-565... .M.L	Muzzle-loading ordnance	
UF560-565... .N	Nordenfelt ordnance	
UF560-565... .Q.F	Quick-firing ordnance	
UF560	Ordnance material (gen.)	355.82+, 623.4+
UF563	Ordnance material (U.S.: gen.)	355.820973, 623.40973

UF563.A4-8	Handbooks, Gun (U.S.: artillery)	
UF563.A4.1+	Gun handbooks (U.S.: by mm. or cm. then date)	
UF563.A5	Handbooks, Gun (U.S.: by inches)	
UF563.A5.2.95in.Mt.	Mountain guns (U.S.: handbooks: 2.95)	
UF563.A6	Handbooks, Gun (U.S.: by pounds)	
UF563.A7-8	Handbooks, Gun (U.S.: by class or type: sometimes use	

UF563.A4-6 with measure. & alphab. symbol: e.g.

UF563.A5.12 in.M for 12 mortar... or ... Mt. for mountain)

UF563.A7	Coast guns (U.S.: handbooks)	
UF563.A75	Mortars (U.S.: handbooks)	
UF563.A76	Railway gun matériel (U.S.: handbooks)	
UF563.A8	Subcaliber guns (U.S.: handbooks)	
UF563.A9-Z	United States ordnance (gen.)	
UF565.A-Z	Ordnance material (countries besides U.S.)	
UF565.F8	Ordnance material (Fr.)	
UF565.G3	Ordnance material (Ger.)	
UF565.G7	Ordnance material (G.B.)	
UF565.J3	Ordnance material (Japan)	
UF565.R9	Ordnance material (Rus.)	
UF620.A2	Machine guns (gen.)	623.4424
UF620.A3-Z	Machine guns (specific types)	
UF620.B6	Browning machine guns	
UF620.C6	Colt machine guns	
UF620.G3	Gatling machine guns	
UF620.G6	Goriunov machine guns	
UF620.H8	Hotchkiss machine guns	
UF620.L5	Lewis machine guns	
UF620.M4	Maxim machine guns	
UF620.N8	Nordenfelt machine guns	
UF620.S8	Sten machine guns	
UF620.T5	Thompson machine guns	
UF620.U6	United States automatic machine guns	
UF620.V4	Vickers machine guns	
UF625	Antiaircraft guns & defenses (SEE ALSO UG730+)	358.13
UF628	Antitank guns	623.42, .44, .4518
UF630	Guns (misc. types: mil. sci.)	
UF640	Gun carriages, caissons, limbers, etc. (gen.)	623.43
UF643	Caissons, gun carriages, etc. (U.S.: gen.)	
UF650	Gun carriages, Disappearing	
UF652	Gun carriages, Self-propelled (plus track-layer tractors & other self-contained)	
UF655	Railway gun cars (SEE ALSO UF563.A76, UF565)	358.22
UF660	Cupolas, Revolving (& other portable gun shelters)	
UF670-675	Firing instructions, Artillery	
UF700	Ammunition, Artillery	358.825, 623.45
UF740-745	Cartridges	623.455
UF750-770	Projectiles, Artillery	623.451
UF750	Artillery projectiles (gen.)	
UF753	Projectiles, Artillery (U.S.)	
UF760	Shells & shrapnel	623.4513-4518
UF765	Grenades	623.45114
UF767	Bombs & projectiles, Aircraft (inclu. std. & nuclear)	623.451
UF770	Bullets	623.455
UF780	Firing devices (primers, percussion caps, etc.)	
UF800	Gunnery, Artillery (gen.)	623.55

UF805	Aerial observations (artillery)	
UF810	Firing tests (artillery)	
UF820-830	Ballistics 623.51+	
UF820	Projectile velocities & motions (gen.)	623.51
UF823	Ballistics, Interior 623.513	
UF825	Ballistics, Exterior 623.514	
UF830.A-Z	Ballistic instruments	
UF840	Photography, Ballistic (inclu. photochronography)	
UF845	Binoculars & telescopes, Military	
UF848-856	Fire control, Artillery (inclu. instruments)	
UF848	Artillery fire control (inclu. instruments: gen.)	623.558
UF849-856	Instruments, Artillery (specific types)	
UF849	Optical instruments & tools, Artillery	
UF850.A2	Range finders, Artillery (gen.)	623.46
UF850.A3-Z	Artillery range finders (particular types)	
UF850.A9	Azimuth instrument (artillery)	
UF850.D4	Depression range finder	
UF850.W3	Watkin range finder	
UF853	Position finders (artillery)	623.46
UF854	Sights, Firearm	
UF855	Telescopic sights (artillery)	
UF856.A-Z	Artillery instruments (misc.)	
UF857	Range tables, Artillery	
UF860-880	Military explosives, unguided rockets, etc.	
UF860	Explosives, Military (gen.) 623.452	
UF870	Explosions, powder force, etc.	
UF880	Rockets, Unguided (mil. sci.: SEE UG1310-1315 for guided	
	rockets) 623.4543	
UF890	Tests, Ordnance	
UF900	Resistance to projectiles (artillery)	
UF910	Bulletproof clothing, materials, etc.	
UG	MILITARY ENGINEERING, AIR FORCES, & AIR WARFARE 358.2,	
	623, 358.4 (air forces etc.)	
UG1-620	ENGINEERING, MILITARY	
UG1	Periodicals & associations (mil. engineering)	
UG6	Museums & exhibitions (mil. engineering)	
UG7	Military engineering (collections)	
UG15	Engineering, Military (gen. hist.) 358.2, .209	
UG21-124	Engineering, Military (by country or area)	
UG23-25	Engineering, Military (U.S.) 358.20973	
UG23	Military engineering (U.S.: gen.)	
UG55-95	Engineering, Military (Eur.) 358.2094	
UG55	Military engineering (Eur.: gen.)	
UG57	Engineering, Military (G.B.)	
UG57.Z6.1st+	Military engineering (G.B.: by #'d regiment)	
UG71	Engineering, Military (Fr.)	
UG73	Engineering, Military (Ger.)	
UG73.Z6.1st+	Military enginering (Ger.: by #'d regiment)	
UG85	Engineering, Military (Rus.: Eur.)	

UG99-113	Engineering, Military (Asia)	
UG99	Military engineering (Asia: gen.)	
UG101	Engineering, Military (China)	
UG105	Engineering, Military (Japan)	
UG105.Z6.1st+	Military engineering (Japan: by #'d regiment)	
UG121-122.5	Engineering, Military (Australia + New Z.)	
UG125.1st+	Military engineering (U.S.: by #'d regiment)	
UG127	Biography, Military engineering (collective)	
UG128.A-Z	Biography, Military engineering (indiv.: SEE ALSO UG21-124)	
UG130-135	Laws (engineer corps)	
UG133	Laws (engineer corps: U.S.: PREFER KF7335.E5)	
UG145	Engineering, Military (gen.: pubn. 1801+)	
UG150-155	Manuals (mil. engineering)	
UG153	Military engineering manuals (U.S.)	
UG156	Engineering, Military (essays & lectures)	
UG157	Instruction (mil. engineering)	
UG160-302	TACTICS & REGULATIONS (mil. engineering: by place)	
UG160	Tactics & regulations (mil. engineering: U.S.)	
UG163	Tactics & regulations (mil. engineering: Can.)	
UG215-269	Tactics & regulations (mil. engineering: Eur.)	
UG215	Regulations & tactics (mil. engineering: Eur.: gen.)	
UG228	Tactics & regulations (mil. engineering: Fr.)	
UG231	Tactics & regulations (mil. engineering: Ger.)	
UG234	Tactics & regulations (mil. engineering: G.B.)	
UG252	Tactics & regulations (mil. engineering: Rus.)	
UG270-280	Tactics & regulations (mil. engineering: Asia)	
UG270	Regulations & tactics (mil. engineering: Asia: gen.)	
UG271	Tactics & regulations (mil. engineering: China)	
UG277	Tactics & regulations (mil. engineering: Japan)	
UG295-298	Tactics & regulations (mil. engineering: Australia & New Z.)	
UG320-325	Maneuvers (mil. engineering)	
UG323	Military engineering maneuvers (U.S.)	
UG330	Roads (mil. engineering)	623.62
UG335	Bridges (mil. engineering)	623.67
UG340	Tunnels (mil. engineering)	623.68
UG343	Ice excavation, tunnels, rooms, etc. (mil. engineering)	
UG345	Railroads, armored trains, etc. (mil. engineering)	623.63
UG350	Harbors, canals, dams (mil. engineering)	623.64
UG360-390	Field engineering (mil.)	
UG360	Military engineering (field: gen.)	
UG365	Camp-making (mil. sci.)	355.412, .544, .71
UG370	Demolitions (mil. engineering)	623.4545, 358.23
UG375	Obstacles (mil. engineering)	355.544
UG380	Intrenching tools (mil.)	
UG385	Ferrying (mil. engineering)	
UG390	Field engineering (misc. topics)	

UG400-442	Fortification	
UG401	Fortification (gen.: pubn. 1801+)	355.544, 623.1
UG403	Field fortification	
UG405	Fortification, Permanent	
UG407	Entanglements & misc. fortification	
UG408-409	Steel & iron land defenses	
UG410-442	Fortifications (by place)	623.19+, 355.45-47+
UG410-412	Fortified defenses (U.S.)	623.1973, 355.4773
UG410	Defenses, Fortified (U.S.: gen.)	623.1973, 355.4773
UG411.A-Z	Fortifications (U.S.: by state or region)	623.1974-1979+, 355.450974+, .4774+
UG411.P2	Pacific Coast (U.S.: fortifications)	
UG412.A-Z	Fortifications (U.S.: by town or place)	
UG412.K4	Key West, Fl. (fortifications)	
UG412.N5	New York City (fortifications)	
UG412.P3	Panama Canal (fortifications)	
UG412.S3	San Diego, Calif. (fortifications)	
UG413-415	Fortified defenses (Can.)	
UG422-424	Fortified defenses (W. Indies)	
UG428-430	Fortified defenses (Eur.)	
UG428	Defenses, Fortified (Eur.: gen.)	623.194, 355.474
UG429.A-Z	Fortifications (Eur.: by region or country)	
UG429.G3	Fortified defenses (Ger.)	
UG430.A-Z	Fortifications (Eur.: by town or place)	
UG431-433	Fortified defenses (Asia)	623.195
UG432.A-Z	Fortifications (Asia: by country)	
UG432.J3	Fortified defenses (Japan)	623.1952
UG432.P5	Fortified defenses (Philip.)	
UG437-439	Fortified defenses (Australia)	
UG440-442	Fortified defenses (Pacific islands)	
UG443-449	Attack, defense, & siege	
UG444	Defense, attack, & siege (gen.: pubn. 1789+)	355.4+
UG446	Trench warfare	355.44
UG446.5	Tanks, armored cars, etc. (attack, defense, & siege: SEE ALSO UE159-302 for armored cavalry)	355.422, 357.5, 358.18
UG447-447.6	Chemical warfare (inclu. flames)	623.4516
UG447	Flame & chemical weapons (gen.)	358.34
UG447.5.A-Z	Gas warfare (by chem. name)	623.4516
UG447.5.M8	Mustard gas	623.4516
UG447.6	Gas masks (mil.)	
UG447.65	Incendiary weapons	
UG447.7	Smoke screens & tactics	
UG447.8	Biological & bacterial warfare	
UG448	Coast defenses (SEE UG410-442 for specific places)	358.16, 355.45
UG449	Camouflage (SEE ALSO V215 for naval)	358.3, 623.77
UG450	Mechanical engineering (mil. applications)	
UG455	Weights & measures (mil. metrology)	
UG465-465.5	Geology & seismology, Military	
UG460	Architecture, Military	623.1
UG467	Meteorology, Military	
UG468	Hydrology, Military	
UG470-474	Military surveying, mapping, & topography	
UG470	Surveying, mapping, & topography (military: gen.)	623.71
UG472	Mapping & surveying, Military (U.S.)	
UG473.A-Z	Topography & mapping, Military (places except U.S.)	

```
UG475          Surveillance, Military          355.413, 358.45
UG476          Photography, Military          623.72
UG480          Electricity (mil. uses)          623.76
UG485          Electronics, Military          623.732+
UG490          Mines, Land (inclu. countermeasures)          623.45115
UG500-565   Technical troops & other special corps
UG500               Technical troops & artificers (gen.)          358.2-3
UG503               Artificers, Military (U.S.: ALSO tech. troops)
UG503               Sappers & bridge troops (U.S.)
UG505.A-Z          Military artificers & technical troops (places besides U.S.)
UG510          Bridge troops & sappers (gen.)
UG520-525   Railroad troops
UG530-535   Pioneer troops
UG550-555   Mining & torpedo troops
UG550          Torpedo & mining troops
UG560-565          Electricians, Military
UG570-582          Signaling, Military          358.24, 623.73+, 355.85
UG570-575          Signal corps & troops
UG573               Signal corps & troops (U.S.)
UG580          Military signaling (gen.)
UG582.A-Z   Signaling, Military (particular types)
UG582.H2    Hand signaling (mil.)
UG582.H4    Heliograph (mil. signal.)
UG582.S4          Semaphores (mil.)
UG582.S68         Sound signaling (mil.)
UG582.V5    Visual signaling (mil.)
UG590-613.5    Telecommunications, Military
UG590          Telephone, radio, & telegraph (military: gen.)          623.732-7345
UG600-605   Telegraph, Military (inclu. telegraph troops)
UG603          Military telegraph & troops (U.S.)
UG607          Submarine cables (mil.)
UG610          Telephone, Military (gen.)
UG610.3            Military telephone (U.S.)
UG610.5.A-Z       Telephone, Military (places besides U.S.)
UG611          Radio, Military (gen.)
UG611.3       Military radio (U.S.)
UG612          Radar, Military (gen.)          623.7348
UG612.3            Military radar (U.S.)
UG612.5.A-Z    Radar, Military (places except U.S.)
UG612.5.G7    Radar, Military (G.B.)
UG615          Motor vehicles, Military (gen.)          623.747, 355.83, 357.5+
UG618          Vehicles, Motor (mil.: U.S.)
UG620.A-Z   Military motor vehicles (places besides U.S.)
```

UG622-1425	AIR FORCES & AIR WARFARE	358.4, 623.74-746
UG622	Periodicals & associations (air forces)	358.005-006
UG623	Conferences (air forces)	
UG623.3.A1	Museums, Air force (inclu. exhibitions: gen.)	623.74074, 358.40074
UG623.3.A2-Z	Air museums & exhibitions (by country or area)	
UG623.3.x2.A-Z	Exhibitions & museums, Air force (by place within country)	
UG624	Air warfare & forces (collected works: gen.)	
UG625	Air forces & warfare (hist.: gen.)	358.4009
UG626	Biography, Air force (collective)	358.400922
UG626.2.A-Z	Biography, Air force (individual)	358.400924
UG627	Air forces & warfare (essays & lectures)	
UG628	Dictionaries & encyclopedias (air forces & warfare)	358.4003
UG630	Air warfare & forces (gen.)	358.4
UG633	Air forces (U.S.: gen.)	358.400973
UG634.5.A-Z	Air bases & fields (U.S.: by name)	
UG634.A-W	Air forces (U.S.: by state)	
UG635.A-Z	Air forces (places besides U.S.)	
UG635.A8	Air forces (Australia)	
UG635.F8	Air forces (Fr.)	
UG635.G3	Air forces (Ger.)	
UG635.G322.T3	Tempelhof Airfield (Berlin, Ger.)	
UG635.G7	Air forces (G.B.)	
UG635.I8	Air forces (It.)	
UG635.J3	Air forces (Japan)	
UG635.R9	Air forces (Rus.)	
UG635.S65	Air forces (Sov.Un.)	
UG635.x2.A-Z	Airfields & bases (countries besides U.S.: by name of base)	
UG637-639	Education & training, Air force	358.415+
UG637	Training & education, Air force (gen.)	
UG638-638.8	Air force training & education (U.S.)	
UG638	Flight training, Air force (U.S.: gen.: inclu. other educ.)	358.4150973
UG639.A-Z	Training & education, Air force (places besides U.S.)	
UG640	Research, Aeronautical (mil.: gen.)	358.407, .40072+
UG643	Aeronautical research, Military (U.S.: gen.)	358.4070973
UG643.5.A-W	Military research, Aeronautical (U.S.: by state of origin)	
UG644.A-Z	Research, Aeronautical (mil.: by company or establishment)	
UG645.A-Z	Research, Aeronautical (mil.: places besides U.S.)	
UG645.G3	Aeronautical research, Military (Ger.)	
UG670	Manuals & regulations, Air force (gen.)	
UG673	Regulations & manuals, Air force (U.S.)	
UG675.A-Z	Air force manuals & regulations (places except U.S.)	
UG675.G3	Air force regulations & manuals (Ger.)	
UG700-705	Tactics, Air warfare (bombing, strafing, dog fighting, air mining, etc.)	358.4142, .43
UG700	Air force tactics (gen.)	
UG703	Bombing, dog fighting, other air tactics (U.S.)	
UG705.A-Z	Dog fighting, bombing, other air tactics (countries besides U.S.)	
UG730-735	Defenses, Air (SEE ALSO UF625 for antiaircraft & UA926+ for civil defense)	358.4145, .13
UG733	Air defenses (U.S.)	358.41450973
UG735.A-Z	Defenses, Air (places besides U.S.)	
UG760-765	Reconnaisance, Aerial	358.45
UG763	Aerial reconnaisance (U.S.)	

UG770-1045	ORGANIZATION (air forces)	
UG770-775	Administration (air forces: structure & personnel: gen.)	358.41, .413, .416+
UG773	Personnel & administration (air forces: U.S.)	
UG790	Officers, Air force (gen.) 358.41331-41332	
UG793	Officers, Air force (U.S.)	
UG795.A-Z	Air force officers (countries except U.S.)	
UG795.G3	Officers, Air force (Ger.)	
UG820-825	Airmen & non-commissioned air officers 358.41338	
UG823	Officers, Non-commissioned (air: U.S.: inclu. airmen)	
UG825.A-Z	Non-commissioned officers, Air force (countries besides U.S.)	
UG850-855	Reserves, Air force	
UG853	Air National Guard (U.S.)	
UG880-885	Recruiting, enlistment, etc. (air forces)	
UG880	Enlistment, recruiting, etc. (air forces: gen.)	
UG940-945	Pay & benefits (air forces) 358.41135, .4164	
UG943	Benefits, pay, allowances (air forces: U.S.)	
UG970	Leaves, furloughs, etc. (air forces: gen.)	
UG973	Furloughs, leaves, etc. (air forces: U.S.)	
UG980-985	Medical services (air forces) 358.41345	
UG990-995	Recreation, social work, etc. (air forces)	
UG990	Social work, recreation, etc. (air forces: U.S.)	
UG1000-1005	Chaplains, Air force	
UG1020-1025	Police, Air force	
UG1040-1045	Prisons, Air force	
UG1100-1425	EQUIPMENT & SUPPLIES (air force)	
UG1100-1105	Supplies & equipment (air force: gen.) 358.418	
UG1120	Procurement & contracts, Air force (gen.) 358.41621	
UG1123	Contracts & procurement, Air force (U.S.)	
UG1130-1185	Personnel, Air force	
UG1130-1135	Air force personnel (gen.) 358.4161	
UG1140-1145	Barracks & quarters, Air force 358.4171	
UG1143	Quarters & barracks, Air force (U.S.)	
UG1160-1165	Uniforms, Air force 358.4114	
UG1180-1185	Insignia, badges, etc. (air force)	
UG1200-1405	Operational equipment, Air force (airplanes, bombs, guns, vehicles)	
UG1200	Air force equipment (gen.: planes, bombs, etc.) 358.418, .412	
UG1203	Equipment, Air force (gen.: planes, bombs, etc.: U.S.) 358.4180973	
UG1220	Airships or dirigibles (gen.) 623.743	
UG1225.A-Z	Dirigibles (places outside U.S.)	
UG1225.G3	Dirigibles (Ger.)	
UG1230-1235	Helicopters, Military 623.746047	
UG1240-1245	Airplanes, Military 623.746, 358.418	
UG1240	Airplanes (air force: gen.)	
UG1242.A-Z	Airplanes (air force: by type)	
UG1242.A25	Antisubmarine aircraft	
UG1242.A28	Attack planes	
UG1242.B6	Bombers (air force) 623.7463, 358.42	
UG1242.F5	Fighter planes 623.7464, 358.43	
UG1242.R4	Reconnaisance planes 623.7467, 358.45	
UG1242.S3	Seaplanes (air force) 629.133347, 623.7466-7467	
UG1242.T7	Transport planes (air force)	

UG1243	Air force planes (U.S.: PREFER UG1242 for particular types)
	358.40973, .4140973, .414773, 623.740973, .7460973
UG1245.A-Z	Air force planes (countries besides U.S.)
UG1245.F8	Air force planes (Fr.) 358.400944
UG1245.G3	Air force planes (Ger.) 358.400943, .414743, 623.740943
UG1245.G7	Air force planes (G.B.) 358.400941, .414741-414742,
	623.740941, .7460941
UG1245.I8	Air force planes (It.) 358.400945
UG1245.J3	Air force planes (Japan) 358.400952, .414752, 623.740952
UG1245.R9	Air force planes (Rus.) 358.400947
UG1270-1275	Ordnance, Air force (gen.) 358.4182, 623.45+
UG1273	Air force ordnance (gen.: U.S.)
UG1280-1285	Bombs, Air force 358.418251, 623.451
UG1282.A-Z	Air force bombs (by specific type)
UG1282.A8	Atomic bombs (SEE ALSO U264) 358.41825119, 623.45119
UG1282.F7	Fragmentation bombs (aerial) 623.4514
UG1282.I6	Incendiary bombs (aerial) 623.4516
UG1310-1315	Rockets & missiles, Air force 623.451, .4519, .4543
UG1312.A-Z	Missiles & rockets, Air force (by particular type)
UG1312.V2	V-2 rocket
UG1313	Rockets, Air force (U.S.)
UG1315.A-Z	Rockets, Air force (places except U.S.)
UG1315.G3	Rockets, Air force (Ger.)
UG1340-1345	Guns, Aircraft 623.7461
UG1340	Aircraft guns & small weapons (gen.)
UG1370-1375	Balloons & kites, Air force 623.741-744
UG1400-1405	Vehicles, Motor (air force: ground)
UG1420	Radar & electronics, Air force (gen.) 623.7348, .7467
UG1423	Electronics & radar, Air force (U.S.)
UG1425.A-Z	Air force radar & electronics (places besides U.S.)
UG1425.G7	Radar & electronics, Air force (G.B.)
UH	MILITARY SERVICES (misc.)
UH20	Chaplains or religious officials, Military (gen.) 355.347
UH23	Chaplains, Military (U.S.) 355.3470973
UH25.A-Z	Religious officials, Military (countries except U.S.)
UH30-35	Cyclists, Military
UH30	Bicyclists, Military (gen.) 357.52
UH40-45	Bands & music, Military
UH40	Music & bands, Military (gen.)
UH60-65	Banking services, Military
UH80-85	Postal service, Military 355.69
UH87-100	Animals, Military
UH87	Military animals (gen.) 355.24
UH90	Pigeons, Military (for communications: SEE ALSO D639.P45 for WWI &
	D810.P53 for WWII)
UH100	Dogs, Military
UH201-570	MEDICAL & RELIEF SERVICES, MILITARY
UH201-515	SANITARY & MEDICAL SERVICES, MILITARY
UH201	Periodicals & associations (military medical services)
UH206	Museums, Military medical (inclu. exhibitions)

UH215-324	MEDICAL SERVICES, MILITARY (hist., statistics, etc.: gen. & by place)
UH215	Military medical services (hist., statistics, etc.: includes sanitary services: gen.) 355.345
UH223-225	Medical services, Military (U.S.) 355.3450973
UH223.A1-29	Reports, Official (military medical: U.S.: serial)
UH223.A1-49	Medical services, Military (U.S.: official reports)
UH223.A3-39	Reports, Official (military medical: U.S.: monographic)
UH223.A4-49	Statistics, Official (military medical: U.S.)
UH223.A5	Statistics (militray medical: U.S.: unofficial)
UH223.A6-Z	Medical services, Military (U.S.: unofficial)
UH224	Military medical services (U.S.: by time period or date: SEE ALSO particular wars)
UH224.1917-18	Medical services, Military (U.S.: WWI)
UH224.1941-45	Medical services, Military (U.S.: WWII)
UH226-227	Medical services, Military (Can.)
UH255-295	Medical services, Military (Eur.)
UH255	Medical services, Military (Eur.: gen.) 355.345094
UH256	Military medical services, Military (Eur.: by date or period)
UH256.1914-18	Medical services, Military (Eur.: WWI)
UH256.1939-45	Medical services, Military (Eur.: WWII)
UH257	Medical services, Military (G.B.: gen.) 355.3450941
UH258	Military medical services (G.B.: by period or date)
UH271-272	Medical services, Military (Fr.)
UH273-274	Medical services, Military (Ger.) 355.3450943
UH285-286	Medical services, Military (Rus.)
UH286.5	Medical services, Military (Scandin.)
UH299-313	Medical services, Military (Asia)
UH299	Military medical services (Asia: gen.)
UH301-302	Medical services, Military (China)
UH305-306	Medical services, Military (Japan) 355.3450952
UH309-310	Medical services, Military (Rus.: Asia)
UH313.A-Z	Medical services, Military (misc. Asian lands)
UH313.P5	Medical services, Military (Philippines)
UH315-319	Medical services, Military (Africa)
UH317-318	Medical services, Military (Egypt)
UH321-322	Medical services, Military (Australia)
UH322.5	Medical services, Military (New Z.)
UH323-324	Medical services, Military (Pac. islands)
UH341	Biography, Military medical (collective, inclu. nurses) 355.3450922
UH347.A-Z	Medical biography, Military (indiv.: by name) 355.3450924
UH390-396	Medicine, Military (gen., hdbks., etc.)
UH390	Military medicine (gen.: inclu. hdbks., manuals, etc.) 616.98023
UH393	Medicine, Military (U.S.: official manuals etc.)
UH394	Medicine, Military (U.S.: unofficial manuals etc.)
UH395.A-Z	Medicine, Military (places besides U.S.: manuals etc.)
UH396	First-aid manuals, Soldiers' (SEE ALSO UH393-395)
UH398	Medical schools, Army (U.S.: gen.)
UH398.5.A-Z	Army medical schools (U.S.: by region or state)
UH399.5-7	Research & laboratories, Medical (mil.)
UH399.A-Z	Medical schools, Army (places besides U.S.)
UH400-485	Organization (mil. medical: inclu. services)
UH400	Military medical services (gen.: inclu. organization, surgeons, etc.)
UH420-425	Pharmacy services, Military

UH430-435	Dentistry, Military	
UH440-445	Supplies, Medical & surgical (mil.)	355.88
UH450-455	Bacteriology, Military (inclu. vaccination)	
UH460-485	Hospital services, Military	
UH470	Hospitals, Military (gen.)	355.72
UH473-474	Military hospitals (U.S.: SEE ALSO D629.U6-8 & D807.U6-87 for WWI & II)	
UH475.A-Z	Hospitals, Military (except U.S.)	
UH487	Cookery & diet, Medical (mil.)	
UH490	Nurses & nursing, Military (gen.)	355.345
UH493	Military nursing (U.S.)	
UH495.A-Z	Nursing & nurses, Military (besides U.S.)	
UH500-505	Ambulances, Military (plus transport)	623.74724
UH500	Transport, Medical (mil.: gen.)	
UH510-515	Equipment, Medical corps	
UH510	Medical corps equipment (gen.)	
UH520-560	Relief societies (mil.: inclu. care of sick & wounded)	361.05, .77
UH520	Wounded, Care of (mil.: inclu. relief societies: gen.)	361.05, .77, .9, 940.477+
UH523	Sick & wounded, Care of (mil.: relief societies, etc.: U.S.: gen.)	
UH524.A-Z	Relief societies (mil.: U.S. by state or region)	
UH525.A-Z	Relief societies (mil.: besides U.S.: by place)	
UH531-533	Geneva & Hague conventions (PREFER JX5136 & JX5243) 341.6+, .65	
UH531	Hague & Geneva conventions (official works: by date: PREFER JX5136 & JX5243)	
UH533	Treatment of prisoners (Geneva & Hague conven.: unofficial: PREFER JX5136 & JX5243)	
UH534	Congresses, International (relief, sick, wounded, etc.: misc.: by date)	
UH535	Red Cross (gen.: wartime)	940.4771, .54771
UH537.A	American Red Cross	
UH537.A-Z	Red Cross (by country or region)	
UH543-545	Relief associations (besides U.S.)	
UH560	Employment for crippled soldiers & sailors (PREFER UB360-366)	355.1154-1156
UH570	Dead, Treatment of	
UH600-629	Hygiene & sanitation, Military	
UH600	Sanitation & hygiene, Military	
UH603	Military hygiene & sanitation (U.S.)	
UH605.A-Z	Hygiene & sanitation, Military (besides U.S.)	
UH611	Tropical hygiene (mil. sci.)	
UH623	Handbooks & manuals (mil. hygiene: Eng. & Am.)	
UH625	Manuals & handbooks (mil. hygiene: not Eng. or Am.)	
UH627	Research, Physiological (mil. hygiene)	
UH629	Mental health, psychiatry, etc. (mil.: gen.)	
UH629.3	Psychiatry, Military (U.S.: inclu. mental health)	
UH629.5.A-Z	Hygiene, Mental (besides U.S.)	
UH630	Moral & health protection (mil.: alcoholism, drug abuse, prostitution, venereal diseases, etc. & work vs.)	
UH650-655	Veterinary services (mil.)	355.345
UH700-705	Press & public relns. (mil.)	
UH700	Media & public relns. (mil.: gen.)	070.433, .449, 355.342
UH703	War correspondents & public relns. (mil.: U.S.)	
UH705.A-Z	Public relations & press (mil.: places besides U.S.)	
UH705.G3	Radio, media, & public relns. (mil.: Ger.)	
UH705.J3	Newspapers, media, & public relns. (mil.: Japan)	

UH720-725	Nonmilitary use of armed forces	
UH723	Civic programs (armed forces: U.S.)	
UH750	Social work, Military (gen.)	355.34, .346-347
UH755	Welfare services, Military (U.S.: gen.)	
UH760	Social welfare services, Military (U.S. Army)	
UH769.A-Z	Military social & welfare services (countries besides U.S.)	
UH800-910	Recreation & information services, Military	
UH800	Military recreation & information services (gen.)	355.346
UH805	Information & recreation, Military (U.S.: gen.)	355.3460973
UH810-815	Recreation & information services, Military (U.S. Army)	
UH819.A-Z	Recreation & information services, Military (besides U.S.)	
UH820	Movie services, Military (gen.)	
UH825	Motion-picture services, Military (U.S.: gen.: inclu. armed forces)	
UH826	Military movie services (U.S. Army)	
UH829.A-Z	Movie services, Military (by place except U.S.)	
UH850	Radio services, Military (gen.)	
UH855	Radiobroadcasting services, Military (U.S.: gen., inclu. armed forces)	
UH857	Military radio services (U.S. Army)	
UH859.A-Z	Radio services, Military (by place except U.S.)	
UH859.F8	Radiobroadcasting, Military (Fr.)	
UH859.G3	Radiobroadcasting, Military (Ger.)	
UH859.J3	Radiobroadcasting, Military (Japan)	
UH900-910	Recreation, Military (off-post)	
UH905	Canteens (Off-post mil. recreation: U.S.)	
V	Naval science (gen.)	359, 623, 629
V-VM	NAVAL SCIENCE, NAVIGATION, & SHIPBUILDING	
VA	Navies (organiz. & world status)	
VB	Naval administration	
VC	Maintenance, Naval	
VD	Seamen, Naval	
VE	Marines	
VF	Ordnance, Naval	
VG	Naval science (misc. services: medical etc.)	
VK	Navigation & merchant marine	
VM	Naval architecture & shipbuilding	
V1-995+	NAVAL SCIENCE (gen.)	359, 623.8
V1	Periodicals & associations (naval: in English)	359.005, .006+
V7	Conferences (naval sci.)	359.0060+, .0063
V9	Almanacs, Naval (official)	359.00202
V10	Yearbooks, Naval (unofficial)	
V11.A-Z	Yearbooks, Naval (official: ALSO lists: by country: SEE ALSO VA #s if dept. reports involved)	359.0025+, .005
V11.U6	Lists, Naval (U.S.: ALSO official yearbooks)	
V13.A1	Museums, Naval (gen.: inclu. exhibitions)	359.0074
V13.A2-Z	Naval museums & exhibitions (by country)	359.00740+
V13.x2.A-Z	Exhibitions & museums, Naval (by country then city)	
V15-17	Naval science (collected works: monographic)	
V19	Speeches & essays (naval sci.: gen.)	
V23	Dictionaries & encyclopedias (naval sci.: gen.)	359.003
V24	Dictionaries (naval sci.: multi-ling.)	

V25-64	Naval science (history, antiquities, & biog.: gen., during peace & war: SEE ALSO D-F #s for specific countries, wars, etc.)	
V25	Philosophy, Naval (e.g. theory of naval sea power)	
V27	Navies (gen. hist.)	359.009, .409, .47
V29-41	Naval science (ancient hist.)	359.00901
V43-46	Naval science (medieval hist.)	359.00902
V47-53+	Naval science (modern hist.: 17th-20th c.)	359.00903
V51	Naval science (19th c.)	359.009034
V53	Naval science (20th c.)	359.00904, .40904
V55.A-Z	Naval science (by region or country)	359.47+
V55.A65	Navies (America)	359.477, .1812
V55.A75	Navies (Asia)	359.475
V55.E8	Navies (Europe)	359.474
V61-64	Biography, Naval (SEE ALSO D-F #s for indiv. biog's. from particular countries)	
V61	Naval biography (collective)	359.00922
V62	Naval biography (U.S.: collective)	359.00922
V63.A-Z	Biography, Naval (U.S.: by name)	359.00924, .3310924, 940.410924, .450924, .540924, .5420924, .5450924
V64.A-Z	Biography, Naval (places besides U.S.: by place)	
V64.x2.A-Z	Naval biography (places except U.S.: by person's name after country name)	
V66	Navy clubs (U.S.)	
V67.A-Z	Clubs, Navy (Am. besides U.S.)	
V68	Clubs, Navy (G.B.)	
V69.A-Z	Clubs, Navy (besides U.S. & G.B.: by country)	
V101	Naval science (gen.: pubn. thru 1800)	
V103	Naval science (gen.: pubn. 1801+)	
V107	Naval science (pop. works)	359
V110-145	Handbooks, Naval	
V110	Handbooks, Seamen's (gen.)	359.00202
V113	Seamen's handbooks (U.S. Navy)	
V115.A-Z	Naval handbooks (seamen's: places besides U.S.)	
V115.G3	Seamen's handbooks (Ger.)	
V115.G7	Seamen's handbooks (G.B.)	
V115.J3	Seamen's handbooks (Japan)	
V115.R9	Seamen's handbooks (Rus.)	
V120-125	Handbooks, Petty officers'	
V120	Petty officers' handbooks (gen.)	
V123	Naval petty officers' handbooks (U.S.)	
V130-135	Handbooks, Naval officers'	359.3320202
V133	Naval officers' handbooks (U.S.)	
V135.A-Z	Officers' handbooks, Naval (places besides U.S.)	
V140-145	Handbooks, Naval reserve	
V160	Strategy, Naval (gen.: pubn. thru 1800)	
V163	Naval strategy (gen.: pubn. 1801+)	359.03, .43
V165	Naval strategy (gen. special)	
V167	Tactics, Naval (gen.)	359.42
V169	Naval tactics (gen. particular)	
V175	Landing ops. & field service tactics (naval: inclu. shore srvc., small arms instruc., etc.)	355.41, .422
V178	Boat attack (naval tactics)	359.32, .42
V179	Logistics, Naval	359.41
V180	Blockades, Naval	355.44, 359.42-43, 940.452, .5452
V182	Convoys, Naval	359.4-43

V185	Security, Naval
V190	Patrols & reconnaisance, Naval 359.413
V200	Coast defense, Naval (SEE ALSO UG410-442) 359.45
V210	Submarine warfare (gen.) 359.3257, .42-43
V214	Antisubmarine warfare 359.3254, .42-43
V215	Camouflage, Marine 623.77
V220	Bases, ports, & docks (naval: gen.: SEE ALSO VA67-750 for specific countries) 359.7
V230	Yards, Navy (gen.: SEE ALSO VA67-750 for particular places) 359.7
V240	Coaling stations, Naval (gen.: SEE ALSO VA67-750)
V245	Maneuvers, Naval (SEE U260-262 for combined — army, navy, air forces — or amphibious warfare ops.) 359.52
V250	War games, Naval 359.52
V252	Training, Simulated (navies)
V253	Imaginary naval battles & wars 359.47
V260	Training, Physical (navies: gen.) 359.54
V263-264	Physical training (navies: U.S.)
V265.A-Z	Training, Physical (navies: countries besides U.S.)
V267-268	Sports in navies
V270	Orders, Transmission of (navies) 359.27, .85
V280-285	Signaling, Naval (gen.) 359.27, .983
V283	Naval signaling (U.S.)
V300	Flags, Naval & marine (gen.: SEE ALSO VK385) 359.15
V303	Naval flags (U.S.: inclu. marine)
V305.A-Z	Flags, Naval & marine (besides U.S.)
V305.G7	Naval flags (G.B.)
V305.J3	Naval flags (Japan)
V310	Ceremonies, honors, & salutes (navies: gen.) 359.17, .1349
V380-385	Safety measures, Naval (inclu. educ.)
V390	Research, Naval (gen.) 359.07
V393	Research, Naval (U.S.: gen.) 359.070973
V393.5.A-W	Naval research (U.S.: by state)
V394.A-Z	Naval research (U.S.: by special establishment locale)
V395.A-Z	Research, Naval (countries besides U.S.)
V396	Oceanography, Military (gen.) 359.982, 551.46, 620.4162
V396.3-4	Military oceanography (U.S.)
V396.5.A-Z	Oceanography, Military (places besides U.S.)
V400-695	EDUCATION, NAVAL
V400	Naval education & training (gen.) 359.007
V401	Education, Naval (hist.: gen.)
V404	Training & education, Naval (modern hist.: gen.)
V409	Education, Naval (hist.: 20th c.)
V411-438	Education, Naval (U.S.)
V411	Naval education (U.S.: gen.) 359.0071073, .0071173, .50973, .550973
V415.A1	U.S. Naval Academy (Act of incorp.: PREFER KF7353.55)
V415.A1-R4+	U.S. Naval Academy (Annapolis) 359.0071173
V415.C3-6	Regulations (U.S. Naval Acad.)
V415.C3-H5	U.S. Naval Academy (admin.)
V415.E1-4	Reports, Official (U.S. Naval Acad. Superinten.: annual)
V415.E5	U.S. Naval Academy (Cong. docs.: gen.: by date)
V415.E9	Hazing (U.S. Naval Acad.: Cong. docs.)
V415.F3.A-Z	Commencement addresses (U.S. Naval Acad.: by speaker)
V415.F5.A-Z	Speeches (U.S. Naval Acad.: misc.: by speaker)
V415.F7	Reports, Official & unoff. (U.S. Naval Acad.)

V415.H3-39	Registers, Official (U.S. Naval Acad.: annual)
V415.H5	U.S. Naval Academy (registers, unoff.)
V415.J1-7	Student publications (U.S. Naval Acad.)
V415.K1-4	Publications, Graduate (U.S. Naval Acad.)
V415.K4	Class histories (U.S. Naval Acad.: by date)
V415.L1	Annapolis (U.S. Naval Acad.: gen. hist's. & other titles)
V415.L1-P1	U.S. Naval Academy (hist. & descrip.)
V415.L3	Pictorials (U.S. Naval Acad.)
V415.M1.A-Z	Biography (U.S. Naval Acad.: by name)
V415.P1	Annapolis (U.S. Naval Acad.: life & conditions)
V415.R1-4	Examinations (U.S. Naval Acad.)
V420	Naval War College (U.S.) 359.550973, .0071173
V425.A-Z	Training schools, Naval (misc.)
V426	Naval Reserve Officers' Training Corps (U.S.: N.R.O.T.C.) 359.2232
V430	Schools, Private naval (U.S.)
V433	Training stations, Naval (U.S.: gen.) 359.50973, .70973
V434.A-Z	Naval training stations (U.S.: by place)
V434.G7	Great Lakes Naval Training Station (Ill.)
V434.H2	Hampton Roads Naval Training Station (Va.)
V435	Training ships (U.S. Navy: gen.)
V436.A-Z	Naval training ships (U.S.: by name)
V437	Training & education, Naval (U.S. Coast Guard) 359.9707
V440-444	Education, Naval (Can.)
V500-623	Education, Naval (Eur.)
V500	Naval education (Eur.: gen.)
V510-530	Education, Naval (G.B.)
V510	Naval education (G.B.: gen.) 359.0071141, .50941, .550941, .007041
V511-512	British naval education (special topics)
V513	Examinations (G.B. Royal Navy)
V515.A1	Dartmouth (Royal Naval College: Act of incorp.)
V515.A1-R1+	Royal Naval College (Dartmouth)
V515.C1-K3	G.B. Royal Naval College, Dartmouth (admin.)
V515.E1-49	Reports, Official (Royal Naval Coll., Dart.: annual)
V515.F3.A-Z	Speeches (Royal Naval Coll., Dart.: by speaker)
V515.H1-5	Registers, Official & unoff. (Royal Naval Coll., Dart.)
V515.K3	Class histories (Royal Naval Coll., Dart.: by date)
V515.L1	Royal Naval College (Dartmouth: hist.)
V515.M1.A-Z	Biography (Royal Naval Coll., Dart.: by name)
V515.P1	Royal Naval College (Dartmouth: life, pictorials, etc.)
V520.A1-R1+	Royal Naval College (Greenwich: set up like V515)
V522-525	Training & education, Naval (G.B.: stations, ships, engin. schools, etc.)
V522.5.A-Z	Training stations, Naval (G.B.: by place)
V522.5.P6	Portsmouth, Eng. (Royal Naval Barracks)
V565-569	Education, Naval (Fr.)
V570-574	Education, Naval (Ger.)
V570	Naval education (Ger.: gen.) 359.007043, .50943
V574.A-Z	Schools, Naval (Ger.)
V574.A2-65	German naval education (main school)
V574.A7-Z	Naval schools (Ger.: by name or place)
V585-589	Education, Naval (It.)
V600-604	Education, Naval (Rus.)

V625-650	Education, Naval (Asia)
V625	Naval education (Asia: gen.)
V630-634	Education, Naval (China)
V640-644	Education, Naval (Japan)
V640	Naval education (Japan: gen.) 359.007052, .0071152, .50952, .550952
V650.A-Z	Education, Naval (Asia: misc. countries)
V650.P5	Education, Naval (Philippines)
V690-694	Education, Naval (Australia) 359.007094
V694.1-5	Education, Naval (New Z.)
V701-716	Naval observations (wartime: PREFER D-F areas)
V713	Observations, Naval (Russo-Japanese War, 1904-5) 952.031, 359.4752, .4747
V715	Observations, Naval (WWI) 940.45-453
V716	Observations, Naval (WWII) 940.545-5459
V720-743	Naval life & customs
V720	Customs, Naval (gen.) 359.1
V735-743	Naval life & customs (modern)
V735	Life & customs, Naval (modern: gen.) 359.10904
V736	Naval life & customs (modern: U.S.) 359.10973
V737	Naval life & customs (modern: G.B.) 359.10941
V739	Naval life & customs (modern: Ger.) 359.10943
V741	Naval life & customs (modern: Rus.) 359.10947
V743.A-Z	Naval life & customs (modern: misc. countries)
V743.J3	Naval life & customs (modern: Japan)
V745	Curiosities, Naval 359.00207, .002
V750-995+	WARSHIPS (construction, armament, types, etc.: SEE VA for status & organiz. of specific navies around the world)
V750	Ships, Naval (gen.: SEE here for earlier works on battleships & V815 for later works)
V765-767	Vessels, Naval war (modern period) 623.80904
V799	Construction of warships (1860-1900: armored vessels)
V800	Construction of warships (1901+) 623.825, 359.325+
V805	Construction of warships (materials: gen.)
V805.3	Construction of warships (materials: U.S.)
V805.5.A-Z	Construction of warships (materials: besides U.S.)
V810	Damage control (warships) 623.888
V815-895	Warships (types) 623.825-826, 359.83, .325-326
V815	Battleships (gen.: construc., armament, etc.: SEE V750 for earlier titles) 623.8252, .81252, 359.3252
V815.3	Battleships (U.S.) 623.82520973, 359.32520973
V815.5.A-Z	Battleships (besides U.S.: by place)
V815.5.G3	Battleships (Ger.) 623.82520943
V815.5.G7	Battleships (G.B.) 623.82520941
V815.5.J3	Battleships (Japan) 623.82520952
V820	Cruisers (gen.: tech. info.) 623.8253, .81253, 359.3253
V820.3	Cruisers (U.S.)
V820.5.A-Z	Cruisers (besides U.S.)
V820.5.G7	Cruisers (G.B.)
V825	Destroyers (gen.) 623.8254, .81254, 359.3254
V825.3	Destroyers (U.S.)
V825.5.A-Z	Destroyers (besides U.S.: by place)
V825.5.J3	Destroyers (Japan)
V826	Frigates & corvettes (gen.) 623.8254
V826.3	Frigates (U.S.)
V826.5.A-Z	Corvettes & frigates (besides U.S.)

V830-838	Torpedo boats	623.8258, 359.3258
V830	P.T. boats (gen.)	
V833	Torpedo boats (U.S.)	
V835.A-Z	Torpedo boats (places besides U.S.)	
V835.G3	Torpedo boats (Ger.)	
V837-838	Torpedo boat service	
V840	Torpedo boat destroyers	623.8254
V850	Torpedoes (gen.: inclu. propelling or launching devices)	623.4517, 359.82517
V855.A-Z	Torpedoes (types or devices: by name)	
V855.G7	Graydon aerial torpedo thrower	
V855.W5	Whitehead torpedo	
V856	Minelaying, minesweeping, submarine mines, etc. (gen.)	623.2, .26, .263, .36, .45115, .8262, 359.825115, .3262
V856.5.A-Z	Minesweeping, minelaying, sub. mines, etc. (by place)	
V856.5.U6-7	Submarine mines, minelaying, minesweeping, etc. (U.S.)	
V857	Submarines (gen.: SEE ALSO V210-14 for sub warfare & VM365-7 for construc.)	623.8257, .82572, .81257, 359.3257
V858	Submarines (U.S.)	623.82570973, 359.32570973
V859.A-Z	Submarines (besides U.S.)	
V859.G3	Submarines (Ger.)	623.82570943
V859.J3	Submarines (Japan)	623.82570952
V860	Turrets, Revolving (naval sci.: inclu. monitors)	
V865	Naval vessels (auxiliary: fleet trains, repair & supply ships, etc.)	623.826, 359.326
V870	Naval vessels, Unarmored	
V874	Aircraft carriers (gen.)	623.8255, 359.3255
V874.3	Aircraft carriers (U.S.)	623.82550973, .81255, 359.32550973
V874.5.A-Z	Carriers, Aircraft (besides U.S.)	
V874.5.G7	Aircraft carriers (G.B.)	623.82550941
V874.5.J3	Aircraft carriers (Japan)	623.82550952
V875.A-Z	Aircraft carriers (special topics)	
V875.A36	Aircraft launching & recovery equipment (carriers)	
V875.F5	Flight decks (aircraft carriers)	
V880	Vedettes, scout & dispatch boats, other minor craft (gen.)	
V885	Minesweepers (SEE ALSO V856)	623.8262
V890	Floating batteries	
V895	Naval vessels (misc., non-major: inclu. landing craft)	
V900-925	Armor plate (naval sci.)	
V900	Armor plate (naval sci.: gen.)	623.81821, .8251
V903	Armor, Naval (U.S.)	623.82510973
V905.A-Z	Naval armor (places besides U.S.)	
V907.A-Z	Plating, Armor (naval sci.: special type)	
V907.K7	Krupp armor plating (naval sci.)	
V910-915	Testing (naval armor: SEE ALSO VF540)	
V913	Naval armor testing (U.S.)	
V950	Armament, Naval (gen.)	623.8251
V960	Naval armament (installation)	
V980	Equipment, Naval (misc.)	

VA	NAVIES (organiz. & world status)
VA10	Naval status (world: gen.) 359, .03
VA20-25	Costs, Naval (budgets etc.)
VA25	Budgets, Naval (gen.) 359.622
VA40	Navies (of the world: gen.) 359, .03, .009, 623.82509
VA41	World navies (pop. works)
VA42	Pictorials (world navies)
VA45	Reserves, Naval (gen.) 359.37+
VA48	Mobilizaton, Naval (gen.) 359.28
VA49-750+	NAVAL STATUS (worldwide: place by place)
VA49	Periodicals & associations (naval: U.S.) 359.005-007+
VA50	Naval status (U.S.: gen.) 359.030973, .4773
VA52-395	NAVAL STATUS (U.S.)
VA52-79	U.S. Navy (SEE ALSO E182)
VA52.A1-89	Reports, Official (U.S. Navy Dept.)
VA52.A1-19	U.S. Navy Dept. (official docs.: gen.)
VA52.A2-29	Secretary of the Navy (U.S.: official docs.)
VA52.A6-67	Reports, Official (U.S. Navy Bur's. of Navigation, Personnel)
VA52.A68-69	Material, Naval (U.S. Navy. Office of: reports)
VA52.A7-79	Naval ops. (U.S. Navy. Office of: reports)
VA53	Reports, Congressional (U.S. Navy: official & others)
VA54	Speeches (U.S. Navy)
VA55	U.S. Navy (gen.) 359.00973, .30973, .4773
VA58	U.S. Navy (gen.: 1881-1970 coverage) 359.00973
VA59	Pictorials (naval: U.S.) 359.3250973
VA60	Budgets, Naval (U.S.) 359.6220973
VA61	Ships (U.S. Navy: lists) 359.32, .320222
VA62-74	U.S. Navy (placement & stations)
VA62	U.S. Navy (distribution: gen.) 359.4773, .31
VA62.5	Naval districts (U.S.: gen.) 359.70973
VA62.7.1st+	Naval districts (U.S.: by #)
VA63.A-Z	Fleets, squadrons, etc. (U.S. Navy: by name) 359.310973
VA63.A83	Atlantic Fleet (U.S.)
VA63.N8	North Atlantic Fleet (U.S.)
VA63.P2	Pacific Fleet (U.S.)
VA65.A-Z	Ships (U.S. Navy: by name) 359.32520973-.32560973
VA65.A75	Arizona (battleship: U.S.)
VA65.C3	California (battleship: U.S.)
VA65.M8	Missouri (battleship: U.S.) 359.32520973
VA65.S28	Saratoga (aircraft carrier: U.S.) 359.32550973
VA66.A-Z	U.S. Navy (misc. units: by name)
VA66.C6-65	Construction Battalions (U.S. Navy) 359.33+, .90973
VA67-68	Naval bases, ports, docks, etc. (U.S.)
VA67	Ports, bases, docks, etc. (U.S. Navy: gen.) 359.70973, 940.4530973 (WWI), .54530973 (WWII), .545973 (WWII)
VA68.A-Z	Bases, ports, etc. (U.S. Navy: by place)
VA69	Naval yards & stations (U.S.: gen.) 359.70973, 623.830973
VA70.A-Z	Yards & stations, Naval (U.S.: by place)
VA70.N5	New London Naval Station (U.S.: Conn.)
VA70.N7	Norfolk Navy Yard (U.S.: Va.)
VA70.P5	Philadelphia Navy Yard (U.S.: Penn.)
VA70.P8	Portsmouth Navy Yard (U.S.: N.H.)
VA73	Naval coaling stations (U.S.: gen.) 359.70973, .750973
VA77	Mobilization (U.S. Navy) 359.280973

VA79	Supply vessels, transports, service craft, etc. (U.S. Naval Auxiliary Service)
VA80-390	RESERVES, NAVAL (U.S.)
VA80	Naval reserves (U.S.: gen.) 359.370973
VA90-387	MILITIA, NAVAL (U.S.: state by state)
VA100-107	Reserves, Naval (U.S.: Calif.)
VA100	Naval reserves (U.S.: Calif.: gen.) 359.3709794
VA101	Reports, Official (naval reserves: U.S.: Calif.)
VA102	Registers & lists (naval reserves: U.S.: Calif.)
VA103.1st+	Reserves, Naval (U.S.: Calif.: special groups by #)
VA104.A-Z	Reserves, Naval (U.S.: Calif.: special groups by name)
VA105.A-Z	Ships (Calif. naval reserves: by name)
VA107	Reserves, Naval (U.S.: Calif.: misc. topics)
VA140-147	Reserves, Naval (U.S.: Florida)
VA158-158.7	Reserves, Naval (U.S.: Hawaii)
VA160-167	Reserves, Naval (U.S.: Ill.)
VA240-247	Reserves, Naval (U.S.: Mississ.)
VA250-257	Reserves, Naval (U.S.: Missouri)
VA280-287	Reserves, Naval (U.S.: N.Y.)
VA350-357	Reserves, Naval (U.S.: Texas)
VA370-377	Reserves, Naval (U.S.: Wash.)
VA380-387	Reserves, Naval (U.S.: Wisc.)
VA390	Waves (U.S. naval reserves for women & other non-local U.S. naval res.)
VA400-402	Naval status (Can.)
VA400	Canada (naval status: gen.) 359.030971, .4771
VA402.5	Latin America (naval status)
VA415-445	Naval status (S.Am.)
VA415	South America (naval status: gen.) 359.03098
VA416	Argentina (naval status) 359.030982
VA440	Uruguay (naval status)
VA450-619	NAVAL STATUS (Eur.)
VA450	Europe (naval status: gen.) 359.03094, .474
VA452-467	Naval status (G.B.)
VA452	Periodicals & associations (naval: G.B.)
VA453	Primary sources, documents (naval: G.B.)
VA454	G.B. Royal Navy (gen.) 359.0309441, .30941, .4741-4742, .00941
VA455	Budgets, Naval (G.B.)
VA456	Ships (G.B. Royal Navy: lists) 359.325+, .320941
VA457.A-Z	Fleets, squadrons, etc. (G.B.: by name) 359.310941
VA458.A-Z	Ships (G.B. Royal Navy: by name) 359.320941, .3252+-.326+
VA458.A7	Ark Royal (aircraft carrier: G.B.)
VA458.H6	Hood (battle cruiser: G.B.)
VA458.I55	Invincible (aircraft carrier: G.B.)
VA458.P75	Prince of Wales (battleship: G.B.)
VA459	Naval bases, ports, docks, etc. (G.B.)
VA459.A1	Ports, bases, docks, etc. (G.B. Royal Navy: gen.) 359.70941, 940.4530941 (WWI), .54530941 (WWII)
VA459.A3-Z	Bases, ports, etc. (G.B. Royal Navy: by place)
VA459.H55	Hong Kong Naval Base (Royal Navy)
VA459.S5	Singapore Naval Base (Royal Navy) 940.5453095952, .5453095957(WWII)
VA460	Naval yards & stations (G.B.) 359.70941
VA463	Mobilization, Naval (G.B.) 359.280941
VA464	Reserves, Naval (G.B.)

```
VA480-489    Belgium (naval status)
VA490-499    Denmark (naval status)
VA500-509        Naval status (Fr.)
VA503.A1-49      Ships (Fr. Navy: lists)      359.320944, .3250944
VA503.A5-Z       France (naval status: gen.)      359.030944, .4744
VA510-519    Naval status (Ger.)
VA510            Periodicals & associations (naval: Ger.)
VA511            Budgets, Naval (Ger.)
VA512                Primary sources, documents (naval: Ger.)
VA513.A1-49      Ships (Ger. Navy: lists)      359.320943, .3250943
VA513.A5-Z       Germany (naval status: gen.)   359.030943, .00943, .30943, .4743
VA514.A-Z    Fleets, squadrons, etc. (Ger.: by name)      359.310943
VA515.A-Z        Ships (Ger. Navy: by name)      359.320943, .3252+-.326+
VA515.B4         Bismarck (battleship: Ger.)
VA515.G          Graf Spee, Admiral (cruiser, armoured: Ger.)
VA515.P73        Prinz Eugen (cruiser, heavy: Ger.)      359.32530943
VA515.S          Scharnhorst (battle cruisers: Ger.: WWI & II)
VA516.A1     Naval bases, ports, docks, etc. (Ger.: gen.)      359.70943,
                                      940.4530943 (WWI), .54530943 (WWII)
VA516.A3-Z   Ports, bases, docks, etc. (Ger. Navy: by name)
VA516.K4     Kiel Naval Base (Ger.)
VA518            Mobilization, Naval (Ger.)      359.290943
VA519            Reserves, Naval (Ger.)      359.370943
VA520-529        Greece (naval status)
VA530-539        Netherlands (naval status)
VA540-549        Naval status (It.)
VA543.A5-Z       Italy (naval status: gen.)      359.030945, .00945, .30945, .4745
VA550-559        Norway (naval status)      359.0309481
VA570-579    Naval status (Rus.)
VA573.A5-Z   Russia (naval status: gen.)      359.030947, .00947, .4747
VA580-589    Spain (naval status)
VA590-599    Sweden (naval status)
VA620-667    NAVAL STATUS (Asia)
VA620        Asia (naval status: gen.)      359.03095
VA630-639        China (naval status)      359.030951
VA650-659        Naval status (Japan)
VA653.A1-49      Ships (Japan. Imper. Navy: lists)      359.30952, .320952,
                                      .3252+-326+
VA653.A5-Z   Japan (naval status: gen.)   359.030952, .00952, .30952, .4752
VA654.A-Z    Fleets, squadrons, etc. (Japan: by name)      359.310952
VA655.A-Z        Ships (Japan. Imper. Navy: by name)   359.320952, .3252+-.326+
VA655.A43        Akagi (aircraft carrier: Japan)
VA655.Y25        Yamato (battleship: Japan)      359.32520952
VA656        Naval bases, ports, docks, etc. (Japan. Imper. Navy)      359.70952,
                                      940.54530952 (WWII)
VA658            Mobilization, Naval (Japan)      359.280952
VA667.A-Z    Naval status (Asia: misc. countries)
VA667.P5     Philippines (naval status)      359.0309599
VA670-700    Africa (naval status)
VA690            Egypt (naval status)      359.030962
VA700.S52    South Africa (naval status)      359.030968
```

VA710-719	Naval status (Australia)	
VA713.A1-49	Ships (Australia. Navy: lists)	359.30994, .320994, .3250994
VA713.A5-Z	Australia (naval status: gen.)	359.030994, .00994, .4794
VA715.A-Z	Ships (Australia. Navy: by name)	359.32520994-.3260994
VA716	Naval bases, ports, docks, etc. (Australia)	359.70994
VA720-729	Naval status (New Z.)	
VA723.A1-49	Ships (New Z. Navy: lists)	359.309931
VA723.A5-Z	New Zealand (naval status: gen.)	359.0309931, .009931, .47931

VB	ADMINISTRATION, NAVAL (command, personnel, law, etc.)	
VB15	Administration, Naval (gen. hist.)	359.6, .1-3
VB21-124	NAVAL ADMINISTRATION (by country)	
VB23	Naval administration (U.S.)	359.60973
VB26	Naval administration (Can.)	
VB55-96	Naval administration (Eur.)	
VB55	Administration, Naval (Eur.: gen.)	359.6094
VB57	Naval administration (G.B.)	359.60941, .30941
VB71	Naval administration (Fr.)	359.60944
VB73	Naval administration (Ger.)	359.60943, .30943
VB79	Naval administration (It.)	359.60945
VB85	Naval administration (Rus.)	359.60947
VB99-113	Naval administration (Asia)	
VB99	Administration, Naval (Asia: gen.)	359.6095
VB105	Naval administration (Japan)	359.60952, .30952
VB121	Naval administration (Australia)	359.60994
VB122.5	Naval administration (New Z.)	
VB145	Naval administration (gen.: pubn. 1801-1970)	359.6, .3
VB170-187	Naval administration (civil sections)	
VB170	Civil depts. (naval admin.: gen.)	
VB180-187	Civilian personnel (naval admin.)	
VB180	Personnel, Civilian (naval admin.: gen.)	
VB183	Employees, Civilian (naval admin.: U.S.)	
VB185.A-Z	Civilian personnel (naval admin.: places besides U.S.)	
VB190	Admirals, commanders, etc. (admin.: inclu. duties)	
VB200-205	Naval command and leadership	
VB200	Command of ships (naval admin.: gen.)	359.33, .6, 158.4, 350.00323
VB203	Leadership (naval admin.: U.S.)	
VB205.A-Z	Leadership (naval admin.: besides U.S.)	
VB210	Headquarters, Naval (ops. inclu. aides)	
VB220-225	Inspection, Naval (inclu. inspectors)	
VB230-254	Intelligence, Naval	
VB230	Naval intelligence (gen.)	359.3432
VB231.A-Z	Intelligence, Naval (by country)	359.343209+
VB231.G3	Naval intelligence (Ger.)	359.34320943
VB231.G7	Naval intelligence (G.B.)	359.34320941
VB231.U6-7	Naval intelligence (U.S.)	359.34320973
VB240	Attachés, Naval	
VB250	Espionage & spies (naval admin.)	359.3432-3433
VB252	Propaganda & psych. warfare (naval sci.: gen.)	359.3434
VB253	Propaganda & psych. warfare (naval sci.: U.S.)	359.34340973
VB254.A-Z	Psychological warfare & propaganda (naval sci.: places besides U.S.)	
VB255	Orders, passes, field correspondence (naval admin.)	
VB257	Personnel administration (naval sci.: gen.)	359.61
VB258	Naval personnel (admin.: U.S.)	359.610973
VB259	Career guidance (naval sci.)	

VB260-275	Enlisted personnel (naval sci.: inclu. recruitment, enlistment, promotion, discharge, etc.)
VB260	Recruitment, enlistment, promotion, discharge (naval sci.: enlisted personnel: gen.) 359.223, .338, .11+
VB263	Promotion, discharge, recruitment, enlistment (naval sci.: enlisted personnel: U.S.) 359.2230973, .3380973
VB264.A-Z	Enlistment, recruitment, promotion, discharge (Naval sci.: U.S.: by region or state)
VB265.A-Z	Discharge, promotion, recruitment, enlistment (naval sci.: places besides U.S.)
VB265.G3	Enlisted personnel (naval sci.: Ger.: inclu. enlistment, promotion, etc.) 359.2230943
VB270-275	Recruits, Naval (inclu. medical & mental examinations) 359.2236
VB277	Demobilization, Naval (inclu. civil employ.) 359.29, .1154
VB278	Crippled sailors, Employment of (PREFER UB360-366)
VB280-285	Pensions, disability benefits, etc. (naval admin.) 359.115-1156
VB283	Disability benefits, pensions, etc. (naval admin.: U.S.)
VB290-295	Homes, Sailors' (SEE ALSO UB380-385)
VB300-305	Cemeteries (naval) 351.86, .866
VB303-304	Naval cemeteries (U.S.)
VB307	Warrant officers (naval: gen.) 359.332
VB308	Officers, Warrant (naval: U.S.) 359.3320973
VB309.A-Z	Naval warrant officers (besides U.S.)
VB310-315	Officers, Naval (inclu. appt., promo., rank, retire., etc.)
VB310	Rank, appointment, promotion, retirement, etc. (naval officers: gen.) 359.332, .331
VB313	Officers, Naval (U.S.: gen.) 359.3320973, .3310973
VB314.A-Z	Biography, Naval (U.S.: by name) 359.3310973, .3310924
VB314.H25	Halsey, William F., 'Bull', Admiral (U.S. Navy)
VB315.A-Z	Naval officers (except U.S.)
VB315.G7	Officers, Naval (G.B.) 359.3320941
VB315.J3	Officers, Naval (Japan)
VB315.R9	Officers, Naval (Rus.)
VB320-325	Minorities & women (navies)
VB320	Women & minorities (navies: gen.) 359.22
VB323	Women & minorities (U.S. Navy: gen.)
VB324.A-Z	Minorities (U.S. Navy: by group)
VB324.A47	Afro-Americans (U.S. Navy)
VB324.I5	Indians (U.S. Navy: native-Am's.)
VB324.W65	Women (U.S. Navy)
VB330-335	Badges, brevets, medals of honor, rewards, etc. (navies)
VB330	Medals, badges, brevets, etc. (navies: gen.) 359.1342
VB333	Brevets, badges, medals, etc. (U.S. Navy: inclu. Navy Cross) 359.13420973
VB335.A-Z	Rewards, badges, brevets, medals (navies: except U.S.)
VB340-345	Pensions, Survivors' (naval)
VB350-785	NAVAL LAW
VB350	Law, Naval (gen.) 359.13, 343.01+
VB353	International naval law
VB360-785	NAVAL LAW (by area or country)
VB360-369	Naval law (U.S.: PREFER KF7345-7375)
VB360	Law, Naval (U.S.) 343.7301
VB363	Regulations, Naval (U.S.)
VB365	General orders (naval: U.S.)
VB370-379	Naval law (Can.)

VB530-699	European naval law	
VB530	Naval Law (Eur.: gen.)	
VB570-579	Naval Law (FR.)	
VB580-589	Naval Law (Ger.)	
VB590-599	Naval Law (G.B.: PREFER KD6128-6158)	343.4101
VB650-659	Naval law (Rus.)	
VB700-799	Asian naval law	
VB700	Naval law (Asia: gen.)	
VB710-719	Naval law (China)	
VB730-739	Naval law (Japan)	343.5201
VB775	Naval law (Australia)	
VB777	Naval law (New Z.)	
VB790-925	Naval justice (admin. of)	
VB790	Justice, Naval (gen.: inclu. judiciary)	343.014, .0146
VB793	Judiciary, Naval (U.S.: inclu. overall naval justice)	
VB795.A-Z	Naval justice (places besides U.S.)	
VB800	Courts-martial, Naval (gen.)	343.0146
VB803	Courts-martial, Naval (U.S.: PREFER KF7646-7650)	
VB805.A-Z	Courts-martial, Naval (besides U.S.: by place)	
VB806	Cases (courts-martial, naval: U.S.: PREFER KF7646-7650)	
VB807.A-Z	Cases (courts-martial, naval: besides U.S.: by place)	
VB810-815	Courts of inquiry, Naval	343.0143
VB813	Inquiry, Courts of (naval: U.S.: PREFER KF7646-7650)	
VB814.A-Z	Cases (courts of inquiry, naval: U.S.: PREFER KF #s)	
VB815.A-Z	Courts of inquiry, Naval (besides U.S.)	
VB840-845	Naval discipline	359.13
VB843	Discipline, Naval (U.S.)	359.130973
VB845.A-Z	Discipline, Naval (besides U.S.)	
VB845.G7	Discipline, Naval (G.B.)	
VB850-880	Offenses & crimes, Naval	
VB850	Crimes, Naval (gen.) 359.1334	
VB853	Naval crimes (U.S.)	
VB855.A-Z	Naval crimes (except U.S.)	
VB855.G3	Naval crimes (Ger.)	
VB855.G7	Naval crimes (G.B.)	
VB855.J3	Naval crimes (Japan)	
VB860	Mutiny (naval: gen.)	359.1334
VB863	Mutiny (naval: U.S.)	
VB865.A-Z	Mutiny (naval: except U.S.)	
VB867.A-Z	Naval mutiny (by ship)	
VB870-875	Desertion (naval)	359.1334
VB873	Naval desertion (U.S.)	
VB880	Looting & other naval crimes	
VB890-910	Prisoners, prisons, punishments (naval)	
VB890	Naval prisons & prisoners (gen.)	344.03548
VB893	Prisons & prisoners, Naval (U.S.)	344.035480973
VB895.A-Z	Prisons & prisoners, Naval (except U.S.: by place)	
VB895.G7	Prisons & prisoners, Naval (G.B.)	
VB895.R9	Prisons & prisoners, Naval (Rus.)	
VB910	Corporal punishment (naval)	364.67, 343.0146, 359.13325

VB920	Shore patrol (gen.)	359.13323, .34
VB923	Shore patrol (U.S.)	
VB925.A-Z	Police, Naval (besides U.S.)	
VB925.G3	Shore patrol (Ger.)	
VB925.G7	Shore patrol (G.B.)	
VB955	Administration, Naval (misc. topics)	

VC	MAINTENANCE, NAVAL 359.6-8
VC10	Naval maintenance (gen.) 359.6
VC20-258	ORGANIZATION (naval maintenance: by place)
VC20-65	Maintenance, Naval (U.S.)
VC20	Naval maintenance (U.S.: gen.) 359.60973
VC25-38	Reports, Official (naval maint.: U.S.)
VC39	Reports, Unofficial (naval maint.: U.S.)
VC40-41	Reserves, Naval (U.S.: maint. & organ.) 359.370973
VC50-65	Pay & allowances (U.S. Navy) 359.135, .640973
VC54-60	Handbooks & tables (naval pay & allowances: U.S.)
VC54	Allowances & pay (U.S. Navy: tables inclu. interest)
VC60	Handbooks & manuals (U.S. Navy: Pay & allowances)
VC64	Reports, Unofficial (naval pay etc.: U.S.)
VC90-93	Maintenance, Naval (Can.)
VC160-229	Maintenance, Naval (Eur.)
VC160	Naval maintenance (Eur.: gen.)
VC176-179	Maintenance, Naval (Fr.)
VC180-183	Maintenance, Naval (Ger.) 359.60943
VC180	Supplies, Naval (Ger.) 359.80943
VC181	Pay & allowances (Ger. Navy)
VC182	Reserves, Naval (Ger.: maint. & organ.) 359.370943
VC183.A-Z	Maintenance, Naval (Ger.: by region or area)
VC184-187	Maintenance, Naval (G.B.) 359.60941
VC196-199	Maintenance, Naval (It.)
VC208-211	Maintenance, Naval (Rus.)
VC230-245	Maintenance, Naval (Asia)
VC230	Naval maintenance (Asia: gen.)
VC235	Maintenance, Naval (China)
VC241	Maintenance, Naval (Japan) 359.60952
VC255-256	Maintenance, Naval (Australia) 359.60944
VC256.5	Maintenance, Naval (New Z.)
VC260-268	Supplies & stores, Naval (inclu. stds., procure., storage, etc.)
VC260	Naval supplies & stores (gen.) 359.8, .62
VC263-264	Stores & supplies, Naval (U.S.) 359.80973
VC265.A-Z	Procurement (naval supplies: except U.S.)
VC265.G7	Naval stores & supplies (G.B.)
VC266	Supplies & stores, Naval (management methods) 359.62
VC267.A-Z	Contracts & claims, Naval (supplies: by place)
VC267.U6-7	Naval contracts (supplies: U.S.)
VC268.A-Z	Commandeering, compensation, etc. (naval: by country or place)
VC270-279	Equipment, fuel, supplies, etc. (ships)
VC270	Naval equipment & supplies (gen.: for ships) 359.8
VC273-274	Ships' stores & equipment (U.S.)
VC275.A-Z	Ships' stores & equipment (except U.S.)
VC276	Fuel supplies & costs, Naval
VC276.A1	Naval fuel (gen.: ALSO costs etc.) 359.83, 623.874, .415
VC276.A3-49	Fuel, Naval (U.S.) 359.83
VC276.A5-Z	Fuel, Naval (other than U.S.)

VC279.A-Z	Supplies & stores, Naval (misc.)
VC279.C3	Cables (naval supplies)
VC279.H45	Hemp (naval supplies)
VC279.R6	Rope (naval supplies)
VC279.R8	Rubber (naval supplies)
VC279.T5	Timber (naval supplies)
VC279.T6	Tools (naval supplies)
VC280-345	Clothing, Naval (inclu. related items)
VC280-285	Naval clothing & personal equipment (overall)
VC300-345	Naval uniforms, badges, shoes, etc.
VC300	Uniforms, Naval (gen.) 359.14, .81
VC303	Naval uniforms (U.S.: gen.) 359.140973, .81
VC305.A-Z	Uniforms, Naval (besides U.S.)
VC307	Foul-weather gear, Naval (plus other special clothing) 359.81
VC310	Shoes & footwear, Naval
VC320	Headgear, Naval
VC330	Tailoring (naval clothing)
VC340	Binoculars (naval clothing: inclu. other misc. accessories)
VC345	Insignia & badges (naval clothing) 359.1342
VC350-410	Subsistence & provisions, Naval (inclu. rations, galleys, water, etc.)
VC350	Provisions & subsistence, Naval (gen.) 359.81
VC353-354	Naval provisions & subsistence (U.S.) 359.810973
VC355.A-Z	Naval provisions & subsistence (countries besides U.S.)
VC355.G3	Provisions & subsistence, Naval (Ger.)
VC355.J3	Provisions & subsistence, Naval (Japan)
VC355.R9	Provisions & subsistence, Naval (Rus.)
VC360-365	Rations, Naval
VC370-375	Cookery, Naval 359.81
VC380-385	Officers' clubs & messes, Naval
VC380	Messes & clubs, Naval officers' (gen.) 359.346
VC383	Naval officers' clubs (U.S.) 359.3460973
VC384.A-W	Naval officers' clubs (U.S.: by state)
VC390-395	Canteens & ship exchanges
VC390	Ship exchanges & canteens (gen.) 359.341
VC398	Galleys & equipment (naval sci.)
VC400	Refrigeration (naval sci.) 623.8535
VC410	Water supplies, Naval (inclu. preservation, purification, etc.: SEE VM503 for onboard storage) 623.854
VC412-425	Navy yards, shore facilities, stations, etc.
VC412	Shore facilities, yards, stations (navies: gen.) 359.7, 623.83
VC414	Yards, stations, shore facilities (navies: U.S.: gen.) 359.70973
VC415.A-W	Stations, shore facilities, yards (navies: U.S.: by state)
VC415.C2	Naval stations & shore facilities (U.S.: Calif.)
VC415.F5	Naval stations & shore facilities (U.S.: Fl.)
VC415.H2	Naval stations & shore facilities (U.S.: Haw.)
VC416.A-Z	Naval stations & shore facilities (countries besides U.S.)
VC416.G3	Naval stations & shore facilities (Ger.)
VC417	Maintenance & repair, Naval (yards etc.)
VC417.5	Sanitation & refuse (naval sci.)
VC418	Power systems, Electric (naval sci.)
VC420-425	Barracks, quarters, housing (naval)
VC420	Quarters & barracks, Naval (gen.) 359.71
VC423-424	Naval quarters & barracks (U.S.)
VC425.A-Z	Housing & barracks, Naval (places besides U.S.)
VC430	Laundries, Naval

VC500-505	Accounting & accounts, Naval (inclu. ships' records)	359.622
VC503-504	Ships' records & accounts (U.S.)	
VC530-580	Transport, Naval	
VC530-535	Transportation, Naval (gen.) 359.83, .27	
VC533	Naval transport (U.S.)	
VC537	Shipment & packing (naval sci.)	
VC550-555	Personnel transport (navies)	
VC553	Transport, Personnel (navies: U.S.)	
VC570-575	Motor transport (naval sci.)	
VC573	Transport, Motor (navies: U.S.)	
VC580	Railroads (naval transp.)	

VD	SEAMEN, NAVAL (enlisted personnel in gen.: drill, way of life, etc.)	
VD7	Enlisted personnel, Naval (gen.: nonperiodical collections)	
VD15	Naval seamen (gen. hist.: enlisted way of life etc.) 359.338, .12	
VD21-124	NAVAL SEAMEN (by area or country)	
VD23-25	Sailors, Navy (U.S.)	
VD23	Seamen, Naval (U.S.: gen.) 359.3380973, .120973	
VD24.A-W	Naval seamen (U.S.: by state)	
VD25.A-Z	Enlisted personnel, Naval (U.S.: by city)	
VD26-27	Sailors, Navy (Can.)	
VD55-96	Sailors, Navy (Eur.)	
VD55	Seamen, Naval (Eur.: gen.) 359.338094, .12094	
VD57-64	Sailors, Navy (G.B.)	
VD57	Seamen, Naval (G.B.: gen.) 359.3380941, .120941	
VD59	Naval seamen (G.B.: Eng. & Wales)	
VD61	Naval seamen (G.B.: Scot.)	
VD63	Naval seamen (G.B.: N. Ire.)	
VD64.A-Z	Enlisted personnel, Naval (G.B.: by city or other div.)	
VD71-72	Sailors, Navy (Fr.) 359.3380944	
VD73-74	Sailors, Navy (Ger.)	
VD73	Seamen, Naval (Ger.: gen.) 359.3380943, .120943	
VD74.A-Z	Naval seamen (Ger.: by locality)	
VD76.5	Sailors, Navy (Ire.)	
VD85-86	Sailors, Navy (Rus.) 359.3380947	
VD99-113	Sailors, Navy (Asia)	
VD99	Seamen, Naval (Asia: gen.) 359.338095, .12095	
VD101	Sailors, Navy (China)	
VD105-106	Sailors, Navy (Japan)	
VD105	Seamen, Naval (Japan: gen.) 359.3380952, .120952	
VD121-122	Sailors, Navy (Australia) 359.3380994	
VD122.5	Sailors, Navy (New Z.)	
VD145	Seamen, Naval (gen.: pubn. 1801-1970)	
VD146	Sailors, Navy (gen.: pubn. 1970+)	
VD150	Manuals (naval seamen: gen.: SEE ALSO V110+ & V120+) 359.00202, .40202	
VD153	Manuals (naval seamen: U.S.) 359.402020973	
VD155.A-Z	Manuals (naval seamen: places except U.S.)	
VD157	Tactics & maneuvers, Naval (PREFER V167-178 & V245) 359.415, .4152	

VD160-302	NAVAL DRILLS (seamen: by country or area: includes watch, station, quarter, fire)	
VD160-162	Drills, Naval (U.S.)	
VD160	Watch drills, Naval (U.S.: gen.: ALSO quarter, station, other)	
		359.50973, .1330973, .133220973
VD163	Quarter drills, Naval (Can.: ALSO watch, station, other)	
VD215-269	Drills, Naval (Eur.)	
VD215	Station drills, Naval (Eur.: gen.: ALSO quarter, watch, etc.)	
VD228	Fire drills, Naval (Fr.: ALSO quarter, watch, station, etc.)	
VD231	Drills, Naval (Ger.)	359.50943
VD234	Drills, Naval (G.B.)	359.50941
VD252	Drills, Naval (Rus.)	
VD270-280	Drills, Naval (Asia)	
VD270	Naval drills (Asia: gen.)	
VD271	Drills, Naval (China)	
VD277	Drills, Naval (Japan)	359.50952
VD295	Drills, Naval (Australia)	359.50994
VD298	Drills, Naval (New Z.)	
VD320	Manual of arms (naval seamen)	359.5470202, .8240202
VD330-335	Shooting (naval seamen: inclu. marksmanship, regs., etc.)	
VD333	Marksmanship (naval seamen: U.S.)	
VD340-345	Bayonet drill (naval seamen)	
VD350-355	Equipment (naval seamen)	
VD360-365	Arms, Small (navies: gen. & by place)	359.824, .8242
VD360-390	Small arms (navies)	
VD363	Naval small arms (U.S.)	359.8240973
VD370	Rifles, carbines, etc. (navies)	359.82425
VD380	Bayonets (navies)	359.8241
VD390	Revolvers & pistols (navies)	359.8243
VD400-405	Small boat service (inclu. armament)	359.3258
VD430	Seamen, Naval (misc. subjects)	
VE	MARINES	359.96
VE7	Marines (collected, nonserial titles)	
VE15	Marines (gen. hist.)	359.96, .9609
VE21-124	MARINES (by geographic area)	
VE21	Marines (Am.)	
VE22	Marines (N. Am.)	
VE23	U.S. Marine Corps	359.960973
VE23.A1.A-Z	Periodicals (U.S. Marines)	359.96097305
VE23.A13-14	U.S. Marine Corps League	
VE23.A2-79	Reports, Official (U.S. Marines)	
VE23.A2	Reports, Official (U.S. Marines: annual)	
VE23.A25	Regulations, Marine (U.S.)	
VE23.A3-32	U.S. Marine Corps (official hist's.)	
VE23.A33	Registers (U.S. Marines)	
VE23.A48	Manuals (U.S. Marines)	
VE23.A5	U.S. Marine Corps (official monographs)	
VE23.A6	Recruiting literature (U.S. Marines: by date)	
VE23.A8-Z	U.S. Marine Corps (gen.)	
VE23.22.1st+	Divisions (U.S. Marines: by #)	
VE23.25.1st+	Marine regiments (U.S.: by #)	
VE23.3	Reserves, Marine (U.S.)	
VE23.4	Women's reserve, Marine (U.S.)	
VE25	Biography (U.S. Marines: PREFER E #s)	

VE26	Marines (Can.)	
VE55-96	Marines (Eur.)	
VE55	European marines (gen.)	
VE57-64	Marines (G.B.)	
VE57	British marines (gen.)	359.960941
VE59	Marines (Eng. & Wales)	
VE61	Marines (Scot.)	
VE73	Marines (Ger.)	
VE79	Marines (It.)	
VE85	Marines (Rus.)	
VE99-113	Marines (Asia)	
VE99	Asian marines (gen.)	
VE105	Marines (Japan)	359.960952
VE121-122.5	Marines (Australia & New Z.)	
VE145	Marines (gen.: pubn. 1801-1970)	359.9609
VE146	Marines (gen.: pubn. 1970+)	359.9609
VE150	Manuals & handbooks (marines: gen.)	359.960202
VE153	Handbooks & manuals (marines: U.S.)	
VE155.A-Z	Manuals & handbooks (marines: places besides U.S.)	
VE155.G7	Handbooks & manuals (marines: G.B.)	
VE157	Maneuvers & tactics (marines)	359.9642, .9652
VE160-302	MARINE DRILLS (by place)	
VE160-162	Drill regulations, Marine (U.S.)	
VE160	Drills, Marine (U.S.: gen.)	359.965, .9654
VE215-269	Drills, Marine (Eur.)	
VE215	Marine drills (Eur.: gen.)	
VE231	Drills, Marine (Ger.)	
VE234	Drills, Marine (G.B.)	
VE270-280	Drills, Marine (Asia)	
VE270	Marine drills (Asia: gen.)	
VE277	Drills, Marine (Japan)	
VE295	Drills, Marine (Australia)	
VE320	Manual of arms (marines)	359.968240202
VE330-335	Shooting (marines: inclu. marksmanship, training, etc.)	
VE330	Training (shooting: marines: gen.) 359.96547	
VE333	Marksmanship (marines: U.S.)	359.96547
VE340	Bayonet drill (marines)	359.96547
VE350-355	Equipment (marines)	
VE360-390	Small arms (marines)	
VE360	Arms, Small (marines (gen.)	359.96824, 623.44
VE370	Rifles (marines)	359.9682425, 623.4425
VE380	Bayonets (marines) 623.441	
VE390	Pistols & revolvers (marines)	359.968243
VE400-405	Uniforms, Marine	359.9614
VE403	Marine uniforms (U.S.)	359.96140973
VE410	Shore service (marines)	
VE420-425	Barracks & quarters, Marine	
VE420	Marine barracks & quarters (gen.)	359.961292, .9671
VE422	Quarters & barracks, Marine (U.S.: gen.)	359.96710973
VE424.A-Z	Barracks & quarters, Marine (U.S.: by place)	
VE424.C2	Barracks & quarters, Marine (U.S.: Calif.)	359.967109794

VE430-435	Training camps, Marine 359.967+	
VE432	Marine training camps (U.S.: gen.) 359.9670973	
VE434.A-Z	Camps, Marine training (U.S.: by place)	
VE434.C2 or P...	Camp Pendleton (Calif.: U.S. Marines)	
VE434.S6	Marine camps (South Carolina: training) 359.96709757	
VE480	Records & accounting (marines)	
VE490	Pay & allowances (marines) 359.9664	
VE500	Marines (misc. subjects: not A-Z)	
VF	ORDNANCE, NAVAL 359.82, 623.8251	
VF1	Periodicals & associations (naval ordnance)	
VF6.A1	Museums & exhibitions (naval ordnance: gen.)	
VF6.A2-Z	Exhibitions & museums (naval ordnance: by place or country)	
VF7	Naval ordnance (nonperiodical collections)	
VF15	Ordnance, Naval (gen. hist's.) 359.8209	
VF21-124	NAVAL ORDNANCE (by country or place)	
VF23	Ordnance, Naval (U.S.) 359.820973, 623.82510973	
VF55-96	Ordnance, Naval (Eur.) 359.82094	
VF55	Naval ordnance (Eur.: gen.)	
VF57	Ordnance, Naval (G.B.) 359.820941	
VF71	Ordnance, Naval (Fr.)	
VF73	Ordnance, Naval (Ger.) 359.820943	
VF79	Ordnance, Naval (It.)	
VF85	Ordnance, Naval (Rus.)	
VF99-113	Ordnance, Naval (Asia)	
VF99	Naval ordnance (Asia: gen.)	
VF105	Ordnance, Naval (Japan) 359.820952	
VF121	Ordnance, Naval (Australia)	
VF145	Ordnance, Naval (gen. pubns. 1801+) 359.82	
VF147	Naval ordnance (special overall)	
VF150-155	Handbooks & manuals (naval ordnance)	
VF150	Ordnance, Naval (handbooks & manuals: gen.)	
VF153	Manuals & handbooks (naval ordnance: U.S.)	
VF155.A-Z	Manuals & handbooks (naval ordnance: places besides U.S.)	
VF160-302	NAVAL ORDNANCE DRILLS (by place)	
VF160	Drills, Naval ordnance (U.S.: gen.)	
VF215-269	Drills, Naval ordnance (Eur.)	
VF215	Ordnance drills, Naval (Eur.: gen.)	
VF228	Drills, Naval ordnance (Fr.)	
VF231	Drills, Naval ordnance (Ger.)	
VF234	Drills, Naval ordnance (G.B.)	
VF252	Drills, Naval ordnance (Rus.)	
VF270-280	Drills, Naval ordnance (Asia)	
VF277	Drills, Naval ordnance (Japan)	
VF295	Drills, Naval ordnance (Australia)	
VF310-315	Target practice, Naval	
VF310	Naval target practice (gen.) 623.553	
VF313	Gunnery practice, Naval (U.S.) 623.5530973	
VF315.A-Z	Naval gunnery practice (places except U.S.)	
VF315.G7	Gunnery practice, Naval (G.B.) 623.5530941	
VF320-325	Artillery equipment, Naval	
VF323	Naval artillery equipment (U.S.)	
VF325.A-Z	Equipment, Naval artillery (places other than U.S.)	
VF330-335	Shore service	

VF346-348	Weapons systems, Naval
VF347	Naval weapons systems
VF350-375	Ordnance & arms, Naval (in sum)
VF350-355	Arms & ordnance, Naval (gen.) 359.82, 623.418
VF350	Naval ordnance & arms (gen.)
VF353	Naval arms & ordnance (gen.: U.S.)
VF357	Instruction (naval ordnance)
VF360	Research (naval ordnance: gen.) 359.82072
VF360.3	Ordnance research, Naval (U.S.)
VF360.5.A-Z	Naval research (ordnance: places besides U.S.)
VF370-375	Ordnance & arms, Naval (manufacture)
VF370	Manufacture (naval ordnance & arms: gen.)
VF373	Naval ordnance & arms (manufacture: U.S.)
VF380-385	Ordnance magazines & facilities (navies)
VF380	Magazines, Ordnance (navies: gen.) 359.75
VF390-395	Ordnance proper (navies)
VF390	Naval ordnance material (gen.) 623.418
VF393	Ordnance material (navies: U.S.)
VF393.A1-3	Ordnance proper (navies: U.S.: documents)
VF393.A4-6	Manuals, Naval ordnance (U.S.: by mm., cm., inches, or lbs.)
VF393.A5.5	5 in. guns, Naval (U.S.: manuals)
VF393.A7-Z	Ordnance proper (navies: U.S.: gen.)
VF395.A-Z	Naval ordnance material (besides U.S.)
VF410.A2	Machine guns, Naval (gen.) 623.4424
VF410.A3-Z	Naval machine guns (special by name)
VF418	Antiaircraft guns, Naval 359.981
VF420	Ordnance material (misc.)
VF430	Gun carriages, Naval 623.43
VF440	Turrets & cupolas, Naval
VF450-455	Firing instructions, Naval
VF460	Ammunition, Naval 359.825, 623.45
VF470	Cartridges, Naval 359.8255
VF480-500	Projectiles, Naval
VF480	Naval projectiles (gen.) 359.8251, 623.451
VF490	Shells & shrapnel, Naval
VF500	Bullets (navies) 359.8255, 623.455
VF509	Depth charges, Naval 623.45115, .4517
VF520-530	Fire control, Naval gunnery (inclu. instruments)
VF520	Instruments, Naval gunnery 623.558
VF530	Radar equipment, Naval 623.557
VF540	Tests, Ordnance & firing (navies)
VF550	Range tables, Naval ordnance 623.5530212
VF580	Ordnance, Naval (misc. topics)
VG	NAVAL SERVICES (misc.)
VG20-25	Chaplains or religious officials, Naval
VG20	Naval chaplains (gen.) 359.347
VG23	Chaplains, Naval (U.S.) 359.3470973
VG25.A-Z	Religious officials, Naval (places besides U.S.)
VG30-35	Bands & music, Naval (SEE ALSO ML1300-1354)
VG33	Music & bands, Naval (U.S.) 359.340973, .170973
VG50-55	Coast guard & coast signal service 359.97
VG50	Signal service, Coast (plus coast guard: gen.)
VG53	U.S. Coast Guard 359.970973
VG55.A-Z	Coast guard & coast signal service (places besides U.S.)

VG60-65	Postal service, Naval	359.341
VG70-85	Telecommunications, Naval	359.415, .85, 623.856, .73
VG70-75	Telegraph, Naval	
VG73	Naval telegraph (U.S.)	359.4150973
VG76-78	Telegraph, radar, & radio communications (navies: wireless)	
VG76	Communications, Naval (inclu. radio, radar, wireless telegraph: gen.)	
		623.8564, .734
VG77	Radio, radar, & wireless telegraph (navies: U.S.)	623.85640973
VG78.A-Z	Radar, radio, & wireless telegraph (navies: besides U.S.)	
VG80-85	Telephone, Naval	623.85645
VG83	Naval telephone (U.S.)	
VG86-88	Underwater demolition teams (navies)	
VG86	Frogmen (navies: gen.)	359.984
VG87	Naval underwater teams (U.S.: inclu. demolition)	359.9840973
VG88.A-Z	Navy frogmen (besides U.S.)	
VG90-95	Air forces & warfare, Naval	359.94, 358.4
VG90	Air warfare & forces, Naval (gen.)	358.4, 359.3255, 623.746
VG93-94	Naval aviation (U.S.)	358.40973
VG93	Aviation, Naval (U.S.: gen.)	
VG94.A-Z	Air forces, Naval (U.S.: by area or state)	
VG94.5.A-Z	Air fields & stations, Naval (U.S.: by name)	
VG94.5.P4	Pensacola Naval Air Station (Flor.)	
VG94.6.A-Z	Units, Naval air (U.S.: by name: inclu. organizations)	
VG94.7.A-Z	Air reserves, Naval & marine (U.S.)	
VG95.A-Z	Aviation, Naval (places besides U.S.)	
VG95.G3	Naval aviation (Ger.)	
VG95.J3	Naval aviation (Japan)	
VG100-475	MEDICAL SERVICES, NAVAL (SEE ALSO UH201-515)	
VG100	Periodicals & associations (naval medical services)	
VG115	Naval medical services (gen.)	359.345, .72, 616.98024
VG121-224	NAVAL MEDICAL SERVICES (by place)	
VG123	Medical services, Naval (U.S.)	359.3450973
VG155-196	Medical services, Naval (Eur.)	
VG157	Medical services, Naval (G.B.)	
VG173	Medical services, Naval (Ger.)	
VG185	Medical services, Naval (Rus.)	
VG199-213	Medical services, Naval (Asia)	
VG205	Medical services, Naval (Japan)	
VG221	Medical services, Naval (Australia)	
VG226	Biography, Naval medical (gen.)	
VG227.A1	Medical biography, Naval (U.S.: collective)	
VG227.A2-Z	Naval medical biography (U.S.: indiv.)	
VG228.A-Z	Biography, Naval medical (places besides U.S.)	
VG230-235	Instruction (naval medicine)	
VG240-245	Research & laboratories, Naval medical	
VG260-265	Surgeons, Naval	359.345, 616.98024, 617.99
VG263	Naval surgeons (U.S.)	
VG270-275	Dispensaries, Naval	
VG280-285	Dentistry, Naval	
VG290-295	Supplies, Medical & surgical (navies)	
VG310-325	Hospital corps, Naval	
VG310	Naval hospital corps (gen.)	
VG320	Hospital corps, Naval (U.S.)	
VG325.A-Z	Hospital corps, Naval (places besides U.S.)	

VG350-355   Nurse corps, Naval
VG350   Naval nurse corps (gen.)   359.345, 610.7349, .7361, 616.98024
VG353   Nurse corps, Naval (U.S.)
VG410-450   Hospital services & hospitals, Naval (SEE ALSO D #s for
                    particular wars)
VG410   Hospital services, Naval (gen.)   359.72
VG420-425   Hospital services, Naval (U.S.)
VG420   Hospitals, Naval (gen.)
VG424.A-Z   Naval hospitals (U.S.: by area or state)
VG425.A-Z   Hospitals, Naval (U.S.: by town)
VG430.A-Z   Naval hospitals (places except U.S.)
VG450   Hospital ships   623.8264, 359.3264
VG457   Red Cross at sea
VG460-466   Handbooks, Medical & surgical (navies)
VG460   Medical & surgical handbooks (navies: gen.)   359.3450202,
                                            610.0202, 617.0260202
VG463   Surgical & medical handbooks (navies: U.S.)
VG465.A-Z   Manuals, medical & surgical (navies: besides U.S.)
VG466   First-aid handbooks, Naval
VG470-475   Health, hygiene, & sanitation (navies)
VG470   Naval health, hygiene, & sanitation (gen.)
VG471   Hygiene, health, & sanitation (navies: special: tropics, drinking water,
                    alcohol problem, venereal diseases, diet, etc.)
VG473   Health, hygiene, & sanitation (navies: U.S.)
VG475.A-Z   Sanitation, health, & hygiene (navies: places besides U.S.)
VG478   Rehabilitation of disabled sailors (PREFER UB360+)
VG500-505   Press & public relns. (navies)
VG500   Media & public relns. (navies: gen.)   359.342, 070.433, .439
VG503   War correspondents & public relns. (navies: U.S.)
VG505.A-Z   Newspapers, media, & public relns. (navies: besides U.S.)
VG590-595   Civil engineering (navies: SEE ALSO VA66.C6+)
VG590   Engineering, Civil (navies: gen.)
VG593   Naval engineering (civil: U.S.)
VG600-605   Artisans, Naval (carpenters' mates, painters, etc.)
VG600   Artificers, Naval (gen.: inclu. carpenters' mates etc.)
VG603   Carpenters & other naval artisans (U.S.)
VG610-615   Aerographers (naval weather & surf forecaster)
VG610   Weather forecaster, Naval (gen.)
VG613   Forecaster, Weather (navies: U.S.)
VG800-805   Machinists, Naval
VG900-905   Yeomen & clerks, Naval
VG903   Clerks & yeomen, Naval (U.S.)
VG920-925   Surveyors, draftsmen, & engineering aids (navies)
VG920   Draftsmen & surveyors, Naval (gen.)
VG950-955   Boatswains
VG953   Boatswains' mates (U.S.)
VG1010-1015   Photographers, Naval
VG1020   Photographic interpretation (navies)
VG1030-1035   Instrumentmen, Naval

VG2000-2005	Social welfare services, Naval
VG2000	Social work, Naval (gen.)
VG2003	Welfare services, Naval (U.S.)
VG2005.A-Z	Naval welfare services (places besides U.S.)
VG2020-2029	Recreation & information services, Naval
VG2020	Naval recreation & information services (gen.) 359.346
VG2025-2026	Information & recreation services, Naval (U.S.: gen.) 359.3460973
VG2029	Recreation & information services, Naval (places besides U.S.)

VK	MARINE NAVIGATION & MERCHANT MARINE
VK1	Periodicals & associations (marine navig. & merch. marine)
VK5	Conferences (marine navig. & merch. marine)
VK6	Museums & exhibitions (marine navig. & merch. marine)
VK7-8	Nautical almanacs & yearbooks
VK7	Almanacs & yearbooks, Nautical (American: inclu. abridged)
VK8	Yearbooks & almanacs, Nautical (non-American)
VK15	Merchant marine & navigation (gen. hist's.)
VK18	Navigation, Marine (gen. hist's.: modern: inclu. merch. marine)
VK20	Merchant marine & navigation (20th c.: hist. & conditions)
VK21-124	Merchant marine & navigation (hist. & conditions: by area or country)
VK139-140	Biography (merch. marine)
VK145	Marine navigation & merchant marine (gen.: pubn. 1801+) 623.89
VK147	Merchant marine & navigation (gen. special)
VK149	Nautical life (merchant marine: pop. titles)
VK155	Handbooks & manuals (marine navig. & merch. marine) 623.890202
VK160	Merchant marine (occupation) 387.0023
VK199	Accidents, Marine
VK200	Safety, Marine
VK205	Masters' manuals (merch. marine: inclu. command of ships)
VK221	Manning of vessels (merch. marine)
VK233	Watch duty (merch. duty)
VK321-369+	Harbors & ports 387.1+
VK358	Terminals, Marine (bunkers, coal supplies, repairs, etc.)
VK371-378	Collisions & avoidance, High seas
VK381-397	Signaling, Merchant marine (flags, lights, codes, radio, etc.)
VK383	Fog signals (merch. marine)
VK385	Flag signals (merch. marine)
VK387	Light signals (merch. marine)
VK391	Code signals (merch. marine)
VK397	Wireless signals (merch. marine)
VK401-529	Instruction (merch. marine)
VK401	Merchant marine & navigation (study & teaching: gen.)
VK421-524	Marine navigation (instruction: by locale: inclu. merch. marine)
VK423	Merchant marine & navigation (instruction: U.S.)
VK457	Navigation, Marine (instruction: G.B.: inclu. merch. marine)
VK531-537	Training (marine navig. & merch. marine)
VK541-547	Seamanship (marine navig. & merch. marine) 623.88
VK545	Warship handling (plus other seamanship topics) 623.8825

VK549-572	Marine navigation science	
VK549	Navigation, Marine (science: hist.)	527.094, 387.155
VK555	Science of marine navigation (gen.: pubn. 1801+)	623.81
VK560	Electronics, Marine navigation	623.893
VK561.A1	Loran tables (marine navig.: ca. 1932+: gen.)	
VK561.A2-Z	Loran tables (marine navig.: by region)	
VK561.A6	Coasts, Asian (Loran tables)	
VK561.A7	Atlantic Ocean (Loran tables)	
VK561.P3	Pacific Ocean (Loran tables)	
VK561.U5	Coasts, United States (Loran tables)	
VK561.U53-54	East Coast (U.S.: Loran tables)	
VK561.U57	West Coast (U.S.: Loran tables)	
VK563-567+	Tables, Nautical	623.8920212
VK563	Nautical tables (gen.: inclu. azimuth)	
VK565	Latitude & longitude (marine navig.: inclu. tables)	
VK567	Longitude & time at sea (marine navig.: inclu. tables)	
VK570	Optimum ship routing	
VK571	Great circle routing (marine navig.)	
VK572	Dead reckoning (naut. navig.)	623.8923
VK573-587	Instruments, Nautical	
VK573	Nautical instruments (gen.)	623.894, .863
VK575-584	Instruments, Nautical (special)	
VK575	Chronometers, Nautical (PREFER QB107)	
VK577	Compasses (sea, air, or land: inclu. gyro type)	623.82
VK579	Distance finders (inclu. tables etc.)	
VK581	Logs, Nautical	
VK583	Sextants & quadrants	527.028, 623.894
VK584.A-Z	Nautical instruments (misc.)	
VK584.A7	Artificial horizon	
VK584.A8	Automatic pilot (marine navig.)	
VK584.G8	Gyroscopic devices (marine navig.)	
VK584.S6	Sounding apparatus	
VK587	Chart use, Nautical (plus other misc. topics on naut. instruments)	
VK588-597	Hydrography, Marine	
VK591	Marine hydrography & surveying (gen.)	
VK593	Surveying, Hydrographic (gen. special)	
VK600-794	TIDE & CURRENT TABLES	
VK602	Current & tide tables (gen.: pubn. 1801+)	623.8949
VK603	Tables, Tide & current (collections)	
VK607-794	TIDE & CURRENT TABLES (by area)	
VK610-680	Atlantic Ocean (all & east: tide & current tables)	
VK610	Tide & current tables (Atlantic Ocean: all & east: gen.)	623.894909163
VK611	North Atlantic (tide & current tables)	623.8949091631
VK615-626	North Sea & Baltic (tide & current tables)	
VK627-638	British Isles (tide & current tables)	
VK639-644	English Channel (tide & current tables)	
VK645	Coasts, French (gen. & Eng. Ch.: tide & current tables)	
VK651	Gibraltar Strait (tide & current tables)	
VK653-674	Mediterranean Sea (tide & current tables)	
VK685-701	Indian Ocean (tide & current tables)	
VK702-711	Coasts, Asian (tide & current tables)	
VK702	Asian coasts (tide & current tables)	
VK709	Japanese Islands (tide & current tables)	
VK710	Malaysia & Singapore (tide & current tables)	
VK711	Philippine Islands (tide & current tables)	

```
VK715-756   Pacific Ocean & islands (tide & current tables)
VK715       Tide & current tables (Pac. Ocean & islands: gen.)   623.894909164
VK717       Current & tide tables (North Pacific)
VK725       Tide & current tables (South Pacific)
VK747       West Coast (U.S.: tide & current tables)   623.8949091643
VK759-792   Current & tide tables (Atlantic Ocean: west)
VK771-777       Caribbean Sea & Gulf of Mexico (tide & current tables)
VK775           Gulf of Mexico (tide & current tables)
VK777           Florida Keys & Strait & Windward Passage (tide & current tables)
VK781           East Coast (U.S.: tide & current tables)   623.8949091634
VK793       Coasts, United States (tide & current tables)
VK798-997   SAILING DIRECTIONS & PILOT GUIDES
VK799       Tables, Nautical navigation (distances etc.)   623.8920212
VK802       Pilot guides & sailing directions (gen.: pubn. 1801+)   623.8922, .8929+
VK803       Sailing & pilot guides (official: British)
VK804-997   PILOT & SAILING GUIDES (by area)
VK804       American waters (gen.: pilot & sailing guides)   623.89297
VK810-880   Atlantic Ocean (all & east: pilot & sailing guides)
VK810       Pilot & sailing guides (Atl. Ocean: all & east: gen.)   623.8929163
VK811-814.5     North Atlantic (pilot & sailing guides)
VK813           Convoy lanes (N. Atlantic: pilot & sailing guides)
VK815-826       North Sea & Baltic (pilot & sailing guides)
VK827-84        British Isles & English Channel (pilot & sailing guides)
                                            623.892916336, .8929422
VK845       Coasts, French (gen. & Eng. Ch.: pilot & sailing guides)
                                            623.8929442 (Normandy)
VK851       Gibraltar Strait (pilot & sailing & guides)   623.8929448, .89294689
VK853-874   Mediterranean Sea (pilot & sailing guides)   623.89291638, .8929448
VK881       East Indies (pilot & sailing guides: Eng. to India etc.)
VK885-901   Indian Ocean (pilot & sailing guides)
VK902-911   Coasts, Asian (pilot & sailing guides)
VK902           Asian coasts (pilot & sailing guides: gen.)
VK909           Japanese Islands (pilot & sailing guides)   623.892952
VK911           Philippine Islands (pilot & sailing guides)   623.8929599
VK915-956   Pacific Ocean & islands (pilot & sailing guides)
VK915       Pilot & sailing guides (Pac. Ocean & islands: gen.)   623.8929164
VK917       North Pacific (pilot & sailing guides)   623.89291644-89291646
VK925       South Pacific (pilot & sailing guides)   623.89291646-89291649
VK927-929   Australia & New Zealand (pilot & sailing guides)
VK931       East Indies & Indonesia (pilot & sailing guides: from U.S.)
VK933.A-Z   Pilot & sailing guides (Pac. islands: misc.)
VK933.C27       Caroline Islands (pilot & sailing guides)
VK933.H3        Hawaiian Islands (pilot & sailing guides)
VK933.M27       Mariana Islands (pilot & sailing guides)
VK933.S65       Solomon Islands (pilot & sailing guides)
VK933.T79       Truk Islands (pilot & sailing guides)
VK941-956   West Coast (Am.: plus E. Pac.: pilot & sailing guides)
VK941       Pilot & sailing guides (E. Pac. & Am. W. Coast: gen.)
VK943       Bering Strait & Alaska coast (pilot & sailing guides)
VK945       Canada (W. coast: pilot & sailing guides)
VK947       West Coast (U.S.: pilot & sailing guides)   623.892916432
VK951-952       Central America (pilot & sailing guides)
VK959-992   Atlantic Ocean (West: pilot & sailing guides)
VK959           Pilot & sailing guides (W. Atlantic: gen.)
VK961-968       South American coasts (gen. & east: pilot & sailing guides)
```

VK969-970   Mexican & Central American coasts (pilot & sailing guides)
VK970.A-Z   Pilot & sailing guides (C. Am.: by locality)
VK970.P2   Panama Canal (pilot & sailing guides)
VK971-973   Caribbean Sea & West Indies (pilot & sailing guides)
VK973.A-Z   West Indies (pilot & sailing guides: by island[s])
VK975-977   Gulf of Mexico (pilot & sailing guides)
VK977   Florida Keys & Strait & Windward Passage (pilot & sailing guides)
VK981   East Coast (U.S.: pilot & sailing guides)
VK985   Canada (E. coast: pilot & sailing guides)
VK993   Coasts, United States (pilot & sailing guides)
VK1000-1249   LIGHTHOUSES, BEACONS, FOGHORNS, ETC. (inclu. buoys & lightships)
VK1010   Beacons, foghorns, lighthouses, etc. (gen.)   623.8942, 387.155
VK1015   Foghorns, beacons, lighthouses, etc. (hist's.)
VK1021-1124   LIGHTHOUSES, BEACONS, FOGHORNS, ETC. (by area)
VK1023-1025   United States (lighthouses, beacons, foghorns, etc.)
VK1024   Lighthouses, beacons, foghorns, etc. (U.S.: by area)
VK1055-1096   Europe (lighthouses, beacons, foghorns, etc.)
VK1055   Lighthouses, beacons, foghorns, etc. (Eur.: gen.)
VK1057-1064   Great Britain (lighthouses, beacons, foghorns, etc.)
VK1071-1072   France (lighthouses, beacons, foghorns, etc.)
VK1073-1074   Germany (lighthouses, beacons, foghorns, etc.)
VK1079-1080   Italy (lighthouses, beacons, foghorns, etc.)
VK1085-1086   Russia (Eur.: lighthouses, beacons, foghorns, etc.)
VK1086.5   Scandinavia (lighthouses, beacons, foghorns, etc.)
    623.89420948
VK1099-1113   Asia (lighthouses, beacons, foghorns, etc.)
VK1101-1102   China (lighthouses, beacons, foghorns, etc.)
VK1105-1106   Japanese Islands (lighthouses, beacons, foghorns, etc.)
    623.89420952
VK1109-1110   Russia (Asia: lighthouses, beacons, foghorns, etc.)
VK1111-1112   Turkey & Asia Minor (lighthouses, beacons, foghorns, etc.)
VK1115-1119   Africa (lighthouses, beacons, foghorns, etc.)
VK1121-1122   Australia (lighthouses, beacons, foghorns, etc.)   623.89420994
VK1122.5   New Zealand (lighthouses, beacons, foghorns, etc.)
    623.894209931
VK1123-1124   Pacific Ocean & islands (lighthouses, beacons, foghorns, etc.)
    623.8942099+, .894209164+
VK1150-1249   LISTS (beacons, foghorns, lighthouses, etc.)
VK1150   Beacons, foghorns, lighthouses, etc. (lists: gen.: inclu. Br. Admiralty)   623.8944
VK1151-1185   Europe (lighthouses, beacons, foghorns, etc.: lists)
VK1151   Lighthouses, beacons, foghorns, etc. (Eur.: gen.: lists)
    623.8944094
VK1153-1159   Great Britain & Ireland (lighthouses, beacons, foghorns, etc.: lists)
    623.89440941
VK1173   France (lighthouses, beacons, foghorns, etc.: lists)
    623.89440944
VK1176   Mediterranean Sea (lighthouses, beacons, foghorns, etc.: lists)
    623.8944091638
VK1190-1199   Africa (lighthouses, beacons, foghorns, etc.: lists)
VK1198   Egypt (lighthouses, beacons, foghorns, etc.: lists)
VK1203-1209   Asia (lighthouses, beacons, foghorns, etc.: lists)
VK1207   Japanese Islands (lighthouses, beacons, foghorns, etc.: lists)
    623.89440952

VK1211-1212	Australia & New Zealand (lighthouses, beacons, foghorns, etc.: lists) 623.89440993-89440994
VK1214-1223	Pacific Ocean & islands (lighthouses, beacons, foghorns, etc.: lists) 623.894409164
VK1239-1240	West Indies (lighthouses, beacons, foghorns, etc.: lists)
VK1241-1246	Lighthouses, beacons, foghorns, etc. (N. Am.: lists) 623.8944097
VK1243	United States (lighthouses, beacons, foghorns, etc.: lists)
VK1250-1299	SHIPWRECKS & FIRES (PREFER D-F #s for specific wars)
VK1250	Fires & shipwrecks (gen.) 910.453
VK1255.A-Z	Shipwrecks (by name)
VK1257.A-Z	Fires, Nautical (by name of ship)
VK1259	Abandoning ship (plus other misc. marine topics of disaster)
VK1265	Disasters, Submarine
VK1270-1294	Shipwrecks (by area)
VK1270-1273	Shipwrecks (U.S.)
VK1280-1282	Shipwrecks (Eur.)
VK1286	Shipwrecks (Asia)
VK1289-1294	Shipwrecks (Australia & Oceania)
VK1299	Icebergs
VK1300-1491	SAVING LIFE & PROPERTY (marine navig.)
VK1300-1481	Lifesaving, Marine
VK1315	Marine lifesaving (hist's.)
VK1321-1424	Nautical lifesaving (by area)
VK1445-1447	Survival after shipwrecks (plus other misc. lifesaving topics) 623.865
VK1460-1481	Lifesaving apparatus & stations (marine navig.)
VK1460-1461	Equipment, Lifesaving (marine navig.: gen.) 623.865
VK1462-1463	Lifesaving on ships
VK1473	Lifeboats 623.829
VK1477	Life preservers
VK1479	Rockets, signal (marine lifesaving)
VK1481.A-Z	Lifesaving equipment (special: by name)
VK1481.S4	Shark protection
VK1491	Salvage, Marine
VK1500-1661	PILOTS & PILOTING, NAUTICAL
VK1515	Nautical pilots & piloting (gen. hist's.) 623.8922, .892209
VK1521-1624	PILOTING & PILOTS, NAUTICAL (by area) 623.291-89299
VK1523-1525	Piloting, Nautical (U.S.) 623.2973
VK1555-1596	Piloting, Nautical (Eur.) 623.294
VK1599-1613	Piloting, Nautical (Asia)
VK1621-1624	Piloting, Nautical (Australia & the Pac.)
VK1645-1661	Pilots & piloting, Nautical (gen.)
VM	NAVAL ARCHITECTURE & MARINE ENGINEERING
VM1-565	NAVAL ARCHITECTURE & SHIPBUILDING (SEE ALSO V750-995+ for construction & armament of warships)
VM1	Periodicals & associations (naval architec.: Eng.)
VM5	Conferences (naval architec.)
VM6	Museums & exhibitions (naval architec.)
VM7	Architecture, Naval (collected, nonperiodical works)
VM12	Directories (naval architec.)

VM15-124	Naval architecture (hist.)	
VM15	Shipbuilding, Naval (gen. hist.)	
VM18	Naval architecture (hist.: modern: gen.)	
VM19	Naval architecture (hist.: 19th c.)	
VM20	Naval architecture (hist.: 20th c.)	
VM21-124	Naval shipbuilding (hist.: by area or country)	
VM23-25	Shipbuilding, Naval (hist.: U.S.)	623.80973
VM55-96	Shipbuilding, Naval (hist.: Eur.)	
VM55	Naval shipbuilding (hist.: Eur.: gen.)	623.8094
VM57-64	Shipbuilding, Naval (hist.: G.B.)	623.80941
VM71-72	Shipbuilding, Naval (hist.: Fr.)	623.80944
VM73-74	Shipbuilding, Naval (hist.: Ger.)	623.80943
VM79-80	Shipbuilding, Naval (hist.: It.)	623.80945
VM85-86	Shipbuilding, Naval (hist.: Rus.)	623.80947
VM99-113	Shipbuilding, Naval (hist.: Asia)	
VM99	Naval shipbuilding (hist.: Asia: gen.)	623.8095
VM105-106	Shipbuilding, Naval (hist.: Japan)	623.80952
VM121-122	Shipbuilding, Naval (hist.: Australia)	623.80994
VM122.5	Shipbuilding, Naval (hist.: New Z.)	
VM139-140	Biography (naval architec.)	
VM142-148	Naval architecture (gen.)	623.81
VM142-145	Wooden ships (naval architec.)	623.81
VM146-147	Metal ships (naval architec.)	623.8182
VM148	Concrete ships (naval architec.)	
VM151	Handbooks, tables, etc. (ship calculations: naval architec.)	
		623.810202, .810212
VM153	Tonnage tables (naval architec.)	
VM155	Measurement of ships (naval architec.)	
VM156-163	Theory & principles (naval architec.)	
VM165-276	Instruction (naval architec.)	
VM165	Naval shipbuilding (instruc.: gen.)	623.8107
VM171-274	Instruction (naval architec.: by place)	
VM173	Shipbuilding, Naval (instruc.: U.S.)	
VM205	Shipbuilding, Naval (instruc.: Eur.: gen.)	
VM207	Shipbuilding, Naval (instruc.: G.B.)	
VM223	Shipbuilding, Naval (instruc.: Ger.)	
VM255	Shipbuilding, Naval (instruc.: Japan)	
VM271	Shipbuilding, Naval (instruc.: Australia)	
VM275-276	Schools (naval architec.: special)	
VM293	Standards (naval architec.)	
VM295-296	Contracts & specifications (naval architec.)	
VM295	Specifications & contracts (naval architec.: gen.)	
VM297	Designs, drawings, blueprints (naval architec.)	623.812
VM297.5	Blueprints, drawings, designs (naval architec.: laying out)	
VM298	Models, Ship	623.8201, 745.5928
VM298.5-301.	Shipbuilding industry	
VM298.5	Industry, Shipbuilding (gen.)	338.476238, 387.5+
VM298.6	Shipbuilding industry (U.S.)	387.50973
VM298.7.A-Z	Shipbuilding industry (places besides U.S.)	
VM298.7.G7	Shipbuilding industry (G.B.)	
VM301.A-Z	Shipyards & shipbuilding companies (by name)	
VM307	Pictorials (ships)	387.2+
VM308	Figureheads, ornaments, decorations on ships	

VM321-349	Small craft
VM321	Small craft (gen.)
VM321.5	Boatyards, Small craft (gen.)
VM321.52.A-Z	Boatyards, Small craft (by name)
VM322	Maintenance & repair (small craft)
VM331	Yachts (small craft: gen.)
VM341	Motorboats & launches (small craft: gen.)
VM351	Rowboats, small sailboats, etc.
VM365-367	Submarine boats
VM365	Submarine boats (gen.) 359.3257, 623.8257
VM367.A-Z	Equipment (submarine boats: special)
VM367.P4	Periscopes (submarine architec.)
VM367.S7	Batteries, Storage (submarine architec.)
VM378-466	Vessels (naval architec.: by use)
VM380	Warships (naval architec.: PREFER V750-995+) 623.825, 359.32
VM381-383	Passenger ships (naval architec.)
VM383.A-Z	Liners, Passenger (by name)
VM383.B7	Bremen (pass. ship)
VM383.N6	Normandie (pass. ship)
VM383.Q4	Queen Mary (pass. ship)
VM385.A-Z	Steamship lines (by co. name)
VM391-395	Freighters (naval architec.) 623.8245, 387.544
VM397	Coast guard vessels (naval architec.: by type) 623.8245, 359.9732
VM451	Icebreakers (naval architec.) 623.828
VM455	Tankers (naval architec.) 623.8245, 387.544
VM457	Ore carriers 623.8245, 387.544
VM469.5	Pontoons & pontoon gear (naval architec.)
VM471-479	Electricity (naval architec. & engin.) 623.8503, .852, .8726
VM473	Electricity (naval architec. & engin.: U.S. Navy)
VM480	Electronics, Marine (radar, radio, sonar, etc.: naval architec. & engin.) 623.8504, .734+, .8564-85648
VM480.3	Radar, radio, sonar, etc. (naval architec.: U.S. Navy)
VM480.5.A-Z	Sonar, radio, radar, etc. (naval architec.: places except U.S.)
VM480.5.G7	Radio, radar, sonar, etc. (naval architec.: G.B.)
VM481-482	Heating, ventilation, & sanitation (naval architec. & engin.)
VM481	Sanitation, heating, & ventilation (naval architec. & engin.) 623.853-54
VM483	Disinfection & fumigation (naval engin.)
VM485	Cold storage (naval architec. & engin.)
VM491-493	Lighting (naval architec. & engin.)
VM501	Plumbing (naval architec. & engin.)
VM503-505	Water supply (naval architec. & engin.) 623.854
VM511	Hammocks, berths, etc. (naval architec.)
VM521	Propulsion (naval architec. & engin.: gen.) 623.87
VM565	Steerage, Nautical
VM600-989	MARINE ENGINEERING
VM600-605	Engineering, Marine (gen.) 623.87
VM607	Handbooks, tables, etc. (marine engin.) 623.870202
VM615	Marine engineering (hist.: gen.)
VM621-724	Engineering, Marine (hist.: by place)
VM623-625	Marine engineering (hist.: U.S.)
VM655	Marine engineering (hist.: Eur.)
VM657	Marine engineering (hist.: G.B.) 623.870941-870942
VM671	Marine engineering (hist.: Fr.)
VM673	Marine engineering (hist.: Ger.) 623.870943
VM679	Marine engineering (hist.: It.)

VM685	Marine engineering (hist.: Rus.)	
VM699	Marine engineering (hist.: Japan)	623.870952
VM721	Marine engineering (hist.: Australia)	
VM725-728	Instruction (marine engin.)	623.8707
VM727	Marine engineering (instruction: U.S.)	
VM728.A-Z	Instruction (marine engin.: places except U.S.)	
VM731-779	Marine engines	
VM731	Engines, Marine (gen.)	623.872
VM740	Turbines, Marine	623.87233
VM741-750	Boilers, Marine	623.873
VM751-759	Propulsion & resistance (marine engin.)	
VM751	Resistance & propulsion (marine engin.: gen.)	
VM753-757	Propellers (marine engin.)	623.81473
VM770	Diesel, oil, & gas engines (marine engin.)	623.8723
VM773	Electric propulsion (marine engin.)	623.8726
VM779	Fuels, Marine engine	623.874
VM781-861	Ships' appliances (engin.)	
VM781	Appliances, Ships' (engin.: gen.)	623.86
VM791	Anchors, cables, etc. (marine engin.)	
VM815	Lights, Ships' (engin.)	
VM821	Pumps, Marine (engin.)	
VM841-845	Steering gear, Marine (engin.)	
VM851	Hatchways, ladders, other special fittings (marine engin.)	
VM880	Ship trials (gen.)	
VM881.A-Z	Trials, Ship (by name of vessel)	
VM901-965	Maintenance & building devices & procedures, Marine (engin.)	
VM901	Shipbuilding & maintenance appliances & activities (engin.: gen.: SEE TC361 & 363 for dry & floating docks)	
VM951	Fouling, corrosion, etc. (marine engin.)	
VM961	Scraping, painting, etc. (marine engin.)	
VM965	Welding & cutting, Underwater (marine engin.)	
VM975-989	Diving (marine engin.: SEE GV840.S78 for skindiving)	
VM977	Diving (marine engin.: hist.)	627.7209, 623.8257 (subs.), 359.3257 (subs.—naval ops.), 797.23 (scuba)
VM980	Biography (divers: marine engin.)	
VM981	Diving (marine engin.: gen.)	627.72
VM985-989	Diving (marine engin.: special types)	

Z	BIBLIOGRAPHY	010
Z1236	Bibliographies (U.S.: hist.)	016.97309
Z1244	Bibliographies (U.S.: hist.: 1900-45)	016.9730904, .97309044 (WWII)
Z1249.M5	Bibliographies (mil. hist.: U.S.)	016.3550973, .35500973,
Z1249.N3	Bibliographies (naval hist.: U.S.)	016.3590973, .35900973, .35930973, .3593310924
Z2016-2020+	Bibliographies (G.B.: hist.)	016.941-942
Z2021.N3	Bibliographies (naval hist.: G.B.)	016.3590941
Z2237	Bibliographies (Ger.: hist.)	016.94309
Z2241.M5	Bibliographies (mil. hist.: Ger.)	016.3550943
Z2506-2510+	Bibliographies (Rus.: hist.)	016.94709
Z3306-3308	Bibliographies (Japan: hist.)	016.95209
Z3308.M5	Bibliographies (naval hist.: Japan)	016.3590952
Z6207.E8 or .W7	Bibliographies (WWI)	016.9403
Z6207.W8	Bibliographies (WWII)	016.94053-94054, .36
Z6616	Bibliographies (naval sci. & hist.)	016.35909, .35900722
Z6724	Bibliographies (mil. sci. & hist.)	016.35509, 355.009, .0009

II. DEWEY DECIMAL CLASSIFICATION SYSTEM (DDC)

Dewey Decimal Classification numbers consist of three digits followed in some instances by a decimal point and one or more digits beyond the decimal. These added numerals may represent divisions of the higher subject unique to that class. They may ALSO be repeating subdivisions taken from the ends of other specified numbers or from certain standard or geographic tables. The complete call numbers end with a letter and number usually for the author's last name.

The basic concept of the Dewey class system is to divide all knowledge into 1000 hierarchical categories running from 000 through 999. Each group of 100 numbers then represents a related area of research. For instance, the 900's belong to the class of History and Geography. Within each set of 100 or 10 or even within single numbers users can find associated material extending out to the third digit and beyond the decimal point as well.

Dewey numbers differ from Library of Congress numbers in several ways, some of which are discussed in the LC introduction. DDC uses digits sometimes succeeded by decimalized numbers for the classification scheme, whereas LC employs letters followed by numerals possibly followed by more letter-number subject subdivisions. Dewey has fewer basic numbers and tries to keep allied material closer together in a tighter overall schema. Further, DDC call numbers utilized in many libraries tend to have fewer identification lines than LC but may well have longer ones if many numbers past the decimal are applied. Incidentally, remember to look at the earlier digits past the decimal to keep proper order rather than going by total number of digits. Therefore, 355.34 shelves AFTER 355.338.

Since many DDC libraries try to avoid overlong numbers traveling six or more digits past the decimal, one can generally count on Dewey numbers to show less specificity in practice than their LC counterparts. The obvious hierarchical nature of the Dewey system, however, makes it more mnemonic for some people and may appear to bring related titles more closely together on the shelves.

Because of its relatively tight character, DDC has not always comfortably incorporated new subject concepts or historical developments. The hierarchical logic of the scheme and its available subdivisions has nevertheless made it a popular model of both sophistication and simplicity. Basic Dewey numbers are definitely easier than LC numbers to remember.

Most public libraries utilize the Dewey system of classification and shelving. In addition, some academic libraries use Dewey or have a split collection, with newer titles probably ordered by LC.

This part of the classification section consists of an outline of the primary Dewey groups followed by an extensive listing of pertinent military, engineering, and historical areas. Brief descriptions of each number are given, and similar Library of Congress numbers follow when available or relevant.

A single index to both Dewey and LC class numbers can be found after the Dewey listings. As mentioned before, certain topics do not easily translate from LC to DDC. Also, while each book or resource item can obviously receive only one call number in the cataloging process, every item may well receive several subject or other headings. Furthermore, subject and corporate headings may provide the greatest focus for certain specific matters. Therefore, readers should check the overall classification index as well as the LC headings section after it in order to find the most leads.

DEWEY CLASS NUMBERS: DESCRIPTIONS: POSSIBLE LC CLASS NUMBERS

000-099	General works	
010	Bibliography	Z; sometimes D-F, U-V, or other subject classes
016	Bibliographies (specific subjects)	Z; sometimes D-F, U-V, or other subject classes
100-199	Philosophy & psychology	B-BD, BH-BJ, BF
200-299	Religion	BL-BX
300-399	Social sciences	G-H, J-L, U-V
355-358	Military science	U
359	Naval science	V
400-499	Language	P
500-599	Sciences (pure) & math	Q
600-699	Technology, medicine, engineering, agriculture, management	T, R, QA76, S, H
620	Engineering	T
623	Military & marine engineering	UG, VM
629.13	Aeronautics	
700-799	Arts, architecture, music, sports, & recreation	N, NB-NX, NA, M, GV
800-899	Literature	P
900-999	Geography & history	G, D-F
940.3-.499	European War (1914-18)	D501-680
940.53-5499	World War II (1939-45)	D731-838

010-019	Bibliographies (inclu. partic. kinds, subjects, etc.)	Z
016	BIBLIOGRAPHIES [SEE ALSO subject #'s like 359+, 940+, etc.]	
016.355	Bibliographies (mil. sci. & hist.)	Z6724
016.359	Bibliographies (naval sci. & hist.)	Z6616
016.9403	Bibliographies (WWI)	Z6207.E8 or .W7
016.94053-94054	Bibliographies (WWII)	Z6207.W8
016.94109	Bibliographies (G.B.: hist.)	Z2016-2020+
016.94309	Bibliographies (Ger.: hist.)	Z2237
016.94709	Bibliographies (Rus.: hist.)	Z2506-2510+
016.95209	Bibliographies (Japan: hist.)	Z3306-3308
016.97309	Bibliographies (U.S.: hist.)	Z1236-1245+

300-399	Social sciences	G-H, J-L, U-V
300-309	Social sciences (gen.)	H1-99
320-329	Political science	J
330-339	Economics	HB-HJ
340-349	Law	K
350-359	Public administration	H-J
355-359	Military & naval science	U, V
370-379	Education	L
380-389	Commerce, communications, & transport	HF, HE

355-358	Military forces & science	U
356-359	Warfare & military forces (types)	UD-UG, V
358.41	Air warfare (gen.)	
359	Naval science	V

355	MILITARY SCIENCE & ORGANIZATION (ALSO armed forces, ground forces, etc.: officers' hdbks. here at 355) U, U21+
355.003	Dictionaries & encyclopedias (mil. sci.) U24-25
355.0082	Women in armed forces
355.0092	Biography, Military U51-55
355.02	War & warfare U21, U21.2, U102
355.021	Warfare (summary topics) U161-162, UA10
355.0213	Militarism & antimilitarism (inclu. mil.-indus. complex) JX1952, JX1963, UA23, U21.5, JF195.C5
355.0215	Limited war (ALSO older titles on total war) UA11+, U21+, UA11
355.022	Sociological factors of war [SEE ALSO 303.66 & 306.2]
355.023	Economic factors of war [PREFER 355.02] HB195, HC65, JX1953
355.027	War (causes) U21.2, HB195, JX1952
355.0272	Causes of war (political)
355.0273	Causes of war (economic) HB195
355.0274	Causes of war (sociological)
355.0275	Causes of war (psychological)
355.028	War (aftermath: occupation, reconstruc., etc.)
355.03	Military status (gen.: inclu. policy)
355.031	Alliances, Military
355.032	Military missions & attachés
355.033	Military status (gen. hist.) D25, U21+, U27, UA15
355.033001-033005	Military status (hist. periods)
355.033004	Military status (20th c.) U42
355.0330041	Military status (1900-1919)
355.0330043	Military status (1930-39)
355.0330044	Military status (1940-49)
355.03301-03309	Military status (by area or country)
355.03304	Europe (mil. status)
355.033043	Germany (mil. status)
355.033052	Japan (mil. status) UA845+
355.033073	United States (mil. status) UA23
355.033094	Australia (mil. status) UA870+
355.0332+	Military capability
355.033244	France (mil. capabil.)
355.033251	China (mil. capabil.)
355.033273	United States (mil. capabil.)
355.0335+	Policy, Military
355.033541-033542	Great Britain (mil. policy) UA647+, UA647-668
355.033543	Germany & Central Europe (mil. policy) UA710+, UA710-719
355.033547	Russia (mil. policy) UA770+
355.033551 (China)-033552 (Japan)	Japan & China (mil. policy) UA830, UA835+, UA845+
355.033573	United States (mil. policy)
355.033594	Australia (mil. policy) UA870-874
355.07	Research & development, Military
355.1	MILITARY LIFE, CUSTOMS, & POSTMILITARY BENEFITS U750, U22
355.11	Military life (service periods, promotion, vet. benefits, etc.)
355.112	Promotion & demotion (mil.) UB320+
355.113	Leaves, furloughs, other inactive periods (mil.)
355.114	Discharge, retirement, other termination (mil.) UB320+
355.115	Veterans' benefits UB356-405, UB356-358
355.1151	Pensions, Veterans' [PREFER now 331.25291355]

355.12	Living conditions, Military	U750-773, U750, U765
355.123	Morale, Military	U22
355.129	Military living conditions (partic. situations)	U765+
355.1292	Basic training (mil. living conditions: ALSO regular quarters)	
355.1293	Transport & maneuvers (mil. living conditions)	
355.1294	Combat conditions (mil. life)	
355.1295	Military prison life (SEE ALSO 365.48)	
355.1296	Prisoner-of-war camps (mil. life: SEE ALSO 365.45)	UB800-805
355.13	Conduct & rewards, Military	U765+
355.133	Discipline & conduct, Military (regulation)	
355.1332	Punishment & enforcement, Military	
355.13323	Military police & conduct enforcement	
355.13325	Military prisons (SEE ALSO 365.48)	UB800-805
355.1334	Mutinies & military offenses (SEE 364.138 for war crimes)	UB780+
355.1336	Etiquette, Military	U765+
355.134	Rewards & privileges, Military	UB430-435
355.1342	Medals, decorations, badges, etc. (mil. rewards)	
355.1349	Gun salutes & other military rewards (misc.: USE 355.134 with 1989+ pubns.)	
355.135	Salaries, Military (SEE ALSO 355.64)	UC70-75 (U.S.), UC91-258 (other places), UC180-183 (Ger.), UC184-187 (G.B.), UC241 (Japan)
355.14	Uniforms, Military (inclu. insignia, etiquette of, etc.)	UC480-535, UC483 (U.S.)
355.15	Colors & standards, Military	UC590-595, U360-365
355.16	Celebrations & commemorations, Military	
355.17	Ceremonies, Military	U350-355
355.2	RESOURCES, MILITARY	UA18, UA10
355.21	Military resources (prep., review, preserv.)	
355.22	Human resources (mil.)	UA17.5, UB320+, UB340+
355.223	Recruitment & enlistment, Military	
355.2232	Training, Reserve	
355.2234	Qualifications, Service (mil.)	
355.2236	Commissioning, registration, classification, exams, etc. (mil. manpower procure.)	UB330+, U400+
355.22362	Enlistment, Military	UB320-325, UB323 (U.S.)
355.22363	Draft, Military	UB340-345, UB343 (U.S.)
355.224	Conscientious objectors	UB341-342
355.225	Universal service & training (mil. resources)	UB350-355
355.23	Civilian personnel (mil. resources)	
355.24	Raw materials (mil. resources)	HC110.A-Z, UA18, UA929.5+
355.242	Metals (mil. raw materials)	
355.243	Minerals (non-metal: mil. raw materials)	
355.245	Agricultural products (mil. raw materials)	UA929.95.A35
355.26	Industrial resources (mil. use)	UA18, UA929.5+, HC106+
355.27	Communication & transport (mil. resources)	UA940-945, UA929.95.T7, UC10+, UC270-275
355.28	Mobilization (mil. resources: inclu. requisition, commandeering, voluntary, etc.)	UA910-915, UA913 (U.S.)
355.29	Demobilization (mil. resources: gen.)	UA917

355.3	MILITARY PERSONNEL (inclu. organization; readiness of partic. groups) UA15+, UA23-39+ (U.S.)
355.309	Organization (mil. personnel: hist. & geog. treatment)
355.31	Military units (types: armies, div's., regiments, co's., mil. districts, etc.) UA, UA23-39+ (U.S.), UA646-829 (Eur.), UA830-853 (Asia), UA870-876 (Australia-Pac.)
355.33	Hierarchy, Military (mil. personnel) UA, UB410-415, UB210
355.33041	Line functions (mil. organiz.)
355.33042	Staff functions (mil. organiz.)
355.331	General & flag officers (above army col. or navy capt.) UB200, UB210
355.332	Officers, Commissioned & warrant UB407-415
355.338	Enlisted personnel (inclu. non-coms) UB320, U765+
355.34	Noncombat services (mil.: inclu. soc. srvcs., dependent srvcs., civil activ's., etc.)
355.341	Supply & administrative services, Military (canteens, post-ex's., messes, etc.: SEE ALSO 355.6 & .71) UC, UC750-755, UH80-85
355.342	Public information & relations (mil.) UH700-705, UH703 (U.S.)
355.343	Espionage & unconventional warfare (mil.: SEE ALSO 327.12) UB250-290
355.3432	Intelligence & military espionage (inclu. cryptanalysis, data analysis, etc.) UB250-251, UB251.A-Z (by country), UB270-271, UB271.A-Z (by place), UB271.x2.A-Z (by spy), UB271.R92.S565 (R. Sorge)
355.3433	Counterintelligence (mil.)
355.3434	Psychological warfare & propaganda (mil.: ALSO use 355.34 for propag.) UB275-277, UB276 (U.S.), UB277.A-Z (except U.S.)
355.3437	Subversion & sabotage (mil.) UB273-274UB275-277, UB276 (U.S.), UB277.A-Z (except U.S.)
355.345	Medical & health services, Military UH201-629, UH215, UH223-225 (U.S.)
355.346	Recreation services, Military (inclu. sports, arts, music, libraries, clubs, etc.) UH800-910, UH800, UH805 (U.S.)
355.347	Religious & counseling services, Military UH20-25
355.348	Women's military units UA565.W6 (U.S. Wac's)
355.35	Combat units (by service field) UA
355.351	Home guards & frontier troops UA42 (U.S. Nat. Guard)
355.352	Expeditionary & colonial forces UA14, UA668 (G.B.), UA709 (Fr.), UA719 (Ger.), UA849 (Jp.)
355.356	Allied forces (inclu. various multi-nat. & combined ops.) UA12 (U.S.), UA15, U260 (comb. ops.)
355.357	International forces (PERHAPS PREFER 355.356)
355.359	Foreign legions
355.37	Reserves, Army UA, UA42 (U.S.), UA50-549 (U.S.: by state), UA661 (G.B.)
355.4	STRATEGY & MILITARY OPS. (plans, attack, defense, etc.) UA11, UA23 (U.S.), U27, U42-43, U102, U161-167
355.409	Military ops. (hist's. & types of persons: SEE ALSO 355.47 for geog. treat.) U27-43
355.41	Support & logistics, Military (logistics, camouflage, p.o.w. care, etc.) U168, UC260-270
355.411	Logistics & troop movement

355.412	Encampments	U180-185
355.413	Reconnaisance & patrols	U220

355.415   Troop support (communication, supply, medical, p.o.w.'s, etc.:
         ALSO use 355.41 for newer titles on p.o.w. care)
                 UC260-267, UA940-945

355.42   Tactics, Military   U164-167.5, U165

355.422   Military tactics (partic. kinds: commando, retreats, blitz, landings,
         attacks & counters, etc.)

355.423   Tactics, Military (in different terrains, climates, weathers)
         U167.D4 (desert), .F6 (forest), .J8 (jungle), .W5 (winter)

355.424   Animals, Use of (mil. sci.)

355.425   Guerrilla tactics (SEE 355.0218 for guer. war)   U240

355.426   Urban warfare tactics   U167.5.S7

355.43   Nuclear ops., Military (also gen. strategy: USE 355.4 for post-'88 titles
         on gen. strategy)   U161-163

355.44   Siege warfare   UG443-449

355.45   Home defense (coasts, frontiers, other valuable redoubts)
         UA (gen.), UG410-442 (fortific's.), UG410-412 (U.S.),
         UG428-430 (Eur.), UG429.G7 (G.B.)

355.46   Combined ops., Military (2 or more types of forces)

355.47   Geography, Military (tactical & strategic)   UA985-997

355.473	United States (mil. geog.)	UA993
355.474	Europe (mil. geog.)	UA990, UA995.E
355.4741-4742	Great Britain (mil. geog.)	UA995.G7
355.4743	Germany & Central Europe (mil. geog.)	UA995.G3
355.4747	Russia (mil. geog.)	UA995.R9
355.4751	China (mil. geog.)	UA995.C
355.4752	Japan (mil. geog.)	UA995.J2
355.47599	Philippines (mil. geog.)	
355.4761-4762	Tunisia & Egypt (mil. geog.)	
355.477287	Panama (mil. geog.: SEE ALSO .47862)	
355.478	South America (mil. geog.)	
355.4793	Melanesia & New Zealand (mil. geog.)	
355.47935	Solomon Islands (mil. geog.)	UA995.S
355.4794	Australia (mil. geog.)	UA995.A
355.4795	New Guinea (mil. geog.)	
355.4796	Micronesia & Polynesia (mil. geog.)	
355.47966	Caroline Islands	
355.47967	Mariana Islands (mil. geog.)	UA995.M
355.47969	Hawaiiian Islands (mil. geog.)	UA995.H
355.48	Analysis, Military (real & mock events)	UA719-740+, U161-167+
355.49	Occupation & government, Military	D802 (WWII)

355.5   TRAINING & EDUCATION, MILITARY   U400-717, U400 (gen.),
         U403 (modern), U408 (U.S.), U410 (West Pt.), U510-549 (G.B.)

355.50973   Education & training, Military (U.S.)

355.52   Military maneuvers   U250-255

355.54   Basic training (mil.: inclu. drills, survival exercises, etc.)
         U400-717, U765-773, U320-325

355.544   Encampment & field training (mil.)   U180-185, UG400-409+

355.547   Small arms & bayonet training   UD380-415, U169

355.548   Hand-to-hand combat & self-defense (training: inclu. unarmed &
         knife fighting)   U167.5.H3, U262

355.55   Training, Officer (mil. sci.)   U400-717 (educ.)

355.56   Training, Technical (mil. sci.)

355.6	MILITARY ADMINISTRATION UB-UC	
355.61	Personnel administration, Military (civilian & mil.) UB160-165, UB180-197, UB410-415 (officers), UB320-338	
355.62	Administration, Military supply & finance UC260-267, UA	
355.621	Supply administration (mil.) UC260-267	
355.6211	Contract administration (mil.) UC267	
355.6212	Procurement (mil. supplies) UC263-267, HD3858-3860	
355.6213	Supplies, Military (use & disposal)	
355.622	Financial administration (mil.) UB150-155, UC263-267, UA21-876, UA910-915	
355.63	Military inspection UB240-245	
355.64	Salaries & wages, Military (admin.: SEE ALSO 355.135) UC70-75	
355.65-66	Clothing, food, & equipment (mil. admin.: PREFER 355.81) UC460-535, UC700-735	
355.67	Housing administration (mil.: SEE ALSO 355.71 & .12 [gen.]) UC400-440	
355.693	Mail, Military	
355.699	Graves registration & military burial	
355.7	MILITARY INSTALLATIONS & LAND (inclu. bases, forts, camps, posts, etc.) UA26+ (U.S.), UC400-405, UA600-876	
355.709	Military bases, camps, forts, reservations, etc. (geog. & hist. applic.)	
355.71	Quarters, Military (barracks, p.o.w. camps etc. on-site) UC400-405	
355.72	Medical installations, Military UH470-475	
355.73	Artillery installations (arsenals, depots, target ranges, schools, etc.) UF540-545	
355.74	Engineering installations, Military	
355.75	Supply depots, Military UC260-269	
355.79	Land (mil. bases, reservations, etc.)	
355.8	EQUIPMENT & SUPPLIES, MILITARY U800+, UC260-267	
355.81	CLOTHING, FOOD, CAMP EQUIPMENT, ETC. (SEE ALSO .65-66) UC460-465+, UC700-705	
355.82	Ordnance UF520-780, U800-823+	
355.821	Artillery (gen.)	
355.8212	Artillery, Field UF400-405	
355.8217	Artillery, Coast UF450-455	
355.8218	Artillery, Naval (SEE ALSO 359.8218) VF320-325	
355.822	Artillery (specific pieces)	
355.823	Gun mounts	
355.824	Small arms UF520-537+	
355.82424	Automatic firearms (rifles, machine guns, etc.) UF620	
355.82425	Rifles UD390-395	
355.8243	Revolvers & pistols UD410-415	
355.825	Bombs, ammunition, etc.	
355.82511	Grenades, mines, etc.	
355.825114	Grenades, Hand & rifle UF765	
355.825115	Mines (mil. equip.) UG490	
355.825119	Nuclear weapons UG1282.A8	
355.82516	Chemical & biological weapons (projectiles etc.) UG447-447.8	
355.8252	Explosives UF860-880	
355.82542	Detonators	
355.82543	Rockets, Tactical	
355.82545	Demolition charges	
355.8255	Ammunition, Small arms	

355.82594	Biological agents (mil.)
355.826	Sighting apparatus & other ordnance access. UF848-856
355.83	Transport equipment & supplies, Military (vehicles, fuel, trains, etc.)
	UC270-360, UC270-275, UC340-345, UC260-267, UG615-620
355.85	Communication equipment, Military UG570-613, UA940-945
355.88	Medical supplies UH440-445

356-357	Land forces warfare UD-UF
356	FOOT FORCES WARFARE UD, U14-43, UA
356.1	INFANTRY UD, UD15, UD21-124 (by place), UD144-145+, UA
356.11	Motorized infantry (pubns. before 1989 may inclu. regular infan. also)
	U167.5.M6, UD15, UD21-124+, UA
356.15	Irregular troops (guerrillas, brigands, etc.) U240, U167.5.A-Z
356.16	Troops, Special-purpose U167.5.A-Z
356.162	Snipers, bazookamen, machine-gunners, & other special-weapon
	troops U167.5.A-Z, UD390+, UF620
356.164	Troops, Ski & mountain UD470-475, U167.5.W5
356.166	Paratroops UD480-485, UD483 (U.S.), UG630-635
356.167	Rangers & commandos U262
356.18	Infantry (gen.) UD160-302, UD160 (U.S.)
356.181	Life & customs (infantry)
356.1814	Uniforms, Infantry
356.183	Tactics & operations, Infantry
356.184	Training (infantry) U400-714 (educ.), U320-325
356.186	Equipment & supplies (infantry) UD380+, UC260-267, UC460+
356.187	Installations, Infantry UC400-405, U180-185
356.189	Organization & personnel (infantry)

357	MOUNTED FORCES & WARFARE UE, UE15, UE21-124,
	UE23 (U.S.), UE57 (G.B.), UE65 (Austria), UD450-455
357.043	Organization & personnel (cavalry: inclu. specific units)
357.1	CAVALRY, HORSE UE15, UE21-124, UE150+, UA
357.184	Horse cavalry (gen. & ops.) UE150-475, UE150+, UE157+
357.5	CAVALRY, MECHANIZED UE147-149, UE150-155 (manuals),
	UE159, UE160-302 (by place)
357.52	Bicycle troops (mech. cav.) UH30-35
357.53	Motorcycle troops (mech. cav.) UC347
357.54	Mechanized cavalry (jeep, truck, other large-motor vehicle troops)
	UC340-345, UG615-620
357.58	Mechanized cavalry (gen. & ops.) UE147-155, UE159,
	UE160-302 (by place)

358	SPECIALIZED FORCES & WARFARE (armored land, technical land, &
	air) UE-UG
358.1	ARTILLERY, LAND MISSILE FORCES, & ARMORED WARFARE
	UF, UF15, UF21-124, UE147, UA32-33 (U.S.), UA
358.12	Army artillery (inclu. field & antitank) UF400-405, UF15,
	UF21-124 (by place), UF150-157+ (manuals & tactics)
358.13	Artillery, Antiaircraft (land) UF625
358.16	Artillery, Coast UF450-455
358.17	Missile forces & warfare (land: may be mostly post-WWII)
	UG1310-1315
358.171	Guided missile forces (land: gen.)
358.175	Rocket forces (land: types)
358.18	Armored forces & warfare (tanks, armored cav., etc.) UG446.5, UE147

358.2	ENGINEER FORCES, ARMY	UG15, UG21-124 (by place), UG23 (U.S.),UG500-620
358.22	Construction & maintenance (army engineers)	UG360-390+, UG15-124
358.23	Bomb disposal & demolition (army engineers)	UG370, UG550-555
358.24	Communications, signaling, & cryptography forces (mil. engineers)	UG570-611.5, UA940-945, UB290 (cryp.)
358.25	Transportation services (mil. engineers)	UC270-275, UG345 (rail)
358.3	TECHNICAL FORCES (chem., biol., & radiation warfare: pre-1989 titles may cover camouflage construc. & war matériel manufac.)	
358.34	Chemical warfare	UG447-447.6
358.38	Biological warfare	UG447.8
358.39	Nuclear warfare	UF767, U162, U165, UA
358.4	AERIAL WARFARE & AIR FORCES (inclu. naval av. for works prior to 1989--SEE 359.94 after 1988)	UG622-1425, UG630, UG633-634 (U.S.), UG635.A-Z (places besides U.S.), VG90-95 (naval av.)
358.403	Air forces (policy & status)	UG630-635, UA
358.407	Research & development (air forces equip. & supplies)	
358.41	Air warfare (gen.)	
358.411	Air force life & customs	U750-773, UG770-775, UG1130-1135
358.41112	Promotion & demotion (air forces)	UB320-325, UB410-415
358.4112	Living conditions (air forces)	
358.4113	Conduct, discipline, & reward (air forces: etiquette, enforcement, punishments, etc.)	UB790-795, UB430-435
358.4114	Uniforms, Air force	UG1160-1165
358.412	Resources, Air force	UG630+, UG1100+
358.4122	Human resources (air forces: enlistment etc.)	UG880-885
358.4124-4126	Industrial resources & raw materials (air forces)	UG1100-1105, UG630+
358.4127	Communication & transport (air force resources)	UC330-335, UA940-945
358.413	Structure & personnel, Air force	UG770-775, UG1130-1135
358.4131	Air force units (types)	
358.4133	Hierarchy, Air force	UG770-775
358.41331	General officers (air forces)	UG790-795
358.41332	Commissioned & warrant officers, Air force	UG820-825
358.41338	Enlisted personnel & non-coms, Air force	UG820-825
358.4134	Noncombat services (air forces)	
358.41343	Unconventional warfare (air forces: intelligence, propaganda, etc.)	
358.41345	Medical & health services, Air force	UH201-655
358.41348	Women in air forces	
358.41356	Allied forces (air)	UG625, UG630+
358.4137	Reserves, Air force	UG850-855
358.414	Air force ops. (gen.)	UG630, UG633-635, UG700-765
358.41409	Air warfare (hist.: gen.)	UG625
358.4141	Logistics & support, Air force	UG1100-1105
358.41415	Troop support (air forces)	UG700-705, UG260
358.4142	Tactics, Air force	UG700-705
358.4143	Strategy, Air force	U162-163, UG633-635
358.4145	Home defense, Air force	UG730-735, UG630-635
358.4147	Geography, Air warfare	UG633-635, UA
358.41474	Europe (air war geog.)	
358.414741	Great Britain (air war geog.)	UG635.G7
358.414743	Germany (air war geog.)	UG635.G3
358.414747	Russia (air war geog.)	

358.41475	Asia (air war geog.)
358.414751	China (air war geog.)
358.414752	Japan (air war geog.)
358.414773	United States (air war geog.) UG633
358.41479	Pacific (air war geog.)
358.4148	Analysis, Air warfare (real & imagined) UG630-635
358.415	Training & education, Air force UG637-639
358.4152	Maneuvers, Air force (training)
358.4155	Training, Officer (air forces)
358.4156	Training, Technical (air forces)
358.416	Air force administration UG770-775, UG1100-1135, UG630-635
358.4161	Air force personnel UG1130-1135
358.4162	Finances & supplies (air force admin.) UG1100-1105, UG1100-1425
358.416212	Equipment & supply procurement (air forces) UG1120-1125, UG1123 (U.S.)
358.4164	Wages & salaries, Air force UG940-945, UC74 (U.S.), UC90+
358.4165-4166	Clothing, food, & equipment (air forces) UG1100-1105, UG1160-1165, UC460-465, UC700-705
358.4167	Housing administration (air forces) UG1140-1145
358.417	Bases & fields, Air force UG634.5.A-Z (U.S.: by name), UG635.A-Z (other countries)
358.4171	Barracks & quarters, Air force UG1140-1145
358.418	Matériel & equipment, Air force UG1100-1425+, UG1100-1105
358.4182	Ordnance, Air force UG1270-1275
358.4183-4184	Combat & support aircraft UG1240-1245, UG1242.A-Z (by type), UG1243 (U.S.), UG633-635, VG90-95 (naval), TL685+
358.42	Bomber forces & ops. UG1242.B6, UG633-635, UG633 (U.S.), TL685.3, TL686.A-Z (by co. or name)
358.43	Pursuit & fighter forces & ops. (air) UG1242.F5, UG633 (U.S.), UG635.A-Z (places except U.S.), TL685.3, TL686.A-Z (by co. or name)
358.44	Transport groups (air forces) UC330-335, UG633-635, UG1242.T
358.45	Reconnaissance forces, Air (inclu. antisub. work) UG760-765, UG1242.R4
358.46	Air force communications & ops. UA940-945, UG611-612.5
358.47	Engineering services (air forces)
359	NAVAL FORCES & WARFARE V-VM, V27-55, V101-109
359.001	Theory & philosophy (naval warfare)
359.003	Dictionaries & encyclopedias (naval forces) V23
359.009+	Sea forces & warfare (hist.) VA, D-F, VA10, VA25-55
359.00941-00942	Great Britain (naval hist.) VA452-467, DA70-89
359.00943	Germany (naval hist.) VA510-519
359.00952	Japan (naval hist.) VA650-659
359.0092	Biography, Naval V61-64, V63.A-Z (U.S.: by name), V64.A-Z (other countries)
359.00973	United States (naval hist.) VA49-395, VA50-70, E182, E746 (20th c.)
359.03+ (country #s follow)	Policy & status, Naval VA
359.030941	Great Britain (naval policy & status)
359.030952	Japan (naval policy & status)
359.030973	United States (naval policy & status)
359.07	Research & development (naval equip. & supplies) V390-395

359.1	LIFE & CUSTOMS, NAVAL	V720-743, V110-145
359.11	Service periods (navies)	
359.112	Promotion & demotion (navies)	
		VB260-275, VB307-315
359.113	Furloughs, leaves, other inactive periods (navies)	
		VB260-275, VB307-315
359.114	Retirement, resignation, other service termination (navies)	
359.12	Living conditions (navies)	V720-743, V720 (gen.), V735 (modern),
		V736 (U.S.), V737 (G.B.)
359.123	Morale (navies)	
359.129	Living conditions (navies: partic. situations)	
359.1292	Naval living conditions (training or perm. bases)	
359.1294	Battle conditions, Naval	
359.13	Conduct & rewards, Naval	VB840-845, VB843 (U.S.)
359.133	Regulation of conduct, Naval	
359.1332	Discipline & enforcement (naval conduct)	VB850-855, VB890-925
359.13323	Enforcement (naval conduct)	
359.13325	Punishments (naval conduct)	
359.1334	Mutiny & other naval offenses	VB850-880
359.1336	Etiquette, Naval	V720-743, VB260-265, VB307-315
359.134	Rewards (navies: inclu. privileges, citations, medals, etc.)	
		VB330-335
359.1342	Medals, decorations, other reward insignia (navies)	
359.14	Naval uniforms (insignia, service, etiquette, etc.)	VC300-345
359.15	Colors & standards (navies)	V300-305
359.16	Commemorations & celebrations (navies)	V310
359.17	Naval ceremonies	V310
359.2	RESOURCES, NAVAL	
		VB, VB21-124 (by place), VB23 (U.S.), VB144-146,
		VA49-750 (by place), VA50-80+ (U.S.)
359.21	Naval resources (preparation, eval., preserv.)	
359.22	Human resources (navies)	
359.223	Recruitment & enlistment (navies)	VB260-315
359.2232	Training, Naval reserve	V400-695
359.2234	Qualifications (naval personnel)	
359.2236	Commissioning, draft, examination, registration, other methods of	
	naval personnel procurement	VB260-275 (enlisted pers.),
		VB307-315 (officers)
359.22362	Voluntary enlistment (navies)	
359.22363	Conscription or draft (navies)	
359.229	Women in naval forces	VA49-750, VA390.W (U.S. Waves)
359.23	Civilian personnel (navies)	VB170-187
359.24	Raw materials (naval resources)	VC260-267, VF390+
359.26	Industrial resources (navies)	
359.27	Communication & transport (naval resources)	VC530-580 (trans.),
		VB255, VG70-85, V270
359.28	Naval mobilization	VA48, VA77-750, VA77 (U.S.)
359.29	Naval demobilization	VB277, UA917

359.3	ORGANIZATION & PERSONNEL, NAVAL VA, VA50 (U.S.), VB21-124
359.31	Squadrons, fleets, flotillas, etc. (naval units) VA, VA63.A-Z (U.S.), VB200-205
359.32	Ships & crews (naval forces) V750-895, V750, VA (indiv. ships)
359.325	Ships, Powered (as units: group op. in squadrons etc., crew duties & life, hist's. of indiv. ships in most cases: SEE ALSO 359.83 & .835-836 for ships as equip.: PREFER .325+ when in doubt) V750, V765-767, V799-800
359.3251	Naval armor & ordnance V900-905, V950-980, VF, VF23 (U.S.)
359.3252	Battleships (units) V750, V765-767, V799-800, VA, VA65.A-Z (U.S.: by name)
359.3253	Cruisers (in units) V820-820.5, VA65.A-Z (U.S.: by name)
359.3254	Destroyer escorts & destroyers (units) V825-825.5, VA65 (U.S.)
359.3255	Aircraft carriers (units: SEE ALSO 359.9435 for pubns. after 1988) V874-875, V874.3 (U.S.), V874.5.A-Z (other places), VA65.A-Z (U.S.: by name)
359.3256	Landing craft (navies: units) V895
359.3257	Naval submarines (units: SEE ALSO 359.933 after 1988) V857-859, V858 (U.S.), V859.A-Z (other countries), VA65.A-Z (U.S.: by name), VM365-367 (construc.)
359.32572	Submarines, Diesel & electric (navies: units)
359.3258	Combat vessels, Small (P.T.'s etc.: units) V830-840, V880-885
359.326	Support vessels, Naval (units) V865
359.3262	Minesweepers & minelayers (navies: units) V885, V856+
359.3263	Coast guard vessels (units) VM397
359.3264	Military transport vessels & hospital ships (units: SEE ALSO 359.9853 for transp. ships on pubns. after 1988) VA79 (transports), VG450 (hosp. ships)
359.3265	Military supply ships (freighters, tankers, etc.: units: SEE ALSO 359.9853 after 1988) VA79
359.33	Hierarchy, Naval V110-145, VA, VB21-124, VB23 (U.S.), VB257-258.5, VB203
359.33041	Line positions (naval hier.)
359.33042	Staff positions (naval hier.)
359.331	Flag officers, Naval (above captain) VB190, VB200-205, VB310-315
359.332	Officers, Commissioned & warrant (navies) VB307-315
359.338	Enlisted personnel & non-coms, Naval VB260-275
359.34	Non-combat services, Naval VG1-2029+, VC10-580+
359.341	Supply services, Naval (canteens, post exch's, messes, etc.) VC, VC10, VC20-258 (overall by place), VC20-65 (U.S.), VC260-410
359.342	Public relations & information (navies) VG500-505
359.343	Unconventional warfare (navies) VB230-250
359.3432	Intelligence, Naval VB230-250, VB230, UB250-271
359.3433	Counterintelligence, Naval
359.3434	Naval propaganda & psychological warfare UB275-277
359.3437	Sabotage, Naval VG86-88 (underwater demolition), UB273-274
359.345	Medical & nursing services (navies) VG100-475, VG115, VG121-224 (overall by place), VG123 (U.S.), VG350-355 (nurse corps)
359.346 etc.)	Recreation services, Naval (sports, arts, music, dancing, libraries, VG2020-2029, UH800-910
359.347	Religious & counseling services, Naval VG20-25, VG2000
359.348	Women's naval units (gen.) VA
359.351	Home guard naval forces VA45
359.356	Allied naval forces (inclu. various coalition forces) VA40-42, VA, U260
359.37	Reserves, Naval VA45, VA, VA80+

359.4	STRATEGY & NAVAL OPS. (SEE ALSO 359.43 for strategic works
	prior to1989) V27-55, V101-107, VA, VA10, VA50-750
359.409	Naval ops. (hist's.: gen.) V27-55
359.41	Support & logistics, Naval V179, VC10
359.411	Logistics, Naval V179
359.413	Reconnaissance, Naval V190
359.415	Troop support, Naval
359.42	Tactics, Naval V167-178
359.43	Strategy, Naval (PREFER 359.4 with titles after 1988) V160-165
359.45	Home defense, Naval VA45, V200
359.46	Combined ops., Naval (2 or more types of forces)
359.47	Geography, Naval (strategic & tactical) UA985-997, VA160-178,
	VA49-750 (by place)
359.474	Europe (naval geog.) VA450
359.4741-4742	Great Britain (naval geog.) VA452-467, VA454 (gen.)
359.4743	Germany (naval geog.) VA510-519, VA513 (gen.)
359.4744	France (naval geog.) VA500-509
359.4745	Italy (naval geog.) VA540-549
359.4747	Russia (naval geog.) VA570-579
359.4748	Scandinavia (naval geog.) VA619.S, VA590599 (Sweden)
359.4749	Europe (naval geog.: misc. areas: Greece etc.)
359.475	Asia (naval geog.) VA620-639
359.4751	China (naval geog.) VA630-639
359.4752	Japan (naval geog.) 650-659
359.47598	Indonesia & Borneo (naval geog.) VA667.I or .B
359.47599	Philippines (naval geog.) VA667.P, VA750.P
359.477287	Panama (naval geog.) VA407.P
359.47729	West Indies (naval geog.) VA409-410
359.4773	United States (naval geog.) VA49-395, VA50 (gen.)
359.4774-4779	United States (naval geog.: partic. states) VA90-387
359.47759	Florida (naval geog.) VA140-147
359.4779	Pacific Coast (naval geog.) VA50
359.47794	California (naval geog.) VA100-107
359.479	Pacific (naval geog.) VA710-750, VA730
359.4793	New Zealand (naval geog.) VA720-729
359.47935	Solomon Islands (naval geog.) VA750.S
359.47936	Bismarck Islands (naval geog.) VA750.B
359.4794	Australia (naval geog.) VA710-719
359.4795	New Guinea (Papua: naval geog.) VA750.N, VA667.N
359.47965	Micronesia (naval geog.) VA750.M
359.47969	Hawaiian Islands (naval geog.) VA750.H, VA158-158.7
359.48	Analysis, Naval warfare (real & imagined battles, campaigns, etc.)
	V25-55,V160-178
359.5	TRAINING & EDUCATION, NAVAL V400-695 (by place),
	V411-438 (U.S.), V260-265
359.52	Maneuvers, Naval (training) V245
359.54	Basic training (naval) V260-265
359.55	Training, Officer (navies) V400-695, V411-438 (U.S.: Annapolis etc.),
	VB307-315
359.56	Training, Technical (navies)

359.6	ADMINISTRATION, NAVAL	VB, VB15, VB21-124 (by place), VB23 (U.S.), VC (maint.), VC10, VC20-258 (by place), VC20-65 (U.S.)
359.61	Personnel administration, Naval (civilian & mil.) VB257-258.5	
359.62	Administration, Naval supply & finance	VC10, VC20-258 (by place), VC20-65 (U.S.)
359.621	Supply administration (navies)	VC260-267, VC263 (U.S.)
359.6211	Contract administration (navies)	VC267
359.6212	Procurement (naval supples &equip.)	
359.622	Financial administration (navies)	VC20-258, VC500-505, VA
359.63	Naval inspection VB220-225	
359.64	Salary & wage administration, Naval	VC50-258, VC50-65 (U.S.)
359.65-66	Food, clothing, & equipment (naval admin.: SEE ALSO 359.81) VC280-285+, VC283 (clothing: U.S.), VC350-355 (food etc.), VC353 (U.S.)	
359.67	Housing administration (navies) VC420-425	
359.69	Burial services, graves registration, & naval military mail	
359.693	Mail, Military (navies)	
359.699	Graves registration & burial services (navies)	
359.7	BASES & STATIONS, NAVAL	V220 (gen.), VA67-750 (by place), VA69-70 (U.S.), VA459-461 (G.B.), VA516-517 (Ger.), VA576-577 (Rus.), VA656-657 (Japan), VC412-425 (maint.: gen.)
359.709+	Naval installations (hist. & geog. works)	
359.70941-70942	Naval bases & stations (in G.B.)	
359.70943	Naval bases & stations (in Ger.)	
359.70944	Naval bases & stations (in Fr.)	
359.70945	Naval bases & stations (in It.)	
359.70947	Naval bases & stations (in Rus.)	
359.70952	Naval bases & stations (in Japan)	
359.709599	Naval bases & stations (in Philip.)	
359.70973	Naval bases & stations (in U.S.)	
359.70993	Naval bases & stations (in New Z.)	
359.71	Quarters, barracks, etc. (navies) VC420-425	
359.72	Medical facilities, Naval	VG410-450, VG420 (U.S.), VG430 (G.B.)
359.73	Ordnance facilities, Naval VF380-385	
359.74	Engineering facilities, Naval	VM621-724, VM623 (U.S.), VC590-595
359.75	Supply depots, Naval VC260-265	
359.79	Land (naval bases etc.) VC412-416	
359.8	EQUIPMENT & SUPPLIES, NAVAL (develop., procure., issue, util., shipping, etc.) VC, VF, VC10, VC20-258, VC20 (U.S.: gen.), VC260-267, VF145, VF21-124, VF23 (ordnance: U.S.), VF57 (G.B.), VF73 (Ger.), VF105 (Japan), VF71 (Fr.)	
359.81	Clothing, equipment, food, & office supplies (navies: SEE ALSO 359.65-66) VC280-345 (clothing & equip.), VC350-410 (food etc.)	
359.82	Ordnance, Naval	
359.8218	Artillery, Naval	
359.825	Ammunition (navies)	
359.8251	Delivery or charge-holding devices (naval ammun.)	
359.825115	Mines (naval ammun.)	
359.82513	Shells, Naval artillery	
359.8254	Depth charges	
359.826	Sighting & range apparatus (naval ordnance)	

359.83	Transport equipment & supplies, Naval (inclu. fuel, vehicles, ships [gen.], etc.) VC530-580, VC270-279, VC276, V750-895, UC320-325
359.835-836	Warships (as equip.: develop., operation, tech. effectiveness: SEE ALSO 359.32+ for ships as units or indiv. ships)
359.8351	Armor & weapons, Naval
359.8352	Battleships (as equip.)
359.8353	Cruisers (as equip.)
359.8354	Destroyers (as equip.)
359.8355	Carriers, Aircraft (as equip.: SEE ALSO 359.94835 with works after 1988)
359.8357	Submarines, Naval (as equip.: SEE ALSO 359.93832 for titles after 1988)
359.85	Communication equipment, Naval VG70-85
359.88	Medical supplies, Naval VG290-295

359.9	SPECIALIST FORCES, NAVAL
359.93	Submarine forces & warfare
359.933	Submarines, Naval (as units: SEE 359.3257 for titles prior to 1989)
359.938	Equipment & supplies (naval submarines)
359.93832	Submarines, Conventionally-powered (navies: as equip.: SEE 359.8357 for works before 1989)
359.94	Naval air forces & warfare (SEE 358.4 for titles before 1989) VG90-95
359.943	Naval aviation units
359.9434	Flights, groups, squadrons, wings, etc. (naval aviation)
359.9435	Carriers, Aircraft (as units: SEE 359.3255 for works before 1989)
359.948	Equipment & supplies (naval aviation)
359.94834	Aircraft, Naval
359.94835	Aircraft carriers (as equip.: SEE ALSO 359.8355 on titles before 1989)

359.96 (add to .96 those #s after 355 in 355.1-.8)	
	MARINES & marine warfare VE, VE7-500+, VE15 (gen.), VE21-124 (by place), VE23 (U.S.), VE57 (G.B.), VE145-146, VG90-95 (aviation)
359.961	Life & customs (marines) VE, VE21-124, V735-743
359.9612	Living conditions (marines) VE420-425
359.962	Resources (marines) VA-VC
359.963	Organization & personnel (marines) VB21-124
359.9631	Military units (marines)
359.9633	Hierarchy (marines)
359.964	Marine military ops. VE21-124 (by place)
359.9642	Tactics (marines) VE157
359.9643	Strategy (marines) VE21-124 (by place), VE144-146
359.9647+	Geography, Marine military (strategic & tactical) VE21-124, VA
359.96479+	Pacific (marine mil. geog.) VE123, VA730
359.965	Training (marines) VE430-435, V411-695, VE422 (U.S.)
359.966	Administration (marines) VB21-124
359.967	Bases & camps (marines) VE21-124, VE23-25 (U.S.), VA67-68, VG90-95 (marine av.)
359.968	Matériel & equipment (marines) VE350-390, VF (ordnance)

359.97	Coast guard (SEE ALSO 363.286 for U.S.C.G.) VG50-55, VG53 (U.S.)	
359.98	Technical forces, Naval (engineering, communic's., etc.)	
359.9812	Artillery services, Naval	
359.982	Engineering services, Naval	
359.983	Communications services, Naval VG70-85	
359.984	Underwater reconnaissance & demolition (navies: inclu. frogmen)	
		VG86-88 (demo.), VG190 (recon.)

600-699	Technology, medicine, engineering, agriculture, management	
		T, R, QA76, S, H
620	Engineering T	
623	Military & marine engineering UG, VM	
623.8	Naval engineering & seamanship VM, VK	
629.13	Aeronautics	

623	ENGINEERING, MILITARY & NAUTICAL UG, VM (naval), V,	
		UG15 (mil.: gen.), UG21-124 (mil.: by place),
		UG23 (U.S.), V750-895 (vessels)
623.003	Dictionaries & encyclopedias (mil. & naut. engineering: SEE ALSO 603)	
		UG144-147
623.009+	Military & nautical engineering (hist. & biog. works: overall)	
		UG400-401
623.04	Military & nautical engineering (overall topics)	
623.042	Engineering, Military & nautical (optical) UG476, UG487	
623.043	Engineering, Military & nautical (electronic) UG480-485	
623.044	Engineering, Military & nautical (nuclear)	
623.045	Engineering, Military & nautical (mechanical) UG450	
623.047	Engineering, Military & nautical (construction) UG460	
623.1	Fortifications (mil. engineering) UG400-442	
623.1-7	Military engineering UG	
623.12	Military fortifications, Permanent (engineering: for titles after 1988 SEE	
	ALSO 623.1) UG405	
623.15	Military fortifications, Temporary (engineering) UG403	
623.19	Fortifications (mil. engineering: by place: for works prior to 1989 SEE	
	ALSO 623.109) UG410-442	
623.1944	Maginot Line (Fr.: fortific's.: engineering) UG429.F, UG430.M	
623.262	Mine laying & sweeping (mil. engnrg.: land) UG490	
623.263	Mine sweeping & laying (mil. engineering: marine) V856-856.5	
623.27	Demolition (mil. engineering) UG37	
623.3	Engineering, Defense UG400-442	
623.31	Defenses, Direct-invasion (barriers, flooding, traps, etc.)	
		UG375, UG403, UG407-409, UG448 (coast)
623.36	Countermining (defense engineering: SEE ALSO 623.3) UG490	
623.37	Warning systems (defense engineering: SEE 623.737 for titles	
	after 1988)	
623.38	Bunkers, caves, shelters (defense engineering: protective construc.)	
623.4	ORDNANCE (engineering & design) UF520-910+,	
		UF520-525 (gen.), UF523 (U.S.), VF (naval), VF1-580,
		VF21-124 (by place), VF23 (U.S.)
623.41	Artillery (design) UF, UF1-910+, UF15 (gen.), UF144-145 (gen.),	
		UF21-124 (by place), UF23 (U.S.), VF320-325 (naval)
623.412	Field & rail artillery (design) UF400-405, UF490-495 (rail)	
623.417	Coastal artillery (design) UF450-455	
623.418	Naval artillery (design) VF320-325, VF323 (U.S.)	
623.419	Artillery (misc.: design: for space artil. after 1988)	

623.42	Cannons, howitzers, mortars, small rockets, other specific artillery (design)	
623.43	Gun mounts (design)	
623.44	Side arms & misc. weapons (design)	UD380-425
623.441	Knives, bayonets, swords, etc. (design) UD420-425, UD400 (bayonets)	
623.442	Firearms, Portable (design) UG520-525, UD380-385+	
623.4424	Automatic weapons (machine & submach. guns, auto. rifles, etc.: design) UD390-395, UF620 (mach. g's.)	
623.4425	Rifles & carbines (design) UD390-395	
623.4426	Bazookas, grenade & rocket launchers, etc. (design) UF628-630	
623.443	Military pistols & revolvers (design) UD410-415	
623.444	Sidearms, Modern (design: SEE ALSO 623.441 or .44) UD420-425, UD400	
623.445	Flame throwers, tear-gas devices, smoke mortars, other chemical weapons (design) UG447-447.5	
623.45	Ammunition & other ruinous media (design) UF700-770	
623.451	Shells, bombs, missiles, other delivery units with charges (design) UF750-755	
623.4511	Grenades, mines, nuclear weapons (design)	
623.45114	Grenades, Hand or rifle (design) UF765	
623.45115	Mines (design) UG490, V856-856.5 (naval)	
623.45119	Nuclear weapons (design) UF767, UG1282.A8 or .H, QC773.A1 or .H	
623.4513	Artillery shells & other projectiles (design) UF750-760, VF480 (naval)	
623.4514	Shrapnel & other antipersonnel devices (design) UF760-765, VF490	
623.4516	Chemical & biological weapons (design) UG447-447.6 (chem.), UG447 (gen.), UG447.5.A-Z (type gas), UG447.8 (bio.)	
623.4517	High-explosive devices (torpedoes, blockbusters, etc.: design) V850-855 (torpedoes), UF860-870	
623.4518	Armor-piercing shells & devices (design)	
623.4519	Guided missiles (design) UG1310-1315	
623.45195	Missiles, Surface-to-surface (design)	
623.452	Explosives (design) UF860-870	
623.4526	Gunpowder, cordite, & other explosives (design: inclu. propellant types) UF870	
623.4527	High explosives (design: inclu. dynamite, nitro, TNT) TP285, TP270-295	
623.4542	Detonators (design: fuses, percus. caps, primers, etc.) UF780, VF510	
623.4543	Rockets (tactical: design) UF880	
623.4544	Charges, Demolition (destructors, bangalore torpedoes, etc.: design) UG370, UF860	
623.455	Small-arms ammunition (bullets, bazooka rockets, etc.: design) UF700, UF740-745, UF770, TS538, VF500	
623.459	Nonexplosive agents (tear gas etc.: design) UF780	
623.4592	Gases, poisons, other chemical agents (design)	
623.4594	Biological agents (ammunition: design)	
623.4595	Heat or other radiations (ammunition: design)	
623.46	Ranging & sighting apparatus (ordnance: design) UF848-856, VF520	
623.48	Maintenance & repair (ordnance) UF350-355, UF550-560	

623.5	BALLISTICS & GUNNERY (engineering)	UF800-830, UF820
623.51	Ballistics (engineering) UF820-830	
623.513	Ballistics, Interior (within bore)	UF823
623.514	Ballistics, Exterior (environmental)	UF825
623.516	Ballistics, Terminal (effects on targets)	
623.55	Gunnery (engineering) UF800-805, VF144-302	
623.551	Gunnery, Land (engineering) UF800-805	
623.553	Gunnery, Naval (engineering) VF144-302, VF145 (gen.), VF150-	
	155 (hdbks.), VF160-302 (drill bks.), VF160 (U.S.)	
623.555	Gunnery, Aircraft (engineering)	
623.557	Target detection & selection (inclu. radar & other methods: engineering:	
	USE 623.46 for ranging & siting apparatae)	
623.558	Firing & fire control (mil. engineering) UF848-856, UF848 (gen.),	
	UF850.A-Z (range finders), VF520-530 (naval)	
623.57	Recoil (mil. engineering)	
623.6	MILITARY TRANSPORT ENGINEERING UC, UC10, UC270-360,	
	UC270-275 (gen.)	
623.61	Land transport (mil. engineering)	
623.62	Construction, Road (mil. engineering) UG330	
623.63	Military railroads & rolling stock (engineering) UC310-315,	
	UF490-495 (r.r. artil.), UG345 (engnrg.)	
623.64	Naval facilities (bases, docks, artificial harbors, etc.: design)	
	V220-230, VA69-750 (by place), VA67-70 (U.S.), VM301	
623.66	Air force facilities UG633-635, UG21-124 (engnrg. by place),	
	UG360-390 (field engnrg.)	
623.6613	Air bases (mil. design) UG633-634.5 (U.S.), UG635 (other lands)	
623.663	Runways (mil. airfields: design)	
623.666	Air traffic control (mil. engineering)	
623.668	Fire-fighting (mil. airfields)	
623.67	Military bridges (design) UG335, UC320-325	
623.68	Military tunnels (design) UG340	
623.7	MILITARY ENGINEERING (misc.)	
623.71	Reconnaisance & intelligence topography (mil. engineering) UG470-474	
623.72	Photography, Military (mil. engineering) UG476	
623.73	Communications technology (mil. engineering) UG590-613.5, UG580,	
	UG590, UG570-575	
623.731	Signals, Visual (mil. engineering) UG582.V5	
623.7312	Semaphore, flag signals, & heliograph (mil. engineering)	
	UG582.S4, UG580, UG582, VK385, V300-305	
623.7313	Pyrotechnic signal devices (mil. engineering) UG580, UF860	
623.7314	Blinkers & electrooptical signal devices (mil. engineering)	
	UG580, UG614-614.5, VK387	
623.732	Telegraphy, Wire (mil. engineering) UG600-607	
623.733	Telephony, Wire (mil. engineering) UG610-610.5	
623.734	Radio & radar (mil. engineering) UG611-612.5	
623.7341	Shortwave radio (mil. engineering)	
623.7342	Radiotelegraphy (mil. engineering) UG600-607, VG76-78	
623.7345	Telephones, Radio (mil. engineering) UG611 (gen.), UG611.3 (U.S.),	
	UG611.5.A-Z (other lands), VG76-85	
623.7348	Radar (mil. engineering) UG612 (gen.), UG612.3 (U.S.),	
	UG612.5.A-Z (other places), UG612.5.G7 (G.B.), VG76-78	
623.735	Television (mil. engineering) UG613-613.5	
623.737	Air-raid warning systems (design: SEE 623.37 for titles prior to 1989)	
	UG730-735	

623.74	Vehicles, Military (design: inclu. combat & support v's. & neces. ordnance)	UC270-275+
623.741	Aircraft (lighter-than-air: mil. design)	UG1310-1375
623.742	Balloons, Military (design)	UG1370-1375
623.743	Dirigibles (mil. engineering)	TL659, UG1220-1225
623.7435	Airships, Rigid (mil. engineering)	
623.7436-7437	Airships, Semirigid & nonrigid (mil. engineering)	
623.744	Barrage ballons & nets (design)	UG1370-1375, UG730-735, UF625
623.746	Aircraft (heavier-than-air: mil. engineering)	UG1240-1245, UG630-635, TL685.3, VG90-95
623.746042	Prop-driven aircraft (mil. design)	
623.746044	Jet aircraft (mil. design)	
623.746047	Helicopters, Military (design)	TL716
623.746048	Piloting (gen.: mil. engineering: SEE ALSO 623.7463 [bombers] or other types)	TL710+, UG670-675 (manuals), UG700-705 (tactics)
623.746049	Aircraft components (cabins, engines, fuselages, instruments, wings, etc.)	TL672-683
623.7461	Ordnance, Aircraft (design)	UG1270-1275, UF530-537
623.7462	Training planes (design)	
623.7463	Bombers & fighter-bombers (mil. engineering)	TL685.3, TL686.A-Z (by manufac. or model), UG1242.B6
623.7464	Planes, Fighter (design)	TL685.3, TL686.A-Z (by manufac. or model), UG1242.F5
623.7465	Cargo & personnel transport planes (design)	TL685.7
623.7466	Rescue aircraft (mil. engineering)	
623.7467	Planes, Reconnaisance (mil. design)	UG1242.R4
623.7469	Guided aircraft (pilotless: mil. design)	UG1310-1315
623.747	Land vehicles, Motorized (mil. design)	UC270-275, UC340-345
623.7472	Personnel transport vehicles (land: mil. design)	
623.74722	Jeeps (mil. design)	
623.74723	Buses (mil. design)	
623.74724	Ambulances (mil. design)	UH500-505
623.7474	Supply transport vehicles (land: mil. design)	
623.7475	Armored cars & other combat vehicles (land: design)	
623.74752	Tanks (design)	UG446.5
623.75	Safety & sanitation (mil. engineering)	UH600-629.5, U380-385, VC417.5, VG470-475, VM481-482, V380-386
623.751	Water supply (mil. engineering)	UC780, VC410, VM503-505
623.753	Sewage disposal (mil. design)	UC430, VM481, VM503
623.754	Garbage disposal (mil. engineering)	
623.76	Electrical engineering (mil.)	UG480, VM471-479
623.77	Engineering, Camouflage (mil.)	UG449, UG1240-1245 (air forces), V215 (ships)
623.8	NAUTICAL ENGINEERING & SEAMANSHIP	VM (architec.), VK (navig.)
623.81	Naval design	VM, V750-995 (warships), VM15-20 (hist.), VM21-124 (by place), VM23 (U.S.), VM57 (G.B.), VM146 (metal ships), VM156 (theory), V750, V765, V800
623.812	Ships (design)	VM297, V765
623.812045	Submersibles (naval design)	
623.8125	Warships (powered: design)	V750, V765-767, V799-800
623.81255	Carriers, Aircraft (design)	V874-875
623.81257	Submarines (naval: design)	V858-859, VM365-367

623.814	Naval design (components & details)	VM, VM156
623.8144	Hull design (naval architec.)	VM156
623.8147	Powerplants (naval design)	VM731+
623.817	Structural theory & design (naval architec.)	VM156-163
623.818	Structural design (naval architec.: specific materials)	
623.81821	Structural design (naval architec.: steel)	VM146
623.819	Tests (naval architec.)	
623.82	Nautical craft & types	VM, VM145
623.82001	Theory & philosophy (nautical craft)	VM156
623.8201	Model ships	
623.8202	Small craft (naut. engineering)	VM320-361, VM321, VM331, VM341
623.8205	Submersibles (naut. engineering)	VM365-367
623.8208	Maintenance & repair (naut. engineering: SEE ALSO 623.00288 after 1988)	VM763 (engines)
623.821-829	Seacraft, Modern (specific types: engineering)	
623.823	Power-driven craft (naut. engineering)	VM315
623.824	Merchant ships, Powered (engineering)	
623.8243	Passenger ships (engineering)	VM381-385, VM383.A-Z (by ship name), VM385.A-Z (by co.)
623.8245	Cargo ships, freighters, & tankers (engineering)	VM391-395, VM455-459, VM455 (tankers)
623.825	Warships, Fuel-powered (engineering)	V750, V765, V797-799
623.8251	Naval ordnance (engineering)	VF, VF21-124 (by place), VF23 (U.S.), VF350-355
623.8252	Battleships (engineering)	V750
623.8253	Cruisers (naval engineering)	V820-820.5
623.8254	Destroyer escorts (d.e.'s) & destroyers (naval engineering)	V825-825.3
623.8255	Aircraft carriers (engineering)	V874-874.5
623.8256	Landing craft (naval engineering)	V895
623.8257	Submarines, Naval (engineering)	VM365-367, V857-859
623.82572	Naval submarines (diesel- & electric-powered: engineering)	
623.8258	Combat craft, Light (torpedo boats etc.: engineering)	V830-835 (p.t.'s), V880
623.826	Support ships (naval engineering)	V865
623.8262	Minelayers & minesweepers (naval engineering)	V885 (sweepers), V856-856.5 (both)
623.8263	Coast guard craft (engineering: also police boats, revenue cutters, etc.)	VM397
623.8264	Transport ships & hospital ships (naval engineering)	UC320-325, VG450 (hosp. ships)
623.8265	Supply ships (naval engineering)	V865
623.828	Lightships, icebreakers, other misc. ships (engineering)	VM451 (icebreakers)
623.829	Lifeboats & other manually-driven vessels (engineering)	VK1473, VM351, VM360 (inflatable)
623.83	Dry docks, shipyards, etc. (naval engineering)	VM301
623.84	Ship hulls (naut. engineering)	VM156
623.848	Hulls (special construc.: anti-fire & -shock, corrosion-resistant, etc.)	
623.85	Engineering systems (naut. craft: mech., electric, water, etc.)	VM471-505
623.8501	Mechanical systems (naut. craft: engineering)	
623.8503	Electrical systems (naut. craft: engineering)	VM471-475
623.8504	Electronic systems (naut. craft: engineering)	VM480-480.5
623.852	Electric lighting (naut. craft: engineering)	VM491-493

| 623.853 | Cooling & heating (naut. craft: engineering) | VM481 |
| 623.854 | Water & sanitation (naut. craft: engineering) | VM503-505 (water), VM481-483 (san.) |

623.853   Cooling & heating (naut. craft: engineering)   VM481
623.854   Water & sanitation (naut. craft: engineering)   VM503-505 (water),
           VM481-483 (san.)
623.8542   Water, Potable (naut. craft: engineering)
623.8543   Water, Sea (naut. craft: engineering)
623.8546   Sanitation (naut. craft: engineering)   VM481-483
623.856   Communications systems, Naval (engineering)   VG70-85, VB255
623.8561   Communication systems, Naval (visual: design)   V280-305
623.85612   Communication systems, Naval (flag & semaphore: design)
           V280-285, V300-305 (flags), VK385
623.85613   Communication systems, Naval (pyrotechnical: design)
623.85614   Communication systems, Naval (blinkers & electrooptical: design)
623.8564   Communication systems, Naval (radar & radiocommun.: design)
           VG76-78, UG610
623.85641   Communication systems, Naval (shortwave radio: design)
623.85642   Communication systems, Naval (radio telegraph: design)   VG70-75
623.85645   Communication systems, Naval (radio telephone: design)   VG80-85
623.85648   Communication systems, Naval (radar: design)   UG612-612.5, UG612.3 (U.S.)
623.86   Gear, equipment, & outfitting (nautical: engineering)   VM781-861, VM781 (gen.)
623.862   Rigging & gear, Nautical (anchors, masts, rope, rudders, sails, etc.: design)   VM791 (anchors), VC279.R6 (rope)
623.863   Instruments, Nautical (design)   VK573-587
623.865   Safety equipment, Nautical (fire-fighting, life-saving, etc.: design)   VK1258, VK1460-1481
623.866   Furniture (naut. design)
623.87   Power plants (marine engineering)   VM600-779, VM600, VM623 (U.S.), VM657 (G.B.), VM673 (Ger.), VM705 (Japan)
623.872   Engines, Marine (types: design)   VM731-779, VM731
623.8722   Steam engines (marine engineering)   VM741-749, TJ735-740
623.8723   Internal combustion engines (marine engineering)   VM770
623.87233   Gas-turbine engines (marine engineering)   VM740, TJ778
623.87234   Spark-ignition engines (marine engineering)
623.87236   Diesel engines (marine engineering)   VM770
623.87237   Cylinders, valves, etc. (internal combustion engines: marine engineering)   VM769
623.8726   Electric engines (marine engineering)   VM773
623.873   Engine auxiliaries (marine engineering: boilers, blowers, pumps, propellers, etc.)   VM753-757 (propellers), VM741-750 (boilers), VM821 (pumps), VM781+
623.874   Engine fuels, Marine   VM779
623.88   Seamanship   VK1-587+, VK541-547
623.881   Handling of nautical craft (gen.)   VK541
623.8812   Small craft (naut. handling)   VK543, GV811
623.8814   Handling of nautical craft (powered)   VK541, VK145, VK205, VB200-205
623.8825   Warships, Fuel-powered (handling)   VB200-205
623.88252   Battleships (handling)   V750
623.88253   Cruisers (handling)   V820-820.5
623.88254   Destroyers (handling)   V825-825.5
623.88255   Aircraft carriers (handling)   V874-875
623.88257   Submarines (navies: handling)   V857-859, V210-214

623.888	Safety technology, Marine (plus other misc. topics)	
623.8881	Loading & unloading nautical craft (plus cargo handling)	VK235
623.8882	Knots & splices (naut. ropes & cables)	VM533
623.8884	Collision & grounding, Nautical (prevention)	VK371-378
623.8885	Wrecks, Nautical (research)	VK1250+
623.8886	Fire-fighting, Nautical (technology)	VK1258
623.8887	Rescue ops., Nautical	VK1321-1424, VK1323 (U.S.), VK1445 (gen.)
623.89	Course navigation (marine: inclu. celestial)	VK549-572+
623.892	Geonavigation, Marine	
623.8920212	Tables, formulae, statistics (marine geonavigation)	
623.8922	Piloting & pilot guides, Nautical	VK1500-1661, VK1523- 1525 (U.S.), VK1645 (gen.), VK798-803
623.8923	Dead reckoning (naut. navig.)	VK572
623.8929	Harbor piloting (inclu. approach)	VK321-369.8
623.89291-89299	Pilot guides (geog. treatment) VK804-997	
623.892941-892942	British Isles (pilot guides)	VK827-838.5
623.892943	Germany (pilot guides)	VK822, VK824
623.892947	Russia (pilot guides)	VK809, VK821, VK870, VK910 (Siberia)
623.892951	China (pilot guides)	VK902-907
623.892952	Japan (pilot guides)	VK909
623.892973	United States (pilot guides: gen.)	VK993
623.892974-892979	United States (pilot guides: specific areas)	
	VK947-948 (W. Coast), VK981-982 (E. Coast)	
623.8929759	Florida (pilot guides: Key West etc.)	VK977
623.893	Navigational aids, Marine (electronic)	VK560
623.8932	Navigational aids, Marine (radio: beacons, compasses, loran, radio, etc.)	VK560-561, VG76-85
623.8933	Navigational aids, Marine (radar & microwave) VK560-561, VG76-78	
623.8938	Navigational aids, Marine (sonar & other sound-ranging)	
	VK388, VK560, VM480-480.5	
623.894	Geonavigational aids, Marine (misc. non-electronic)	
623.8942	Lighthouses	VK1000-1249 (gen. & by place), VK1010, VK1021-1124, VK1023-1025 (U.S.), VK1243 (U.S.: lists)
623.8943	Lightships	VK1010, VK1021-1124
623.8944	Beacons, buoys, etc. (marine navig.)	VK1000-1249, VK1010, VK1021-1124, VK1023-1025 (U.S.)
623.8945	Light lists (marine navig.)	VK1150-1246, VK1150, VK1151-1185 (Eur.), VK1203-1209 (Asia), VK1211-1223 (Australia & Pac.), VK1241-1246 (N.Am.)
623.8949	Tide & current tables	VK600-794, VK602 (gen.), VK610- 650 (Atl.: E.), VK628-644 (Brit. Isles & Eng. Ch.), VK653- 674 (Medit.), VK702-711 (China, Japan, Asian coasts), VK715-756 (Pac.), VK727-733 (Australia & Oceania), VK741 (Am. W. Coast), VK759-792 (Atl: W., U.S., Carib.)
629.13	AERONAUTICS	
629.1309	Flight (gen. hist.)	
629.13091+	Transoceanic flights	
629.130915	Trans-Pacific flights	
629.13092	Fliers (biog.)	
629.132	Aeronautics (principles)	
629.1323	Aerodynamics	
629.1324	Meteorology, Aviation	

```
629.1325      Flying
629.13251         Navigation, Aerial
629.13252         Piloting, Aerial
629.1325212       Takeoff (aviation)
629.1325213       Landing (aviation)
629.133+      Aircraft (types)
629.13324         Dirigibles
629.13334         Airplanes
629.133343        Propeller-driven airplanes
629.133347        Seaplanes
629.133348        Amphibious planes
629.133349        Jet airplanes
629.133352        Helicopters
629.134       Aircraft parts & components
629.13432     Wings, Aircraft
629.13434     Fuselages, Aircraft
629.134351            Fuels, Aircraft
629.134352-134354+      Engines, Aircraft
629.1346                 Maintenance & repair, Aircraft
629.135              Instrumentation, Aircraft
629.1351      Navigational instruments (air.)
629.1352      Flight instruments
629.136       Airports
629.1363      Runways, Airport
629.1366      Air traffic control systems
629.1368      Fire-fighting equipment, Airport


900-999+      HISTORY & GEOGRAPHY      G (geog.), D-F
900-909       Geography & history (gen.)     G, C-D
910-919       Geography & travel      G, D-F
920-929       Biography (sometimes placed with country #s or topical #s in 930-999 or
                   000 999)                         C-F
930-939       Ancient history      C-F
940-949       Europe      D-DR
940.3-.499        Great War (1914-18)      D501-680
940.53-5499       Second World War (1939-45)      D731-838
950-959       Asia      DS
960-969       Africa      DT
970-979       North America & America   E-F
980-989       South America   F
990-999       History (misc. areas: Oceania, Atlantic islands, Arctic, extraterr.
                   worlds, etc.)      C-F, G, Q
993-996           Oceanica   DU


900-909       GEOGRAPHY & HISTORY (gen.)      G, C-D
903           Dictionaries & encyclopedias (history: gen.)      D9
909.8         World history (gen.: 1800-)      D299, D395
909.82        1900-1999 (20th c.: gen. hist.)      D421, D443
909.821           1900-1919 (gen. hist.)      D421, D521 (WWI: gen.)
909.822           1920-1929 (gen. hist.)      D653, D655-659, D720,
                                              D723-728 (1919-39)
909.823           1930-1939 (gen. hist.)   D720, D723-728
909.824           1940-1949 (gen. hist.)      D743 (WWII: gen.), D825, D840
```

910-919	TRAVEL & GEOGRAPHY	G (geog.), D-F (descr. & travel)
912	MAPS & ATLASES G	
912.4	Europe (maps & atlases)	G1796+
912.5	Asia (maps & atlases)	G2200+
912.73	United States (maps & atlases)	G1200+, G1201
912.9	Pacific Ocean area (maps & atlases)	G2860-3012
913-919	GEOGRAPHY & TRAVEL (by locale)	
914	EUROPE (geog. & travel)	D901-980, D907 (gen.), D921 (1901-50)
914.1	Great Britain & Ireland (geog. & travel)	DA11, DA600-668, DA969-987 (Ire.)
914.2	England (geog. & travel)	DA600-668, DA600 (gen.), DA630 (1901-45)
914.3	Central Europe & Germany (geog. & travel)	DD21-43, DB21-27, D901-980
914.31-35	Germany (geog. & travel)	DD21-43, DD42 (1919-45)
914.36	Austria (geog. & travel)	DB21-27, DB26 (1901-45)
914.37	Czechoslovakia (geog. & travel)	DB191 (titles prior to 1979-80), DB2020
914.38	Poland (geog. & travel)	DK407 (1867-1945)
914.39	Hungary (geog. & travel)	DB916-917
914.4	France (geog. & travel)	DC28-45
914.5	Italy (geog. & travel)	DG428-429
914.581-582	Sicily (geog. & travel)	DG864
914.585	Malta (geog. & travel)	DG989
914.6	Spain & Portugal (geog. & travel)	DP42, DP525 (Port.)
914.7	Soviet Union & Eur. Russia (geog. & travel)	DK27
914.76	White Russia & Western U.S.S.R. (geog. & travel)	
914.77	Black Sea area (geog. & travel)	DK511.C7
914.771	Ukraine (geog. & travel)	
914.79	Caucasus (geog. & travel)	
914.8	Scandinavia (geog. & travel)	DL10
914.81-84	Norway (geog. & travel)	DL418
914.891-895	Denmark (geog. & travel)	DL118
914.897	Finland (geog. & travel: SEE ALSO 914.71 for earlier works) DK450, DL1015.2 (books cataloged after 1969-70)	
914.92	Holland (geog. & travel)	DJ39
914.931-934	Belgium (geog. & travel)	DH433
914.94	Switzerland (geog. & travel)	DQ24
914.95	Greece (geog. & travel)	DF726
914.96	Balkan Peninsula (geog. & travel)	DR15, DR1221 (later works)
914.965	Albania (geog. & travel)	DR701.S5, DR917 (later books)
914.971-976	Yugoslavia (geog. & travel)	DR309, DR1221 (later books)
914.977	Bulgaria (geog. & travel)	DR60 (1879-1950)
914.98	Rumania (geog. & travel)	DR209 (1866-1950)
914.99	Crete & Aegean Islands (geog. & travel)	DF901.C8 (Crete), .C9 (Cyclades), DS52-53, DS53.A-Z (by island), DS53.R4-6 (Rhodes)
915	ASIA (geog. & travel)	DS9 (1901-50)
915.1	China (geog. & travel)	DS710 (1901-48)
915.18	Manchuria (geog. & travel)	DS784
915.19	Korea (geog. & travel)	DS902
915.2	Japan (geog. & travel)	DS810 (1901-45)
915.3	Arabian Peninsula (geog. & travel)	DS207
915.4	India, Pakistan, & Ceylon (geog. & travel)	DS335, DS413
915.5	Persia (geog. & travel)	DS258

915.6	Middle East (geog. & travel)	DS49-49.5
915.61-66	Turkey & Cyprus (geog. & travel)	DR428, DS54 (Cyprus)
915.67	Iraq (geog. & travel)	DS70.6, DS79+
915.69	Mediterranean, Eastern (geog. & travel)	DS44, DS49, D972-973
915.691	Syria (geog. & travel)	DS94
915.694	Palestine (geog. & travel)	DS107.3
915.7	Siberia & Asiatic Russia (geog. & travel)	DK755, DK584 (C.Asia)
915.9	Southeast Asia (geog. & travel)	DS508
915.91	Burma (geog. & travel)	DS485.B74-892, DS527.6 (later bks.)
915.97	Vietnam (geog. & travel)	DS556.36
915.98	Indonesia (geog. & travel)	DS619
915.99	Philippines (geog. & travel)	DS659
915.991	Luzon (geog. & travel)	DS688.L9
915.997	Mindanao (geog. & travel)	DS688.M2
916	AFRICA (geog. & travel)	DT55 (1901-50)
916.1	Tunisia & Libya (geog. & travel)	
916.2	Egypt & Sudan (geog. & travel)	DT55 (Egypt), DT124
916.3	Ethiopia (geog. & travel)	DT378
916.4	Africa, Northwest (geog. & travel: Morocco, Canary Islands, etc.)	
		DT165, DT310 (Mor.)
916.5	Algeria (geog. & travel)	DT280
917	NORTH AMERICA (geog. & travel)	E41, E27
917.1	Canada (geog. & travel)	F1015
917.2	Mexico & Central America (geog. & travel)	F1215 (Mexico),
		F1432 (C.Am.)
917.29	Bermuda & West Indies (geog. & travel)	F1611
917.3	United States (geog. & travel: overall)	E169 (1914-45)
917.4-9	United States (geog. & travel: states, areas, & towns)	
917.4	New England & Middle Atlantic states (geog. & travel)	F2.3, F4,
		F9 (1865-1950), F106 (Mid.Atl.)
917.5	South Atlantic states & Florida (geog. & travel)	F106,
		F207.3 (S.Atl.), F309.3 (Fla.)
917.53	District of Columbia (geog. & travel)	F192.3, F194, F199
917.59	Florida (geog. & travel)	F309.3, F316
917.6	Gulf Coast & South Central states (geog. & travel)	F296 (Gulf), F396
917.64	Texas (geog. & travel)	F384.3, F391
917.7	Great Lakes & North Central states (geog. & travel)	F477.3 (Old NW.),
		F551 (Lakes area in gen.), F484.5
917.8	Great Plains & American West (geog. & travel)	F591
917.9	Pacific Coast & Far West (U.S.: geog. & travel)	F851
917.94	California (geog. & travel)	F859.3, F861, F866 (hist.: 1869-1950)
918	SOUTH AMERICA (geog. & travel)	F2211, F2223, F2236-2237
919	PACIFIC OCEAN & MISC. (geog. & travel)	DU22
919.31	New Zealand (geog. & travel)	DU411
919.32-37	Melanesia (geog. & travel)	
919.35	Solomon Islands (geog. & travel)	
919.36	Bismarck Archipelago (geog. & travel)	
919.4	Australia (geog. & travel)	DU104
919.5	New Guinea (geog. & travel)	DU740
919.6	Pacific Ocean areas (misc.: geog. & travel)	
919.65	Micronesia (geog. & travel)	DU500
919.66-67	Caroline & Mariana Islands (geog. & travel)	
919.68	Gilbert, Marshall, & related islands (geog. & travel)	
919.69	Hawaiian Islands (geog. & travel)	DU623

920-929	BIOGRAPHY & GENEALOGY	CT (gen. or collec.), D-F, other specific classes for specialists or famous people in those areas
920	BIOGRAPHY (gen.: SOMETIMES '92' or 'B' are used, followed by particular individuals in alphabetical order by last name. These may also be placed in specific discipline number areas followed by the standard subdivision, '092'. So, 355.0092 is for mil. biog.)	
923	BIOGRAPHY (social sciences: gov., law, commerce, etc.)	
923.1	HEADS OF STATE (biog.)	
923.14	Europe (biog.: heads of state)	D107
923.141-142	Great Britain (biog.: heads of state)	
923.143	Germany (biog.: heads of state)	
923.144	France (biog.: heads of state)	
923.145	Italy (biog.: heads of state)	
923.147	Russia (biog.: heads of state)	
923.15	Asia (biog.: heads of state)	DS32 (collective)
923.151	China (biog.: heads of state)	
923.152	Japan (biog.: heads of state)	
923.173	United States (biog.: heads of state)	E176.1 (Presidents: collective)
923.5	MILITARY BIOGRAPHY (SEE ALSO 355.0092, 940.3+, .53+, etc.)	
		U51-55
923.54	Biography, Military (Eur.)	
923.541-542	Military biography (G.B.)	DA54 (collec.), DA69.3.A-Z (20th c.: indiv.), DA89.1.A-Z (naval: 20th c.: indiv.), U55.G7
923.543	Military biography (Ger.)	DD100 (group)
923.547	Military biography (Rus.)	DK50.5-8
923.55	Military biography (Asia)	
923.551	Military biography (China)	DS738 (group)
923.552	Military biography (Japan)	DS838-839
923.573	Military biography (U.S.)	E181 (mil.: collec.), E182 (naval: collec.), U52-53
929	GENEALOGY	
929.7	Royal houses (genealogy)	
929.72	Genealogy (royal houses: G.B.: hist. treatment poss. or in 941+) DA28.1-.35, CS418-424	
940-949	EUROPE & THE WORLD WARS	D-DR, D501-651, D731-838
940	EUROPE & W. EUROPE (gen.)	D-DR
940.092	Biography (Eur.: group)	D106-110 (group)
940.2	Western Europe & Europe (1453+)	D208, D217
940.28	Europe (1789-1914)	D299, D359 (1801-1914)
940.288	Europe (1900-14)	D424, D443 (pol. & dipl.)
940.3-.499	WORLD WAR I (1914-18)	D501-680
940.3	European War (1914-18: gen.)	D521
940.31	First World War (econ., polit., social hist.)	D443, D453, D511-523, D610
940.311	Causes (WWI)	D511
940.3112	Causes (WWI: polit. & dipl.)	D610-621, D610
940.3113	Causes (WWI: econ.)	D635
940.3114	Causes (WWI: psychological & social)	
940.312	Peace efforts (WWI: preserve or restore)	D613, D641-644+ (armistice)

940.314	Results (WWI: dipl., econ., & polit.: SEE ALSO specific country #s)
	D511-20, D511, D610-611, D643-644+
940.3141	Conferences & treaties (WWI) D642-647
940.3142	Treaties (WWI: results) D511-20
940.31422	Reparations (WWI) D648-649
940.31424	Post-WWI territorial questions D650, D651.A-Z
940.31426	Mandates (post-WWI) D651
940.3144	Post-WWI reconstruction D652-659, D653 (gen.), D657-658 (U.S.),
	D659.A-Z (other places)
940.315	Social groups (WWI) D639.A-Z
940.31503	Ethnic or racial groups (WWI)
940.315042	World War I & women D639.W7, JX1965
940.3152	Religious groups & officials (WWI) D639.R4, D622 (Cath. Church)
940.3155	Scientists (WWI) D639.S2
940.3159	Refugees (WWI) D637, D638.A-Z (by place)
940.316	Noncombatants, pacifists, sympathizers, etc. (WWI)
940.3161	Orphans, children, similar noncombatants (WWI) D639.C4
940.3162	Pacifists (WWI) D613, UB342.A-Z (by place)
940.3163	Sympathizers, Enemy (WWI) D570.8.A6 (U.S.), D636.A-Z (by locale)
940.32	Diplomatic history (WWI) D610-621, D610 (gen.)
940.322	Allies & associates (WWI: dipl. hist.) D511, D459 (Triple Entente)
940.324	Central Powers (WWI: dipl. hist.) D511, D458 (Triple Alliance)
940.325	Neutrals (WWI: dipl. hist.) D611, D639.N
940.332	Allies (WWI: gen. particip.) D544
940.334	Central Powers (WWI: gen. particip.) D531
940.335	Neutrals (WWI: gen. particip.) D639.N, D615 (Belgium),
	D611
940.34-39	World War I (gen. particip.: by country: inclu. mobilization)
940.341-342	World War I (gen. particip.: G.B.) D546, DA577
940.343	World War I (gen. particip.: Ger.) D531, DD228.8
940.344	World War I (gen. particip.: Fr.) D548, DC387
940.345	World War I (gen. particip.: It.) D569, DG570
940.347	World War I (gen. particip.: Rus.) D550, DK264.8
940.371	World War I (gen. particip.: Can.) D547.C2
940.373-379	World War I (gen. particip.: U.S.) D570
940.3931	World War I (gen. particip.: New Z.: SEE ALSO 940.393 for titles
	after 1988) D547.N5
940.394	World War I (gen. particip.: Australia) D547.A8
940.4	Military history (WWI) D521 (gen.), D529-608
940.4003	Encyclopedias & dictionaries (WWI)
	D510, D521, D523
940.4005	Magazines & serial pubns. (WWI) D501
940.4006	Societies & associations (WWI)
	D502, D504 (congresses)
940.40074	Exhibitions, museums, etc. (WWI) D503
940.401	Strategy (WWI) D521, D530, D550
940.4012	Strategy (WWI: Allies) D544, D570
940.4013	Strategy (WWI: Central Powers) D531
940.402	World War I (mobilization: SEE 940.34-39 for particular countries)
940.403	Racial minorities (WWI: soldiers) D547.N4 (blacks: G.B.),
	D570.8.I6 (Indians: U.S.), D639.N4 (blacks)
940.405	Repression & atrocities (WWI) D625 (gen.),
	D626.A-Z (by place)

940.409	Military history (WWI: by place)	
940.40941-40942	Great Britain (WWI: mil. hist.)	D546-547
940.40943	Germany & Austria (WWI: mil. hist.)	D531-538 (Ger.),
		D531 (gen.), D539 (Austria)
940.40944	France (WWI: mil. hist.)	D548-549
940.40945	Italy (WWI: mil. hist.)	D569
940.40947	Russia (WWI: mil. hist.)	D550
940.409571	Military history (WWI: Can.)	D547.C2
940.40973	Military history (WWI: U.S.)	D570
940.40993	Military history (WWI: New Z.: SEE ALSO 940.409931 for titles	
	earlier than 1989)	D547.N5
940.40994	Military history (WWI: Australia)	D547.A8
940.41	World War I (mil. units & ops.: gen.)	D521
940.412-413+	Military history (WWI: units & ops.: by country: inclu. structure,	
	hist., registers, etc.)	D532-578, D608
940.412+	World War I (Allies & associates: mil. units & ops.)	D544-550,
		D569-570
940.41241	Military history (WWI: units & ops.: G.B.)	D546-546.55+, D547
940.413+	World War I (Central Powers: mil. units & ops.)	D531-540, D566
940.41343	Military history (WWI: units & ops.: Ger.)	D531-538
940.414	Fronts (WWI: Eur.)	D521, D530 (W.), D550 (E.)
940.4147	Fronts (WWI: Rus. & E. in gen.)	D550, D551 (Rus.-Ger.-Austrian),
		D556 (Rus.-Austrian), D560 (Balkan)
940.42	Battles & campaigns, Land (WWI: 1914-16)	
940.43	Battles & campaigns, Land (WWI: 1917-18)	
940.439	World War I (Armistice)	D641
940.44	Battles & campaigns, Aerial (WWI)	D600-607
940.449	Aerial ops. (WWI: particular countries)	
940.44941	Aerial ops. (WWI: G.B.)	D602
940.44943	Aerial ops. (WWI: Ger.)	D604
940.44973	Aerial ops. (WWI: U.S.)	D606, D570.6-7 (squadrons)
940.45	Battles & campaigns, Naval (WWI)	D580-595, D580 (gen.)
940.451	World War I (submarine ops.)	D590-595, D590 (gen.)
940.4512	Submarine ops. (WWI: Ger.)	D591 (gen.),
		D592.A-Z (by ship, battle, etc.)
940.4513	Submarine ops. (WWI: Allies)	D590
940.4516	World War I (antisub. ops.)	D580-589, D590
940.452	Blockades & blockade-running (WWI)	D581
940.453+	Naval bases (WWI)	D581-589
940.45341	Naval bases (WWI: in G.B.)	
940.459	World War I (naval ops.: particular countries)	D580-589
940.45941	Naval ops. (WWI: G.B.)	D581-582, VA458
940.45943	Naval ops. (WWI: Ger.)	D581-582
940.45973	Naval ops. (WWI: U.S.)	D589.U5-8
940.45994	Naval ops. (WWI: Australia)	D589.A
940.46	Commemorations, celebrations, & memorials (WWI: gen.)	
		D663-680, D663 (gen.)
940.465	Cemeteries & monuments (WWI)	D639.D4 (cem's.),
	D663-680 (mon's.), D675.W2 (Tomb of Unkn. Soldier: Wash. D.C.)	
940.46547	Monuments & cemeteries (WWI: Rus.)	D680.R
940.467	Rolls of honored & dead (WWI)	D609, D609.A2 (gen.)
940.46741	Honored & dead (WWI: G.B.: rolls)	D609.G7
940.46743	Honored & dead (WWI: Ger.: rolls)	D609.G3

940.47   Social services, prisons, & medical services (WWI)
940.472   Prisoner-of-war camps & internment (WWI)   D627
940.47241-47242   P.O.W. camps & internment centers (WWI: in G.B.)   D627.G7
940.47243   P.O.W. camps & internment centers (WWI: in Ger.)   D627.G3
940.47247   P.O.W. camps & internment centers (WWI: in Rus.)   D627.R9
940.47273   Internment centers & P.O.W. camps (WWI: in U.S.)   D627.U6+
940.475   World War I (medical srvcs.)   D628 (gen.), D629.A-Z (by country),
                                               D630.A-Z (biog.)
940.4752   Sanitary control (WWI: med. srvcs.)
940.47547   Medical services (WWI: Rus.)   D629.R9
940.47573   Medical services (WWI: U.S.)   D629.U6-8
940.4763+   Hospitals (WWI: in particular places)   D629.A-Z
940.4764-4769 Hospitals (WWI: operated by particular countries)
940.477   Welfare & relief services (WWI)   D637-638
940.4778+   Welfare & relief services (WWI: provided by specific countries)
                                               D638.A-Z
940.477841   Welfare & relief services (WWI: by G.B.)   D638.G7
940.4779+   Welfare & relief services (WWI: in specific places)   D638.A-Z,
                 D657-658 (Reconstruc. in U.S.), D659.A-Z (by place)
940.477943   Relief & welfare services (WWI: in Ger.)   D638.G3, D659.G3
940.477947   Relief & welfare services (WWI: in Rus.)   D638.R9, D659.R9
940.48   World War I (misc. topics)
940.481+   Personal accounts, Allied (WWI)   D640, D570.9 (U.S.)
940.482+   Personal accounts, Central Power (WWI)   D640, D531-540
940.483+   Allies (WWI: mil. & naval life & customs)   D544
940.48373   Military & naval life & customs (WWI: U.S.)   D570,
                 D589.U6-7 (naval), D606 (aerial)
940.484   Central Powers (WWI: mil. & naval life & customs)
940.48443   Military & naval life & customs (WWI: Ger.)   D532-538,
                 D581-582 (naval), D604 (aerial)
940.485   Unconventional warfare (WWI: espionage, intell., infilt., sabotage, etc.)
                                               D639.S7-8
940.486   Unconventional warfare, Allied (WWI: espionage, intell., infilt.,
                 sabotage, etc.)
940.48641   Intelligence, espionage, & unconventional warfare (WWI: G.B.)
940.487   Unconventional warfare, Central Power (WWI)
940.48743   Intelligence, espionage, & unconventional warfare (WWI: Ger.)
                                               D619.3-5 (in U.S.)
940.488   News & propaganda (WWI)   D639.P6-7, D631-633, D619.3
940.4886   Propaganda, Allied (WWI)
940.488673   Propaganda, American (WWI: U.S.)   D632, D639.P7.U5+
940.4887   Propaganda, Central Power (WWI)
940.488743   Propaganda, German (WWI)   D639.P7.G3, D619.3 (in U.S.)
940.4889+   News & propaganda (WWI: in specific countries)
940.488943   News & propaganda (WWI: in Ger.)
940.488947   News & propaganda (WWI: in Rus.)

940.5   Europe (20th c. or 1918-)   D424-425, D720 (1919-39),
                                               D431-443, D551, D720-728
940.51   Europe (1918-29)
940.52   Europe (1930-39)

174

```
940.53-5499     WORLD WAR II (1939-45)      D731-838
940.53          World War II (1939-45: gen.: inclu. overall works on Sino-Japanese
                   War [1937-45])      D743
940.531         Second World War (econ., polit., social hist.)      D421, D443,
                                                              D720-728, D743, D748
940.5311        Causes (WWII: gen.)      D741 (gen.), D742.A-Z (by country), D720-728
940.53112           Causes (WWII: dipl. & polit.)      D741-742, D443, D727, D748
940.53113           Causes (WWII: econ.)      D741-742, D720-728, D421, D800
940.53114           Causes (WWII: psychological & social)      D741-742, D726, D421
940.5312        Peace efforts (WWII: preserve or restore)      D749, D748-754
940.5314        Results (WWII: dipl., econ, & polit.: SEE ALSO specific country #s)
                        D743, D748-754, D825-829 (Reconstruction),
                        D814-821 (peace, reparations, terr. ?s, etc.), D840+
940.53141           Conferences & treaties (WWII)
940.53142           Treaties (WWII: results)
940.531422      Reparations (WWII)
940.531424          Post-WWII territorial questions
940.531425          New countries (post-WWII: formation)
940.531426      Mandates (post-WWII)
940.53144       Post-WWII reconstruction      D824-829, D825 (gen.),
                        D827-828 (U.S.), D829.A-Z (by country, nationality, etc.)
940.5315+       Social groups (WWII)
940.531503          Ethnic or racial groups (WWII)
940.531503924       Jews (WWII: SEE ALSO 940.5315296)      D810.J4, D804.G4,
                                                              D829.J4, DS135
940.53150396073         Afro-Americans (WWII)      E185, D810.N4
940.5315042         World War II & women      D810.W7
940.5315062         Wealthy & upper classes (WWII)      D800
940.5315097         Journalists & publishers (WWII)      D798 (gen.),
                                                              D799.A-Z (by place)
940.53152           Religious groups & officials (WWII)      D810.C5-68
940.5315296         Jewish groups (WWII: SEE ALSO 940.531503924)
                                                              D810.J4
940.5315355         Military personnel (WWII)
940.5315372         Teachers (WWII)      D810.E2-5
940.53155        Scientists (WWII)      D810.S2
940.53156        Scientists, Applied (WWII)
940.531562          Engineers (WWII)      D795
940.531563          Farmers (WWII)      HD9006 (U.S.)
940.53157        Artists (WWII)      D810.A7
940.531578          Musicians (WWII)      D810.A7 or .M
940.5315791-5315793     Entertainers (WWII)      D810.E8
940.5315796         Athletes (WWII)      D810.E8
940.53158        Writers (WWII)      D810.A7
940.53159        Refugees (WWII)      D808, D809.A-Z (by place)
940.5316         Noncombatants, pacifists, sympathizers, etc. (WWII)
940.53161           Orphans, children, similar noncombatants (WWII)
                                                              D810.C4
940.53162           Pacifists (WWII)      D810.C82, UB342.A-Z (by place)
940.53163           Sympathizers, Enemy (WWII)
                                    D769.8.A6 (U.S.), D801.A2 (gen.),
                                    D801.A3-Z (by place except U.S.)
```

940.5317	Concentration camps, internment centers, labor camps (WWII)
940.531709+	Internment centers, labor & concentration camps (WWII: geog. treatment: by controlling country: SEE 940.5472+ for works prior to 1989 on intern. ctrs.)
940.53170943	Labor camps, internment centers, concentration camps (WWII: Ger.)
940.53174-53179	Concentration camps & internment centers (WWII: by location)
940.5317438	Auschwitz Concentration Camp (Poland)
940.531779487	Manzanar Internment Camp (Calif.)
940.5318	Holocaust (WWII: inclu. exterm. camps)
940.532	World War II (dipl. hist.) D748-754, D748 (gen.)
940.5322+	Allies & anti-Axis exile govs. or nat. groups (WWII: dipl. hist.) D748
940.532241	Diplomacy (WWII: G.B.) D750
940.532244	Diplomacy (WWII: Fr.) D752
940.532247	Russia (WWII: dipl. hist.) D754.R9 or .S65 (Sov. U.)
940.5322481	Norway (WWII: dipl. hist.) D754.N8
940.5322493	Belgium (WWII: dipl. hist.) D754.B
940.5322495	Greece (WWII: dipl. hist.) D754.G
940.5322497	Diplomacy (WWII: Yug.) D754.Y
940.532251	China (WWII: dipl. hist.) D754.C5
940.532254	India (WWII: dipl. hist.) D754.I4
940.5322599	Philippines (WWII: dipl. hist.: puppet gov. might be with Axis Powers at 940.5324599) D754.P5
940.532268	South Africa (WWII: dipl. hist.) D754.S
940.532271	Canada (WWII: dipl. hist.) D754.C2
940.532273	Diplomacy (WWII: U.S.) D753
940.532282	Argentina (WWII: dipl. hist.) D754.A
940.5322892	Paraguay (WWII: dipl. hist.: might ALSO be with Neutrals at 940.5325892) D754.P
940.5322931	New Zealand (WWII: dipl. hist.: titles after 1988 may be at 940.532293) D754.N45
940.532294	Australia (WWII: dipl. hist.) D754.A8
940.5324+	Axis Powers (WWII: dipl. hist.) D748
940.532443	Diplomacy (WWII: Ger.) D751
940.532444	Vichy France (WWII: dipl. hist.: perhaps ALSO 940.532544) D752
940.532445	Italy (WWII: dipl. hist.) D754.I8
940.5325	Neutrals (WWII: dipl. hist.)
940.5325415	Diplomacy (WWII: Ire.: could ALSO be at 940.5322415 with Allies or at .5324415 with Axis) D754.I5-7
940.5325485	Diplomacy (WWII: Sweden) D754.S8
940.5325494	Switzerland (WWII: dipl. hist.) D754.S9
940.532572	Mexico (WWII: dipl. hist.: could be with Allies at 940.532272) D754.M
940.532581	Brazil (WWII: dipl. hist.) D754.B
940.532582	Argentina (WWII: dipl. hist.: might ALSO be at 940.532482 with Axis) D754.A7
940.5325895	Uruguay (WWII: dipl. hist.: could ALSO be at 940.5324895 with Axis) D754.U

940.533	World War II (gen. particip.: country groups, inclu. nat. groups, pro- & anti-Axis nat. groups, mobilization)	
940.5332	United Nations (WWII: Allies: gen. particip.)	D743, D748
940.5334	Axis (WWII: gen. particip.)	D743, D748
940.5335	Neutral nations (WWII: gen. particip.)	D743, D749
940.5336	Occupied countries (WWII: gen. particip.)	D802.A2
940.5337	Captured nations (WWII: Axis-occup'd.: gen. particip.)	
940.5338	Captured nations (WWII: Allied-occup'd.: gen. particip.)	
940.534-539	World War II (gen. particip.: by country: inclu. exile govs., undergr. move's., pro- & anti-Axis nat. groups, mobilization, etc.)	
940.5341-5342	British Isles (WWII: gen. particip.)	
940.5341	World War II (gen. particip.: G.B.)	D750, D759, DA587
940.53411	Scotland (WWII: gen. particip.)	
940.53415	Ireland (WWII: gen. particip.)	
940.5342	England & Wales (WWII: gen. particip.)	
940.53421	World War II (gen. particip.: London, Eng.)	D760.8.L7, DA684
940.534234	Channel Islands (Eng.: WWII: gen. particip.)	DA670.C4, .J5 (Jersey), .G8-9 (Guernsey)
940.5343	World War II (gen. particip.: Ger.)	D751, D757, DD253-256.5
940.53436	World War II (gen. particip.: Austria & Liech.)	D765.4 (Austria), DB99, D765.45.L (Liech.), DB540.5
940.53437	Czechoslovakia (WWII: gen. particip.)	D765.5, DB215.3, DB2205-2211, DB2206
940.53438	Poland (WWII: gen. particip.)	D765, DK441
940.53439	World War II (gen. particip.: Hungary)	D765.56, DB955
940.5344	World War II (gen. particip.: Fr. & Monaco)	D752, D761, DC397
940.534436	World War II (gen. particip.: Paris, Fr. area)	D762.P3, DC737+
940.5345	World War II (gen. particip.: It.)	D763.I8, DG571-572
940.5345634	Vatican City (Rome: WWII: gen. particip.)	D763.I82.V or .R, D810.C6, DG800
940.5346	Spain (WWII: gen. particip.)	D754.S7, DP270-271
940.53469	Portugal (WWII: gen. particip.)	D754.P8, DP680
940.5347	World War II (gen. particip.: Rus.)	D764, D754.R9 or .S65, DK267-273, DK273
940.53481	World War II (gen. particip.: Nor.)	D763.N6-62, DL532
940.53485	Sweden (WWII: gen. particip.)	D754.S8, DL868.5-870
940.53489	World War II (gen. particip.: Denmark & Fin.)	D763.D4-42, DL256 (Den.)
940.534897	World War II (gen. particip.: Finland: SEE ALSO 940.53471 for some works before 1980) D754.F5, D765.3, DK459.45+, DL1090-1105+ (works after about 1980), DL1090, DL1097	
940.53492	Holland (WWII: gen. particip.)	DL763.N4-42, DJ287
940.53493	World War II (gen. particip.: Belgium)	D763.B4-42, DH687
940.534935	World War II (gen. particip.: Luxemb.)	D763.L9, DH916
940.53494	Switzerland (WWII: gen. particip.)	D754.S9, DQ201
940.53495	World War II (gen. particip.: Greece)	D766.3-32, DF726
940.534965	World War II (gen. particip.: Albania)	D766.7.A4, DR701.S8-86, DR974 (later works after 1980?)
940.53497	World War II (gen. particip.: Yug.)	D766.6-62, DR366, DR1289 (later works after 1980?)
940.534977	World War II (gen. particip.: Bulg.)	D766.7.B8, DR89-90
940.53498	World War II (gen. particip.: Rumania)	D766.4, DR264-267
940.53499	Greek Isles (WWII: gen. particip.)	DF901.C9 (Cyclades)
940.534998	World War II (gen. particip.: Crete)	D766.7.C7, DF901. C86

940.535	World War II (gen. particip.: Asia)	
940.5351	World War II (gen. particip.: China)	D767.3, DS777.518-533
940.53512	Hong Kong (WWII: gen. particip.)	DS796.H7
940.5351249	Formosa (WWII: gen. particip.)	DS895.F75,
		DS799.69-72 (pubns. 1970+)
940.53517	Mongolia (WWII: gen. particip.)	DS793.M7
940.53518	Manchuria (WWII: gen. particip.)	DS784
940.53519	Korea (WWII: gen. particip.) DS916	
940.5352	World War II (gen. particip.: Japan)	D767.2-25, DS888.5-889
940.5354	World War II (gen. particip.: India)	D767.6, D767.63 (Free India),
		DS413
940.5355	World War II (gen. particip.: Iran)	D766.7.I55, DS317-318
940.53561	Turkey (WWII: gen. particip.)	D766.7.T8, DR590
940.535645	Cyprus (WWII: gen. particip.)	DS54.8
940.53567	World War II (gen. particip.: Iraq)	D766.7.I57, DS79.53
940.53569	World War II (gen. particip.: Syria)	D766.7.S9, DS98
940.535694	World War II (gen. particip.: Israel)	D766.7.P (Palestine), D766.7.I7
940.5357	Siberia (WWII: gen. particip.: more likely with Russia at 940.5347)	
		D764, D767, DK766
940.53591	World War II (gen. particip.: Burma)	D767.6, DS485.B89,
		DS530 (later titles post 1970?)
940.53593	Thailand (WWII: gen. particip.)	DS585
940.53594	Laos (WWII: gen. particip.)	DS555.36
940.535951	Malaysia (WWII: gen. particip.)	D767.5, DS596,
		DS598-599 (local, A-Z)
940.535952	World War II (gen. particip.: Singapore: SEE 940.535957 for later titles)	
		D767.5, DS598.S7
940.5359527	Singapore (WWII: gen. particip.: SEE 940.535952 for earlier titles)	
		D767.5, DS598.S7
940.53597	Vietnam (Annam: WWII: gen. particip.)	D767.45, DS556.36,
		DS549 (earlier works)
940.53598	Indonesia & Malay Archipelago (WWII: gen. particip.)	
		D767.7 (Dutch E. Indies), DS643.5, DS643
940.535983	Borneo (WWII: gen. particip.)	D767.7, DS646.3
940.53599	World War II (gen. particip.: Philippines)	D767.4, DS686.3-4
940.53611	World War II (gen. particip.: Tunisia)	D766.99.T8, DT264
940.53612	World War II (gen. particip.: Libya)	D766.93, DT235
940.5362	World War II (gen. particip.: Egypt)	D766.9, DT107.82
940.5364	World War II (gen. particip.: Morocco)	D766.99.M8, DT324
940.5365	World War II (gen. particip.: Algeria)	D766.99.A4-6, DT295
940.5368	World War II (gen. particip.: S. Africa)	D766.97, DT779.7
940.5371	World War II (gen. particip.: Can.)	D768.15, F1034
940.5373	World War II (gen. particip.: U.S.)	D769, E806-813, E806 (gen.)
940.5374-5379	United States (WWII: gen. particip.: by area or state)	
		D769.85.A-Z, D769.87-88, F1-951+
940.53747	World War II (gen. particip.: U.S.: N.Y.)	D769.85.N4-5, F124
940.53794	California (WWII: gen. particip.)	D769.85.C2-21, F866
940.5393	Melanesia (WWII: gen. particip.)	DU940
940.53931	World War II (gen. particip.: New Z.: SEE ALSO 940.5393 for works	
	after 1988)	D767.85-852, DU411
940.53932	New Caledonia (WWII: gen. particip.)	DU720
940.53934	New Hebrides (WWII: gen. particip.)	DU760
940.53935	World War II (gen. particip.: Solomon Is.)	D767.98, DU850
940.53936	Bismarck Archipelago (WWII: gen. particip.)	DU550-553
940.5394	World War II (gen. particip.: Australia)	D767.8-82, DU116

940.5395	World War II (gen. particip.: New Guinea)	D767.95, DU740-746
940.53965	Micronesia (WWII: gen. particip.)	DU500
940.53966	World War II (gen. particip.: Caroline Is.)	DU565-567
940.53967	World War II (gen. particip.: Guam & the Marianas)	D767.G or .M,
		DU647 (Guam), DU645 (Marianas)
940.53968	Micronesia, Eastern (Ellice, Gilbert, Marshall Is.: WWII: gen. particip.)	
	D767.917 (Gilb's.), D767.99.M3 (Marshalls), DU500 (Micro.),	
	DU590 (Ell. Is.), DU615 (Gilb's.), DU710 (Marshalls)	
940.54	Military history (WWII)	D743
940.54003	Encyclopedias & dictionaries (WWII)	D740
940.54005	Magazines & serial pubns. (WWII)	D731
940.54006	Societies & associations (WWII)	D732, D734
940.5401	Strategy (WWII)	D743
940.54012	Strategy (WWII: Allies)	
940.54013	Strategy (WWII: Axis)	
940.5402	World War II (mobilization: SEE 940.534-539 for particular countries)	
		D800, HC, HF, HJ
940.5403	Afro-Americans & American Indians as troops (WWII)	
		D810.N4, D810.I5
940.5404	Minorities, Ethnic (WWII: as troops)	D769.88.A-Z,
		D769.88.M4 (Mex.-Am's.)
940.5405	Repression & atrocities (WWII)	D803, D804.A-Z (by country)
940.54094-54099	Military history (WWII: by place)	D757-769
940.540941-540942	Military history (WWII: G.B.)	D759-760
940.540943	Military history (WWII: Ger.)	D757
940.5409436	Military history (WWII: Austria)	D765.4
940.5409437	Czechoslovakia (WWII: mil. hist.)	D765.5
940.5409438	Poland (WWII: mil. hist.)	D765
940.5409439	Military history (WWII: Hungary)	D765.56
940.540944	Military history (WWII: Fr.)	D761
940.540945	Military history (WWII: It.)	D763.I8-817
940.540947	Military history (WWII: Rus.)	D764
940.5409471	Military history (WWII: Fin.: SEE 940.54094897 for newer	
	titles)	D765.3
940.5409481	Military history (WWII: Norway)	D763.N6-613
940.5409489	Military history (WWII: Denmark)	D763.D4
940.54094897	Finnish military history (WWII: SEE ALSO 940.5409471 for	
	earlier works)	D765.3
940.5409492	Holland (WWII: mil. hist.)	D763.N4-41
940.5409493	Military history (WWII: Belgium)	D763.B4
940.54094935	Military history (WWII: Luxemb.)	D763.L9
940.5409495	Military history (WWII: Greece)	D766.3
940.5409497	Military history (WWII: Yug.)	D766.6-613
940.54094977	Military history (WWII: Bulg.)	D766.7.B8
940.5409498	Military history (WWII: Rumania)	D766.4
940.540951	Military history (WWII: China)	D767.3
940.540952	Military history (WWII: Japan)	D767.2
940.540954	Military history (WWII: India)	D767.6,
		D767.63 (Free India, 1943-45)
940.5409561	Military history (WWII: Turkey)	D766.7.T8
940.5409591	Military history (WWII: Burma)	D767.6
940.5409595	Malaysia (WWII: mil. hist.)	D767.5
940.54095957	Military history (WWII: Singapore)	
940.5409598	Indonesia (WWII: mil. hist.)	D767.7
940.5409599	Military history (WWII: Philip. Is.)	D767.4

940.540962	Military history (WWII: Egypt)	D766.9
940.540968	Military history (WWII: S. Africa)	D766.97
940.540971	Military history (WWII: Can.)	D768.15
940.540973	Military history (WWII: U.S.)	D769, D769.25-4 (armies, div's., regt's.), D769.45-598 (naval particip., units, ops.)
940.54097308664	Homosexuals (WWII: U.S.: armed forces)	
940.5409931	Military history (WWII: New Z.: SEE ALSO 940.540993 for titles prior to 1989)	D767.85
940.540994	Military history (WWII: Australia)	D767.8
940.541	World War II (mil. units & ops.: gen.)	D743
940.5412-5413+	Military history (WWII: units & ops.: by country: inclu. structure, history, registers, & service records)	
940.5412+	World War II (Allies & United Nations: mil. units & ops.)	
940.541241	Military history (WWII: units & ops.: G.B.)	D759.5-760.A-Z
940.5412411	Military history (WWII: units & ops.: Scot.)	D760.S
940.541242	England (WWII: mil. units & ops.)	D759.5-63+, D760.A-Z
940.541244	Military history (WWII: units & ops.: Fr.)	D761.1-9
940.5412481	Military history (WWII: units & ops.: Norway)	D763.N61-613
940.5412493	Military history (WWII: units & ops.: Belgium)	D763.B4
940.5412495	Military history (WWII: units & ops.: Greece)	D766.3
940.5412497	Military history (WWII: units & ops.: Yug.)	D766.61-613
940.541251	Military history (WWII: units & ops.: China)	D767.3
940.541254	Military history (WWII: units & ops.: India)	D767.6, D767.63 (Free India, 1943-45)
940.5412591	Military history (WWII: units & ops.: Burma)	D767.6
940.5412599	Military history (WWII: units & ops.: Phil. Is.)	D767.4
940.541268	Military history (WWII: units & ops.: S. Africa)	D766.97
940.541271	Military history (WWII: units & ops.: Can.)	D768.15
940.541273	Military history (WWII: units & ops.: U.S.)	D769.25-4, D769.5-555 (naval), D769.585-598 (Coast Guard etc.), D769.73-76+ (transport, ordnance, supplies)
940.541274-541279	Military history (WWII: units & ops.: U.S.: particular areas or states)	D769.85.A-Z
940.5412931	Military history (WWII: units & ops.: New Z.: SEE ALSO 940.541293 for works before 1989)	D767.85
940.541294	Military history (WWII: units & ops.: Australia)	D767.8
940.5413+	World War II (Axis Powers: mil. units & ops.)	
940.541343	Military history (WWII: units & ops.: Ger.)	D757.1-.85
940.541345	Military history (WWII: units & ops.: It.)	D763.I81-813, D763.I815-817 (Corpo Volontari Della Liberta)
940.54134897	Military history (WWII: units & ops.: Fin.)	D765.3
940.5413498	Military history (WWII: units & ops.: Rum.)	D766.4
940.541352	Military history (WWII: units & ops.:Japan)	D767.2
940.542	Battles & campaigns (WWII: by theatre)	D756-769
940.5421	Theatres, Battle (WWII: Eur.)	D743, D756 (W.), D764 (E.)
940.5423	Theatres, Battle (WWII: Afr. & Mid. E.)	D766.8 (Afr.), D766 (Balkans, E. Medit., Near E.)
940.5425	Theatres, Battle (WWII: E. Ind., S.E. Asian, E. Asia: SEE ALSO 951.042 for pre-1941 Sino-Jpn. conflict)	D767, D767.6 (India-Burma), D767.35 & D767.45 (Cochin China, Fr. Indoch.)
940.5426	Theatres, Battle (WWII: Pacific)	D767 (gen.), D767.9+ (Pac. Is.)
940.5428	Theatres, Battle (WWII: Am.)	D768 (gen.), D768.18-3 (Latin Am.), D769 (U.S.)
940.5429	Theatres, Battle (WWII: misc.)	

940.544	Battles & campaigns, Aerial (WWII: inclu. comb. air & naval ops. as well as antiaircraft defenses)	D785-792, D785 (gen.)
940.5441	Aerial ops. (WWII: particular srvcs.: scouting, artil. supp., bombing, close air supp., antisub. ops., balloon barrage, coast patrols, etc.)	
940.5442	Air battles & campaigns (WWII)	D785+
940.5443+	Air bases (WWII: by area or place)	
940.544342	Air bases (WWII: in Eng.)	D786
940.544343	Air bases (WWII: in Ger.)	D787
940.544347	Air bases (WWII: in Rus.)	
940.544351	Air bases (WWII: in China)	
940.544352	Air bases (WWII: in Japan)	D792.J3
940.544373	Air bases (WWII: in U.S.)	D790
940.544394	Air bases (WWII: in Australia)	
940.5449+	Aerial ops. (WWII: by country: inclu. specific craft, units, fliers)	
940.544941-544942	Aerial ops. (WWII: G.B.: R.A.F. etc.)	D786
940.544943	Aerial ops. (WWII: Ger.: Luftwaffe etc.)	D787
940.544945	Aerial ops. (WWII: It.)	D792.I8
940.544947	Aerial ops. (WWII: Rus.)	D792.R9 or .S65
940.544951	Aerial ops. (WWII: China)	D792.C5
940.544952	Aerial ops. (WWII: Japan)	D792.J3
940.544971	Aerial ops. (WWII: Can.)	
940.544973	Aerial ops. (WWII: U.S.: Army Air Corps, Navy, Marines, etc.)	D790
940.544994	Aerial ops. (WWII: Australia)	D792.A8
940.545	Battles & campaigns, Naval (WWII: SEE ALSO 940.542 for ops. by theatre)	D770-784, D770 (gen.), D773 (U.S.: gen.), D774.A-Z (U.S.: by ship, battle, etc.), D769.45-598 (U.S.: by fleet, squadron, base, etc.)
940.5451+	World War II (submarine ops.: SEE ALSO 940.542 for ops. by theatre)	D780-784, D780 (gen.), D781-782 (Ger.), D783 (U.S.), D784.A-Z (other lands)
940.54516	World War II (antisub. ops.)	D780, D770-784
940.5451941	Submarine ops. (WWII: G.B.)	D784.G7
940.5451943	Submarine ops. (WWII: Ger.)	D781-782
940.5451945	Submarine ops. (WWII: It.)	D784.I8
940.5451952	Submarine ops. (WWII: Japan)	D784.J3
940.5451973	Submarine ops. (WWII: U.S.)	D783
940.5452	Blockades & blockade-running (WWII)	D770, D771 (Anglo-Grmn.), D773 (U.S.)
940.5453+	Naval bases (WWII)	D769.54-542 (U.S.), D770-784 (other lands)
940.545341	Naval bases (WWII: in G.B.)	
940.5453411	Scapa Flow Naval Base (G.B.: Scot.: WWII)	
940.5453343	Naval bases (WWII: in Ger.)	
940.545344	Naval bases (WWII: in Fr.)	
940.545345	Naval bases (WWII: in It.)	
940.545352	Naval bases (WWII: in Japan)	
940.545373	Naval bases (WWII: in U.S.)	
940.5453755	Naval bases (WWII: in U.S.: Va.)	
940.5453794	Naval bases (WWII: in U.S.: Calif.)	
940.54537946	Naval bases (WWII: in U.S.: Calif.: S.F. Bay Area)	
940.5453794985	Naval bases (WWII: in U.S.: Calif.: San Diego)	

| 940.5459+ | World War II (naval ops.: particular countries) | D770-784 |

940.545941-545942 Naval ops. (WWII: G.B. Royal Navy) D771-772, D767
(Pac.), DA89, DA89.1.A-Z (biog's.), DA566.5 (20th c.)

940.545943	Naval ops. (WWII: Ger.)	D771-772, DD106
940.545944	Naval ops. (WWII: Fr.)	D779.F8, DC53, DC368
940.545945	Naval ops. (WWII: It.)	D775, DG486
940.545952	Naval ops. (WWII: Japan)	D777, VA653, DS890.A-Z (biog.)
940.545971	Naval ops. (WWII: Can.)	D779.C2, F1028.5
940.545973	Naval ops. (WWII: U.S.: U.S.N., Marines, Coast Guard)

D773-774, D769.45-598 (fleets etc.), E746

940.5459931 Naval ops. (WWII: New Z.: SEE ALSO 940.545993 for earlier titles
prior to 1989) D779.N45

940.545994	Naval ops. (WWII: Australia)	D779.A8, DU112.4
940.546	Commemorations, celebrations, & memorials (WWII: gen.)	D830-838
940.5465	Cemeteries & monuments (WWII)	D833-838 (celebrations,

monuments, etc.), D810.D4 (dead, cemeteries, etc.)

| 940.546542 | Cemeteries & monuments (WWII: Eng.) | D838.G6 (gen.), |

.G7.A-Z (local, by place)

940.546543	Monuments & cemeteries (WWII: Ger.)	D838.G3
940.546544	Monuments & cemeteries (WWII: Fr.)	D838.F8
940.546547	Monuments & cemeteries (WWII: Rus.)	D838.R9 or .S65
940.546551	Monuments & cemeteries (WWII: China)	D838.C5
940.546552	Monuments & cemeteries (WWII: Japan)	D838.J3
940.546573	Cemeteries & monuments (WWII: U.S.)	D833-836,

D833 (gen.), D835.A-W (by state), D836.A-Z (by town)

940.5465753 Monuments & cemeteries (WWII: U.S.: Wash. D.C.)

D835.D6, D836.W

| 940.546594 | Monuments & cemeteries (WWII: Australia) | D838.A8 |
| 940.5465969 | Monuments & cemeteries (WWII: Hawaiian Is.) |

D835.H, D838.H

940.5467	Rolls of honored & dead (WWII)	D797
940.546741	Honored & dead (WWII: G.B.: rolls)	D797.G7
940.546743	Honored & dead (WWII: Ger.: rolls)	D797.G3
940.546744	Honored & dead (WWII: Fr.: rolls)	D797.F8
940.546747	Honored & dead (WWII: Rus.: rolls)	D797.R9
940.546752	Honored & dead (WWII: Japan: rolls)	D797.J3
940.546773	Honored & dead (WWII: U.S.: rolls)	D797.U6-7
940.547	Social services, prisons, & medical services (WWII)

D805-809

940.5472+ Prisoner-of-war camps & internment centers (WWII: SEE ALSO
940.5317+ for post-1988 titles on internment camps) D805

940.547241	P.O.W. camps & internment centers (WWII: run by G.B.)	D805.G7
940.547243	P.O.W. camps & internment centers (WWII: run by Ger.)	D805.G3
940.547247	P.O.W. camps & internment centers (WWII: run by Rus.)	D805.R9
940.547252	P.O.W. camps & internment centers (WWII: run by Japan)

D805.J3

940.547273 P.O.W. camps & internment centers (WWII: run by U.S.)

D805.U5-6

| 940.5473 | Prisoner exchanges (WWII) | D805 |

940.5475	World War II (medical srvcs.)	D806-807, D806 (gen.)
940.54752	Sanitary control (WWII)	
940.54753	Ambulance services (WWII)	
940.54754-54759	Medical services (WWII: particular countries)	D807.A-Z
940.547541	Medical services (WWII: G.B.)	D807.G7
940.547543	Medical services (WWII: Ger.)	D807.G3
940.547547	Medical services (WWII: Rus.)	D807.R9
940.547552	Medical services (WWII: Japan)	D807.J3
940.547573	United States medical services (WWII)	D807.U6-87,

.U6 (gen.), .U62.A-Z (by state),
.U72-73 (Army hospitals), .U85-87 (Navy hospitals)

940.5476	Medical services (WWII: hospitals)	D806
940.547634-547639	Hospitals (WWII: in particular places)	D807.A-Z
940.5476341-5476342	Hospitals (WWII: in G.B.)	D807.G7
940.5476343	Hospitals (WWII: in Ger.)	D807.G3
940.5476344	Hospitals (WWII: in Fr.)	D807.F8
940.5476351	Hospitals (WWII: in China)	D807.C5
940.5476352	Hospitals (WWII: in Japan)	D807.J3
940.5476373	Hospitals (WWII: in U.S.)	D807.U6-87
940.5476394	Hospitals (WWII: in Australia)	D807.A8
940.54764-54769	Hospitals (WWII: operated by particular countries)	D807.A-Z
940.547641	Medical services (WWII: hospitals, British)	D807.G7
940.547643	Medical services (WWII: hospitals, German) ·	D807.G3
940.547647	Medical services (WWII: hospitals, Russian)	D807.R9
940.547652	Medical services (WWII: hospitals, Japanese)	D807.J3
940.547673	Medical services (WWII: hospitals, United States)	D807.U6-87
940.5477	Welfare & relief services (WWII)	D808-809
940.54771	Red Cross (WWII)	D806-807
940.547784-547789	Welfare & relief services (WWII: provided by specific countries)	D809.A-Z
940.5477841	Welfare & relief services (WWII: by G.B.)	D809.G7
940.5477873	Welfare & relief services (WWII: by U.S.)	D809.U5
940.5477894	Welfare & relief services (WWII: by Australia)	D809.A8
940.547794-547799	Welfare & relief services (WWII: in particular countries)	D809.A-Z
940.5477943	Relief & welfare & services (WWII: in Ger.)	D809.G3
940.5477944	Relief & welfare & services (WWII: in Fr.)	D809.F8
940.5477947	Relief & welfare & services (WWII: in Rus.)	D809.R9
940.5477951	Relief & welfare & services (WWII: in China)	D809.C5
940.5477952	Relief & welfare & services (WWII: in Japan)	D809.J3
940.54779599	Relief & welfare & services (WWII: in Philip. Is.)	D809.P5
940.5478	Religious services (WWII)	D810.C35-6 (chaplains),

.C5 (churches: gen.), .C53-68 (alphab. by denom.)

940.548	World War II (misc. topics)	
940.5481+	Personal accounts, Allied (WWII)	D811
940.548141	Personal accounts, British (WWII)	
940.548142	Personal accounts, English (WWII)	
940.548144	Personal accounts, French (WWII)	
940.548147	Personal accounts, Russian (WWII)	
940.548173	Personal accounts, American (WWII: U.S.)	
940.548194	Personal accounts, Australian (WWII)	
940.5482+	Personal accounts, Axis (WWII)	D811
940.548243	Personal accounts, German (WWII)	
940.548245	Personal accounts, Italian (WWII)	
940.548252	Personal accounts, Japanese (WWII)	

940.5483+	Allies (WWII: mil. & naval life & customs)	U750, U765+, V720 (naval), V735+
940.548341	Military & naval life & customs (WWII: G.B.)	U767, V737
940.548347	Military & naval life & customs (WWII: Rus.)	U771, V741
940.548373	Naval & military life & customs (WWII: U.S.)	U766, V736
940.5484+	Axis (WWII: mil. & naval life & customs)	U750, U765+, V720 (naval), V735+
940.548443	Military & naval life & customs (WWII: Ger.)	U769, V739
940.548452	Military & naval life & customs (WWII: Japan)	U773, V743.J3
940.5485	Unconventional warfare (WWII: inclu. espionage, infilt., intelligence, subversion) D810.S7 (gen.), .S8.A-Z (by spy), D802(underground), D802.F8 (Fr. undergr.), UB250-274, UB273-274 (sabo.), UB251.A-Z (intell., by country), UB271.A-Z (espion., by country respons.), VB230-250 (naval intell. & espionage)	
940.5486+	Unconventional warfare, Allied (WWII: inclu. espionage, infilt., intelligence, subversion)	
940.548641	Intelligence, espionage, & unconventional warfare (WWII: G.B.) D810.S7, UB251.G7, UB271.G7, VB230-250	
940.548644	Sabotage, espionage, & unconventional warfare (WWII: Fr.) D802.F8 (underground), D810.S7+, UB271.F8	
940.548647	Infiltration, espionage, & unconventional warfare (WWII: Rus.) UB251.R9, UB271.R9	
940.548673	Intelligence, espionage, & unconventional warfare (WWII: U.S.) D810.S7+, UB251.U5, UB271.U5, VB230-250 (naval)	
940.548694	Espionage, intelligence, & unconventional warfare (WWII: Australia)	
940.5487+	Unconventional warfare, Axis (WWII: inclu. espionage, intelligence, infiltration, subversion)	
940.548743	Intelligence, espionage, & unconventional warfare (WWII: Ger.) D810.S7+, UB251.G3, UB271.G3	
940.548745	Espionage, intelligence, & unconventional warfare (WWII: It.)	
940.548752	Espionage, intelligence, & unconventional warfare (WWII: Japan) UB251.J3, UB271.J3, VB230-250	
940.5488	News & propaganda (WWII) D810.P6 (gen.), .P7.A-Z (by country)	
940.54886	Propaganda, Allied (WWII)	
940.5488641	Propaganda, British (WWII) D810.P7.G7	
940.5488644	Propaganda, French (WWII) D810.P7.F8	
940.5488647	Propaganda, Russian (WWII: after 21 June 1941) D810.P7.R9 or .S65	
940.5488673	Propaganda, American (WWII: U.S.) D810.P7.U6	
940.54887+	Propaganda, Axis (WWII)	
940.5488743	Propaganda, German (WWII) D810.P7.G3	
940.5488744	Propaganda, French (WWII: Vichy) D810.P7.F8	
940.5488745	Propaganda, Italian (WWII) D810.P7.I8	
940.5488747	Propaganda, Russian (WWII: prior to 22 June 1941) D810.P7.R9	
940.5488752	Propaganda, Japanese (WWII) D810.P7.J3	

940.54889+	News & propaganda (WWII: in specific places)	
940.5488941-5488942	News & propaganda (WWII: in G.B.)	
940.5488943	News & propaganda (WWII: in Ger.)	
940.5488944	News & propaganda (WWII: in Fr.)	
940.5488945	News & propaganda (WWII: in It.)	
940.5488947	News & propaganda (WWII: in Rus.)	
940.5488951	News & propaganda (WWII: in China)	
940.5488952	News & propaganda (WWII: in Japan)	
940.54889599	News & propaganda (WWII: in Philip. Is.)	
940.5488972	News & propaganda (WWII: in Can.)	
940.5488973	News & propaganda (WWII: in U.S.)	D753.3
940.5488994	News & propaganda (WWII: in Australia)	
940.549	Humor, comics, pictorials, & miscellanea (WWII)	D743.9, D745
940.5494	Anecdotes (WWII)	D743.9
940.5496-5497	Comics, caricatures, humor (WWII)	

941	BRITAIN & BRITISH ISLES	DA
941.003	Encyclopedias & dictionaries (G.B.)	DA34
941.081	Britain (19th c. & Victorian era of 1837-1901)	DA550-566,
		DA550 (gen.)
941.082	Britain (20th c. & Edward VII era of 1901-1910)	
	DA567-570 (Ed. VII), DA570 (gen.), DA566 (20th c.: gen.)	
941.083	Britain (1910-36: George VI)	DA573-578, DA576 (gen.),
		DA577 (WWI era), DA578 (1920-39)
941.084	Britain (1936-45: WWII era)	DA580-587, DA586 (gen.),
		DA587 (WWII period)
941.1	SCOTLAND	DA750-890, DA760 (gen.)
941.1083	Scotland (1910-36)	DA821
941.1084	Scotland (1936-45))	DA821
941.34	Edinburgh, Scot.	DA890.E2-4
941.5	IRELAND (overall)	DA900-995, DA910 (gen.)
941.508	Ireland (19th-20th c.)	DA950-965+
941.5082	Ireland (20th c.)	DA959-965
941.50821	Ireland (1900-20)	DA960
941.50822	Ireland (1921-49)	DA963
941.6	Northern Ireland	DA990.U45-46
941.7	Eire (Republic of Ireland)	DA963

942	ENGLAND & WALES	DA20-745, DA20-690 (Eng.), DA700-45 (Wales)
942.083	England (1910-36)	DA576
942.084	England (1936-45)	DA586-587
942.1	London, Eng.	DA675-689, DA677 (gen.)
942.1084	London, Eng. (1936-45)	DA684
942.34	Channel Islands (G.B.)	DA670.C4
942.341	Jersey (G.B.: island)	
942.342	Guernsey (G.B.: island)	
942.9	Wales	

943   GERMANY & CENTRAL EUROPE   DD (Ger.), DB (Austria, Hung.,
                                           Czech.), DK401-441 & DK4010-4800 (Pol.)
943.0004924   Jews (Central Eur.)
943.004924   Jews (Ger.)   DS135.G3-5
943.084   Germany (1888-1918: Fred. & William II eras)   DD224-232,
                           DD228 (gen.), DD228.8 (WWI era), DD448 (Prussia)
943.085   Weimar Republic (Ger.: 1918-33)   DD233-251, DD237 (gen.),
                           DD251 (Hindenb. era), DD453 (Prussia)
943.086   Germany (1933-45: 3rd Reich)   DD253-256, DD256 (WWII period),
                           DD256.5 (gen.: post-war pubn. dates), DD454 (Prussia)
943.155   Berlin, Ger.   DD851-900, DD860 (gen.)
943.155086   Berlin, Ger. (1933-45)   DD880
943.3   Bavaria   DD801.B31-55
943.4   Rhine River Valley   DD801.R7-76
943.42   Saar (Ger.)   DD801.S13
943.48   Black Forest (Ger.)   DD801.B63-65
943.6   AUSTRIA   DB1-170+
943.605   Austria (20th c. & 1919-)   DB91 (20th c.), DB96 (1918-)
943.6051   Austrian Republic (1919-38)   DB96-98
943.6052   Anschluss & WWII Period (Austria: 1938-55)   DB99 (1938-45),
                           DB99.1 (Allied occup., 1945-55)
943.613   Vienna, Austria   DB841-860, DB847 (gen.)
943.648   LIECHTENSTEIN   DB540.5
943.7   CZECHOSLOVAKIA   DB191-217 (older works),
                   DB2000-3150 (newer)
943.7024   Czechoslovakia (19th c.: 1815-1918)   DB214, DB2176
943.703   Czechoslovakia (1918-45)   DB215-215.3, DB2186-2211,
                           DB2186 (gen.), DB2196 (1918-39), DB2206 (1939-45)
943.8   POLAND   DK401-441 (older titles), DK4010-4800 (titles 1970+?),
                   DK414, DK4140
943.803   Poland (1795-1918: foreign rule)   DK434.9, DK4349, DK439
943.804   Polish Republic (1918-39)   DK440, DK4400
943.805   Poland (1939-)   DK441
943.8053   Poland (1939-45: WWII era)   DK441, DK4410
943.84   Warsaw, Pol. (area)   DK651.W2, DK4610-4645
943.9   HUNGARY   DB901-975+, DB906, DB925
943.905   Hungary (20th c.: 1918-)   DB947-950, DB947 (gen.),
                           DB950.A-Z (biog.)
943.9051   Hungary (1918-41)   DB955
943.9052   Hungary (1942-56)   DB956

944   FRANCE   DC
944.08   France (1870- & 20th c.: 3d, 4th, 5th Repub's.)   DC289+, DC335+
944.081   France (1870-1945: 3d Repub.)   DC335
944.0814   France (1914-18: WWI era)   DC387
944.0815   France (1918-39)   DC389-396
944.0816   France (1939-45: WWII period)   DC397
944.1   Brittany   DC611.B841-915
944.2   Normandy area (Fr.)   DC611.N841-899
944.36   Paris, Fr. (area)   DC701-790, DC707 (gen.),
                           DC735 (1871-1914), DC737 (1914-)
944.89   Pyrenees region   DC611.P981-992
944.949   MONACO   DC941-947

945	ITALY DG	
945.09	Italy (1870- & 20th c.) DG555-575+, DG555, DG570 (WWI era)	
945.091	Italy (1918-46: SEE ALSO 963.056 for Italo-Eth. War of 1935-6)	
		DG566-575, DG571-572 (Fascist period),
		DG572 (WWII time)
945.632	Rome, It. DG803-818, DG808, DG813 (1871-)	
945.634	Vatican City DG800	
945.8	Sicily DG869	
945.85	MALTA DG994	

946	IBERIAN PENINSULA & SPAIN	
		DP, DP1-402+ (Sp.), DP501-900+ (Port.)
946.08	Spain (1868-) DP222 (1868-86), DP233 (1886- & 20th c.)	
946.081	Spain (1931-39: 2d Repub.: inclu. Civil War, 1936-39) DP250-269,	
		DP254 (gen.), DP269 (Civil War)
946.082	Spain (1939-75: Franco period) DP270	
946.0824	Spain (1939-49)	
946.41	Madrid, Sp. (area) DP350-374, DP361	
946.79	ANDORRA DC921-930	
946.89	GIBRALTAR (Br. colony) DP302.G31-41	
946.9	PORTUGAL DP501-900+	
946.904	Portugal (1910-) DP675	
946.9042	Portugal (1926-68) DP680	
946.942	Lisbon, Port. DP752-776, DP764	
946.99	Azores DP702.A81-99, .A9 (19th-20th c.)	

947	UNION OF SOVIET SOCIALIST REPUBLICS (Russia)	
		DK, DK1-275, DK501-973+
947.08	Russia (1855-) DK219+, DK220-221	
947.083	Russia (1894-1918: NIcholas II: perhaps SEE ALSO 952.031 for Russo-	
	Jpn. War) DK251-264.3, DK258, DK260-262,	
		DS516-517 (R-J War)
947.084	Russia (20th c. & 1917-: Communist period) DK246	
947.0841	Soviet Union (1917-24: Rev. period & Lenin era) DK265 (Rev.),	
		DK265-266.5+
947.0842	Soviet Union (1924-53: Stalin era: might ALSO try 948.97032 for	
	Russo-Finnish War) DK267-273, DK267 (gen.),	
	DK459.5 (R-F War), DL1095-1105 (R-F War: later works)	
947.1	FINLAND (SEE ALSO 948.97 for works after 1970 or so)	
		DK445-465, DL1002-1180+ (pubns. 1970+)
947.23	Archangel, Rus.	
947.31	Moscow, Rus. DK591-609, DK601 (hist. to 1950)	
947.45	Leningrad, Rus. DK541-579, DK568 (1801-)	
947.65	Belorussia DK511.W5 (White Russia)	
947.7	Black Sea region (Rus.) DK509	
947.71	Little Russia (Ukraine) DK508	
947.717	Odessa & Crimea areas (Rus.) DK511.C7	
947.85	Volgograd, Rus. (ALSO Tsaritsyn or Stalingrad) DK651.S7	
947.87	Ural Mts. region (Rus.) DK511.U7	
947.9	Caucasus area (Rus.) DK511.C1-35	
947.95	Georgian Republic (U.S.S.R.) DK511.G3-47, .G47 (gen. hist., 1917-)	

948	NORTHERN EUROPE & Scandinavia	DL
948.08	Scandinavia & N. Europe (20th c.: 1905-)	DL83-87+
948.081	Scandinavia & N. Europe (1905-19)	DL83
948.082	Scandinavia & N. Europe (1920-29)	DL83
948.083	Scandinavia & N. Europe (1930-39)	DL83
948.084	Scandinavia & N. Europe (1940-49)	DL83 (1901-45)
948.1	NORWAY DL401-596, DL448 (gen.)	
948.104	Norway (20th c.: 1905-) DL527+	
948.1041	Norway (1905-45) DL530-532	
948.2	Oslo, Nor. (area) DL581	
948.4	Norway, Central & Northern	
948.5	SWEDEN DL601-991+, DL648	
948.505	Sweden (20th c.: 1905-) DL860+	
948.5051	Sweden (1905-45) DL860-868	
948.7	Stockholm, Swe. (area) DL976	
948.9	DENMARK & FINLAND	
948.9	DENMARK (overall) DL101-291+, DL148	
948.905	Denmark (1906-) DL250 (20th c.)	
948.9051	Denmark (1906-45) DL253-257	
948.97	FINLAND DK445-465 (mostly pre-1970 pubns.),	
	DL1002-1180+ (1970+ titles)	
948.9702	Finland (1809-1917) DK458, DL1065	
948.9703	Finland (1917-) DK459, DL1066.5	
948.97031	Finland (1917-39) DK459, DL1084	
948.97032	Finland (1939-45: WWII era: inclu. Russo-Finnish War: SEE ALSO	
	947.0842 for R-F War) DK459.45-5+, DL1090-1105+,	
	DL1090 (gen.)	
948.971	Helsingfors, Fin. (Helsinki: area) DK465.H5, DL1175,	
	DL1175.48 (1917-)	
948.977	Lapland (Fin.) DL971.L2, DL1170.L2	
949	EUROPE (misc. areas: Iceland, Belg., Switz., Greece, etc.)	
949.12	ICELAND DL301-398+, DL375 (1918-)	
949.2	HOLLAND (NETHERLANDS) DJ, DJ109 (gen.)	
949.207	Holland (20th c.) DJ216 (19th-20th c.)	
949.2071	Holland (1890-1948: Q. Wilhelmina era) DJ281-287,	
	DJ281 (gen.), DJ285 (WWI time), DJ287 (WWII	
era)		
949.3	BELGIUM DH401-811+, DH521	
949.304	Belgium (1909-) DH677 (20th c.)	
949.3041	Belgium (1909-34: Albert I) DH681-685, DH681, DH682 (WWI)	
949.3042	Belgium (1934-51: Leopold III) DH687-689, DH687	
949.35	LUXEMBOURG DH901-925, DH916 (1815-)	
949.4	SWITZERLAND DQ, DQ54	
949.407	Switzerland (20th c.) DQ201	
949.4072	Switzerland (1918-45)	
949.47	Alpine region (Switz.) DQ820-841, DQ823	
949.5	GREECE DF, DF757	
949.506	Greece (1821-1924: Monarchy) DF802	
949.507	Greece (20th c.: 1924-) DF833 (20th c.), DF838 (WWI)	
949.5073	Greece (1924-35: Republic) DF848	
949.5074	Greece (1935-67: Monarchy) DF849	
949.512	Athens, Gr. DF915-936, DF925 (1901-)	
949.55	Ionian Sea islands DF901.I57-69	

949.6	BALKAN PENINSULA (inclu. Balkan Wars of 1912-13)	DR1-48,
		DR45 (20th c.), DR46 (Balkan Wars)
949.65	ALBANIA	DR701.S49-86 (known as Scutari for earlier works),
	DR701.S5, DR941-979+ (for later works), DR941 (gen.)
949.6502	Albania (1912-46)	DR701.S6 (1914-17), .S85 (1939-43),
		DR971, DR972 (WWI), DR975 (WWII)
949.7	YUGOSLAVIA (overall)	DR301-396+ (earlier books), DR1202-1307+
949.7+	YUGOSLAVIA & BULGARIA
949.701	Yugoslavia (to 1918)	DR317, DR1274
949.702	Yugoslavia (20th c. & 1918-)	DR357, DR1274, DR1282
949.7021	Yugoslavia (1918-39: Kingdom)	DR366, DR1289
949.7022	Yugoslavia (1939-45: WWII era)	DR369, DR1297-1298)
949.71	SERBIA (inclu. Belgrade)	DR301-396, DR1932-2125+
949.71015	Serbia (1878-1918: Independence)	DR351-363, DR2006-2032
949.7102	Serbia (1918-)	DR366, DR2034
949.72	CROATIA (inclu. Dalmatia, Istria, Slavonia)	DB361-380, DR1502-1645
949.73	Slovenia	DR381.S6, DR1352-1485+
949.74	Yugoslavia (central republics: Bosnia, Herzegovina, Montenegro)
949.742	HERCEGOVINA (Herzegovina) & BOSNIA	DB231-250 (Bos.),
		DB521-540 (Her.), DR1652-1785
949.745	MONTENEGRO	DR101-196, DR1802-1928
949.76	MACEDONIA	DR701.M13-42, DR2152-2285+
949.77	BULGARIA	DR51-98
949.7702	Bulgaria (1878-1946)	DR85-93, DR89 (1918-43)
949.8	ROMANIA (Rumania)	DR201-296
949.802	Romania (1861-1947: Monarchy)	DR250-266, DR250,
		DR263 (1914-18), DR264 (1918-44)
949.9	Aegean Sea islands	DS52
949.98	CRETE	DF901.C78-89, .C86 (1898-)
950-959	Asia	DS
950	ASIA (gen.)	DS, DS5, DS33
950.3	Asia (1480-1905)	DS33
950.4	Asia (20th c.)	DS35
950.41	Asia (1905-45)	DS35
951	CHINA (plus surrounding areas)	DS701-796+, DS706, DS735
951.003	Dictionaries & encyclopedias (China)	DS705
951.03	China (1644-1912: inclu. Sino-Japanese War, 1894-5: SEE ALSO
	952.03 for Sino-Jpn. War of 1894-5)	DS764.4-767.7
951.04	China (1912-49)	DS773.83-777.544, DS774
951.041	China (1912-27)	DS776.4-777.462, DS776.4
951.042	China (1927-49: Nationalist rule: inclu. Sino-Jpn. conflict of 1937-45:
	SEE ALSO 940.53 for Sino-Jpn. War of 1937-45)
		DS777.47-544, DS777.47
951.13	Kiangsu Province (China: inclu. Nanking & Shanghai)	DS793.K
951.156	Peking, China	DS795
951.222	Kiangsi Province (China)
951.245	Fukien Province (China)
951.249	FORMOSA (Taiwan)	DS895.F7-77 (books prior to about 1970),
		DS798.92-799.99+
951.24904	Formosa (1895-1945: Japanese period)	DS895.F75,
		DS799.69-72, DS799.7 (gen.)
951.25	HONG KONG	DS796.H7
951.2504	Hong Kong (1843-1945)	DS796.H757

951.3	China (Southwestern)	
951.35	Yunnan Province (China)	
951.38	Chungking, China (plus Szechwan Province)	
951.38	Szechwan Province (China: inclu. Chungking)	DS793.S8
951.5	TIBET DS785	
951.7	MONGOLIA DS793.M7	
951.8	MANCHURIA DS781-784+, DS784 (1932-45)	
951.9	KOREA DS901-935, DS916 (20th c.)	

952	JAPAN DS801-897+	
952.03	Japan (1868-1945: Imperial power) DS881.9	
952.032	Japan (1912-26: Taisho or Yoshihito era) DS885.8-888, DS886 (gen.)	
952.033	Japan (1926-88: Showa or Hirohito period: inclu. Sino-Jpn. conflict of 1937-41: PREFER 951.042 for Sino-Jpn. War of 1937-41) DS888.15-890+, DS888.2, DS888.5 (1926-45)	
952.1	Honshu (Japan)	
952.135	Tokyo, Japan DS896, DS896.64 (1867-1945), DS897.T6 (for earlier works)	
952.19	Hiroshima, Japan	
952.191	Kyoto, Japan: USE 952.1864 with books after about 1988)	
952.3	Shikoku (Japan)	
952.4	Hokkaido (Japan)	
952.7	Kurile Islands (Japan or Russia)	
952.81	Ryukyu Islands (Japan: inclu. Okinawa: try 952.29 for titles after 1988)	
952.85	Bonin Islands (Japan: SEE 952.28 for works after 1988)	

953	ARABIAN PENINSULA DS201-248+, DS244 (1914-)	
954	Southern Asia & India DS335-498+	
954	INDIA (overall) DS436	
954.03	India (1785-1947: British rule) DS463-480, DS463 (gen.)	
954.0356	India (1905-16) DS480.2-3	
954.0357	India (1916-26) DS480.4-6	
954.0358	India (1926-36) DS480.7-8	
954.0359	India (1936-47: Gov'ships. of Linlithgow, Wavell, Mountbatten) DS480.82-83	
954.14	Calcutta, India (area) DS486.C2	
954.93	Ceylon DS488-490, DS489.5 (gen. hist.)	

955	PERSIA (Iran) DS251-325, DS272	
955.05	Iran (1906-) DS298, DS313-318+	
955.051	Iran (1906-25) DS315-316	
955.052	Iran (1925-41: Reza Shah era) DS317	
955.053	Iran (1941-ca. 1978) DS318	
956	MIDDLE EAST (NEAR EAST) DS41-326	
956.02	Near East (1900-18) DS62.4	
956.03	Middle East (1918-45) DS62.4	
956.1	TURKEY & CYPRUS DR401-741, DS47-53, DS54 (Cyp.)	
956.1	TURKEY (overall) DR440	
956.102	Turkey (1918-45) DR589-590	
956.1024	Turkey (1923-38: Kemal Ataturk era) DR590, DR592 (biogs.), DR592.K4(Ataturk)	
956.1025	Turkey (1938-50: Ismet Inonu rule) DR590, DR592	
956.45	CYPRUS DS54	
956.4503	Cyprus (1878-1960: British rule) DS54.8	

956.7	IRAQ DS67-79, DS70.9	
956.703	Iraq (1553-1920: Ottoman rule)	DS77
956.704	Iraq (1920-: Mandate & independence)	DS79
956.9	MEDITERRANEAN REGION (EASTERN)	DS80-151+, DS62
956.91	SYRIA DS92-99, DS95.5	
956.9103	Syria (1516-1920: time of Ottomans)	DS97.5-6
956.9104	Syria (1920-: Mandate & independence)	DS98+
956.94	ISRAEL & PALESTINE DS101-131+, DS116-117, DS123	
956.9403	Palestine (640-1917) DS124-125, DS125.5 (WWI yrs.)	
956.9404	Israel (1917-48: Brit. rule) DS126, DS126.3 (WWII era)	
957	SIBERIA DK751-781, DK761	
959	SOUTHEAST ASIA DS521-689+, DS518 (1904-45: Far E. ?), DS525, DS541	
959.05	Asia, Southeast (20th c.) DS526.6-7+	
959.051	Southeast Asia (1900-41) DS518, DS526.6 (newer titles), DS549	
959.052	Southeast Asia (1941-45: Japanese occup.) DS549, DS526.6	
959.1	BURMA DS485.B79-892, DS527-530 (newer works), DS528.5	
959.104	Burma (1886-1948: British rule) DS485.B89, DS530-530.32	
959.3	SIAM (THAILAND) DS561-589, DS571	
959.304	Siam (20th c.) DS578	
959.3043	Siam (1935-46: time of Rama VIII) DS585	
959.4	LAOS DS555, DS557.L2 (earlier books)	
959.5	MALAYSIA DS591-599, DS592, DS596	
959.503	Malaysia (to 1946) DS596, DS596.6	
959.52	SINGAPORE DS598.S7	
959.5203	Singapore (to 1946)	
959.6	CAMBODIA DS554, DS554.7	
959.7	FRENCH INDOCHINA & VIETNAM DS531-558	
959.703	French Indochina (to 1949) DS556.8-83	
959.8	INDONESIA & MALAY ARCHIPELAGO DS611-649	
959.802	Indonesia (1602-1945: Dutch period) DS642-643	
959.8022	Indonesia (1798-1945) DS643	
959.81	Sumatra (Indon.) DS646.1-15, DS646.129	
959.82	Java (Indon.) DS646.17-29, DS646.2	
959.83	BORNEO DS646.3-38, DS646.3	
959.9	PHILIPPINE ISLANDS DS651-689, DS655, DS668	
959.903	Philippine Islands (1898-1946: U.S. era) DS679-686.4, DS685	
959.9032	Philippine Islands (1901-35) DS685	
959.9035	Philippine Islands (1935-46: Commonwealth)) DS686-686.4	
959.91	Luzon (Philip.: inclu. Manila & Bataan) DS688.L9	
959.95	Visayan Islands (Philip.: inclu. Cebu, Leyte, Negros, etc.) DS688.B6 (Bisayas)	
959.98	Mindanao (Philip.) DS688.M2	
960-969	Africa DT	
960	AFRICA (gen.) DT, DT3 (gen.), DT20 (gen. hist.)	
960.31	Africa (1900-45) DT29	
961	NORTH AFRICA DT160-346	
961.03	North Africa (1830-1950: Eur. era) DT176	
961.1	TUNISIA DT241-269, DT254	
961.104	Tunisia (1881-1956) DT264	

961.2	LIBYA	DT211-239, DT224
961.203	Libya (1911-52: Ital. rule)	DT235
962	EGYPT & SUDAN	DT43-159
962	EGYPT (overall)	DT43-107, DT115-154, DT77
962.04	Egypt (1882-1922: Brit. protec.)	DT107-107.8, DT107 (gen.)
962.05	Egypt (1922-: Independence)	DT107.8+
962.051	Egypt (1922-36: Fuad I)	DT107.8
962.052	Egypt (1936-52: Faruk I)	DT107.82
962.4	SUDAN	DT108 (older works), DT154.1-159
963	ETHIOPIA (Abyssinia)	DT371-398, DT381
963.05	Ethiopia (1896-1941 & 20th c.)	DT386-387.9, DT386
963.055	Ethiopia (1930-74: Haile Selassie era)	DT387.7-387.92
963.056	Ethiopia (1935-6: Italo-Eth. War: SEE ALSO 945.091 for Italo-Eth. War of 1935-6)	DT387.8
963.057	Ethiopia (1936-41: Ital. rule)	DT387.9
963.06	Ethiopia (1941-: Independence)	DT387.9

964	NORTHWEST AFRICA, Morocco, & offshore islands	
964	MOROCCO (in sum)	DT301-330, DT305, DT314
964.04	Morocco (1900-56)	DT324
964.3	Casablanca, Mor. (area)	DT329.C3
964.8	SPANISH WEST AFRICA	
964.9	CANARY ISLANDS	DP302.C36-51
965	ALGERIA	DT271-299, DT275, DT284
965.04	Algeria (1900-62: last of Fr. rule)	DT295 (older titles), DT294.5-295.3
966	SAHARA DESERT & West Africa	
967.6	EAST AFRICA (Uganda & Kenya)	DT421-435+ (newer titles), DT431
967.62	KENYA	DT434.E2, DT433.5-434, DT433.522, DT433.557
967.6203	Kenya (1895-1963: Brit. rule)	DT433.57-577
967.8103	ZANZIBAR (1890-1963)	DT435, DT449.Z2-29 (newer works), DT449.Z28
967.8202	GERMAN WEST AFRICA (1884-1916)	DT444, DT447 (newer books)
967.8203	Tanganyika (1916-61: Brit. era)	DT444, DT447
968	AFRICA, SOUTHERN	DT730-990+, DT732-733
968	SOUTH AFRICA (overall)	DT751-944, DT766
968.05	South Africa (1910-61: Union)	DT779
968.052	South Africa (1910-19: Louis Botha)	DT779.5
968.055	South Africa (1939-48: Jan Christiaan Smuts: 2d era)	DT779.7
968.9	NORTHERN RHODESIA (Zambia), Rhodesia (Zimbabwe), & Nyasaland (Malawi)	DT858-865 (Malawi, Nyasaland, Br. Central Afr. Protec.), DT946-965 (Rhodesia), DT963 (Zambia)
969.1	MADAGASCAR	DT469.M21-38

970-979	North America & America	E-F
970	NORTH AMERICA (gen.)	E-F1392+, E11-45, E31-45
970.05	North America (1900-)	E45, E18.85
970.051	North America (1900-18)	
970.052	North America (1918-45)	
971	CANADA	F1001-1140
971.06	Canada (20th c. & 1911-)	F1034
971.061	Canada (1911-21)	
971.062	Canada (1921-35)	
971.063	Canada (1935-57)	
971.0632	Canada (1935-48: 2d prime min'ship. of Wm. Lyon Mackenzie King)	
971.1	British Columbia	F1086-1089.7, F1089 (gen.)
971.3	Ontario (Can.)	F1056-1059.7, F1058 (gen.)
971.4	Quebec	F1051-1055
971.6	Nova Scotia	F1036-1040, F1038 (gen.)
971.8	Newfoundland	F1121-1139
972	CARIBBEAN, MEXICO, & CENTRAL AMERICA	F1201-1392 (Mex.), F1421-2175
972	MEXICO (overall)	F1201-1392, F1208, F1226
972.082	Mexico (1917-64)	F1234-1235
972.8	CENTRAL AMERICA	F1421-1577, F1436
972.805	Central America (1900-)	F1438-1439
972.87	PANAMA	F1561-1577, F1566
972.87051	Panama (1904-45)	F1566.5
972.875	Panama Canal & Zone	F1569.C2
972.9	WEST INDIES	F1601-2175+, F1608, F1621
972.9051	West Indies (1902-45)	F1623
972.91	CUBA	F1751-1849, F1758, F1776
972.9106	Cuba (1899-)	F1787-1788
972.92	JAMAICA	F1861-1896, F1881
972.95	PUERTO RICO	F1951-1983, F1971
972.983	TRINIDAD & TOBAGO	F2016 (Windward Is.), F2116 (Tob.), F2121 (Trin.)
973	UNITED STATES	E-F975+, E178 (gen.)
973.03	Encyclopedias & dictionaries (U.S.)	E174
973.05	Serials & periodicals (U.S.)	E171
973.06	Clubs & societies (U.S.)	E172
973.9	United States (20th c.)	E740-749, E741
973.91	United States (1901-53)	E741, E740-816
973.913	United States (1913-21: Woodrow Wilson)	E765-783, E766, E780 (WWI era)
973.914	United States (1921-23: Warren G. Harding era)	E783-786, E785
973.915	United States (1923-29: Calvin Coolidge)	E791-796, E791
973.916	United States (1929-33: Herbert C. Hoover)	E796-805, E801
973.917	United States (1933-45: Franklin D. Roosevelt)	E805-812, E806

974-979	UNITED STATES (local: regions, states, towns, etc.: note that Hawaii is placed at 996.9)	F1-900+
974	New England & Middle Atlantic states	F1-105 (New Eng.), F106-205 (Mid. At.), F1-15, F106
974.042	New England & Middle Atlantic states (1918-45)	F9 (New Eng.), F106 (Mid. At.)
974.1	Maine	F16-30, F19 (gen.), F25 (1865-1950)
974.4	Massachusetts	F61-75, F64
974.7	New York	F116-130, F119
974.7042	New York (1918-45)	F124 (1865-1950)
974.71	New York City, N.Y.	F128, F128.3
974.721	Long Island, N.Y.	F127.L8
974.8	Pennsylvania	F146-160, F149
974.811	Philadelphia, Penn.	F158
974.9	New Jersey	F131-145
975	South Atlantic states	F206-295, F206-220, F209, F215 (1865-)
975.3	District of Columbia	F191-205, F194
975.303	Washington, D.C. (1865-1933)	F198-199
975.304	Washington, D.C. (1933-)	F199+
975.5	Virginia	F221-235, F226, F231 (1865-1950)
975.8	Georgia	F281-295, F286
975.9	Florida	F306-320, F311
975.9062	Florida (1918-45)	F316
975.9381	Miami, Florida	F319.M6
975.941	Florida Keys	F317.M7 (Monroe Co.)
976	South Central states & Gulf Coast	F296-475, F296-395 (Gulf), F296-301, F396-475 (Old S.W.), F396
976.3	Louisiana	F366-380, F369
976.4	Texas	F381-395, F386
976.4062	Texas (1918-45)	F391
976.4139	Galveston, Texas (area)	F392.G25
976.496	El Paso, Texas (area)	F392.E45, F394.E4
976.7	Arkansas	F406-420
976.9	Kentucky	F446-460
977	North Central states	F476-705, F476-590 (Old N.W.), F476-485, F591-705 (Trans-Miss.), F591-596
977.1	Ohio	F486-500, F491
977.3	Illinois	F536-550, F541, F546 (1865-1950)
977.311	Chicago, Ill.	F548
977.4	Michigan (inclu. Lakes Mich. & Huron)	F561-575, F566
977.49	Lake Superior & Upper Peninsula (Mich.)	F572.N8 (N. Penin.), F552 (Lake Sup.)
977.8	Missouri	F461-475, F466
978	Western states	F591-785, F591-596, F591
978.1	Kansas	F676-690
978.4	North Dakota	F631-645
978.6	Montana	F726-740
978.8	Colorado	F771-785, F776
978.883	Denver, Colo.	F784.D4
978.9	New Mexico	F791-805, F796

979	Great Basin & Pacific Coast states	F786-915, F786-850 (New S.W.), F786-788, F851-915 (Pac. states), F851
979.03	Pacific Coast & Great Basin (U.S.: 20th c.)	F786, F852
979.1	Arizona F806-820	
979.3	Nevada F836-850	
979.4	California F856-870, F861 (gen.)	
979.405	California (1900-) F866 (1869-1950)	
979.4052	California (1918-45) F866	
979.454	Sacramento, Calif. F869.S12	
979.46	San Francisco Bay area F868.S156	
979.461	San Francisco, Calif. F869.S3	
979.49	California, Southern F867	
979.491	Santa Barbara County (Calif.) F868.S23	
979.493	Los Angeles County (Calif.) F868.L8	
979.494	Los Angeles, Calif. F869.L8	
979.495	San Bernardino County (Calif.) F868.S14	
979.498	San Diego County (Calif.) F868.S15	
979.5	Oregon F871-885	
979.7	Washington F886-900, F891	
979.77	Puget Sound area (Wash.) F897.P9	
979.777	Seattle, Wash. (area) F897.K4, F899.S4	
979.8	Alaska F901-915	
979.804	Alaska (1912-59: U.S. Territory) F909	
979.84	Aleutian Islands & Southwestern Alaska F951	
980-989	South America F	
980	SOUTH AMERICA (overall: inclu. Latin Am. in gen.) F2201-3799+, F2201-2239, F2231 (GEN.)	
980.033	South America (1918-49) F2236, F2237 (1939-)	
981	BRAZIL F2501-2659, F2521	
981.061	Brazil (1930-54) F2538	
982	ARGENTINA F2801-3021+, F2831 (gen.)	
982.06	Argentina (20th c.) F2847-2849+	
982.061	Argentina (1910-46) F2848	
982.11	Buenos Aires, Arg. (area) F3001	
983	CHILE F3051-3285, F3081 (gen.)	
985	PERU F3401-3619, F3431	
987	VENEZUELA F2301-2349, F2321	
989.2	PARAGUAY F2661-2699	
989.5	URUGUAY F2701-2799, F2721 (gen.)	
989.5063	Uruguay (1933-51) F2728	
989.513	Montevideo, Urug. F2781	

990-999	History (misc. areas: Oceania, Atlantic islands, Arctic, extraterr.
	worlds, etc.) C-F, G, Q
990	OCEANICA & other misc. areas (SEE ALSO 995 for gen. works after
	about 1988) DU, DU28.3
993-996	OCEANIA DU
993	NEW ZEALAND & MELANESIA (overall: SEE ALSO 993.1 for N.Z. titles
	before 1989, 995 for Mel. after about 1988) DU400-490+
993.03	New Zealand (1908-: Dominion: SEE ALSO 993.103 for works
	before 1989)
993.032	New Zealand (1918-45: SEE ALSO 993.1032 for titles before
	about 1989)
993.1	NEW ZEALAND (PREFER 993 after 1988) DU400-430
993.103	New Zealand (1908-: Dominion: PREFER 993.03+ for titles after
	1988) DU420-421
993.1031	New Zealand (1908-18)
993.1032	New Zealand (1918-45)
993.12	North Island (New Z.)
993.122	Auckland, New Z. (area) DU430.A79
993.15	South Island (New Z.)
993.155	Christchurch, New Z. (area) DU430.C5
993.2-993.7	MELANESIA (PREFER 995 after 1988) DU490 (gen.)
993.2	NEW CALEDONIA (try ALSO 993.97 after 1988) DU720
993.4	NEW HEBRIDES (SEE ALSO 995.95 for books after 1988) DU760
993.5	SOLOMON ISLANDS (ALSO try 995.93 for works dated after 1988)
	DU850
993.6	BISMARCK ARCHIPELAGO (inclu. New Britain [Rabaul] & New Ireland:
	PREFER 995.8 for pubn. dates after 1988) DU550-553,
	DU553.N35 (New Brit.)
993.95	VANUATU (New Hebrides: SEE ALSO 993.4 to find works on New
	Hebrides prior to 1989) DU760
993.97	NEW CALEDONIA (SEE ALSO 993.2 for works before 1989) DU720
994	AUSTRALIA DU80-398, DU450-480, DU110 (gen.)
994.04	Australia (1901-45) DU116
994.041	Australia (1901-22)
994.042	Australia (1922-45)
994.1	Australia, Western DU350-380
994.11	Perth, Australia (area) DU378
994.2	Australia, Central DU300-330, DU390+
994.29	Northern Territory (Australia) DU392-398
994.295	Darwin & N. District (Australia) DU398.D3
994.3	Queensland (Australia: inclu. Great Barrier Reef) DU250-280
994.31	Brisbane, Australia DU278
994.4	New South Wales (Australia) DU150-180, DU170
994.41	Sydney, Australia (area) DU178
994.5	Victoria (Australia) DU200-230, DU220
994.51	Melbourne, Australia DU228
994.6	Tasmania DU450-480, DU470
994.7	Capital Territory (Australia) DU145
994.71	Canberra, Australia DU145

995	MELANESIA, NEW GUINEA, & OCEANIA (SEE ALSO 993.2-7 for titles on Mel. & New G. before 1989; 990 for gen. titles on Oceania prior to 1989) DU739-746, DU739	
995	NEW GUINEA (overall)	
995.1-7	New Guinea	
995.3	Papua New Guinea & New Guinea region	
995.303	Papua New Guinea (inclu. Kokoda Trail, Port Moresby, Owen Stanley Range, etc.: 1942-45: WWII era)	
995.403	Papua Territory (1942-45: WWII period)	
995.603	New Guinea (Highlands region: 1942-45: WWII era)	
995.703	New Guinea (Northern coastal region: inclu. Lae, Huon Penin., Madang, Wewak, etc.: 1942-45: WWII era)	
995.8	Bismarck Archipelago (SEE ALSO 993.6 for books before 1989)	
995.803	Bismarck Archipelago (1942-45: WWII period) DU550-553	
995.92	Solomon Islands (Northern: inclu. Buka, Bougainville, etc.)	
995.93	SOLOMON ISLANDS(SEE ALSO 993.5 for works prior to about 1989) DU850	
996	POLYNESIA & other Pacific areas DU510 (Poly.: gen.)	
996.1	PACIFIC, SOUTHWEST CENTRAL (plus isolated S.E. islands)	
996.11	FIJI ISLANDS DU600	
996.12	FRIENDLY ISLANDS (Tonga) DU880	
996.13	SAMOA, AMERICAN DU819.A1, DU810-819, DU815	
996.14	SAMOA, WESTERN DU819.A2, DU810-819, DU815	
996.4	LINE ISLANDS (Pacific)	
996.5	MICRONESIA DU500 (gen.)	
996.6	PALAU & CAROLINE ISLANDS DU560-568, DU5630565	
996.7	MARIANAS (Ladrone Islands: inclu. Guam) DU640-648, DU643-645	
996.8	MICRONESIA, EASTERN	
996.81	KIRIBATI (inclu. Gilbert Is.) DU615	
996.82	TUVALU (Ellice Is.) DU590	
996.83	MARSHALL ISLANDS DU710	
996.85	NAURU (Pleasant Island)	
996.9	PACIFIC, NORTH CENTRAL (inclu. Hawaiian Is.)	
996.9	HAWAIIAN ISLANDS (overall) DU620-629, DU625	
996.903	Hawaiian Islands (1898-1959: U.S. Terr.) DU627.5	
996.91	Hawaii (island) DU628.H28	
996.921	Maui (Haw. Is.) DU628.M3	
996.93	Oahu (Haw. Is.) DU628.O3	
996.931	Honolulu, Haw. DU629.H7	
996.941	Kauai (Haw. Is.) DU628.K3	
996.99	Baker, Johnston, Palmyra, Midway, & other outlying Hawaiian Islands DU629.M (Midway), DU650	
997	ATLANTIC OCEAN ISLANDS	
997.1	Falkland Islands (S. Atl. Ocean: G.B.) F3031	
997.3	Saint Helena (Atl. Ocean) DT671.S2	
998-998.8	ARCTIC ISLANDS	
998.2	GREENLAND	
998.9	ANTARCTICA	

III. INDEX TO LIBRARY OF CONGRESS & DEWEY CLASSIFICATION

Following is a unified index to both of the preceding classification sections--
Library of Congress and Dewey. Words and phrases are followed by either
LC, Dewey, or sometimes both kinds of numbers. Since this listing was
generated by alphabetizing a combined LC/Dewey database, one might find
either form given first. Entries missing one or the other of the types do so
because exact translations could not be found or do not exist. A similar
warning as in other sections: do not use this part of the book alone for
complete knowledge of a topical area. Class index entries, class numbers and
ranges, and subject/corporate phrases from the different sections should all
be consulted for the most thorough group of control points.

INDEX WORDS/PHRASES: POSSIBLE CLASS NUMBERS (LC AND/OR DEWEY)

5 in. guns, Naval (U.S.: manuals)   VF393.A5.5
1900-1999 (20th c.: gen. hist.)   909.82   D421, D443
1900-1919 (gen. hist.)   909.821   D421, D521 (WWI: gen.)
1920-1929 (gen. hist.)   909.822   D653, D655-659, D720, D723-728 (1919-39)
1930-1939 (gen. hist.)   909.823   D720, D723-728
1940-1949 (gen. hist.)   909.824   D743 (WWII: gen.), D825, D840

AACHEN, Ger. (Aix-la-Chapelle)   DD901.A25-28
Abandoning ship (plus other misc. marine topics of disaster)   VK1259
Abyssinia (19th -20th c.)   DT386   963.03-05+
Accidents, Marine   VK199
Accounting & accounts, Military (inclu. records, muster rolls, etc.)   UB160-165
Accounting & accounts, Naval (inclu. ships' records)   VC500-505   359.622
Addis Ababa, Eth.   DT390.A3
Adelaide, Australia   DU328   994.231
Aden   DS247.A2
Adjutant generals' offices   UB170-175
Administration (air forces: structure & personnel: gen.)   UG770-775   358.41,
                                                                    .413, .416+
Administration (marines)   359.966   VB21-124
ADMINISTRATION, MILITARY   UB
Administration, Military (Asia: gen.)   UB99
Administration, Military (command, intelligence, law, etc.)   UB   355, .6
Administration, Military (Eur.: gen.)   UB55
Administration, Military (G.B.: gen.)   UB57   355.60941, 354.41066
Administration, Military (gen. hist.)   UB15
Administration, Military supply & finance   355.62   UC260-267, UA
Administration, Military (U.S.: gen.)   UB23
ADMINISTRATION, NAVAL   359.6   VB, VB15, VB21-124 (by place),
            VB23 (U.S.), VC (maint.), VC10, VC20-258 (by place), VC20-65 (U.S.)
Administration, Naval (Asia: gen.)   VB99   359.6095
Administration, Naval (command, personnel, law, etc.)   VB
Administration, Naval (Eur.: gen.)   VB55   359.6094
Administration, Naval (gen. hist.)   VB15   359.6, .1-3
Administration, Naval (misc. topics)   VB955
Administration, Naval supply & finance   359.62   VC10, VC20-258 (by
                                                        place), VC20-65 (U.S.)

Admirals, commanders, etc. (admin.: inclu. duties)   VB190
Admiralty Islands   DU520   993.7
Adriatic coast (Yug.)   DR1350.A35
Advanced guard   U167.5.A35
Adventists (WWII)   D810.C53
Aegean islands   DS52-53   949.9
Aegean Sea   DR701.A5
Aegean Sea islands   949.9   DS52
Aerial observations (artillery)   UF805
AERIAL OPS. (Sp. Civil War, 1936-39)   DP269.4
Aerial ops. (WWI: G.B.)   940.44941   D602
Aerial ops. (WWI: gen.)   D600
Aerial ops. (WWI: Ger.)   940.44943   D604
Aerial ops. (WWI: particular countries)   940.449
Aerial ops. (WWI: U.S.)   940.44973   D606, D570.6-7 (squadrons)
AERIAL OPS. (WWII: Australia)   940.544994   D792.A8
Aerial ops. (WWII: by country: inclu. specific craft, units, fliers)   940.5449+
Aerial ops. (WWII: Can.)   940.544971
Aerial ops. (WWII: China)   940.544951   D792.C5
Aerial ops. (WWII: G.B.: R.A.F. etc.)   940.544941-544942   D786
Aerial ops. (WWII: gen.)   D785   940.544
Aerial ops. (WWII: Ger.: Luftwaffe etc.) 940.544943   D787
Aerial ops. (WWII: It.)   940.544945   D792.I8
Aerial ops. (WWII: Japan)   940.544952   D792.J3
Aerial ops. (WWII: misc. countries)   D792.A-Z
Aerial ops. (WWII: particular srvcs.: scouting, artil. supp., bombing, close air supp.,
          antisub. ops., balloon barrage, coast patrols, etc.)   940.5441
Aerial ops. (WWII: Rus.)   940.544947   D792.R9 or .S65
Aerial ops. (WWII: U.S.: Army Air Corps, Navy, Marines, etc.)   940.544973
                                                                                                            D790
Aerial reconnaisance (U.S.)   UG763
Aerial warfare & air forces   358.4 (inclu. naval av. for works prior to 1989--SEE
          359.94 after 1988)   UG622-1425, UG630, UG633-634 (U.S.),
          UG635.A-Z (places besides U.S.), VG90-95 (naval av.)
Aerodynamics   629.1323
Aeronautics   629.13
Aeronautics (principles)   629.132
AFRICA   960-969   DT
Africa (1884-1945: gen.)   DT29   960.23-31
Africa (1900-45)   960.31   DT29
Africa (gen.)   960   DT, DT3 (gen.), DT20 (gen. hist.)
Africa (geog. & travel)   916   DT55 (1901-50)
Africa (lighthouses, beacons, foghorns, etc.)   VK1115-1119
Africa (lighthouses, beacons, foghorns, etc.: lists)   VK1190-1199
Africa (mil. status: gen.)   UA855   355.03306
Africa (naval status)   VA670-700
Africa, Northwest (geog. & travel: Morocco, Canary Islands, etc.)   916.4
                                                                                            DT165, DT310 (Mor.)
Africa (overall)   DT1-38   960
Africa (post-WWI territorial ?s)   D651.A4
Africa, Southern   968   DT730-990+, DT732-733

Africa (WWII)   D766.8-99
Africa (WWII: by country)   D766.9-99
Africa (WWII: dipl. history)   D754.A34
Africa (WWII: gen.)   D766.8   940.536, .5423, 960.31
Africa (WWII: misc. countries: by name)   D766.99.A-Z
Afro-Americans & American Indians as troops (WWII)   940.5403   D810.N4,
                                                                                     D810.I5

Afro-Americans (armed forces)   UB418.A47
Afro-Americans (U.S. Navy)   VB324.A47
Afro-Americans (WWII)   940.53150396073   E185, D810.N4
Agricultural products (mil. raw materials)   355.245   UA929.95.A35
Agriculture (defense)   UA929.95.A35
Agriculture, forestry, hunting   S   630-639, 574, 581, 799
AIR BASES & fields (U.S.: by name)   UG634.5.A-Z
Air bases (mil. design)   623.6613   UG633-634.5 (U.S.), UG635 (other lands)
Air bases (WWII: by area or place)   940.5443+
Air bases (WWII: in Australia)   940.544394
Air bases (WWII: in China)   940.544351
Air bases (WWII: in Eng.)   940.544342 D786
Air bases (WWII: in Ger.)   940.544343 D787
Air bases (WWII: in Japan)   940.544352 D792.J3
Air bases (WWII: in Rus.)   940.544347
Air bases (WWII: in U.S.)   940.544373 D790
Air battles & campaigns (WWII)   940.5442   D785+
Air defenses (U.S.)   UG733   358.41450973
Air fields & stations, Naval (U.S.: by name)   VG94.5.A-Z
AIR FORCE administration   358.416   UG770-775, UG1100-1135, UG630-635
Air force bombs (by specific type)   UG1282.A-Z
Air force communications & ops.   358.46   UA940-945, UG611-612.5
Air force equipment (gen.: planes, bombs, etc.)   UG1200   358.418, .412
Air force facilities   623.66   UG633-635, UG21-124 (engnrg. by place),
                                                     UG360-390 (field engnrg.)
Air force history (G.B.)   DA89.5-6
Air force life & customs   358.411   U750-773, UG770-775, UG1130-1135
Air force manuals & regulations (places except U.S.)   UG675.A-Z
Air force officers (countries except U.S.)   UG795.A-Z
Air force ops. (gen.)   358.414   UG630, UG633-635, UG700-765
Air force ops. (WWI)   D600-607   940.44
Air force ops. (WWII)   D785-792   940.544
Air force ordnance (gen.: U.S.)   UG1273
Air force personnel   358.4161   UG1130-1135
AIR FORCE PLANES (countries besides U.S.)   UG1245.A-Z
Air force planes (Fr.)   UG1245.F8   358.400944
Air force planes (G.B.)   UG1245.G7   358.400941, .414741-414742,
                                                     623.740941, .7460941
Air force planes (Ger.)   UG1245.G3   358.400943, .414743, 623.740943
Air force planes (It.)   UG1245.I8   358.400945
Air force planes (Japan)   UG1245.J3   358.400952, .414752, 623.740952
Air force planes (Rus.)   UG1245.R9   358.400947
Air force planes (U.S.: PREFER UG1242 for particular types)   UG1243
                                                     358.40973, .4140973, .414773, 623.740973, .7460973
Air force radar & electronics (places besides U.S.)   UG1425.A-Z
Air force regulations & manuals (Ger.)   UG675.G3

Air force tactics (gen.)   UG700
Air force training & education (U.S.)   UG638-638.8
Air force units (types)   358.4131
AIR FORCES & air warfare   UG622-1425   358.4, 623.74-746
Air forces & warfare (essays & lectures)   UG627
Air forces & warfare (hist.: gen.)   UG625   358.4009
Air forces & warfare, Naval   VG90-95   359.94, 358.4
Air forces (Australia)   UG635.A8
Air forces (Fr.)   UG635.F8
Air forces (G.B.)   UG635.G7
Air forces (Ger.)   UG635.G3
Air forces (It.)   UG635.I8
Air forces (Japan)   UG635.J3
Air forces, Naval (U.S.: by area or state)   VG94.A-Z
Air forces (places besides U.S.)   UG635.A-Z
Air forces (policy & status)   358.403   UG630-635, UA
Air forces (Rus.)   UG635.R9
Air forces (Sov.Un.)   UG635.S65
Air forces (U.S.: by state)   UG634.A-W
Air forces (U.S.: gen.)   UG633   358.400973
Air museums & exhibitions (by country or area)   UG623.3.A2-Z
Air National Guard (U.S.)   UG853
Air-raid warning systems (design)   623.737 (SEE 623.37 for titles prior to 1989)
          UG730-735
Air raids (WWI)   940.442   D600-607
Air reserves, Naval & marine (U.S.)   VG94.7.A-Z
Air traffic control (mil. engineering)   623.666
Air transport, Military   UC330-335   358.44
AIR WARFARE   D437   358.41409, 358.41447
Air warfare & forces (collected works: gen.)   UG624
Air warfare & forces (gen.)   UG630   358.4
Air warfare & forces, Naval (gen.)   VG90   358.4, 359.3255, 623.746
Air warfare (gen.)   358.41
Air warfare (hist.: gen.)   358.41409   UG625
Airborne & parachute troops   UD480-485   356.166
Airborne troop battalions etc. (WWII: U.S.: by #)   D769.346.1st-
Airborne troops (WWII: G.B.)   D759.6
Airborne troops (WWII: Ger.)   D757.6
Airborne troops (WWII: U.S.: gen.)   D769.345
Aircraft (heavier-than-air: mil. engineering)   623.746   UG1240-1245,
          UG630-635, TL685.3, VG90-95
Aircraft (lighter-than-air: mil. design)   623.741   UG1310-1375
AIRCRAFT CARRIERS (as equip.)   359.94835 (SEE ALSO .8355 on titles
          before 1989)
Aircraft carriers (engineering)   623.8255   V874-874.5
Aircraft carriers (G.B.)   V874.5.G7   623.82550941
Aircraft carriers (gen.)   V874   623.8255, 359.3255
Aircraft carriers (handling)   623.88255   V874-875
Aircraft carriers (Japan)   V874.5.J3   623.82550952
Aircraft carriers (special topics)   V875.A-Z
Aircraft carriers (U.S.)   V874.3   623.82550973, .81255, 359.32550973
Aircraft carriers (units)   359.3255 (SEE ALSO .9435 for pubns. after 1988)
          V874-875, V874.3 (U.S.), V874.5.A-Z (other places), VA65.A-Z (U.S.: by name)

Aircraft components (cabins, engines, fuselages, instruments, wings, etc.)
                623.746049   TL672-683
Aircraft guns & small weapons (gen.)   UG1340
Aircraft instrumentation (flight)   629.1352
Aircraft instrumentation (navig.)   629.1351
Aircraft launching & recovery equipment (carriers)   V875.A36
Aircraft, Naval   359.94834
Aircraft parts & components   629.134
Aircraft (types: engineering)   629.133+
Airfields & bases (countries besides U.S.: by name of base)   UG635.x2.A-Z
Airmen & non-commissioned air officers   UG820-825   358.41338
Airplanes   629.13334 (engineering)
Airplanes (air force: by type)   UG1242.A-Z
Airplanes (air force: gen.)   UG1240
Airplanes, Military   UG1240-1245   623.746, 358.418
Airports (engineering)   629.136
Airships or dirigibles (gen.)   UG1220   623.743
Airships, Rigid (mil. engineering)   623.7435
Airships, Semirigid & nonrigid (mil. engineering)   623.7436-7437
Akagi (aircraft carrier: Japan)   VA655.A43
Alabama   F321-335   976.1
Alabama (to 1950)   F326
Alaska   979.8   F901-915
Alaska (1894-1959)   F909   979.803-804
Alaska (1912-59: U.S. Territory)   979.804   F909
Alaska area   F901-951   979.8
ALBANIA   949.65 DR701.S49-86 (known as Scutari for earlier works),
            DR701.S5, DR941-979+ (for later works), DR941 (gen.)
Albania (1912-46)   949.6502   DR701.S6 (1914-17), .S85 (1939-43),
            DR971, DR972 (WWI), DR975 (WWII)
Albania (1912-44)   DR970-975
Albania (1912-44: gen.)   DR971
Albania (1912-18)   DR972, DR46+ (Balkan War etc.)
Albania (1914-17: Kingdom)   DR701.S6   949.6502
Albania (1917-25)   DR701.S7   949.6502
Albania (1925-39)   DR974   949.6501-6502
Albania (1925-39: Zog I)   DR701.S8   949.6502
Albania (1939-44)   DR975
Albania (1939-43: Ital. rule)   DR701.S85 949.6502
Albania (1944-)   DR977 949.6502-6503
Albania (1946-: Republic)   DR701.S86
Albania (gen.)   DR941
Albania (geog. & travel)   914.965   DR701.S5, DR917 (later books)
Albania (post-WWI territorial ?s)   D651.A5
Albania (Scutari) DR701.S49-86 (SEE ALSO DR941-979 for later titles)   949.65
Albania (WWII)   D766.7.A4
Albany, N.Y.   F129.A3
Alberta F1075-1080   971.23
Aleutian Islands & Bering Sea   F951 (SEE D769.87.A4 for 1939-45 & Jpn.
        occupation)   979.84, 940.096451, 909.096451824
Aleutian Islands & Southwestern Alaska   979.84   F951
Aleutian Islands (WWII)   PREFER D769.87.A4, but sometimes D767.913
Aleuts (WWII)   D810.A53
Alexander, Harold Rupert (G.B.: 20th c. mil. biog.)   DA69.3.A57
Alexandria, Egypt   DT154.A4

Alfonso XIII (Sp.: King, 1886-1931)   DP238
ALGERIA   DT271-299, DT275, DT284   965
Algeria (1900-62: last of Fr. rule)   965.04   DT295 (older titles), DT294.5-295.3
Algeria (1901+)   DT295 (for newer works SEE DT294.5-295.3)   965.04+
Algeria (1901-62)   DT294.5-295.3 (for older titles use DT295)
Algeria (1901-45)   DT294.5-7   965.04 (1900-62)
Algeria (geog. & travel)   916.5   DT280
Algeria (mil. status)   UA858   355.033065
Algeria (WWII)   D766.99.A6
Algiers, Alg.   DT299.A5   965.3
ALIEN ENEMIES (WWI)   D636
Alien enemies (WWII)   D801   940.5315, .53163
Alien enemies (WWII: by country)   D801.A3-Z
Alien enemies (WWII: Fr.)   D801.F8
Alien enemies (WWII: gen.)   D801.A2   940.5315, .53163
Alien enemies (WWII: U.S.: inclu. Japanese relocation centers: SEE ALSO D753.8.
    For alien property custody SEE JX5313.U6)   D769.8.A6   940.5315+,
                                                                        .547273, .53163
Alliances, Military   355.031
Allied forces (air)   358.41356   UG625, UG630+
Allied forces (inclu. various multi-nat. & combined ops.)   355.356   UA12 (U.S.),
                                                                        UA15, U260 (comb. ops.)
Allied intervention (Rus. Rev.: by country)   DK265.42.A-Z
Allied naval forces (inclu. various coalition forces)   359.356   VA40-42, VA, U260
ALLIES & Allied military ops (WWI: gen.)   D544   940.412+, .414, .42-3, 944.0814
Allies & anti-Axis exile govs. or nat. groups (WWII: dipl. hist.)   940.5322+   D748
Allies & associates (WWI: dipl. hist.)   940.322   D511, D459 (Triple Entente)
Allies (WWI: gen. particip.)   940.332   D544
Allies (WWI: mil. & naval life & customs)   940.483+   D544
Allies (WWII: mil. & naval life & customs)   940.5483+   U750, U765+,
                                                                        V720 (naval), V735+
Allowances & pay (U.S. Navy: tables inclu. interest)   VC54
Almanacs & yearbooks, Nautical (American: inclu. abridged)   VK7
Almanacs, annuals, etc., Military (countries besides U.S.)   U10.A-Z
Almanacs, annuals, etc., Military (G.B.)   U10.G7
Almanacs, annuals, etc., Military (U.S.)   U9
Almanacs, Naval (official)   V9   359.00202
Alpine region (Switz.)   949.47   DQ820-841, DQ823
Alps   DQ820-829   949.47
Alsace, Fr. (WWI)   D545.A55 (SEE ALSO DD801.A57)
Alsace-Lorraine (Ger.)   DD801.A31-69
Alsace-Lorraine (WWII: occupied terr.)   D802.A45
Ambulance services (WWII)   940.54753
Ambulances (mil. design)   623.74724   UH500-505
Ambulances, Military (plus transport)   UH500-505   623.74724
America (1901-)   E18.185   970.05
America & American neutrality (WWII: dipl. history)   D752.8
America & North America (gen.), United States   E   970, 973
America (gen.)   E1-143   970
America (mil. status: gen.)   UA21   355.03301812
Americal Division (WWII: U.S.)   D769.295.A5

AMERICAN literature in English   PS   810-819
American military ops. & U.S. (WWI: gen. unofficial)   D570.A5-Z   940.373,
                                                         41273, .40973, 327.73
American Red Cross   UH537.A
American Samoa   DU819.A1   996.13
American waters (gen.: pilot & sailing guides)   VK804   623.89297
Americanization, civilization, etc. (U.S.)   E169.1
Americans (in Arg.)   F3021.A5
Americans (in Brazil)   F2659.A5
Americans (in Peru)   F3619.A5
Americas (WWII)   D768-769
Ammunition & other ruinous media (design)   623.45   UF700-770
Ammunition (navies)   359.825
Ammunition, Artillery   UF700   358.825, 623.45
Ammunition, Naval   VF460   359.825, 623.45
Ammunition, Small arms   355.8255
Amphibious ops.   U261   359.83, .96
Amphibious planes   629.133348
Amsterdam, Neth.   DJ411.A5-59
Analysis, Air warfare (real & imagined)   358.4148   UG630-635
Analysis, Military (real & mock events)   355.48   UA719-740+, U161-167+
Analysis, Naval warfare (real & imagined battles, campaigns, etc.)   359.48
                                                         V25-55, V160-178
Anarchism & anarchists (WWII)   D810.A6
Anarchists (Rus. Rev., 1917-21)   DK265.9.A5
Anchors, cables, etc. (marine engin.)   VM791
Ancient history   930-939   C-F
Andalusia (Sp.)   DP302.A41-55
Andaman & Nicobar Islands   DS491.A5-6
Andes   F2212
Andorra   946.79   DC921-930
Andorra (modern hist.)   DC928
Anecdotes (WWII)   940.5494
Angkor, Cam.   DS558.A6
ANGLO-Egyptian Sudan (1899-1955)   DT108.6   962.403
Anglo-French & Allied military ops (WWI)   D544-549+
Anglo-German naval conflict & blockade (WWII: gen.)   D771   940.545, .5452
Anglo-Italian naval conflict (WWII: gen.)   D775   940.545941, .545945
Anglo-Saxon supremacy   D446
Anglo-Soviet Treaty (26 May 1942)   D749.5.A5
Angola (Portuguese West Africa)   DT591-617   967.3
Animals (WWI: use of)   D639.A65
Animals (WWII: inclu. use of dogs, horses, etc.)   D810.A65
Animals, Military   UH87-100
Animals, Use of (mil. sci.)   355.424
Annam (Fr. protectorate only)   DS559.92.A5
Annam (Vietnam: gen.)   DS556.5
Annapolis (U.S. Naval Acad.: gen. hist's. & other titles)   V415.L1
Annapolis (U.S. Naval Acad.: life & conditions)   V415.P1
Annual registers (20th c.: politics and diplomacy)   D440
Anschluss & WWII Period (Austria: 1938-55)   943.6052   DB99 (1938-45),
                                                         DB99.1 (Allied occup., 1945-55)

Antarctica   998.9

ANTI-aircraft artillery (WWII: Ger.)   D757.4.A-53
Anti-aircraft artillery (WWII: U.S.: gen.)   D769.342
Anti-aircraft artillery battalions (WWII: U.S.: by #)   D769.343.1st-
Anti-aircraft Command (WWII: G.B.)   D759.523
Anti-aircraft, Light Artillery regiments (WWII: G.B.)   D759.527
Anti-guerrilla warfare   U241
Anti-Semitism   DS145
Anti-Soviet propaganda (1925-53: gen.)   DK272.5
Antiaircraft (U.S.: N.Y. army reserves)   UA367.7-75
Antiaircraft artillery (U.S.: Calif. army reserves) UA97.7-75
Antiaircraft guns & defenses   UF625 (SEE ALSO UG730+)   358.13
Antiaircraft guns, Naval   VF418   359.981
Antilles (Greater: gen. hist. of the chain)   F1741   972.9
Antilles (Lesser: gen.)   F2001   972.9
Antisubmarine & submarine ops. (WWII: gen.)   D780   940.54516
Antisubmarine aircraft   UG1242.A25
Antisubmarine warfare   V214   359.3254, .42-43
Antitank guns   UF628   623.42, .44, .4518
Antwerp area (Bel.)   DH801.A6-69
Antwerp, Bel.   DH811.A55-68
Appliances, Ships' (engin.: gen.)   VM781   623.86
Arabian Desert (Egypt)   DT137.A7
Arabian Penninsula   953   DS201-248+, DS244 (1914-)
Arabian Peninsula (gen.)   DS223
Arabian Peninsula (geog. & travel)   915.3   DS207
Archangel & northern Russia (WWI)   D559
Archangel (Rus.)   DK511.A5
Archangel, Rus.   947.23
Architecture, Military   UG460   623.1
Architecture, Naval (collected, nonperiodical works) VM7
Arctic areas (WWII: Greenland etc.)   D763.5
Arctic islands   998-998.8
ARGENTINA   F2801-3021+, F2831 (gen.)   982
Argentina (1810-)   F2846   982.03+
Argentina (20th c.)   982.06   F2847-2849+
Argentina (1910-46)   982.061   F2848
Argentina (1910-43)   F2848   982.06
Argentina (1943-: Inclu. Perón regime & biog.)   F2849   982.061-062
Argentina (gen.)   F2831
Argentina (mil. status)   UA613-615   355.033082
Argentina (naval status)   VA416   359.030982
Argentina (WWII: dipl. hist.)   940.532282, .532582 (might ALSO be at .532482
              with Axis)   D754.A7
Arizona   979.1   F806-820
Arizona (battleship: U.S.)   VA65.A75
Ark Royal (aircraft carrier: G.B.)   VA458.A7, D772.A66 (WWII)
Arkansas   976.7   F406-420
Arkansas (battleship: U.S.: WWII)   D774.A7
Arkansas (WWII: Reconstruction)   D828.A8-81
Arlington National Cemetery (Arlington, Va.)   F234.A7
Armament (modern: Asia: by country)   U821.A-Z
Armament (modern: Eur.: by place)   U820.A-Z
Armament (modern: gen.)   U815
Armament (modern: U.S.)   U818
Armament, Naval (gen.)   V950   623.8251

Armenia   DK509 (gen. titles), DS161-199 (earlier titles), DK680-689 (later
           works)   956.62
Armenia (1901-)   DS195   956.6202
Armenian S. S. R. (1920+)   DK687+
Armenians (WWII: U.S.)   D769.88.A7
ARMIES & navies (of the world)   UA15
Armies etc. (WWI: U.S.)   D570.25-.358   940.412+, .44973, .45
Armies etc. (WWII: G.B.: by #)   D759.5.1st-   940.541241-541242
Armies etc. (WWII: U.S.)   D769.25-4
Armies etc. (WWII: U.S.: misc.)   D769.4
Armies (organiz., descrip., & world status)   UA   355
Armies (U.S.: by #/author)   UA27.3.1st-
Armies (WWII: Fr.)   D761.1   940.541244
Armies (WWII: Ger.)   D757.1   940.541343
Armies (WWII: U.S.: by # or author)   D769.26
Armistice (WWII: by country)   D813.A-Z   940.5314, .532+
Armistice (WWII: Fr.)   D813.F7
Armistice (WWII: gen.)   D812   940.5314, .532+
Armistice (WWII: Germ.)   D813.G3
ARMOR & CAVALRY UE (SEE ALSO UA for specific armies) 357-358.1
Armor & cavalry (Asia)   UE99-113
Armor & cavalry (Australia & New Z.)   UE121-122.5   357.099+
Armor & cavalry (China)   UE101
Armor & cavalry (essays & speeches)   UE149
Armor & cavalry (Eur.)   UE55-95
Armor & cavalry (Fr.)   UE71   357.0944
Armor & cavalry (G.B.)   UE57-64
Armor & cavalry (G.B.: by date)   UE58
Armor & cavalry (gen. hist.: inclu. several countries) UE15 357.09, .109, 358.1809
Armor & cavalry (Ger.)   UE73   357.0943
Armor & cavalry (It.)   UE79
Armor & cavalry (Japan)   UE105   357.0952
Armor & cavalry manuals (U.S.)   UE153-154
Armor & cavalry (Rus.: Asia)   UE109
Armor & cavalry (Rus.: Eur.)   UE85   357.0947
Armor & cavalry (U.S.)   UE23   357.0973
Armor & weapons, Naval   359.8351
Armor plate (naval sci.)   V900-925
Armor plate (naval sci.: gen.)   V900   623.81821, .8251
Armor, Naval (U.S.)   V903   623.82510973
Armor-piercing shells & devices (design)   623.4518
ARMORED cars & other combat vehicles (land: design)   623.7475
Armored divisions (WWII: U.S.)   D769.305-307
Armored divisions (WWII: U.S.: by #)   D769.3053
Armored divisions (WWII: U.S.: gen.)   D769.305
Armored divisions etc. (WWII: G.B..)   D759.528
Armored forces & warfare (tanks, armored cav., etc.)   358.18 UG446.5, UE147
Armored regiments (WWII: U.S.: by #)   D769.3055.1st-
Armored units & cavalry (Ger.)   UA714   357.10943, .50943, 358.180943
Armored units & cavalry (It.)   UA744
Armored units & cavalry (Rus.)   UA774
Armored units & cavalry (U.S.: inclu. mechanized: gen.) UA30 357.10973
Armories, arsenals, magazines (gen.)   UF540

ARMS & armor (hist.)   U799-897
Arms & ordnance, Naval (gen.)   VF350-355   359.82, 623.418
Arms (gen.: pubn. dates 1801+)   U800.A3-Z   355.8, 623.4
Arms manuals (infantry)   UD320-325
Arms, Small (infantry: gen.)   UD380
Arms, Small (marines (gen.)   VE360   359.96824, 623.44
Arms, Small (navies: gen. & by place)   VD360-365   359.824, .8242
ARMY artillery (inclu. field & antitank)   358.12   UF400-405, UF15,
        UF21-124 (by place), UF150-157+ (manuals & tactics)
Army corps (WWII: Fr.)   D761.15
Army corps (WWII: Ger.)   D757.2
Army corps (WWII: U.S.)   D769.27
Army hospitals (WWII: U.S.: evacuation: by #)   D807.U722.1st-
Army hospitals (WWII: U.S.: general: by #)   D807.U72.1st-
Army medical schools (U.S.: by region or state)   UH398.5.A-Z
Army posts (Fr.: by place)   UA702.32.A-Z
Army posts (Fr.: gen.)   UA702.3
Army posts (U.S.: by place)   UA26.A7-Z
Army posts (U.S.: gen.)   UA26.A1-6
Army reserves (U.S.)   UA42
Army staffs (U.S.)   UB223
Army War College (U.S.)   U413
Arnhem, Neth.   DJ411.A8
Arras, Battle of (1940)   D756.5.A78
Arsenals, armories, etc. (U.S.: gen.)   UF543
Art (WWII)   D810.A7
Artificers, Military (U.S.: ALSO tech. troops)   UG503
Artificers, Naval (gen.: inclu. carpenters' mates etc.)   VG600
Artificial horizon   VK584.A7
ARTILLERY   UA (for specific armies & units), UF   358.1+, 355.82+
Artillery & rifle ranges   U300-305
Artillery, Antiaircraft (land)   358.13   UF625
Artillery (Asia)   UF99-113
Artillery (Asia: gen.)   UF99
Artillery (Australia & New Z.)   UF121-122.5
Artillery batteries (U.S.: by #/author)   UA33.1st-
Artillery (by place)   UF21-121 (SEE ALSO UA for particular armies)
Artillery (China)   UF101
Artillery, Coast   355.8217, 358.16   UF450-455
Artillery (design)   623.41   UF, UF1-910+, UF15 (gen.), UF144-145 (gen.),
        UF21-124 (by place), UF23 (U.S.), VF320-325 (naval)
Artillery equipment, Naval   VF320-325
Artillery, Field   355.8212   UF400-405
Artillery, Field (U.S.)   UF403-404
Artillery fire control (inclu. instruments: gen.)   UF848   623.558
Artillery (Fr.)   UF71   358.120944
Artillery (G.B.)   UA658   358.10941, .120941
Artillery (G.B.: by date periods)   UF58
Artillery (G.B.: gen.)   UF57   358.120941
Artillery (G.B.: WWII)   UF58.1939-45
Artillery (gen. hist.)   UF15   358.109, .1209, 355.82, .821
Artillery (Ger.)   UA715, UF73   358.120943
Artillery, Howitzer & mortar (places besides U.S.)   UF475.A-Z
Artillery installations (arsenals, depots, target ranges, schools, etc.)   355.73
        UF540-545

Artillery instruments (misc.)   UF856.A-Z
Artillery (It.)   UA745, UF79
Artillery (Japan)   UF105   358.120952
Artillery, Land missile forces & armored warfare   358.1   UF, UF15,
                                    UF21-124, UE147, UA32-33 (U.S.), UA
Artillery manuals (U.S.)   UF153-154
Artillery (misc.: design)   623.419 (for space artil. after 1988)
Artillery, Mountain (U.S.)   UF443-444
Artillery museums & exhibitons (gen.)   UF6.A1.A-Z   358.12
Artillery, Naval   359.8218, 355.8218   VF320-325
Artillery (Norway)   UF81
Artillery projectiles (gen.)   UF750
Artillery (pubn. 1801+)   UF145   358.12
Artillery, Railway (U.S.: gen.)   UF493
Artillery range finders (particular types)   UF850.A3-Z
Artillery (Rus.)   UA775
Artillery (Rus.: Eur.)   UF85
Artillery, Seacoast (U.S.)   UF453-454
Artillery services, Naval   359.9812
Artillery shells & other projectiles (design)   623.4513   UF750-760, VF480 (naval)
Artillery, Siege (gen.)   UF460
Artillery (specific pieces)   355.822
Artillery (titles in collections)   UF7
Artillery (U.S.)   UF23   358.120973, .10973, 355.820973
Artillery (U.S.: Calif. reserves: gen., inclu. field)   UA96
Artillery (U.S.: gen.)   UA32   358.10973, .120973
Artillery (U.S.: N.Y. reserves)   UA366-367.75
Artillery (WWII: Fr.)   D761.6
Artillery (WWII: G.B.)   D759.52
Artillery (WWII: Ger.)   D757.4.A-5
Artillery (WWII: Rus.)   D764.52
Artisans, Naval (carpenters' mates, painters, etc.)   VG600-605
Artists (WWII)   940.53157   D810.A7
Arts & architecture (visual, decorative & applied)   N   700-709, 720-769
Arts, architecture, music, sports, & recreation   700-799   N, NB-NX, NA, M, GV
ASIA   DS   950-959, DS5, DS33
Asia (1480-1905)   950.3   DS33
Asia (20th c.)   DS35   950.4
Asia (1905-45)   950.41   DS35
Asia (air war geog.)   358.41475
Asia & the Pacific Theatre   D767-767.99
Asia (biog.: heads of state)   923.15   DS32 (collective)
Asia (geog. & travel)   915   DS9 (1901-50)
Asia (lighthouses, beacons, foghorns, etc.)   VK1099-1113
Asia (lighthouses, beacons, foghorns, etc.: lists)   VK1203-1209
Asia (maps & atlases)   912.5   G2200+
Asia (mil. status: gen.)   UA830   355.03305, .03325, .03355
Asia (naval geog.)   359.475   VA620-639
Asia (naval status: gen.)   VA620   359.03095
Asia, Russian   DK750
Asia, Southeast (20th c.)   959.05   DS526.6-7+
Asia, Southeast (newer titles)   DS521-526+
Asia, Soviet Central   DK845-973   958

ASIAN coasts (pilot & sailing guides: gen.)   VK902
Asian coasts (tide & current tables)   VK702
Asian infantry (gen.)   UD99   356.1095
Asian marines (gen.)   VE99
Asian military law   UB685-710
Asian naval law   VB700-799
ASSOCIATIONS, periodicals, conferences (Russo-Fin. War, 1939-40)   DL1095
Associations, periodicals, societies (U.S.: 20th c.)   E740
Associations, periodicals, societies (U.S.: army reserves)   UA42.A6.A-Z
Associations, societies (U.S.)   E172
Associations, societies (WWII)   D732
Associations, societies (WWII: U.S.)   D769.A1-15
Associations, societies (WWII: Yug.)   D766.6.A1-5
Astor, Nancy W. Langhorne, Viscountess (G.B.: 1910-36 era)   DA574.A8
Astrology (WWII)   D810.A75
Athenia (WWII: steamship)   D772.A7
Athens, Gr.   DF915-936, DF925 (1901-)   949.512
Athens, Gr. (1910-)   DF925
Athens, Gr. (WWII)   D766.32.A8
Athletes (WWII)   940.5315796   D810.E8
ATLANTIC Charter (Newfoundland: 14 Aug. 1941)   D734.A7-8
Atlantic Coast (S.Am.)   F2214   980.009821, .009636
Atlantic Coast (U.S.: Maine to Flor.)   F106   974-975
Atlantic Declaration ('Charter': 14 Aug. 1941)   D735.A7
Atlantic Fleet (U.S.)   VA63.A83
Atlantic Ocean (all & east: pilot & sailing guides)   VK810-880
Atlantic Ocean (all & east: tide & current tables)   VK610-680
Atlantic Ocean (Loran tables)   VK561.A7
Atlantic Ocean (West: pilot & sailing guides)   VK959-992
Atlantic Ocean Islands   997
Atomic bombs   UG1282.A8, U264   358.41825119, 623.45119
Atomic weapons   U264, UG1282.A8
Atrocities (Sp. Civil War, 1936-39)   DP269.5-55
Atrocities, war crimes, trials (WWI)   D625-626
Atrocities, war crimes, trials (WWI: Ger. & Central Powers)   D626.G3
Atrocities, war crimes, trials (WWII)   D803-804
Atrocities, war crimes, trials (WWII: Ger.)   D804.G4
Attachés, Military   UB260
Attachés, Naval   VB240
Attack & defense plans (gen.)   UA920   355.0330+, .0332+, .0335+, .4+
Attack, defense, & siege   UG443-449
Attack planes   UG1242.A28
Auckland, N.Z.   DU430.A8   993.122
Auckland, N.Z. (area)   993.122   DU430.A79
Auschwitz Concentration Camp (Poland)   940.5317438

AUSTRALIA   DU80-398, DU450-480, DU110 (gen.)   994
Australia (1901-45: Commonwealth)   DU116   994.04
Australia (1901-22)   994.041
Australia (1922-45)   994.042
Australia & Anzacs (WWI)   D547.A8
Australia & Australian military ops. (WWII)   D767.8-82
Australia & New Zealand (lighthouses, beacons, foghorns, etc.: lists)
                          VK1211-1212   623.89440993-89440994
Australia & New Zealand (pilot & sailing guides)   VK927-929
Australia. Army (descrip. & hist.)   UA872   355.00994, .30994, .310994
Australia. Army (special branches by name)   UA873.A-Z
Australia, Central   994.2   DU300-330, DU390+
Australia (gen.)   DU110   994
Australia (geog. & travel)   919.4   DU104
Australia (lighthouses, beacons, foghorns, etc.)   VK1121-1122   623.89420994
Australia (mil. geog.)   355.4794   UA995.A
Australia (mil. policy)   355.033594   UA870-874
Australia (mil. status)   355.033094   UA870+
Australia (mil. status)   UA870   355.033094, .033294, .033594
Australia (mil. status: states, territories, localities)   UA874.A-Z
Australia (naval geog.)   359.4794   VA710-719
Australia (naval status: gen.)   VA713.A5-Z   359.030994, .00994, .4794
Australia, New Zealand, Tasmania   DU80-480
Australia, Western   994.1   DU350-380
Australia (WWII: dipl. hist.)   940.532294   D754.A8
Australian aerial ops. (WWII)   D792.A8   940.544994
Australian military ops. & Australia (WWII: gen.)   D767.8   940.532294, .5394,
                          .540994, .541294, .5426, 994.042
Australian naval ops. (WWII)   D779.A8   940.545994
AUSTRIA   DB1-860   943.6
Austria (1801-)   DB38   943.604
Austria (20th c.)   DB91-99+   943.605
Austria (20th c.: gen.)   DB91
Austria (20th c. & 1919-)   943.605   DB91 (20th c.), DB96 (1918-)
Austria (1914-18: WWI era)   DB86.7
Austria (1916-18: Emp. Karl I: gen.)   DB92
Austria (1918-: Republic)   DB96   943.6051
Austria (1938-1945: Ger. annex.)   DB99   943.6052
Austria & Austria-Hungary (mil. status)   UA670   355.0330436
Austria & Austro-Hungarian Empire (gen.)   DB17
Austria, Czechoslovakia, Hungary   DB   943.6-943.9
Austria (geog. & travel)   914.36   DB21-27, DB26 (1901-45)
Austria-Hungary. Army (gen.)   UA672   355.309436
Austria, Hungary, Czechoslovakia   DB   943.6-9
Austria (naval status)   VA470-479   359.2809436
Austria (post-WWI territorial ?s)   D651.A95
Austria (WWII: gen.)   D765.4   940.53436, 943.6052
Austrian question (20th c.)   DB48
Austrian Republic (1919-38)   943.6051   DB96-98
Automatic firearms (rifles, machine guns, etc.)   355.82424   UF620
Automatic pilot (marine navig.)   VK584.A8
Automatic weapons (machine & submach. guns, auto. rifles, etc.: design)
                          623.4424   UD390-395, UF620 (mach. g's.)
Auxiliaries, Army (U.S.)   UA565.A-Z
Auxiliary Territorial Service (WWII: G.B.)   D760.A8

Aviation, Naval (places besides U.S.)   VG95.A-Z
Aviation, Naval (U.S.: gen.)   VG93
Axis (Ger.-Italy: 1919-39)   D728   940.51-52
Axis (WWII: gen. particip.)   940.5334   D743, D748
Axis (WWII: mil. & naval life & customs)   940.5484+   U750, U765+,
                                                V720 (naval), V735+
Axis Powers (WWII: dipl. hist.)   940.5324+   D748
Azerbaijan S.S.R.   DK690-699
Azerbaijan S.S.R. (1917+)   DK697.3-5
Azimuth instrument (artillery)   UF850.A9
Azores   DP702.A81-99, .A9 (19th-20th c.)   946.99
Azores (19th & 20th c.)   DP702.A9   946.99

BACTERIAL & biological warfare   UG447.8
Bacteriology, Military (inclu. vaccination)   UH450-455
Baden military ops. (WWI)   D533
Badges, brevets, medals of honor, rewards, etc. (navies)   VB330-335
Badges, insignia, etc. (mil.: SEE ALSO UB430+ for decorations)   UC530-535
Badoglio, Pietro (It.: 1900-46 period)   DG575.B2
Baguio, Philip.   DS689.B2
Bahama Islands   F1650-1660   972.96
Bahamas (gen. hist.)   F1656-1657
Bahrein   DS247.B2-28
Baker, Johnston, Palmyra, Midway, & other outlying Hawaiian Islands   996.99
                                        DU629.M (Midway), DU650
Bakeries (mil.)   UC730-735
Baku (Rus.: prov.)   DK511.B2
Baku, Rus.   DK699.2-39
Balbo, Italo (It.: 1900-46 period)   DG575.B3
Baldwin, Stanley, 1st Earl (G.B.: 20th c.)   DA566.9.B15
Balfour, Arthur James Balfour, 1st Earl of (G.B.: 20th c.)   DA566.9.B2
Bali (Indon.)   DS647.B2   959.86
Balikpapan, Br. N. Borneo   DS646.335.B24
BALKAN conflict (WWI)   D560-565
Balkan Peninsula (inclu. Balkan Wars of 1912-13)   949.6   DR1-48,
                                DR45 (20th c.), DR46 (Balkan Wars)
Balkan Peninsula (1913-19)   DR47
Balkan Peninsula (1919-45)   DR48
Balkan Peninsula & Eastern Europe (1901-: gen.)   DR45
Balkan Peninsula, Eastern Europe DR (titles written prior to about 1978-79)
                                949.6-949.8, 943.7-943.9, 947, 947.8, 956
Balkan Peninsula (geog. & travel)   914.96   DR15, DR1221 (later works)
Balkan States (mil. status: descrip. & hist.)   UA822
Balkan States (mil. status: gen.)   UA820   355.0330496
Balkan War (1912-13)   DR46   949.6
Balkans & Near East (WWII: misc. countries: by name)   D766.7.A-Z
Balkans, Near East, Eastern Mediterranean (WWII)   D766-766.79

Ballistic instruments   UF830.A-Z
BALLISTICS   UF820-830   623.51+
Ballistics & gunnery (engineering)   623.5   UF800-830, UF820
Ballistics (engineering)   623.51   UF820-830
Ballistics, Exterior   UF825   623.514
Ballistics, Exterior (environmental)   623.514   UF825
Ballistics, Interior   UF823   623.513
Ballistics, Interior (within bore)   623.513   UF823
Ballistics, Terminal (effects on targets)   623.516
Balloons & kites, Air force   UG1370-1375   623.741-744
Balloons, Military (design)   623.742   UG1370-1375
Baltic provinces (post-WWI territorial ?s)   D651.B2
Baltic Sea (mil. status)   UA646.53   355.033016334, .4716334, 359.4716334
Baltic States   DK502.3-505
Baltic States (gen.)   DK502.7
Baltic States (WWII: occupied terr.)   D802.B3
Bands & music, Military   UH40-45
Bands & music, Naval (SEE ALSO ML1300-1354)   VG30-35
Bandung, Java   DS646.29.B23
Bangkok, Thai.   DS589.B2
Banking services, Military   UH60-65
Baptists (WWII)   D810.C56
Barbary States   DT181-346   961.1-2, 964-965, 966
Barbary States (19th-20th c.)   DT204   961.023-03+
Barcelona, Sp.   DP402.B2-3
BARRACKS & camps, Military (gen.)   UC400   355.412, .7
Barracks & quarters, Air force   UG1140-1145   358.4171
Barracks & quarters, Marine   VE420-425
Barracks & quarters, Marine (U.S.: by place)   VE424.A-Z
Barracks & quarters, Marine (U.S.: Calif.)   VE424.C2   359.967109794
Barracks, quarters, housing (naval)   VC420-425
Barrage balloons & nets (design)   623.744   UG1370-1375, UG730-735,
                                                    UF625
Baruch, Bernard (U.S.: 20th c.)   E748.B32
BASES & camps (marines)   359.967   VE21-124, VE23-25 (U.S.), VA67-68,
                                                    VG90-95 (marine av.)
Bases & fields, Air force   358.417   UG634.5.A-Z (U.S.: by name),
                                                    UG635.A-Z (other countries)
Bases & stations, Naval   359.7   V220 (gen.), VA67-750 (by place),
                VA69-70 (U.S.), VA459-461 (G.B.), VA516-517 (Ger.),
        VA576-577 (Rus.), VA656-657 (Japan), VC412-425 (maint.: gen.)
Bases, ports, & docks (naval: gen.: SEE ALSO VA67-750 for specific countries)
                                        V220   359.7
Bases, ports, etc. (G.B. Royal Navy: by place)   VA459.A3-Z
Bases, ports, etc. (U.S. Navy: by place)   VA68.A-Z
Basic training (mil.: inclu. drills, survival exercises, etc.)   355.54   U400-717,
                                                    U765-773, U320-325
Basic training (mil. living conditions: ALSO regular quarters)   355.1292
Basic training (naval)   359.54   V260-265
Bataan (Luzon, Philip.)   DS688.B2   959.91
Batavia, Java (Djakarta)   DS646.29.B3
Bath, Eng. (WWII)   D760.8.B3
Batteries, Storage (submarine architec.)   VM367.S7

Battle conditions, Naval   359.1294
Battle of the Atlantic, freedom of the seas, general naval ops. (WWII)   D770
                                                                     940.545
Battlefield guides (WWI: gen.: SEE ALSO specific battles)   D528
Battlefield guides (WWII: gen.: particular battles at D756.5 etc.)   D747
BATTLES & campaigns, Aerial (WWI)   940.44   D600-607
Battles & campaigns, Aerial (WWII: inclu. comb. air & naval ops. as well as
    antiaircraftdefenses)   940.544   D785-792, D785 (gen.)
Battles & campaigns, Naval (WWI)   940.45   D580-595, D580 (gen.)
Battles & campaigns, Naval (WWII)   940.545 (SEE ALSO .542 for ops. by
       theatre)   D770-784, D770 (gen.), D773 (U.S.: gen.), D774.A-Z (U.S.: by
       ship, battle, etc.), D769.45-598 (U.S.: by fleet, squadron, base, etc.)
Battles & campaigns (WWII: by theatre)   940.542   D756-769
Battles & local history (Russo-Fin. War, 1939-40)   DL1103.A-Z
Battles, campaigns, etc. (Sino-Jpn. Confl., 1937-45: by name)   DS777.5316.A-Z
Battles, campaigns, sieges (Russo-Polish, other Polish conflicts, 1918-21: by
    name)   DK4407.A-Z
Battles, campaigns, sieges (Sp. Civil War, 1936-39: by name)   DP269.2.A-Z
Battles, campaigns, sieges (WWII: Rus., Eastern front: by place)   D764.3.A-Z
Battles, campaigns, sieges (WWII: West: by place)   D756.5.A-Z
BATTLESHIPS (as equip.)   359.8352
Battleships (besides U.S.: by place)   V815.5.A-Z
Battleships (engineering)   623.8252   V750
Battleships (G.B.)   V815.5.G7   623.82520941
Battleships (gen.: construc., armament, etc.: SEE V750 for earlier titles)
                                V815   623.8252, .81252, 359.3252
Battleships (Ger.)   V815.5.G3   623.82520943
Battleships (handling)   623.88252   V750
Battleships (Japan)   V815.5.J3   623.82520952
Battleships (U.S.)   V815.3   623.82520973, 359.32520973
Battleships (units)   359.3252   V750, V765-767, V799-800, VA,
                            VA65.A-Z (U.S.: by name)
Bavaria   DD801.B31-55   943.3
Bavaria (1939-45)   DD801.B422
Bayonet drill   UD340-345
Bayonet drill (marines)   VE340   359.96547
Bayonet drill (naval seamen)   VD340-345
Bayonets   UD400
Bayonets (marines)   VE380   623.441
Bayonets (navies)   VD380   359.8241
Bayreuth, Ger.   DD901.B4
Bazookas, grenade & rocket launchers, etc. (design)   623.4426   UF628-630
Beacons, buoys, etc. (marine navig.)   623.8944   VK1000-1249, VK1010,
                            VK1021-1124, VK1023-1025 (U.S.)
Beacons, foghorns, lighthouses, etc. (gen.)   VK1010   623.8942, 387.155
Beacons, foghorns, lighthouses, etc. (lists: gen.: inclu. Br. Admiralty)   VK1150
                                     623.8944
Beatty, David Beatty, 1st Earl (G.B.: 20th c. naval biog.)   DA89.1.B4
Beaverbrook, William Maxwell Aitken, Baron (G.B.: 20th c.)   DA566.9.B37
Beck, Josef (Pol.: 1918-45 era)   DK440.5.B4, DK4420.B4
Belfast, N. Ire. (WWII)   D760.8.B4
Belgian Congo   DT641-665   967.5
Belgian Congo (WWII)   D766.95
Belgian military ops. (WWII: gen.)   D763.B4

BELGIUM   DH418-811+, DH521   949.3
Belgium (20th c.)   DH677   949.304
Belgium (1909-)   949.304   DH677 (20th c.)
Belgium (1909-34: Albert I)   949.3041   DH681-685, DH681, DH682 (WWI)
Belgium (1914-18: WWI)   DH682
Belgium (1920-)   DH683
Belgium (1934-51: Leopold III)   949.3042   DH687-689, DH687
Belgium & Belgian military ops. (WWII)   D763.B4-42   940.3493, 949.3
Belgium & Luxembourg   DH401-925
Belgium (geog. & travel)   914.931-934   DH433
Belgium (mil. status)   UA680-689   355.0330493
Belgium (naval status)   VA480-489
Belgium (post-WWI territorial ?s)   D651.B3
Belgium (WWII: dipl. hist.)   940.5322493   D754.B
Belgrade, Serbia (Yug.)   DR2106-2124
Belgrade, Yug.   DR386
Belgrade, Yug. (WWII)   D766.62.B4
Belorussia   947.65   DK511.W5 (White Russia)
Ben-Gurion, David (Palestine: 19th-20th c.)   DS125.3.B37
Benefits, pay, allowances (air forces: U.S.)   UG943
Benes, Edward (Czech.: era of 1918-)   DB2191.B45
Bengal (E. Pak.)   DS485.B39-492
Bengal (W. Pak.)   DS485.B493   954.14
Berchtesgaden, Ger. DD901.B443
Bergen (Nor.: area)   DL576.B4
Bergen, Nor.   DL596.B4
Bering Strait & Alaska coast (pilot & sailing guides)   VK943
BERLIN, Ger.   943.155   DD851-900, DD860 (gen.)
Berlin, Ger. (1914-21)   DD879
Berlin, Ger. (1922-45)   DD880   943.155086
Berlin, Ger. (1933-45)   943.155086   DD880
Berlin, Ger. (districts, sections)   DD883
Berlin, Ger. (gen.)   DD860   943.155
Berlin, Ger. (WWII)   D757.9.B4   943.155086
Bermuda & West Indies (geog. & travel)   917.29   F1611
Bermuda (gen. hist.) F1636-1637
Bermuda Islands   F1630-1640   972.99
Bern, Swit.   DQ401-420   949.45
Bernadotte af Wisborg, Folke, greve (Swe.: 1907-50 period)   DL870.B47
BIBLIOGRAPHIES (inclu. partic. kinds, subjects, etc.)   010-019, 016 (SEE ALSO
                              subject #'s like 359+, 940+, etc.)   Z
Bibliographies (G.B.: hist.)   Z2016-2020+   016.941-942, .94109
Bibliographies (Ger.: hist.)   Z2237   016.94309
Bibliographies (Japan: hist.)   Z3306-3308   016.95209
Bibliographies (mil. hist.: Ger.)   Z2241.M5   016.3550943
Bibliographies (mil. hist.: U.S.)   Z1249.M5   016.3550973, .35500973,
Bibliographies (mil. sci. & hist.)   Z6724   016.355, .35509, 355.009, .0009
Bibliographies (naval hist.: G.B.)   Z2021.N3   016.3590941
Bibliographies (naval hist.: Japan) Z3308.M5   016.3590952
Bibliographies (naval hist.: U.S.)   Z1249.N3   016.3590973, .35900973,
                              .35930973, .3593310924
Bibliographies (naval sci. & hist.)   Z6616   016.359, .35909, .35900722
Bibliographies (Rus.: hist.)   Z2506-2510+   016.94709
Bibliographies (specific subjects)   016   Z (sometimes D-F, U-V, or other
                              subject classes)

214

Bibliographies (U.S.: hist.)   Z1236-1245+, Z1236   016.97309
Bibliographies (U.S.: hist.: 1900-45)   Z1244   016.9730904, .97309044 (WWII)
Bibliographies (WWI)   Z6207.E8 or .W7   016.9403
Bibliographies (WWII)   Z6207.W8   016.94053-94054, .36
Bibliography   Z (sometimes D-F, U-V, or other subject classes)   010
Bibliography & library science   Z (bibliog's. sometimes classed with A-Z subject #s)
                                  010-028+
Bicycle troops (mech. cav.)   357.52   UH30-35
Bicyclists, Military (gen.)   UH30   357.52
Billeting   UC410
Binoculars & telescopes, Military   UF845
Binoculars (naval clothing: inclu. other misc. accessories)   VC340
BIOGRAPHY & genealogy   920-929   CT (gen. or collec.), D-F, other specific
                         classes for specialists or famous people in those areas
Biography (20th c.: collective: gen.)   D412   920.02
Biography (20th c.: individual or memoir by name)   D413.A-Z
Biography (20th c.: memoirs and collective)   D412-412.8
Biography (1945-: collective)   D839.5
Biography (1945-: individual by name)   D839.7.A-Z (SEE ALSO DA-F
                                         country & era #s)
Biography, Air force (collective)   UG626   358.400922
Biography, Air force (G.B.: collective)   DA89.6.A1
Biography, Air force (G.B.: inclu. memoirs)   DA89.6.A-Z
Biography, Air force (individual)   UG626.2.A-Z   358.400924
Biography (Australia: 1901-45)   DU116.2 (SEE DU114 for earlier pubns.)
Biography (Australia: by name)   DU114.A3-Z (SEE ALSO DU116.2 for later works)
Biography (Australia: collective)   DU114.A2
Biography (Austria: 20th c.: by name: inclu. memoirs)   DB98.A-Z
Biography (Bel.: 1909-34)   DH685.A-Z
Biography (Bel.: 1934-51)   DH689.A-Z
Biography (Bulg.: 1879-1943: inclu. memoirs)   DR85.5.A-Z
BIOGRAPHY (CHINA: 20th c. & 1912-49: collective: SEE paric. era for indiv.)
                                         DS776
Biography (China: 1912-49 period: except Sun Yat Sen)   DS777.15.A-Z
Biography (China: 1928-37 era: collective)   DS777.487
Biography (China: 1928-37 era: indiv. inclu. memoirs)   DS777.488.A-Z
Biography (China: 1937-45)   DS777.5194-5
Biography (China: 1949+)   DS778.A-Z
Biography (collective: WWII)   D736 (for individuals SEE DA-F class numbers for
                         person's country: SEE ALSO D811 for personal narratives)
                         940.5481-5482 (ALSO country numbers ended sometimes by 0922-0924)
Biography (Czech.: 1918-)   DB2191.A-Z
Biography (Czech.: 1918-39)   DB2200-2201.A-Z
Biography (Czech.: 1939-45: by name)   DB2821.A-Z
Biography (Czech.: 1939-45: inclu. memoirs)   DB2211.A-Z
Biography (Den.: 1912-47)   DL257.A-Z
Biography (divers: marine engin.)   VM980
Biography (Egypt: 1879-1952)   DT107.2.A-Z
Biography (Eur.: group)   940.092   D106-110 (group)
Biography (Fin.: 20th c.)   DK461.A-Z
Biography (Fin.: 1918-39)   DL1088-1088.5
Biography (Fin.: 1939-45)   DL1093-1093.5
Biography (Formosa: 1895-1945)   DS799.72.A-Z

Biography (Fr.: 1871-1940: by name: inclu. memoirs & autobiog.)   DC342.8.A-Z
Biography (Fr.: 1871-1940: collective)   DC342
Biography (Fr.: 20th c.: by name)   DC373.A-Z
Biography (Fr.: 20th c.: collective)   DC371
BIOGRAPHY (G.B.: 20th c.: collective)   DA566.9.A1
Biography (G.B.: 20th c.: inclu. memoirs)   DA566.9.A-Z   941.0820922-24
Biography (G.B.: 1910-36: collective)   DA574.A1
Biography (G.B.: 1910-36: inclu. memoirs)   DA574.A-Z
Biography (G.B.: 1910-36: various royalty)   DA574.A2-45
Biography (G.B.: 1937-52: collective)   DA585.A1
Biography (G.B.: 1937-52: inclu. memoirs)   DA585.A-Z
Biography (G.B.: 1937-52: misc. royalty)   DA585.A5.A-Z
Biography (gen.)   920 (sometimes '92' or 'B' are used, followed by particular
                individuals in alphabetical order by last name. These may ALSO be
                placed in specific discipline number areas followed by the standard
                subdivision, '092'. So, 355.0092 is for mil. biog.)
Biography (Ger.: 1888-1918+: by name)   DD231.A-Z
Biography (Ger.: 1918-48: group)   DD243
Biography (Ger.: 1918-48: inclu. memoirs: by name)   DD247.A-Z
Biography (Ger.: mostly pre-WWI: by name)   DD219.A-Z
Biography (Greece: 20th c.)   DF836.A-Z
Biography (Hawaii: 1891-1959: inclu. memoirs)   DU627.7.A-Z
Biography (Hung.: 20th c.: by name, inclu. memoirs)   DB950.A-Z
Biography (India: 1901-: collective)   DS481.A1
Biography (India: 1901-: inclu. memoirs)   DS481.A-Z
Biography (Iraq: 1919-: by name)   DS79.8.A-Z
Biography (It.: 1871-1947: collec.)   DG574
Biography (It.: 1871-1941)   DG556.A-Z
Biography (It.: 1900-46: by name, inclu. memoirs)   DG575.A-Z
BIOGRAPHY (JAPAN: 20th c.: collective)   DS885.5.A1
Biography (Japan: 20th c.: inclu. memoirs: SEE ALSO DS890)   DS885.5.A-Z
Biography (Japan: 1926-89: collective)   DS890.A1
Biography (Japan: 1926-89: inclu. memoirs: SEE ALSO DS885.5)   DS890.A-Z
Biography (Japan: 1926-89: royal family)   DS889.7-9
Biography (Japan: collective)   DS834
Biography (Japan: Imperial family & rulers)   DS834.1
Biography (Korea: 20th c.: inclu. memoirs)   DS916.5.A-Z
Biography (merch. marine)   VK139-140
BIOGRAPHY, MILITARY   U51-55 (SEE ALSO D-F war & country #s)
                355.0092, .00922-00924, .3310922-0924,
Biography, Military engineering (collective)   UG127
Biography, Military engineering (indiv.)   UG128.A-Z (SEE ALSO UG21-124)
Biography, Military (Eur.)   923.54
Biography, Military (except U.S.: group by place)   U54.A-Z
Biography, Military (except U.S.: individual)   U55.A-Z
Biography, Military (G.B.: 20th c.: collective)   DA69.3.A1
Biography, Military (G.B.: 20th c.: inclu. memoirs)   DA69.3.A-Z 355.3310922-24
Biography, Military (G.B.: collective)   DA54
Biography, Military (Ger.: collective: gen.)   DD100.A2
Biography, Military (Ger.: collective: officers)   DD100.A3-Z
Biography, Military (It.: collective)   DG481
Biography, Military medical (collective, inclu. nurses)   UH341   355.3450922
Biography, Military (Rus.: collective)   DK50.5-8
Biography, Military (U.S.: individual)   U53.A-Z   355.330973
Biography (Montenegro: 1918-45)   DR1890-1891

Biography (N. Viet.: 1945-: inclu. memoirs)   DS560.72.A-Z
BIOGRAPHY, NAVAL   359.0092   V61-64 (SEE ALSO D-F #s for indiv. biog's.
     from particular countries), V63.A-Z (U.S.: by name), V64.A-Z (other countries)
Biography (naval architec.)   VM139-140
Biography, Naval (G.B.: 20th c.: by name)   DA89.1.A-Z
Biography, Naval (G.B.: 20th c.: collective)   DA89.1.A1
Biography, Naval (G.B.: collective)   DA74
Biography, Naval medical (gen.)   VG226
Biography, Naval medical (places besides U.S.)   VG228.A-Z
Biography, Naval (places besides U.S.: by place)   V64.A-Z
Biography, Naval (U.S.: by name)   V63.A-Z   359.00924, .3310924,
                    940.410924, .450924, .540924, .5420924, .5450924
Biography, Naval (U.S.: by name)   VB314.A-Z   359.3310973, .3310924
Biography (Neth.: by name)   DJ283.A-Z
Biography (New Z.: inclu. memoirs: by name)   DU422.A-Z
Biography (Nor.: 20th c.)   DL529.A-Z
Biography (Nor.: 20th c.: collective)   DL529.A1
Biography (Palestine: 19th-20th c.)   DS125.3.A-Z
Biography (Palestine: 19th-20th c.: collective)   DS125.3.A2
Biography (Philip.: 1935-46: collective)   DS686.2.A2
Biography (Philip.: 1935-46: inclu. memoirs)   DS686.2.A-Z
Biography (Pol.: 1918-: collective)   DK440.5.A1
Biography (Pol.: 1918-: inclu. memoirs)   DK440.5.A-Z
Biography (Pol.: 1918-45: by name, inclu. memoirs)   DK4420.A-Z
Biography (Pol.: 1918-45: collec.)   DK4419
Biography (Port.: 1910-)   DP676.A-Z
Biography (Royal Naval Coll., Dart.: by name)   V515.M1.A-Z
Biography (Rum.: 1914-27)   DR262.A-Z
Biography (Rus.: 1894-1917: by name, inclu. memoirs)   DK254.A-Z
Biography (Rus.: 1894-1917: collective)   DK253
Biography (Rus.: 1925-53: collective)   DK268.A1
Biography (Rus.: 1925-53: inclu. memoirs: by name)   DK268.A2-Z
Biography (Serbia: 1903-18)   DR2031
Biography (Serbia: 1918-45)   DR2038
Biography (social sciences: gov., law, commerce, etc.)   923
Biography   920-929 (sometimes placed with country #s or topical #s in
                    930-999 or 000-999)   C-F
Biography (Sp.: 1886-1931)   DP235-236
Biography (Sp.: 1931-39: collective)   DP260
Biography (Sp.: 1939-)   DP271.A-Z
Biography (Sp.: 1931-39: by name: inclu. memoirs)   DP264.A-Z
Biography (Swe.: 1907-50: by name)   DL870.A-Z
Biography (Swe.: 1907-50: collec.)   DL869
Biography (Swit.: 20th c.)   DQ206-207
Biography (Tur.: 1909-: inclu. memoirs)   DR592.A-Z
Biography (U.S.: 20th c.: by name)   E748.A-Z
Biography (U.S.: 20th c.: collective)   E747
Biography (U.S. Marines)   VE25 (PREFER E #s)
Biography (U.S. Mil. Acad.: by name)   U410.M1.A1-Z
Biography (U.S. Naval Acad.: by name)   V415.M1.A-Z
Biography (Viet.: by name: inclu. memoirs: Ho Chi Minh at DS560.72.H6)
                                                            DS558.83.A-Z
Biography (Viet.: collective)   DS558.82
Biography (WWI: collective)   D507   940.3092, .481-2. Also use country #'s

Biography (Yug.: 20th c.)   DR359.A-Z
Biography (Yug.: 20th c.: collective)   DR359.A2
Biography (Yug.: 1918-45)   DR1293-1294
Biography (Yug.: 1918-45: by name, inclu. memoirs)   DR1294.A-Z
Biography (Yug.: 1934-45+)   DR1300-1305
Biological agents (ammunition: design) 623.4594
Biological agents (mil.)   355.82594
Biological warfare   358.38   UG447.8
Birkenhead, Frederick E. S., 1st Earl of (G.B.: 20th c.)   DA566.9.B5
Bisayas (Visayan Islands, Philip.)   DS688.B6   959.95
BISMARCK Archipelago (inclu. New Britain [Rabaul] & New Ireland)
                993.6 (PREFER 995.8 for pubn. dates after 1988), 995.8 (SEE ALSO
                993.6 for books before 1989)   DU550-553, DU553.N35 (New Brit.)
Bismarck Archipelago (1942-45: WWII period)   995.803   DU550-553
Bismarck Archipelago (gen.)   DU550   993.6
Bismarck Archipelago (geog. & travel)   919.36
Bismarck Archipelago (WWII: gen. particip.)   940.53936   DU550-553
Bismarck (battleship: Ger.: WWII)   D772.B5, VA515.B4
Bismarck Islands (naval geog.)   359.47936   VA750.B
Bismarck Islands (WWII)   D767.99.B46
Bismarck Sea, Battle of (1943-44)   D774.B48
BLACK Forest (Ger.)   943.48   DD801.B63-65
Black Sea area (geog. & travel)   914.77   DK511.C7
Black Sea region   DJK61-66
Black Sea region (Rus.)   947.7   DK509
Blacks (in U.S.)   E185   973.0496
Blacks (WWI: Negroes)   D639.N4
Blacks (WWII: Negroes)   D810.N4
Blacks as soldiers & seamen (U.S.)   E185.63
Blamey, Thomas, Sir (Australia)   DU114.B52
Blinkers & electrooptical signal devices (mil. engineering)   623.7314   UG580,
                UG614- 614.5, VK387
Blitzkrieg (lightning war)   U167.5.L5
Blockades & blockade-running (WWI)   940.452   D581
Blockades & blockade-running (WWII)   940.5452   D770, D771 (Anglo-
                Grmn.), D773 (U.S.)
Blockades, Naval   V180   355.44, 359.42-43, 940.452, .5452
Blueprints, drawings, designs (naval architec.: laying out)   VM297.5
Blum, Léon (Fr.: 20th c.)   DC373.B5
Boat attack (naval tactics)   V178   359.32, .42
Boatswains   VG950-955
Boatswains' mates (U.S.) VG953
Boatyards, Small craft (by name)   VM321.52.A-Z
Boatyards, Small craft (gen.)   VM321.5
Boilers, Marine   VM741-750   623.873
Boise (cruiser: U.S.: WWII)   D774.B6
Bolivia   F3301-3359   984
Bolivia (1938-)   F3326   984.051
Bomb disposal & demolition (army engineers)   358.23   UG370, UG550-555
Bomb reconnaissance (WWII)   D810.B66
Bomb shelters (plus other special civil defense topics like psych. aspects)   UA926.5
Bombay, India   DS486.B7

Bomber forces & ops.   358.42   UG1242.B6, UG633-635, UG633 (U.S.),
        TL685.3, TL686.A-Z (by co. or name)
Bombers & fighter-bombers (mil. engineering)   623.7463   TL685.3,
        TL686.A-Z (bymanufac. or model), UG1242.B6
Bombers (air force)   UG1242.B6   623.7463, 358.42
Bombing, dog fighting, other air tactics (U.S.)   UG703
Bombs, Air force   UG1280-1285   358.418251, 623.451
Bombs, ammunition, etc.   355.825
Bombs & projectiles, Aircraft (inclu. std. & nuclear)   UF767   623.451
Bonin Islands (Japan)   DS895.B6   952.85 (SEE .28 for works after 1988)
Borneo   959.83   DS646.3-38, DS646.3
Borneo & the Dyaks   DS646.3-38   959.53-55, .83
Borneo (WWII: gen. particip.)   940.535983   D767.7, DS646.3
Bose, Subhas Chandra (India: 1901+ era)   DS481.B6
Bosnia & Bosnia-Herzegovina (20th c.)   DB250
Bosnia & Hercegovina (1914-18: WWI)   DR1732
Bosnia & Hercegovina (1918-45)   DR1733-1741
Bosnia & Hercegovina (1941-45: Axis occup.)   DR1741
Bosnia & Hercegovina (Herzegovina)   DR1652-1785 (SEE ALSO DR357 etc.)
        949.742
Boston, Mass. (1865-1950)   F73.5
Bougainville (WWII)   D767.982.B5, D767.99.B54
Boxer Rebellion (China: 1899-1901)   DS770-772   951.03
Boy Scouts (WWII)   D810.B7
Boys (armed forces)   UB418.B69
Brandenburg, Ger.   DD901.B65
BRAZIL   F2501-2659, F2521   981
Brazil (1822-)   F2535   981.04+
Brazil (1889-)   F2537   981.05+
Brazil (1930-54)   981.061   F2538
Brazil (1930-54)   F2538   981.06-061
Brazil (gen.)   F2521
Brazil (mil. status)   UA619-621
Brazil (WWII)   D768.3   940.5381, .544381, 981.061
Brazil (WWII: dipl. hist.)   940.532581   D754.B
Breech-loading ordnance   UF560-565... .B.L.
Bremen, Ger.   DD901.B71-79
Bremen (pass. ship)   VM383.B7
Brest, Fr.   DC801.B83
Brest, Fr. (WWI: U.S. training camp)   D570.37.B7
Brest-Litovsk, Russia (WWI: treaty: 3 Mar. 1918)   D614.B6
Brest-Litovsk, Ukraine (WWI: treaty: 9 Feb. 1918)   D614.B5
Brevets, badges, medals, etc. (U.S. Navy: inclu. Navy Cross)   VB333
        359.13420973
Briand, Aristide (Fr.: 20th c.)   DC373.B7
Bridge troops & sappers (gen.)   UG510
Bridges (London, Eng.: inclu. London Bridge)   DA689.B8
Bridges (mil. engineering)   UG335   623.67
Brisbane, Australia   DU278   994.31
Bristol, Eng. (WWII)   D760.8.B7

BRITAIN (19th c. & Victorian era of 1837-1901) 941.081   DA550-566, DA550 (gen.)
Britain (20th c. & Edward VII era of 1901-1910)   941.082
                    DA567-570 (Ed. VII), DA570 (gen.), DA566 (20th c.: gen.)
Britain (1910-36: George VI)   941.083   DA573-578, DA576 (gen.),
                                              DA577 (WWI era), DA578 (1920-39)
Britain (1936-45: WWII era)   941.084   DA580-587, DA586 (gen.),
                                              DA587 (WWII period)
Britain & British Isles   941   DA
Britain, Battle of (1940)   D756.5.B7
BRITISH aerial ops. (WWI)   D602   940.44941
British aerial ops. (WWII)   D786   940.544941
British air force history (gen.)   DA89.5   358.400941
British armament (modern)   U820.G3
British Central Africa (1901-52)   DT855   968.97
British Columbia   F1086-1089.7, F1089 (gen.)   971.1
British Columbia (gen. hist.)   F1088
British East Africa & East Africa   DT421-435   967.6
British East Indies   DS648 (SEE DS646.3 for Borneo)
British Empire   DA10-18
British Empire & Britain (WWI: by place or name) D547.A-Z
British Empire (gen.)   DA16   909.824+
British engineering ops. (WWII)   D795.G7
British espionage (gen.)   UB271.G7   327.120941
British (in Arg.)   F3021.B86
British (in S.Am.)   F2239.B8
British (in U.S.)   E184.B7
British infantry (gen.)   UD57   356.10941
British Isles & English Channel (pilot & sailing guides)   VK827-844
                                    623.892916336, .8929422
British Isles (pilot guides)   623.892941-892942   VK827-838.5
British Isles (tide & current tables)   VK627-638
British Isles (WWII: gen. particip.)   940.5341-5342
British marines (gen.)   VE57   359.960941
BRITISH MILITARY education (special time periods)   U511
British military history (gen.)   DA50   355.00941
British military ops. & Great Britain (WWII: gen.)   D759   940.54091, .5341-
                                              5342, 942.084
British military ops., British Empire, & England (WWI)   D546-547.8+, D547.A-Z+
British military ops. (WWI: gen.)   D546.A2-Z   354.42066, 940.48341, .412+,
                                              941.083
British military ops. (WWII: special by group or region)   D760.A-Z   940.5412
British naval education (special topics)   V511-512
British naval history (gen.)   DA70   359.00941
British naval ops. & Anglo-German naval conflict (WWI: by battle, ship, etc.)
                                              D582.A-Z
British North Borneo   DS646.33-34   959.53
British prisons & prisoners (WWII)   D805.G7
British public opinion (WWII)   D810.P85.G7
British Somaliland   DT406   967.73-7305+
British South Africa   DT751-848   968-968.7
British submarine ops. (WWII: G.B.)   D784.G7
British West Africa   DT491-518   966, 966.4-51, .7, .81, .9
British West Indies   F2131-2133   972.9, .973
Brittany (Fr.)   DC611.B841-915   944.1
Browning machine guns   UF620.B6

Brunei   DS646.35   959.55
Brüning, Heinrich (Ger.: 1918-48 era)   DD247.B7
Brussels, Bel.   DH802-809
Brussels, Bel. (20th c.)   DH807.5
Bucharest, Rum.   DR286   949.82
Budapest, Hun. (20th c.)   DB872
Budapest, Hun. (WWII)   D765.562.B8
Budgets, Naval (G.B.)   VA455
Budgets, Naval (gen.)   VA25   359.622
Budgets, Naval (Ger.)   VA511
Budgets, Naval (U.S.)   VA60   359.6220973
Buenos Aires (Arg.: prov.)   F2861
Buenos Aires, Arg.   F3001   982.11
Buenos Aires, Arg. (area)   982.11   F3001
Buffalo, N.Y.   F129.B8
Buildings (London, Eng.)   DA686-687
Buildings (London, Eng.: by name)   DA687.A-Z
Buildings, Public (Berlin, Ger.)   DD896
Buildings (Washington, D.C.)   F204.A-Z
Bukowina (20th c.)   DB280
BULGARIA   DR51-98   949.77
Bulgaria (1878-1946)   949.7702   DR85-93, DR89 (1918-43)
Bulgaria (1879-1943)   DR85   949.7702
Bulgaria (1912-13: Balkan War period)   DR87.7
Bulgaria (1914-18: WWI)   DR87.8
Bulgaria (1918-43: Boris III era)   DR89
Bulgaria (1943-: inclu. regency of Simeon II, 1943-46)   DR90
Bulgaria (geog. & travel)   914.977   DR60 (1879-1950)
Bulgaria (mil. status)   UA824   355.03304977
Bulgaria (post-WWI territorial ?s)   D651.B8
Bulgaria (WWII)   D766.7.B8
Bulge, Battle of the (Ardennes: 1944-45)   D756.5.A7
Bulletproof clothing, materials, etc.   UF910
Bullets   UF770   623.455
Bullets (navies)   VF500   359.8255, 623.455
Bunkers, caves, shelters (defense engineering: protective construc.)   623.38
Bunks & bedding (mil.)   UC550-555
Burial services, graves registration, & naval military mail   359.69
BURMA   959.1   DS485.B79-892, DS527-530 (newer works), DS528.5
Burma (1851-1947)   DS485.B89   959.104
Burma (1885-1945)   DS530
Burma (1886-1948: British rule)   959.104   DS485.B89, DS530-530.32
Burma & India (WWII)   D767.6
Burma (gen.)   DS527.4
Burma (geog. & travel)   915.91   DS485.B74-892, DS527.6 (later bks.)
Burma (mil. status)   UA853.B9
Buses (mil. design)   623.74723
Bushido (Jpn. custom)   DS827.B98

CABLES (naval supplies)   VC279.C3
Cadiz, Sp.   DP402.C2-3
Caen, Fr.   DC801.C11
Cairo, Egypt   DT139-152   962.16
Cairo, Egypt (gen. hist. & descrip.)   DT143
Caissons, gun carriages, etc. (U.S.: gen.)   UF643

Calais, Battle of (1940)   D756.5.C2
Calcutta, India   DS486.C2
Calcutta, India (area)   954.14   DS486.C2
CALIFORNIA   F856-870, F861 (gen.)   979.4
California (1869-1950)   F866 (SEE D570.85.C2-21 for 1914-18 war years &
                          D769.85.C2-21 for 1939-45)   979.404-4053
California (1900-)   979.405   F866 (1869-1950)
California (1918-45)   979.4052   F866
California (battleship: U.S.)   VA65.C3
California (gen.)   F861   979.4
California (geog. & travel)   917.94   F859.3, F861, F866 (hist.: 1869-1950)
California National Guard (gen.)   UA90
California (naval geog.)   359.47794   VA100-107
California, Southern   979.49   F867
California (WWII: gen. particip.)   940.53794   D769.85.C2-21, F866
California (WWII: gen.)   D769.85.C2   979.4052
Cambodia   DS554 (newer works), DS554.7, DS557.C2 (older titles)   959.6
Cambodia (1863-1954)   DS554.7-73   959.603
Camel batteries   UF420
Camel troops & camelry   UE500
Camels, elephants, etc. (mil. transp.)   UC350
Cameroon (mil. status)   UA859
Cameroons (German West Africa) & Togoland   DT561-584   966.6695, .81, 967.1
Camouflage UG449, V215 (naval) 358.3, 623.77
Camouflage, Marine   V215   623.77
Camouflage (WWII)   D810.C2
Camp-making (mil. sci.)   UG365   355.412, .544, .71
Camp Pendleton (Calif.: U.S. Marines)   VE434.C2 or P...
Camps & barracks, Military   UC400-440
Camps, Marine training (U.S.: by place)   VE434.A-Z
Camps, Training (armor & cavalry: U.S.)   UE433-434
CANADA   F1001-1140+   971
Canada (1867+)   F1033   971.05+
Canada (20th c. & 1911-) 971.06   F1034
Canada (1911-21)   971.061
Canada (1914+)   F1034 (SEE ALSO D768.15 for 1939-45 war years)
                   971.061+
Canada (1921-35)   971.062
Canada (1935-57)   971.063
Canada (1935-48: 2d prime min'ship. of Wm. Lyon Mackenzie King)   971.0632
Canada (E. coast: pilot & sailing guides)   VK985
Canada (gen.)   F1026
Canada (geog. & travel) 917.1   F1015
Canada (mil. status: gen.)   UA600   355.033271, .033571, .033071
Canada (naval status: gen.)   VA400   359.030971, .4771
Canada (W. coast: pilot & sailing guides)   VK945
Canada (WWI)   D547.C2
Canada (WWII)   D768.15   940.5371, .532271, .540971, .541271, 971.063
Canada (WWII: dipl. hist.)   940.532271   D754.C2
Canadian aerial ops. (WWII)   D792.C2-29
Canadian naval ops. (WWII)   D779.C2-29
Canal Zone & Panama Canal   F1569.C2   972.875
Canary Islands   DP302.C36-51   964.9
Canberra, Australia 994.71   DU145
Canberra, Australia (inclu. Capital Territory)   DU145

Cannons, howitzers, mortars, small rockets, other specific artillery (design)
623.42
Canteens & post exchanges, Military (U.S.)   UC753
Canteens & ship exchanges   VC390-395
Canteens (mil. equip.)   UC529.C2
Canteens (off-post mil. recreation: U.S.)   UH905
Canton, China   DS796.C2
Cape Verde Islands   DT671.C2   966.58
Cape York Peninsula (Queens., Aust.)   DU280.C3
Capital Territory (Australia)   994.7   DU145
Captured nations (WWII: Allied-occup'd.: gen. particip.)   940.5338
Captured nations (WWII: Axis-occup'd.: gen. particip.)   940.5337
Carbines, rifles, etc.   UD390
Career guidance (naval sci.)   VB259
Cargo & personnel transport planes (design)   623.7465   TL685.7
Cargo ships, freighters, & tankers (engineering)   623.8245   VM391-395,
VM455-459, VM455 (tankers)
Caribbean, Mexico, & Central America   972   F1201-1392 (Mex.), F1421-2175
Caribbean Sea & Gulf of Mexico (tide & current tables)   VK771-777
Caribbean Sea & West Indies (pilot & sailing guides)   VK971-973
Caribbean Sea Area   F2161-2175   972.9, 909.096365
Caribbean Sea area (1811-)   F2175   972.904-905
Carol II (Rum.: King, 1930-40)   DR266
Caroline & Mariana Islands (geog. & travel)   919.66-67
Caroline Islands   DU560-568   355.47966, 996.6
Caroline Islands (gen.)   DU565
Caroline Islands (modern hist.)   DU567
Caroline Islands (pilot & sailing guides)   VK933.C27
Caroline Islands (WWII)   D767.99.C3
Carpathian Mts. region   DJK71-75
Carpathian Mts. (Uk.)   DK508.9.C37
Carpenters & other naval artisans (U.S.)   VG603
Carriers, Aircraft (as equip.)   359.8355 (SEE ALSO .94835 with works after 1988)
Carriers, Aircraft (as units)   359.9435 (SEE .3255 for works before 1989)
Carriers, Aircraft (besides U.S.)   V874.5.A-Z
Carriers, Aircraft (design)   623.81255   V874-875
Cartography (WWII)   D810.C26
Cartridges   UF740-745   623.455
Cartridges, Naval   VF470   359.8255
Casablanca, Mor.   DT329.C3   964.3
Casablanca, Mor. (area)   964.3   DT329.C3
Cases (courts of inquiry, naval: U.S.)   VB814.A-Z (PREFER KF #s)
Cases (courts of inquiry: by place: SEE KF7642 etc. for U.S.)   UB867.A-Z
Cases (courts-martial, mil.: by place)   UB857.A-Z (for U.S. SEE KF7642,
7652, etc.)
Cases (courts-martial, naval: besides U.S.: by place)   VB807.A-Z
Cases (courts-martial, naval: U.S.)   VB806 (PREFER KF7646-7650)
Catalonia (Sp.)   DP302.C57-69
Catalonia (Sp. Civil War, 1936-39)   DP269.27.C3
Catholic Church (WWI)   D622
Catholic Church (WWII)   D810.C6
Caucasus area (Rus.)   DK511.C1-35   947.9
Caucasus (geog. & travel)   914.79

CAUSES, aims, results (WWI)   D511-520   940.31-2
Causes, aims, results (WWI: gen.) D511   940.311, .314
Causes, aims, results (WWII: by country)   D742.A-Z   940.534-539
Causes, aims, results (WWII: gen.)   D741   940.5311, 327+
Causes (WWI)   940.311   D511
Causes (WWI: econ.)   940.3113   D635
Causes (WWI: polit. & dipl.)   940.3112   D610-621, D610
Causes (WWI: psychological & social)   940.3114
Causes (WWII: dipl. & polit.)   940.53112   D741-742, D443, D727, D748
Causes (WWII: econ.)   940.53113   D741-742, D720-728, D421, D800
Causes (WWII: gen.)   940.5311   D741 (gen.), D742.A-Z (by country), D720-728
Causes (WWII: psychological & social)   940.53114   D741-742, D726, D421
Causes of war (economic)   355.0273   HB195
Causes of war (political)   355.0272
Causes of war (psychological) 355.0275
Causes of war (sociological) 355.0274
CAVALRY & armor (Asia: gen.)   UE99   357.095
Cavalry & armor (by place)   UE21-124 (SEE ALSO UA for specific units)
Cavalry & armor (collections)   UE7
Cavalry & armor (Eur.: gen.)   UE55   357.094
Cavalry & armor (G.B.: gen.)   UE57   357.0941
Cavalry & armored regiments (U.S.: by #/author) UA31.1st-
Cavalry (armored & mechanized)   UE
Cavalry (Austria & Austria-Hung.)   UA674
Cavalry divisions (WWII: U.S.: 1st)   D769.308
Cavalry (G.B.)   UA654-657   357.10941
Cavalry groups etc. (WWII: U.S.: by #)   D769.325.1st-
Cavalry, Horse   357.1   UE15, UE21-124, UE150+, UA
Cavalry horses (gen.)   UE460
Cavalry installations (horse)   357.187   UE350, UE430-435, UC400-405, UA
Cavalry, Mechanized   357.5   UE147-149, UE150-155 (manuals), UE159,
                UE160-302 (by place)
Cavalry (WWII)   D794
Cavalry (WWII: G.B.)   D759.54
Cavalry (WWII: Rus.)   D764.54
Cavalry (WWII: U.S.: gen.)   D769.32
Cebu (Philip.)   DS688.C4   959.95
Cebu, Philip. (town)   DS689.C5
Celebes   DS646.4   959.84
Celebrations & commemorations, Military   355.16
Celebrations, memorials, monuments (WWII: U.S.: gen.)   D833   940.546573
CEMETERIES & graves, Military   UB390-397
Cemeteries & monuments (WWI)   940.465   D639.D4 (cem's.), D663-
                680 (mon's.), D675.W2 (Tomb of Unkn. Soldier: Wash. D.C.)
Cemeteries & monuments (WWII)   940.5465   D833-838 (celebrations,
                monuments, etc.), D810.D4 (dead, cemeteries, etc.)
Cemeteries & monuments (WWII: Eng.)   940.546542   D838.G6 (gen.),
                .G7.A-Z (local, by place)
Cemeteries & monuments (WWII: U.S.)   940.546573 D833-836, D833 (gen.),
                D835.A-W (by state), D836.A-Z (by town)
Cemeteries (naval)   VB300-305   351.86, .866
Censorship, news media, etc. (WWII: by country)   D799.A-Z
Censorship, press, publicity (WWI: gen.)   D631 (SEE ALSO D639.P6-7 for
                propaganda)   940.315097

224

CENTRAL Africa   DT351-364   967
Central America   F1421-1577, F1436   972, 972.8+
Central America (1821-1950)   F1438   972.804-805
Central America (1900-)   972.805   F1438-1439
Central America (mil. status: by country)   UA607.A-Z
Central America (pilot & sailing guides)   VK951-952
Central Asia & Tibet (pubns. to 1950: gen.)   DS785.A5-Z   951.5, 958 (C. Asia)
Central Asia (Rus, Rev., 1917-21)   DK265.8.S63
Central Asian question (19th c.)   D378
Central Asian question (20th c.)   D471-72
Central Asian question (20th c.: by country)   D472.A-Z
Central Asian question (1914-)   D471
Central Australia   DU390   994.2
Central Europe & Germany (geog. & travel)   914.3   DD21-43, DB21-27, D901-980
Central Powers (WWI: dipl. hist.)   940.324   D511, D458 (Triple Alliance)
Central Powers (WWI: gen. particip.)   940.334   D531
Central Powers (WWI: mil. & naval life & customs)   940.484
Cephalonia, Gr. (WWII)   D766.32.C4
Ceremonies, honors, & salutes (navies: gen.)   V310   359.17, .1349
Ceremonies, Military   355.17   U350-355
Ceylon   DS488-490, DS489.5 (gen. hist.)   954.93
Chamberlain, Austen, Sir (G.B.: 20th c.)   DA566.9.C43
Channel Islands (Eng.: WWII: gen. particip.)   940.534234   DA670.C4,
                                                .J5 (Jersey), .G8-9 (Guernsey)
Channel Islands (G.B.)   DA670.C4   942.34
Chaplain Corps (WWII: U.S. Army)   D769.375
CHAPLAINS, Air force   UG1000-1005
Chaplains, Military (U.S.)   UH23   355.3470973
Chaplains, Naval (U.S.)   VG23   359.3470973
Chaplains or religious officials, Military (gen.)   UH20   355.347
Chaplains or religious officials, Naval   VG20-25
Chaplains (WWII: by country)   D810.C36.A-Z
Chaplains (WWII: gen.)   D810.C35   940.5478
Chaplains (WWII: U.S.)   D810.C36.U6 (SEE ALSO D769.375 & D769.59)
Charges, Demolition (destructors, bangalore torpedoes, etc.: design)   623.4544
                                                UG370, UF860
Charities, refugees, relief work (WWI: gen.)   D637   940.477+
Charities, refugees, relief work (WWII: by country)   D809.A-Z   940.54778+
Chart use, Nautical (plus other misc. topics on naut. instruments)   VK587
Chasseurs & Chasseurs Alpine (WWII: Fr.)   D761.5
Chemical & biological weapons (design)   623.4516   UG447-447.6 (chem.),
                            UG447 (gen.), UG447.5.A-Z (type gas), UG447.8 (bio.)
Chemical & biological weapons (projectiles etc.)   355.82516   UG447-447.8
Chemical Corps battalions etc. (WWII: U.S.: by type, sub-arranged by # if applic.)
                                                D769.353.A-Z
Chemical Corps (WWII: U.S.: gen.)   D769.35
Chemical industry (defense)   UA929.95.C5
Chemical warfare   358.34   UG447-447.6
Chemical warfare (inclu. flames)   UG447-447.6   623.4516
Chesapeake Bay region (Va.)   F232.C43
Chiang Kai Shek (China: 1887-1975: SEE DS778.M3 for Mao Tse Tung)
                                                DS777.488.C5
Chicago, Ill.   F548   977.311
Chicago, Ill. (1892-1950)   F548.5   977.31103-033

Children & orphans (WWI)   D639.C4   940.53161
Children & orphans (WWII)   D810.C4
Chile   F3051-3285, F3081 (gen.)   983
Chile (1921-)   F3099   983.063-064+
Chile (gen.)   F3081
Chile (mil. status)   UA622-624
CHINA   DS701-796+   951
China (1861-1912)   DS761
China (1911-12: Rev.: gen.)   DS773.4
China (1912-49 [Republic] & 20th c. overall)   DS773.83-776, DS774 (gen.)
    951.03-04
China (1912-49)   951.04   DS773.83-777.544, DS774
China (1912-28: gen.)   DS776.4   951.041
China (1912-27)   951.041   DS776.4-777.462, DS776.4
China (1913: 2d Rev.)   DS777.2
China (1927-49: Nationalist rule: inclu. Sino-Jpn. conflict of 1937-45)   951.042
    (SEE ALSO 940.53 for Sino-Jpn. War of 1937-45)   DS777.47-544, DS777.47
China (1928-37: gen.)   DS777.47
China (1928-37: Nationalist rule)   DS777.47-514   951.042
China (1937-45)   DS777.518   951.042
China (1945-49: Republic: gen.)   DS777.535   951.042
China (air war geog.)   358.414751
China & Chinese military ops. (WWII)   D767.3   940.5351, .540951, .5425,
    951.042
China. Army (gen.)   UA837   355.30951, .00951
China (biog.: heads of state)   923.151
China (gen.: pubn. 1801+)   DS735.A3-Z   951
China (geog. & travel)   915.1   DS710 (1901-48)
China (lighthouses, beacons, foghorns, etc.)   VK1101-1102
China (mil. capabil.)   355.033251
China (mil. geog.)   355.4751   UA995.C
China (mil. status)   UA835   355.033051, .033251, .033551
China (naval geog.)   359.4751   VA630-639
China (naval status)   VA630-639   359.030951
China (pilot guides)   623.892951   VK902-907
China (plus surrounding areas)   951   DS701-796+, DS706, DS735
China (post-WWI relns.: Japan)   D651.C6
China (post-WWI relns.: U.S.)   D651.C5
China (post-WWI territorial ?s)   D651.C4-7
China (Southwestern)   951.3
China (WWII: causes, aims, results)   D742.C5
China (WWII: dipl. hist.)   940.532251   D754.C5
Chinese Civil War (1945-49: gen.)   DS777.54
Chinese (in other lands: gen.)   DS732
Chinese-Japanese Conflict (1931-33)   DS777.5   951.042, 952.033
Chinese-Japanese Conflict (1937-45: gen.)   DS777.53   940.53, 951.042,
    952.033
Chinese-Japanese War (1894-5)   DS764.4-767.7   951.03, 952.031
Chinese Revolution (1911-12)   DS773.32-6   951.03
Choiseul (WWII)   D767.982.C4
Christchurch, N.Z.   DU430.C5   993.155
Christchurch, N.Z. (area)   993.155   DU430.C5
Christian Scientists (WWII)   D810.C62
Christian X (Den.: 1912-47 period: also gen. histories of time)   DL255

Chronologies, outlines, syllabi, tables, etc. (20th c.)   D427   909.82, 940.28
Chronologies, tables, outlines (WWII)   D743.5   940.530202
Chronologies (U.S.)   E174.5
Chronometers, Nautical (PREFER QB107)   VK575
Chungking, China (plus Szechwan Province)   951.38
Church of the Brethren (WWII)   D810.C63
Churches (WWII: gen.)   D810.C5
Churchill, Winston Leonard Spencer, Sir (G.B.: 20th c.)   DA566.9.C5
Ciano, Galeazzo, Conte (It.: 1900-46 period)   DG575.C51
Civic programs (armed forces: U.S.)   UH723
CIVIL Affairs Division (WWII: U.S. Army)   D769.309
Civil defense (countries besides U.S.)   UA929.A-Z
Civil defense (G.B.)   UA929.G7
Civil defense (gen.)   UA926.A3-Z (SEE ALSO numbers within wars, such as
                D810.C69 for WWII)
Civil defense (Sov.Un.)   UA929.S65
Civil defense (U.S.: gen.)   UA927
Civil defense (WWII)   D810.C69 (SEE UA926-929 for more technical works)
Civil depts. (naval admin.: gen.)   VB170
Civil engineering (navies)   VG590-595 (SEE ALSO VA66.C6+)
Civil liberties & freedom of speech (WWII: U.S.)   D769.8.C4 (SEE UB342.U5 for
                conscientious objectors)
Civilian personnel (mil. admin.: gen.)   UB180   355.23
Civilian personnel (mil. resources)   355.23
Civilian personnel (naval admin.)   VB180-187
Civilian personnel (naval admin.: places besides U.S.)   VB185.A-Z
Civilian personnel (navies)   359.23 VB170-187
CIVILIZATION, customs, social life (20th c.)   D429 (SEE ALSO CB415, GT146)
                940.5,320.904,327.09
Civilization, customs, social life (1919-39: sometimes Europe alone)   D726
Civilization, customs, social life (Australia)   DU107
Civilization, customs, social life (China: 20th c. & 1912-49)   DS775.2
Civilization, customs, social life (China: gen.)   DS721
Civilization, customs, social life (Fr.: 20th c.)   DC365
Civilization, customs, social life (Fr.: 1901-)   DC33.7
Civilization, customs, social life (G.B.: 20th c.)   DA566.4
Civilization, customs, social life (Ger.)   DD67
Civilization, customs, social life (Ger.: 1918-)   DD239
Civilization, customs, social life (It.: 1816-1945)   DG450
Civilization, customs, social life (Japan: 1868+)   DS822.25
Civilization, customs, social life (Japan: 1912-45)   DS822.4
Civilization, customs, social life (Japan: by special topic) DS827.A-Z
Civilization, customs, social life (Japan: gen.)   DS821
Civilization, customs, social life (Palestine & the Jews)   DS112-113
Civilization, customs, social life (Philip.)   DS663-664
Civilization, customs, social life, races (Pacific)   DU28
Civilization, customs, social life (Rus.: 1925-53)   DK268.3
Civilization, customs, social life (Rus.: gen.)   DK32
Civilization, customs, social life (Serbia: 1918-45)   DR2035
Civilization, customs, social life (Swit.)   DQ36
Civilization, customs, social life (U.S.: gen.)   E161
Civilization, customs, social life (Pol.)   DK411
Class histories (Royal Naval Coll., Dart.: by date)   V515.K3
Class histories (U.S. Naval Acad.: by date)   V415.K4
Classification, Military   UB337

Clerks & yeomen, Naval (U.S.)   VG903
Clothing & equipment, Military   UC460-535
Clothing & equipment, Military (places besides U.S.)   UC465.A-Z
Clothing, equipment, food, & office supplies (navies)   359.81 (SEE ALSO .65-
       66)   VC280-345 (clothing & equip.), VC350-410 (food etc.)
Clothing, food, & equipment (air forces)   358.4165-4166   UG1100-1105,
       UG1160-1165, UC460-465, UC700-705
Clothing, food, & equipment (mil. admin.)   355.65-66 (PREFER .81)   UC460-
       535, UC700-735
Clothing, food, camp equipment, etc.   355.81 (SEE ALSO .65-66)   UC460-465+,
       UC700-705
Clothing, Naval (inclu. related items)   VC280-345
CLUBS & societies (U.S.)   973.06   E172
Clubs, Military (by place, except U.S. & G.B.)   U59.A-Z
Clubs, Military (G.B.)   U58
Clubs, Navy (Am. besides U.S.)   V67.A-Z
Clubs, Navy (besides U.S. & G.B.: by country)   V69.A-Z
Clubs, Navy (G.B.)   V68
Clubs, Officers' (mil.)   UC740-745
Coaling stations, Naval (gen.)   V240 (SEE ALSO VA67-750)
COAST artillery (gen.)   UF450
Coast artillery (U.S.: Calif. reserves)   UA97-97.5
Coast artillery (U.S.: N.Y. reserves)   UA367-367.5
Coast defense, Naval   V200 (SEE ALSO UG410-442)   359.45
Coast defenses   UG448, UG410-442 (specific places)   358.16, 355.45
Coast guard   359.97 (SEE ALSO 363.286 for U.S.C.G.)   VG50-55, VG53 (U.S.)
Coast guard & coast signal service   VG50-55   359.97
Coast guard & coast signal service (places besides U.S.)   VG55.A-Z
Coast guard craft (engineering: ALSO police boats, revenue cutters, etc.)
       623.8263   VM397
Coast Guard Reserve & Women's Reserve (SPARS: WWII: U.S.)   D769.598
Coast Guard Reserve Boat 3070 (WWII)   D783.5.C6
Coast Guard Reserve (WWII: U.S.: temporary inclu. U.S. Volunteer Port Security
       Force)   D769.585
Coast guard vessels (naval architec.: by type)   VM397   623.8245, 359.9732
Coast guard vessels (units)   359.3263   VM397
Coast guns (U.S.: handbooks)   UF563.A7
Coastal artillery (design)   623.417   UF450-455
Coasts, Asian (Loran tables)   VK561.A6
Coasts, Asian (pilot & sailing guides)   VK902-911
Coasts, Asian (tide & current tables)   VK702-711
Coasts, French (gen. & Eng. Ch.: pilot & sailing guides)   VK845
       623.8929442 (Normandy)
Coasts, French (gen. & Eng. Ch.: tide & current tables)   VK645
Coasts, United States (Loran tables)   VK561.U5
Coasts, United States (pilot & sailing guides)   VK993
Coasts, United States (tide & current tables)   VK793
Cochin China (Vietnam: WWII)   D767.35-352
Code signals (merch. marine)   VK391
Cold storage (naval architec. & engin.)   VM485
Coldstream Guards (G.B.)   UA651.C6
Collectibles, relics, trophies (WWII)   D733.5
Collectibles (WWII)   D743.27
College, school, etc. (WWII: U.S.: by name)   D810.E45.A-Z

Collision & grounding, Nautical (prevention)   623.8884   VK371-378
Collisions & avoidance, High seas   VK371-378
Colombia   F2251-2299   986.1+
Colombia (1904-46)   F2277   986.1062-10631
Colonial troops   UA14
Colonial troops (Fr.)   UA709
Colonial troops (G.B.: inclu. natives: gen.)   UA668
Colonial troops (Ger.)   UA719
COLONIES, British   DA10-18 (SEE ALSO JV1000-1099 for other collective
                                   works & D-F for specific colonies)
Colonies, Dutch   DJ500 (PREFER D-F #s for indiv. colonies or JV2500-2599 for
                                   collective)
Colonies, French   DC890 (PREFER D-F for individual colonies or JV1800-1899 for
                                   collective)
Colonies, German   DD905 (PREFER D-F #s for specific colonies or JV2000-2099
                                   for collective)
Colonies, Portuguese   DP802.A-Z (SEE ALSO D-F for indiv. places & JV4200-
                                   4299 for collective works)
Colonies (WWI)   D573-578
Colonies (WWI: G.B.: gen.)   D547.A1
Colonies (WWII: Fr.: gen.)   D761.9.A1
Colonies (WWII: G.B.: gen.)   D760.A1
Colorado   F771-785, F776   978.8
Colorado (WWII: Reconstruction)   D828.C6-61
Colors & standards, Military   355.15   UC590-595, U360-365
Colors & standards (navies)   359.15   V300-305
Colors, flags, standards (mil.: U.S.)   UC593-594
Colt machine guns   UF620.C6
COMBAT & support aircraft   358.4183-4184   UG1240-1245, UG1242.A-Z (by
                                   type), UG1243 (U.S.), UG633-635, VG90-95 (naval), TL685+
Combat conditions (mil. life)   355.1294
Combat craft, Light (torpedo boats etc.: engineering)   623.8258   V830-
                                                   835 (p.t.'s), V880
Combat engineers (WWII: U.S.: gen.)   D769.33
Combat units (by service field)   355.35   UA
Combat vessels, Small (P.T.'s etc.: units)   359.3258   V830-840, V880-885
Combined ops. (joint: air, army, navy)   U260
Combined ops., Military (2 or more types of forces)   355.46
Combined ops., Naval (2 or more types of forces)   359.46
Comics, caricatures, humor (WWII)   940.5496-5497   D743.9, D745
Command & control systems   UB212
Command control   UB200-245   355.41, .33, .6
Command of ships (naval admin.: gen.)   VB200   359.33, .6, 158.4, 350.00323
Commandeering, compensation, etc. (naval: by country or place)   VC268.A-Z
Commando ops. (WWII)   D794.5
Commando tactics   U262   355.425
Commemorations & celebrations (navies)   359.16   V310
Commemorations, celebrations, & memorials (WWI: gen.)   940.46   D663-
                                                   680, D663 (gen.)
Commemorations, celebrations, & memorials (WWII: gen.)   940.546   D830-838
Commencement addresses (U.S. Naval Acad.: by speaker)   V415.F3.A-Z
Commerce, communications, & transport   380-389   HF, HE

Commissioned & warrant officers, Air force   358.41332   UG820-825
Commissioning, draft, examination, registration, other methods of naval personnel
    procurement   359.2236   VB260-275 (enlisted pers.), VB307-315 (officers)
Commissioning, registration, classification, exams, etc. (mil. manpower procure.)
                                              355.2236   UB330+, U400+
Commissions, Military (gen.)   UB870
COMMUNICATION & transport (air force resources)   358.4127   UC330-335,
                                              UA940-945
Communication & transport (mil. resources)   355.27   UA940-945,
                                              UA929.95.T7, UC10+, UC270-275
Communication & transport (naval resources)   359.27   VC530-580 (trans.),
                                              VB255, VG70-85, V270
Communication equipment, Military   355.85   UG570-613, UA940-945
Communication equipment, Naval   359.85   VG70-85
Communication routes (except U.S.)   UA955.A-Z
Communication routes (mil. sci.)   UA950-979
Communication routes (U.S.)   UA953-954
Communication systems, Naval (blinkers & electrooptical: design)   623.85614
Communication systems, Naval (flag & semaphore: design)   623.85612
                                              V280-285, V300-305 (flags), VK385
Communication systems, Naval (pyrotechnical: design)   623.85613
Communication systems, Naval (radar: design)   623.85648
                                              UG612-612.5, UG612.3 (U.S.)
Communication systems, Naval (radar & radiocommun.: design)   623.8564
                                              VG76-78, UG610
Communication systems, Naval (radio telegraph: design)   623.85642   VG70-75
Communication systems, Naval (radio telephone: design)   623.85645   VG80-85
Communication systems, Naval (shortwave radio: design)   623.85641
Communication systems, Naval (visual: design)   623.8561   V280-305
COMMUNICATIONS, Military (U.S.)   UA943-944
Communications, Naval (inclu. radio, radar, wireless telegraph: gen.)   VG76
                                              623.8564, .734
Communications services, Naval   359.983   VG70-85
Communications, signaling, & cryptography forces (mil. engineers)   358.24
                                              UG570-611.5, UA940-945, UB290 (cryp.)
Communications systems, Naval (engineering)   623.856   VG70-85, VB255
Communications technology (mil. engineering)   623.73   UG590-613.5, UG580,
                                              UG590, UG570-575
Communications (WWII)   D810.C7
Compasses (sea, air, or land: inclu. gyro type)   VK577   623.82
Compulsory service & exemption (mil.: besides U.S.)   UB345.A-Z
Comrades of the Great War (G.B.)   D546.A12
CONCENTRATION camps & internment centers (WWII: by location)
                                              940.53174-53179
Concentration camps, internment centers, labor camps (WWII)   940.5317
Concentration camps (Sp. Civil War, 1936-39: outside Sp.)   DP269.67
Concentration camps (WWII)   D803-805
Concentration camps (WWII: by country)   D804.A-Z
Concentration camps (WWII: gen.: atrocities)   D803
Concentration camps (WWII: Ger.)   D804.G3
Concentration camps (WWII: Jpn.)   D804.J3
Concrete ships (naval architec.)   VM148

Corporal punishment & flogging (mil. sci.: gen.)   UB810
Corporal punishment (naval)   VB910   364.67, 343.0146, 359.13325
Corregidor (Philip.)   DS688.C67   959.91
Corsica (Fr.)   DC611.C8-839
Corvettes & frigates (besides U.S.)   V826.5.A-Z
Cossacks (Rus. Rev., 1917-21)   DK265.9.C62
Cossacks (Ukr.)   DK508.55
Cossacks (WWII)   D810.C83
Costs, Military   UA17   355.622
Costs, Naval (budgets etc.)   VA20-25
Council of Foreign Ministers (WWII)   D814.4-47
Council of Foreign Ministers (WWII: gen.)   D814.4
Councils of Defense (WWI: U.S.: by state)   D570.8.C8.A-Z
Counterintelligence (mil.)   355.3433
Counterintelligence, Naval   359.3433
Countermining (defense engineering)   623.36 (SEE ALSO .3)   UG490
Course navigation (marine: inclu. celestial)   623.89   VK549-572+
COURTS-martial, Military   UB855.A-Z (besides U.S., for which SEE KF7625-7659)
Courts-martial, Military (gen.)   UB850   343.0146, 355.13325
Courts-martial, Naval (besides U.S.: by place)   VB805.A-Z
Courts-martial, Naval (gen.)   VB800   343.0146
Courts-martial, Naval (U.S.)   VB803 (PREFER KF7646-7650)
Courts of inquiry, Military (gen.)   UB860
Courts of inquiry, Naval   VB810-815   343.0143
Courts of inquiry, Naval (besides U.S.)   VB815.A-Z
Coventry, Eng.   DA690.C75
Coventry, Eng. (WWII)   D760.8.C6
Crete   DF901.C78-89, .C86 (1898-)   949.98
Crete & Aegean Islands (geog. & travel)   914.99   DF901.C8 (Crete),
        .C9 (Cyclades), DS52-53, DS53.A-Z (by island), DS53.R4-6 (Rhodes)
Crete (WWII)   D766.7.C7
Crimea (Rus.)   DK511.C7   947.717
Crimes, Military (gen.)   UB780   355.1334
Crimes, Naval (gen.)   VB850   359.1334
Crippled sailors, Employment of (PREFER UB360-366)   VB278
CROATIA (inclu. Dalmatia, Istria, Slavonia)   DB361-380, DR1502-1645   949.72
Croatia (1914-18: WWI)   DR1582
Croatia (1918-45)   DR1583-1591
Croatia (1918-45: gen.)   DR1584
Croatia (1941-45: WWII)   DR1591
Croatia (gen.)   DR1510, 1535
Croatia (post-WWI territorial ?s)   D651.C78
CRUISERS (as equip.)   359.8353
Cruisers (besides U.S.)   V820.5.A-Z
Cruisers (G.B.)   V820.5.G7
Cruisers (gen.: tech. info.)   V820   623.8253, .81253, 359.3253
Cruisers (handling)   623.88253   V820-820.5
Cruisers (in units)   359.3253   V820-820.5, VA65.A-Z (U.S.: by name)
Cruisers (naval engineering)   623.8253   V820-820.5
Cruisers (U.S.)   V820.3
Cryptography & ciphers   UB290   358.24
Cryptography (WWI)   D639.C75
Cryptography (WWII)   D810.C88

Cuba   F1751-1849, F1758, F1776   972.91
Cuba (1899-)   972.9106   F1787-1788
Cuba (1933-)   F1788   972.91063
Cuba (gen.)   F1776
Cullum's Register (U.S. Mil. Acad.)   U410.H5
Cupolas, Revolving (& other portable gun shelters)   UF660
Curiosities, Military (inclu. collector's hdbks.)   U790
Curiosities, Naval   V745   359.00207, .002
Current & tide tables (Atlantic Ocean: west)   VK759-792
Current & tide tables (gen.: pubn. 1801+)   VK602   623.8949
Current & tide tables (North Pacific)   VK717
Current events yrbks. (20th c.: nonserial: includes pictorial titles: by time then
            author)   D410.5
Customs & laws of war (inclu. treatment of prisoners)   UB485 (SEE ALSO JX)
Customs, Military (gen.)   U750
Customs, Naval (gen.)   V720   359.1
Cyclists, Military   UH30-35
Cylinders, valves, etc. (internal combustion engines: marine engineering)
                    623.87237   VM769
Cyprus   DS54   956.45
Cyprus (1878-1960: British rule)   956.4503   DS54.8
Cyprus (WWII: gen. particip.)   940.535645   DS54.8
Czech military ops. (WWII: gen.)   D765.5
CZECHOSLOVAKIA (inclu. Bohemia, Moravia, Slovakia)   DB191-217 (earlier titles),
            DB2000-3150+ (for most titles cataloged after 1979)   943.7
Czechoslovakia   DB2000-2299   943.7+
Czechoslovakia (1801-1976 pubns.)   DB2062
Czechoslovakia (20th c.)   DB215   943.7024-703+
Czechoslovakia (to 1918)   943.702
Czechoslovakia (1918-)   DB2185-2232+
Czechoslovakia (1918-: gen.)   DB2186
Czechoslovakia (1918-45)   943.703   DB215-215.3, DB2186-2211,
            DB2186 (gen.), DB2196 (1918-39), DB2206 (1939-45)
Czechoslovakia (1918-39)   DB2195-2202   943.703
Czechoslovakia (1918-39: gen.)   DB2196
Czechoslovakia (1939-45: Ger. occup.)   DB215.3, DB2205-2211   943.703
Czechoslovakia (1939-45: Ger. occup.: gen.)   DB2206
Czechoslovakia & Czech military ops. (WWII)   D765.5-55   940.53437, 943.703
Czechoslovakia (gen.)   DB2011
Czechoslovakia (geog. & travel)   914.37   DB191 (titles prior to 1979-80), DB2020
Czechoslovakia (mil. status)   UA829.C95   355.0330437
Czechoslovakia (post-WWI territorial ?s)   D651.C9
Czechoslovakia (WWII: dipl. history)   D754.C95
Czechoslovakia (WWII: gen. particip.)   940.53437   D765.5, DB215.3,
                    DB2205-2211, DB2206
Czechoslovakia (WWII: mil. hist.)   940.5409437   D765.5
Czechoslovakian military ops. (WWI)   D539.5.C8
Czechs (in Pol.)   DK4121.5.C9

DALADIER, Édouard (Fr.: 20th c.)   DC373.D3
Dallas, Texas   F394.D2
Dalmatia (20th c.)   DB420
Dalmatia (Yug.: local Croatia)   DR1620-1630   949.72
Damage control (warships)   V810   623.888

Danube River Valley (gen.)   DJK76
Danube River Valley (Yug.)   DR1350.D35
Danzig   DD901.D2-29
Danzig (19th-20th c.)   DD901.D28
Danzig, Pol. (1919-45: time of free city)   DK4673
Danzig, Pol. (Gdansk)   DK4650-4685
Dardanelles (Tur.)   DR701.D2
Dartmouth (Royal Naval College: Act of incorp.)   V515.A1
Darwin & N. District (Australia)   994.295   DU398.D3
Darwin, Australia   DU398.D3   994.295
Davao (Philip.)   DS688.D3
Dawes Plan (WWI)   D649.G3.A4-5
De Gaulle, Charles (Fr.: 20th c.)   DC373.G3
DEAD reckoning (naut. navig.)   623.8923   VK572
Dead reckoning (naut. navig.)   VK572   623.8923
Dead, Treatment of   UH570
Dead, wounded, decorated (WWI: lists: U.S.)   D609.U6-7
Dead, wounded, decorated (WWII: Australia)   D797.A8
Dead, wounded, decorated (WWII: South Australia)   D797.A83
Dead, wounded, decorated (WWII: U.S.: Calif.)   D797.U62.C2
Dead, wounded, decorated (WWII: U.S.: gen.)   D797.U6   940.546773
Dead, wounded, decorated (WWII: U.S.: special)   D797.U7
Dead (WWI: burial, cemeteries, etc.)   D639.D4
Dead (WWII: treatment, cemeteries, etc.)   D810.D4
Death (Jpn. custom)   DS827.D4
Decorations, Military (gen.)   UB430
DEFENSE & attack plans (U.S.)   UA923   355.033073, .4773
Defense, attack, & siege (gen.: pubn. 1789+)   UG444   355.4+
Defense, Civil (U.S. states, cities, etc.)   UA928-928.5.A-Z
Defense, Industrial (U.S.)   UA929.6-8
Defenses, Air   UG730-735, UF625 (antiaircraft), UA926+ (civil defense)
            358.4145, .13
Defenses, Air (places besides U.S.)   UG735.A-Z
Defenses, Direct-invasion (barriers, flooding, traps, etc.)   623.31   UG375,
            UG403, UG407-409, UG448 (coast)
Defenses, Fortified (Eur.: gen.)   UG428   623.194, 355.474
Defenses, Fortified (U.S.: gen.)   UG410   623.1973, 355.4773
Delivery or charge-holding devices (naval ammun.)   359.8251
Demobilization (by country)   UA917.A3-Z
Demobilization (gen.)   UA917.A2   355.29
Demobilization (mil. resources: gen.)   355.29   UA917
Demobilization, Naval (inclu. civil employ.)   VB277   359.29, .1154
Demolition (mil. engineering)   623.27   UG37
Demolition charges   355.82545
Demolitions (mil. engineering)   UG370   623.4545, 358.23
DENMARK   DL101-291+, DL148(gen.)   948.9
Denmark (20th c.)   DL250   948.905
Denmark (1906-)   948.905   DL250 (20th c.)
Denmark (1906-45)   948.9051   DL253-257
Denmark (1912-47: time of Christian X)   DL255-257   948.9051
Denmark (1914-18: WWI)   DL256
Denmark (1919+)   DL256.5
Denmark & Finland   948.9
Denmark (gen.)   DL109   948.9
Denmark (geog. & travel)   914.891-895   DL118

Denmark (mil. status)   UA690-699   355.0330489
Denmark (naval status)   VA490-499
Denmark (WWII: gen.)   D763.D4
Dentistry, Military   UH430-435
Dentistry, Naval   VG280-285
Denver, Colo.   978.883   F784.D4
Deportation (WWII)   D810.D5
Depression range finder   UF850.D4
Depth charges   359.8254
Depth charges, Naval   VF509   623.45115, .4517
DESCRIPTION & travel (Africa: 1901-50)   DT12   916.0431-0432
Description & travel (Algeria: 1901-50)   DT280
Description & travel (Arabian Penin.: 1801-1950)   DS207
Description & travel (Arg.: 1806-1950)   F2815   918.2043-2062
Description & travel (Asia: 1901-50)   DS9   915.044
Description & travel (Australia: 1901-50)   DU104   919.4044
Description & travel (Austria: 1901-45)   DB26
Description & travel (Barbary States: 1901-50)   DT190
Description & travel (Bel.: 1831-1945)   DH433
Description & travel (Bel. & Holl.: 1901-50)   DH39
Description & travel (Brazil: 1890-1950)   F2515   918.1045-1061
Description & travel (Brit. Empire)   DA11
Description & travel (Bulg.: 1879-1950)   DR60
Description & travel (Burma: 1824-1945)   DS527.6
Description & travel (Can.: 1867-1950)   F1015   917.1045-1063
Description & travel (Carib. Sea: 1811-)   F2171
Description & travel (Caroline Islands)   DU563
Description & travel (Chile: 1810-1950)   F3063   918.3044-30643
Description & travel (China: 1901-48)   DS710   915.1043-1044
Description & travel (Cuba: 1898-)   F1765   917.291046
Description & travel (Czech.: 1901-45)   DB2020
Description & travel (Den.: 1901-50)   DL118
Description & travel (Dutch E. Ind. & Indon.: 1801-1945)   DS619
Description & travel (E. Eur. & Balkan Penin.: 1901-50)   DR15
Description & travel (Eastern Europe: 1901-50)   DJK17
Description & travel (Egypt & Egyp. Sudan: 1901-50)   DT55   916.2044-2045
Description & travel (Ethiopia: 1901-50)   DT378
Description & travel (Europe: 1901-1950)   D921   914.045
Description & travel (Far East, E. & SE.Asia: 1901-50)   DS508   915.0441
Description & travel (Fin.: 1901-44)   DL1015.2
Description & travel (Fin.: 1945-80)   DL1015.3
Description & travel (Formosa: to 1945)   DS799.15   915.1249044
Description & travel (Fr.: 1871-1945)   DC28
Description & travel (Fr. Indoch.: 1788-1950)   DS534   915.97043
Description & travel (G.B.: 1901-45)   DA630   914.1-2, 914.10482
Description & travel (Ger.: 1919-45)   DD42   914.3009042
Description & travel (Hawaiian Is.: to 1950)   DU623   919.69043
Description & travel (India, pre-1947 Pak.)   DS413
Description & travel (Iran: 1801-1950)   DS251
Description & travel (It.: 1919-44)   DG429
Description & travel (Jam.: 1811-1950)   F1871
Description & travel (Japan: 1901-45)   DS810   915.2043
Description & travel (Java, Indon.: 1801-1945)   DS646.2
Description & travel (Latin Am.: 1811-1950)   F1409   918.042-043
Description & travel (Libya: 1901-50)   DT220

Description & travel (Lux.: to 1945)   DH906
Description & travel (Mex.: 1867-1950)   F1215   917.2048+
Description & travel (Mid. East, SW. Asia: 1901-50)   DS49   915.6044
Description & travel (Montenegro: 1860-1950)   DR109
Description & travel (Morocco: 1901-50)   DT310
Description & travel (N. Africa: 1901-50)   DT165   916.2043
Description & travel (New. Z.: 1840-1950)   DU411   919.31042-310435
Description & travel (Neth.: 1901-45)   DJ39
Description & travel (Nor.)   DL418
Description & travel (Pacific: 1898-1950)   DU22
Description & travel (Palestine: 1901-50)   DS107.3
Description & travel (Paris, Fr.: ALSO gen. hist.)   DC707
Description & travel (Peru: 1820-1950)   F3423
Description & travel (Philip.: 1898-1945)   DS659   915.99043
Description & travel (Pol.: 1867-1945)   DK407
Description & travel (Pol.: 1867-1944)   DK4070
Description & travel (Port.: 1816-1950)   DP525
Description & travel (Puerto R.: 1898-)   F1965
Description & travel (Rum.: 1866-1950)   DR209
Description & travel (Rus.: 1901-44)   DK27   914.70904
Description & travel (S.Am.: 1811-1950)   F2223
Description & travel (Scan., N. Eur., Fin.: 1901-50)   DL10
Description & travel (SE. Asia: 1901-50)   DS522.4 (for earlier books SEE DS525)
                                                                               915.9045+
Description & travel (Siberia: 1801-1945)   DK755
Description & travel (Sp.: 1901-50)   DP42
Description & travel (Swe.: 1901-50)   DL618
Description & travel (Swit.: 1901-50)   DQ24
Description & travel (Thai.: 1801-1950)   DS565
Description & travel (Tunisia: 1901-50)   DT250
Description & travel (Tur.: 1901-50)   DR428
Description & travel (Viet.: 1801-1954)   DS556.36   915.97043
Description & travel (W.Ind.: 1810-1950)   F1611   917.29044-045
Description & travel (Yug.: 1860-1944)   DR309
Description & travel (Yug.: 1901-44)   DR1221   914.971+
Description (Rome, It.: 1861-1950)   DG806
Description, travel, civilization, customs (U.S.: 1866-1913)   E168
Description, travel, civilization, customs (U.S.: 1914-45)   E169   917.3049
Desert warfare   U167.5.D4
Desertion (mil.)   UB788
Desertion (naval)   VB870-875   359.1334
Designs, drawings, blueprints (naval architec.)   VM297   623.812
DESTROYER escorts (d.e.'s) & destroyers (naval engineering)   623.8254
                                                                               V825-825.3
Destroyer escorts (d.e.'s) & destroyers (units)   359.3254   V825-825.5, VA65 (U.S.)
Destroyers (as equip.)   359.8354
Destroyers (besides U.S.: by place)   V825.5.A-Z
Destroyers (gen.)   V825   623.8254, .81254, 359.3254
Destroyers (handling)   623.88254   V825-825.5
Destroyers (Japan)   V825.5.J3
Destroyers (U.S.)   V825.3
Destruction & pillage (WWII)   D810.D6 (SEE ALSO D785.U58-63 for U.S. Strategic
                                                                               Bombing Survey)
Deterrence   U162.6

Detonators   355.82542
Detonators (design: fuses, percus. caps, primers, etc.)   623.4542   UF780,
                                                                      VF510
Deutsches Jungvolk (Nazi Party)   DD253.49
Deutschland (submarine: Ger.: WWI)   D592.D4
Devonshire Regiment (WWII: G.B.)   D760.D4
Dewey, Thomas (U.S.: 20th c.)   E748.D48
Dictionaries (20th c. history)   D419   909.8203, 320.03, 320.904
DICTIONARIES & ENCYCLOPEDIAS (air forces & warfare)   UG628   358.4003
Dictionaries & encyclopedias (artillery)   UF9   358.1203
Dictionaries & encyclopedias (China)   951.003   DS705
Dictionaries & encyclopedias (history: gen.)   903   D9
Dictionaries & encyclopedias (mil. & naut. engineering)   623.003 (SEE ALSO 603)
                                                                      UG144-147
Dictionaries & encyclopedias (mil. sci.)   U24-25   355.003
Dictionaries & encyclopedias (naval forces)   359.003   V23
Dictionaries & encyclopedias (naval sci.: gen.)   V23   359.003
Dictionaries & encyclopedias (U.S.)   E174   973.03
Dictionaries & encyclopedias (WWI: includes 'Times' index and chronology)   D510
Dictionaries & encyclopedias (WWII)   D740   940.5303
DICTIONARIES, CHRONOLOGIES, ETC. (Asia)   DS31
Dictionaries, chronologies, etc. (China)   DS733
Dictionaries, chronologies, etc. (G.B.)   DA34
Dictionaries, chronologies, etc. (Japan)   DS833
Dictionaries, chronologies, etc. (military history: world)   D25.A2
Dictionaries, chronologies, etc. (Palestine, the Jews)   DS114
Dictionaries, chronologies, etc. (Rus.)   DK36
Dictionaries, gazeteers, guidebooks (Japan)   DS805
Dictionaries, guidebooks, etc. (Far East, E. & SE.Asia)   DS504
Dictionaries, Military (G.B.)   DA52
Dictionaries, Naval (G.B.)   DA72
Dictionaries (naval sci.: multi-ling.)   V24
Dieppe, Fr.   DC801.D56
Dieppe Raid (1942)   D756.5.D5
Diesel engines (marine engineering)   623.87236   VM770
Diesel, oil, & gas engines (marine engin.)   VM770   623.8723
Dinaric Alps (Yug.)   DR1350.D55
DIPLOMACY (20th c.)   D451-457
Diplomacy (20th c.: gen. special)   D455
Diplomacy (20th c.: gen.)   D453   909.82, 327.3-9, 320.9
DIPLOMACY & POLITICS (Africa: 19th-20th c.: gen.)   DT31.5
Diplomacy & politics (Bel.: gen.)   DH566
Diplomacy & politics (Bulg.)   DR72
Diplomacy & politics (Ger.: 1918-)   DD240-241
Diplomacy & politics (Ger.: gen.)   DD112   320.943, 327.43+
Diplomacy & politics (India, pre-1947 Pak.: 20th c.)   DS448
Diplomacy & politics (Iran)   DS274
Diplomacy & politics (Iraq: gen.)   DS70.95
Diplomacy & politics (It.)   DG491-499
Diplomacy & politics (Japan)   DS840-849   320.952, 327.52
Diplomacy & politics (Lux.)   DH908.5
Diplomacy & politics (Neth.: 1795-20th c.)   DJ147
Diplomacy & politics (Nor.: gen.)   DL458
Diplomacy & politics (Pacific: gen.: inclu. colonial rule)   DU29
Diplomacy & politics (Pol.)   DK418, DK4178.5-4185

237

Diplomacy & politics (Port.)   DP555-557   320.9469, 327.469+
Diplomacy & politics (Rum.)   DR226
Diplomacy & politics (Rus.-Jpn. War, 1904-5)   DS517.13
Diplomacy & politics (Saudi Arabia: gen.)   DS227
Diplomacy & politics (Serbia: gen.)   DR1975
Diplomacy & politics (Sp.)   DP83-86
Diplomacy & politics (Sp.: 1931-39)   DP257-258
Diplomacy & politics (Swe.)   DL658-659
Diplomacy & politics (Swe.: 1907-50)   DL867.5   948.5051-2
Diplomacy & politics (Swit.)   DQ68-76   320.9494, 327.4940+
Diplomacy & politics (Swit.: 1798-20th c.)   DQ75
Diplomacy & politics (Syria: gen.)   DS95.5
Diplomacy & politics (Tur.: 1918-)   DR477   327.5610+, 320.9561
Diplomacy & politics (Yug.)   DR326
Diplomacy & politics (Yug.: 1918-45)   DR367.A-Z
DIPLOMACY (Arg.: gen.)   F2833
Diplomacy (Australia: gen.)   DU113   327.94
Diplomacy (Brazil: gen.)   F2523   327.81
Diplomacy (Can.: gen.)   F1029   327.71
Diplomacy (Chile: gen.)   F3083
Diplomacy (China: gen.)   DS740.4   327.51
Diplomacy (Cuba: gen.)   F1776.2
Diplomacy (Den.: gen.)   DL159
Diplomacy (Fin.: gen.)   DL1046   327.4897
Diplomacy (Formosa: gen.)   DS799.625
Diplomacy (Fr.: gen.)   DC55
Diplomacy (G.B.: gen.)   DA45   327.41+
Diplomacy (Ger.: 1888-1918: gen.)   DD228.6   327.43+
Diplomacy (Greece: gen.)   DF785
Diplomacy (Hung.: gen.)   DB926
Diplomacy (Ire.: 20th c.)   DA964.A-Z
Diplomacy (Japan: gen.)   DS845   327.52
Diplomacy (Latin Am.: gen.)   F1415   327.8
Diplomacy (Liech.: gen.)   DB893
Diplomacy (Mex.: gen.)   F1228
Diplomacy (N. Viet.)   DS560.68
Diplomacy (Paraguay)   F2682
Diplomacy (Peru: gen.)   F3433
Diplomacy (Rus.)   DK65-69
Diplomacy (Sp.: 1814-20th c.) DP85.8
Diplomacy (U.S.: gen.)   E183.7 327.73
Diplomacy (Ukr.: gen.)   DK508.56
Diplomacy (Urug.: gen.)   F2722
Diplomacy (Venez.: gen.) F2321.2
Diplomacy (Viet.: gen.)   DS556.57
Diplomacy (W.Ind.: gen.)   F1621.5

Diplomacy (WWI)   D610-621   940.32
Diplomacy (WWII)   D748-754   940.532+, .5322-5325, 327.+
Diplomacy (WWII: Fr.)   940.532244   D752
Diplomacy (WWII: G.B.)   940.532241   D750
Diplomacy (WWII: gen.)   D748
Diplomacy (WWII: Ger.)   940.532443   D751
Diplomacy (WWII: Ire.)   940.5325415 (could ALSO be at .5322415 with Allies or at
                         .5324415 with Axis)   D754.I5-7
Diplomacy (WWII: misc. countries or areas) D754.A-Z
Diplomacy (WWII: Sweden)   940.5325485   D754.S8
Diplomacy (WWII: U.S.)   940.532273   D753
Diplomacy (WWII: Yug.)   940.5322497   D754.Y
Diplomatic history (WWI) 940.32   D610-621, D610 (gen.)
Directories (naval architec.)   VM12
Dirigibles   629.13324
Dirigibles (Ger.)   UG1225.G3
Dirigibles (mil. engineering)   623.743   TL659, UG1220-1225
Dirigibles (places outside U.S.)   UG1225.A-Z
Disability benefits, pensions, etc. (naval admin.: U.S.)   VB283
Disabled American Veterans of the World War (WWI)   D570.A15.D5
Disabled veterans (U.S.: rehab.)   UB363-364
Disarmament (WWI: Ger.)   D650.D5
Disarmament (WWII)   D820.D5
Disasters, Submarine   VK1265
Discharge, promotion, recruitment, enlistment (mil. sci.: countries besides U.S.)
                                               UB325.A-Z
Discharge, promotion, recruitment, enlistment (naval sci.: places besides U.S.)
                                               VB265.A-Z
Discharge, retirement, other termination (mil.)   355.114   UB320+
Discipline & conduct, Military (regulation)   355.133
Discipline & enforcement (naval conduct)   359.1332   VB850-855, VB890-925
Discipline, Military (U.S.)   UB793 (SEE ALSO KF7590)
Discipline, Naval (besides U.S.)   VB845.A-Z
Discipline, Naval (G.B.)   VB845.G7
Discipline, Naval (U.S.)   VB843   359.130973
Disinfection & fumigation (naval engin.) VM483
Dispensaries, Naval   VG270-275
Distance finders (inclu. tables etc.)   VK579
District of Columbia   975.3   F191-205, F194
District of Columbia (geog. & travel)   917.53   F192.3, F194, F199
Diving (marine engin.)   VM975-989 (SEE GV840.S78 for skindiving),
                         VM981 (gen.)   627.72 (gen.)
Diving (marine engin.: hist.)   VM977   627.7209, 623.8257 (subs.),
                         359.3257 (subs.-naval ops.), 797.23 (scuba)
Diving (marine engin.: special types)   VM985-989

Division of the Philippines (U.S. Army)   UA27.P5
DIVISIONS etc. (WWII: Australia)   D767.813   940.541294
Divisions etc. (WWII: Bel.)   D763.B41
Divisions etc. (WWII: Czech.)   D765.53
Divisions etc. (WWII: Dutch: by #)   D763.N41.1st-
Divisions etc. (WWII: Fin.)   D765.32
Divisions etc. (WWII: Ital.: by #)   D763.I81.1st-
Divisions etc. (WWII: Ital.: by name or author)   D763.I813.A-Z
Divisions etc. (WWII: Japan)   D767.23
Divisions etc. (WWII: New Z.)   D767.851   940.5412931
Divisions etc. (WWII: Nor.: by #)   D763.N61.1st-
Divisions etc. (WWII: Nor.: by name or author)   D763.N613.A-Z
Divisions etc. (WWII: Pol.)   D765.13
Divisions etc. (WWII: Rum.)   D766.413
Divisions etc. (WWII: Rus.: by #)   D764.5.1st-   940.541247
Divisions etc. (WWII: U.S.)   D769.29-309
Divisions etc. (WWII: U.S.: by #)   D769.3.1st-
Divisions etc. (WWII: U.S.: by name)   D769.295.A-Z
Divisions etc. (WWII: U.S.: gen.)   D769.29
Divisions etc. (WWII: Yug.: by #)   D766.61.1st-
Divisions etc. (WWII: Yug.: by name)   D766.613.A-Z
Divisions (U.S. Army: by place)   UA27.A-Z
Divisions (U.S. Marines: by #)   VE23.22.1st+
Divisions (U.S.: by #/author)   UA27.5.1st-
Divisions (WWII: Fr.)   D761.2
Dnepropetrovsk (Uk.)   DK508.9.D64
Documentary films, slides, etc. (WWI: catalogs)   D522.22
Documentary films, slides, etc. (WWII: catalogs)   D746.3 (older titles),
          D743.22 (newer titles)
Dog fighting, bombing, other air tactics (countries besides U.S.)   UG705.A-Z
Dogs, Military   UH100
Dogs (mil. transp.)   UC355 (SEE ALSO UH100)   355.424
Dollfuss, Englebert (Austria)   DB98.D6
Dominican Republic   F1931-1941   972.93
Don River Valley (Rus.)   DK511.D7
Donovan, William, 1883-1959 (WWII: spy)   D810.S8.D55
Dover, Eng. (WWII)   D760.8.D6
Downing St. (London, Eng.: No. 10)   DA687.D7
Draft & exemption (mil.: Japan)   UB345.J3
Draft & exemption (mil.: U.S.)   UB343-344   355.2236306073
Draft, Military   355.22363   UB340-345, UB343 (U.S.)
Draftsmen & surveyors, Naval (gen.)   VG920
Dreams (WWI)   D639.D7
Dresden, Ger.   DD901.D71-79
DRILL camps, instruction bases, maneuver grounds (gen.)   U290
Drill camps, maneuver grounds, etc. (U.S.: by name)   U294.5.A-Z
Drill regulations (armor & cavalry: U.S. reserves)   UE161
Drill regulations (artillery: U.S. reserves: by state)   UF162.A-W
Drill regulations (infantry: U.S. reserves)   UD161
Drill regulations, Marine (U.S.)   VE160-162
Drill regulations, Naval (U.S. reserves)   VD161
Drills, maneuvers, & tactics (artillery: by place)   UF160-302

DRILLS, MARINE (Asia)   VE270-280
Drills, Marine (Australia)   VE295
Drills, Marine (Eur.)   VE215-269
Drills, Marine (G.B.)   VE234
Drills, Marine (Ger.)   VE231
Drills, Marine (Japan) VE277
Drills, Marine (U.S.: gen.)   VE160   359.965, .9654
DRILLS, NAVAL (Asia)   VD270-280
Drills, Naval (Australia)   VD295   359.50994
Drills, Naval (China)   VD271
Drills, Naval (Eur.)   VD215-269
Drills, Naval (G.B.)   VD234   359.50941
Drills, Naval (Ger.)   VD231   359.50943
Drills, Naval (Japan)   VD277   359.50952
Drills, Naval (New Z.)   VD298
DRILLS, NAVAL ORDNANCE (Asia)   VF270-280
Drills, Naval ordnance (Australia)   VF295
Drills, Naval ordnance (Eur.)   VF215-269
Drills, Naval ordnance (Fr.)   VF228
Drills, Naval ordnance (G.B.)   VF234
Drills, Naval ordnance (Ger.)   VF231
Drills, Naval ordnance (Japan) VF277
Drills, Naval ordnance (Rus.)   VF252
Drills, Naval ordnance (U.S.: gen.)   VF160
Drills, Naval (Rus.)   VD252
Drills, Naval (U.S.)   VD160-162
Drills, tactics, & maneuvers (armor & cavalry: Eur.)   UE215-269
Drills, tactics, & maneuvers (infantry: U.S.)   UD160-162
Dry docks, shipyards, etc. (naval engineering)   623.83   VM301
Dunkirk, Battle of (1940)   D756.5.D8
Düsseldorf, Ger.   DD901.D95
DUTCH East Indies & Indonesia   DS611-649
Dutch East Indies & Indonesia (WWII)   D767.7   940.53598, .5425, 959.8022
Dutch East Indies (WWII: Reconstruction)   D829.D8
Dutch military ops. (WWII: gen.)   D763.N4
Dutch New Guinea (West)   DU744-744.5   995.1
Dutch West Indies   F2141   972.986
Dyak Islands & Borneo (gen.)   DS646.3   959.53, .83
Dzerzhinsky, Feliks (Rus.: 1925-53 era)   DK268.D9

EAST Africa   DT365-469   967.6, 963
East Africa (to 1960)   DT431
East Africa (1884-1960: gen.)   DT365.7   967.6
East Africa (Uganda & Kenya)   967.6   DT421-435+ (newer titles), DT431
East Africa (WWII)   D766.84   940.53676, 967.6
East African islands   DT469.A-Z
East Coast (U.S.: Loran tables)   VK561.U53-54
East Coast (U.S.: pilot & sailing guides)   VK981
East Coast (U.S.: tide & current tables)   VK781   623.8949091634
East Downing, Eng. (WWII)   D760.8.E3
East Indies & Indonesia (pilot & sailing guides: from U.S.)   VK931
East Indies (pilot & sailing guides: Eng. to India etc.)   VK881

Eastern Asia (history & foreign relns.: inclu. SE. Asia)   DS518-518.9
Eastern Europe (1815-1918)   DJK48
Eastern Europe (1918-45)   DJK49
Eastern Europe & Balkan Peninsula   DR (SEE DJK for gen. bks. on E. Eur. after
                about 1977-78)   949.6-8
Eastern Europe   DR (pubns. prior to 1978 & specific countries), DJK (titles after
                about 1977-78)   943.7-943.9, 947, 947.8, 949.6-949.84
Eastern Front (WWI)   D550-569
Eastern Front (WWII)   D764-766.7
Eastern Orthodox Church (WWII)   D810.C6745
Eastern question (1801-1914/20)   D371-379   949, 320.956, 327.41-42
Eastern question (20th c.)   D461-475   320.95, 956.03, 325.342
Eastern question (20th c.: by country)   D469.A-Z
Eastern question (20th c.: gen.)   D463
Eastern question (general: 19th c.)   D374
Ebert, Friedrich (Ger.: 1918-48 era)   DD247.E2
Economic aspects (Rus. Rev., 1917-21)   DK265.9.E2
Economic factors of war   355.023 (PREFER 355.02)   HB195, HC65, JX1953
Economic matters (Sp. Civil War, 1936-39)   DP269.8.E2
Economic matters (WWI: commerce, finance, mail)   D635 (SEE ALSO HC56,
                HF3030, HJ236, HJ8011)
Economic matters (WWII: commerce, mail, finance, monetary & fiscal planning, etc.
                in gen.)   D800 (SEE ALSO HC, HF, HJ for specific places)
Economics   330-339   HB-HJ
Ecuador   F3701-3799   986.6
Ecuador (1895-1944)   F3737   986.607-6072
Eden, Anthony (G.B.: 20th c.)   DA566.9.E28
Edinburgh, Scot.   941.34   DA890.E2-4
EDUCATION   L   370-379
Education & employment of veterans (U.S.)   UB357-358   355.1150973
Education & training, Air force   UG637-639   358.415+
Education & training, Military (U.S.)   355.50973
EDUCATION, MILITARY   U400-714   355.07
Education, Military (Asia)   U635-660
Education, Military (Australia)   U700-704   355.0071094
Education, Military (Austria-Hung.: gen.)   U550
Education, Military (Balkan States)   U625
Education, Military (China)   U640-644   355.0071051
Education, Military (Eur.)   U505-630   355.007104+
Education, Military (Fr.)   U565-569
Education, Military (G.B.)   U510-549.3
Education, Military (gen.: pubns. 1801+)   U405
Education, Military (Ger.)   U570-574   355.0071043
Education, Military (It.)   U585-589
Education, Military (Japan)   U650-654   355.0071052
Education, Military (New Z.)   U705-709
Education, Military (Nor.)   U590-594
Education, Military (Rus.)   U600-604   355.0071047
Education, Military (Tur.)   U620-624
Education, Military (U.S.)   U407-439

EDUCATION, NAVAL   V400-695
Education, Naval (Asia)   V625-650
Education, Naval (Asia: misc. countries)   V650.A-Z
Education, Naval (Australia)   V690-694   359.007094
Education, Naval (Can.)   V440-444
Education, Naval (China)   V630-634
Education, Naval (Eur.)   V500-623
Education, Naval (Fr.)   V565-569
Education, Naval (G.B.)   V510-530
Education, Naval (Ger.)   V570-574
Education, Naval (hist.: 20th c.)   V409
Education, Naval (hist.: gen.)   V401
Education, Naval (It.)   V585-589
Education, Naval (Japan)   V640-644
Education, Naval (New Z.)   V694.1-5
Education, Naval (Philippines)   V650.P5
Education, Naval (Rus.)   V600-604
Education, Naval (Turkey)   V650.T9
Education, Naval (U.S.)   V411-438
Education (WWI)   D639.E2-6
EDUCATION (WWII)   D810.E2-5
Education (WWII: gen.)   D810.E2
Education (WWII: Missouri)   D810.E4.M8-81
Education (WWII: U.S.)   D810.E3-46
Education (WWII: U.S.: by state)   D810.E4.A-W
Education (WWII: U.S.: gen.)   D810.E3
Education (WWII: Wisconsin)   D810.E4.W6-61
Edward VII (G.B.: King: 1901-1910)   DA567
Edward VIII (G.B.: King: 1936)   DA580
EGYPT   UA865   355.033062
Egypt (1879-1952)   DT107   962.03-052
Egypt (1882-1922: Brit. protec.)   962.04   DT107-107.8, DT107 (gen.)
Egypt (1914-17: Hussein Kamil)   DT107.7   962.04
Egypt (1917-36: Fuad I)   DT107.8   962.04-051
Egypt (1922-: Independence)   962.05   DT107.8+
Egypt (1922-36: Fuad I)   962.051   DT107.8
Egypt (1936-52: Faruk I)   DT107.82   962.052
Egypt & Sudan   962   DT43-159
Egypt & Sudan (geog. & travel)   916.2   DT55 (Egypt), DT124
Egypt & the Egyptian Sudan   DT43-154   962
Egypt (gen.)   DT43-107, DT77, DT115-154   962
Egypt (lighthouses, beacons, foghorns, etc.: lists)   VK1198
Egypt (naval status)   VA690   359.030962
Egypt (WWI)   D568.2
Egypt (WWII)   D766.9   940.5423, .5362, 962.052
Egyptian Sudan (inclu. Anglo-Egyptian)   DT108, DT154.1-159 (newer titles)   962.4
Eire (Republic of Ireland)   941.7   DA963
Eisenhower, Dwight D. (U.S.: 1953-61)   E836   973.9210924, 940.540973,
                                          355.0024
El Paso, Texas   F394.E4
El Paso, Texas (area)   976.496   F392.E45, F394.E4

ELECTRIC engines (marine engineering)   623.8726   VM773
Electric lighting (naut. craft: engineering)   623.852   VM491-493
Electric plants (defense)   UA929.95.E4
Electric propulsion (marine engin.)   VM773   623.8726
Electrical engineering (mil.)   623.76   UG480, VM471-479
Electrical systems (naut. craft: engineering)   623.8503   VM471-475
Electricians, Military   UG560-565
Electricity (mil. uses)   UG480   623.76
Electricity (naval architec. & engin.)   VM471-479   623.8503, .852, .8726
Electricity (naval architec. & engin.: U.S. Navy)   VM473
Electronic systems (naut. craft: engineering)   623.8504   VM480-480.5
Electronics & radar, Air force (U.S.)   UG1423
Electronics, Marine (radar, radio, sonar, etc.: naval architec. & engin.)   VM480
                                                   623.8504, .734+, .8564-85648
Electronics, Marine navigation   VK560   623.893
Electronics, Military   UG485   623.732+
Elephant batteries   UF430
Elizabeth (G.B.:1937-52 royal biog.: Consort of George VI)   DA585.A2
Elks, Benevolent...Order of (WWII)   D810.E6
Ellice Islands   DU590   996.81
Ellice Islands (WWII)   D767.99.E55
Emigrés, Russian (1925-53)   DK269
Employees, Civilian (naval admin.: U.S.)   VB183
Employment & education of veterans (countries except U.S.)   UB359.A-Z
Employment for crippled soldiers & sailors   UB360-366 (PREFER), UH560
                                                   355.1154-1156
Encampment & field training (mil.)   355.544   U180-185, UG400-409+
Encampments   355.412   U180-185
Encampments   U180-185   355.412
Encyclopedias & dictionaries (G.B.)   941.003   DA34
Encyclopedias & dictionaries (U.S.)   973.03   E174
Encyclopedias & dictionaries (WWI)   940.4003   D510, D521, D523
Encyclopedias & dictionaries (WWII)   940.54003   D740
Enforcement (naval conduct)   359.13323
Engine auxiliaries (marine engineering: boilers, blowers, pumps, propellers, etc.)
                   623.873   VM753-757 (propellers),
                   VM741-750 (boilers), VM821 (pumps), VM781+
Engine fuels, Marine   623.874   VM779
Engineer battalions etc. (WWII: U.S.: by #)   D769.335.1st-
Engineer battalions etc. (WWII: U.S.: by name)   D769.337.A-Z
Engineer forces, Army   358.2   UG15, UG21-124 (by place), UG23 (U.S.),
                   UG500-620
ENGINEERING   620   T
Engineering facilities, Naval   359.74   VM621-724, VM623 (U.S.), VC590-595
Engineering installations, Military   355.74
Engineering ops. (WWII)   D795
Engineering ops. (WWII: by country)   D795.A3-Z
Engineering ops. (WWII: gen.)   D795.A2
Engineering services (air forces)   358.47
Engineering services, Naval   359.982
Engineering systems (naut. craft: mech., electric, water, etc.)   623.85   VM471-505
Engineering, Camouflage (mil.)   623.77   UG449, UG1240-1245 (air forces),
                   V215 (ships)
Engineering, Civil (navies: gen.)   VG590
Engineering, Defense   623.3   UG400-442

Engineering, Marine (gen.)   VM600-605   623.87
Engineering, Marine (hist.: by place)   VM621-724
ENGINEERING, MILITARY   UG1-620
Engineering, Military & nautical   623   UG, VM (naval), V, UG15 (mil.: gen.),
          UG21-124 (mil.: by place), UG23 (U.S.), V750-895 (vessels)
Engineering, Military & nautical (construction)   623.047   UG460
Engineering, Military & nautical (electronic)   623.043   UG480-485
Engineering, Military & nautical (mechanical)   623.045   UG450
Engineering, Military & nautical (nuclear)   623.044
Engineering, Military & nautical (optical)   623.042   UG476, UG487
Engineering, Military (Asia)   UG99-113
Engineering, Military (Australia + New Z.)   UG121-122.5
Engineering, Military (by country or area)   UG21-124
Engineering, Military (China)   UG101
Engineering, Military (essays & lectures)   UG156
Engineering, Military (Eur.)   UG55-95   358.2094
Engineering, Military (Fr.)   UG71
Engineering, Military (G.B.)   UG57
Engineering, Military (gen. hist.)   UG15   358.2, .209
Engineering, Military (gen.: pubn. 1801+)   UG145
Engineering, Military (Ger.)   UG73
Engineering, Military (Japan)   UG105
Engineering, Military (Rus.: Eur.)   UG85
Engineering, Military (U.S.)   UG23-25   358.20973
Engineers (WWII)   940.531562   D795
Engineers (WWII: G.B.)   D759.55
Engineers (WWII: Ger.)   D757.8
Engines, Aircraft   629.134352-134354+
Engines, Marine (gen.)   VM731   623.872
Engines, Marine (types: design)   623.872   VM731-779, VM731
ENGLAND   DA20-690
England (1485-)   DA300
England (1702-)   DA470
England (1837-1901: Queen Victoria)   DA550-565   941.08
England (20th c.: misc. overall)   DA566-566.9
England (1901-10: King Edward VII)   DA567-570   941.082
England (1910-36)   942.083   DA576
England (1910-36: King George V)   DA573-578   941.083
England (1936-45)   942.084   DA586-587
England (1936: King Edward VIII)   DA580-583   941.084
England (1937-52: King George VI)   DA584-589   941.084
England & Wales   942   DA20-745, DA20-690 (Eng.), DA700-45 (Wales)
England & Wales (WWII: gen. particip.)   940.5342
England (gen.)   DA30   941, 942
England (geog. & travel)   914.2   DA600-668, DA600 (gen.), DA630 (1901-45)
England (WWII: mil. units & ops.)   940.541242   D759.5-63+, D760.A-Z
English Channel (tide & current tables)   VK639-644
English literature   PR   820-829
English poetry, satire, etc. (WWI)   D526.2 (PREFER PR, PS)
English poetry, satire, etc. (WWII)   D745.2 (PREFER PR, PS)

ENLISTED personnel & non-coms, Air force   358.41338   UG820-825
Enlisted personnel & non-coms, Naval   359.338   VB260-275
Enlisted personnel (inclu. non-coms)   355.338   UB320, U765+
Enlisted personnel, Naval (G.B.: by city or other div.)   VD64.A-Z
Enlisted personnel, Naval (gen.: nonperiodical collections)   VD7
Enlisted personnel (naval sci.: Ger.: inclu. enlistment, promotion, etc.) VB265.G3
                                                              359.2230943
Enlisted personnel (naval sci.: inclu. recruitment, enlistment, promotion, discharge,
            etc.)   VB260-275
Enlisted personnel, Naval (U.S.: by city)   VD25.A-Z
Enlistment, Military   355.22362   UB320-325, UB323 (U.S.)
Enlistment, recruiting, etc. (air forces: gen.)   UG880
Enlistment, recruitment, promotion, discharge (mil. sci.: U.S) UB323   355.20973
Enlistment, recruitment, promotion, discharge (Naval sci.: U.S.: by region or state)
                                                              VB264.A-Z
Entanglements & misc. fortification   UG407
Enterprise (aircraft carrier: U.S.: WWII)   D774.E5
Entertainers (WWII)   940.5315791-5315793   D810.E8
Entertainment, recreation, hospitality (WWII: civilian services for military)   D810.E8
Envelopment (mil. sci.)   U167.5.E57
EQUIPMENT & clothing, Military (gen.)   UC460
Equipment, Air force (gen.: planes, bombs, etc.: U.S.)   UG1203   358.4180973
EQUIPMENT & SUPPLIES (air force)   UG1100-1425
Equipment & supplies (horse cavalry)   357.188   UE440-445, UC260-267
Equipment & supplies (infantry)   356.186   UD380+, UC260-267, UC460+
Equipment & supplies, Military   355.8   U800+, UC260-267
Equipment & supplies (naval aviation)   359.948
Equipment & supplies, Naval (develop., procure., issue, util., shipping, etc.)
            359.8   VC, VF, VC10, VC20-258, VC20 (U.S.: gen.),
            VC260-267, VF145,   VF21-124, VF23 (ordnance: U.S.),
            VF57 (G.B.), VF73 (Ger.), VF105 (Japan), VF71 (Fr.)
Equipment & supplies (naval submarines)   359.938
Equipment & supply procurement (air forces)   358.416212   UG1120-1125,
                                                              UG1123 (U.S.)
Equipment, fuel, supplies, etc. (ships)   VC270-279
Equipment, Infantry   UD370-375
Equipment, Lifesaving (marine navig.: gen.)   VK1460-1461   623.865
Equipment (marines)   VE350-355
Equipment, Medical corps   UH510-515
Equipment, Military (countries except U.S.)   UC525.A-Z
Equipment, Military (gen.)   UC520   355.8
Equipment, Military (special: by name)   UC529.A-Z
Equipment, Naval artillery (places other than U.S.)   VF325.A-Z
Equipment, Naval (misc.)   V980
Equipment (naval seamen)   VD350-355
Equipment (submarine boats: special)   VM367.A-Z
Eritrea   DT391-398   963.5
Escort carriers (WWII: U.S.)   D769.52.E7   940.545

ESPIONAGE & spies (mil. admin.)   UB270-271
Espionage & spies (naval admin.)   VB250   359.3432-3433
Espionage & unconventional warfare (mil.)   355.343 (SEE ALSO 327.12)
                                            UB250-290
Espionage (by country responsible)   UB271.A-Z (SEE D-F #s for other cases in
                                         particular countries or particular wars)
Espionage, conspiracy, propaganda in U.S. (WWII)   D753.3
Espionage, intelligence, & unconventional warfare (WWII: Australia)   940.548694
Espionage, intelligence, & unconventional warfare (WWII: It.)   940.548745
Espionage, intelligence, & unconventional warfare (WWII: Japan)   940.548752
                                            UB251.J3, UB271.J3, VB230-250
Espionage, secret service, intelligence (WWII: gen.: spies)   D810.S7
Espionage, secret service, spies (WWI)   D639.S7-8
Espionage, spies (Sp. Civil War, 1936-39)   DP269.8.S4
Espionage (U.S.: gen.)   UB271.U6   327.120973
Essen, Ger.   DD901.E75
Essex (aircraft carrier: U.S.: WWII)   D774.E7
Essex, Eng. (WWII)   D760.8.E7
Estonia   DK511.E4-8, DK503 (later pubns.)   947.41
Estonia (1918-40)   DK503.74-746
Estonia (1940+)   DK503.75-77
Estonia (gen.)   DK511.E6, DK503 (later pubns.)
Ethics, religious questions (WWII)   D744.4
Ethics, prophecy, religious questions (WWI)   D524
ETHIOPIA (Abyssinia)   963   DT371-398, DT381
Ethiopia (1889-1928: inclu. 1895-6 conflict w. Italy)   DT387-387.6   963.043-054
Ethiopia (1896-1941 & 20th c.)   963.05   DT386-387.9, DT386
Ethiopia (1928-74: Haile Selassie)   DT387.7   963.055-06
Ethiopia (1930-74: Haile Selassie era)   963.055   DT387.7-387.92
Ethiopia (1935-6: Italo-Eth. War)   963.056 (SEE ALSO 945.091 for Italo-Eth. War of
                                         1935-6)   DT387.8
Ethiopia (1936-41: Ital. rule)   963.057   DT387.9
Ethiopia (1941-: Independence)   963.06   DT387.9
Ethiopia & Ethiopian military ops. (WWII)   D766.92   940.5423
Ethiopia (geog. & travel)   916.3   DT378
Ethiopia (mil. status)   UA860   355.033063
Ethnic groups (Sp.-Am. War: U.S.: participation)   E725.A-Z
Ethnic or racial groups (WWI)   940.31503
Ethnic or racial groups (WWII)   940.531503
Etiquette, Military   355.1336   U765+
Etiquette, Naval   359.1336   V720-743, VB260-265, VB307-315
EUROPE   940-949   D-DR
Europe (1789-1914)   940.28   D299, D359 (1801-1914)
Europe (1801-1914)   D359   940.28
Europe (20th c.)   D424   940.288-5
Europe (1900-14)   940.288   D424, D443 (pol. & dipl.)
Europe (20th c. or 1918-)   940.5   D424-425, D720 (1919-39), D431-443, D551,
                                         D720-728
Europe (1918-29)   940.51
Europe (1930-39)   940.52
Europe (1945-)   D1051+   940.55+
Europe (air war geog.)   358.41474
Europe & the World Wars   940-949   D-DR, D501-651, D731-838
Europe and Turkey   DA-DR   940's, 956.1
Europe & W. Eur. (gen.)   940   D-DR

Europe (biog.: heads of state)   923.14   D107
Europe, Eastern (gen.)   DJK38
Europe (gen.)   D51-838, D901+   940-949
Europe (geog. & travel)   914   D901-980, D907 (gen.), D921 (1901-50)
Europe (lighthouses, beacons, foghorns, etc.)   VK1055-1096
Europe (lighthouses, beacons, foghorns, etc.: lists)   VK1151-1185
Europe (maps & atlases)   912.4   G1796+
Europe (mil. geog.)   355.474   UA990, UA995.E
Europe (mil. status)   355.03304
Europe (mil. status)   UA646   355.03304, .03324, .03354
Europe (misc. areas: Iceland, Belg., Switz., Greece, etc.)   949
Europe (naval geog.)   359.474   VA450
Europe (naval geog.: misc. areas: Greece etc.)   359.4749
Europe (naval status: gen.)   VA450   359.03094, .474
Europe, Northern (plus Scandinavia and Finland)   DL1-87+
European aerial ops. (WWII: U.S. bombing survey)   D785.U6
European Gypsies (by place)   DX211-275
European infantry (gen.)   UD55   356.1094
European marines (gen.)   VE55
European military law   UB590-684
European naval law   VB530-699
European War (1914-18)   940.3-.499   D501-680
European War (1914-18: gen.)   940.3   D521
Evangelical and Reformed Church (WWII)   D810.C64
Examinations (G.B. Royal Navy)   V513
Examinations (U.S. Naval Acad.)   V415.R1-4
Examinations, questions, etc. (WWII)   D743.6
Exemption & draft (mil.: Ger.)   UB345.G3
Exercises, problems, etc. (artillery)   UF148
Exeter, Eng. (WWII)   D760.8.E88
Exhibitions & museums, Air force (by place within country)   UG623.3.x2.A-Z
Exhibitions & museums, Military (by country)   U13.A2-Z   355.00740+
Exhibitions & museums, Naval (by country then city)   V13.x2.A-Z
Exhibitions & museums (naval ordnance: by place or country)   VF6.A2-Z
Expeditionary & colonial forces   355.352   UA14, UA668 (G.B.), UA709 (Fr.),
                                        UA719 (Ger.), UA849 (Jp.)
Explosions, powder force, etc.   UF870
Explosives   355.8252   UF860-880
Explosives (design)   623.452   UF860-870
Explosives, Military (gen.)   UF860   623.452
Extermination & concentration camps (WWII: prisons & prisoners) D805

FALKLAND Islands   F3031   997.11
Falkland Islands (S. Atl. Ocean: G.B.)   997.1   F3031
FAR East (1904-45: inclu. Far Eastern question)   DS518 (SEE ALSO DU29)
                                        327.5, 950.41
Far East, Eastern & Southeastern Asia   DS501-935+   950-952, 958-959
Far East (WWII: Reconstruction)   D829.E2
FAR EASTERN question (China: 1861-1945)   DS740.63
Far Eastern question (France)   DS518.2
Far Eastern question (G.B.)   DS518.4
Far Eastern question (Ger.)   DS518.3
Far Eastern question (misc. countries)   DS518.9.A-Z (SEE DS845 for Japan,
                                        DS740.63 for China)
Far Eastern question (Netherlands)   DS518.5

Far Eastern question (Port.)   DS518.6
Far Eastern question (Russia)   DS518.7
Far Eastern question (U.S.)   DS518.8
Farley, James (U.S.: 20th c.)   E748.F24
Farmers (WWII)   940.531563   HD9006 (U.S.)
Fascism (1919-39)   D726.5 (SEE ALSO JC481 and 'D' numbers for Italy, Ger.)
          320.533, 321.94094
Fashion (WWI)   D639.F3
Ferdinand (Rum.: King, 1914-27: also works on era)   DR261
Ferrying (mil. engineering)   UG385
FIELD & rail artillery (design)   623.412   UF400-405, UF490-495 (rail)
Field artillery (gen.)   UF400   358.12
Field artillery groups etc. (WWII: U.S.: by #)   D769.34.1st-
Field artillery (places besides U.S.)   UF405.A-Z
Field artillery (U.S.: N.Y. reserves: also gen. artil.)   UA366
Field engineering (mil.)   UG360-390
Field engineering (misc. topics)   UG390
Field fortification   UG403
Field hospitals (WWII: U.S.: by #)   D807.U73.1st-
Field kits & equip. (mil.)   UC540-585
Field kits & equip. (mil.: U.S.)   UC543-544
Field ovens (mil.)   UC730
Field service, Infantry   UD440-445
Field service (mil. sci.)   U170-175
Fighter planes   UG1242.F5   623.7464, 358.43
Figureheads, ornaments, decorations on ships   VM308
Fiji Islands   DU600   996.11
Films, lantern slides, etc.: (WWI)   D527.3
Finances & supplies (air force admin.)   358.4162   UG1100-1105, UG1100-1425
Financial administration (mil.)   355.622   UB150-155, UC263-267, UA21-876,
          UA910-915
Financial administration (navies)   359.622   VC20-258, VC500-505, VA
FINLAND   DK445-465 (pre-1970 pubns.), DL1002-1180+ (pubns. from around
          1970 on)   947.1, 948.97 (works after 1970 or so)
Finland (20th c.)   DL1066.5   948.9703
Finland (20th c.: inclu. Revolution, 1917-18)   DK459   948.9703
Finland (1917-)   948.9703   DK459, DL1066.5
Finland (1917-39)   948.97031   DK459, DL1084
Finland (1918-39)   DL1084   948.97031
Finland (1939-)   DK459.45   948.97032
Finland (1939-45)   DL1090-1105+   948.97032
Finland (1939-45: gen.)   DL1092
Finland (1939-45: WWII era: inclu. Russo-Finnish War)   948.97032 (SEE ALSO
          947.0842 for R-F War)   DK459.45-5+, DL1090-1105+, DL1090 (gen.)
Finland (1945-)   DL1125
Finland & Finnish military ops. (WWII)   D765.3-35   940.53471, 534897,
          .54094897, 948.97032
Finland (gen.)   DL1032   948.97
Finland (geog. & travel)   914.897 (SEE ALSO .71 for earlier works)   DK450,
          DL1015.2 (books cataloged after 1969-70)
Finnish military history (WWII)   940.54094897 (SEE ALSO .5409471 for earlier
          works)   D765.3
Finnish military ops. (WWII: gen.)   D765.3

FIRE control, Artillery (inclu. instruments)   UF848-856
Fire control, Naval gunnery (inclu. instruments)   VF520-530
Fire drills, Naval (Fr.: also quarter, watch, station, etc.)   VD228
Fire-fighting equipment, Airport   629.1368
Fire-fighting (mil. airfields)   623.668
Fire-fighting, Nautical (technology)   623.8886   VK1258
Firearms, Portable (design)   623.442   UG520-525, UD380-385+
Firedrake (WWII: destroyer)   D772.F5
Fires & shipwrecks (gen.)   VK1250   910.453
Fires (mil. qtrs.)   UC425
Fires, Nautical (by name of ship)   VK1257.A-Z
FIRING & fire control (mil. engineering)   623.558   UF848-856, UF848 (gen.),
                                        UF850.A-Z (range finders), VF520-530 (naval)
Firing (armor & cavalry)   UE400-405
Firing devices (primers, percussion caps, etc.)   UF780
Firing instructions, Artillery   UF670-675
Firing instructions, Naval   VF450-455
Firing or sharpshooting (infantry: gen.)   UD330
Firing tests (artillery)   UF810
First-aid handbooks, Naval   VG466
First-aid manuals, Soldiers'   UH396 (SEE ALSO UH393-395)
First World War (econ., polit., social hist.)   940.31   D443, D453, D511-523, D610
Flag officers, Naval (above captain)   359.331   VB190, VB200-205, VB310-315
Flag signals (merch. marine)   VK385
Flags, colors, standards (mil.)   UC590-595
Flags, Naval & marine (besides U.S.)   V305.A-Z
Flags, Naval & marine (gen.)   V300 (SEE ALSO VK385)   359.15
Flame & chemical weapons (gen.)   UG447   358.34
Flame throwers, tear-gas devices, smoke mortars, other chemical weapons (design)
                                        623.445   UG447-447.5
Flanders area (Bel.)   DH801.F4-49
FLEETS (WWII: U.S. Navy: by #)   D769.5.1st-
Fleets, squadrons, etc. (G.B.: by name)   VA457.A-Z   359.310941
Fleets, squadrons, etc. (Ger.: by name)   VA514.A-Z   359.310943
Fleets, squadrons, etc. (Japan: by name)   VA654.A-Z   359.310952
Fleets, squadrons, etc. (U.S. Navy: by name)   VA63.A-Z   359.310973
Fleets, squadrons, etc. (WWII: U.S. Navy)   D769.5-539
Fliers (biog.)   629.13092
Flight decks (aircraft carriers)   V875.F5
Flight (gen. hist.)   629.1309
Flight training, Air force (U.S.: gen.: inclu. other educ.)   UG638   358.4150973
Flights, groups, squadrons, wings, etc. (naval aviation)   359.9434
Floating batteries   V890
Flogging & corp. punish. (countries besides U.S.)   UB815.A-Z
Florence, It.   DG760
FLORIDA   F306-320, F311   975.9
Florida (1865-1950)   F316   975.906
Florida (1918-45)   975.9062   F316
Florida (geog. & travel)   917.59   F309.3, F316
Florida Keys   975.941   F317.M7 (Monroe Co.)
Florida Keys & Strait & Windward Passage (pilot & sailing guides)   VK977
Florida Keys & Strait & Windward Passage (tide & current tables)   VK777
Florida Keys (Monroe County, Fl.)   F317.M7

Florida (naval geog.)   359.47759   VA140-147
Florida (pilot guides: Key West etc.)   623.8929759   VK977
Florida (WWII)   D769.85.F5-51
Flying   629.1325
Fog signals (merch. marine)   VK383
Foghorns, beacons, lighthouses, etc. (hist's.)   VK1015
Food, clothing, & equipment (naval admin.)   359.65-66 (SEE ALSO .81)
          VC280-285+, VC283 (clothing: U.S.), VC350-355 (food etc.), VC353 (U.S.)
Food, cooking, water, etc.   UC700-780   355.65-66, .81
Foot forces warfare   356   UD, U14-43, UA
Forecaster, Weather (navies: U.S.)   VG613
FOREIGN legions   355.359
Foreign participation (Rus. Rev., 1917-21: by country)   DK265.9.F52.A-Z
Foreign participation (Sp. Civil War, 1936-39: by country)   DP269.47.A-Z
Foreign participation (Sp. Civil War, 1936-39: Ger.)   DP269.47.G3
Foreign participation (Sp. Civil War, 1936-39: It.)   DP269.47.I8
Foreign participation (Sp. Civil War, 1936-39: Rus.)   DP269.47.R8-9
Foreign participation (Sp. Civil War, 1936-39: U.S.)   DP269.47.U6-7
Foreign population war effort (WWII: U.S.)   D769.8.F6
FOREIGN RELNS. & politics (1945-)   D843
Foreign relns. & politics (Fr.: 20th c.)   DC369   944.08
Foreign relns. & politics (G.B.: 20th c.)   DA566.7
Foreign relns. & politics (Malta)   DG991-991.6
Foreign relns. & politics (Scan., N. Eur., Fin.: gen.)   DL55
Foreign relns. (Africa-Fr.: 19th-20th c.)   DT33.5
Foreign relns. (Africa-G.B.: 19th-20th c.)   DT32.5   960.23-3, 325.3+
Foreign relns. (Africa-Ger.: 19th-20th c.)   DT34.5
Foreign relns. (Africa-It.: 19th-20th c.)   DT35.5
FOREIGN RELNS. (ARG.-Fr.)   F2833.5.F8
Foreign relns. (Arg.-G.B.)   F2833.5.G7
Foreign relns. (Arg.-Ger.)   F2833.5.G3   327.82043
Foreign relns. (Arg.-It.)   F2833.5.I8
Foreign relns. (Arg.-Japan)   F2833.5.J3
Foreign relns. (Arg.-partic. lands)   F2833.5.A-Z   327.820+
Foreign relns. (Arg.-U.S.)   F2833.5.U6-7
Foreign relns. (Asia-particular other areas or countries)   DS33.4.A-Z
Foreign relns. (Australia-G.B.)   DU113.5.G7   327.94041
Foreign relns. (Australia-Japan)   DU113.5.J3   327.94052
Foreign relns. (Australia-other specific lands)   DU113.5.A-Z   327.940+
Foreign relns. (Australia-U.S.)   DU113.5.U6-7   327.94073
Foreign relns. (Austria: by other country)   DB49.A-Z
Foreign relns. (Bel.-Fr.)   DH569.F8
Foreign relns. (Bel.-Ger.)   DH569.G3
Foreign relns. (Bel.: by country)   DH569.A-Z
Foreign relns. (Brazil-G.B.)   F2523.G7
Foreign relns. (Brazil-Ger.)   F2523.G3
Foreign relns. (Brazil-other lands)   F2523.A-Z
Foreign relns. (Bulg.-Ger.)   DR73.G3   327.4977043
Foreign relns. (Bulg.-Rus.)   DR73.R9
Foreign relns. (Bulg.-specific countries)   DR73.A-Z
Foreign relns. (Cambodia: plus gen. hist.)   DS554.5-58

FOREIGN RELNS. (CAN.-Fr.)   F1029.5.F8   327.71044
Foreign relns. (Can.-G.B.)   F1029.5.G7   327.71041
Foreign relns. (Can.-Ger.)   F1029.5.G3   327.71043
Foreign relns. (Can.-It.)   F1029.5.I8
Foreign relns. (Can.-Japan)   F1029.5.J3
Foreign relns. (Can.-other places) F1029.5.A-Z   327.710+
Foreign relns. (Can.-Rus.)   F1029.5.R9   327.71047
Foreign relns. (Can.-U.S.)   F1029.5.U6-7   327.71073
Foreign relns. (Chile-Ger.)   F3083.5.G3
Foreign relns. (Chile-Japan)   F3083.5.J3
Foreign relns. (Chile-other places) F3083.5.A-Z
Foreign relns. (Chile-U.S.)   F3083.5.U6-7
FOREIGN RELNS. (CHINA: 20th c. & 1912-49)   DS775.8
Foreign relns. (China & other lands: by name)   DS740.5.A-Z   327.510+
Foreign relns. (China-G.B.)   DS740.5.G5-6
Foreign relns. (China-Ger.)   DS740.5.G2-3   327.51043
Foreign relns. (China-Hong Kong)   DS740.5.G6.H6
Foreign relns. (China-Japan)   DS740.5.G6.J3   327.51052
Foreign relns. (China-Sov. Un.)   DS740.5.S65   327.51047
Foreign relns. (China-U.S.)   DS740.5.U6-7 (PREFER E183.8.C5)   327.51073
Foreign relns. (Cuba-G.B.)   F1776.3.G7
Foreign relns. (Cuba-Ger.)   F1776.3.G3
Foreign relns. (Cuba-other places) F1776.3.A-Z
Foreign relns. (Cuba-U.S.)   F1776.3.U6-7
Foreign relns. (Czech.: 1918-: gen.)   DB2189
Foreign relns. (Czech: 1918-39)   DB2199
Foreign relns. (Czech.: 1939-45)   DB2209
Foreign relns. (Czech.: by country)   DB2078.A-Z
Foreign relns. (Den.-G.B.)   DL159.5.G7
Foreign relns. (Den.-Ger.)   DL159.5.G3
Foreign relns. (Den.-other lands)   DL159.5.A-Z
Foreign relns. (Eastern Europe)   DJK43-44
Foreign relns. (Egypt & various countries)   DT82.5.A-Z   327.620+
Foreign relns. (Egypt-G.B.)   DT82.5.G7   327.62041
Foreign relns. (Egypt-Ger.)   DT82.5.G3   327.62043
Foreign relns. (Fin. & other partic. lands)   DL1048.A-Z
Foreign relns. (Fin.-Ger.)   DL1048.G3
Foreign relns. (Fin.-Rus.)   DL1048.R9
Foreign relns. (Fin.-Sov. Un.)   DL1048.S65
Foreign relns. (Formosa-Japan)   DS799.63.J3
Foreign relns. (Formosa-other places)   DS799.63.A-Z
Foreign relns. (Formosa: 1895-1945)   DS799.718
FOREIGN RELNS. (FR.: 19th-20th c.)   DC58
Foreign relns. (Fr.-G.B.)   DC59.8.G7   327.44041
Foreign relns. (Fr.-Ger.)   DC59.8.G3   327.44043
Foreign relns. (Fr.-Rus.)   DC59.8.R9
Foreign relns. (Fr.-Sov.Un.)   DC59.8.S65
Foreign relns. (Fr.: by country)   DC59.8.A-Z   327.440+
Foreign relns. (G.B.-Fr.)   DA47.1   327.41044
Foreign relns. (G.B.-Ger.)   DA47.2   327.41043
Foreign relns. (G.B.-misc. countries: SEE E183.8 for U.S.)   DA47.9.A-Z
Foreign relns. (G.B.-other countries)   DA47   327.410+
Foreign relns. (G.B.-Rus.)   DA47.65   327.41047

```
FOREIGN RELNS. (GER.: 19th-20th c.)        DD117        327.43+
Foreign relns. (Ger.: 1918-: by country)        DD241.A-Z
Foreign relns. (Ger.-Albania: 1918-)        DD241.A5
Foreign relns. (Ger.-Argen.: 1918-)        DD241.A7
Foreign relns. (Ger.-Austria: 1918-)        DD241.A9
Foreign relns. (Ger.-Bel.: 1918-)        DD241.B4
Foreign relns. (Ger.-Brazil: 1918-)        DD241.B7
Foreign relns. (Ger.-Bulg.: 1918-)        DD241.B8
Foreign relns. (Ger.: by country)        DD120.A-Z        327.430+
Foreign relns. (Ger.-Can.: 1918-)        DD241.C2-29
Foreign relns. (Ger.-Czech.: 1918-)        DD241.C95
Foreign relns. (Ger.-Den.: 1918-)        DD241.D3
Foreign relns. (Ger.-Egypt: 1918-)        DD241.E3
Foreign relns. (Ger.-Fin.: 1918-)        DD241.F5
Foreign relns. (Ger.-Fr.)        DD120.F8        327.43044
Foreign relns. (Ger.-Fr.: 1918-)        DD241.F8
Foreign relns. (Ger.-G.B.)        DD120.G7        327.43041
Foreign relns. (Ger.-G.B.: 1888-1918)        DD228.7.G7
Foreign relns. (Ger.-G.B.: 1918-)        DD241.G7
Foreign relns. (Ger.-Greece: 1918-)        DD241.G8
Foreign relns. (Ger.-Hung.: 1918-)        DD241.H9
Foreign relns. (Ger.-India: 1918-)        DD241.I4
Foreign relns. (Ger.-Ire.)        DD120.I6
Foreign relns. (Ger.-Ire.: 1918-)        DD241.I6
Foreign relns. (Ger.-It.)        DD120.I8
Foreign relns. (Ger.-It.: 1918-)        DD241.I8
Foreign relns. (Ger.-Japan)        DD120.J3        327.43052
Foreign relns. (Ger.-Japan: 1918-)        DD241.J3
Foreign relns. (Ger.-Neth.: 1918-)        DD241.N4
Foreign relns. (Ger.-Nor.: 1918-)        DD241.N8
Foreign relns. (Ger.-Pol.: 1918-)        DD241.P7
Foreign relns. (Ger.-Port.: 1918-)        DD241.P8
Foreign relns. (Ger.-Rum.: 1918-)        DD241.R8
Foreign relns. (Ger.-Rus.)        DD120.R9        327.43047
Foreign relns. (Ger.-Rus.: 1918-)        DD241.R9
Foreign relns. (Ger.-Sov. Un.)        DD120.S65
Foreign relns. (Ger.-Sp.: 1918-)        DD241.S7
Foreign relns. (Ger.-Swe.: 1918-)        DD241.S8
Foreign relns. (Ger.-Swit.: 1918-)        DD241.S9
Foreign relns. (Ger.-Syria: 1918-)        DD241.S95
Foreign relns. (Ger.-Tur.: 1918-)        DD241.T8
Foreign relns. (Ger.-U.S.)        DD120.U6-7
Foreign relns. (Ger.-U.S.: 1918-)        DD241.U6-69+
Foreign relns. (Ger.-Uruguay: 1918-)        DD241.U7+
Foreign relns. (Ger.-Yug.: 1918-)        DD241.Y8
Foreign relns. (Greece: by country)        DF787.A-Z
Foreign relns. (Greece-G.B.)        DF787.G7
Foreign relns. (Greece-Ger.)        DF787.G3
Foreign relns. (Greece-It.)        DF787.I8
Foreign relns. (Hung.-Ger.)        DB926.3.G3
Foreign relns. (Hung.-other lands)        DB926.3.A-Z
Foreign relns. (Hung.-Sov. Un.)        DB926.3.S65
Foreign relns. (India-Ger.)        DS450.G3        327.54043
Foreign relns. (India-Japan)        DS450.J3        327.54052
Foreign relns. (India-other specific places)        DS450.A-Z        327.540+
```

Foreign relns. (Indon.-Japan)   DS640.J3
Foreign relns. (Indon.-other countries) DS640.A-Z
Foreign relns. (Iran-G.B.)   DS274.2.G7   327.55042
Foreign relns. (Iran-Ger.)   DS274.2.G3   327.55043
Foreign relns. (Iran-other countries)   DS274.2.A-Z   327.550+
Foreign relns. (Iran-Rus.)   DS274.2.R9 327.55047
Foreign relns. (Iran-U.S.)   DS274.2.U6-7   327.55073
Foreign relns. (Iraq-G.B.)   DS70.96.G7
Foreign relns. (Iraq-Ger.)   DS70.96.G3
Foreign relns. (Iraq-other specific places)   DS70.96.A-Z
Foreign relns. (Ire.: 20th c.: gen.)   DA964.A2
Foreign relns. (Ire.-G.B.: 20th c.)   DA964.G7
Foreign relns. (Ire.-Ger.: 20th c.)   DA964.G3
FOREIGN RELNS. (IT.: 1861-1945)   DG498
Foreign relns. (It.-Alb.)   DG499.A5
Foreign relns. (It.: by country) DG499.A-Z 327.450+
Foreign relns. (It.-Eth.)   DG499.E7
Foreign relns. (It.-Fr.)   DG499.F8
Foreign relns. (It.-G.B.)   DG499.G7
Foreign relns. (It.-Ger.)   DG499.G3
Foreign relns. (It.-Japan) DG499.J3
Foreign relns. (It.-Rus.)   DG499.R9
Foreign relns. (It.-Sov.Un.)   DG499.S65
Foreign relns. (It.-Swit.)   DG499.S9
Foreign relns. (It.-U.S.)   DG499.U6-7
Foreign relns. (It.-Yug.)   DG499.Y8
FOREIGN RELNS (JAPAN-Asia)   DS849.A75   327.5205
Foreign relns. (Japan-Australia)   DS849.A8   327.52094
Foreign relns. (Japan-Burma)   DS849.B9
Foreign relns. (Japan-Cambodia)   DS849.C15
Foreign relns. (Japan-China)   DS849.C5   327.52051
Foreign relns. (Japan-G.B.)   DS849.G7   327.52041
Foreign relns. (Japan-Ger.)   DS849.G3   327.52043
Foreign relns. (Japan-India)   DS849.I4
Foreign relns. (Japan-Indoch.)   DS849.I45
Foreign relns. (Japan-Indonesia)   DS849.I5
Foreign relns. (Japan-It.)   DS849.I8
Foreign relns. (Japan-Korea)   DS849.K5
Foreign relns. (Japan-Malayas)   DS849.M3
Foreign relns. (Japan-New Zea.)   DS849.N45
Foreign relns. (Japan-other places)   DS849.A-Z   327.520+
Foreign relns. (Japan-Philip.)   DS849.P5   327.520599
Foreign relns. (Japan-Rus.)   DS849.R9   327.52047
Foreign relns. (Japan-Sov. Un.)   DS849.S65 327.52047
Foreign relns. (Japan-Thai.)   DS849.T4
Foreign relns. (Japan-U.S.)   DS849.U6-7   327.52073
Foreign relns. (Japan-Viet.)   DS849.V5
Foreign relns. (Korea-China)   DS910.2.C5   327.519051
Foreign relns. (Korea-Japan)   DS910.2.J3   327.519052
Foreign relns. (Korea-other lands)   DS910.2.A-Z   327.5190+
Foreign relns. (Korea-Rus.)   DS910.2.R9
Foreign relns. (Laos: also gen. hist.)   DS555.5-58

FOREIGN RELNS. (LATIN AM. & other places except U.S.)   F1416.A-Z   327.80+
Foreign relns. (Latin Am.-Fr.)   F1416.F8
Foreign relns. (Latin Am.-G.B.)   F1416.G7
Foreign relns. (Latin Am.-Ger.)   F1416.G3   327.8043
Foreign relns. (Latin Am.-It.)   F1416.I8
Foreign relns. (Latin Am.-Japan)   F1416.J3   327.8052
Foreign relns. (Latin Am.-Rus.)   F1416.R9
Foreign relns. (Latin Am.-U.S.)   F1418   327.8073
Foreign relns. (Libya & other particular places)   DT227.5.A-Z
Foreign relns. (Libya-Ger.)   DT227.5.G3
Foreign relns. (Libya-It.)   DT227.5.I8
Foreign relns. (Liech.: by country)   DB894.A-Z
Foreign relns. (Liech.-Ger.)   DB894.G3
Foreign relns. (Lux.: by country)   DH908.6.A-Z
Foreign relns. (Lux.-Ger.)   DH908.6.G3
Foreign relns. (Mex.-Ger.)   F1228.5.G3   327.72043
Foreign relns. (Mex.-Japan)   F1228.5.J3   327.72052
Foreign relns. (Mex.-other places)   F1228.5.A-Z   327.720+
Foreign relns. (Mex.-Rus.)   F1228.5.R9   327.72047
Foreign relns. (Mex.-Sov.Un.)   F1228.5.S65   327.72047
Foreign relns. (Mex.-U.S.)   F1228.5.U6-7   327.72073
Foreign relns. (Mid. East, SW. Asia: by specific country)   DS63.2.A-Z   327.560+
Foreign relns. (Morocco-Fr.)   DT317.5.F8
Foreign relns. (Morocco-Ger.)   DT317.5.G3
Foreign relns. (Morocco-other specific places)   DT317.5.A-Z
Foreign relns. (N. Viet.-other countries)   DS560.69.A-Z
Foreign relns. (N. Zea.-Japan)   DU421.5.J3   327.931052
Foreign relns. (N. Zea.-other specific places)   DU421.5.A-Z   327.9310+
Foreign relns. (N. Zea.-U.S.)   DU421.5.U6-7   327.931073
Foreign relns. (Neth.: by country)   DJ149.A-Z
Foreign relns. (Neth.-Ger.)   DJ149.G3
Foreign relns. (Nor.-G.B.)   DL459.G7
Foreign relns. (Nor.-Ger.)   DL459.G3
Foreign relns. (Nor.-other specific countries)   DL459.A-Z   327.4810+
Foreign relns. (Nor.-Swe.)   DL459.S8
Foreign relns. (Pacific-Fr.)   DU50
Foreign relns. (Pacific-G.B.)   DU40
Foreign relns. (Pacific-Ger.)   DU60
Foreign relns. (Pacific-Sp.)   DU65
Foreign relns. (Pacific-U.S.)   DU30
Foreign relns. (Paraguay-Ger.)   F2682.G3   327.892043
Foreign relns. (Paraguay-other places)   F2682.A-Z
Foreign relns. (Peru-Ger.)   F3434.G3
Foreign relns. (Peru-Japan)   F3434.J3
Foreign relns. (Peru-other places)   F3434.A-Z
Foreign relns. (Peru-U.S.)   F3434.U6-7
Foreign relns. (Philip.: by country)   DS673.A-Z   327.5990+
Foreign relns. (Philip.-Japan)   DS673.J3   327.599052
Foreign relns. (Philip.-U.S.)   DS673.U6-7   327.599073

```
FOREIGN RELNS. (POL.: 1918-45)      DK4402.5
Foreign relns. (Pol.: by country)          DK418.5.A-Z
Foreign relns. (Pol.-Fr.)          DK418.5.F8, DK4185.F8 (newer titles)
Foreign relns. (Pol.-G.B.)      DK418.5.G7
Foreign relns. (Pol.: gen.)      DK4180
Foreign relns. (Pol.-Ger.)      DK418.5.G3 (earlier titles), DK4185.G3
Foreign relns. (Pol.-Rus.)          DK418.5.R9, DK4185.R9 (later works)
Foreign relns. (Pol.: with particular countries)      DK4185.A-Z
Foreign relns. (Port.-G.B.)      DP557.G7
Foreign relns. (Port.-Ger.)      DP557.G3
Foreign relns. (Port.-other countries: by name)      DP557.A-Z
Foreign relns. (Port.-Sp.)      DP557.S7
Foreign relns. (Port.-U.S.)      DP557.U6-7
Foreign relns. (Rum. & partic. countries)          DR229.A-Z
Foreign relns. (Rum.-Ger.)      DR229.G3      327.498043
Foreign relns. (Rum.-Rus.)      DR229.R9
FOREIGN RELNS. (RUS. & non-U.S. Am. countries)  DK69.3.A-Z
Foreign relns. (Rus.-Asia: gen.: pubns. 1801-)    DK68.A3-Z
Foreign relns. (Rus.-Asian countries by name)    DK68.7.A-Z
Foreign relns. (Rus.-Balkan Penin.)          DK67.4
Foreign relns. (Rus.-Bulg.)      DK67.5.B8
Foreign relns. (Rus.-Can.)      DK69.3.C2-29
Foreign relns. (Rus.-Cath. Church)      DK67.3
Foreign relns. (Rus.-China)      DK68.7.C5          327.47051
Foreign relns. (Rus.-Czech.)      DK67.5.C95
Foreign relns. (Rus.-Europe)      DK67
Foreign relns. (Rus.-Fin.)      DK67.5.F5
Foreign relns. (Rus.-Fr.)      DK67.5.F8
Foreign relns. (Rus.-G.B.)      DK67.5.G7
Foreign relns. (Rus.: gen.)      DK66          327.47
Foreign relns. (Rus.-Ger.)      DK67.5.G3
Foreign relns. (Rus.-Greece)      DK67.5.G8
Foreign relns. (Rus.-Hung.)      DK67.5.H9
Foreign relns. (Rus.-India)      DK68.7.I4
Foreign relns. (Rus.-Iran)      DK68.7.I55
Foreign relns. (Rus.-It.)      DK67.5.I8
Foreign relns. (Rus.-Japan)      DK68.7.J3      327.47052
Foreign relns. (Rus.-Mex.)      DK69.3.M6
Foreign relns. (Rus.: particular areas)      DK67-69      327.470+
Foreign relns. (Rus.-Pol.)      DK67.5.P7
Foreign relns. (Rus.-Rum.)      DK67.5.R8
Foreign relns. (Rus.-specific Eur. countries)      DK67.5.A-Z
Foreign relns. (Rus.-Swe.)      DK67.5.S8
Foreign relns. (Rus.-Tur.)      DK68.7.T8
Foreign relns. (Rus.-U.S.)      DK69 (PREFER E183.8.R9)      327.47073
Foreign relns. (Rus.-Yug.)      DK67.5.Y8
Foreign relns. (Saudi Arab. Penin.: G.B.)    DS228.G7
Foreign relns. (Saudi Arab. Penin.: Ger.)    DS228.G3
Foreign relns. (Saudi Arabia-specific countries)  DS228.A-Z
Foreign relns. (Serbia-other specific places)    DR1976.A-Z
Foreign relns. (Slovakia: 1918-)      DB2809
Foreign relns. (Slovakia: 1939-45)      DB2819
```

```
FOREIGN RELNS. (SP.-Fr.: 1931-39)     DP258.F8
Foreign relns. (Sp.-Ger.)              DP86.G3      327.46043
Foreign relns. (Sp.-Ger.: 1931-39)     DP258.G3
Foreign relns. (Sp.-It.)               DP86.I8
Foreign relns. (Sp.-It.: 1931-39)      DP258.I8
Foreign relns. (Sp.-Port.: 1931-39)   DP258.P8
Foreign relns. (Sp.-Rus.)              DP86.R9      327.46047
Foreign relns. (Sp.-Rus.: 1931-39)     DP258.R9
Foreign relns. (Sp.-Sov. Un.)          DP86.S65
Foreign relns. (Sp.-Sov. Un.: 1931-39)       DP258.S65
Foreign relns. (Sp.-specific lands: 1931-39)    DP258.A-Z
Foreign relns. (Sp.-U.S.: 1931-39)       DP258.U6-7
Foreign relns. (Sp.: with partic. countries)  DP86.A-Z   327.460+
FOREIGN RELNS (SWE.-Fin.)              DL659.F5
Foreign relns. (Swe.-G.B.)             DL659.G7
Foreign relns. (Swe.-Ger.)             DL659.G3
Foreign relns. (Swe.-Nor.)             DL659.N8
Foreign relns. (Swe.-other lands: by name)  DL659.A-Z   327.485+
Foreign relns. (Swe.-Rus.)                   DL659.R9
Foreign relns. (Swe.-Sov. Un.)         DL659.S65
Foreign relns. (Swe.-U.S.)             DL659.U6-7
Foreign relns. (Swe.: 1818-20th c.)    DL658.8
FOREIGN RELNS. (SWIT.-Fr.)             DQ76.F8
Foreign relns. (Swit.-G.B.)            DQ76.G7
Foreign relns. (Swit.-Ger.)            DQ76.G3      327.494043
Foreign relns. (Swit.-It.)             DQ76.I8      327.494045
Foreign relns. (Swit.-Rus.)            DQ76.R9
Foreign relns. (Swit.-specific countries)    DQ76.A-Z   327.4940+
Foreign relns. (Swit.-U.S.)            DQ76.U6-7   327.494073
Foreign relns. (Syria-Fr.)             DS95.6.F8
Foreign relns. (Syria-G.B.)            DS95.6.G7
Foreign relns. (Syria-Ger.)            DS95.6.G3
Foreign relns. (Syria-other countries)  DS95.6.A-Z   327.56910+
Foreign relns. (Thai.-Japan)           DS575.5.J3
Foreign relns. (Thai.-other places)    DS575.5.A-Z
Foreign relns. (Tunisia-It.)           DT257.5.I8
Foreign relns. (Tunisia-other lands: by name)    DT257.5.A-Z
Foreign relns. (Tur.-G.B.)             DR479.G7
Foreign relns. (Tur.-Ger.)             DR479.G3
Foreign relns. (Tur.-particular countries)   DR479.A-Z
Foreign relns. (Tur.-Rus.)             DR479.R9
Foreign relns. (Ukr.: by country)      DK508.57
FOREIGN RELNS. (U.S.: 1865-1900: gen.)    E661.7 (SEE ALSO E183.8.A-Z)
Foreign relns. (U.S.: 1897-1901: gen.)    E713
Foreign relns. (U.S.: 20th c.: gen.)   E744      327.73
Foreign relns. (U.S.: 1913-21)         E768
Foreign relns. (U.S.-China)            E183.8.C5   327.73051
Foreign relns. (U.S.-Fr.)              E183.8.F8   327.73044
Foreign relns. (U.S.-G.B.)       E183.8.G7         327.73041
Foreign relns. (U.S.-Ger.)       E183.8.G3         327.73043
Foreign relns. (U.S.-It.)        E183.8.I8         327.73045
Foreign relns. (U.S.-Japan)            E183.8.J3   327.73052
Foreign relns. (U.S.-other places)  E183.8.A-Z    327.730+
Foreign relns. (U.S.-Russia)           E183.8.R9   327.73047
Foreign relns. (U.S.-Sov.Un.)          E183.8.S65  327.73047
```

Foreign relns. (Urug. & other partic. places: by name)   F2722.5.A-Z
Foreign relns. (Urug.-Ger.)   F2722.5.G3   327.895043
Foreign relns. (Urug.-It.)   F2722.5.I8
Foreign relns. (Venez. & other places)   F2321.3.A-Z
Foreign relns. (Venez.-Ger.)   F2321.3.G3
Foreign relns. (Viet.-Fr.)   DS556.58.F8
Foreign relns. (Viet.-Japan)   DS556.58.J3
Foreign relns. (Viet.-other countries: by place)   DS556.58.A-Z
Foreign relns. (W.Ind.-G.B.)   F1622.5.G7
Foreign relns. (W.Ind.-Ger.)   F1622.5.G3
Foreign relns. (W.Ind.-partic. places)   F1622.5.A-Z
Foreign relns. (W.Ind.-U.S.)   F1622
FOREIGN RELNS (YUG.: 1918-45)   DR1292
Foreign relns. (Yug.-G.B.: 1918-45)   DR367.G7
Foreign relns. (Yug.: gen.)   DR1257-1258
Foreign relns. (Yug.-Ger.: 1918-45)   DR367.G3
Foreign relns. (Yug.-It.: 1918-45)   DR367.I8
Foreign relns. (Yug.-Rus.: 1918-45)   DR367.R9
Foreign relns. (Yug.-specific countries)   DR327.A-Z
Foreign relns. (Yug.-U.S.: 1918-45)   DR367.U6-7
Forest fighting   U167.5.F6
FORMOSA (Taiwan)   951.249   DS895.F7-77 (books prior to about 1970),
                           DS798.92-799.99+ (many post-1969 pubns.)
Formosa (19th-20th c.)   DS895.F75   951.24903-24904
Formosa (1895-1945)   DS799.69-72   951.24904
Formosa (1895-1945: Japanese period)   951.24904   DS895.F75,
                               DS799.69-72, DS799.7 (gen.)
Formosa (gen.)   DS799.5   951.249
Formosa (WWII: gen. particip.)   940.5351249   DS895.F75,
                               DS799.69-72 (pubns. 1970+)
Fortification   UG400-442
Fortification (gen.: pubn. 1801+)   UG401   355.544, 623.1
Fortification, Permanent   UG405
FORTIFICATIONS (Asia: by country)   UG432.A-Z
Fortifications (by place)   UG410-442   623.19+, 355.45-47+
Fortifications (Eur.: by region or country)   UG429.A-Z
Fortifications (Eur.: by town or place)   UG430.A-Z
Fortifications (mil. engineering)   623.1   UG400-442
Fortifications (mil. engineering: by place)   623.19 (for works prior to 1989 SEE
                               ALSO .109)   UG410-442
Fortifications (U.S.: by state or region)   UG411.A-Z   623.1974-1979+,
                               355.450974+, .4774+
Fortifications (U.S.: by town or place)   UG412.A-Z
FORTIFIED defenses (Asia)   UG431-433   623.195
Fortified defenses (Australia)   UG437-439
Fortified defenses (Can.)   UG413-415
Fortified defenses (Eur.)   UG428-430
Fortified defenses (Ger.)   UG429.G3
Fortified defenses (Japan)   UG432.J3   623.1952
Fortified defenses (Pacific islands)   UG440-442
Fortified defenses (Philip.)   UG432.P5
Fortified defenses (U.S.)   UG410-412   623.1973, 355.4773
Fortified defenses (W. Indies)   UG422-424
Fortress & garrison artillery (U.S.: gen.)   UF483
Foul-weather gear, Naval (plus other special clothing)   VC307   359.81

Fouling, corrosion, etc. (marine engin.)   VM951
Fragmentation bombs (aerial)   UG1282.F7   623.4514
FRANCE   DC   944
France (1515-)   DC110
France (1870- & 20th c.: 3d, 4th, 5th Repub's.)   944.08   DC289+, DC335+
France (1870-1945: 3d Repub.)   944.081   DC335
France (1871-1940: 3rd Repub.)   DC334-354+
France (20th c.: overall)   DC361-373, DC361   944.081
France (1913-20: era of Pres. Raymond Poincaré)   DC385
France (1914-18: WWI era)   DC387   944.0814
France (1918-39)   944.0815   DC389-396
France (1919-40: Reconstruc.)   DC389-396
France (1924-31: Gaston Doumergue)   DC394
France (1932-40: Albert F. Lebrun)   DC396
France (1939-45: WWII period: inclu. Pétain collab.)   DC397   944.0816
France & French military ops. (WWI: gen.)   D548   940.344, .412+
France & French military ops. (WWII)   D761-762
France. Army (gen.)   UA702   355.00944, .30944
France. Army (infantry, cavalry, armor, artillery)   UA703-705
France (biog.: heads of state)   923.144
France (gen. hist., culture)   DC17
France (gen. hist.: pubn. 1815-)   DC38
France (geog. & travel)   914.4   DC28-45
France (lighthouses, beacons, foghorns, etc.)   VK1071-1072
France (lighthouses, beacons, foghorns, etc.: lists)   VK1173   623.89440944
France (mil. capabil.)   355.033244
France (mil. status: gen.)   UA700   355.033044
France (naval geog.)   359.4744   VA500-509
France (naval status: gen.)   VA503.A5-Z   359.030944, .4744
France (post-WWI relns.: U.S.: inclu. defensive alliance bet. Fr., U.S., G.B.)
    D651.F6.A2-Z
France (post-WWI territorial ?s)   D651.F5-7
France (post-WWI territorial ?s: gen.)   D651.F5
France (WWI: causes, aims, results)   D516
France (WWI: mil. hist.)   940.40944   D548-549
France (WWI: Reconstruction)   D659.F8
France (WWII: causes, aims, results)   D742.F8
France (WWII: dipl. history)   D752   940.532244
Franco Bahamonde, Francisco (Sp.: 1931-39 period)   DP264.F7
Frankfurt, Ger.   DD901.F71-79
Franz Ferdinand (Austria: Archduke)   DB89.F7
Franz Joseph I (Austria: Emp.: 1848-1916)   DB87
Fraternities (WWII: U.S. educ.: by name)   D810.E46.A-Z
Free French, France Combattante, French Volunteer Force (WWII)   D761.9.F7
Free India (Azad Hind: WWII: 1943-45: includes Indian National Army)   D767.63
Freedom of the seas & naval ops. (gen.: WWI)   D580
Freighters (naval architec.)   VM391-395   623.8245, 387.544
Fremantle. Australia   DU380.F8
FRENCH aerial ops. (WWI)   D603   940.44944
French aerial ops. (WWII)   D788   940.544944
French Canadians   F1027
French Equatorial Africa (WWII)   D766.96
French Foreign Legion (WWI)   D548.35

French (in Arg.)   F3021.F8
French (in Brazil)   F2659.F8
French (in S.Am.)   F2239.F8
French (in U.S.)   E184.F8
French (in Urug.)   F2799.F7
FRENCH INDOCHINA   DS531-560   959.4, 959.6-7
French Indochina (to 1949)   959.703   DS556.8-83
French Indochina (1884-1945)   DS549   959.703
French Indochina & Vietnam   959.7   DS531-558
French Indochina (gen.)   DS541
French Indochina (WWII)   D767.45   940.53597, 959.703
French military history (gen.)   DC45   355.00944, .033044
French military ops. & France (WWI)   D548-549
French military ops. & France (WWII: gen.)   D761   940.5344, .540944,
                                                       944.0815-0816
French military ops. (WWII: misc.)   D761.9.A-Z
French mission to U.S. (WWI)   D570.8.M6.F4
French naval history (gen.)   DC50
French poetry, satire, etc. (WWI)   D526.3
French poetry, satire, etc. (WWII)   D745.3
French prisons & prisoners (WWII)   D805.F8
French Somaliland (Djibouti or Afars & Issas)   DT411   967.71-7104+
French West Africa   DT521-553   966, 966.1-3, .52, .68, .81
French West Indies   F2151   972.976
Friendly Islands (Tonga)   996.12   DU880
Frigates & corvettes (gen.)   V826   623.8254
Frigates (U.S.)   V826.3
Frogmen (navies: gen.)   VG86   359.984
Fronts (WWI: Eur.)   940.414   D521, D530 (W.), D550 (E.)
Fronts (WWI: Rus. & E. in gen.)   940.4147   D550, D551 (Rus.-Ger.-Austrian),
                                      D556 (Rus.-Austrian), D560 (Balkan)
FUEL & light (mil. qtrs.)   UC420
Fuel, Naval (other than U.S.)   VC276.A5-Z
Fuel, Naval (U.S.)   VC276.A3-49   359.83
Fuel supplies & costs, Naval   VC276
Fuel supplies (WWII)   D810.F83
Fuels, Aviation   629.134351
Fuels, Marine engine   VM779   623.874
Fukien Province (China)   951.245
Furloughs   UB420-425
Furloughs, leaves, etc. (air forces: U.S.)   UG973
Furloughs, leaves, other inactive periods (navies)   359.113   VB260-275,
                                                        VB307-315

Furnishings (mil. qtrs.)   UC415
Furniture (naut. design)   623.866
Fuselages, Aircraft   629.13434

GALICIA (20th c.)   DB500
Galicia (Pol.)   DK4600.G34
Galicia (Pol.: Polish wars, 1918-21)   DK4407.G3
Galleys & equipment (naval sci.)   VC398
Gallipoli & the Dardanelles (WWI)   D568.3
Gallipoli (Tur.)   DR701.G3
Galveston, Texas (area)   976.4139   F392.G25
Gandhi, Mohandas (India: 1901+ era)   DS481.G3

Garand rifle   UD395.G4
Garbage disposal (mil. engineering)   623.754
Garner, John Nance (U.S.: 20th c.)   E748.G23
Garrison & fortress artillery (gen.)   UF480
Gas masks (mil.)   UG447.6
Gas-turbine engines (marine engineering)   623.87233   VM740, TJ778
Gas warfare (by chem. name)   UG447.5.A-Z   623.4516
Gas warfare (WWI)   D607.5 (PREFER UG447)
Gases, poisons, other chemical agents (design)   623.4592
Gatling machine guns   UF620.G3
Gdansk, Pol. (Danzig: gen.)   DK4670
Gear, equipment, & outfitting (nautical: engineering)   623.86   VM781-861,
    VM781 (gen.)

Genealogy   929
Genealogy (royal houses: G.B.)   929.72 (hist. treatment poss. or in 941+)
    DA28.1-.35, CS418-424
GENERAL & flag officers (above army col. or navy capt.)   355.331   UB200, UB210
General officers (air forces)   358.41331   UG790-795
General orders (naval: U.S.)   VB365
General orders (Rus. military: collections)   UB657
General staff & headquarters (WWI: U.S.)   D570.25.A-Z
General staff & headquarters (WWII: U.S.)   D769.25
General works (gen. almanacs, encyclopediae, etc.)   A   000-099
Generals, marshals, commanders (admin.: duties etc.)   UB200   355.331
Geneva & Hague conventions   UH531-533 (PREFER JX5136 & JX5243)   341.6+, .65
Geneva, Swit.   DQ441-460   949.45
GEOGRAPHY, Air warfare   358.4147   UG633-635, UA
Geography & history   900-999   G, D-F
Geography & history (gen.)   900-909   G, C-D
Geography & travel   910-919   G, D-F
Geography & travel (by locale)   913-919
Geography, anthropology, sports, & recreation   G   910-919, 301, 790's
Geography, Marine military (strategic & tactical)   359.9647+   VE21-124, VA
Geography, Military (gen. inclu. Eur.)   UA990   355.47
Geography, Military (tactical & strategic)   355.47   UA985-997
Geography, Naval (strategic & tactical)   359.47   UA985-997, VA160-178,
    VA49-750 (by place)
Geology & seismology, Military   UG465-465.5
Geonavigation, Marine   623.892
Geonavigational aids, Marine (misc. non-electronic)   623.894
George V (G.B.: King: 1910-36)   DA573
George VI (G.B.: King: 1937-52)   DA584
Georgia   F281-295, F286   975.8
Georgia (Rus.)   DK511.G3-47 (earlier pubns.), DK670-679
Georgia, Transcaucasia (post-WWI territorial ?s)   D651.G2
Georgian Republic (U.S.S.R.)   947.95   DK511.G3-47, .G47 (gen. hist., 1917-)
Georgian S. S. R. (1801-1921)   DK677.4-6
Georgian S. S. R. (1921+)   DK677.7-9+
Germ warfare (WWII: bacterial)   D810.B3

GERMAN aerial ops. (WWI)   D604   940.44943
German aerial ops. (WWII)   D787   940.544943
German-Anglo naval conflict & blockade (WWII: by battle, ship, etc.)   D772.A-Z
                                                          940.545941-43
German armament (modern)   U820.G7
German Austria & Bavaria   DD791-800
German culture (in other lands: gen.)   DD68
German East Africa (gen.: later Tanganyika)   DT444
German East Africa (post-WWI territorial ?s)   D651.A41
German East Indies   DS649
German engineering ops. (WWII)   D795.G3
German espionage (gen.)   UB271.G3   327.120943
German field artillery   UF405.G3
German marching (mil.)   UD315.G3
German military education (special times)   U571
German military history (gen.)   DD101   355.00943
German military ops. (WWI: West & overall)   D531-538
German military ops. (WWII: gen.)   D757   940.5343, .54013, .5413, .5421,
                                                          943.086
German naval education (main school)   V574.A2-65
German New Guinea (N.E.)   DU742 (SEE ALSO DU550+ for Bismarck Arch.)
                                                          993.6, 995
German poetry, satire, etc. (WWI)   D526.5
German poetry, satire, etc. (WWII)   D745.5
German prisons & prisoners (WWII)   D805.G3
German propaganda (1933-45: in other countries: gen.)   DD254
German ski troops   UD475.G3   356.1640943
German Southwest Africa (post-WWI territorial ?s)   D651.A42
German submarine ops. (WWI: gen.)   D591   940.4512
German submarine ops. (WWII: by battle, ship, etc.) D782.A-Z
German submarine ops. (WWII: gen.)   D781
German West Africa (1884-1916)   967.8202   DT444, DT447 (newer books)
GERMANS (in Arg.)   F3021.G3
Germans (in Bolivia)   F3359.G3
Germans (in Brazil)   F2659.G3
Germans (in C.Am.)   F1440.G3
Germans (in Calif.)   F870.G3
Germans (in Can.)   F1035.G3
Germans (in Chile)   F3285.G3
Germans (in Mex.)   F1392.G4
Germans (in N.Y.)   F130.G3
Germans (in other lands: gen.)   DD119.3
Germans (in Paraguay)   F2699.G3
Germans (in Peru)   F3619.G3
Germans (in Pol.)   DK4121.5.G4
Germans (in S.Am.)   F2239.G3
Germans (in U.S.)   E184.G3
Germans (in Urug.)   F2799.G3

GERMANY   DD   943
Germany (1519-)   DD175
Germany (1871-1918: New Empire)   DD217-231   943.08
Germany (1888-1918: Kaiser Wilhelm II era)   DD228-231 943.084
Germany (20th c.: gen.)   DD232
Germany (1914-1918: WWI period)   DD228.8   943.08
Germany (1918-: revolution & Republic)   DD233-251+   943.085
Germany (1918-: revolution & Republic: gen.)   DD237
Germany (1918: Revolution)   DD248
Germany (1919-25: Ebert period)   DD249
Germany (1925-34: Hindenburg era)   DD251 943.085
Germany (1930-45: postwar titles) DD256.5
Germany (1930-45, 1933-45: eras of Hitler & National Socialism)   DD252-256
                                                943.086
Germany (1933-45: 3rd Reich)   943.086   DD253-256, DD256 (WWII period),
                    DD256.5 (gen.: post-war pubn. dates), DD454 (Prussia)
Germany (1939-45: WWII period)   DD256
Germany (1945-: Allied occupation)   DD257
Germany (1945-: Reunification ?)   DD257.25
Germany (air war geog.)   358.414743   UG635.G3
Germany & Austria (WWI: mil. hist.)   940.40943   D531-538 (Ger.), D531 (gen.),
                                          D539 (Austria)
Germany & Central Europe   943   DD (Ger.), DB (Austria, Hung., Czech.),
                    DK401-441 & DK4010-4800 (Pol.)
Germany & Central Europe (mil. geog.)   355.4743   UA995.G3
Germany & Central Europe (mil. policy)   355.033543   UA710+, UA710-719
Germany & German military ops. (WWII)   D757-757.9
Germany & Prussia   DD   943
Germany. Army (gen.)   UA712   355.00943, .30943, .310943
Germany. Army (local)   UA718.A-Z
Germany. Army (special units: by name)   UA716.A-Z
Germany (biog.: heads of state)   923.143
Germany (gen. hist., culture, etc.) DD17
Germany (gen.: pubn. 1801-)   DD89
Germany (geog. & travel)   914.31-35   DD21-43, DD42 (1919-45)
Germany (lighthouses, beacons, foghorns, etc.)   VK1073-1074
Germany (mil. status)   355.033043
Germany (mil. status: gen.)   UA710   355.033043, .033243, .033543
Germany (naval geog.)   359.4743   VA510-519, VA513 (gen.)
Germany (naval hist.)   359.00943   VA510-519
Germany (naval status: gen.)   VA513.A5-Z   359.030943, .00943, .30943, .4743
Germany (pilot guides)   623.892943   VK822, VK824
Germany (post-WWI territorial ?s)   D651.G3
Germany (WWI: causes, aims, results)   D515
Germany (WWI: Reconstruction)   D659.G3
Germany (WWII: causes, aims, results)   D742.G3
Germany (WWII: dipl. history)   D751   940.532443
Gibraltar   DP302.G31-41
Gibraltar (Br. colony)   946.89   DP302.G31-41
Gibraltar Strait (pilot & sailing & guides)   VK851   623.8929448, .89294689
Gibraltar Strait (tide & current tables)   VK651
Gilbert Islands (inclu. Tarawa & Makin Atolls)   DU615 996.81
Gilbert Islands (WWII)
Gilbert Islands (WWII)   D767.917, D767.99.G38
Gilbert, Marshall, & related islands (geog. & travel)   919.68

Girl Scouts (WWII)   D810.G57
Gobi (China)   DS793.G6
Goebbels, Joseph (Ger.: 1918-48 era)   DD247.G6
Göring, Hermann (Ger.: 1918-48 era)   DD247.G67
Goriunov machine guns   UF620.G6
Governments in exile (WWII)   D639.G6
Graf Spee, Admiral (armoured cruiser: Ger.: WWII)   D772.G7, VA515.G
Grain industry (defense)   UA929.95.G7
Granada (Sp.)   DP302.G51-65
Graves registration & burial services (navies)   359.699
Graves registration & military burial   355.699
Graydon aerial torpedo thrower   V855.G7
Great Basin & Pacific Coast states   979   F786-915, F786-850 (New S.W.),
                                             F786-788, F851-915 (Pac. states), F851

GREAT BRITAIN DA 941-942
Great Britain (1837-1901: gen.)   DA550   941.08
Great Britain (20th c.: gen.)   DA566   941.082
Great Britain (1901-10: gen.)   DA570
Great Britain (1910-36)   DA576
Great Britain (1914-19: WWI era)   DA577
Great Britain (1920-39)   DA578
Great Britain (1936)   DA583
Great Britain (1937-52)   DA586
Great Britain (1939-45: WWII era)   DA587
Great Britain (air war geog.)   358.414741   UG635.G7
Great Britain & British military ops. (WWII)   D759-760
Great Britain & Ireland (geog. & travel)   914.1   DA11, DA600-668, DA969-
                                                       987 (Ire.)
Great Britain & Ireland (lighthouses, beacons, foghorns, etc.: lists)
                                   VK1153-1159   623.89440941
Great Britain. Army   UA649-668
Great Britain. Army (gen.)   UA649   355.00941, .310941
Great Britain (biog.: heads of state)   923.141-142
Great Britain. Fifth Army (WWI)   D546.5.5th
Great Britain (lighthouses, beacons, foghorns, etc.)   VK1057-1064
Great Britain (mil. geog.)   355.4741-4742   UA995.G7
Great Britain (mil. policy)   355.033541-033542   UA647+,UA647-668
Great Britain (mil. status)   UA647   355.033041
Great Britain (naval geog.)   359.4741-4742   VA452-467, VA454 (gen.)
Great Britain (naval hist.)   359.00941-00942   VA452-467, DA70-89
Great Britain (naval policy & status)   359.030941
Great Britain (post-WWI relns.: countries other than U.S.)   D651.G7
Great Britain (post-WWI relns.: U.S.: inclu. defensive alliance w. Fr., U.S.)   D651.G6
Great Britain (post-WWI territorial ?s)   D651.G5-7
Great Britain (post-WWI territorial ?s: gen.)   D651.G5
Great Britain. Royal Naval College, Dartmouth (admin.)   V515.C1-K3
Great Britain. Royal Navy (gen.)   VA454   359.0309441, .30941,
                                              .4741-4742, .00941
Great Britain (WWI: causes, aims, results)   D517
Great Britain (WWI: mil. hist.)   940.40941-40942   D546-547
Great Britain (WWI: Reconstruction)   D659.G7
Great Britain (WWII: causes, aims, results)   D742.G7
Great Britain (WWII: dipl. history)   D750   940.532241
Great circle routing (marine navig.)   VK571

Great Lakes & North Central states (geog. & travel)   917.7   F477.3 (Old NW.),
                                                    F551 (Lakes area in gen.), F484.5
Great Lakes (U.S.)   F551-556   977
Great Lakes Naval Training Station (Ill.)   V434.G7
Great Plains & American West (geog. & travel)   917.8   F591
Great War (1914-18)   940.3-.499   D501-680
Greater Antilles (Cuba, Haiti, Puerto Rico, Jamaica, etc.)   F1741-1991 972.9, .91-95
GREECE   949.5   DF, DF757
Greece (1821-1924: Monarchy)   949.506   DF802
Greece (20th c.: gen.)   DF833   949.507
Greece (20th c.: 1924-)   949.507   DF833 (20th c.), DF838 (WWI)
Greece (1914-18: WWI)   DF838   949.506
Greece (1924-35: Republic)   949.5073   DF848
Greece (1935-47: George II era)   DF849   949.5074
Greece (1935-67: Monarchy)   949.5074   DF849
Greece & unredeemed Greeks (post-WWI territorial ?s)   D651.G8
Greece (gen.)   DF751   949.5
Greece (geog. & travel)   914.95   DF726
Greece (mil. status)   UA720-729   355.0330495
Greece (modern)   DF701-951+
Greece (naval status)   VA520-529
Greece (WWII: gen.)   D766.3   940.53495, 949.5074
Greek Isles (WWII: gen. particip.)   940.53499   DF901.C9 (Cyclades)
Greenland   998.2
Grenades   UF765   623.45114
Grenades, Hand & rifle   355.825114 UF765
Grenades, Hand or rifle (design)   623.45114   UF765
Grenades, mines, etc.   355.82511
Grenades, mines, nuclear weapons (design)   623.4511
Grey, Edward (G.B.: 20th c.)   DA566.9.G8
Guadalajara, Battle of (Sp. Civil War: 1937)   DP269.2.G8
Guadalcanal (WWII)   D767.982.G92, D767.99.G88
Guam (Mariana Is.)   DU647   996.7
Guam (WWII)
Guam (WWII)   D767.99.G9, D767.99.M272.G9
Guam (WWII: U.S. naval base)   D769.542.G9
Guernsey (G.B.: island)   942.342
Guerrilla tactics   355.425 (SEE 355.0218 for guer. war)   U240
Guerrilla warfare & small wars   U240   355.02184, 356.15
Guiana (Brit., Dutc, & Fr.)   F2351-2471   988
Guidebooks (Berlin, Ger.)   DD859
Guidebooks (G.B.)   DA650
Guidebooks (Ger.)   DD16
Guidebooks (London, Eng.)   DA679   914.21
Guidebooks (Paris, Fr.)   DC708
Guided aircraft (pilotless: mil. design)   623.7469   UG1310-1315
Guided missile forces (land: gen.)   358.171
Guided missiles (design)   623.4519   UG1310-1315
Guides & marching (mil.)   UD313-314

GULF Coast & South Central states (geog. & travel)   917.6   F296 (Gulf), F396
Gulf Coast (Florida)   F317.G8
Gulf Coast (Texas)   F392.G9
Gulf of Mexico (pilot & sailing guides)   VK975-977
Gulf of Mexico (tide & current tables)   VK775
Gulf states (U.S.: gen.)   F296   976
Gulf states, Mississippi Valley, Middle West, & Texas   F296-395   975.9-976.4, 976.7-9
GUN carriages, caissons, limbers, etc. (gen.)   UF640   623.43
Gun carriages, Disappearing   UF650
Gun carriages, Naval   VF430   623.43
Gun carriages, Self-propelled (plus track-layer tractors & other self-contained)   UF652
Gun handbooks (U.S.: by mm. or cm. then date)   UF563.A4.1+
Gun mounts   355.823
Gun mounts (design)   623.43
Gun salutes & other military rewards (misc.)   355.1349 (use 355.134 with 1989+ pubn.)
GUNNERY (engineering)   623.55   UF800-805, VF144-302
Gunnery practice, Naval (G.B.)   VF315.G7   623.5530941
Gunnery practice, Naval (U.S.)   VF313   623.5530973
Gunnery, Aircraft (engineering)   623.555
Gunnery, Artillery (gen.)   UF800   623.55
Gunnery, Land (engineering)   623.551   UF800-805
Gunnery, Naval (engineering)   623.553   VF144-302, VF145 (gen.), VF150-155 (hdbks.), VF160-302 (drill bks.), VF160 (U.S.)
Gunpowder, cordite, & other explosives (design: inclu. propellant types)   623.4526   UF870
Guns (gen.)   U880   623.4
Guns (misc. types: mil. sci.)   UF630
Guns, Aircraft   UG1340-1345   623.7461
Gustav V (Swe.: King, 1907-50)   DL867
Gvardia (WWII: Rus.: by #)   D764.6.G8.1st-
Gvardia (WWII: Rus.: gen.)   D764.6.G7
Gynecology (WWI)   D639.G8
Gypsies   DX1-301
Gypsies in Czechoslovakia   DX222
Gypsies in Europe (gen. & elsewhere)   DX145
Gypsies in Germany   DX229
Gypsies in Russia (inclu. Poland & Lith.)   DX241
Gypsies (WWII)   D810.G9
Gyroscopic devices (marine navig.)   VK584.G8

HAAKON VII (Nor.: King, 1905-57)   DL530
Hácha, Emil (Czech.: 1939-45 period)   DB2211.H33
Hague & Geneva conventions (official works: by date)   UH531 (PREFER JX5136 & JX5243)
Haiti   F1900-1940   972.94
Haiti (1915-50)   F1927   972.9405-9406
Halsey, William F., 'Bull', Admiral (U.S. Navy)   VB314.H25
Hamburg, Ger. (WWII)   D757.9.H3
Hammocks, berths, etc. (naval architec.)   VM511
Hampton Roads Naval Training Station (Va.)   V434.H2
Hancock (aircraft carrier: U.S.: WWII)   D774.H3

Hand signaling (mil.)   UG582.H2
Hand-to-hand combat & self-defense (training: inclu. unarmed & knife fighting)
                                    355.548   U167.5.H3, U262
HANDBOOKS & manuals (marine navig. & merch. marine)   VK155   623.890202
Handbooks & manuals (marines: G.B.)   VE155.G7
Handbooks & manuals (marines: U.S.)   VE153
Handbooks & manuals (mil. hygiene: Eng. & Am.)   UH623
Handbooks & manuals (naval ordnance)   VF150-155
Handbooks & manuals, Soldiers'   U110-145   355.00202
Handbooks & manuals, Soldiers' (by place except U.S.)   U115.A-Z
Handbooks & manuals (U.S. Navy: Pay & allowances)   VC60
Handbooks & tables (naval pay & allowances: U.S.)   VC54-60
Handbooks, Gun (U.S.: artillery)   UF563.A4-8
Handbooks, Gun (U.S.: by class or type)   UF563.A7-8 (sometimes use UF563.A4-
                                    6 with measure. & alphab. symbol: e.g. UF563.A5.12
                                    in.M for 12 in. mortar or ... Mt. for mountain)
Handbooks, Gun (U.S.: by inches)   UF563.A5
Handbooks, Gun (U.S.: by pounds)   UF563.A6
Handbooks, Infantry (U.S.)   UD153
Handbooks, Medical & surgical (navies)   VG460-466
Handbooks, Naval   V110-145
Handbooks, Naval officers'   V130-135   359.3320202
Handbooks, Naval reserve   V140-145
Handbooks, Officers'   U130-135
Handbooks, Petty officers'   V120-125
Handbooks, Seamen's (gen.)   V110   359.00202
Handbooks, tables, etc. (marine engin.)   VM607   623.870202
Handbooks, tables, etc. (ship calculations: naval architec.)   VM151
                                    623.810202, .810212
Handling of nautical craft (gen.)   623.881   VK541
Handling of nautical craft (powered)   623.8814   VK541, VK145, VK205,
                                    VB200-205
Hankow, China   DS796.H3
Hanoi, Viet.   DS558.H3 (earlier titles), DS560.92.H3
Harbor piloting (inclu. approach)   623.8929   VK321-369.8
Harbors & ports   VK321-369+   387.1+
Harbors, canals, dams (mil. engineering)   UG350   623.64
Harvard Univ. (WWII)   D810.E45.H38
Hatchways, ladders, other special fittings (marine engin.)   VM851
Havana, Cuba   F1799.A-Z   972.9123
Havana Province (Cuba)   F1791-1799
Hawaii (1900-59: U.S. Territory)   DU627.5.A6-Z   996.903
Hawaii (island)   DU628.H25-28   996.91
Hawaii (WWII: U.S. naval base)   D769.542.H38
HAWAIIAN ISLANDS   DU620-629   996.9
Hawaiian Islands (1898-1959: U.S. Terr.)   996.903   DU627.5
Hawaiian Islands (annex. to U.S.)   DU627.4
Hawaiian Islands (gen.)   DU620-629, DU625   996.9
Hawaiian Islands (geog. & travel)   919.69   DU623
Hawaiian Islands (mil. geog.)   355.47969   UA995.H
Hawaiian Islands (naval geog.)   359.47969   VA750.H, VA158-158.7
Hawaiian Islands (pilot & sailing guides)   VK933.H3
Hawaiian Islands (WWII)   D767.92, D769.87.H3   940.539969, 996.903
Hazing (U.S. Naval Acad.: Cong. docs.)   V415.E9
Headgear, Naval   VC320

Headquarters, Military   UB230-235
Headquarters, Naval (ops. inclu. aides)   VB210
Heads of state (biog.)   923.1
Health, hygiene, & sanitation (navies)   VG470-475
Health, hygiene, & sanitation (navies: U.S.)   VG473
Heat or other radiations (ammunition: design)   623.4595
Heating, ventilation, & sanitation (naval architec. & engin.)   VM481-482
Heidelberg, Ger.   DD901.H55-59
Helena (cruiser: U.S.: WWII)   D774.H4
Helicopters   629.133352
Helicopters, Military   UG1230-1235   623.746047
Helicopters, Military (design)   623.746047   TL716
Heliograph (mil. signal.)   UG582.H4
Helmets, hats, etc. (mil.)   UC500-505
Helsingfors, Fin. (Helsinki: area)   948.971   DK465.H5, DL1175,
    DL1175.48 (1917-)
Helsinki, Fin.   DL1175   948.971
Helsinki, Fin. (1917-)   DL1175.48
Helsinki, Fin. (gen.)   DL1175.42
Hemp (naval supplies)   VC279.H45
Hercegovina & Bosnia (1918-45: gen.)   DR1734
Hercegovina (Herzegovina) & Bosnia   949.742   DB231-250 (Bos.), DB521-
    540 (Her.), DR1652-1785
Herzegovina (20th c.)   DB540
Herzegovina (Hercegovina) & Bosnia (gen.)   DR1660, 1685
Hess, Rudolf (Ger.: 1918-48 era)   DD247.H37
Hierarchy, Air force   358.4133   UG770-775
Hierarchy (marines)   359.9633
Hierarchy, Military (mil. personnel)   355.33   UA, UB410-415, UB210
Hierarchy, Naval   359.33   V110-145, VA, VB21-124, VB23 (U.S.),
    VB257-258.5, VB203
High-explosive devices (torpedoes, blockbusters, etc.: design)   623.4517
    V850-855 (torpedoes), UF860-870
High explosives (design: inclu. dynamite, nitro, TNT)   623.4527   TP285,
    TP270-295
Highland Division (WWII: G.B.: 51st)   D759.5.51st
Highways (U.S.)   UA963-964
Hilo, Haw.   DU629.H5
Hindenburg, Paul von (Ger.: 1888-1918+ period)   DD231.H5
Hirohito (Japan: Emperor, 1926-89)   DS889.8
Hiroshima, Japan   DS897.H48   952.19
Hiroshima, Japan (WWII)   D767.25.H6
Hispanic-Americans (armed forces)   UB418.H57
Historiography (WWI)   D522.42
Historiography (WWII)   D743.42
HISTORY (1945-)   D839-845+
History & geography   900-999+   G (geog.), D-F
History (auxiliary: civilization, gen. archaeology, heraldry, gen. biography) C 900-
    909, 920-929, 930-939+
History (gen., Eastern Hemisphere, Oceania)   D   909, 930-969, 990-996
History (gen., world wars, Eur. overall, etc.)   D1-1075+   909, 940, 950
History (misc. areas: Oceania, Atlantic islands, Arctic, extraterr. worlds, etc.)
    990- 999   C-F, G, Q
Hitler, Adolf (Ger.: 1918-48 era)   DD247.H5
Hitler Youth (Hitlerjugend)   DD253.5

Ho Chi Minh (N. Viet.)   DS560.72.H6
Hobart, Australia (Tasmania)   DU480.H6   994.61
Hokkaido (Japan)   DS895.H6   952.4
HOLLAND (NETHERLANDS)   949.2   DJ, DJ109 (gen.)
Holland (1890-1948: Queen Wilhelmina era)   949.2071   DJ281-287,
          DJ281 (gen.), DJ285 (WWI time), DJ287 (WWII era)
Holland (20th c.)   949.207   DJ216 (19th-20th c.)
Holland (geog. & travel)   914.92   DJ39
Holland (WWII: gen. particip.)   940.53492   DL763.N4-42, DJ287
Holland (WWII: mil. hist.)   940.5409492   D763.N4-41
Holocaust (WWII: inclu. exterm. camps)   940.5318
Holy See (1870-)   DG799
Home defense (coasts, frontiers, other valuable redoubts)   355.45   UA (gen.),
    UG410-442 (fortific's.), UG410-412 (U.S.), UG428-430 (Eur.), UG429.G7 (G.B.)
Home defense, Air force   358.4145   UG730-735, UG630-635
Home defense, Naval   359.45   VA45, V200
Home guard naval forces   359.351   VA45
Home guards & frontier troops   355.351   UA42 (U.S. Nat. Guard)
Homes, Sailors'   VB290-295 (SEE ALSO UB380-385)
Homosexuals (WWII: U.S.: armed forces)   D769.2   940.54097308664
Honan (China)   DS793.H5
Hong Kong   DS796.H7   951.25
Hong Kong (1843-1945)   951.2504   DS796.H757
Hong Kong Naval Base (Royal Navy)   VA459.H55
Hong Kong (WWII: gen. particip.)   940.53512   DS796.H7
Honolulu, Haw.   996.931   DU629.H7
Honolulu, Haw.   DU629.H7   996.931
HONORED & dead (WWI: G.B.: rolls)   940.46741   D609.G7
Honored & dead (WWI: Ger.: rolls)   940.46743   D609.G3
Honored & dead (WWII: Fr.: rolls)   940.546744   D797.F8
Honored & dead (WWII: G.B.: rolls)   940.546741   D797.G7
Honored & dead (WWII: Ger.: rolls)   940.546743   D797.G3
Honored & dead (WWII: Japan: rolls)   940.546752   D797.J3
Honored & dead (WWII: Rus.: rolls)   940.546747   D797.R9
Honored & dead (WWII: U.S.: rolls)   940.546773   D797.U6-7
Honshu (Japan)   952.1
Hood (battle cruiser: G.B.)
Hood (WWII: battle cruiser: G.B.)   D772.H6, VA458.H6
Hoover, Herbert (U.S.: Pres., 1929-33)   E802
Hopkins, Harry (U.S.: 20th c.)   E748.H67
Hornet (aircraft carrier: U.S.: WWII)   D774.H6
Horse artillery   UF410
Horse cavalry (gen. & ops.)   357.184   UE150-475, UE150+, UE157+
Horses & mules, Military   UC600-695
Horses, Artillery   UF370
Horses, Cavalry   UE460-475
Horthy, Miklós (Hung.: 20th c.)   DB950.H6

HOSPITAL corps, Naval   VG310-325
Hospital corps, Naval (places besides U.S.)   VG325.A-Z
Hospital corps, Naval (U.S.)   VG320
Hospital services & hospitals, Naval   VG410-450 (SEE ALSO D #s for
                                                                           particular wars)
Hospital services, Military   UH460-485
Hospital services, Naval (gen.)   VG410   359.72
Hospital services, Naval (U.S.)   VG420-425
Hospital ships   VG450   623.8264, 359.3264
Hospital ships (WWII: U.S.: by name)   D807.U74.A-Z
HOSPITALS, medical services, etc. (WWII: gen.)   D806   940.5475
Hospitals, medical services, Red Cross (WWI: gen.)   D628
Hospitals, Military (except U.S.)   UH475.A-Z
Hospitals, Military (gen.)   UH470   355.72
Hospitals, Naval (gen.)   VG420
Hospitals, Naval (U.S.: by town)   VG425.A-Z
Hospitals (WWI: in particular places)   940.4763+   D629.A-Z
Hospitals (WWI: operated by particular countries)   940.4764-4769
HOSPITALS (WWII: in Australia)   940.5476394   D807.A8
Hospitals (WWII: in China)   940.5476351   D807.C5
Hospitals (WWII: in Fr.)   940.5476344   D807.F8
Hospitals (WWII: in G.B.)   940.5476341-5476342   D807.G7
Hospitals (WWII: in Ger.)   940.5476343   D807.G3
Hospitals (WWII: in Japan)   940.5476352   D807.J3
Hospitals (WWII: in particular places)   940.547634-547639   D807.A-Z
Hospitals (WWII: in U.S.)   940.5476373   D807.U6-87
Hospitals (WWII: operated by particular countries)   940.54764-54769   D807.A-Z
Hotchkiss machine guns   UF620.H8
Hotchkiss ordnance   UF560-565... .H.
Housing administration (air forces)   358.4167   UG1140-1145
Housing administration (mil.)   355.67 (SEE ALSO .71 & .12 [gen.])   UC400-440
Housing administration (navies)   359.67   VC420-425
Housing & barracks, Naval (places besides U.S.)   VC425.A-Z
Houston, Texas   F394.H8   976.41411
Howitzers & mortars   UF470-475
Howitzers & mortars (Fr.)   UF475.F8
Howitzers & mortars (G.B.)   UF475.G7
Howitzers & mortars (Japan)   UF475.J3
Hudson River (N.Y.)   F127.H8
Hull, Cordell (U.S.: 20th c.)   E748.H93
Hull design (naval architec.)   623.8144   VM156
Hulls (special construc.: anti-fire & -shock, corrosion-resistant, etc.)   623.848
Human resources (air forces: enlistment etc.)   358.4122   UG880-885
Human resources (mil.)   355.22   UA17.5, UB320+, UB340+
Human resources (navies)   359.22
Humor, comics, pictorials, & miscellanea (WWII) 940.549   D743.9, D745
Hunan (China)   DS793.H7

Hungarian military ops (WWI)   D540
HUNGARY   943.9   DB901-975+, DB906, DB925
Hungary (20th c.)   DB947-957+   943.9043+
Hungary (20th c.: gen.)   DB947
Hungary (1914-18: WWI era)   DB953   943.9043
Hungary (20th c.: 1918-)   943.905   DB947-950, DB947 (gen.), DB950.A-Z (biog.)
Hungary (1918-45)   DB955   943.9051-2
Hungary (1918-41)   943.9051   DB955
Hungary (1942-56)   943.9052   DB956
Hungary (gen.)   DB906   943.9
Hungary (gen.: pubn. dates 1801+)   DB925
Hungary (geog. & travel)   914.39   DB916-917
Hungary, Liechtenstein   DB861-975+
Hungary (mil. status)   UA829.H9   355.0330439
Hungary (post-WWI territorial ?s)   D651.H7
Hungary (WWII: gen.)   D765.56   940.53439, 943.905
Hydrography, Marine   VK588-597
Hydrology, Military   UG468
Hygiene & sanitation, Military   UH600-629
Hygiene & sanitation, Military (besides U.S.)   UH605.A-Z
Hygiene, health, & sanitation (navies: special: tropics, drinking water, alcohol
                    problem, venereal diseases, diet, etc.)   VG471
Hygiene, Mental (besides U.S.)   UH629.5.A-Z

IBERIAN Peninsula   DP   946
Iberian Peninsula & Spain   946   DP, DP1-402+ (Sp.), DP501-900+ (Port.)
Ice excavation, tunnels, rooms, etc. (mil. engineering)   UG343
Icebergs   VK1299
Icebreakers (naval architec.)   VM451   623.828
Iceland   949.12   DL301-398+, DL375 (1918-)
Iceland (1801-1918)   DL365
Iceland (1918-)   DL375   949.1204
Ickes, Harold (U.S.: 20th c.)   E748.I28
Ickes, Harold (U.S.: 20th c.: works)   E742.5.I25
Illinois   977.3   F536-550, F541, F546 (1865-1950)
Illinois (1865-1950)   F546   977.303
Imaginary naval battles & wars   V253   359.47
Imperial War Museum (London, G.B.)   U13.G72.L69
Incendiary bombs (aerial)   UG1282.I6   623.4516
Incendiary weapons   UG447.65
Indemnity & reparations (WWI: gen.)   D648   940.31422
Indemnity & reparations (WWII: gen.)   D818
Indemnity (Sino-Jpn. Confl., 1937-45)   DS777.533.I53

INDIA   954   DS436, DS401-481
India (1761-1947: Brit. rule)   DS463-480.83   954.03
India (1785-1947: British rule) 954.03   DS463-480, DS463 (gen.)
India (1914-19)   DS480.4   954.0356-0357
India (1916-26)   954.0357   DS480.4-6
India (1916-21: Viscount of Chelmsford)   DS480.5
India (1919-47)   DS480.45   954.035+
India (1926-36)   954.0358   DS480.7-8
India (1931-36: Marquis of Willingdon)   DS480.8
India (1936-47: Gov'ships. of Linlithgow, Wavell, Mountbatten)   954.0359
                                                        DS480.82-83
India (1936-43: Marquis of Linlithgow)   DS480.82   954.0359
India (1943-47: Earl of Wavell)   DS480.83   954.0359
India & Burma (WWII)   D767.6-63   940.5425, .5354, 954.0359
India (mil. status)   UA840-844   355.033054
India (overall) & pre-1947 Pakistan   DS401-481   954
India, Pakistan, & Ceylon (geog. & travel)   915.4   DS335, DS413
India, Pakistan, Ceylon, Burma, etc.   DS376-498   954, 959.1
India (WWII: dipl. hist.)   940.532254   D754.I4
INDIAN Ocean islands   DS491.A-Z
Indian Ocean (pilot & sailing guides)   VK885-901
Indian Ocean region & Southern Asia (gen.) DS335
Indian Ocean (tide & current tables)   VK685-701
Indians as soldiers (WWI: U.S.)   D570.8.I6
Indians (N. Am.)   E77-99   970.00497, .1-5, 973.0497
Indians (U.S. Navy: native-Am's.)   VB324.I5
Indians (WWII)   D810.I5
Indochina   DS521-560   959-959.7
INDONESIA (1602-1945: Dutch period)   959.802   DS642-643
Indonesia (1798-1945)   959.8022   DS643
Indonesia (1798-1942: colonial era)   DS643   959.8022
Indonesia (1942-45: Japanese occupation)   DS643.5   959.8022
Indonesia & Borneo (naval geog.)   359.47598   VA667.I or .B
Indonesia & Malay Archipelago   959.8   DS611-649
Indonesia & Malay Archipelago (WWII: gen. particip.)   940.53598
                  D767.7 (Dutch E. Indies), DS643.5, DS643
Indonesia (geog. & travel)   915.98   DS619
Indonesia (mil. status)   UA853.I5
Indonesia (WWII: mil. hist.)   940.5409598   D767.7
Induction & exemption (mil.)   UB340   355,22363, .225
INDUSTRIAL defense (by specific industry)   UA929.95.A-Z (SEE ALSO H
                                                industry #s)
Industrial defense (gen.)   UA929.5   355.28, .26
Industrial defense (places besides U.S.)   UA929.9.A-Z
Industrial mobilization (by country)   UA18.A3-Z (SEE ALSO D-F for specific wars)
Industrial resources & raw materials (air forces)   358.4124-4126
                                      UG1100-1105, UG630+
Industrial resources (mil. use)   355.26   UA18, UA929.5+, HC106+
Industrial resources (navies)   359.26
Industry, Shipbuilding (gen.)   VM298.5   338.476238, 387.5+

INFANTRY   356.1   UD, UD15, UD21-124 (by place), UD144-145+, UA
Infantry arms (small: U.S.)   UD383-384
Infantry (Asia)   UD99-113
Infantry (Australia)   UD121   356.10994
Infantry (Austria)   UD65   356.109436
Infantry (Austria & Austria-Hung.)   UA673
Infantry (Can.)   UD26
Infantry (China)   UD101   356.10951
Infantry (collections)   UD7
Infantry (Eur.)   UD55-95
Infantry (Fr.)   UD71   356.10944
Infantry (G.B.)   UA650-653, UD57-64
Infantry (G.B.: by date)   UD58
Infantry (G.B.: gen.)   UA650   356.10941
Infantry (gen.)   356.18   UD160-302, UD160 (U.S.)
Infantry (gen. hist.)   UD15   356.09, 109, 355.009
Infantry (gen.: pubn. 1801+)   UD145   356.1
Infantry (Ger.)   UA713.A1-Z9.A-Z, UD73   356.10943
Infantry (Ger.: by group name)   UA713.Z9.A-Z
Infantry (Ger.: by regiment #)   UA713.Z6.1st-
Infantry (Ger.: gen.)   UA713.A6-Z4
Infantry (hist.: by area or country regardless of specific unit)   UD21-124 (SEE
                                                      ALSO UA)
Infantry (It.)   UA743, UD79   356.10945
Infantry (Japan)   UD105   356.10952
Infantry manuals (gen.)   UD150   356.10202
Infantry, Mounted (U.S.)   UD453-454
Infantry (New Z.)   UD122.5
Infantry regiments etc. (WWII: U.S.: by #)   D769.31.1st-
Infantry regiments (G.B.: by name)   UA651.A-Z
Infantry regiments (Sp.-Am. War: U.S.: by #)   E725.4.1st-
Infantry regiments (U.S.: by #/author)   UA29.1st-
Infantry (Rus.)   UA773.A1-Z9.A-Z
Infantry (Rus.: Asian)   UD109
Infantry (Rus.: by group name)   UA773.Z9.A-Z
Infantry (Rus.: by regiment #)   UA773.Z6.1st-
Infantry (Rus.: Eur.)   UD85   356.10947
Infantry (Rus.: gen.)   UA773.A6-Z4
Infantry tactics & maneuvers (Asia: gen.)   UD270
Infantry tactics & maneuvers (Eur.: gen.)   UD215
Infantry tactics & maneuvers (U.S.: gen.)   UD160
Infantry (tactics, use, gen. hist's.)   UD (SEE ALSO UA for specific armies)   356
Infantry (U.S.)   UD23   356.10973
Infantry (U.S.: Calif. reserves)   UA93-94
Infantry (U.S.: gen.)   UA28   356.10973
Infantry (U.S.: N.Y. reserves)   UA363-364
Infantry (WWI: U.S.)   D570.33 (newer bks. may use A1 or #'s as in D570.27)
INFANTRY (WWII: Fr.)   D761.3
Infantry (WWII: G.B.)   D759.53
Infantry (WWII: Ger.)   D757.3
Infantry (WWII: Ger.: by author, division, name, etc.)   D757.32.A-Z
Infantry (WWII: Rus.)   D764.53
Infantry (WWII: U.S.: regiments, combat teams, etc.: by #)   D769.31.1st-
Infiltration, espionage, & unconventional warfare (WWII: Rus.)   940.548647
                                                      UB251.R9, UB271.R9

Information & recreation, Military (U.S.: gen.)   UH805   355.3460973
Information & recreation services, Naval (U.S.: gen.) VG2025-2026   359.3460973
Information security (mil. data: gen.)   UB246
Inquiry, Courts of (mil.: by country)   UB865.A-Z
Inquiry, Courts of (naval: U.S.)   VB813 (PREFER KF7646-7650)
Insignia & badges (naval clothing) VC345   359.1342
Insignia, badges, etc. (air force)   UG1180-1185
Insignia, badges, etc. (mil.: U.S.)   UC533
Inspection, Military   UB240-245
Inspection, Naval (inclu. inspectors)   VB220-225
Inspection (small arms: infantry)   UD382
Installations, Infantry   356.187   UC400-405, U180-185
INSTRUCTION camps, maneuver grounds, etc. (U.S.)   U293
Instruction (marine engin.)   VM725-728   623.8707
Instruction (marine engin.: places except U.S.)   VM728.A-Z
Instruction (merch. marine)   VK401-529
Instruction (mil. engineering)   UG157
Instruction (naval architec.)   VM165-276
Instruction (naval architec.: by place)   VM171-274
Instruction (naval medicine)   VG230-235
Instruction (naval ordnance)   VF357
Instruction (ordnance & small arms)   UF527
Instruction (WWII)   D743.4
Instrumentation, Aircraft   629.135
Instrumentmen, Naval   VG1030-1035
Instruments, Artillery (specific types)   UF849-856
Instruments, Nautical   VK573-587
Instruments, Nautical (design)   623.863   VK573-587
Instruments, Nautical (special)   VK575-584
Instruments, Naval gunnery   VF520   623.558
INTELLIGENCE & military espionage (inclu. cryptanalysis, data analysis, etc.)
    355.3432   UB250-251, UB251.A-Z (by country), UB270-271,
    UB271.A-Z (by place), UB271.x2.A-Z (by spy), UB271.R92.S565 (R. Sorge)
Intelligence, espionage, & unconventional warfare (WWI: G.B.)   940.48641
Intelligence, espionage, & unconventional warfare (WWI: Ger.)   940.48743
    D619.3-5 (in U.S.)
Intelligence, espionage, & unconventional warfare (WWII: G.B.)   940.548641
    D810.S7, UB251.G7, UB271.G7, VB230-250
Intelligence, espionage, & unconventional warfare (WWII: Ger.)   940.548743
    D810.S7+, UB251.G3, UB271.G3
Intelligence, espionage, & unconventional warfare (WWII: U.S.)   940.548673
    D810.S7+, UB251.U5, UB271.U5, VB230-250 (naval)
Intelligence, Military   UB250-271
Intelligence, Military (by country)   UB251.A-Z
Intelligence, Naval   359.3432   VB230-254, VB230, UB250-271
Intelligence, Naval (by country)   VB231.A-Z   359.343209+
Inter-allied Military Commission of Control in Germany (WWI)   D650.I6
Inter-war period (1919-39: essays, minor works)   D725
Inter-war period (1919-39: gen.)   D720   940.5-.52
Inter-war period (1919-39: special)   D723
Internal combustion engines (marine engineering)   623.8723   VM770
International forces   355.357 (perhaps PREFER 355.356)
International military law   UB481 (PREFER JX areas)   341.6
International naval law   VB353

Internment centers & P.O.W. camps (WWI: in U.S.)   940.47273   D627.U6+
Internment centers, labor & concentration camps (WWII: geog. treatment: by
                    controlling country)   940.531709+ (SEE .5472+ for
                    works prior to 1989 on intern. ctrs.)
Intrenching tools (mil.)   UG380
Invincible (aircraft carrier: G.B.: WWII)   VA458.I55
Ionian Sea islands   949.55   DF901.I57-69
IRAN (Persia)   DS251-325   955
Iran (1794-1925: Kajar dynasty: gen.)   DS298
Iran (1906-)   955.05   DS298, DS313-318+
Iran (1906-25)   955.051   DS315-316
Iran (1909-25: Ahmed era)   DS315   955.05-051
Iran (1925-41: Pahlavi family: Reza Shah era)   DS317   955.052
Iran (1941-78?: Pahlavi: Mohammed Reza)   DS318   955.053
Iran (WWII)   D766.7.I55
IRAQ   956.7   DS67-79, DS70.9
Iraq (1517-1918: Turkish period)   DS77   956.703
Iraq (1919-)   DS79   956.704
Iraq (1920-: Mandate & independence)   956.704   DS79
Iraq (1921-33: Faisal I)   DS79.5
Iraq (1933-39: Ghazi I)   DS79.52
Iraq (1939-58: Faisal II)   DS79.53   956.7042
Iraq (geog. & travel)   915.67   DS70.6, DS79+
Iraq (WWII)   D766.7.I57
IRELAND   941.5   DA900-995, DA910 (gen.)
Ireland (19th-20th c.)   941.508   DA950-965+
Ireland (20th c.)   DA959-965, DA959   941.5082
Ireland (1900-20)   941.50821   DA960
Ireland (1901-22)   DA960
Ireland (1914-21)   DA962
Ireland (1921-49)   941.50822   DA963
Ireland (1922-: Irish Free State, Eire, etc.)   DA963
Ireland (WWI)   D547.I6
Ireland (WWII: dipl. history: gen.)   D754.I5
Ireland (WWII: gen. particip.)   940.53415
Irish Free State (WWII: dipl. history)   D754.I6
Irish Guards (WWII: G.B.)   D760.I7
Irish troops (G.B.)   UA665
Irregular troops (guerrillas, brigands, etc.)   356.15   U240, U167.5.A-Z
Israel (inclu. Palestine)   956.94   DS101-131+, DS116-117, DS123
Israel (70 A.D.+)   DS123
Israel (1917-48: Brit. rule)   956.9404   DS126, DS126.3 (WWII era)
Israel & the Jews (1939-45: WWII era)   DS126.3 (PREFER D810.J4 to cover
    titles on ethnicgroup)
Istanbul, Tur. (Constantinople)   DR716-739   956.3

ITALIAN aerial ops. (WWII)   D792.I8
Italian-Anglo naval conflict (WWII: by battle, ship, etc.)   D775.5.A-Z
Italian East Africa & Northeast Africa   DT367   963
Italian military history (gen.)   DG482   355.00945
Italian military ops (WWI: gen.)   D569.A2   940.4145
Italian military ops. (WWII: gen.)   D763.I8
Italian poetry, satire, etc. (WWII)   D745.7.I8
Italian Somaliland   DT416   967.73-7305+
Italians (in Arg.)   F3021.I8
Italians (in N.Y.)   F130.I8
Italians (in Paraguay)   F2699.I8
Italians (in S.Am.)   F2239.I8
Italians (in U.S.)   E184.I8
Italo-Ethiopian War (1935-6)   DT387.8   963.056
Italo-Ethiopian War (1935-6: gen.)   DT387.8.A8-Z   963.056
ITALY   945   DG
Italy (476-)   DG401-579
Italy (1870- & 20th c.)   945.09   DG555-575+, DG555, DG570 (WWI era)
Italy (1871-1947: gen.)   DG555   945.09
Italy (1871-1947: United Italy: Monarchy)   DG555-575
Italy (1900-46: times of Vittorio Emanuele III, Umberto II)   DG566-575
Italy (1914-18: WWI)   DG570   945.0814
Italy (1918-46)   945.091 (SEE ALSO 963.056 for Italo-Eth. War of 1935-6)
          DG566-575, DG571, DG571-572 (Fascist period), DG572 (WWII time)
Italy (1919-45: Fascism)   DG571   945.0815-0816
Italy (1939-45: WWII era)   DG572   945.0816
Italy & Italian military ops. (WWII)   D763.I8-82   940.40945, .41345, 945.091
Italy & Italian neutrality (WWI: dipl. history)   D617
Italy. Army (gen.)   UA742   355.30945
Italy (biog.: heads of state)   923.145
Italy (gen. hist., culture, etc.)   DG417
Italy (gen.: titles dated after 1800)   DG467
Italy (geog. & travel)   914.5   DG428-429
Italy (lighthouses, beacons, foghorns, etc.)   VK1079-1080
Italy (mil. status)   UA740   355.033045
Italy (naval geog.)   359.4745   VA540-549
Italy (naval status: gen.)   VA543.A5-Z   359.030945, .00945, .30945, .4745
Italy (post-WWI relns.: U.S.)   D651.I7
Italy (post-WWI territorial ?s: inclu. Fiume)   D651.I6-8
Italy, Sicily, Sardinia, Malta   DG 945
ITALY (WWI)   D569   940.4145
Italy (WWI: causes, aims, results: includes Treaty of London, 1915)   D520.I7
Italy (WWI: mil. hist.)   940.40945   D569
Italy (WWI: Reconstruction)   D659.I8
Italy (WWII: dipl. hist.)   940.532445   D754.I8
Italy (WWII: dipl. history)   D754.I8
Italy (WWII: religious & ethical ?'s)   D744.5.I8
Iwo Jima (WWII)   D767.99.I9

JAMAICA   972.92   F1861-1896, F1881
Jamaica (1810-1953)   F1886   972.92034-9205
Jamaica (gen.)   F1881
JAPAN   DS801-897+   952
Japan (1868+: modern era)   DS881.85+   952.03
Japan (1868-1945: Imperial power)   952.03   DS881.9
Japan (20th c.)   DS885   952.03-04
Japan (1912-26: special topics: inclu. large earthquakes like 1923)   DS888
Japan (1912-26: Taisho or Yoshihito era)   952.032   DS885.8-888, DS886 (gen.)
Japan (1914-18: WWI era)   DS887   952.032
Japan (1926-89: Hirohito rule: collected, non-serial works)   DS888.15
Japan (1926-89: Hirohito rule: gen.)   DS888.2
Japan (1926-89: Showa or Hirohito period: inclu. Sino-Jpn. conflict of 1937-41)
                952.033 (PREFER 951.042 for Sino-Jpn. War of 1937-41)
                DS888.15-890+, DS888.2, DS888.5 (1926-45)
Japan (1926-45)   DS888.5   952.033
Japan (1945+: may ALSO cover 1926+)   DS889   952.04
Japan (air war geog.)   358.414752
Japan & China (mil. policy)   355.033551 (China)-033552 (Japan)   UA830,
                                    UA835+, UA845+
Japan & Japanese military ops. (WWII)   D767.2-25
Japan. Army (gen.)   UA847   355.00952, .30952, .310952
Japan. Army (service branches by name)   UA848.A-Z
Japan (biog.: heads of state)   923.152
Japan (gen. & cultural)   DS806
Japan (gen. history, descrip., culture)   DS835
Japan (geog. & travel)   915.2   DS810 (1901-45)
Japan (mil. geog.)   355.4752   UA995.J2
Japan (mil. status)   355.033052   UA845+
Japan (mil. status: gen.)   UA845   355.033052, .033252, .033552
Japan (mil. status: states, provinces, etc.)   UA849.A-Z
Japan (naval geog.)   359.4752   650-659
Japan (naval hist.)   359.00952   VA650-659
Japan (naval policy & status)   359.030952
Japan (naval status: gen.)   VA653.A5-Z   359.030952, .00952, .30952, .4752
Japan (pilot guides)   623.892952   VK909
Japan (post-WWI relns.: U.S.)   D651.J4
Japan (post-WWI territorial ?s)   D651.J3-5
Japan (WWI: causes, aims, results)   D519
Japan (WWII: causes, aims, results)   D742.J3
Japan (WWII: dipl. history)   D754.J3   940.532452
Japan (WWII: religious & ethical ?'s)   D744.5.J3
JAPANESE aerial ops. (WWII)   D792.J3-39   940.544952
Japanese-Americans (WWII)   D753.8 (SEE ALSO D769.8.A6)
Japanese armament (modern)   U821.J3
Japanese engineering ops. (WWII)   D795.J3
Japanese (in Brazil)   F2659.J3
Japanese (in Calif.)   F870.J3
Japanese (in Can.)   F1035.J3
Japanese (in Peru)   F3619.J3
Japanese (in U.S.)   E184.J3

Japanese Islands (lighthouses, beacons, foghorns, etc.)   VK1105-1106
                                                            623.89420952
Japanese Islands (lighthouses, beacons, foghorns, etc.: lists)   VK1207
                                                            623.89440952
Japanese Islands (pilot & sailing guides)   VK909   623.892952
Japanese Islands (tide & current tables)   VK709
Japanese military education (special periods)   U651
Japanese military ops. & Japan (WWII: gen.)   D767.2   940.5352, .540952,
                                                            .541352, 952.033
Japanese military ops. (WWI: gen.)   D571
Japanese naval ops. (WWII: by battle, ship, etc.)   D777.5.A-Z
Japanese naval ops. (WWII: gen.)   D777   940.545952, .5426
Japanese propaganda (1926-89: in other lands: gen.)   DS889.2
Japanese submarine ops. (WWII: by battle, ship, author, etc.)   D783.7.A-Z
Japanese submarine ops. (WWII)   D783.6, D784.J3
Japanese territories (WWII)   D802.J3
Java (Indon.)   959.82   DS646.17-29, DS646.2, DS646.27
Jeeps (mil. design)   623.74722
Jersey (G.B.: island)   942.341
Jerusalem, Pal.   DS109
Jerusalem, Pal. (1917-)   DS109.93
Jet aircraft (mil. design)   623.746044
Jet airplanes (engineering)   629.133349
Jewish groups (WWII)   940.5315296 (SEE ALSO .531503924)   D810.J4
Jewish question   DS141
JEWS & the Holocaust (WWII)   D810.J4
Jews (by country or area)   DS135.A-Z   Usually 004924 after Dewey place #s
Jews (Central Eur.)   943.0004924
Jews (Eng. and G.B.)   DS135.E5-6
Jews (Eur.)   DS135.E8-9   940.04924 (single '0' after decimal in this case)
Jews (Fr.)   DS135.F8-9   944.004924
Jews (Ger.)   DS135.G3-5   943.004924
Jews (Ger.: 19th-20th c.)   DS135.G33
Jews (Ger.: gen.)   DS135.G3.A5-Z
JEWS (IN Arg.)   F3021.J5
Jews (in Brazil)   F2659.J5
Jews (in Calif.)   F870.J5
Jews (in Chile)   F3285.J4
Jews (in Cuba)   F1789.J4
Jews (in Mex.)   F1392.J4
Jews (in N.Y.)   F130.J5
Jews (in S.Am.)   F2239.J5
Jews (in U.S.)   E184.J5
Jews (in Urug.)   F2799.J4
Jews (It.)   DS135.I8-9   945.004924
Jews, Modern   DS143
Jews (outside Israel: economic, political, social conditions)   DS140-140.5
Jews (outside Israel: gen.)   DS134   909.04924
Jews (outside Palestine)   DS133-151
Jews, Palestine, & Israel (gen. histories)   DS117

Jews (Rus.)   DS135.R9-95   947.004924
Jews (S. Am.)   DS135.S8 (PREFER E #s in most cases)
Jews (Sp.-Am. War, 1898: U.S.)   E725.5.J4
Jews (U.S.)   DS135.U6-7 (PREFER E184.J5 in most cases)   973.004924
Jews (WWI: includes Ukrainian pogroms)   D639.J4 (SEE DS145.P5-7 for Protocols
    of the Wise Men of Zion)
Jews (WWI: peace topic)   D650.J4
Jews (WWII)   940.531503924 (SEE ALSO .5315296)   D810.J4,
    D804.G4, D829.J4, DS135
Jews (WWII: Reconstruction)   D829.J4
Joffre, Joseph J. (Fr.: 1871-1940 era)   DC342.8.J6
JORDAN   DS153-154   956.95
Jordan (1517-1918: Turkish rule)   DS154.4   956.9503
Jordan (1919-)   DS154.5   956.9504
Jordan River (Pal.)   DS110.J6
Joubert de la Ferté, Philip Bennet, Sir (G.B.: air force biog.)   DA89.6.J6
Journalists & publishers (WWII)   940.5315097   D798 (gen.), D799.A-Z (by place)
Judiciary, Military (by country except U.S.)   UB845.A-Z (for U.S. SEE KF7601-7679)
Judiciary, Naval (U.S.: inclu. overall naval justice)   VB793
Jungle warfare   U167.5.J8
Justice, Naval (gen.: inclu. judiciary)   VB790   343.014, .0146
Juvenile works (WWI)   D522.7
Juvenile works (WWII)   D743.7

KAMCHATKA (Sib.)   DK771.K2
Kansas   F676-690   978.1
Kauai (Haw. Is.)   DU628.K3   996.941
Kemal, Mustafa (Tur.: 'Atatürk': 1909- era)   DR592.K4
Kent, Eng. (WWII)   D760.8.K4
Kentucky   976.9   F446-460
Kenya   967.62   DT434.E2 (older titles), DT433.5-434 (newer books),
    DT433.522, DT433.557
Kenya (1895-1963: Brit. era)   DT433.57-433.577   967.6203
Kenya (1920-63)   DT433.575
Kenya (mil. status)   UA860.5   355.03306762
Kerensky, Aleksandr (Rus.: 1894-1917: biog.)   DK254.K3
Key West, Fl. (fortifications)   UG412.K4
Khartoum, Egypt   DT154.K63
Kiangsi (China)   DS793.K4
Kiangsi Province (China)   951.222
Kiangsu Province (China: inclu. Nanking & Shanghai)   951.13   DS793.K
Kiel Naval Base (Ger.)   VA516.K4
Kiev, Rus.   DK651.K37
Kiev, Uk. (Kyiv)   DK508.92-939, DK508.95.K54
King's Own Scottish Borderers (WWI)   D547.K47
Kingston, Jam.   F1895.K5
Kiribati (inclu. Gilbert Is.)   996.81   DU615
Klintsy, Rus. (WWII)   D764.7.K5
Knapsacks (mil. equip.)   UC529.K6
Knives, bayonets, swords, etc. (design)   623.441   UD420-425,
    UD400 (bayonets)
Knots & splices (naut. ropes & cables)   623.8882   VM533
Knox, W. Frank (U.S.: 20th c.)   E748.K55
Konoye, Fumimaro, Prince (Japan: 20th. c.)   DS885.5.K6

KOREA   DS901-935+   951.9
Korea (20th c.)   DS916   951.903-904
Korea (1945+)   DS917
Korea (gen.)   DS907
Korea (geog. & travel)   915.19   DS902
Korea (WWII)   D767.255   940.53519
Korea (WWII: gen. particip.)   940.53519   DS916
Krakow, Pol. (Cracow)   DK4700-4735
Krupp armor plating (naval sci.)   V907.K7
Kurile Islands (Japan or Russia)   DS895.K9   957.7
Kuwait   DS247.K8-88
Kwangsi (China)   DS793.K6
Kwangtung (China)   DS793.K7
Kweichow (China)   DS793.K8
Kyoto, Japan   DS897.K8   952.191 (use 952.1864 with books after about 1988)

LABOR camps, internment centers, concentration camps (WWII: Ger.)
                                          940.53170943
Labor (WWI)   D639.L2
Labrador   F1135-1139
Ladrone Islands (Marianas: gen.)   DU645
Lake Baikal (Sib.)   DK771.B3
Lake Superior & Upper Peninsula (Mich.)   977.49   F572.N8 (N. Penin.),
                                          F552 (Lake Sup.)
Lanai (Haw. Is.)   DU628.L3   996.923
LAND forces warfare   356-357   UD-UF
Land (mil. bases, reservations, etc.)   355.79
Land (naval bases etc.)   359.79   VC412-416
Land transport (mil. engineering)   623.61
Land vehicles, Motorized (mil. design)   623.747   UC270-275, UC340-345
Landing (aviation)   629.1325213
Landing craft (naval engineering)   623.8256   V895
Landing craft (navies: units)   359.3256   V895
Landing maneuvers & debarkation   U200
Landing ops. & field service tactics (naval: inclu. shore srvc., small arms
                                instruc., etc.)   V175   355.41, .422
Language   400-499   P
Languages & literatures   P   400-499, 800-899
Laos   959.4   DS555, DS557.L2 (earlier books)
Laos (1893-1954)   DS555.7-73   959.403+
Laos (WWII: gen. particip.)   940.53594   DS555.36
Lapland (Fin.)   948.977   DL971.L2, DL1170.L2
LATIN AMERICA & the West Indies   F1201-3799+   972, 980-989
Latin America (1898-)   F1414   980.032+
Latin America (gen.)   F1401-1419   980
Latin America (mil. status: gen.)   UA602.3   355.03328, .03308
Latin America (naval status)   VA402.5
Latin America (WWII)   D768.18   940.538, .53228, .53248, .53258, 980.033
Latitude & longitude (marine navig.: inclu. tables)   VK565
Latrines & sewers (mil. qtrs.)   UC430
Lattre de Tassigny, Jean Joseph (Fr.: 20th c.)   DC373.L33

LATVIA   DK511.L15-18 (earlier pubns.), DK504 (later works)   947.43
Latvia (1800-1918)   DK504.73
Latvia (1914-18: WWI)   DK511.L178
Latvia (1918-)   DK511.L18
Latvia (1918-40)   DK504.74-76
Latvia (1940+)   DK504.77-79
Latvia (WWII: occupied terr.)   D802.L3
Laundries, Military   UC440
Laundries, Naval   VC430
Laurel, José P. (Philip.: 1935-46 period)   DS686.2.L3
Laval, Pierre (Fr.: 20th c.)   DC373.L35
LAW   K   340, 342-349
Law, Military (gen.: pubn. 1801+)   UB465   343.01
Law, Military (Rus.: commentaries, digests, etc.)   UB655.A7-Z
Law, Naval (gen.)   VB350   359.13, 343.01+
Law, Naval (U.S.)   VB360   343.7301
Laws (engineer corps)   UG130-135
Laws (engineer corps: U.S.)   UG133 (PREFER KF7335.E5)
Laws, Ordnance   UF130-135
Lawyers (WWII)   D810.L4
Leadership, Military   UB210
Leadership (naval admin.: besides U.S.)   VB205.A-Z
Leadership (naval admin.: U.S.)   VB203
League of Nations Commission of Enquiry (Manchuria: Lytton Commission)
                                                                                    DS783.7.L4-45
Leaves, furloughs, etc. (air forces: gen.)   UG970
Leaves, furloughs, other inactive periods (mil.)   355.113
Lebanon   DS80-90   956.92
Lebanon (1861-1918: close of Turkish era)   DS85
Lebanon (1919-)   DS86   956.92034+
Leeward Islands (inclu. St. Thomas, Virgin Islands, etc.)   F2006   972.97
Legislative compendia (WWI: U.S.)   D570.A3
Legislative compendia (WWII: U.S.)   D769.A3
Lend-lease, mutual aid (WWII: U.S.-G.B.)   D753.2.G7
Lend-lease, mutual aid (WWII: U.S.-Rus.)   D753.2.R9
LENIN Vladimir Ilich (Rus.: 1894-1917: biog. & works)   DK254.L3-46
Leningrad area (Rus.)   DK511.L195
Leningrad, Rus.   947.45   DK541-579, DK568 (1801-)
Leningrad, Rus. (Rev., 1917-21)   DK265.8.L195
Leningrad, Siege of (WWII)   D764.3.L4
Leningrad, U.S.S.R.   DK541-579   947.45
Lesser Antilles & Caribbes   F2001-2151   972.9, .97-98
Lesser Antilles (by political group)   F2131-2151
Lesser Antilles (indiv. islands in alphab. order)   F2033-2129
Levant (WWII: dipl. history)   D754.L4
Lewis machine guns   UF620.L5
Lexington (aircraft carrier: U.S.: 1st with name: WWII)   D774.L4
Libraries (WWI)   D639.L5 (PREFER Z675.W2)
Libya   961.2   DT211-239, DT224
Libya (1911-52: Ital. rule)   961.203   DT235
Libya (1912-45)   DT235   961.203
Libya (mil. status)   UA868   355.0330612
Libya (WWII)   D766.93   940.5423, 961.203
Liechtenstein   DB540.5 (older titles), DB881-898   943.648
Liechtenstein (gen. hist. & descr.)   DB886, 891

Li`ege, Bel.   DH811.L5
Li`ege, Bel. (WWI)   D542.L5
LIFE & customs (infantry)   356.181
Life & customs (marines)   359.961   VE, VE21-124, V735-743
Life & customs, Military (modern: gen.)   U765   355.1
Life & customs, Naval   359.1   V720-743, V110-145
Life & customs, Naval (modern: gen.)   V735   359.10904
Life preservers   VK1477
Lifeboats   VK1473   623.829
Lifeboats & other manually-driven vessels (engineering)   623.829   VK1473,
                                          VM351, VM360 (inflatable)
Lifesaving apparatus & stations (marine navig.)   VK1460-1481
Lifesaving equipment (special: by name)   VK1481.A-Z
Lifesaving on ships   VK1462-1463
Lifesaving, Marine   VK1300-1481
Light lists (marine navig.)   623.8945   VK1150-1246, VK1150,
                        VK1151-1185 (Eur.), VK1203-1209 (Asia), VK1211-
                              1223 (Australia & Pac.), VK1241-1246 (N.Am.)
Light signals (merch. marine)   VK387
LIGHTHOUSES   623.8942   VK1000-1249 (gen. & by place), VK1010,
                  VK1021-1124, VK1023-1025 (U.S.), VK1243 (U.S.: lists)
Lighthouses, beacons, foghorns, etc. (by area)   VK1021-1124
Lighthouses, beacons, foghorns, etc. (Eur.: gen.)   VK1055
Lighthouses, beacons, foghorns, etc. (Eur.: gen.: lists)   VK1151   623.8944094
Lighthouses, beacons, foghorns, etc. (inclu. buoys & lightships)   VK1000-1249
Lighthouses, beacons, foghorns, etc. (N. Am.: lists)   VK1241-1246   623.8944097
Lighthouses, beacons, foghorns, etc. (U.S.: by area)   VK1024
Lighting (naval architec. & engin.)   VM491-493
Lights, Ships' (engin.)   VM815
Lightships   623.8943   VK1010, VK1021-1124
Lightships, icebreakers, other misc. ships (engineering)   623.828
                                          VM451 (icebreakers)
Lille, Fr. (WWI)   D545.L5
Limited war   355.0215 (also older titles on total war)   UA11+, U21+, UA11
Line functions (mil. organiz.)   355.33041
Line Islands (Pacific)   996.4
Line positions (naval hier.)   359.33041
Liners, Passenger (by name)   VM383.A-Z
Lisbon, Port.   DP752-776, DP764   946.942
Lisbon, Port. (1840-1950)   DP764
LISTS & registers (Calif. Nat. Guard)   UA92
Lists & registers (N.Y. Nat. Guard)   UA362
Lists & registers (U.S. Army: vets.)   UA37
Lists & registers (WWI: decorated, dead, wounded)   D609   940.467
Lists & registers (WWII: decorated, dead, wounded)   D797 (SEE ALSO D796 for
      newer titles)   940.5467
Lists (beacons, foghorns, lighthouses, etc.)   VK1150-1249
Lists, Naval (U.S.: also official yearbooks)   V11.U6
Literature   800-899   P
Literature (gen. & gen. collections)   PN   800-809

LITHUANIA   DK511.L2-28 (earlier pubns.), DK505   947.5
Lithuania (1800-1918)   DK505.73
Lithuania (1914-19)   DK511.L26
Lithuania (1918-40)   DK505.74-76
Lithuania (1919-)   DK511.L27
Lithuania (1940+)   DK505.77-79
Lithuania (post-WWII territorial ?s)   D821.L5
Lithuania (WWII: Reconstruction)   D829.L5
Little Entente (1919)   D460
Little Russia (Ukraine)   947.71   DK508
Litvinov, Maksim M. (Rus.: 1925-53 era)   DK268.L5
Liverpool, Eng. (WWII)   D760.8.L6
Living conditions (air forces)   358.4112
Living conditions (marines)   359.9612   VE420-425
Living conditions, Military   355.12   U750-773, U750, U765
Living conditions (navies)   359.12   V720-743, V720 (gen.), V735 (modern),
                              V736 (U.S.), V737 (G.B.)
Living conditions (navies: partic. situations)   359.129
Lloyd George, David (G.B.: 20th c.)   DA566.9.L5
Loading & unloading nautical craft (plus cargo handling)   623.8881   VK235
Local government (WWII: U.S.)   D769.8.L6
LOCAL HISTORY (Algeria: towns etc.)   DT299.A-Z
Local history (Arabian Penin.: cities)   DS248.A-Z
Local history (Arabian Penin.: regions, sultanates, etc.: by place)   DS247.A-Z
Local history (Arg.: provinces, regions, etc.: alphab. order)   F2850-2991
Local history (Arg.: towns etc.)   F3011.A-Z
Local history (Armenian S. S. R.)   DK689
Local history (Australia)   DU145-398
Local history (Bel.: provinces, regions, etc.)   DH801.A-Z
Local history (Bel.: towns except Brussels)   DH811.A-Z
Local history (Bismarck Arch.: islands, groups, etc. by name)   DU553.A-Z
Local history (Br. Colum.: towns, cities, etc.)   F1089.5.A-Z
Local history (Br. N. Borneo)   DS646.335.A-Z
Local history (Brazil: regions, states, etc.)   F2541-2636+
Local history (Bulg.)   DR95-98
Local history (Calif.: regions, counties, etc.)   F868.A-Z
Local history (Calif.: towns etc.)   F869.A-Z
Local history (Caroline Islands: islands, groups, towns, etc.)   DU568.A-Z
Local history (China: cities & towns)   DS796.A-Z
Local history (China: dependencies, provinces, areas, etc.)   DS793.A-Z
Local history (Croatia)   DR1620-1636+
Local history (Den.: counties, islands, regions)   DL271.A-Z
Local history (Den.: towns etc.)   DL291
Local history (Dutch E. Ind.: islands, regions, etc.)   DS647.A-Z
Local history (Egypt: cities, towns, other)   DT154.A-Z
Local history (Egypt: provinces, regions, etc.)   DT137.A-Z
Local history (Eng.: towns besides London)   DA690.A-Z   942.2+
Local history (Ethiopia: kingdoms, regions, towns, etc.)   DT390.A-Z   963.056
Local history (Eur. Russia, Poland: provinces, governments, regions, etc.)
                                              DK511.A-Z
Local history (Fin.: regions, provinces, etc.)   DL1170.A-Z
Local history (Fin.: towns except Helsinki)   DL1180.A-Z
Local history (Florida: regions, counties, etc.)   F317.A-Z
Local history (Florida: towns etc.)   F319.A-Z

Local history (Fr. Indoch.: regions: earlier titles: by place)   DS557.A-Z
Local history (Fr. Indoch.: towns: earlier works)   DS558.A-Z
Local history (Fr.: north, east, Riviera, etc.)   DC601-609+
Local history (Fr.: regions, prov.'s, depts., etc.: by name)   DC611.A-Z
Local history (Fr.: towns besides Paris)   DC801.A-Z
Local history (G.B.: counties, regions, etc.: by name)   DA670.A-Z   942+
Local history (Ger.: areas, towns except Berlin)   DD901.A-Z
Local history (Ger.: large areas)   DD701-800
Local history (Ger.: provinces, regions, states, etc.)   DD801.A-Z
Local history (Greece: regions, islands, provinces, etc.)   DF901.A-Z
Local history (Hawaii: islands, counties, etc.)   DU628.A-Z
Local history (Hawaii: towns, volcanoes, etc.)   DU629.A-Z
Local history (Ice.)   DL396-398
Local history (Ice.: towns etc.)   DL398.A-Z
Local history (India, Burma, etc.)   DS486.A-Z
Local history (India, Pak., Burma, Ceylon, Indian Ocean islands, etc.)   DS485-498
Local history (Indian region kingdom, states, etc.)   DS485.A-Z
Local history (It.: large areas, cities)   DG600-980
Local history (It.: non-metro. towns, provinces, etc.)   DG975.A-Z
Local history (Jam.: regions, islands, etc.)   F1891.A-Z
Local history (Jam.: towns etc.)   F1895.A-Z
Local history (Japan: islands, provinces, regions)   DS895.A-Z
Local history (Japan: towns & cities)   DS897.A-Z
Local history (Java, Indon.)   DS646.29.A-Z
Local history (Libya)   DT238-239
Local history (Libya: towns etc.)   DT239.A-Z
Local history (London, Eng.)   DA675-689   942.1
Local history (Malay Penin.: protectorates, regions, settlements)   DS598.A-Z
Local history (Malay Penin.: towns etc.)   DS599.A-Z
Local history (Mariana Is.: islands, towns, etc.)   DU648.A-Z
Local history (Mex.: cities, towns, etc. except for Mex. City)   F1391.A-Z
Local history (Morocco: cities, towns, etc.)   DT329.A-Z
Local history (N. Australia: regions, towns, etc.)   DU398.A-Z
Local history (N. Viet.: cities etc.)   DS560.92.A-Z
Local history (N. Viet.: regions etc.)   DS560.9.A-Z
Local history (N. Zea.: regions, towns, dependencies, etc. except Wellington)
                                                        DU430.A-Z
Local history (N.Y.: cities, towns, etc. except N.Y.C.)   F129.A-Z
Local history (N.Y.: regions, counties, etc.)   F127.A-Z
Local history (Neth.: islands, provinces, regions, etc.)   DJ401.A-Z
Local history (Neth.: towns, cities, etc.)   DJ411.A-Z
Local history (New Mex.: towns etc.)   F804.A-Z
Local history (New S. Wales, Aust.: towns, regions, etc. except Sydney)
                                                        DU180.A-Z
Local history (Nor.: counties, regions, etc.)   DL576.A-Z
Local history (Nor.: towns, villages, etc.)   DL596.A-Z
Local history (Palestine: regions, towns, etc.)   DS110.A-Z
Local history (Pan.: provinces, regions, etc.)   F1569.A-Z
Local history (Paris, Fr.)   DC701-790+   944.36
Local history (Philip.: islands, provinces, regions)   DS688.A-Z
Local history (Philip.: towns & cities)   DS689.A-Z
Local history (Pol.)   DK4600-4800
Local history (Pol.: provinces)   DK4600.A-Z
Local history (Port.: regions, provinces, areas)   DP702.A-Z
Local history (Prus.: provinces, regions, etc.)   DD491.A-Z

Local history (Puerto R.: regions, towns, etc.)   F1981.A-Z
Local history (Queens., Aust.: all except Brisbane)   DU280.A-Z
Local history (Rum.)   DR281-296
Local history (Rus. Rev., 1905-6: by place)   DK264.2.A-Z
Local history (Rus. Rev., 1917-21: by place)   DK265.8.A-Z
Local history (Rus.: towns other than Moscow in Eur., Pol. areas)   DK651.A-Z
Local history (Russia)   DK501-973+
Local history (S. Australia except Adelaide)   DU330.A-Z
Local history (S.Am.: regions)   F2212-2217
Local history (Samoan Is.: partic. islands, towns, etc.)   DU819.A3-Z
Local history (Scotland: counties, regions, etc.)   DA880.A-Z
Local history (Serbia)   DR2075-2125
Local history (Siberia: provinces, regions, etc.)   DK771.A-Z
Local history (Siberia: towns etc.)   DK781.A-Z
Local history (Sp. Civil War, 1936-39: by place name)   DP269.27.A-Z
Local history (Sp.: provinces, regions, etc.)   DP302.A-Z
Local history (Sp.: towns except Madrid)   DP402.A-Z
Local history (Sumatra, Indon.)   DS646.15.A-Z
Local history (Swe.)   DL971-991
Local history (Swit.: cantons, cantonal capitals)   DQ301-800
Local history (Swit.: lakes, peaks, regions)   DQ841.A-Z (SEE ALSO DQ820+ for
                                                         more Alps #s)
Local history (Swit.: towns except cantonal capitals)   DQ851.A-Z (SEE DQ301-
                                                         800 for canton capitals)
Local history (Tasmania: regions, towns, etc.)   DU480.A-Z
Local history (Texas: regions, counties, etc.)   F392.A-Z
Local history (Texas: towns etc.)   F394.A-Z
Local history (Thai.)   DS588-589
Local history (Tur.: Eur. regions: by name)   DR701.A-Z
Local history (Ukraine: regions, oblasts, etc.)   DK508.9.A-Z
Local history (Ukraine: towns etc.)   DK508.95.A-Z
Local history (Victoria, Aust.: all except Melbourne)   DU230.A-Z
Local history (Viet.: cities, towns, etc.)   DS559.93.A-Z
Local history (Viet.: regions, protectorates, etc.)   DS559.92.A-Z
Local history (Virginia: regions, counties, etc.)   F232.A-Z
Local history (Virginia: towns etc.)   F234.A-Z
Local history (W. Australia except Perth)   DU380.A-Z
Local history (Washington, D.C.: cemeteries, churches, hotels, statues, parks,
                                    circles, streets, etc.)   F203
Local history (Wash. state: regions, counties, etc.)   F897.A-Z
Local history (Wash. state: towns etc.)   F899.A-Z
Local history (WWI: Calif.)   D570.85.C21.A-Z
Local history (WWI: England: by place)   D547.8.A-Z
Local history (WWI: Ger.: by place)   D538.5.A-Z
LOCAL HISTORY (WWII: Australia: by place)   D767.82.A-Z   994.1-8
Local history (WWII: Austria)   D765.45.A-Z
Local history (WWII: Bel.)   D763.B42
Local history (WWII: Calif.: by place)   D769.85.C21.A-Z
Local history (WWII: Cochin China: by place)   D767.352.A-Z
Local history (WWII: Czech.)   D765.55.A-Z
Local history (WWII: Den.: by place)   D763.D42.A-Z
Local history (WWII: Fin.)   D765.35.A-Z

Local history (WWII: Fr.: by place)   D762.A-Z   944.1-9+
Local history (WWII: G.B.: by place)   D760.8.A-Z   941.084, 942.084,
                                                        942.1-9+, 940.5341-5342+
Local history (WWII: Ger.: by place)   D757.9.A-Z 940.5343+, 943.1-9+
Local history (WWII: Greece)   D766.32.A-Z
Local history (WWII: Hung.)   D765.562.A-Z
Local history (WWII: It.: by place)   D763.I82.A-Z
Local history (WWII: Japan: by place)   D767.25.A-Z
Local history (WWII: Neth.: by place)   D763.N42.A-Z
Local history (WWII: New Britain)   D767.99.N415.A-Z
Local history (WWII: New Z.)   D767.852.A-Z
Local history (WWII: Nor.: by place)   D763.N62.A-Z
Local history (WWII: Pol.)   D765.2.A-Z
Local history (WWII: Rum.)   D766.42.A-Z
Local history (WWII: Rus.: by place)   D764.7.A-Z
Local history (WWI: U.S.: by state)   D570.85.A-W   974-979
Local history (WWII: U.S.: by state)   D769.85.A-W, F1-951+
Local history (WWII: Yug.)   D766.62.A-Z
Local history (Yug.)   DR381-396
Local history (Yug.: provinces, regions, etc.)   DR381.A-Z
Local history (Yug.: regions not limited to partic. sections or old republics)
                                                        DR1350.A-Z
Local history (Yug.: sections & old republics: Slovenia, Bosnia, Montenegro, etc.)
                                                        DR1352-2285+
Lodge, Henry Cabot (U.S.: 1865-1900 era)   E664.L7
Lodz Voivodeship (Pol.)   DK4600.L63
Logistics & support, Air force 358.4141   UG1100-1105
Logistics & troop movement   355.411
Logistics (mil. sci.)   U168   355.411
Logistics, Naval   V179   359.411
Logs, Nautical   VK581
Lombardy & Milan, It.   DG651-662
LONDON, Eng.   942.1   DA675-689, DA677 (gen.)
London, Eng. (1901-50)   DA684   942.1082
London, Eng. (1936-45)   942.1084   DA684
London, Eng. (boroughs, streets, etc.)   DA685.A-Z
London, Eng. (gen.)   DA677   942.1
London, Eng. (WWI)   D547.8.L7
London, Eng. (WWII)   D760.8.L7   942.1084, 940.534421
Long Island (N.Y.)   F127.L8   974.721
Long March (China: 1934-35: Communists)   DS777.5132-5139
Long March (China: 1934-35: Communists: gen.)   DS777.5134
Longitude & time at sea (marine navig.: inclu. tables)   VK567
Looting & other mil. crimes   UB789
Looting & other naval crimes   VB880
Lop-nor (China: lake)   DS793.L6
Loran tables (marine navig.: by region)   VK561.A2-Z
Loran tables (marine navig.: ca. 1932+: gen.)   VK561.A1
Los Alamos, New Mex.   F804.L6
Los Angeles, Calif.   F869.L8   979.494
Los Angeles County (Calif.)   F868.L8   979.493
Louisiana   F366-380, F369   976.3
Low Countries   DH-DJ
Lucerne, Lake (Swit.)   DQ841.L8
Lucerne, Swit.   DQ501-520   949.45

Ludendorff, Erich (Ger.: 1888-1918+ period)   DD231.L8
Lutheran Church (WWII)   D810.C66
LUXEMBOURG   949.35   DH901-925, DH916 (1815-)
Luxembourg (WWII: Grand Duchy)   D763.L9
Luxemburg   DH901-925
Luxemburg (1815-)   DH916
Luxemburg (gen.)   DH908   949.35
Luxemburg (gen. hist., culture, etc.)   DH905
Luzon (geog. & travel)   915.991   DS688.L9
Luzon (Philip.: inclu. Manila & Bataan)   959.91   DS688.L9
Lvov, Siege of (Polish wars, 1918-21)   DK4407.L9
Lyons, Fr.   DC801.L96-988
Lytton Commission (Manchuria: League of Nations Commission of Enquiry: summary
    & var. reports)   DS783.7.L45

M1 rifle   UD395.M17
Macao   DS796.M2   951.26
MacDonald, James Ramsay (G.B.: 20th c.)   DA566.9.M25
MACEDONIA   DR701.M13-42, DR2152-2285+   949.76
Macedonia (1912-45)   DR2230
Macedonia (1912-19)   DR2237
Macedonia (1919-45)   DR2240
Macedonia (1941-45: WWII)   DR2242
Macedonia (gen., descrip., culture, hist.)   DR2160, 2185
Macedonia (WWII: occupied terr.)   D802.M15
Machine-gun warfare   U167.5.M3
Machine guns (gen.)   UF620.A2   623.4424
Machine guns, Naval (gen.)   VF410.A2   623.4424
Machine guns (specific types) UF620.A3-Z
Machinists, Naval   VG800-805
Madagascar   DT469.M21-38   969.1
Madagascar (WWII)   D766.99.M3
Madeira Is.   DP702.M11-23
Madrid, Sp.   DP350-374   946.41
Madrid, Sp. (1801-1950)   DP361
Madrid, Sp. (area)   946.41   DP350-374, DP361
Madrid, Sp. (Civil War, 1936-39)   DP269.27.M3
Magazines & serial pubns. (WWI)   940.4005   D501
Magazines & serial pubns. (WWII)   940.54005   D731
Magazines, armories, etc. (countries except U.S.)   UF545.A-Z
Magazines, Ordnance (navies: gen.)   VF380   359.75
Maginot Line (Fr.: fortific's.: engineering)   623.1944   UG429.F, UG430.M
Mail, Military   355.693
Mail, Military (navies)   359.693
Maine   974.1   F16-30, F19 (gen.), F25 (1865-1950)
Maine (1865-1950)   F25
Maine (gen.)   F19

MAINTENANCE & building devices & procedures, Marine (engin.)   VM901-965
Maintenance & repair (aircraft)   629.1346
Maintenance & repair (naut. engineering)   623.8208 (SEE ALSO .00288 after
                                                 1988)   VM763 (engines)
Maintenance & repair, Naval (yards etc.)   VC417
Maintenance & repair (ordnance)   623.48   UF350-355, UF550-560
Maintenance & repair (small craft)   VM322
MAINTENANCE & TRANSPORT (mil.: Asia) UC234-245
Maintenance & transport (mil.: Australia)   UC255
Maintenance & transport (mil.: Can.)   UC90-93
Maintenance & transport (mil.: Eur.)   UC158-233
Maintenance & transport (mil.: G.B.)   UC184-187
Maintenance & transport (mil.: Ger.)   UC180-183
Maintenance & transport (mil.: Japan)   UC241
Maintenance & transport (mil.: New Z.)   UC256.5
Maintenance & transport (mil.: Pac. islands)   UC257-258
Maintenance & transport (mil.: Rus.)   UC208-211
Maintenance & transport (mil.: U.S.)   UC20-88
Maintenance & transport (mil.: U.S.: by time period)   UC23
Maintenance & transport, Military   UC
MAINTENENCE, NAVAL   VC   359.6-8
Maintenance, Naval (Asia)   VC230-245
Maintenance, Naval (Australia)   VC255-256   359.60944
Maintenance, Naval (Can.)   VC90-93
Maintenance, Naval (China)   VC235
Maintenance, Naval (Eur.)   VC160-229
Maintenance, Naval (Fr.)   VC176-179
Maintenance, Naval (G.B.)   VC184-187   359.60941
Maintenance, Naval (Ger.)   VC180-183   359.60943
Maintenance, Naval (Ger.: by region or area)   VC183.A-Z
Maintenance, Naval (It.)   VC196-199
Maintenance, Naval (Japan)   VC241   359.60952
Maintenance, Naval (New Z.)   VC256.5
Maintenance, Naval (Rus.)   VC208-211
Maintenance, Naval (U.S.)   VC20-65
Malacca, Malay Penin.   DS599.M3
MALAY Archipelago & Indonesia   DS600-605   959.8
Malay Archipelago (gen.)   DS603
Malay Peninsula, Malaya, & the Straits   DS591-599   959.5
Malay Peninsula (to 1946)   DS596.5   959.503
Malay Peninsula (WWII)   D767.5   959.503
Malaya & Malay Peninsula (gen.)   DS596
Malaya (mil. status)   UA853.M3
Malaya (WWII: occupied terr.)   D802.M2
Malaysia   959.5   DS591-599, DS592, DS596
Malaysia & Singapore (tide & current tables)   VK710
Malaysia (to 1946)   959.503   DS596, DS596.6
Malaysia (WWII: gen. particip.)   940.535951   D767.5, DS596, DS598-
                                                 599 (local, A-Z)
Malaysia (WWII: mil. hist.)   940.5409595   D767.5
Maldive Islands   DS491.M3

MALTA   945.85   DG994
Malta & Maltese Islands   DG987-999
Malta (1798-1964: Brit. era)   DG992.7
Malta (1802-1947)   DG993
Malta (20th c.)   DG994
Malta (gen.)   DG990
Malta (geog. & travel)   914.585   DG989
Malta (WWII)   D763.M3
Manchester, Eng. (WWII)   D760.8.M3
Manchoukuo (1932-45: P'u-i era)   DS784
Manchuria   951.803-804   DS781-784.2+, DS784 (1932-45)
Manchuria (19th-20th c.)   DS783.7
Manchuria (geog. & travel)   915.18   DS784
Manchuria (WWII: gen. particip.)   940.53518   DS784
Manchuria (WWII: occupied terr.)   D802.M25
Mandates (post-WWI)   940.31426   D651
Mandates (post-WWII)   940.531426
MANEUVERS, Air force (training)   358.4152
Maneuvers & tactics (armor & cavalry: Asia)   UE270-280
Maneuvers & tactics (armor & cavalry: by place) UE160-302
Maneuvers & tactics (artillery: Asia)   UF270-280
Maneuvers & tactics (artillery: Eur.)   UF215-269
Maneuvers & tactics (marines)   VE157   359.9642, .9652
Maneuvers, drills, & tactics (artillery: gen.)   UF157
Maneuvers, drills, & tactics (infantry: gen.)   UD157   356.18, 355.42
Maneuvers (mil. engineering)   UG320-325
Maneuvers (mil. sci.)   U250-255
Maneuvers (mil. sci.: gen.)   U250   355.52
Maneuvers (mil. sci.: places besides U.S.)   U255.A-Z
Maneuvers (mil. sci.: U.S.)   U253
Maneuvers, Naval   V245, U260-262 (combined — army, navy, air forces — or
                    amphibious warfare ops.)   359.52
Maneuvers, Naval (training)   359.52   V245
Manila, Philip.   DS689.M2   959.91
Mannerheim, Carl (Fin.: 20th c.)   DK461.M32
Manning of vessels (merch. marine)   VK221
Manpower (by country)   UA17.5.A3-Z
Manpower (gen.)   UA17.5.A2   355.22, .61
Manual of arms (infantry: U.S.)   UD323-324
Manual of arms (marines)   VE320   359.968240202
Manual of arms (naval seamen)   VD320   359.5470202, .8240202
MANUALS & handbooks (marines: gen.)   VE150   359.960202
Manuals & handbooks (marines: places besides U.S.)   VE155.A-Z
Manuals & handbooks (mil. hygiene: not Eng. or Am.)   UH625
Manuals & handbooks (naval ordnance: places besides U.S.)   VF155.A-Z
Manuals & handbooks (naval ordnance: U.S.)   VF153
Manuals & handbooks, Soldiers' (U.S.)   U113
Manuals & regulations, Air force (gen.)   UG670
Manuals, Armor & Cavalry   UE150-155
Manuals (artillery)   UF150-155   358.120202
Manuals, Infantry   UD150-155
Manuals, Infantry (places besides U.S.)   UD155.A-Z
Manuals, medical & surgical (navies: besides U.S.)   VG465.A-Z
Manuals (mil. engineering)   UG150-155

Manuals, Naval ordnance (U.S.: by mm., cm., inches, or lbs.)   VF393.A4-6
Manuals (naval seamen: gen.)   VD150, V110+, V120+ (SEE ALSO V110+ &
                    V120+)   359.00202, .40202
Manuals (naval seamen: places except U.S.)   VD155.A-Z
Manuals (naval seamen: U.S.)   VD153   359.402020973
Manuals (U.S. Marines)   VE23.A48
Manufacture (naval ordnance & arms: gen.)   VF370
Manufacture (ordnance & small arms: gen.)   UF530   623.4+, 338.476234
Manufacture (small arms & ordnance: U.S.: by state)   UF534.A-W
Manufacturers (small arms & ordnance)   UF537.A-Z
Manzanar Internment Camp (Calif.)   940.531779487
Mao Tse Tung (China: 1893-1976: SEE DS777.488.C5 for Chiang Kai Shek)
                                        DS778.M3

Map maneuvers & problems   U312
Mapping & surveying, Military (U.S.)   UG472
Maps & atlases   912   G
Maps & atlases (WWI)   D522.3, G1037 (PREFER)
Maps & atlases (WWII)   D743.3, G1038 (PREFER)
Marblehead (cruiser: WWII)   D774.M3
Marching & guides (countries except U.S.)   UD315.A-Z
Marching & guides (mil.: gen.)   UD310
Marco Polo Bridge Incident (Sino-Jpn. Confl.: 1937)   DS777.533.M3
MARIANA ISLANDS (Ladrones: inclu. Guam)   DU640-648, DU643-5 996.7
Mariana Islands (mil. geog.)   355.47967   UA995.M
Mariana Islands (pilot & sailing guides)   VK933.M27
Mariana Islands (WWII: by specific is.)   D767.99.M272.A-Z, D767.99.A-Z (direct
                                        alternatives, e.g. D767.99.G9 for Guam)
Mariana Islands (WWII: gen.)   D767.99.M27
Marianas (Ladrone Islands)   996.7   DU640-648, DU643-645
MARINE barracks & quarters (gen.)   VE420   359.961292, .9671
Marine camps (South Carolina: training)   VE434.S6   359.96709757
Marine Corps divisions (WWII: U.S.: by #)   D769.37.1st-
Marine Corps regiments (WWII: U.S.: by #)   D769.372.1st-
Marine Corps (WWII: U.S.: gen.)   D769.369
Marine drills (Asia: gen.)   VE270
Marine drills (by place)   VE160-302
Marine drills (Eur.: gen.)   VE215
MARINE ENGINEERING   VM600-989
Marine engineering (hist.: Australia)   VM721
Marine engineering (hist.: Eur.)   VM655
Marine engineering (hist.: Fr.)   VM671
Marine engineering (hist.: G.B.)   VM657   623.870941-870942
Marine engineering (hist.: gen.)   VM615
Marine engineering (hist.: Ger.)   VM673   623.870943
Marine engineering (hist.: It.)   VM679
Marine engineering (hist.: Japan)   VM699   623.870952
Marine engineering (hist.: Rus.)   VM685
Marine engineering (hist.: U.S.)   VM623-625
Marine engineering (instruction: U.S.)   VM727
Marine engines   VM731-779
Marine hydrography & surveying (gen.)   VK591
Marine lifesaving (hist's.)   VK1315
Marine military ops.   359.964   VE21-124 (by place)

Marine navigation & merchant marine   VK
Marine navigation & merchant marine (gen.: pubn. 1801+)   VK145   623.89
Marine navigation (instruction: by locale: inclu. merch. marine)   VK421-524
Marine navigation science   VK549-572
Marine regiments (U.S.: by #)   VE23.25.1st+
Marine training camps (U.S.: gen.)   VE432   359.9670973
Marine uniforms (U.S.)   VE403   359.96140973
MARINES   VE   359.96
Marines (Am.)   VE21
Marines & marine warfare   359.96 (add to .96 those #s after 355 in 355.1-.8)
    VE, VE7-500+,VE15 (gen.), VE21-124 (by place), VE23 (U.S.),
    VE57 (G.B.), VE145-146, VG90-95 (aviation)
Marines (Asia)   VE99-113
Marines (Australia & New Z.)   VE121-122.5
Marines (by geographic area)   VE21-124
Marines (Can.)   VE26
Marines (collected, nonserial titles)   VE7
Marines (Eng. & Wales)   VE59
Marines (Eur.)   VE55-96
Marines (G.B.)   VE57-64
Marines (gen. hist.)   VE15   359.96, .9609
Marines (gen.: pubn. 1801-1970)   VE145   359.9609
Marines (gen.: pubn. 1970+)   VE146   359.9609
Marines (Ger.)   VE73
Marines (It.)   VE79
Marines (Japan)   VE105   359.960952
Marines (misc. subjects: not A-Z)   VE500
Marines (N. Am.)   VE22
Marines (Rus.)   VE85
Marines (Scot.)   VE61
Marines (WWI: U.S.: inland ops.)   D570.348
Marines (WWII: U.S.: land ops. only)   D769.369-372 (SEE D767, D769.45, D774,
    D790, U-V for naval or aerial ops.)
Maritime Provinces (Can.: Atlantic coast)   F1035.8   971.5-8
Marksmanship (marines: U.S.)   VE333   359.96547
Marksmanship (naval seamen: U.S.)   VD333
Marquesas Islands   DU700   996.31
Marseilles, Fr.   DC801.M34-38
Marshall Islands (inclu. Kwajalein Atoll)   DU710   996.83
Marshall Islands (WWII)   D767.99.M3
Marshall Islands (WWII: occupied terr.)   D802.M3
Maryland (battleship: U.S.: WWII)   D774.M35
Masaryk, Jan (Czech.: era of 1918-)   DB2191.M37
Masaryk, Tomas G. (Czech.: era of 1918-)   DB2191.M38
Massachusetts   974.4   F61-75, F64
Massachusetts   F61-75   974.4
Massachusetts (1865-1950)   F70 (SEE D570.85.M4-41 for war years, 1914-18
    & D769.85.M4-41 for 1939-45)   974.404-043
Masters' manuals (merch. marine: inclu. command of ships)   VK205
Material, Naval (U.S. Navy. Office of: reports)   VA52.A68-69
Matériel & equipment (marines)   359.968   VE350-390, VF (ordnance)
Matériel & equipment, Air force   358.418   UG1100-1425+, UG1100-1105
Maui (Haw. Is.)   996.921   DU628.M3
Maui (Haw. Is.)   DU628.M3   996.921
Maurras, Charles M. (Fr.: 20th c.)   DC373.M3

Mauser rifle   UD395.M3
Maxim machine guns   UF620.M4
May 4th Movement (China: 20th c.)   DS777.43
Measurement of ships (naval architec.)   VM155
Mecca, Saudi Arabia   DS248.M4
Mechanical engineering (mil. applications)   UG450
Mechanical systems (naut. craft: engineering)   623.8501
Mechanized & armored cavalry   UE147   357.5, 358.18
Mechanized cavalry (gen. & ops.)   357.58   UE147-155, UE159,
                                   UE160-302 (by place)
Mechanized cavalry (jeep, truck, other large-motor vehicle troops)   357.54
                                   UC340-345, UG615-620
MEDALS, badges, brevets, etc. (navies: gen.)   VB330   359.1342
Medals, badges, decorations (WWII: by country)   D796.5.A-Z
Medals, badges, decorations (WWII: inclu. individual s & lists)   D796 (SEE ALSO
                                   D797 for older works)
Medals, decorations, badges, etc. (mil. rewards)   355.1342
Medals, decorations, etc. (mil.: U.S.)   UB433
Medals, decorations, other reward insignia (navies)   359.1342
Media & public relns. (mil.: gen.)   UH700   070.433, .449, 355.342
Media & public relns. (navies: gen.)   VG500   359.342, 070.433, .439
MEDICAL & health services, Air force   358.41345   UH201-655
Medical & health services, Military   355.345   UH201-629, UH215,
                                   UH223-225 (U.S.)
Medical & mental examinations (mil. recruits)   UB330-336
Medical & nursing services (navies)   359.345   VG100-475, VG115, VG121-
                                   224 (overall by place), VG123 (U.S.), VG350-355 (nurse corps)
Medical & relief services, Military   UH201-570
Medical & surgical handbooks (navies: gen.)   VG460   359.3450202,
                                   610.0202, 617.0260202
Medical biography, Military (indiv.: by name)   UH347.A-Z   355.3450924
Medical biography, Naval (U.S.: collective)   VG227.A1
Medical care for retired military   UB448-449
Medical care of veterans   UB368-369   355.115
Medical corps equipment (gen.)   UH510
Medical facilities, Naval   359.72   VG410-450, VG420 (U.S.), VG430 (G.B.)
Medical installations, Military   355.72   UH470-475
Medical schools, Army (places besides U.S.)   UH399.A-Z
Medical schools, Army (U.S.: gen.)   UH398
Medical services (air forces)   UG980-985   358.41345
MEDICAL SERVICES & RED CROSS (WWI: G.B.)   D629.G7
Medical services & Red Cross (WWI: U.S.: gen.)   D629.U6
Medical services & Red Cross (WWII: Australia)   D807.A8
Medical services & Red Cross (WWII: G.B)   D807.G7
Medical services & Red Cross (WWII: Hawaiian Islands)   D807.H3
Medical services & Red Cross (WWII: U.S.)   D807.U6-89
Medical services & Red Cross (WWII: U.S.: gen.)   D807.U6   940.547673
Medical services, hospitals, Red Cross (WWI)   D628-630   940.475+, .477+
Medical services, hospitals, Red Cross (WWII)   D806-807

MEDICAL SERVICES, MILITARY (Africa)   UH315-319
Medical services, Military (Asia)   UH299-313
Medical services, Military (Australia)   UH321-322
Medical services, Military (Can.)   UH226-227
Medical services, Military (China)   UH301-302
Medical services, Military (Egypt)   UH317-318
Medical services, Military (Eur.)   UH255-295
Medical services, Military (Eur.: gen.)   UH255   355.345094
Medical services, Military (Eur.: WWI)   UH256.1914-18
Medical services, Military (Eur.: WWII)   UH256.1939-45
Medical services, Military (Fr.)   UH271-272
Medical services, Military (G.B.: gen.)   UH257   355.3450941
Medical services, Military (Ger.)   UH273-274   355.3450943
Medical services, Military (hist., statistics, etc.: gen. & by place)   UH215-324
Medical services, Military (Japan)   UH305-306   355.3450952
Medical services, Military (misc. Asian lands)   UH313.A-Z
Medical services, Military (New Z.)   UH322.5
Medical services, Military (Pac. islands)   UH323-324
Medical services, Military (Philippines)   UH313.P5
Medical services, Military (Rus.)   UH285-286
Medical services, Military (Rus.: Asia)   UH309-310
Medical services, Military (Scandin.)   UH286.5
Medical services, Military (Tur.)   UH311-312
Medical services, Military (U.S.)   UH223-225   355.3450973
Medical services, Military (U.S.: official reports)   UH223.A1-49
Medical services, Military (U.S.: unofficial)   UH223.A6-Z
Medical services, Military (U.S.: WWI)   UH224.1917-18
Medical services, Military (U.S.: WWII)   UH224.1941-45
MEDICAL SERVICES, NAVAL   VG100-475 (SEE ALSO UH201-515)
Medical services, Naval (Asia)   VG199-213
Medical services, Naval (Australia)   VG221
Medical services, Naval (Eur.)   VG155-196
Medical services, Naval (G.B.)   VG157
Medical services, Naval (Ger.)   VG173
Medical services, Naval (Japan)   VG205
Medical services, Naval (Rus.)   VG185
Medical services, Naval (U.S.)   VG123   359.3450973
Medical services (WWI: hospitals)   940.476   D628-629
Medical services (WWI: particular countries)   940.4754-4759   D629.A-Z
Medical services (WWI: Rus.)   940.47547   D629.R9
Medical services (WWI: U.S.)   940.47573   D629.U6-8
MEDICAL SERVICES (WWII: G.B.)   940.547541   D807.G7
Medical services (WWII: Ger.)   940.547543   D807.G3
Medical services (WWII: hospitals)   940.5476   D806
Medical services (WWII: hospitals, British)   940.547641   D807.G7
Medical services (WWII: hospitals, German)   940.547643   D807.G3
Medical services (WWII: hospitals, Japanese)   940.547652   D807.J3
Medical services (WWII: hospitals, Russian)   940.547647   D807.R9
Medical services (WWII: hospitals, United States)   940.547673   D807.U6-87
Medical services (WWII: Japan)   940.547552   D807.J3
Medical services (WWII: particular countries)   940.54754-54759   D807.A-Z
Medical services (WWII: Rus.)   940.547547   D807.R9
Medical supplies   355.88   UH440-445
Medical supplies, Naval   359.88   VG290-295

MEDICINE   610-619   R
Medicine, Military (gen., hdbks., etc.)   UH390-396
Medicine, Military (places besides U.S.: manuals etc.)   UH395.A-Z
Medicine, Military (U.S.: official manuals etc.)   UH393
Medicine, Military (U.S.: unofficial manuals etc.)   UH394
Medicine, psychiatry, & nursing   R   610-619, 649
MEDITERRANEAN Region (Eastern)   956.9   DS80-151+, DS62
Mediterranean Sea (lighthouses, beacons, foghorns, etc.: lists)   VK1176
                                          623.8944091638
Mediterranean Sea (mil. status)   UA646.55   355.03301638, 359.471638
Mediterranean Sea (pilot & sailing guides)   VK853-874   623.89291638, .8929448
Mediterranean Sea (tide & current tables)   VK653-674
Mediterranean, Eastern (geog. & travel)   915.69   DS44, DS49, D972-973
MEETINGS (CNCL. FOR. MIN.: Berlin: 1954: 25Jan.-18 Feb.)   D814.47
Meetings (Cncl. For. Min.: London: 1945: 11 Sept.-2 Oct.)   D814.413
Meetings (Cncl. For. Min.: London: 1947: 25 Nov.-16 Dec.)   D814.45
Meetings (Cncl. For. Min.: Moscow: 1945: 16-26 Dec.)   D814.415
Meetings (Cncl. For. Min.: Moscow: 1947: 10 Mar.-24 Apr.)   D814.44
Meetings (Cncl. For. Min.: New York: 1946: Nov.-Dec.)   D814.43
Meetings (Cncl. For. Min.: Paris: 1946: Apr.)   D814.42
Meetings (Cncl. For. Min.: Paris: 1946: 15 June-July)   D814.425
Meetings (Cncl. For. Min.: Paris: 1949: 23 May-20 June)   D814.46
MEETINGS (NAZI PARTY: Ger.: 1923)   DD253.28.1923
Meetings (Nazi Party: Ger.: 1926)   DD253.28.1926
Meetings (Nazi Party: Ger.: 1927)   DD253.28.1927
Meetings (Nazi Party: Ger.: 1929)   DD253.28.1929
Meetings (Nazi Party: Ger.: 1933-38)   DD253.28.1933-38
Meetings (Nazi Party: Ger.: gen.)   DD253.27
MELANESIA   993.2-993.7 (PREFER 995 after 1988)   DU490 (gen.)
Melanesia & New Zealand (mil. geog.)   355.4793
Melanesia (gen)   DU490 (SEE DU520-950 for specific islands, groups, atolls, etc.)
                                          993, 993.2-7, 996.1
Melanesia (geog. & travel)   919.32-37
Melanesia, New Guinea & Oceania   995 (SEE ALSO 993.2-7 for titles on Mel. &
                    New G. before 1989; 990 for gen. titles on Oceania
                    prior to 1989)   DU739-746, DU739
Melanesia (WWII: gen. particip.)   940.5393   DU940
Melbourne, Australia   DU228   994.51
Melbourne, Australia (WWII)   D767.82.M44   994.51
Memorials, monuments, celebrations (WWI: gen.)   D663 (SEE ALSO D503 for
                                          museums & NA9325 for fine arts)
Memorials, monuments, celebrations (WWII: G.B.: local: by place)   D838.G7.A-Z
Memorials, monuments, celebrations (WWII: gen.)   D830   940.5465
Memorials, monuments, celebrations (WWII: misc.)   D831
Memorials, monuments, celebrations (WWII: U.S.)   D833-836   940.546573
Mennonites (WWII)   D810.C665
Mental & medical examinations (mil. recruits: gen.)   UB330   355.2236
Mental health, psychiatry, etc. (mil.: gen.)   UH629

MERCHANT MARINE & navigation (20th c.: hist. & conditions)   VK20
Merchant marine & navigation (gen. hist's.)   VK15
Merchant marine & navigation (gen. special)   VK147
Merchant marine & navigation (hist. & conditions: by area or country) VK21-124
Merchant marine & navigation (instruction: U.S.)   VK423
Merchant marine & navigation (study & teaching: gen.)   VK401
Merchant marine (occupation)   VK160   387.0023
Merchant ships, Powered (engineering)   623.824
Messes & clubs, Naval officers' (gen.)   VC380   359.346
Messing (mil.: cooking: U.S.)   UC723
Metal ships (naval architec.)   VM146-147   623.8182
Metals (mil. raw materials)   355.242
Meteorology, Aviation   629.1324
Meteorology, Military   UG467
Methodist Church (WWII)   D810.C67
Meuse, Battle of the (Monthermé: 1940)   D756.5.M4
Mexican-Americans (WWII: as troops)   D769.88.M4   940.5404
Mexican & Central American coasts (pilot & sailing guides)   VK969-970
MEXICO   F1201-1392   972.72.7
Mexico (1910-46)   F1234   972.081-082
Mexico (1917-64)   972.082   F1234-1235
Mexico & Central America (geog. & travel)   917.2   F1215 (Mexico), F1432 (C.Am.)
Mexico (mil. status)   UA603-605
Mexico (overall)   972   F1201-1392, F1208, F1226
Mexico (WWII)   D768.2   940.5372
Mexico (WWII: dipl. hist.)   940.532572 (could be with Allies at .532272)   D754.M
Mexico City area (Mex.)   F1386   972.53
Miami, Florida   975.9381   F319.M6
Michael (Rum.: regent period, 1927-3; King, 1940-47)   DR265
Michigan (inclu. Lakes Mich. & Huron)   F561-575, F566   977.4
MICRONESIA   996.5   DU500 (gen.)
Micronesia & Polynesia (mil. geog.)   355.4796
Micronesia, Eastern   996.8
Micronesia, Eastern (Ellice, Gilbert, Marshall Is.: WWII: gen. particip.)
                    940.53968   D767.917 (Gilb's.),
                    D767.99.M3 (Marshalls), DU500 (Micro.), DU590 (Ell. Is.),
                    DU615 (Gilb's.), DU710 (Marshalls)
Micronesia (gen.)   DU500 (SEE DU520-950 for particular islands, island
                    groups, atolls, etc.)   996.5-68
Micronesia (geog. & travel)   919.65   DU500
Micronesia (naval geog.)   359.47965   VA750.M
Micronesia (WWII: gen. particip.)   940.53965   DU500
MIDDLE Atlantic states & District of Columbia   F116-205
Middle East (Near East)   956   DS41-326
Middle East (1918-45)   956.03   DS62.4
Middle East & Southwestern Asia   DS41-329   953, 955, 956
Middle East (geog. & travel)   915.6   DS49-49.5
Middle West & Mississippi River Valley (1865-1950)   F354   977.03
Midway, Battle of (1942)   D774.M5
Midway Islands (Haw. Is.)   DU628.M5   996.99
Midway Islands (WWII)   D767.94
Mihailovic, Draza (Yug.: 1918-45 era)   DR359.M5, DR1294.M54
Milan, It.   DG660-662

Militarism & antimilitarism (inclu. mil.-indus. complex)   355.0213   JX1952,
                                        JX1963, UA23, U21.5, JF195.C5
MILITARY ADMINISTRATION   355.6   UB-UC
Military administration (Africa)   UB115-119
Military administration (Asia)   UB99-113
Military administration (Australia)   UB121-122   354.94066
Military administration (Belg.)   UB67-68
Military administration (by country)   UB21-124
Military administration (Can.)   UB26-27
Military administration (China)   UB101-102   354.51066
Military administration (civil sections)   UB180-197
Military administration (Den.)   UB69-70
Military administration (Eur.)   UB55-95
Military administration (Fr.)   UB71-72   354.44066
Military administration (G.B.)   UB57-64
Military administration (G.B.: by time period)   UB58.1900+
Military administration (G.B.: Eng. & Wales)   UB59
Military administration (G.B.: Scot.)   UB61
Military administration (gen.: pubn. 1801-1970)   UB145   355.6
Military administration (gen.: pubn. 1971+)   UB146   355.6
Military administration (Ger.)   UB73-74   354.43066, 355.60943
Military administration (Greece)   UB75-76
Military administration (India)   UB103-104
Military administration (It.)   UB79-80
Military administration (Japan)   UB105-106   354.52066, 355.60952
Military administration (Lat.Am.)   UB27.5-54
Military administration (misc. Asian lands)   UB113.A-Z
Military administration (misc. Eur. lands)   UB95.A-Z
Military administration (New Z.)   UB122.5
Military administration (Norway)   UB81-82
Military administration (Pac. islands)   UB123-124
Military administration (Pol.)   UB95.P7
Military administration (Rus.: Asia & Sib.)   UB109-110
Military administration (Rus.: Eur.)   UB85-86   354.47066
Military administration (Scan.: gen.)   UB86.5
Military administration (Sp.)   UB87-88
Military administration (U.S.)   UB23-25   353.6, 355.60973
Military administration (U.S.: by state)   UB24.A-W
Military air transport (U.S.)   UC333-334   358.440973
Military & marine engineering   623   UG; VM
Military & nautical engineering (hist. & biog. works: overall)   623.009+   UG400-401
Military & nautical engineering (overall topics)   623.04
MILITARY & NAVAL HISTORY (Arg.)   F2832
Military & naval history (Brazil)   F2522
Military & naval history (Cuba)   F1776.1
Military & naval history (G.B.: 20th c.)   DA566.5
Military & naval history (Mex.)   F1227.5
Military & naval history (Philip.: inclu. battles vs. Sp. & U.S.)   DS682-684 (PREFER
                E717.7 for Battle of Manila Bay [1898] & U.S.-Sp. naval confront.)

MILITARY & NAVAL LIFE & customs (WWI: Ger.)   940.48443   D532-538,
                                               D581-582 (naval), D604 (aerial)
Military & naval life & customs (WWI: U.S.)   940.48373   D570, D589.U6-7 (naval),
                                               D606 (aerial)
Military & naval life & customs (WWII: G.B.)   940.548341   U767, V737
Military & naval life & customs (WWII: Ger.)   940.548443   U769, V739
Military & naval life & customs (WWII: Japan) 940.548452   U773, V743.J3
Military & naval life & customs (WWII: Rus.)   940.548347   U771, V741
Military & naval science   355-359   U, V
Military animals (gen.)   UH87   355.24
Military artificers & technical troops (places besides U.S.)   UG505.A-Z
Military barracks & camps (U.S.)   UC403-404   355.70973
Military bases, camps, forts, reservations, etc. (geog. & hist. applic.)   355.709
MILITARY BIOGRAPHY   923.5 (SEE ALSO 355.0092, 940.3+, .53+, etc.)   U51-55
Military biography (Asia)   923.55
Military biography (China)   923.551   DS738 (group)
Military biography (G.B.)   923.541-542   DA54 (collec.), DA69.3.A-Z (20th c.:
                                indiv.), DA89.1.A-Z (naval: 20th c.: indiv.), U55.G7
Military biography (Ger.)   923.543   DD100 (group)
Military biography (Japan)   923.552   DS838-839
Military biography (Rus.)   923.547   DK50.5-8
Military biography (U.S.)   923.573   E181 (mil.: collec.), E182 (naval:
                                collec.), U52-53
Military biography (U.S.: collective)   U52
Military bridges (design)   623.67   UG335, UC320-325
Military capability   355.0332+
Military clothing & equipment (U.S.)   UC463-464
Military clubs (U.S.)   U56
Military commissions (by country except U.S., for which SEE KF7661)   UB875.A-Z
Military communications (except U.S.: by country)   UA945.A-Z
Military communications (gen.)   UA940   355.27, .41, .6
Military construction (U.S.: gen.)   UC46 (SEE ALSO UG for engineer., VC420+ &
                                VG590+ for naval)   358.22
Military crimes (countries outside U.S.)   UB785.A-Z
Military crimes (U.S.)   UB783 (SEE ALSO KF7615-7618)
Military decorations, medals, rewards, etc.   UB430-435   355.1342
Military discipline   UB790-795   343.014, .13325
MILITARY EDUCATION & training (gen.)   U400   355.07
Military education (Asia: gen.)   U635
Military education (Can.)   U440-444
Military education (China: gen.)   U640
Military education (Eur.: gen.)   U505
Military education (G.B.: gen.)   U510
Military education (Ger.: gen.)   U570
Military education (Ger.: special topics)   U572.A-Z
Military education (Japan: gen.)   U650
Military education (U.S.: Command & Gen. Staff Coll.)   U415
Military education (U.S.: gen.)   U408   355.0071073

MILITARY ENGINEERING 623.1-7 UG
Military engineering, air forces, & air warfare UG 358.2, 623, 358.4 (air forces etc.)
Military engineering & air forces UG
Military engineering (Asia: gen.) UG99
Military engineering (collections) UG7
Military engineering (Eur.: gen.) UG55
Military engineering (field: gen.) UG360
Military engineering (G.B.: by #'d regiment) UG57.Z6.1st+
Military engineering (Japan: by #'d regiment) UG105.Z6.1st+
Military engineering (misc.) 623.7
Military engineering (U.S.: by #'d regiment) UG125.1st+
Military engineering (U.S.: gen.) UG23
Military engineering maneuvers (U.S.) UG323
Military engineering manuals (U.S.) UG153
Military engineering (Ger.: by #'d regiment) UG73.Z6.1st+
Military equipment (U.S.) UC523-524 355.80973
Military expeditions U265
Military explosives, unguided rockets, etc. UF860-880
Military flags, colors, standards (gen.) UC590 355.15
Military footwear (U.S.) UC493
Military forces & science 355-358 U
Military fortifications, Permanent (engineering) 623.12 (for titles after 1988 SEE
                                                       ALSO .1) UG405
Military fortifications, Temporary (engineering) 623.15 UG403
Military geography UA985-997 355.47+, .0330+, 359.47+
Military geography (except U.S.) UA995.A-Z
Military geography (U.S.) UA993 355.4773, 359.4773
Military headgear UC500
Military headquarters ops. (gen.: inclu. aides, adjutants, etc.) UB230
MILITARY HISTORY (1801-1914/20) D361 355.033003+
Military history (20th c.) D431 355.020904, 355.009, 355,033+
Military history (Australia) DU112.3 355.00994, .033094
Military history (Bel.: 1815-) DH545
Military history (Bel.: gen.) DH540
Military history (Bulg.) DR70
Military history (Can.) F1028 355.00971
Military history (China: 20th c. & 1912-49) DS775.4
Military history (Den.) DL154
Military history (Dutch E. Ind.) DS636
Military history (Egypt) DT81
Military history (Fin.) DL1036-1037 355.0094897
Military history (Formosa: 1895-1945) DS799.714
Military history (Fr. Indoch.) DS544
Military history (Fr.) DC44-47
Military history (Fr.: 1871-1940) DC339
Military history (Fr.: 19th-20th c.) DC47
Military history (Fr.: 20th c.) DC367
Military history (G.B.) DA50-69.3
Military history (G.B.: 20th. c.: gen.) DA69 355.00941, .033041, .033241,
                                                       .033541
Military history (Ger.) DD99-105
Military history (Ger.: 20th c.) DD104 355.00943, .033043, .033242, .033543
Military history (Greece) DF765
Military history (India: 1901-) DS442.6

Military history (It.) DG48-84
Military history (It.: 1792-20th c.) DG484
Military history (Japan: 1868+) DS838.7 355.00952, .033052, .033252, .033552
Military history (Japan: overall) DS838 355.00952
Military history (Malta) DG990.5
Military history (N. Zea.) DU420.5 355.009931
Military history (Neth.) DJ124
Military history (Nor.) DL454 355.009481
Military history (Philip.) DS671 355.009599
Military history (Pol.) DK417 (older titles), DK4170-4178
Military history (Pol.: 1795-1918) DK4173
Military history (Pol.: 1919-) DK4174
Military history (Port.) DP547
Military history (Rum.) DR219
Military history (Rus.: 1917-) DK54 355.00947, .033+
Military history (S. Afr.) DT769 355.00968
Military history (Scan., N. Eur., Fin.) DL52
Military history (Serbia) DR1970
Military history (Sp.: 1808-20th c.) DP78.5 355.00946
Military history (Swe.) DL654
Military history (Swit.) DQ59
Military history (Thai.) DS573
Military history (U.S.) E181 355.00973, .033073
Military history (U.S.: 20th c.: inclu. biog.: more than 1 war) E745 355.00973,
                                                    .033073, .033273, .033573
Military history (Ukr.) DK508.54
Military history (world) D25 355.48, 904.7, 909
MILITARY HISTORY (WWI) 940.4 D521 (gen.), D529-608
Military history (WWI: Australia) 940.40994 D547.A8
Military history (WWI: by place) 940.409
Military history (WWI: Can.) 940.409571 D547.C2
Military history (WWI: New Z.) 940.40993 (SEE ALSO .409931 for titles earlier than
                                    1989) D547.N5
Military history (WWI: U.S.) 940.40973 D570
Military history (WWI: units & ops.: by country: inclu. structure, hist., registers, etc.)
                                    940.412-413+ D532-578, D608
Military history (WWI: units & ops.: G.B.) 940.41241 D546-546.55+, D547
Military history (WWI: units & ops.: Ger.) 940.41343 D531-538
MILITARY HISTORY (WWII) 940.54 D743
Military history (WWII: Australia) 940.540994 D767.8
Military history (WWII: Austria) 940.5409436 D765.4
Military history (WWII: Belgium) 940.5409493 D763.B4
Military history (WWII: Bulg.) 940.54094977 D766.7.B8
Military history (WWII: Burma) 940.5409591 D767.6
Military history (WWII: by place) 940.54094-54099 D757-769
Military history (WWII: Can.) 940.540971 D768.15
Military history (WWII: China) 940.540951 D767.3
Military history (WWII: Denmark) 940.5409489 D763.D4
Military history (WWII: Egypt) 940.540962 D766.9
Military history (WWII: Fin.) 940.5409471 (SEE .54094897 for newer titles)
                                    D765.3
Military history (WWII: Fr.) 940.540944 D761
Military history (WWII: G.B.) 940.540941-540942 D759-760
Military history (WWII: Ger.) 940.540943 D757
Military history (WWII: Greece) 940.5409495 D766.3

Military history (WWII: Hungary)   940.5409439   D765.56
Military history (WWII: India)   940.540954   D767.6, D767.63 (Free India,
                                                   1943-45)
Military history (WWII: It.)   940.540945   D763.I8-817
Military history (WWII: Japan)   940.540952   D767.2
Military history (WWII: Luxemb.)   940.54094935   D763.L9
Military history (WWII: New Z.)   940.5409931 (SEE ALSO .540993 for titles
                                                   prior to 1989)   D767.85
Military history (WWII: Norway)   940.5409481   D763.N6-613
Military history (WWII: Philip. Is.)   940.5409599   D767.4
Military history (WWII: Rumania)   940.5409498   D766.4
Military history (WWII: Rus.)   940.540947   D764
Military history (WWII: S. Africa)   940.540968   D766.97
Military history (WWII: Singapore)   940.54095957
Military history (WWII: Turkey)   940.5409561   D766.7.T8
Military history (WWII: U.S.)   940.540973   D769, D769.25-4 (armies,
                   div's., regt's.), D769.45-598 (naval particip., units, ops.)
MILITARY HISTORY (WWII: UNITS & OPS.: Australia)   940.541294   D767.8
Military history (WWII: units & ops.: Belgium)   940.5412493   D763.B4
Military history (WWII: units & ops.: Burma)   940.5412591   D767.6
Military history (WWII: units & ops.: by country: inclu. structure, history, registers, &
                                   service records)   940.5412-5413+
Military history (WWII: units & ops.: Can.)   940.541271   D768.15
Military history (WWII: units & ops.: China)   940.541251   D767.3
Military history (WWII: units & ops.: Fin.)   940.54134897   D765.3
Military history (WWII: units & ops.: Fr.)   940.541244   D761.1-9
Military history (WWII: units & ops.: G.B.)   940.541241   D759.5-760.A-Z
Military history (WWII: units & ops.: Ger.)   940.541343   D757.1-.85
Military history (WWII: units & ops.: Greece)   940.5412495   D766.3
Military history (WWII: units & ops.: India)   940.541254   D767.6,
                                                   D767.63 (Free India, 1943-45)
Military history (WWII: units & ops.: It.)   940.541345   D763.I81-813,
                   D763.I815-817 (Corpo Volontari Della Liberta)
Military history (WWII: units & ops.: New Z.)   940.5412931 (SEE ALSO .541293
                                   for works before 1989)   D767.85
Military history (WWII: units & ops.: Norway)   940.5412481   D763.N61-613
Military history (WWII: units & ops.: Phil. Is.)   940.5412599   D767.4
Military history (WWII: units & ops.: Rum.)   940.5413498   D766.4
Military history (WWII: units & ops.: S. Africa)   940.541268   D766.97
Military history (WWII: units & ops.: Scot.)   940.5412411   D760.S
Military history (WWII: units & ops.: U.S.)   940.541273   D769.25-4,
                   D769.5-555 (naval), D769.585-598 (Coast Guard
                   etc.), D769.73-76+ (transport, ordnance, supplies)
Military history (WWII: units & ops.: U.S.: particular areas or states)   940.541274-
                                                   541279   D769.85.A-Z
Military history (WWII: units & ops.: Yug.)   940.5412497   D766.61-613
Military history (WWII: units & ops.:Japan)   940.541352   D767.2
Military history (WWII: Yug.)   940.5409497   D766.6-613
Military history (Yug.)   DR319
Military history (Yug.: gen.)   DR1251
Military horses & mules (gen.)   UC600
Military hospitals (U.S.)   UH473-474 (SEE ALSO D629.U6-8 & D807.U6-87 for
                   WWI & II)
Military hygiene & sanitation (U.S.)   UH603

Military information (security: besides U.S.)   UB248.A-Z
Military information (security: U.S.)   UB247
Military inspection   355.63   UB240-245
Military installations & land (inclu. bases, forts, camps, posts, etc.)   355.7
                                          UA26+ (U.S.), UC400-405, UA600-876
Military intelligence (G.B.)   UB251.G7
Military intelligence (gen.)   UB250   355.3432
Military intelligence (Ger.)   UB251.G3   355.34320943
Military justice (admin.: gen.)   UB840   343.0143, .133
Military kits & field equip. (gen.)   UC540   355.81
MILITARY LAW   UB461-736
Military law (Asia)   UB685
Military law (Australia)   UB730-734
Military law (Austria)   UB600-604
Military law (Balkan states)   UB680-683
Military law (Can.)   UB505-509
Military law (China)   UB690-694
Military law (Eur.: gen.)   UB590
Military law (Fr.)   UB615-619
Military law (G.B.)   UB625-629 (PREFER KD6000-6355)   343.010941
Military law (Ger.)   UB620-624   343.010943
Military law (Japan)   UB700-704   343.010952
Military law (New Z.)   UB734.5
Military law (Phil. Islands)   UB705-709
Military law (Rus.: gen.)   UB655   343.010947
Military law (Rus.: statutes & compil's.)   UB655.A2
Military law (Tur.)   UB675-679
Military law (U.S.)   UB500-504 (PREFER KF7201-7755)   343.010973,
                            .0106073
MILITARY LIFE & CUSTOMS   U750-773   355.1
Military life & customs (modern: Fr.)   U768
Military life & customs (modern: G.B.)   U767   355.10941
Military life & customs (modern: Ger.)   U769   355.10943
Military life & customs (modern: It.)   U770
Military life & customs (modern: misc. countries besides U766-771)   U773
Military life & customs (modern: Rus.)   U771   355.10947
Military life & customs (modern: U.S.)   U766   355.10973
Military life, customs, & postmilitary benefits   355.1   U750, U22
Military life (service periods, promotion, vet. benefits, etc.)   355.11
Military living conditions (partic. situations)   355.129   U765+
MILITARY MAINTENENCE & TRANSPORT (Asia: gen.)   UC234
Military maintenance & transport (Eur.: gen.)   UC158
Military maintenance & transport (gen.)   UC10   355.6-8
Military maintenance & transport (U.S.: gen.)   UC20
Military maintenance & transport (U.S.: WWI era)   UC23.1917-1918
Military maintenance & transport (U.S.: WWII era)   UC23.1941-1945
Military maneuvers   355.52   U250-255

MILITARY MEDICAL SERVICES (Asia: gen.)   UH299
Military medical services (G.B.: by period or date)   UH258
Military medical services (gen.: inclu. organization, surgeons, etc.)   UH400
Military medical services (hist., statistics, etc.: includes sanitary services: gen.)
                                                    UH215   355.345
Military medical services (U.S.: by time period or date: SEE ALSO particular wars)
                                                            UH224
Military medical services, Military (Eur.: by date or period)   UH256
Military medicine (gen.: inclu. hdbks., manuals, etc.)   UH390   616.98023
Military missions   UA16
Military missions & attachés   355.032
Military motor vehicles (places besides U.S.)   UG620.A-Z
Military movie services (U.S. Army)   UH826
Military museums & exhibitions (gen.)   U13.A1
Military nursing (U.S.)   UH493
Military observations (collected: 2 or more wars)   U719
Military oceanography (U.S.)   V396.3-4
Military officers (except U.S.: by country)   UB415.A-Z
MILITARY OPS. (hist's. & types of persons)   355.409 (SEE ALSO 355.47 for
                                           geog. treat.)   U27-43
Military ops. (Russo-Fin. War, 1939-40)   DL1099
Military ops. (Sp. Civil War, 1936-39: gen. titles on the war)   DP269.A56-Z
Military ops. (WWII: West: gen.)   D530   940.41+, .421, .424, .4272, .431, .434
Military ops. (WWII: West: gen. special)   D756.3
Military ops. (WWII: West: gen.)   D756
Military personnel (inclu. organization; readiness of partic. groups)   355.3
                                           UA15+, UA23-39+ (U.S.)
Military personnel (WWII)   940.5315355
Military pistols & revolvers (design)   623.443   UD410-415
Military planning   U150-155
Military police & conduct enforcement   355.13323
Military police (gen.)   UB820   355.13323
Military Police (MP's: WWII: U.S.)   D769.775
Military police (WWI: U.S.)   D570.35
Military prison life   355.1295 (SEE ALSO 365.48)
Military prisons   355.13325 (SEE ALSO 365.48)   UB800-805
Military prisons & prisoners (gen.)   UB800   365.48, 355.13325, 344.03548
Military prisons (outside U.S.)   UB805.A-Z
Military quarters & camps (besides U.S.)   UC405.A-Z
Military radar (U.S.)   UG612.3
Military radio (U.S.)   UG611.3
Military radio services (U.S. Army)   UH857
Military railroads & rolling stock (engineering)   623.63   UC310-315, UF490-
                                           495 (r.r. artil.), UG345 (engnrg.)
Military railroads (U.S.: gen.)   UC313   355.830973
Military recreation & information services (gen.)   UH800   355.346
Military research, Aeronautical (U.S.: by state of origin)   UG643.5.A-W
Military research (U.S.)   U393
Military resources (prep., review, preserv.)   355.21

MILITARY SCIENCE   355-358   U
Military science (19th c.)   U41
Military science (20th c.)   U42   355.00904
Military science & engineering   U   355-358, 623
Military science & organization (ALSO armed forces, ground forces, etc.)
                                                    355 (inclu. officers' hdbks.)   U, U21+
Military science (gen.)   U1-900+   355
Military science (gen.: pubn. date 1789-)   U102   355, .43
Military science (history)   U27-45
Military science (history: by country or area)   U43.A-Z
Military science (history: gen.)   U27   355.009
Military science, military engineering, & air forces   U-UH   355-359, 623
Military science (misc. services: medical etc.)   UH
Military science (modern: 1800-)   U39
Military service as a profession   UB147
Military services (misc.)   UH
Military signaling (gen.)   UG580
Military skill (Indians of N. Am.)   E98.M5
Military social & welfare services (countries besides U.S.)   UH769.A-Z
Military sports (by place)   U328.A-Z
Military staffs (countries besides U.S.)   UB225.A-Z
MILITARY STATUS (20th c.)   355.033004   U42
Military status (1900-1919)   355.0330041
Military status (1930-39)   355.0330043
Military status (1940-49)   355.0330044
Military status (Africa)   UA855-868
Military status (Asia)   UA830-853
Military status (Asia: by country except India, China, Japan)   UA853.A-Z
Military status (Australia)   UA870-874
Military status (Balkan States)   UA820-827
Military status (by area or country) 355.03301-03309
Military status (Can.)   UA600-602
Military status (Central Am.)   UA606-608
Military status (China)   UA835-839
Military status (Eur.)   UA646-829
Military status (Fr.)   UA700-709
Military status (G.B.)   UA647-668   355.033041-033042, .033241, .033541
Military status (gen. hist.)   355.033   D25, U21+, U27, UA15
Military status (gen.: inclu. policy)   355.03
Military status (Ger.)   UA710-719
Military status (hist. periods)   355.033001-033005
Military status (It.)   UA740-749
Military status (Japan)   UA845-849
Military status (misc. Eur. countries)   UA829.A-Z
Military status (N. Am.)   UA22-602
Military status (New Z.)   UA874.3-7
Military status (Norway)   UA750-759
Military status (Pacific islands)   UA875-876
Military status (Rus. or Sov.Un.)   UA770-779
Military status (S.Am.)   UA612-645
Military status (U.S.)   UA23-585   355.033273
Military staus (W. Hemis.)   UA21-645
Military status (world: gen.)   UA10   355.03
Military status (worldwide: place by place)   UA21-876+   355.0330+

Military supplies & stores (gen.)   UC260
Military supply ships (freighters, tankers, etc.: units)   359.3265 (SEE ALSO
                                            .9853 after 1988)   VA79
Military surveying, mapping, & topography   UG470-474
Military tactics (partic. kinds: commando, retreats, blitz, landings, attacks &
     counters, etc.)   355.422
Military tactics (special topics: by name)   U167.5.A-Z
Military telegraph & troops (U.S.)   UG603
Military telephone (U.S.)   UG610.3
Military transport engineering   623.6   UC, UC10, UC270-360, UC270-275 (gen.)
Military transport (U.S.)   UC273-274
Military transport vessels & hospital ships (units)   359.3264 (SEE ALSO
                              .9853 for transp. ships on pubns. after 1988)
                              VA79 (transports), VG450 (hosp. ships)
Military tunnels (design)   623.68   UG340
Military uniforms (U.S.)   UC483-484   355.140973
Military units (marines)   359.9631
Military units (types: armies, div's., regiments, co's., mil. districts, etc.)
                    355.31   UA, UA23-39+ (U.S.), UA646-829 (Eur.),
                    UA830-853 (Asia), UA870-876(Australia-Pac.)
Militia (Ger.)   UA717
Militia, Naval (U.S.: state by state)   VA90-387
Militia (U.S.: inclu. Nat. Guard etc.: state by state)   UA50-549
Mindanao (geog. & travel)   915.997   DS688.M2
Mindanao (Philip.)   DS688.M2   959.97-8
Mindoro (Philip.)   DS688.M28   959.93
MINE laying & sweeping (mil. engnrg.: land)   623.262   UG490
Mine sweeping & laying (mil. engineering: marine)   623.263   V856-856.5
Minelayers & minesweepers (naval engineering)   623.8262   V885 (sweepers),
                                            V856-856.5 (both)
Minelaying, minesweeping, submarine mines, etc. (gen.)   V856   623.2, .26,
                              .263, .36, .45115, .8262, 359.825115, .3262
Minerals (non-metal: mil. raw materials)   355.243
MINES (design)   623.45115   UG490, V856-856.5 (naval)
Mines (mil. equip.)   355.825115   UG490
Mines (naval ammun.)   359.825115
Mines, Land (inclu. countermeasures)   UG490   623.45115
Minesweepers   V885 (SEE ALSO V856)   623.8262
Minesweepers & minelayers (navies: units)   359.3262   V885, V856+
Minesweeping, minelaying, sub. mines, etc. (by place)   V856.5.A-Z
Mining & torpedo troops   UG550-555
Minnesota   F601-615   977.6
MINORITIES & women in the armed forces (gen.)   UB416   355.22 (women), .3
Minorities & women in the armed forces (places besides U.S.)   UB419
Minorities & women in the armed forces (U.S.: by group name)   UB418.A-Z
Minorities & women (navies)   VB320-325
Minorities, Ethnic (WWII: as troops)   940.5404   D769.88.A-Z,
                                            D769.88.M4 (Mex.-Am's.)
Minorities (U.S. Navy: by group)   VB324.A-Z
Minsk, Rus.   DK651.M5
Missile forces & warfare (land: may be mostly post-WWII)   358.17   UG1310-1315
Missiles & rockets, Air force (by particular type)   UG1312.A-Z
Missiles, Surface-to-surface (design)   623.45195

Mississippi   F336-350   976.2
Mississippi (WWII)   D769.85.M7
Mississippi Valley & the Midwest   F351-355   976-977
Missouri   977.8   F461-475, F466
Missouri (battleship: U.S.)   VA65.M8   359.32520973
MOBILIZATION   UA910-915
Mobilization (except U.S.: by name of place)   UA915.A-Z
Mobilization (G.B.)   UA915.G7   355.280941
Mobilization (gen.)   UA910   355.28
Mobilization, Industrial (gen.)   UA18.A2   355.28
Mobilization (mil. resources: inclu. requisition, commandeering, voluntary, etc.)
                                    355.28   UA910-915, UA913 (U.S.)
Mobilization, Naval (G.B.)   VA463   359.280941
Mobilization, Naval (Ger.)   VA518   359.290943
Mobilization, Naval (Japan)   VA658   359.280952
Mobilizaton, Naval (gen.)   VA48   359.28
Mobilization (U.S.)   UA913   355.280973
Mobilization (U.S. Navy)   VA77   359.280973
Model ships   623.8201
Models, Military   U311
Models, Ship   VM298   623.8201, 745.5928
Modern history (1453-)   D208   901.93, 909.8+, 940
Modern history (1789-)   D299   909.8+
Modern history (1801-1914/20)   D358   909.81
Modern history (1945-)   D840   909.824-825+
Mohammed V (Tur.: ruler, 1909-18: also titles on era)   DR583
Molokai (Haw. Is.)   DU628.M7   996.924
Molotov, Viacheslav M. (Rus.: 1925-53 era)   DK268.M64
Moluccas   DS646.6   959.85
Monaco   944.949   DC941-947, DC945
Mongolia   DS793.M7 (SEE ALSO DS19-23.1 for Mongols)   951.7
Mongolia (WWII: gen. particip.)   940.53517   DS793.M7
Mongols   DS19-23.1 (SEE ALSO DS793.M7 for Mongolia)
Mons, Bel. (WWI)   D542.M7
Montana   F726-740   978.6
Montego Bay, Jam.   F1895.M6
MONTENEGRO   DR101-196+, DR1802-1928 (SEE ALSO DR357+, DR1214)
                        949.745, .76
Montenegro (1878-1918: Nicholas I)   DR1878-1883
Montenegro (1912-18: Balkan wars & WWI)   DR1883
Montenegro (1914-18: WWI)   DR158
Montenegro (1918-: part of Yug.)   DR159
Montenegro (1918-45)   DR1884-1893
Montenegro (1918-45: gen.)   DR1885
Montenegro (1941-45)   DR1893
Montenegro (gen.)   DR117, DR1810, 1835
Montevideo (steamship: WWII)   D782.M6
Montevideo, Urug.   F2781   989.513
Montgomery, Bernard Law Montgomery, 1st Viscount (G.B.: 20th c. mil. biog.)
                                            DA69.3.M56

Monuments & cemeteries (WWI: Rus.) 940.46547 D680.R
MONUMENTS & CEMETERIES (WWII: Australia) 940.546594 D838.A8
Monuments & cemeteries (WWII: China) 940.546551 D838.C5
Monuments & cemeteries (WWII: Fr.) 940.546544 D838.F8
Monuments & cemeteries (WWII: Ger.) 940.546543 D838.G3
Monuments & cemeteries (WWII: Hawaiian Is.) 940.5465969 D835.H, D838.H
Monuments & cemeteries (WWII: Japan) 940.546552 D838.J3
Monuments & cemeteries (WWII: Rus.) 940.546547 D838.R9 or .S65
Monuments & cemeteries (WWII: U.S.: Wash. D.C.) 940.5465753
                                                 D835.D6, D836.W
Monuments, memorials, celebrations (WWI) D663-680 940.46+
Monuments, memorials, celebrations (WWI: G.B.) D680.G7
Monuments, memorials, celebrations (WWI: U.S.: by city) D675.A-Z
MONUMENTS, MEMORIALS, CELEBRATIONS (WWII: Australia) D838.A8
Monuments, memorials, celebrations (WWII: Fr.: gen.) D838.F8
Monuments, memorials, celebrations (WWII: Fr.: Paris) D838.F8.P3
Monuments, memorials, celebrations (WWII: G.B.: gen.) D838.G6
Monuments, memorials, celebrations (WWII: G.B.: London) D838.G7.L5
Monuments, memorials, celebrations (WWII: Ger.) D838.G3
Monuments, memorials, celebrations (WWII: memorials dedicated to special divisions
                                classed with them) D830-838
Monuments, memorials, celebrations (WWII: N.Z.) D838.N45
Monuments, memorials, celebrations (WWII: outside U.S.: by place) D838.A-Z
Monuments, memorials, celebrations (WWII: Rus.) D838.R9
MONUMENTS, MEMORIALS, CELEBRATIONS (WWII: U.S.: by city) D836.A-Z
Monuments, memorials, celebrations (WWII: U.S.: by state) D835.A-Z
                                                 940.546574-54679+
Monuments, memorials, celebrations (WWII: U.S.: Calif.) D835.C2-21
                                                 940.5465794
Monuments, memorials, celebrations (WWII: U.S.: District of Columbia) D835.D6
Monuments, memorials, celebrations (WWII: U.S.: Ill.) D835.I3-31
Monuments, memorials, celebrations (WWII: U.S.: Los Angeles) D836.L62
Monuments, memorials, celebrations (WWII: U.S.: N.Y.) D835.N4-5
Monuments, memorials, celebrations (WWII: U.S.: New York City) D836.N49
Monuments, statues, memorials (London, Eng.) DA689.M7
Monuments, statues, memorials (Washington, D.C.) F203.4.A-Z
Moral & health protection (mil.: alcoholism, drug abuse, prostitution, venereal
                diseases, etc. & work vs.) UH630
Morale, Military 355.123 U22
Morale (navies) 359.123
Moravia (20th c.) DB2415-2421
Moravia (20th c.: gen.) DB2416
Moreton Bay (Queens., Aust.) DU280.M7
Moroccan question (20th c.) D475 (PREFER DT317)
MOROCCO DT301-330 964
Morocco (19th-20th c.) DT324 964.03-04
Morocco (1900-56) 964.04 DT324
Morocco (gen.) 964 DT301-330, DT305, DT314
Morocco (mil. status) UA867 355.033064
Morocco (WWII) D766.99.M8 940.5364, 964.04
Mortars & howitzers (U.S.: gen.) UF473
Mortars (U.S.: handbooks) UF563.A75

Moscow area (Rus.)   DK511.M6
Moscow, Rus.   DK591-609, DK601 (hist. to 1950)   947.31
Moscow, Rus. (to 1950)   DK601
Moscow, Rus. (Rev., 1917-21)   DK265.8.M6
Moscow, Rus. (WWII)   D764.7.M58
Moslems or Muslims (WWII)   D810.M6 or .M8
Mosley, Oswald, Sir, Baronet (G.B.: 1910-36 biog.)   DA574.M6
Moss, Nor.   DL596.M7
Motion-picture services, Military (U.S.: gen.: inclu. armed forces)   UH825
Motor transport, Artillery   UF390
Motor transport (mil. sci.)   UC340-345   355.83
Motor transport (naval sci.)   VC570-575
Motor vehicles, Military (gen.)   UG615   623.747, 355.83, 357.5+
Motorboats & launches (small craft: gen.)   VM341
Motorcycle troops (mech. cav.)   357.53   UC347
Motorcycles (mil. transp.)   UC347   623.7472
Motorized infantry   356.11 (pubns. before 1989 may inclu. regular infan. ALSO)
                U167.5.M6, UD15, UD21-124+, UA
Motorized units (mil. sci.)   U167.5.M6
MOUNTAIN artillery   UF440-445
Mountain guns (U.S.: handbooks)   UF563.A5.2.95in.Mt. (2.95)
Mountain Province (Philip.)   DS688.M5
Mountain troops (WWII: Ger.)   D757.39
Mountain troops (WWII: Ger.: by author, division, name, etc.)   D757.4.A-Z
Mountain warfare & troops   UD460-465   356.164
Mounted forces & warfare   357   UE, UE15, UE21-124, UE23 (U.S.),
                UE57 (G.B.), UE65 (Austria), UD450-455
Mounted infantry (gen.)   UD450
Movie services, Military (by place except U.S.)   UH829.A-Z
Movie services, Military (gen.)   UH820
Movies & movie propaganda (WWII)   D743.23   791.43+, 940.53+
Movies (WWI)   D522.23
Mozambique (Portuguese East Africa)   DT451-465   967.9
Mukden, China   DS796.M8
Mukden, Manch. (Ch.-Jpn. Confl.:1931: incident)   DS783.8
Mules & horses, Military (places besides U.S.)   UC605.A-Z
Munich Four-power Agreement   DB2202
Munich, Ger.   DD901.M71-95
Munich, Ger. (1871-1950)   DD901.M9
Munich, Ger. (gen.)   DD901.M77
Munich, Ger. (WWII)   D757.9.M9
MUSEUMS, Air force (inclu. exhibitions: gen.)   UG623.3.A1   623.74074,
                358.40074
Museums & exhibitions (marine navig. & merch. marine)   VK6
Museums & exhibitions (mil. engineering)   UG6
Museums & exhibitions (naval architec.)   VM6
Museums & exhibitions (naval ordnance: gen.)   VF6.A1
Museums, Artillery (by city within area, whose 1st letter & shelf # are shown by
                'x' in 'x2')   UF6.x2.A-Z
Museums, Artillery (by country or region)   UF6.A2-Z
Museums, Artillery (inclu. exhibitions)   UF6

MUSEUMS, EXHIBITIONS, ETC. (arms)   U804
Museums, exhibitions, etc. (arms: by country)   U804.A2-Z
Museums, exhibitions, etc. (WWI)   D503
Museums, exhibitions, etc. (WWII)   D733
Museums, exhibitions, etc. (WWII: by country)   D733.A2-Z
Museums, exhibitions, etc. (WWII: gen.)   D733.A1
MUSEUMS, MILITARY (Fr.)   U13.F8
Museums, Military (G.B.)   U13.G7
Museums, Military (inclu. exhibitions)   U13.A-Z   355.0074
Museums, Military medical (inclu. exhibitions)   UH206
Museums, Military (Sov.Un.)   U13.S65
Museums, Military (U.S.)   U13.U6-7   355.0074073
Museums, Naval (gen.: inclu. exhibitions)   V13.A1   359.0074
Music   M   780-789
Music & bands, Military (gen.)   UH40
Music & bands, Naval (U.S.)   VG33   359.340973, .170973
Musicians (WWII)   940.531578   D810.A7 or .M
Mussolini, Benito (It.: 1900-46 period)   DG575.M8
Mustard gas   UG447.5.M8   623.4516
Muster rolls & accounts, Military (gen.: inclu. gen. corresp.: admin.)   UB160
Mutinies & military offenses   355.1334 (SEE 364.138 for war crimes)   UB780+
Mutiny & other naval offenses   359.1334   VB850-880
Mutiny (mil.)   UB787
Mutiny (naval: except U.S.)   VB865.A-Z
Mutiny (naval: gen.)   VB860   359.1334
Mutiny (naval: U.S.)   VB863
Mutual-aid agreements (WWII: U.S.: by country)   D753.2.A-Z
Muzzle-loading ordnance   UF560-565... .M.L.

NAGASAKI, Japan   DS897.N285   952.2
Nagasaki, Japan (WWII)   D767.25.N3
Nagumo, Chuichi, Vice Adm. (Japan: 1926-89 period)   DS890.N23
Namur area (Bel.)   DH801.N2-29
Nanking, China   DS796.N2
Naples, It. (kingdom & later)   DG840-855
National characteristics (Ger.)   DD76
National Home & Vets' Admin. (U.S.: gen.)   UB383
National security (gen.)   UA10.5
National War College (U.S.: Wash., D.C.)   U412
Nationalities & the war (WWII: U.S.: by name)   D769.8.F7.A-Z (for Indians
                                                SEE D810.I5)
Nationalities (WWI: U.S.)   D570.88.A-Z
Nationalities (WWII: population transfers: gen.)   D820.P7
Nationalities (WWII: U.S.)   D769.88.A-Z   940.5315+
Nationalsozialistische Deutsche Arbeiter-Partei (Ger.: 1930-45: gen.)   DD253.25
Nationalsozialistische Frauenschaft   DD253.58
Naturalized subjects in belligerent lands (WWI)   D639.N2-3
Naturalized subjects (WWII: in belligerent countries: by place)
                              D810.N3.A-Z (SEE D753.8 for Japanese-Am's. in
                              U.S., D769.8.A6 for alien enemies in the U.S.)
Naturalized subjects (WWII: in belligerent countries: gen.)   D810.N2
Nauru (Pleasant Island)   996.85

NAUTICAL almanacs & yearbooks   VK7-8
Nautical craft & types   623.82   VM, VM145
Nautical engineering & seamanship   623.8   VM (architec.), VK (navig.)
Nautical instruments (gen.)   VK573   623.894, .863
Nautical instruments (misc.)   VK584.A-Z
Nautical life (merchant marine: pop. titles)   VK149
Nautical lifesaving (by area)   VK1321-1424
Nautical pilots & piloting (gen. hist's.)   VK1515   623.8922, .892209
Nautical tables (gen.: inclu. azimuth)   VK563
NAVAL ADMINISTRATION   VB
Naval administration (Asia)   VB99-113
Naval administration (Australia)   VB121   359.60994
Naval administration (by country)   VB21-124
Naval administration (Can.)   VB26
Naval administration (civil sections)   VB170-187
Naval administration (Eur.)   VB55-96
Naval administration (Fr.)   VB71   359.60944
Naval administration (G.B.)   VB57   359.60941, .30941
Naval administration (gen.: pubn. 1801-1970)   VB145   359.6, .3
Naval administration (Ger.)   VB73   359.60943, .30943
Naval administration (It.)   VB79   359.60945
Naval administration (Japan)   VB105   359.60952, .30952
Naval administration (New Z.)   VB122.5
Naval administration (Rus.)   VB85   359.60947
Naval administration (U.S.)   VB23   359.60973
Naval air forces & warfare   359.94 (SEE 358.4 for titles before 1989)   VG90-95
Naval & military life & customs (WWII: U.S.)   940.548373   U766, V736
Naval & submarine ops. (WWI)   D580-595
Naval & submarine ops. (WWII)   D770-784   940.545
NAVAL ARCHITECTURE & marine engineering   VM
Naval architecture & shipbuilding   VM, VM1-565 (SEE ALSO V750-995+ for
          construction & armament of warships), VM142-148 (gen.)   623.81
Naval architecture (hist.)   VM15-124
Naval architecture (hist.: 19th c.)   VM19
Naval architecture (hist.: 20th c.)   VM20
Naval architecture (hist.: modern: gen.)   VM18
Naval armament (installation)   V960
Naval armor & ordnance   359.3251   V900-905, V950-980, VF, VF23 (U.S.)
Naval armor (places besides U.S.)   V905.A-Z
Naval armor testing (U.S.)   V913
Naval arms & ordnance (gen.: U.S.)   VF353
Naval artillery (design)   623.418   VF320-325, VF323 (U.S.)
Naval artillery equipment (U.S.)   VF323
Naval aviation (Ger.)   VG95.G3
Naval aviation (Japan)   VG95.J3
Naval aviation (U.S.)   VG93-94   358.40973
Naval aviation units   359.943

NAVAL BASES & STATIONS (in Fr.)   359.70944
Naval bases & stations (in G.B.)   359.70941-70942
Naval bases & stations (in Ger.)   359.70943
Naval bases & stations (in It.)   359.70945
Naval bases & stations (in Japan)   359.70952
Naval bases & stations (in New Z.)   359.70993
Naval bases & stations (in Philip.)   359.709599
Naval bases & stations (in Rus.)   359.70947
Naval bases & stations (in U.S.)   359.70973
Naval bases, ports, docks, etc. (Australia)   VA716   359.70994
Naval bases, ports, docks, etc. (G.B.)   VA459
Naval bases, ports, docks, etc. (Ger.: gen.)   VA516.A1   359.70943,
                940.4530943 (WWI), .54530943 (WWII)
Naval bases, ports, docks, etc. (Japan. Imper. Navy)   VA656   359.70952,
                940.54530952 (WWII)
Naval bases, ports, docks, etc. (U.S.)   VA67-68
Naval bases (WWI)   940.453+   D581-589
Naval bases (WWI: in G.B.)   940.45341
NAVAL BASES (WWII)   940.5453+   D769.54-542 (U.S.), D770-784 (other lands)
Naval bases (WWII: in Fr.)   940.545344
Naval bases (WWII: in G.B.)   940.545341
Naval bases (WWII: in Ger.)   940.545343
Naval bases (WWII: in It.)   940.545345
Naval bases (WWII: in Japan)   940.545352
Naval bases (WWII: in U.S.)   940.545373
Naval bases (WWII: in U.S.: Calif.)   940.5453794
Naval bases (WWII: in U.S.: Calif.: S.F. Bay Area)   940.54537946
Naval bases (WWII: in U.S.: Calif.: San Diego)   940.5453794985
Naval bases (WWII: in U.S.: Va.)   940.5453755
Naval bases (WWII: U.S.: by location)   D769.542.A-Z
Naval bases (WWII: U.S.: gen.)   D769.54   940.545373
Naval biography (collective)   V61   359.00922
Naval biography (places except U.S.: by person's name after country name)
                V64.x2.A-Z
Naval biography (U.S.: collective)   V62   359.00922
Naval cemeteries (U.S.)   VB303-304
Naval ceremonies   359.17   V310
Naval Chaplain Corps (WWII: U.S.)   D769.59
Naval chaplains (gen.)   VG20   359.347
Naval clothing & personal equipment (overall)   VC280-285
Naval coaling stations (U.S.: gen.)   VA73   359.70973, .750973
Naval command and leadership   VB200-205
Naval construction battalions (WWII: U.S.)   D769.55-555
Naval construction maintenance (WWII: U.S.: gen.)   D769.554
Naval construction maintenance units (WWII: U.S.:by#)   D769.555.1st-
Naval contracts (supplies: U.S.)   VC267.U6-7
Naval crimes (except U.S.)   VB855.A-Z
Naval crimes (G.B.)   VB855.G7
Naval crimes (Ger.)   VB855.G3
Naval crimes (Japan)   VB855.J3
Naval crimes (U.S.)   VB853
Naval demobilization   359.29   VB277, UA917
Naval desertion (U.S.)   VB873

Naval design   623.81   VM, V750-995 (warships), VM15-20 (hist.),
                      VM21-124 (by place), VM23 (U.S.), VM57 (G.B.),
                      VM146 (metal ships), VM156 (theory), V750, V765, V800
Naval design (components & details)   623.814   VM, VM156
Naval discipline   VB840-845   359.13
Naval districts (U.S.: by #)   VA62.7.1st+
Naval districts (U.S.: gen.)   VA62.5   359.70973
Naval drills (Asia: gen.)   VD270
Naval drills (seamen: by country or area: includes watch, station, quarter, fire)
                                                              VD160-302
NAVAL EDUCATION & training (gen.)   V400   359.007
Naval education (Asia: gen.)   V625
Naval education (Eur.: gen.)   V500
Naval education (G.B.: gen.)   V510   359.0071141, .50941, .550941, .007041
Naval education (Ger.: gen.)   V570   359.007043, .50943
Naval education (Japan: gen.)   V640   359.007052, .0071152, .50952, .550952
Naval education (U.S.: gen.)   V411   359.0071073, .0071173, .50973,
                                                    .550973
Naval engineering & seamanship   623.8   VM, VK
Naval engineering (civil: U.S.)   VG593
Naval equipment & supplies (gen.: for ships)   VC270   359.8
Naval facilities (bases, docks, artificial harbors, etc.: design)   623.64
                      V220-230, VA69-750 (by place), VA67-70 (U.S.), VM301
Naval flags (G.B.)   V305.G7
Naval flags (Japan)   V305.J3
Naval flags (U.S.: inclu. marine)   V303
Naval forces & divisions (WWII: U.S.: by name)   D769.52.A-Z
Naval forces & warfare   359   V-VM, V27-55, V101-109
Naval fuel (gen.: ALSO costs etc.)   VC276.A1   359.83, 623.874, .415
Naval gunnery practice (places except U.S.)   VF315.A-Z
Naval handbooks (seamen's: places besides U.S.)   V115.A-Z
Naval health, hygiene, & sanitation (gen.)   VG470
NAVAL HISTORY (1453-)   D215
Naval history (1801-1914/20)   D362
Naval history (20th c.)   D436   359.409, 904.7, 359.47
Naval history (Australia)   DU112.4   359.00994
Naval history (Can.)   F1028.5   359.00971
Naval history (China: 20th c. & 1912-49)   DS775.5
Naval history (Den.: 19th-20th c.)   DL154.7
Naval history (Dutch E. Ind.)   DS637
Naval history (Fin.)   DL1040-1042
Naval history (Fr.)   DC49-53
Naval history (Fr.: 19th-20th c.)   DC53
Naval history (Fr.: 20th c.)   DC368
Naval history (Fr. Indoch.)   DS545
Naval history (G.B.)   DA70-89
Naval history (G.B.: 20th c.)   DA89   359.00941, .4741
Naval history (Ger.)   DD106   359.00943, .4743
Naval history (Greece)   DF775
Naval history (India)   DS443
Naval history (It.: gen.)   DG486   359.00945
Naval history (Japan: 1868+)   DS839.7   359.00952, .4752
Naval history (Japan: gen.)   DS839   359.00952
Naval history (Malta)   DG990.7
Naval history (Nor.)   DL456

```
Naval history (Philip.)        DS672
Naval history (Pol.)           DK417.7
Naval history (Pol.)           DK4177-4178
Naval history (Port.)          DP551
Naval history (Rum.)           DR225
Naval history (Rus.-Jpn. War, 1904-5)        DS517.1
Naval history (Rus.: 1917-)    DK59      359.00947
Naval history (Scan., N. Eur., Fin.)     DL53
Naval history (Swe.)           DL656
Naval history (Thai.)          DS574
Naval history (U.S.)           E182      359.00973, .4773
Naval history (U.S.: 20th c.)  E746      359.00973, .4773
Naval history (world)          D27       359, 904.7
Naval hospital corps (gen.)        VG310
Naval hospitals (places except U.S.)     VG430.A-Z
Naval hospitals (U.S.: by area or state)  VG424.A-Z
Naval inspection          359.63      VB220-225
Naval installations (hist. & geog. works)    359.709+
Naval intelligence (G.B.)      VB231.G7    359.34320941
Naval intelligence (gen.)      VB230   359.3432
Naval intelligence (Ger.)  VB231.G3    359.34320943
Naval intelligence (U.S.)  VB231.U6-7      359.34320973
Naval justice (admin. of)      VB790-925
Naval justice (places besides U.S.)      VB795.A-Z
NAVAL LAW          VB350-785
Naval law (Asia: gen.)      VB700
Naval law (Australia)       VB775
Naval law (by area or country)     VB360-785
Naval law (Can.)        VB370-379
Naval law (China)       VB710-719
Naval Law (Eur.: gen.)      VB530
Naval Law (FR.)         VB570-579
Naval Law (G.B.)        VB590-599 (PREFER KD6128-6158)     343.4101
Naval Law (Ger.)        VB580-589
Naval law (Japan)       VB730-739       343.5201
Naval law (New Z.)      VB777
Naval law (Rus.)        VB650-659
Naval law (U.S.)        VB360-369 (PREFER KF7345-7375)
NAVAL LIFE & CUSTOMS       V720-743
Naval life & customs (modern)      V735-743
Naval life & customs (modern: G.B.)      V737      359.10941
Naval life & customs (modern: Ger.)      V739      359.10943
Naval life & customs (modern: Japan)     V743.J3
Naval life & customs (modern: misc. countries)    V743.A-Z
Naval life & customs (modern: Rus.)      V741      359.10947
Naval life & customs (modern: U.S.)      V736      359.10973
Naval living conditions (training or perm. bases)    359.1292
Naval machine guns (special by name)   VF410.A3-Z
Naval maintenance (Asia: gen.)     VC230
Naval maintenance (Eur.: gen.)     VC160
Naval maintenance (gen.)       VC10      359.6
Naval maintenance (U.S.: gen.)     VC20      359.60973
Naval medical biography (U.S.: indiv.)     VG227.A2-Z
Naval medical services (by place)      VG121-224
Naval medical services (gen.)      VG115      359.345, .72, 616.98024
```

Naval mobilization   359.28   VA48, VA77-750, VA77 (U.S.)
Naval museums & exhibitions (by country)   V13.A2-Z   359.00740+
Naval mutiny (by ship)   VB867.A-Z
Naval nurse corps (gen.)   VG350   359.345, 610.7349, .7361, 616.98024
Naval observations (wartime)   V701-716 (PREFER D-F areas)
Naval officers (except U.S.)   VB315.A-Z
Naval officers' clubs (U.S.)   VC383   359.3460973
Naval officers' clubs (U.S.: by state)   VC384.A-W
Naval officers' handbooks (U.S.)   V133
NAVAL OPS. (hist's.: gen.)   359.409   V27-55
Naval ops. (Sp. Civil War, 1936-39)   DP269.3-35
Naval ops. (U.S. Navy. Office of: reports)   VA52.A7-79
Naval ops. (WWI)   D580-595   940.45
Naval ops. (WWI: Australia)   940.45994   D589.A
Naval ops. (WWI: G.B.)   940.45941   D581-582, VA458
Naval ops. (WWI: Ger.)   940.45943   D581-582
Naval ops. (WWI: U.S.)   940.45973   D589.U5-8
NAVAL OPS. (WWII)   D770-784
Naval ops. (WWII: Australia)   940.545994   D779.A8, DU112.4
Naval ops. (WWII: Can.)   940.545971   D779.C2, F1028.5
Naval ops. (WWII: Fr.)   940.545944   D779.F8, DC53, DC368
Naval ops. (WWII: G.B. Royal Navy)   940.545941-545942   D771-772,
                D767 (Pac.), DA89, DA89.1.A-Z (biog's.), DA566.5 (20th c.)
Naval ops. (WWII: Ger.)   940.545943   D771-772, DD106
Naval ops. (WWII: It.)   940.545945   D775, DG486
Naval ops. (WWII: Japan)   940.545952   D777, VA653, DS890.A-Z (biog.)
Naval ops. (WWII: misc. countries: by place)   D779.A-Z
Naval ops. (WWII: New Z.)   940.5459931 (SEE ALSO .545993 for earlier titles
                prior to 1989)   D779.N45
Naval ops. (WWII: U.S.: U.S.N., Marines, Coast Guard)   940.545973   D773-774,
                D769.45-598 (fleets etc.), E746

NAVAL ORDNANCE & arms (gen.)   VF350
Naval ordnance & arms (manufacture: U.S.)   VF373
Naval ordnance (Asia: gen.)   VF99
Naval ordnance (by country or place)   VF21-124
Naval ordnance drills (by place)   VF160-302
Naval ordnance (engineering)   623.8251   VF, VF21-124 (by place),
                VF23 (U.S.), VF350-355
Naval ordnance (Eur.: gen.)   VF55
Naval ordnance material (besides U.S.)   VF395.A-Z
Naval ordnance material (gen.)   VF390   623.418
Naval ordnance (nonperiodical collections)   VF7
Naval ordnance (special overall)   VF147
Naval personnel (admin.: U.S.)   VB258   359.610973
Naval petty officers' handbooks (U.S.)   V123
Naval prisons & prisoners (gen.)   VB890   344.03548
Naval projectiles (gen.)   VF480   359.8251, 623.451
Naval propaganda & psychological warfare   359.3434   UB275-277
Naval provisions & subsistence (countries besides U.S.)   VC355.A-Z
Naval provisions & subsistence (U.S.)   VC353-354   359.810973
Naval quarters & barracks (U.S.)   VC423-424
Naval recreation & information services (gen.)   VG2020   359.346
Naval research (ordnance: places besides U.S.)   VF360.5.A-Z
Naval research (U.S.: by special establishment locale)   V394.A-Z
Naval research (U.S.: by state)   V393.5.A-W

Naval Reserve & Women's Reserve (WAVES: WWII: U.S.)   D769.597
Naval Reserve Officers' Training Corps (U.S.: N.R.O.T.C.)   V426   359.2232
Naval reserves (U.S.: Calif.: gen.)   VA100   359.3709794
Naval reserves (U.S.: gen.)   VA80   359.370973
Naval resources (preparation, eval., preserv.)   359.21
Naval schools (Ger.: by name or place)   V574.A7-Z
NAVAL SCIENCE   359   V
Naval science (19th c.)   V51   359.009034
Naval science (20th c.)   V53   359.00904, .40904
Naval science (ancient hist.)   V29-41   359.00901
Naval science (by region or country)   V55.A-Z   359.47+
Naval science (collected works: monographic)   V15-17
Naval science (gen.)   V, V1-995+   359, 623.8
Naval science (gen.: pubn. thru 1800)   V101
Naval science (gen.: pubn. 1801+)   V103
Naval science (history, antiquities, & biog.: gen., during peace & war)   V25-64 (SEE
                            ALSO D-F #s for specific countries, wars, etc.)
Naval science (medieval hist.)   V43-46   359.00902
Naval science (misc. services: medical etc.)   VG
Naval science (modern hist.: 17th-20th c.)   V47-53+   359.00903
Naval science, navigation, & naval architecture   V   359, 623, 629
Naval science, navigation, & shipbuilding   V-VM
Naval science (pop. works)   V107   359
NAVAL SEAMEN (by area or country)   VD21-124
Naval seamen (G.B.: Eng. & Wales)   VD59
Naval seamen (G.B.: N. Ire.)   VD63
Naval seamen (G.B.: Scot.)   VD61
Naval seamen (gen. hist.: enlisted way of life etc.)   VD15   359.338, .12
Naval seamen (Ger.: by locality)   VD74.A-Z
Naval seamen (U.S.: by state)   VD24.A-W
Naval services (misc.)   VG
Naval shipbuilding (hist.: Asia: gen.)   VM99   623.8095
Naval shipbuilding (hist.: by area or country)   VM21-124
Naval shipbuilding (hist.: Eur.: gen.)   VM55   623.8094
Naval shipbuilding (instruc.: gen.)   VM165   623.8107
Naval signaling (U.S.)   V283
Naval small arms (U.S.)   VD363   359.8240973
Naval stations & shore facilities (countries besides U.S.)   VC416.A-Z
Naval stations & shore facilities (Ger.)   VC416.G3
Naval stations & shore facilities (U.S.: Calif.)   VC415.C2
Naval stations & shore facilities (U.S.: Fl.)   VC415.F5
Naval stations & shore facilities (U.S.: Haw.)   VC415.H2

NAVAL STATUS (Asia)   VA620-667
Naval status (Asia: misc. countries)   VA667.A-Z
Naval status (Australia)   VA710-719
Naval status (Can.)   VA400-402
Naval status (Eur.)   VA450-619
Naval status (Fr.)   VA500-509
Naval status (G.B.)   VA452-467
Naval status (Ger.)   VA510-519
Naval status (It.)   VA540-549
Naval status (Japan)   VA650-659
Naval status (New Z.)   VA720-729
Naval status (Rus.)   VA570-579
Naval status (S.Am.)   VA415-445
Naval status (U.S.)   VA52-395
Naval status (U.S.: gen.)   VA50   359.030973, .4773
Naval status (world: gen.)   VA10   359, .03
Naval status (worldwide: place by place)   VA49-750+
Naval stores & supplies (G.B.)   VC265.G7
Naval strategy (gen. special)   V165
Naval strategy (gen.: pubn. 1801+)   V163   359.03, .43
Naval submarines (diesel- & electric-powered: engineering)   623.82572
Naval submarines (units)   359.3257 (SEE ALSO .933 after 1988)
                    V857-859, V858 (U.S.), V859.A-Z (other countries),
                    VA65.A-Z (U.S.: by name), VM365-367 (construc.)
Naval supplies & stores (gen.)   VC260   359.8, .62
Naval surgeons (U.S.)   VG263
Naval tactics (gen. particular)   V169
Naval target practice (gen.)   VF310   623.553
Naval telegraph (U.S.)   VG73   359.4150973
Naval telephone (U.S.)   VG83
Naval training ships (U.S.: by name)   V436.A-Z
Naval training stations (U.S.: by place)   V434.A-Z
Naval transport (U.S.)   VC533
Naval underwater teams (U.S.: inclu. demolition)   VG87   359.9840973
Naval uniforms (insignia, service, etiquette, etc.)   359.14   VC300-345
Naval uniforms (U.S.: gen.)   VC303   359.140973, .81
Naval uniforms, badges, shoes, etc.   VC300-345
Naval vessels (auxiliary: fleet trains, repair & supply ships, etc.)   V865
                    623.826, 359.326
Naval vessels (misc., non-major: inclu. landing craft)   V895
Naval vessels, Unarmored   V870
Naval War College (U.S.)   V420   359.550973, .0071173
Naval warrant officers (besides U.S.)   VB309.A-Z
Naval weapons systems   VF347
Naval welfare services (places besides U.S.)   VG2005.A-Z
Naval yards & stations (G.B.)   VA460   359.70941
Naval yards & stations (U.S.: gen.)   VA69   359.70973, 623.830973
NAVIES (America)   V55.A65   359.477, .1812
Navies (Asia)   V55.A75   359.475
Navies (Europe)   V55.E8   359.474
Navies (gen. hist.)   V27   359.009, .409, .47
Navies (of the world: gen.)   VA40   359, .03, .009, 623.82509
Navies (organiz. & world status)   VA

NAVIGATION, Aerial   629.13251
Navigation & merchant marine   VK
Navigation, Marine (gen. hist's.: modern: inclu. merch. marine)   VK18
Navigation, Marine (instruction: G.B.: inclu. merch. marine)   VK457
Navigation, Marine (science: hist.)   VK549   527.094, 387.155
Navigational aids, Marine (electronic)   623.893   VK560
Navigational aids, Marine (radar & microwave)   623.8933   VK560-561, VG76-78
Navigational aids, Marine (radio: beacons, compasses, loran, radio, etc.)
                                                623.8932   VK560-561, VG76-85
Navigational aids, Marine (sonar & other sound-ranging)   623.8938   VK388,
                                                VK560, VM480-480.5

Navy base hospitals (WWII: U.S.: by #)   D807.U85.1st-
Navy clubs (U.S.)   V66
Navy frogmen (besides U.S.)   VG88.A-Z
Navy mobile base hospitals (WWII: U.S.: by #)   D807.U87.1st-
Navy yards, shore facilities, stations, etc.   VC412-425
Nazi Party (Ger.: 1930-45)   DD253.2-8   329.43, 324.243+, 943.086
Nazi Party (Ger.: admin. offices)   DD253.29-3
Nazi Party (Ger.: branches or gliederungen)   DD253.46-73
Nazi Party (Ger.: geog. divisions)   DD253.39-45
Nazi Party meetings (Ger.: specific by date)   DD253.28.Date
Near East (1900-18)   956.02   DS62.4
Near East & Southwestern Asia (modern)   DS62.4
Near East, Balkans, E. Mediterranean (WWII: gen.)   D766   940.53495+, 949.5+,
                                                956.03, 962.052
Near East, Turkey, Italy, Greece (WWI)   D566-569
Near East (WWII: dipl. history)   D754.N34
Nebeltruppe (WWII: Ger.)   D757.83
Negros Islands (Philip.)   DS688.N5   959.95
Nehru, Jawaharlal (India: 1901+ era)   DS481.N35
NETHERLANDS (HOLLAND)   DJ   949.2
Netherlands (1890-1948: gen. & biogs. of Queen Wilhelmina)   DJ281   949.2071
Netherlands (1914-18: WWI)   DJ285   949.2071
Netherlands (1939-48: inclu. WWII period)   DJ287
Netherlands & Dutch military ops. (WWII)   D763.N4-42   940.3492071, 949.207
Netherlands (mil. status)   UA730-739   355.0330492
Netherlands (naval status)   VA530-539
Neutral nations (WWII: gen. particip.)   940.5335   D743, D749
Neutrality, other special diplomatic history (WWI)   D611
Neutrality, small states, other special diplomatic history (WWII)   D749
Neutrals (WWI: dipl. hist.)   940.325   D611, D639.N
Neutrals (WWI: gen. particip.)   940.335   D639.N, D615 (Belgium), D611
Neutrals (WWII: dipl. hist.)   940.5325
Nevada   979.3   F836-850
New Britain (Bismarck Arch.: inclu. Rabaul)   DU553.N35
New Britain (WWII)   D767.99.N4
New Brunswick   F1041-1045   971.5
New Caledonia   DU720   993.2 (works before 1989), 993.97
New Caledonia (WWII)   D767.99.N42
New Caledonia (WWII: gen. particip.)   940.53932   DU720
New countries (post-WWI: formation)   940.31425   D651
New countries (post-WWII: formation)   940.531425

NEW ENGLAND (1865-1950)   F9   974.04-042
New England & Middle Atlantic states   974   F1-105 (New Eng.),
    F106-205 (Mid. At.), F1-15, F106
New England & Middle Atlantic states (1918-45)   974.042   F9 (New Eng.),
    F106 (Mid. At.)
New England & Middle Atlantic states (geog. & travel)   917.4   F2.3, F4,
    F9 (1865-1950), F106 (Mid.Atl.)
New England (gen. hist.)   F4   974
New England (overall)   F1-15, F4   974
New England states   F6-105   974.1-6
New Georgia (WWII)   D767.982.N34, D767.99.N44
NEW GUINEA   DU740-746   995.1-7, 995
New Guinea (geog. & travel)   919.5   DU740
New Guinea (Highlands region: 1942-45: WWII era)   995.603
New Guinea (mil. geog.)   355.4795
New Guinea (Northern coastal region: inclu. Lae, Huon Penin., Madang, Wewak, etc.:
    1942-45: WWII era)   995.703
New Guinea(overall)   995
New Guinea (Papua: naval geog.)   359.4795   VA750.N, VA667.N
New Guinea (WWI)   D578.N4
New Guinea (WWII)   D767.95   940.5426, .5395
New Hebrides   DU760   993.4, 995.95 (books after 1988)
New Hebrides (WWII)   D767.99.N46
New Hebrides (WWII: gen. particip.)   940.53934   DU760
New Ireland (Bismarck Arch.)   DU553.N4
New Ireland (WWII)   D767.99.N47
New Jersey   F131-145   974.9
New Jersey (1865-1950)   F139 (SEE D570.85.N3-31 for 1914-18 war years &
    D769.85.N3-31 for 1039-45)
New London Naval Station (U.S.: Conn.)   VA70.N5
New Mexico   F791-805, F796   978.9
New Mexico (1848-1950)   F801
New Mexico (WWII)   D769.85.N33-34
New Orleans (cruiser: U.S.: WWII)   D774.N4
New South Wales (Australia)   DU150-180, DU170   994.4
New South Wales (Australia: 1837-1950: gen.)   DU161
NEW YORK   F116-130, F119   974.7
New York (1865-1950)   F124 (SEE D570.85.N4-5 for 1914-18 war years &
    D769.85.N4-5 for 1939-45)   974.704
New York (1918-45)   974.7042   F124 (1865-1950)
New York City area (N.Y.: 1901-50)   F128.5   974.7104-043
New York City (fortifications)   UG412.N5
New York City, N.Y.   F128, F128.3   974.71
New York City, N.Y. (gen.)   F128.3
New York City, N.Y. (sections, suburbs, rivers)   F128.68.A-Z
New York City, N.Y. (streets, bridges, railroads)   F128.67.A-Z
New York (gen.)   F119
New York National Guard (gen.)   UA360
New York (WWI)   D570.85.N4-5
New York (WWII)   D769.85.N4-5   979.7042

NEW ZEALAND   DU400-430   993.1 (PREFER 993 after 1988)
New Zealand (1908-: Dominion)   993.103 (works before 1989), 993.03+ (for titles
                                     after 1988)   DU420-421
New Zealand (1908-18)   993.031, 993.1031 (works prior to about 1989)
New Zealand (1918-45)   993.032, 993.1 (titles before about 1989), 993.1032
New Zealand & Melanesia (overall)   993 (SEE ALSO 995 for Mel. with pubn.
                                     dates after about 1988)   DU400-490+
New Zealand. Army (descrip. & hist.)   UA874.5   355.309931
New Zealand. Army (special sections)   UA874.6.A-Z
New Zealand (gen.)   DU420   993.1-1037+
New Zealand (geog. & travel)   919.31   DU411
New Zealand (lighthouses, beacons, foghorns, etc.)   VK1122.5   623.894209931
New Zealand military ops. (WWII)   D767.85
New Zealand (mil. status: gen.)   UA874.3   355.0330931
New Zealand (naval geog.)   359.4793   VA720-729
New Zealand (naval status: gen.)   VA723.A5-Z   359.0309931, .009931, .47931
New Zealand (WWI)   D547.N5
New Zealand (WWII)   D767.85-852   940.53931, .5409931, .5426, 993.1032
New Zealand (WWII: dipl. hist.)   940.5322931 (titles after 1988 may be at
                                     .532293)   D754.N45
Newfoundland   F1121-1139   971.8, .803 (1934-49)
NEWS & PROPAGANDA (WWI)   940.488   D639.P6-7, D631-633, D619.3
News & propaganda (WWI: in Ger.)   940.488943
News & propaganda (WWI: in Rus.)   940.488947
News & propaganda (WWI: in specific countries) 940.4889+
News & propaganda (WWII)   940.5488   D810.P6 (gen.),
                                     .P7.A-Z (by country)
News & propaganda (WWII: in Australia)   940.5488994
News & propaganda (WWII: in Can.)   940.5488972
News & propaganda (WWII: in China)   940.5488951
News & propaganda (WWII: in Fr.)   940.5488944
News & propaganda (WWII: in G.B.)   940.5488941-5488942
News & propaganda (WWII: in Ger.)   940.5488943
News & propaganda (WWII: in It.)   940.5488945
News & propaganda (WWII: in Japan)   940.5488952
News & propaganda (WWII: in Philip. Is.)   940.54889599
News & propaganda (WWII: in Rus.)   940.5488947
News & propaganda (WWII: in specific places)   940.54889+
News & propaganda (WWII: in U.S.)   940.5488973   D753.3
News media, censorship, etc. (WWII: G.B.)   D799.G7
News media, censorship, etc. (WWII: Ger.)   D799.G3
News media, censorship, etc. (WWII: U.S.)   D799.U6
News media (WWII: gen.)   D798
Newspapers, media, & public relns. (mil.: Japan)   UH705.J3
Newspapers, media, & public relns. (navies: besides U.S.)   VG505.A-Z
Nicaragua (post-WWI territorial ?s)   D651.N5
Nice, Fr. (1860-)   DC989
Nicholas II (Rus.: Czar, 1894-1917)   DK258
Night fighting   U167.5.N5
Nihon Kirisuto Kyodan (WWII: churches)   D810.C674
Nile River (20th c.: descrip. & travel)   DT124   962.044-045
Nitti, Francesco (It. 1900-46 period)   DG575.N5

Noncombat services (air forces)   358.4134
Noncombat services (mil.: inclu. soc. srvcs., dependent srvcs., civil activ's., etc.)
                                                                                  355.34
Non-combat services, Naval   359.34   VG1-2029+, VC10-580+
Noncombatants, pacifists, sympathizers, etc. (WWI)   940.316
Noncombatants, pacifists, sympathizers, etc. (WWII)   940.5316
Non-commissioned officers, Air force (countries besides U.S.)   UG825.A-Z
Nonexplosive agents (tear gas etc.: design)   623.459   UF780
Nonmilitary use of armed forces   UH720-725
Nordenfelt machine guns   UF620.N8
Nordenfelt ordnance   UF560-565... .N.
Norfolk Navy Yard (U.S.: Va.)   VA70.N7
Norfolk, Va.   F234.N8
Normandie (pass. ship)   VM383.N6
Normandy area (Fr.)   944.2   DC611.N841-899
Normandy (Fr.)   DC611.N841-899
Normandy (Fr.: 20th c.)   DC611.N899
NORTH Africa   961   DT160-346
North Africa (1830-1950: Eur. era)   961.03   DT176
North Africa (19th-20th c.)   DT176   961.023-03+
North Africa (Egypt & Barbary States)   DT160-177   961-962
North Africa (WWII)   D766.82   940.5361, .5423, 961.03
NORTH AMERICA   E-F1392+, E11-45, E31-45   . 970
North America (1900-)   970.05   E45, E18.85
North America (1900-18)   970.051
North America (1918-45)   970.052
North America & America   970-979   E-F
North America (gen.)   E45
North America (geog. & travel)   917   E41, E27
North America (mil. status: gen.)   UA22   355.03307
North & South America (WWII: gen.)   D768
North Atlantic Fleet (U.S.)   VA63.N8
North Atlantic (pilot & sailing guides)   VK811-814.5
North Atlantic (tide & current tables)   VK611   623.8949091631
North Carolina   F251-265   975.6
North Carolina (1865-1950)   F259
North Central states   977   F476-705, F476-590 (Old N.W.), F476-485, F591-
                                      705 (Trans-Miss.), F591-596
North Dakota   F631-645   978.4
North Dakota (WWII: Reconstruction)   D828.N9-91
North Island (New Z.)   993.12
North Pacific (pilot & sailing guides)   VK917   623.89291644-89291646
North Sea & Baltic (pilot & sailing guides)   VK815-826
North Sea & Baltic (tide & current tables)   VK615-626
North Sea (mil. status)   UA646.6   355.033016336
North Vietnam (1945-75)   DS560   959.7
North Vietnam (gen.)   DS560.6
Northcliffe, Alfred C. W. Harmsworth, 1st Viscount (G.B.: 20th c.)   DA566.9.N7
Northeast Africa (1900-74)   DT367.75   963.05+
NORTHERN Australia   DU392-398   994.29
Northern Australia (gen. & descrip.)   DU395-396
Northern Europe & Scandinavia   948   DL
Northern Europe (mil. status)   UA646.85   355.033048
Northern Europe, Scandinavia, Finland (1901-45)   DL83   948.08
Northern Expedition (China: 1926-28)   DS777.46

Northern Ireland   941.6   DA990.U45-46
Northern Ireland (WWII: dipl. history)   D754.I7
Northern Rhodesia (Zambia), Rhodesia (Zimbabwe), & Nyasaland (Malawi)
          968.9   DT858-865 (Malawi, Nyasaland, Br. Central
          Afr. Protec.), DT946-965 (Rhodesia), DT963 (Zambia)
Northern Territory (Australia)   994.29   DU392-398
Northwest Africa, Morocco, & offshore islands   964
Northwest (U.S.: Old)   F476-590   977
NORWAY   DL401-596+, DL448 (gen.)   948.1
Norway (20th c.)   DL527   948.104
Norway (20th c.: 1905-)   948.104   DL527+
Norway (1905-57: Haakon VII era)   DL530-533   948.1041-1045
Norway (1914-18)   DL531
Norway (1939-45)   DL532
Norway & Norwegian military ops. (WWII)   D763.N6-62   940.3481, 948.1041
Norway, Central & Northern   948.4
Norway (geog. & travel)   914.81-84   DL418
Norway (mil. status)   UA750   355.0330481
Norway (naval status)   VA550-559   359.0309481
Norway (WWI: dipl. hist.)   D621.S45
Norway (WWII: dipl. hist.)   940.5322481   D754.N8
Norwegian military ops. (WWII)   D763.N6
Nova Scotia   F1036-1040, F1038 (gen.)   971.6
Nuclear ops., Military (also gen. strategy)   355.43 (use .4 for post-'88 titles on
          gen. strategy)   U161-163
Nuclear warfare   358.39   UF767, U162, U165, UA
Nuclear weapons   355.825119   UG1282.A8
Nuclear weapons (design)   623.45119   UF767, UG1282.A8 or .H,
          QC773.A1 or .H
Nuremberg, Ger.   DD901.N91-97
Nuremberg Trial of Major German War Criminals (1945-46)   D804.G42
Nurse corps, Naval   VG350-355
Nurse corps, Naval (U.S.)   VG353
Nurses & nursing, Military (gen.)   UH490   355.345
Nursing & nurses, Military (besides U.S.)   UH495.A-Z
NYASALAND (Malawi, Brit. Cent. Afr. Protec.)   DT858-865

OAHU (Haw. Is.)   DU628.O3   996.93
O'Bannon (destroyer: WWII)   D774.O3
OBSERVATIONS, Military   U719-740+
Observations, Military (Russo-Jpn. War, 1904-5)   U735
Observations, Military (Sino-Jpn. War, 1937-45)   U739.8
Observations, Military (Sp. Civil War, 1936-9)   U739.5
Observations, Military (WWI)   U738
Observations, Military (WWII)   U740
Observations, Naval (Russo-Japanese War, 1904-5)   V713   952.031,
          359.4752, .4747
Observations, Naval (WWI)   V715   940.45-453
Observations, Naval (WWII)   V716   940.545-5459
Obstacles (mil. engineering)   UG375   355.544
Occupation & government, Military   355.49   D802 (WWII)
Occupation, Military (WWI: Rhineland)   D650.M5
Occupational rehabilitation of veterans (by occup.)   UB366.A-Z

OCCUPIED countries (WWII: gen. particip.)   940.5336   D802.A2
Occupied territories (WWI: by country)   D623.A3-Z
Occupied territories (WWI: gen.: includes laws) D623.A2
Occupied territories (WWII: by country, area, etc.)   D802.A3-Z
Occupied territories (WWII: events, laws, etc.)   D802
Occupied territories (WWII: gen.)   D802.A2
Oceania   993-996   DU
Oceania, Australia, New Zealand   DU   990-996
Oceania (mil. status)   UA875   355.03309
Oceania or Pacific Islands (WWII)   D767.9-99
Oceania (Pacific Ocean)   DU   990-996, 909.0964
Oceanica & other misc. areas   990 (SEE ALSO 995 for gen. works after about 1988)
                    DU, DU28.3
Oceanography, Military (gen.)   V396   359.982, 551.46, 620.4162
Oceanography, Military (places besides U.S.)   V396.5.A-Z
Odessa & Crimea areas (Rus.)   947.717   DK511.C7
Odessa, Rus.   DK651.O2
Odessa, Uk.   DK508.95.O33
Offenses & crimes, Military   UB780-789
Offenses & crimes, Naval   VB850-880
OFFICERS, Air force (gen.)   UG790   358.41331-41332
Officers, Air force (Ger.)   UG795.G3
Officers, Air force (U.S.)   UG793
Officers' clubs & messes, Military (U.S.)   UC743
Officers' clubs & messes, Naval   VC380-385
Officers, Commissioned & warrant   355.332   UB407-415
Officers, Commissioned & warrant (navies)   359.332   VB307-315
Officers' handbooks, Naval (places besides U.S.)   V135.A-Z
Officers, Military (G.B.)   UB415.G7   355.3320941
Officers, Military (Ger.)   UB415.G3   355.3320943
Officers, Military (inclu. appt., promo., retire.)   UB410-415
Officers, Military (U.S.)   UB412-414   355.3320973
Officers, Naval (G.B.)   VB315.G7   359.3320941
Officers, Naval (inclu. appt., promo., rank, retire., etc.)   VB310-315
Officers, Naval (Japan)   VB315.J3
Officers, Naval (Rus.)   VB315.R9
Officers, Naval (U.S.: gen.)   VB313   359.3320973, .3310973
Officers, Non-commissioned (air: U.S.: inclu. airmen)   UG823
Officers, Warrant (mil.: gen.)   UB407
Officers, Warrant (naval: U.S.)   VB308   359.3320973
Ohio   F486-500, F491   977.1
Okinawa (Japan)   DS895.O4   952.81
Okinawa (WWII)   D767.99.O45
Oklahoma   F691-705   976.6
Old Northwest (U.S.: 1865-1950)   F484.5   977.03
Oman   DS247.O6-68
Ontario (Can.)   F1056-1059.7, F1058 (gen.)   971.3
Operational equipment, Air force (airplanes, bombs, guns, vehicles)   UG1200-1405
Optical instruments & tools, Artillery   UF849
Optimum ship routing   VK570
Oran, Alg.   DT299.O7

Orders, General (Rus. military: offic. compil's.)   UB657.A5
Orders, passes, field correspondence (mil. sci.)   UB280-285
Orders, passes, field correspondence (naval admin.)   VB255
Orders, Special (Rus. military: collec's. & compil's.)   UB657.A6-7
Orders, Transmission of (navies)   V270   359.27, .85
ORDNANCE   355.82   UF520-780, U800-823+
Ordnance, Air force   358.4182   UG1270-1275
Ordnance, Air force (gen.)   UG1270-1275   358.4182, 623.45+
Ordnance, Aircraft (design)   623.7461   UG1270-1275, UF530-537
Ordnance & arms, Naval (in sum)   VF350-375
Ordnance & arms, Naval (manufacture)   VF370-375
Ordnance & small arms   UF520-537   355.82, 623.4+, .44
Ordnance & small-arms research (U.S.)   UF526.3
Ordnance & small arms (U.S.)   UF523   355.820973
Ordnance battalions etc. (WWII: U.S.: by #)   D769.743.1st-
Ordnance battalions etc. (WWII: U.S.: gen.)   D769.74
Ordnance drills, Naval (Eur.: gen.)   VF215
Ordnance (engineering & design)   623.4   UF520-910+, UF520-525 (gen.),
        UF523 (U.S.), VF (naval), VF1-580, VF21-124 (by place), VF23 (U.S.)
Ordnance facilities, Naval   359.73   VF380-385
Ordnance laws (U.S.: PREFER KF7335   UF133
Ordnance magazines & facilities (navies)   VF380-385
ORDNANCE MATERIAL (by type, mark #, ed. date, etc.)
        UF560-565.A-Z.A-Z(II-IV) etc.
Ordnance material (countries besides U.S.)   UF565.A-Z
Ordnance material (Fr.)   UF565.F8
Ordnance material (G.B.)   UF565.G7
Ordnance material (gen.)   UF560   355.82+, 623.4+
Ordnance material (Ger.)   UF565.G3
Ordnance material (Japan)   UF565.J3
Ordnance material (misc.)   VF420
Ordnance material (navies: U.S.)   VF393
Ordnance material (Rus.)   UF565.R9
Ordnance material (U.S.: gen.)   UF563   355.820973, 623.40973
ORDNANCE, NAVAL   VF   359.82, 623.8251
Ordnance, Naval (Asia)   VF99-113
Ordnance, Naval (Australia)   VF121
Ordnance, Naval (Eur.)   VF55-96   359.82094
Ordnance, Naval (Fr.)   VF71
Ordnance, Naval (G.B.)   VF57   359.820941
Ordnance, Naval (gen. hist's.)   VF15   359.8209
Ordnance, Naval (gen. pubns. 1801+)   VF145   359.82
Ordnance, Naval (Ger.)   VF73   359.820943
Ordnance, Naval (handbooks & manuals: gen.)   VF150
Ordnance, Naval (It.)   VF79
Ordnance, Naval (Japan)   VF105   359.820952
Ordnance, Naval (misc. topics)   VF580
Ordnance, Naval (Rus.)   VF85
Ordnance, Naval (U.S.)   VF23   359.820973, 623.82510973
Ordnance proper   UF560-780
Ordnance proper (navies)   VF390-395
Ordnance proper (navies: U.S.: documents)   VF393.A1-3
Ordnance proper (navies: U.S.: gen.)   VF393.A7-Z
Ordnance research, Naval (U.S.)   VF360.3
Ordnance stores, accounts, etc. (gen.)   UF550

Ore carriers   VM457   623.8245, 387.544
Oregon   979.5   F871-885
ORGANIZATION (air forces)   UG770-1045
Organization & personnel (cavalry: inclu. specific units)   357.043
Organization & personnel (infantry)   356.189
Organization & personnel (marines)   359.963   VB21-124
Organization & personnel, Naval   359.3   VA, VA50 (U.S.), VB21-124
Organization (armor & cavalry: gen.)   UE10
Organization (artillery forces)   UF10
Organization (infantry: gen.)   UD10
Organization (mil. maint. & transport: by country)   UC20-258
Organization (mil. medical: inclu. services)   UH400-485
Organization (mil. personnel: hist. & geog. treatment)   355.309
Organization (naval maintenance: by place)   VC20-258
Orientals (in Calif.)   F870.O6
Orientals (in U.S.)   E184.O6
Orkney Islands (Scot.)   DA880.O5-6
Orphans, children, similar noncombatants (WWI)   940.3161   D639.C4
Orphans, children, similar noncombatants (WWII)   940.53161   D810.C4
Osaka, Japan   DS897.O8   952.183
Oslo, Nor. (area)   948.2   DL581
Oslo, Nor. (Christiana)   DL581   948.2
Oxford and Asquith, Herbert Henry Asquith, 1st Earl of (G.B.: 20th c.)   DA566.9.O7
Oxford University (WWI)   D547.O7

P.O.W. CAMPS & internment centers (WWI: in G.B.)   940.47241-47242   D627.G7
P.O.W. camps & internment centers (WWI: in Ger.)   940.47243   D627.G3
P.O.W. camps & internment centers (WWI: in Rus.)   940.47247   D627.R9
P.O.W. camps & internment centers (WWII: run by G.B.)   940.547241   D805.G7
P.O.W. camps & internment centers (WWII: run by Ger.)   940.547243   D805.G3
P.O.W. camps & internment centers (WWII: run by Japan)   940.547252   D805.J3
P.O.W. camps & internment centers (WWII: run by Rus.)   940.547247   D805.R9
P.O.W. camps & internment centers (WWII: run by U.S.)   940.547273   D805.U5-6
P.T. boats (gen.)   V830
PACIFIC aerial ops. (WWII: U.S. bombing survey)   D785.U63
Pacific (air war geog.)   358.41479
Pacific, Asiatic, & other colonies (WWI: Ger.: gen.)   D577
Pacific Coast & Far West (U.S.: geog. & travel)   917.9   F851
Pacific Coast & Great Basin (U.S.: 20th c.)   979.03   F786, F852
Pacific Coast (naval geog.)   359.4779   VA50
Pacific Coast (S.Am.)   F2213
Pacific Coast (U.S.: fortifications)   UG411.P2
Pacific Fleet (U.S.)   VA63.P2
Pacific Islands, German (post-WWI territorial ?s)   D651.P2
Pacific Islands (mil. status: by island or group name)   UA876.A-Z
Pacific Islands (smaller misc.: by name)   DU950.A-Z
Pacific Islands (WWII: gen.)   D767.9   940.5426, .54439, .544952, .54539, .545952, .5352
Pacific Islands (WWII: misc. by name)   D767.99.A-Z
Pacific (marine mil. geog.)   359.96479+   VE123, VA730
Pacific (naval geog.)   359.479   VA710-750, VA730
Pacific, North Central (inclu. Hawaiian Is.)   996.9
Pacific Northwest (1859-1950)   F852   979.5

PACIFIC OCEAN & islands (lighthouses, beacons, foghorns, etc.) VK1123-1124
                                                     623.8942099+, .894209164+
Pacific Ocean & islands (lighthouses, beacons, foghorns, etc.: lists)
                                     VK1214-1223   623.894409164
Pacific Ocean & islands (pilot & sailing guides)   VK915-956
Pacific Ocean & islands (tide & current tables)   VK715-756
Pacific Ocean & misc. (geog. & travel)   919   DU22
Pacific Ocean area (maps & atlases)   912.9   G2860-3012
Pacific Ocean areas (misc.: geog. & travel)   919.6
Pacific Ocean (Loran tables)   VK561.P3
Pacific Ocean (Oceania: gen.)   DU28.3   990, 990.09, 909.0964
Pacific, Southwest Central (plus isolated S.E. islands)   996.1
Pacific States & Alaska   F851-915+   979
Pacific Theatre & Asia (WWII: gen.)   D767   940.5425-5426
Pacifists (WWI)   940.3162   D613, UB342.A-Z (by place)
Pacifists (WWII)   940.53162   D810.C82, UB342.A-Z (by place)
Packing & shipment (mil. supplies)   UC277
Paderewski, Ignacy Jan (Pol.: 1918-45 era)   DK4420.P3
Page, Walter Hines (U.S.: 1865-1900 era)   E664.P15
Pago Pago, Samoa   DU819.P3
Pakistan (Bengal: East & West)   DS485.B39-493   954.14
Pakistan (pre-1947), India, Ceylon, Burma, etc.   DS401-498   954
Palaces (London, Eng.)   DA689.P17
Palau & Caroline Islands   996.6   DU560-568, DU5630565
Palau Islands (Pelew Is.: WWII)   D767.99.P4
Palawan (Philip.)   DS688.P15   959.94
Palembang, Sumatra   DS646.15.P3
PALESTINE (640-1917)   956.9403   DS124-125, DS125.5 (WWI yrs.)
Palestine (19th-20th c.)   DS125   956.9403-9404
Palestine (1914-18: WWI)   DS125.5   956.9403-9404
Palestine (1919-48: Brit. control)   DS126   956.9404
Palestine (geog. & travel)   915.694   DS107.3
Palestine, Israel, & the Jews   DS101-151   956.94, 909.04924
Palestine (post-WWI territorial ?s)   D651.P3
Palestine (post-WWII territorial ?s)   D821.P3
Palestine (WWI)   D568.7
Palestine (WWII: Israel)   D766.7.I7
Palestine (WWII: Reconstruction)   D829.P3
PAMPHLETS, MINOR WORKS (20th c.)   D416
Pamphlets, minor works (20th c.: diplomacy)   D457
Pamphlets, minor works (20th c.: politics and diplomacy)   D450
Pamphlets, minor works, addresses (Rus.: 1925-53)   DK267.3.1925-1953
Pamphlets, minor works (Jpn. for. relns.)   DS847
Pamphlets, minor works (Jpn. polit. & dipl. hist.)   DS844
Pamphlets, minor works, sermons (Rus. Rev., 1917-21)   DK265.17
Pamphlets, minor works, sermons (Sp. Civil War, 1936-39)   DP269.17
Pamphlets, minor works, sermons (WWI)   D525
Pamphlets, minor works, sermons (WWII)   D743.9
Pamphlets, minor works (WWI: peace)   D646
Pamphlets, minor works (WWI: U.S.)   D570.15
Pamphlets, minor works (WWII: peace)   D816.5
Pamphlets, minor works (WWII: Reconstruction)   D826
Pamphlets, minor works (WWII: U.S.)   D769.15

PANAMA   F1561-1577, F1566   972.87
Panama (1903-52)   F1566.5   972.8705-052
Panama (1904-45)   972.87051   F1566.5
Panama Canal & Zone   972.875   F1569.C2
Panama Canal (fortifications)   UG412.P3
Panama Canal (pilot & sailing guides)   VK970.P2
Panama (mil. geog.)   355.477287 (SEE ALSO .47862)
Panama (mil. status)   UA607.P3
Panama (naval geog.)   359.477287   VA407.P
Panay (Philip.)   DS688.P2   959.95
Panceltism   D448.5
Pangermanism   D447
Panlatinism   D448
Pannonia   DJK77
Panslavism   D449
Panslavism (Eastern question: 19th c.)   D377.3-5
Panzer divisions (by #)   D757.56.1st-
Panzer regiments (by #)   D757.57.1st-
Panzer troops (by author, division, name, etc.)   D757.55.A-Z
Panzer troops (WWII: Ger.)   D757.54-57
Panzer troops (WWII: Ger.: gen.)   D757.54
Papal States   DG791-800+
Papal States (modern)   DG796
Papen, Franz von (Ger.: 1918-48 era)   DD247.P5
Papen, Franz von (WWI: Ger. spy in U.S.)   D619.5.P2
Papua & New Guinea (gen.: inclu. Brit. terr. & Port Moresby, Owen Stanley Mts., Lae,
     Salamaua, etc.)   DU740   995, 995.3
Papua New Guinea & New Guinea region   995.3
Papua New Guinea (inclu. Kokoda Trail, Port Moresby, Owen Stanley Range, etc.:
     1942-45: WWII era)   995.303
Papua Territory (1942-45: WWII period)   995.403
Parachute & airborne troops (gen.)   UD480
Parachute troops (WWII: Brit.)   D759.63
Parachute troops (WWII: Fr.)   D761.7
Parachute troops (WWII: Ger.)   D757.63
Parachute troops (WWII: U.S.)   D769.347
Paraguay   F2661-2699   989.2
Paraguay (1938-)   F2689   989.2071-2072
Paraguay (gen.)   F2681
Paraguay (mil. status)   UA634-636   355.0330892
Paraguay (WWII: dipl. hist.)   940.5322892 (might ALSO be with Neutrals at
                    .5325892)   D754.P
Paratroops   356.166   UD480-485, UD483 (U.S.), UG630-635
Paris, Fr. (1914-21)   DC736
Paris, Fr. (1922-)   DC737+   944.360816
Paris, Fr. (area)   944.36   DC701-790, DC707 (gen.), DC735 (1871-1914),
                    DC737 (1914-)
Paris, Fr. (WWII)   D762.P3   944.360816
Passenger ships (engineering)   623.8243   VM381-385, VM383.A-Z (by ship
                    name), VM385.A-Z (by co.)
Passenger ships (naval architec.)   VM381-383
Passes, orders, field correspondence (mil. sci.: gen.)   UB280
Patrols & reconnaisance, Naval   V190   359.413

PAY & allowances (Ger. Navy)   VC181
Pay & allowances (marines)   VE490   359.9664
Pay & allowances (mil.: G.B.)   UC185
Pay & allowances (U.S. Navy)   VC50-65   359.135, .640973
Pay & benefits (air forces)   UG940-945   358.41135, .4164
Paymaster's Dept. (U.S. Army)   UC70-75
PEACE conferences (WWII: gen.)   D814.56
Peace efforts (WWI: preserve or restore)   940.312   D613, D641-644+ (armistice)
Peace efforts (WWII: preserve or restore)   940.5312   D749, D748-754
Peace (WWI)   D642-651   940.312, .3141
Peace (WWI: gen.)   D644   940.312
Peace (WWII)   D814-821   940.5314, .532+
Peace (WWII: gen.)   D815
Peace (WWII: gen. spec.)   D816
Peace (WWII: special topics)   D820.A-Z
Peiping, China (Peking)   DS795   951.156
Peking, China   951.156   DS795
Penelope (WWII: cruiser)   D772.P4
Pennsylvania   F146-160, F149   974.8
Pennsylvania Ave. (Washington, D.C.)   F203.7.P4
Pennsylvania (1865-1950)   F154
Pensacola, Florida   F319.P4
Pensacola Naval Air Station (Flor.)   VG94.5.P4
Pensions, disability benefits, etc. (naval admin.)   VB280-285   359.115-1156
Pensions, Survivors' (mil.)   UB400-405
Pensions, Survivors' (naval)   VB340-345
Pensions, Veterans'   UB370-375   331.25291355 (PREFER), 355.1151, .64
PERIODICALS & ASSOCIATIONS (air forces)   UG622   358.005-006
Periodicals & associations (armor & cavalry)   UE1
Periodicals & associations (arms & armor: hist.) U799
Periodicals & associations (artillery)   UF1
Periodicals & associations (Ger.: 1918-)   DD233
Periodicals & associations (infantry)   UD1
Periodicals & associations (marine navig. & merch. marine)   VK1
Periodicals & associations (mil. engineering)   UG1
Periodicals & associations (military: in English)   U1   355.005-006
Periodicals & associations (military medical services)   UH201
Periodicals & associations (military: U.S.)   UA23.A1.A-Z
PERIODICALS & ASSOCIATIONS (NAVAL architec.: Eng.)   VM1
Periodicals & associations (naval medical services)   VG100
Periodicals & associations (naval ordnance)   VF1
Periodicals & associations (naval: G.B.)   VA452
Periodicals & associations (naval: Ger.)   VA510
Periodicals & associations (naval: in English)   V1   359.005, .006+
Periodicals & associations (naval: U.S.)   VA49   359.005-007+
Periodicals & associations (WWI: prisons)   D627.A1   940.472+
Periodicals & associations (WWII: prison)   D805.A1
Periodicals & documents (Ger.: Nazi Party)   DD253.2
Periodicals & yearbooks (U.S.)   E171
Periodicals, associations, collections (Ger.: 1930-45)   DD253.A1
Periodicals, associations, yearbooks (20th c.)   D410
Periodicals, associations, yearbooks (It.: 1919-45)   DG571.A1

Periodicals (mil. admin.)   UB1
Periodicals, serials, collections (WWII)   D731
Periodicals (U.S. Marines)   VE23.A1.A-Z   359.96097305
Periodicals (WWII: by country)   D805.A3-Z.A1-19
Periscopes (submarine architec.)   VM367.P4
Persia (Iran)   955   DS251-325, DS272
Persia (1794-1925: Kajar dynasty)   DS298-316   955.04-051
Persia (geog. & travel)   915.5   DS258
Persia (post-WWI territorial ?s)   D651.P4
PERSONAL accounts, Allied (WWI)   940.481+   D640, D570.9 (U.S.)
Personal accounts, Allied (WWII)   940.5481+   D811
Personal accounts, American (WWII: U.S.)   940.548173
Personal accounts, Australian (WWII)   940.548194
Personal accounts, Axis (WWII)   940.5482+   D811
Personal accounts, British (WWII)   940.548141
Personal accounts, Central Power (WWI)   940.482+   D640, D531-540
Personal accounts, English (WWII)   940.548142
Personal accounts, French (WWII)   940.548144
Personal accounts, German (WWII)   940.548243
Personal accounts, Italian (WWII)   940.548245
Personal accounts, Japanese (WWII)   940.548252
Personal accounts, Russian (WWII)   940.548147
Personal accounts (Russo-Fin. War, 1939-40: collective)   DL1102
Personal accounts (Russo-Fin. War, 1939-40: individual)   DL1102.5
Personal accounts (Russo-Polish War, other Polish conflicts of 1918-21)
                                                          DK4406.5
Personal accounts (Sino-Jpn. Confl., 1937-45: collections)   DS777.5314
Personal accounts (Sino-Jpn. Confl., 1937-45: indiv. by name) DS777.5315.A-Z
Personal accounts (Sp. Civil War, 1936-39)   DP269.9
Personal accounts (WWI) D640 (SEE ALSO D570.9 for U.S. soldiers)   940.481+
Personal accounts (WWII)   D811 (SEE ALSO DA-F country #'s for biographies &
                              memoirs)   940.5481-5482+
Personal accounts (WWII: collections)   D811.A2
Personal accounts (WWII: individual: by name) D811.A3-Z
Personal accounts (WWII: noncombatants: by name)   D811.5.A-Z
Personal accounts (WWII: U.S.)   D769.9 (PREFER D811)
PERSONNEL administration, Military (civilian & mil.)   355.61   UB160-165,
                              UB180-197, UB410-415 (officers), UB320-338
Personnel administration, Naval (civilian & mil.)   359.61   VB257-258.5
Personnel administration (naval sci.: gen.)   VB257   359.61
Personnel, Air force   UG1130-1185
Personnel & administration (air forces: U.S.)   UG773
Personnel, Civilian (mil. admin.: U.S.)   UB193
Personnel, Civilian (naval admin.: gen.)   VB180
Personnel transport (navies)   VC550-555
Personnel transport vehicles (land: mil. design)   623.7472
Perth, Australia   DU378   994.11
Perth, Australia (area)   994.11   DU378
Peru   F3401-3619, F3431   985
Peru (1919-)   F3448   985.0631-0632
Peru (gen.)   F3431
Peru (mil. status)   UA637-639
Pétain, Henri Philippe (Fr.: 1871-1940 era)   DC342.8.P4

Peter I Karadordevic (Serbia: ruler, 1903-18: ALSO gen. works on period)
                                                      DR2030
Peter I (Yug.: King, 1903-21: ALSO covers era)   DR360
Peter II (Yug.: monarch, 1934-45)   DR1297
Petrograd, Rus. (1801-)   DK568
Petroleum industry (defense)   UA929.95.P4
Petty officers' handbooks (gen.)   V120
Pharmacy services, Military   UH420-425
Philadelphia Navy Yard (U.S.: Penn.)   VA70.P5
Philadelphia, Penn.   F158   974.811
PHILIPPINE ISLANDS   DS651-689, DS655, DS668   959.9
Philippine Islands (1898-1946: U.S. era)   959.903   DS679-686.4, DS685
Philippine Islands (1901+)   DS685   959.903
Philippine Islands (1901-35)   959.9032   DS685
Philippine Islands (1935-46: Commonwealth)   DS686-686.4   959.9035
Philippine Islands (1935-44: Manuel Quezon era)   DS686.3   959.9035
Philippine Islands (1942-46: Japanese occup. [1942-45] & Osmeña rule [44-46])
                                                        DS686.4
Philippine Islands (gen.: pubn. 1801+)   DS668.A3-Z   959.9
Philippine Islands (pilot & sailing guides)   VK911   623.8929599
Philippine Islands (Sp.-Am. War, 1898: ALSO Battle of Manila Bay)   E717.7
                                                          973.8937
Philippine Islands (tide & current tables)   VK711
Philippine Islands (WWII)   D767.4   940.53599, .5409599, .5425-5426, 959.03
Philippine Sea, Battle of (1944)   D774.P55
PHILIPPINES (geog. & travel)   915.99   DS659
Philippines (mil. geog.)   355.47599
Philippines (mil. status)   UA853.P5   355.0330599
Philippines (naval geog.)   359.47599   VA667.P, VA750.P
Philippines (naval status)   VA667.P5   359.0309599
Philippines (WWII: dipl. hist.)   940.5322599 (puppet gov. might be with Axis Powers
                     at .5324599)   D754.P5
Philosophy & psychology   100-199   B-BD, BH-BJ, BF
Philosophy, Naval (e.g. theory of naval sea power)   V25
Philosophy, psychology, religion   B   100-299
Photographers, Naval   VG1010-1015
Photographic interpretation (navies)   VG1020
Photography, Ballistic (inclu. photochronography)   UF840
Photography, Military   UG476   623.72
Photography, Military (mil. engineering)   623.72   UG476
Photography (WWII)   D810.P4
Physical training (mil. sci.)   U320-325   355.54+
Physical training (navies: U.S.)   V263-264
Pictorial and graphic histories (20th c.)   D426   779.990194, 909.82
PICTORIALS (naval: U.S.)   VA59   359.3250973
Pictorials, satires, etc. (Rus. Rev., 1917-21)   DK265.15
Pictorials, satires, etc. (Sp. Civil War, 1936-39)   DP269.15
Pictorials (ships)   VM307   387.2+
Pictorials (U.S. Mil. Acad.)   U410.L3
Pictorials (U.S. Naval Acad.)   V415.L3
Pictorials (world navies)   VA42
Pictorials (WWI)   D522 (SEE ALSO D527)   940.49
Pictorials (WWII)   D743.2 (SEE ALSO D746)   940.549

Pigeons, Military (for communications: SEE ALSO D639.P45 for WWI & D810.P53
          for WWII)   UH90
Pigeons (WWII)   D810.P53
PILOT & SAILING GUIDES (Atl. Ocean: all & east: gen.)   VK810   623.8929163
Pilot & sailing guides (by area)   VK804-997
Pilot & sailing guides (C. Am.: by locality)   VK970.A-Z
Pilot & sailing guides (E. Pac. & Am. W. Coast: gen.)   VK941
Pilot & sailing guides (Pac. islands: misc.)   VK933.A-Z
Pilot & sailing guides (Pac. Ocean & islands: gen.)   VK915   623.8929164
Pilot & sailing guides (W. Atlantic: gen.)   VK959
Pilot guides & sailing directions (gen.: pubn. 1801+)   VK802   623.8922, .8929+
Pilot guides (geog. treatment)   623.89291-89299   VK804-997
PILOTING, Aerial   629.13252
Piloting & pilot guides, Nautical   623.8922   VK1500-1661, VK1523-1525 (U.S.),
                    VK1645 (gen.), VK798-803
Piloting & pilots, Nautical (by area)   VK1521-1624   623.291-89299
Piloting (gen.: mil. engineering)   623.746048 (SEE ALSO .7463 [bombers] or
          other types)   TL710+, UG670-675 (manuals), UG700-705 (tactics)
Piloting, Nautical (Asia)   VK1599-1613
Piloting, Nautical (Australia & the Pac.)   VK1621-1624
Piloting, Nautical (Eur.)   VK1555-1596   623.294
Piloting, Nautical (U.S.)   VK1523-1525   623.2973
Pilots & piloting, Nautical   VK1500-1661
Pilots & piloting, Nautical (gen.)   VK1645-1661
Pilsudski, Joseph (Pol.: 1918+ biog.)   DK440.5.P5
Pilsudski, Jozef (Pol.: 1918-45 time)   DK4420.P5
Pioneer Corps (WWII: G.B.)   D760.P5
Pioneer troops   UG530-535
Pistols & revolvers (gen.)   UD410   355.8243, 623.443
Pistols & revolvers (marines)   VE390   359.968243
Piston & turboprop airplanes   629.133343
Planes, Fighter (design)   623.7464   TL685.3, TL686.A-Z (by manufac.
          or model), UG1242.F5
Planes, Reconnaisance (mil. design)   623.7467   UG1242.R4
Planning, Military (U.S.)   U153
Plans, Attack & defense (countries except U.S.)   UA925.A-Z
Plating, Armor (naval sci.: special type)   V907.A-Z
Plumbing (naval architec. & engin.)   VM501
Poetry, satire, etc. (WWI)   D526-526.7 (PREFER PQ-PT)
Poetry, satire, etc. (WWII)   D745-745.7 (PREFER PQ-PT)
Poetry, satire, etc. (WWII: languages besides Eng., Fr., Ger.)   D745.7.A-Z
POLAND   DK401-441+ (older titles prior to 1976-77), DK414, DK4010-4800
          (titles 1970+?), DK4140   943.8
Poland (1795-1918)   DK434.9 (older), DK4349-4395   943.803
Poland (1795-1918: foreign rule)   943.803   DK434.9, DK4349, DK439
Poland (1864-1918)   DK4380   943.803
Poland (20th c.)   DK4382
Poland (1914-18: WWI)   DK439 (older works), DK4390   943.803
Poland (1915-18: Austrian occupation)   DK4392

Poland (1918-: Republic: inclu. wars of 1918-21)   DK440   943.804
Poland (1918-45)   DK4397-4420   943.804
Poland (1918-45: gen.)   DK4400
Poland (1918-26)   DK4403.5
Poland (1918-21: wars, inclu. Russo-Polish of 1919-20)   DK4404-4409
Poland (1926-39)   DK4409.5
Poland (1926: Coup)   DK4409.4
Poland (1939-)   943.805   DK441
Poland (1939-45: WWII era)   DK441, DK4410-4420 (newer titles)   943.8053
Poland (1939-45: WWII era: gen., inclu. Ger. occup.)   DK4410
Poland (1939-41: Russ. occup.)   DK4415
Poland (1945-)   DK443
Poland & Polish military ops. (WWII)   D765-765.2+
Poland (gen.)   DK4040
Poland (gen. history, culture, etc.)   DK404
Poland (gen.: pubns. 1801+)   DK414.A3-Z, DK4140 (newer works)
Poland (geog. & travel)   914.38   DK407 (1867-1945)
Poland (mil. status)   UA829.P7   355.0330438
Poland (post-WWI territorial ?s)   D651.P7
Poland (WWII: gen. particip.)   940.53438   D765, DK441
Poland (WWII: mil. hist.)   940.5409438   D765
Poles (in other lands)   DK4122
Police, Air force   UG1020-1025
Police, Military (by country)   UB825.A-Z
Police, Naval (besides U.S.)   VB925.A-Z
Policy & status, Naval   359.03+ (country #s follow)   VA
Policy, Military   355.0335+
Policy, Military (gen.)   UA11
POLISH military history (gen.)   DK4170
Polish military ops. (1918-21, inclu. Russo-Polish conflict)   DK4406
Polish military ops. (WWII: gen.)   D765   940.53438, .5409438, 943.8053
Polish question   DK4182
Polish Republic (1918-39)   943.804   DK440, DK4400
Polish troops (WWII: French Army)   D761.9.P6
Political prisoners (WWI: U.S.)   D570.8.P7
Political prisoners (WWII: U.S.)   D769.8.P7 (SEE ALSO D805.U5 for
                                    prisons & prisoners)
Political science   320-329   J
Political science, international law   J   320-329, 341
POLITICS & DIPLOMACY (20th c.)   D440-460
Politics & diplomacy (20th c.: collected works)   D442
Politics & diplomacy (20th c.: gen. special: projected, possible wars, other polit.
                                    events)   D445
Politics and diplomacy (20th c.: gen.: world pol., Triple Alliance & Entente, etc.)
                    D443   940.5, 320.904, 327.09
Politics & diplomacy (1919-39)   D727   327.0904, .4, 909.822-23, 940.51-52
Politics & diplomacy (Africa: inclu. colonialism)   DT31-38   320.96, 327.6
Politics & diplomacy (Asia: gen.)   DS33.3   320.95, 327.5+
Politics & diplomacy (Austria)   DB46-49
Politics & diplomacy (Egypt: gen.)   DT82
Politics & diplomacy (Fr.)   DC55-59
Politics & diplomacy (Ger.)   DD110-120
Politics & diplomacy (Ger.: 1918-)   DD240
Politics & diplomacy (Indon.: gen.)   DS638
Politics & diplomacy (It.: gen.)   DG491   320.945, 327.45+

Politics & diplomacy (Japan: gen.)   DS841
Politics & diplomacy (Korea)   DS910
Politics & diplomacy (Libya: gen.)   DT227
Politics & diplomacy (Middle East, SW. Asia)   DS63   320.956, 327.56+
Politics & diplomacy (Montenegro: 1918-45)   DR1887
Politics & diplomacy (Morocco: gen.)   DT317
Politics & diplomacy (N. Zea.: gen.)   DU421
Politics & diplomacy (Neth.: gen.)   DJ142
Politics & diplomacy (Palestine, Jews)   DS119-119.8
Politics & diplomacy (Philip.: gen.)   DS672.8   320.9599, 327.599
Politics & diplomacy (Pol.: 1918-45)   DK4402
Politics & diplomacy (Port.: gen.)   DP556
Politics & diplomacy (Rus.)   DK60-63
Politics & diplomacy (Rus.: 1894-1939)   DK63
Politics & diplomacy (Rus.: 1939-)   DK63.3
Politics & diplomacy (Rus.: gen.)   DK61   320.947
Politics & diplomacy (Sp.)   DP84
Politics & diplomacy (Sp.: 1931-39: gen.)   DP257
Politics & diplomacy (Swe.: gen.)   DL658.A3-Z 320.9485, 327.485
Politics & diplomacy (Swit.: gen.)   DQ69
Politics & diplomacy (Thai.)   DS575
Politics & diplomacy (Tunisia: gen.)   DT257
Politics & diplomacy (Yug.: 1918-45)   DR1291
Politics & diplomacy (Yug.: 1918-45: gen.)   DR367.A1
POLITICS (China: 20th c. & 1912-49)   DS775.7
Politics (Czech.: 1939-45)   DB2208.7
Politics (Eastern Europe: gen.)   DJK42
Politics (Eng.: gen.)   DA40
Politics (Eng.: modern)   DA42
Politics (Formosa: 1895-1945)   DS799.716
Politics (Georgian S. S. R.: gen.)   DK676.5-6
Politics (Pol.)   DK4179
Politics (Rus. armed forces, 1917-21)   DK265.9.A6
Politics (Serbia: 1918-45)   DR2036
Politics (Serbia: gen.)   DR1972
POLITICS (U.S.: 20th c.)   E743   320.973, .904
Politics (U.S.: 1920 Pres. campaign)   E783
Politics (U.S.: gen.)   E183   320.973
Politics (U.S.: 1932 Pres. race)   E805
Politics (U.S.: 1936 Pres. race)   E810
Politics (U.S.: 1940 Pres. race)   E811
Politics (U.S.: 1944 Pres. race)   E812
Politics (Ukr.: gen.)   DK508.554
Polynesia & other Pacific areas   996   DU510 (Poly.: gen.)
Polynesia (gen.)   DU510 (SEE DU520-950 for specific island groups, individual
                       islands, atolls, etc.)   996, 996.1-4, .9
Pomerania (Pol.)   DK4600.P67
Ponape (Carolines)   DU568.P7
Pontoons & pontoon gear (naval architec.)   VM469.5
Popular histories (20th c.)   D422
Popular histories (20th c.: Europe) D425
Population transfers (WWII)   D820.P7-72
Population transfers (WWII: by nationality)   D820.P72.A-Z
Population transfers (WWII: Jews)   D820.P72.J

PORT Arthur, Siege of (Rus.-Jpn. War, 1904-5)   DS517.3
Port of London (Eng.)   DA689.P6
Port Royal, Jam.   F1895.P6
Ports, bases, docks, etc. (G.B. Royal Navy: gen.)   VA459.A1   359.70941,
                        940.4530941 (WWI), .54530941 (WWII)
Ports, bases, docks, etc. (Ger. Navy: by name) VA516.A3-Z
Ports, bases, docks, etc. (U.S. Navy: gen.)   VA67   359.70973,
                940.4530973 (WWI), .54530973 (WWII), .545973 (WWII)
Portsmouth Navy Yard (U.S.: N.H.)   VA70.P8
Portsmouth, Eng. (Royal Naval Barracks)   V522.5.P6
PORTUGAL   DP501-900+   946.9
Portugal (20th c.: gen.)   DP672   946.904
Portugal (1910-)   946.904   DP675
Portugal (1910-: Republic)   DP675   946.904
Portugal (1914-18: WWI)   DP677   946.9041
Portugal (1919-)   DP680   946.9041-9042
Portugal (1919: Revolution)   DP678
Portugal (1926-68)   946.9042   DP680
Portugal (mil. status)   UA760-769
Portugal (post-WWI territorial ?s)   D651.P75
Portugal (WWII: gen. particip.)   940.53469   D754.P8, DP680
Portuguese (in Brazil)   F2659.P8
Position finders (artillery)   UF853   623.46
Possessions of the U.S. (WWI)   D570.87.A-Z
POST exchanges & canteens, Military   UC750-755
Post-war era & Reconstruction (WWI)   D652-659   940.3144, .34-39
Post-WWI reconstruction   940.3144   D652-659, D653 (gen.),
                        D657-658 (U.S.), D659.A-Z (other places)
Post-WWI territorial questions   940.31424   D650, D651.A-Z
Post-WWII reconstruction   940.53144   D824-829, D825 (gen.),
                D827-828 (U.S.), D829.A-Z (by country, nationality, etc.)
Post-WWII territorial questions   940.531424
Postal service, Military   UH80-85   355.69
Postal service, Naval   VG60-65   359.341
Posters (WWII)   D743.25 (newer works), D746.5 (older works)   769.4994+
Power-driven craft (naut. engineering)   623.823   VM315
Power plants (marine engineering)   623.87   VM600-779, VM600,
                VM623 (U.S.), VM657 (G.B.), VM673 (Ger.), VM705 (Japan)
Power systems, Electric (naval sci.)   VC418
Powerplants (naval design)   623.8147   VM731+
Prague, Cz. (20th c.)   DB2629
Prague, Cz. (WWII)   D765.55.P7
Presbyterian Church (WWII)   D810.C68
Preservation of maps & charts   UA997
Press & public relns. (mil.)   UH700-705
Press & public relns. (navies)   VG500-505
Press, publicity, censorship (WWI: U.S.)   D632
Press, radio, censorship, propaganda & publicity (WWII: SEE ALSO D746.5 for
                        posters, D753.3 for enemy propaganda in U.S., D810.P6-7
                        for propaganda elsewhere)   D798-799

PRIMARY SOURCES (20th c.: collections) D411
Primary sources (20th c.: diplomacy) D451
Primary sources (20th c.: politics and diplomacy) D441
PRIMARY SOURCES, DOCUMENTS (Australia) DU80
Primary sources, documents (Australia: military status) UA871
Primary sources, documents (Bulg.) DR52
Primary sources, documents (Calif. army reserves) UA91
Primary sources, documents (China: 20th c. & 1912-49) DS773.83
Primary sources, documents, collections (WWII: Reconstruction) D824
Primary sources, documents (Czech.: 1918-) DB2185
Primary sources, documents (Den.) DL103
Primary sources, documents (Dutch E. Ind.) DS613
Primary sources, documents (Eastern Europe: politics) DJK41
Primary sources, documents (Egypt) DT43
Primary sources, documents (Eng.) DA25
Primary sources, documents (Far East, E. & SE.Asia) DS503
Primary sources, documents (Fin.) DL1005
Primary sources, documents (Fin.: 20th c.) DL1066
Primary sources, documents (Fin.: 1939-45) DL1090
Primary sources, documents (Formosa: 1895-1945) DS799.693
Primary sources, documents (Fr.) DC3
Primary sources, documents (Fr.: 1871-1940) DC334
Primary sources, documents (Fr. Indoch.) DS532
Primary sources, documents (G.B.: War Dept., Parliament, other re military)
  UA648
Primary sources, documents (Ger. infantry) UA713.A1-5
Primary sources, documents (Ger.: 1918-) DD234
Primary sources, documents (Ger.: for. relns. & politics) DD110
Primary sources, documents (Hawaiian Is.: 1900-59) DU627.5.A1-5
Primary sources, documents (India, pre-1947 Pak.) DS403
Primary sources, documents (It.) DG403
Primary sources, documents (Italo-Eth. War, 1935-6) DT387.8.A1-7
Primary sources, documents (Japan) DS803, DS840
Primary sources, documents (Jpn. military) UA846
Primary sources, documents (Korea) DS901
Primary sources, documents (N.Y. army reserves) UA361
Primary sources, documents (naval: G.B.) VA453
Primary sources, documents (naval: Ger.) VA512
Primary sources, documents (Nor.) DL403
Primary sources, documents (Palestine & the Jews) DS102
Primary sources, documents (Philip.) DS653
Primary sources, documents (Pol.) DK402
Primary sources, documents (Pol.: 1918-45) DK4397
Primary sources, documents (Port.: 20th c.) DP670
Primary sources, documents (Port.: dipl. & polit. hist.) DP555
Primary sources, documents (Rum.) DR203
Primary sources, documents (Rum.: 1881-1914) DR252
Primary sources, documents (Rum.: 1914-27) DR260
PRIMARY SOURCES, DOCUMENTS (RUS. military) UA771
Primary sources, documents (Rus.) DK3, UA773.A1-5
Primary sources, documents (Rus.: 1894-1917) DK251
Primary sources, documents (Rus.: 1918-) DK266.A3
Primary sources, documents (Rus.: for. relns.) DK65
Primary sources, documents (Rus.: politics & diplomacy) DK60
Primary sources, documents (Russo-Fin. War, 1939-40) DL1096

Primary sources, documents (Serbia: 1918-45)   DR2033
Primary sources, documents (Sino-Jpn. Confl., 1937-45) DS777.52
Primary sources, documents (Sp.: 1931-39)   DP251
Primary sources, documents (Sp.: 1936-39: Civil War)   DP269.A2-55
Primary sources, documents (Sp.: dipl. & polit. hist.) DP83
Primary sources, documents (Swe.)   DL658.A2
Primary sources, documents (Swit.)   DQ3
Primary sources, documents (Swit.)   DQ68
Primary sources, documents (U.S.)   E173
Primary sources, documents (U.S.: 20th c.)   E740.5
Primary sources, documents (Viet.)   DS556.2
Primary sources, documents (WWI)   D505
Primary sources, documents (WWI: peace: collections)   D642
Primary sources, documents (WWII: collection, preservation)   D735.A1
Primary sources, documents (WWII: peace: collections: gen.)   D814
Primary sources, documents (WWII: sometimes by gov. agency, A-Z)   D735
Primary sources, documents (Yug.)   DR1288
Primary sources, documents (Yug.: 1918-45)   DR364
Prince of Wales (battleship: G.B.)   VA458.P75
Princess (aircraft carrier: WWII)   D774.P7
Prinz Eugen (cruiser, heavy: Ger.)   VA515.P73   359.32530943
PRISONER exchanges   940.473
Prisoner exchanges (WWII)   940.5473   D805
Prisoner-of-war camps & internment (WWI)   940.472   D627
Prisoner-of-war camps & internment centers (WWII) 940.5472+ (SEE ALSO .5317+
                    for post-1988 titles on internment camps)   D805
Prisoner-of-war camps (mil. life)   355.1296 (SEE ALSO 365.45)   UB800-805
Prisoners, prisons, punishments (naval)   VB890-910
Prisons, Air force   UG1040-1045
PRISONS & PRISONERS, Naval (except U.S.: by place)   VB895.A-Z
Prisons & prisoners, Naval (G.B.)   VB895.G7
Prisons & prisoners, Naval (Rus.)   VB895.R9
Prisons & prisoners, Naval (U.S.)   VB893   344.035480973
Prisons & prisoners (Sp. Civil War,   1936-39)   DP269.63-65
Prisons & prisoners (WWI: by country)   D627.A3-Z
Prisons & prisoners (WWI: gen.)   D627.A2
Prisons & prisoners (WWII: by country)   D805.A3-Z
Prisons & prisoners (WWII: gen.)   D805.A2
Prisons & prisoners (WWII: inclu. internment camps)   D805   940.5472+
Prisons, Military (U.S.)   UB803 (SEE ALSO KF7675)
Procurement & contracts, Air force (gen.)   UG1120   358.41621
Procurement (mil. supplies)   355.6212   UC263-267, HD3858-3860
Procurement (mil. supplies: countries besides U.S.)   UC265.A-Z
Procurement (naval supples &equip.)   359.6212
Procurement (naval supplies: except U.S.)   VC265.A-Z
Projectile velocities & motions (gen.)   UF820   623.51
Projectiles, Artillery   UF750-770   623.451
Projectiles, Artillery (U.S.)   UF753
Projectiles, Naval   VF480-500
Promotion & demotion (air forces)   358.41112   UB320-325, UB410-415
Promotion & demotion (mil.)   355.112   UB320+
Promotion & demotion (navies)   359.112   VB260-275, VB307-315
Promotion, discharge, recruitment, enlistment (mil. sci.: gen.) UB320   355.2, .61
Promotion, discharge, recruitment, enlistment (naval sci.: enlisted personnel: U.S.)
                    VB263   359.2230973, .3380973

Prop-driven aircraft (mil. design)   623.746042
PROPAGANDA, Allied (WWI)   940.4886
Propaganda, Allied (WWII)   940.54886
Propaganda, American (WWI: U.S.)   940.488673   D632, D639.P7.U5+
Propaganda, American (WWII: U.S.)   940.5488673   D810.P7.U6
PROPAGANDA & PSYCH. WARFARE (Ger.)   UB277.G3   355.34340943
Propaganda & psych. warfare (Japan)   UB277.J3   355.34340952
Propaganda & psych. warfare (mil. sci.: gen.: SEE ALSO BF1045.M55 & HM263 for
                indiv. & social aspects)   UB275   355.3434
Propaganda & psych. warfare (naval sci.: gen.)   VB252   359.3434
Propaganda & psych. warfare (naval sci.: U.S.)   VB253   359.34340973
Propaganda & psych. warfare (Rus.)   UB277.R9   355.34340947
Propaganda & psych. warfare (Sov.Un.)   UB277.S65   355.34340947
Propaganda & psych. warfare (U.S.)   UB276   355.34340973
Propaganda, Anti-Soviet (1925-53: by Ger.)   DK272.7.G3 (SEE ALSO
                DD255.R9)
Propaganda, Anti-Soviet (1925-53: by Japan)   DK272.7.J3
Propaganda, Anti-Soviet (1925-53: by partic. country)   DK272.7.A-Z
Propaganda, Axis (WWII)   940.54887+
Propaganda, British (WWII)   940.5488641   D810.P7.G7
Propaganda, Central Power (WWI)   940.4887
Propaganda, French (WWII)   940.5488644   D810.P7.F8
Propaganda, French (WWII: Vichy)   940.5488744   D810.P7.F8
PROPAGANDA, GERMAN   DD119.5
Propaganda, German (1933-45: by place)   DD255.A-Z
Propaganda, German (1933-45: France)   DD255.F8
Propaganda, German (1933-45: Gt. Brit.)   DD255.G7
Propaganda, German (1933-45: Rus.: SEE ALSO DK272.7.G3)   DD255.R9
Propaganda, German (1933-45: United States)   DD255.U6-7
Propaganda, German (WWI)   940.488743   D639.P7.G3, D619.3 (in U.S.)
Propaganda, German (WWII)   940.5488743   D810.P7.G3
Propaganda, Italian (WWII)   940.5488745   D810.P7.I8
PROPAGANDA, JAPANESE (1926-89: abroad: by place)   DS889.3.A-Z
Propaganda, Japanese (1926-89: China)   DS889.3.C5
Propaganda, Japanese (1926-89: G.B.)   DS889.3.G7
Propaganda, Japanese (1926-89: Indonesia)   DS889.3.I5
Propaganda, Japanese (1926-89: Philip.)   DS889.3.P5
Propaganda, Japanese (1926-89: U.S.)   DS889.3.U6
Propaganda, Japanese (WWII)   940.5488752   D810.P7.J3
Propaganda, Russian (1925-53: internal)   DK269.5
Propaganda, Russian (WWII: prior to 22 June 1941) 940.5488747   D810.P7.R9
Propaganda, Russian (WWII: after 21 June 1941)   940.5488647   D810.P7.R9
                or .S65
PROPAGANDA, SOVIET (1925-53: foreign: by country)   DK272.A-Z
Propaganda, Soviet (1925-53: France)   DK272.F8
Propaganda, Soviet (1925-53: G.B.)   DK272.G7
Propaganda, Soviet (1925-53: Ger.)   DK272.G3
Propaganda, Soviet (1925-53: Japan)   DK272.J3
Propaganda, Soviet (1925-53: U.S.)   DK272.U6-7
Propaganda (WWI: by country)   D639.P7.A-Z
Propaganda (WWI: gen.)   D639.P6 (SEE ALSO D631-633 for press)   940.488+
Propaganda (WWII: by country)   D810.P7.A-Z   940.54886-54889+
Propaganda (WWII: gen.)   D810.P6 (SEE ALSO D798-799 for press)
Propellers (marine engin.)   VM753-757   623.81473
Prophecies (WWII)   D810.P75

Propulsion & resistance (marine engin.)   VM751-759
Propulsion (naval architec. & engin.: gen.)   VM521   623.87
Protest movements (WWI)   D639.P77
Protest movements (WWII)   D810.P76
Protocols of the Wise Men of Zion (WWI: anti-Semitism)   DS145.P49-7
Provisions & subsistence, Naval (gen.)   VC350   359.81
Provisions & subsistence, Naval (Ger.)   VC355.G3
Provisions & subsistence, Naval (Japan)   VC355.J3
Provisions & subsistence, Naval (Rus.)   VC355.R9
Provost-Marshall-General's Bureau (WWII: U.S.: gen.)   D769.77
PRUSSIA (1871-1918: gen.)   DD448
Prussia (1918-45)   DD452-454
Prussia (1918-45: gen.)   DD452
Prussia (1918-33)   DD453
Prussia (1933-45)   DD454
Prussia, East & West (post-WWI territorial ?s)   D651.P89-9
Prussia, East (Pol.)   DK4600.P77
Psychiatry, Military (U.S.: inclu. mental health)   UH629.3
Psychical phenomena (WWI)   D639.P8
Psychological warfare & propaganda (countries except U.S.)   UB277.A-Z
Psychological warfare & propaganda (mil.)   355.3434 (ALSO use 355.34 for
          propag.)   UB275-277, UB276 (U.S.), UB277.A-Z (except U.S.)
Psychological warfare & propaganda (naval sci.: places besides U.S.)   VB254.A-Z
PUBLIC administration   350-359   H-J
Public figures (20th c.: collective biog.: men)   D412.6   920.02, 909.82,
                              940.50922
Public figures (Ger.: 1918-48: men)   DD244
Public information & relations (mil.)   355.342   UH700-705, UH703 (U.S.)
Public opinion (WWI: by place)   D639.P88.A-Z
Public opinion (WWI: gen.)   D639.P87
Public opinion (WWII: by country)   D810.P85.A-Z
Public opinion (WWII: gen.)   D810.P8
Public relations & information (navies)   359.342   VG500-505
Public relations & press (mil.: places besides U.S.)   UH705.A-Z
Public utilities (defense)   UA929.95.P93
Publications, Graduate (U.S. Naval Acad.)   V415.K1-4
Puerto Rico   F1951-1983, F1971   972.95
Puerto Rico (1898-1952)   F1975   972.9504-9505
Puerto Rico (gen.)   F1971
Puerto Rico (WWII)   D769.87.P7
Puget Sound area (Wash.)   979.77   F897.P9
Puget Sound (Wash.)   F897.P9
Pumps, Marine (engin.)   VM821
Punishment & enforcement, Military   355.1332
Punishment, Corporal (U.S.)   UB813
Punishments (naval conduct)   359.13325
Pursuit & fighter forces & ops. (air)   358.43   UG1242.F5, UG633 (U.S.),
          UG635.A-Z (places except U.S.), TL685.3, TL686.A-Z (by co. or name)
Pyrenees (Fr.)   DC611.P981-992
Pyrenees region   944.89   DC611.P981-992
Pyrotechnic signal devices (mil. engineering)   623.7313   UG580, UF860

QUAKERS (WWII: Society of Friends)   D810.C65
Qualifications (naval personnel)   359.2234
Qualifications, Service (mil.)   355.2234
Quarter drills, Naval (Can.: also watch, station, other)   VD163
Quartermaster depots (WWII: U.S.: by #)   D769.73.1st-
Quartermaster's Dept. (U.S.)   UC30-34   355.8
Quarters & barracks, Air force (U.S.)   UG1143
Quarters & barracks, Marine (U.S.: gen.)   VE422   359.96710973
Quarters & barracks, Naval (gen.)   VC420-425, VC420   359.71
Quarters, Military (barracks, p.o.w. camps etc. on-site)   355.71   UC400-405
Quebec   971.4   F1051-1055
Queen Mary (pass. ship)   VM383.Q4
Queen's Westminster and Civil Service Rifles (WWI)   D547.Q3
Queens, princesses, etc. (20th c.: collective biography)   D412.8
Queensland (Australia)   DU250-280   994.3
Queensland (Australia: gen.: inclu. descrip.)   DU260-270
Queensland (Australia: inclu. Great Barrier Reef)   994.3   DU250-280
Quick-firing ordnance   UF560-565... .Q.F.
Quisling, Vidkun (Nor.: 20th c.)   DL529.Q5

RABAUL, New Brit. (WWII)   D767.99.N415.R32
Race problems (WWII)   D810.R3
RACES & ETHNOGRAPHY (Australia)   DU120-122
Races & ethnography (China)   DS730-731
Races & ethnography (Ger.)   DD74
Races & ethnography (N. Zea.)   DU423
Races & ethnography (Philip.)   DS665-666
Races & ethnography (Pol.: by specific element)   DK4121.5.A-Z
Races & ethnography (Pol.: gen.)   DK4120
Races & ethnography (Rus.)   DK33
RACES, ETHNOGRAPHY, RELIGIOUS GROUPS (Arg.)   F3021.A-Z
Races, ethnography, religious groups (Arg.: gen.)   F3021.A1
Races, ethnography, religious groups (Bolivia)   F3359.A-Z
Races, ethnography, religious groups (Brazil)   F2659.A-Z
Races, ethnography, religious groups (C.Am.)   F1440.A-Z
Races, ethnography, religious groups (Calif.)   F870.A-Z
Races, ethnography, religious groups (Calif.: gen.)   F870.A1
Races, ethnography, religious groups (Can.)   F1035.A-Z
Races, ethnography, religious groups (Chile)   F3285.A-Z
Races, ethnography, religious groups (Jam.)   F1896.A-Z
Races, ethnography, religious groups (Mex.)   F1392.A-Z
Races, ethnography, religious groups (N.Y.)   F130.A-Z
Races, ethnography, religious groups (Paraguay)   F2699.A-Z
Races, ethnography, religious groups (Peru)   F3619.A-Z
Races, ethnography, religious groups (S.Am.)   F2239.A-Z
Races, ethnography, religious groups (U.S.: gen.)   E184.A1
Races, ethnography, religious groups (Urug.)   F2799.A-Z
Races, ethnography, religious groups (U.S.)   E184.A-Z   973.04+
Races, ethnography, religious groups (W.Ind.)   F1629.A-Z
Races. ethnography, religious groups (Cuba)   F1789.A-Z
Racial minorities (WWI: soldiers)   940.403   D547.N4 (blacks: G.B.),
                                   D570.8.I6 (Indians:U.S.), D639.N4 (blacks)

RADAR & electronics, Air force (G.B.) UG1425.G7
Radar & electronics, Air force (gen.) UG1420 623.7348, .7467
Radar equipment, Naval VF530 623.557
Radar (mil. engineering) 623.7348 UG612 (gen.), UG612.3 (U.S.),
 UG612.5.A-Z (other places), UG612.5.G7 (G.B.), VG76-78
Radar, Military (G.B.) UG612.5.G7
Radar, Military (gen.) UG612 623.7348
Radar, Military (places except U.S.) UG612.5.A-Z
Radar, radio, & wireless telegraph (navies: besides U.S.) VG78.A-Z
Radar, radio, etc. (WWII) D810.R33
Radar, radio, sonar, etc. (naval architec.: U.S. Navy) VM480.3
RADIO & radar (mil. engineering) 623.734 UG611-612.5
Radio, media, & public relns. (mil.: Ger.) UH705.G3
Radio, Military (gen.) UG611
Radio, radar, & wireless telegraph (navies: U.S.) VG77 623.85640973
Radio, radar, sonar, etc. (naval architec.: G.B.) VM480.5.G7
Radio services, Military (by place except U.S.) UH859.A-Z
Radio services, Military (gen.) UH850
Radiobroadcasting services, Military (U.S.: gen., inclu. armed forces) UH855
Radiobroadcasting, Military (Fr.) UH859.F8
Radiobroadcasting, Military (Ger.) UH859.G3
Radiobroadcasting, Military (Japan) UH859.J3
Radiotelegraphy (mil. engineering) 623.7342 UG600-607, VG76-78
Raids (mil. sci.) U167.5.R34
RAILROAD artillery (gen.) UF490
Railroad troops UG520-525
Railroads, armored trains, etc. (mil. engineering) UG345 623.63
Railroads (defense) UA929.95.R3
Railroads (mil. transp.: gen.) UC310 623.63, 355.83
Railroads (mil. transp.: U.S. regions or states) UC314.A-Z
Railroads (naval transp.) VC580
Railway artillery (countries besides U.S.) UF495.A-Z
Railway artillery (Fr.) UF495.F8
Railway artillery (Ger.) UF495.G3
Railway gun cars UF655 (SEE ALSO UF563.A76, UF565) 358.22
Railway gun matériel (U.S.: handbooks) UF563.A76
Rainbow Division (WWI: U.S.) D570.3.R3
Range finders, Artillery (gen.) UF850.A2 623.46
Range tables, Artillery UF857
Range tables, Naval ordnance VF550 623.5530212
Rangers & commandos 356.167 U262
Ranging & sighting apparatus (ordnance: design) 623.46 UF848-856, VF520
Rangoon, Burma DS486.R25
Rank, appointment, promotion, retirement, etc. (mil. officers: gen.) UB410
 355.332
Rank, appointment, promotion, retirement, etc. (naval officers: gen.) VB310
 359.332, .331
Rasputin, Grigory (Rus.: 1894-1917 biog.) DK254.R3
Rathenau, Walther (Ger.: 1888-1918+ period) DD231.R3
Rations (mil.) UC710-715
Rations, Naval VC360-365
Raw materials (mil. resources) 355.24 HC110.A-Z, UA18, UA929.5+
Raw materials (naval resources) 359.24 VC260-267, VF390+
Rearguard action U215
Recoil (mil. engineering) 623.57

RECONNAISANCE & intelligence topography (mil. engineering)   623.71
                                                              UG470-474
Reconnaisance & patrols   U220   355.413, 358.45
Reconnaisance, Aerial   UG760-765   358.45
Reconnaisance battalions (WWII: U.S.)   D769.3058
Reconnaisance, Cavalry   UE360   355.413, 358.45
Reconnaissance forces, Air (inclu. antisub. work)   358.45   UG760-765,
                                                              UG1242.R4
Reconnaissance, Naval   359.413   V190
Reconnaisance planes   UG1242.R4   623.7467, 358.45
RECONSTRUCTION & post-war era (WWI: gen.)   D653
Reconstruction (Fr.: 1919-40)   DC389, D659.F8   944.0815
Reconstruction (WWI: countries outside U.S.)   D659.A-Z
Reconstruction (WWII)   D824-829
Reconstruction (WWII: gen.)   D825   940.53144
Reconstruction (WWII: outside U.S.: by country, nationality, etc.)   D829.A-Z
Records & accounting (marines)   VE480
RECREATION & information services, Military   UH800-910
Recreation & information services, Military (besides U.S.)   UH819.A-Z
Recreation & information services, Military (U.S. Army)   UH810-815
Recreation & information services, Naval   VG2020-2029
Recreation & information services, Naval (places besides U.S.)   VG2029
Recreation, Military (off-post)   UH900-910
Recreation services, Military (inclu. sports, arts, music, libraries, clubs, etc.)
                               355.346   UH800-910, UH800, UH805 (U.S.)
Recreation services, Naval (sports, arts, music, dancing, libraries, etc.)   359.346
                                                              VG2020-2029, UH800-910
Recreation, social work, etc. (air forces)   UG990-995
Recruiting, enlistment, etc. (air forces)   UG880-885
Recruiting literature (U.S. Marines: by date)   VE23.A6
Recruitment & enlistment, Military   355.223
Recruitment & enlistment (navies)   359.223   VB260-315
Recruitment, enlistment, promotion, discharge (mil. sci.)   UB320-325
Recruitment, enlistment, promotion, discharge (naval sci.: enlisted personnel: gen.)
                               VB260   359.223, .338, .11+
Recruits, Naval (inclu. medical & mental examinations)   VB270-275   359.2236
RED CROSS & medical services (WWI: by country)   D629.A-Z
Red Cross & medical services (WWII: by country)   D807.A-Z   940.54764-69
Red Cross (by country or region)   UH537.A-Z
Red Cross (gen.: wartime)   UH535   940.4771, .54771
Red Cross (WWII)   940.54771   D806-807
Red Cross at sea   VG457
Red Guard (Rus. Rev., 1917-21: Krasnaia Gvardiia)   DK265.9.K73
Reed, Thomas Brackett (U.S.: 1865-1900 era)   E664.R3
Refrigeration (naval sci.)   VC400   623.8535
Refrigerators, Military   UC760
Refugees (WWI)   940.3159   D637, D638.A-Z (by place)
Refugees (WWII)   940.53159   D808, D809.A-Z (by place)
Refugees, relief work, charities (WWI: by country or area)   D638.A-Z
Refugees, relief work, charities (WWII: gen.)   D808   940.5477

REGISTERS & lists (naval reserves: U.S.: Calif.)   VA102
Registers & lists (WWI: decorated, dead, wounded: by country)   D609.A3-Z
Registers & lists (WWII: dead, wounded, decorated: by country)   D797.A3-Z
Registers & lists (WWII: dead, wounded, decorated: gen.)   D797.A2
Registers, Official & unoff. (Royal Naval Coll., Dart.)   V515.H1-5
Registers, Official (U.S. Mil. Acad.)   U410.H3-4
Registers, Official (U.S. Naval Acad.: annual)   V415.H3-39
Registers (U.S. Marines)   VE23.A33
Regulation of conduct, Naval   359.133
REGULATIONS & manuals, Air force (U.S.)   UG673
Regulations & tactics (mil. engineering: Asia: gen.)   UG270
Regulations & tactics (mil. engineering: Eur.: gen.)   UG215
Regulations, Army (Rus.)   UB655.9-656.5
Regulations, Marine (U.S.)   VE23.A25
Regulations, Naval (U.S.)   VB363
Regulations (U.S. Naval Acad.)   V415.C3-6
Rehabilitation of disabled sailors   VG478 (PREFER UB360+)
Rehabilitation of disabled veterans (gen.)   UB360   355.1156, .1154
RELIEF & WELFARE SERVICES (WWI: in Ger.)   940.477943   D638.G3, D659.G3
Relief & welfare services (WWI: in Rus.)   940.477947   D638.R9, D659.R9
Relief & welfare services (WWII: in China)   940.5477951   D809.C5
Relief & welfare services (WWII: in Fr.)   940.5477944   D809.F8
Relief & welfare services (WWII: in Ger.)   940.5477943   D809.G3
Relief & welfare services (WWII: in Japan)   940.5477952   D809.J3
Relief & welfare services (WWII: in Philip. Is.)   940.54779599   D809.P5
Relief & welfare services (WWII: in Rus.)   940.5477947   D809.R9
Relief associations (besides U.S.)   UH543-545
Relief societies (mil.: inclu. care of sick & wounded)   UH520-560   361.05, .77
Relief societies (mil.: besides U.S.: by place)   UH525.A-Z
Relief societies (mil.: U.S. by state or region)   UH524.A-Z
Relief work, refugees, displaced persons, charities (WWII)   D808-809
Relief work, refugees, displaced persons, charities (WWII: Belgium)   D809.B4
Relief work, refugees, displaced persons, charities (WWII: G.B.)   D809.G7
Relief work, refugees, displaced persons, charities (WWII: U.S.: domestic & abroad)
                                                                    D809.U5
Relief work, refugees, etc. (WWI: U.S.)   D638.U5
Religion   200-299   BL-BX
Religion (Sp. Civil War, 1936-39)   DP269.8.R4
Religion (WWII: churches)   D810.C5-68
Religion, Christianity (WWI)   D639.R4   940.478
RELIGIOUS & counseling services, Military   355.347   UH20-25
Religious & counseling services, Naval   359.347   VG20-25, VG2000
Religious & ethical questions (WWII: by country)   D744.5.A-Z
Religious groups & officials (WWI)   940.3152   D639.R4, D622 (Cath. Church)
Religious groups & officials (WWII)   940.53152   D810.C5-68
Religious officials, Military (countries except U.S.)   UH25.A-Z
Religious officials, Naval (places besides U.S.)   VG25.A-Z
Religious services (WWII)   940.5478   D810.C35-6 (chaplains), .C5 (churches:
                                gen.), .C53-68 (alphab. by denom.)

REPARATIONS & indemnity (WWI: by country)   D649.A-Z
Reparations & indemnity (WWII: by country)   D819.A-Z
Reparations (WWI)   940.31422   D648-649
Reparations (WWI: Ger.)   D649.G3
Reparations (WWII)   940.531422
Reparations (WWII: Ger.)   D819.G3
Reparations (WWII: Jp.)   D819.J3
REPORTS, Congressional (U.S. Military Academy: by date)   U410.E5
Reports, Congressional (U.S. Navy: official & others)   VA53
REPORTS, OFFICIAL & unoff. (U.S. Naval Acad.)   V415.F7
Reports, Official (army reserves: U.S.)   UA42.A1-59
Reports, Official (military medical: U.S.: monographic)   UH223.A3-39
Reports, Official (military medical: U.S.: serial)   UH223.A1-29
Reports, Official (naval maint.: U.S.)   VC25-38
Reports, Official (naval reserves: U.S.: Calif.)   VA101
Reports, Official (Royal Naval Coll., Dart.: annual)   V515.E1-49
Reports, Official (U.S. Army: War Dept., Dept. o/t Army, Adj. Gen., Inspec. Gen.,
                      etc.: annual)   UA24.A1-7
Reports, Official (U.S. Dept. Defense: formerly War Dept.)   UA23.2
Reports, Official (U.S. Marines)   VE23.A2-79
Reports, Official (U.S. Marines: annual)   VE23.A2
Reports, Official (U.S. Mil. Acad. Superinten.: annual)   U410.E1
Reports, Official (U.S. Naval Acad. Superinten.: annual)   V415.E1-4
Reports, Official (U.S. Navy Bur's. of Navigation, Personnel)   VA52.A6-67
Reports, Official (U.S. Navy Dept.)   VA52.A1-89
Reports, Official (WWI: military)   D529
Reports, Unofficial (naval maint.: U.S.)   VC39
Reports, Unofficial (naval pay etc.: U.S.)   VC64
Repression & atrocities (WWI)   940.405   D625 (gen.), D626.A-Z (by place)
Repression & atrocities (WWII)   940.5405   D803, D804.A-Z (by country)
Requisitions, Military   UC15
Rescue aircraft (mil. engineering)   623.7466
Rescue & search ops. (WWII: by country)   D810.S45.A-Z
Rescue ops., Nautical   623.8887   VK1321-1424, VK1323 (U.S.), VK1445 (gen.)
RESEARCH, Aeronautical (mil.: by company or establishment)   UG644.A-Z
Research, Aeronautical (mil.: gen.)   UG640   358.407, .40072+
Research, Aeronautical (mil.: places besides U.S.)   UG645.A-Z
Research & development (air forces equip. & supplies)   358.407
Research & development, Military   355.07
Research & development (naval equip. & supplies)   359.07   V390-395
Research & laboratories, Medical (mil.)   UH399.5-7
Research & laboratories, Naval medical   VG240-245
Research, Military   U390-395   355.07
Research, Naval (countries besides U.S.)   V395.A-Z
Research, Naval (gen.)   V390   359.07
Research (naval ordnance: gen.)   VF360   359.82072
Research, Naval (U.S.: gen.)   V393   359.070973
Research, Ordnance & small-arms   UF526
Research, Physiological (mil. hygiene)   UH627

Rewards & privileges, Military   355.134   UB430-435
Rewards, badges, brevets, medals (navies: except U.S.)   VB335.A-Z
Rewards (navies: inclu. privileges, citations, medals, etc.)   359.134   VB330-335
Reykjavik, Ice.   DL398.R5
Reynaud, Paul (Fr.: 20th c.)   DC373.R45
Rhee, Syngman (Korea: 20th c.)   DS916.5.R5
Rhine Province (Prus.)   DD491.R4-52
Rhine River (Ger.)   DD801.R7-76   943.4
Rhine River Valley   943.4   DD801.R7-76
Rhodesia   DT946-965
Ribbentrop, Joachim von (Ger.: 1918-48 era)   DD247.R47
Rifle & artillery ranges (U.S.)   U303
RIFLES   355.82425   UD390-395
Rifles & carbines (design)   623.4425   UD390-395
Rifles, carbines, etc. (infantry)   UD390-395   355.82425, 623.4425
Rifles, carbines, etc. (navies)   VD370   359.82425
Rifles (infantry: by type)   UD395.A-Z
Rifles (marines)   VE370   359.9682425, 623.4425
Riga, Rus.   DK651.R5
Rigging & gear, Nautical (anchors, masts, rope, rudders, sails, etc.: design)
                        623.862   VM791 (anchors), VC279.R6 (rope)
Rio de Janeiro, Br.   F2646   981.53
Rio de Janeiro (Br.: state)   F2611
River & stream crossing (infantry)   UD317
Roads & highways (gen.)   UA960
Roads (mil. engineering)   UG330   623.62
Roads (places outside U.S.)   UA965.A-Z
Robin Moor (steamship: WWII)   D782.R6
Rocket forces (land: types)   358.175
ROCKETS & missiles, Air force   UG1310-1315   623.451, .4519, .4543
Rockets, Air force (Ger.)   UG1315.G3
Rockets, Air force (places except U.S.)   UG1315.A-Z
Rockets, Air force (U.S.)   UG1313
Rockets, signal (marine lifesaving)   VK1479
Rockets, Tactical   355.82543
Rockets, Tactical (design)   623.4543   UF880
Rockets, Unguided (mil. sci.)   UF880 (SEE UG1310-1315 for guided rockets)
                        623.4543
Rocky Mts. area (Mont., Idaho, Wyo., Colo.)   F721-785   978
Rolls of honored & dead (WWI)   940.467   D609, D609.A2 (gen.)
Rolls of honored & dead (WWII)   940.5467   D797
Romania (Rumania)   949.8   DR201-296
Romania (1861-1947: Monarchy)   949.802   DR250-266, DR250,
                        DR263 (1914-18), DR264 (1918-44)
Romania (1944-)   DR267
Rome, It.   945.632   DG803-818, DG808, DG813 (1871-)
Rome, It. (1527-)   DG812
Rome, It. (1871-)   DG813
Rome, It. (476-: gen.)   DG808
Rome, It. (modern era)   DG803-818
Romulo, Carlos P. (Philip.: 1935-46 era)   DS686.2.R6
Roosevelt, Franklin D. (U.S.: 20th c.: works)   E742.5.R5-7
Roosevelt, Franklin D. (U.S.: Pres., 1933-45)   E807
Roosevelt, Franklin D. (U.S.: Pres., 1933-45: family, inclu. Eleanor)   E807.1
Rope (naval supplies)   VC279.R6

Rosenberg, Alfred (Ger.: 1918-48 era)   DD247.R58
Rosters, Officers' (U.S. Mil. Acad.)   U410.H2
Rostov, Rus.   DK651.R7
Rotary International (WWII)   D810.R6
Roten teufel, Die (WWII: Panzer troops)   D757.55.R6
Rowboats, small sailboats, etc.   VM351
ROYAL Armored Corps (WWII: G.B.)   D760.R7
Royal houses (genealogy)   929.7
Royal Military Academy (Woolwich: div'd like U410.A-Z)   U518.A-Z
Royal Military Academy (Woolwich: gen. hist's.)   U518.L1
Royal Military College (Sandhurst)   U520.A-Z
Royal Naval College (Dartmouth)   V515.A1-R1+
Royal Naval College (Dartmouth: hist.)   V515.L1
Royal Naval College (Dartmouth: life, pictorials, etc.)   V515.P1
Royal Naval College (Greenwich: set up like V515)   V520.A1-R1+
Rubber (naval supplies)   VC279.R8
Rudolf (Austria:1848-1916 era: Crown Prince)   DB89.R8
Rulers, kings, etc. (20th c.: collective biography)   D412.7   929.7
RUMANIA (Romania)   DR201-296   949.8
Rumania (1866-1944)   DR250-266
Rumania (1912-13: Balkan War era)   DR258
Rumania (1914-27: Ferdinand)   DR260-263   949.802
Rumania (1914-18: WWI)   DR263
Rumania (1918-44)   DR264-266   949.802
Rumania & Rumanian military ops. (WWII)   D766.4-42   940.53498, 949.802
Rumania (geog. & travel)   914.98   DR209 (1866-1950)
Rumania (mil. status)   UA826   355.0330498
Rumania (post-WWI territorial ?s)   D651.R6
Rumanian military ops. (WWII)   D766.4
Runways, Airport   629.1363
Runways (mil. airfields: design)   623.663
RUSSIA   947 (SEE ALSO DK1-275+)
Russia (1855-)   947.08   DK219+, DK220-221
Russia (1894-1918: Nicholas II)   947.083 (perhaps SEE ALSO 952.031 for Russo-
            Jpn. War)   DK251-264.3, DK258, DK260-262, DS516-517 (R-J War)
Russia (1894-1917)   DK258-260   947.083
Russia (20th c.: gen.)   DK246   947.084
Russia (20th c. & 1917-: Communist period)   947.084   DK246
Russia (1904-17: empire status)   DK262
Russia (1905-6: Revolution: gen.)   DK263
Russia (1914-18: WWI era)   DK264.8   947.083
Russia (1918-: gen.)   DK266.A4-Z
Russia (1925-53: Stalin era: gen.)   DK267   947.0842
Russia (air war geog.)   358.414747
Russia & Eastern Front (WWII: gen.)   D764   940.540947, .532247, .5347,
            .541247,947.0842
Russia. Army (gen.)   UA772   355.30947, .00947
Russia (Asia: lighthouses, beacons, foghorns, etc.)   VK1109-1110
Russia (biog.: heads of state)   923.147
Russia, Eastern & Estonia   DK503 (SEE DK511.E4 for earlier pubns. on Estonia)
            947.41
Russia (Eur.: lighthouses, beacons, foghorns, etc.)   VK1085-1086
Russia, Finland, Poland   DK
Russia (gen.)   DK17

Russia (mil. geog.)   355.4747   UA995.R9
Russia (mil. policy)   355.033547   UA770+
Russia (mil. status)   UA770   355.033047, .033247, .033547
Russia (naval geog.)   359.4747   VA570-579
Russia (naval status: gen.)   VA573.A5-Z   359.030947, .00947, .4747
Russia, Northern   DK501
Russia (pilot guides)   623.892947   VK809, VK821, VK870, VK910 (Siberia)
Russia, Poland, Finland, Soviet Asia   DK
Russia (post-WWI territorial ?s)   D651.R8
Russia, Southern (Black Sea, Caucasus, Armenia, etc.)   DK509
Russia (WWI: causes, aims, results: includes Panslavism)   D514
Russia (WWI: mil. hist.)   940.40947   D550
Russia (WWII: causes, aims, results)   D742.R9
Russia (WWII: dipl. hist.)   940.532247   D754.R9 or .S65 (Sov. U.)
Russia (WWII: occupied terr.)   D802.R8
Russia (WWII: religious & ethical ?'s)   D744.5.R9
RUSSIAN aerial ops. (WWI)   D605
Russian aerial ops. (WWII)   D792.R9
Russian Asia   DK750-973+   957-958
Russian Central Asia (to 1920)   DK858
Russian espionage (gen.)   UB271.R9   327.120947
Russian military history   DK50-54
Russian military ops. and Eastern Front (WWI: gen.)   D550   940.4147, .40947
Russian military ops. (Rev., 1917-21)   DK265.2
Russian military ops. (WWII: special: by region, name, author)   D764.6.A-Z
Russian mission to U.S. (WWI)   D570.8.M6.R7
Russian naval ops. (Rev., 1917-21)   DK265.3
Russian poetry, satire, etc. (WWII)   D745.7.R9
Russian prisons & prisoners (WWII: SEE ALSO D805.S65 for Soviet)   D805.R9
                                                                     940.547247
RUSSIAN REVOLUTION (1905-6)   DK263-264.3
Russian Revolution (1917-21)   DK265-265.9+
Russian Revolution (1917-21: Allied intervention, 1918-20)   DK265.4
Russian Revolution (1917-21: foreign particip.: gen.)   DK265.9.F5
Russian Revolution (1917-21: gen.)   DK265.A56-Z
Russian Revolution (1917-21: special topics)   DK265.9.A-Z
Russian S.F.S.R. (1917-45)   DK510.7-72
Russian S.F.S.R. (Russia)   DK510
Russians (in U.S.)   E184.R9
RUSSO-Austrian conflict (WWI: gen.)   D556
Russo-Finnish War (1939-40)   DK459.5, DL1095-1105+ (might ALSO try
                      DK459.5)   948.97032, 947.0842
Russo-Finnish War (1939-40: gen.)   DL1097
Russo-Finnish War (1939-40: special topics)   DL1105.A-Z
Russo-German conflict (WWI: gen.)   D551
Russo-German naval conflict (WWII: Arctic areas & Baltic)   D772.3
                                                              940.545947, .545943
Russo-Japanese War (1904-5)   DS516-517   952.031, 947.083
Russo-Polish War (1919-20: plus other Polish conflicts of the time)   DK4405
Ruthenia (post-WWII territorial ?s)   D821.R95
Ruthenia (WWII: occupied terr.)   D802.R95
Ryukyu Islands (Japan: inclu. Okinawa)   DS895.R9   952.81 (try .29 for titles
     after 1988) Ryukyu Islands (WWII)   D767.99.R9

SAAR (Ger.)   943.42   DD801.S13
Saar Valley (post-WWI territorial ?s)   D651.S13
Sabotage equipment (mil. sci.)   UB274
Sabotage, espionage, & unconventional warfare (WWII: Fr.)   940.548644
                    D802.F8 (underground), D810.S7+, UB271.F8
Sabotage, intelligence, & unconventional warfare (WWI: Fr.)   940.48644
Sabotage (mil. sci.: gen.)   UB273   355.3437
Sabotage, Naval   359.3437   VG86-88 (underwater demolition), UB273-274
Sacramento, Calif.   979.454   F869.S12
Safety & sanitation (mil. engineering)   623.75   UH600-629.5, U380-385,
                    VC417.5, VG470-475, VM481-482, V380-386
Safety equipment, Nautical (fire-fighting, life-saving, etc.: design)   623.865
                    VK1258, VK1460-1481
Safety, Marine   VK200
Safety measures, Naval (inclu. educ.)   V380-385
Safety technology, Marine (plus other misc. topics)   623.888
Sahara Desert   DT331-346   966
Sahara Desert & West Africa   966
Sahara Desert (gen. hist., descrip. etc.)   DT333
Saigon, Viet.   DS558.S3 (earlier works), DS559.93.S2 (later titles)   959.7
Saigon, Viet. (WWII)   D767.352.S3
Sailing & pilot guides (official: British)   VK803
Sailing directions & pilot guides   VK798-997
Sailing ships, Modern (engineering)   623.822   VM321, VM351
Sailing vessels (handling)   623.8813   VK543
Sailing vessels (naut. engineering)   623.8203   VM156,
                    VM142-145 (wooden), VM331, VM351
SAILORS, NAVY (Asia)   VD99-113
Sailors, Navy (Australia)   VD121-122   359.3380994
Sailors, Navy (Can.)   VD26-27
Sailors, Navy (China)   VD101
Sailors, Navy (Eur.)   VD55-96
Sailors, Navy (Fr.)   VD71-72   359.3380944
Sailors, Navy (G.B.)   VD57-64
Sailors, Navy (gen.: pubn. 1970+)   VD146
Sailors, Navy (Ger.)   VD73-74
Sailors, Navy (Ire.)   VD76.5
Sailors, Navy (Japan)   VD105-106
Sailors, Navy (New Z.)   VD122.5
Sailors, Navy (Rus.)   VD85-86   359.3380947
Sailors, Navy (U.S.)   VD23-25
Saint Helena (Atl. Ocean)   997.3   DT671.S2
Saint Pierre & Miquelon   F1170   971.88
Saipan (Mariana Is.)   DU648.S35
Saipan (WWII)   D767.99.S3
Sakhalin (Siberia)   DK771.S2
Salaries & wages, Military (admin.)   355.64 (SEE ALSO .135)   UC70-75
Salaries, Military   355.135 (SEE ALSO 355.64)   UC70-75 (U.S.),
                    UC91-258 (other places),   UC180-183 (Ger.),
                    UC184-187 (G.B.), UC241 (Japan)
Salary & wage administration, Naval   359.64   VC50-258, VC50-65 (U.S.)
Salvage, Marine   VK1491
Salvation Army (WWI)   D639.S15

Samoa, American   996.13   DU819.A1, DU810-819, DU815
Samoa (modern hist.)   DU817.A6-Z
Samoa, Western   996.14   DU819.A2, DU810-819, DU815
Samoa, Western (post-WWI territorial ?s)   D651.S3
Samoan Islands   DU810-819   996.13-14
Samurai (Jpn. custom)   DS827.S3
SAN Bernardino County (Calif.)   979.495   F868.S14
San Demetrio (WWII: tanker)   D772.S25
San Diego, Calif.   F869.S22   979.498
San Diego, Calif. (fortifications)   UG412.S3
San Diego, Calif. (WWII: U.S. naval base)   D769.542.S345
San Diego County (Calif.)   979.498   F868.S15
San Francisco Bay area   979.46   F868.S156
San Francisco Bay area (Calif.)   F868.S156   979.46
San Francisco, Calif.   F869.S3   979.461
San Juan, P.R.   F1981.S2
San Marino (Republic)   DG975.S2
Sandhurst (Royal Mil. Coll.: descrip. & life)   U520.L1
Sanitary & medical services, Military   UH201-515
Sanitary control (WWI: med. srvcs.)   940.4752
Sanitary control (WWII)   940.54752
Sanitation & hygiene, Military   UH600
Sanitation & refuse (naval sci.)   VC417.5
Sanitation, health, & hygiene (navies: places besides U.S.)   VG475.A-Z
Sanitation, heating, & ventilation (naval architec. & engin.)   VM481   623.853-854
Sanitation (naut. craft: engineering)   623.8546   VM481-483
Santa Barbara County (Calif.)   F868.S23   979.491
Santa Cruz Islands   DU840   993.5
Sappers & bridge troops (U.S.)   UG503
Saragossa, Sp.   DP402.S3-32
Saratoga (aircraft carrier: U.S.: WWII)   D774.S3, VA65.S28   359.32550973
Sarawak   DS646.36-38   959.54
Sardinia   DG975.S29-33
Satire, caricature (G.B.: 20th c.)   DA566.8
Satire, poetry, etc. (WWI: gen.)   D526
Satire, poetry, etc. (WWII: gen.)   D745   940.5481, .5483, misc. 800 literature #s
Saudi Arabia (1914-: gen.)   DS244   953.04-05
Saudi Arabia (1932-: Ibn Saud)   DS244.53   953.052
Saudi Arabia & Arabian Peninsula   DS201-248   953
Saving life & property (marine navig.)   VK1300-1491
Savo Island (aircraft carrier: U.S.: WWII)   D774.S32
Savo Island, Battle of (1942)   D774.S318
Saxony (Prus.)   DD491.S3-39
SCANDINAVIA   DL
Scandinavia & N. Europe (20th c.: 1905-)   948.08   DL83-87+
Scandinavia & N. Europe (1905-19)   948.081   DL83
Scandinavia & N. Europe (1920-29)   948.082   DL83
Scandinavia & N. Europe (1930-39)   948.083   DL83
Scandinavia & N. Europe (1940-49)   948.084   DL83 (1901-45)
Scandinavia (geog. & travel)   914.8   DL10
Scandinavia (lighthouses, beacons, foghorns, etc.)   VK1086.5   623.89420948

Scandinavia (mil. status)   UA646.7   355.033048, .033248, .033548
Scandinavia (naval geog.)   359.4748   VA619.S, VA590599 (Sweden)
Scandinavia, Northern Europe, Finland   DL
Scandinavia (WWI: dipl. hist.)   D621.S3
Scandinavia (WWII: dipl. history)   D754.S29
Scapa Flow Naval Base (G.B.: Scot.: WWII)   940.5453411
Scenic places (London, Eng.: bridges, parks, etc.)   DA689.A-Z
Schacht, Hjalmar Horace Greeley (Ger.: 1918-48 era)   DD247.S335
Scharnhorst (battle cruisers: Ger.: WWI & II)   VA515.S
Schools (naval architec.: special)   VM275-276
Schools, Naval (Ger.)   V574.A-Z
Schools, Private naval (U.S.)   V430
Schuschnigg, Kurt (Austria)   DB98.S3
Schutzstaffel (SS: Nazi Party: gen.)   DD253.6
SCIENCE & technology (WWI)   D639.S2
Science & technology (WWII)   D810.S2
Science of marine navigation (gen.: pubn. 1801+)   VK555   623.81
Sciences (pure) & math   500-599   Q
Sciences (pure), math, & computer science Q   500-599, 611-612
Scientists, Applied (WWII)   940.53156
Scientists (WWI)   940.3155   D639.S2
Scientists (WWII)   940.53155   D810.S2
Scotland   941.1   DA750-890, DA760 (gen.)
Scotland (20th c.)   DA821   941.1082
Scotland (1910-36)   941.1083   DA821
Scotland (1936-45))   941.1084   DA821
Scotland (WWII: gen. particip.)   940.53411
Scottish troops (G.B.)   UA664
Scraping, painting, etc. (marine engin.)   VM961
Scutari (Albania: gen.)   DR701.S5
Sea forces & warfare (hist.)   359.009+   VA, D-F, VA10, VA25-55
Seabees or naval construction battalions (WWII: U.S.: gen.)   D769.55
Seabees (WWII: U.S.: by battalion #)   D769.552.1st-
Seacoast artillery   UF450-455
Seacraft, Modern (specific types: engineering)   623.821-829
Seamanship   623.88   VK1-587+, VK541-547
Seamanship (marine navig. & merch. marine)   VK541-547   623.88
SEAMEN, NAVAL   VD
Seamen, Naval (Asia: gen.)   VD99   359.338095, .12095
Seamen, Naval (enlisted personnel in gen.: drill, way of life, etc.)   VD
Seamen, Naval (Eur.: gen.)   VD55   359.338094, .12094
Seamen, Naval (G.B.: gen.)   VD57   359.3380941, .120941
Seamen, Naval (gen.: pubn. 1801-1970)   VD145
Seamen, Naval (Ger.: gen.)   VD73   359.3380943, .120943
Seamen, Naval (Japan: gen.)   VD105   359.3380952, .120952
Seamen, Naval (misc. subjects)   VD430
Seamen, Naval (U.S.: gen.)   VD23   359.3380973, .120973
Seamen's handbooks (G.B.)   V115.G7
Seamen's handbooks (Ger.)   V115.G3
Seamen's handbooks (Japan)   V115.J3
Seamen's handbooks (Rus.)   V115.R9
Seamen's handbooks (U.S. Navy)   V113
Seaplanes   629.133347
Seaplanes (air force)   UG1242.S3   629.133347, 623.7466-7467
Search & rescue ops. (WWII: gen.)   D810.S42

Seattle, Wash.   F899.S4   979.777
Seattle, Wash. (area)   979.777   F897.K4, F899.S4
Seawolf (submarine: WWII)   D783.5.S4
Second Republic (Sp.: 1931-39: gen.)   DP254
Second World War (1939-45)   940.53-5499   D731-838
Second World War (econ., polit., social hist.)   940.531   D421, D443, D720-728,
                                                                    D743, D748
Secret service, espionage, military intelligence (WWII: spies)   D810.S7-8
                                                                    940.5485-5487+
Secret service, spies (WWI: gen.)   D639.S7
Secretary of the Navy (U.S.: official docs.)   VA52.A2-29
Security (defense info.)   UB246-249
Security, Industrial (defense purposes)   UB249
Security, Naval   V185
Seizure & disposition of German ships (WWI: U.S.)   D570.8.S4
Semaphore, flag signals, & heliograph (mil. engineering)   623.7312   UG582.S4,
                                                                    UG580, UG582, VK385, V300-305
Semaphores (mil.)   UG582.S4
SERBIA (inclu. Belgrade)   DR1932-2125+ (SEE ALSO DR301+ & DR1202 areas)
                                                                    949.71-71022
Serbia (1903-18: Peter I Karadordevic)   DR2030-2032
Serbia (1914-18: WWI)   DR2032
Serbia (1918-)   949.7102   DR366, DR2034
Serbia (1918-45: gen.)   DR2034
Serbia (1918-45: part of Yug.)   DR2033-2040
Serbia (1941-45: WWII era)   DR2040
Serbia (gen. histories)   DR1965
Serbia (gen., descrip., culture, history)   DR1940
Serials & periodicals (U.S.)   973.05   E171
Sermons, minor works, pamphlets (WWI)   D525
Sermons, minor works, pamphlets, (WWII)   D743.9
Service flags (WWI: U.S.)   D570.8.S5
Service flags (WWII: U.S.)   D769.8.S5
Service periods (navies)   359.11
Service squadrons (WWII: U.S.: by #)   D769.537
Service squadrons (WWII: U.S.: gen.)   D769.535
Sevastopol, Rus.   DK651.S45
Sevastopol, Uk.   DK508.95.S49
Seville, Sp.   DP402.S36-48
Sewage disposal (mil. design)   623.753   UC430, VM481, VM503
Sex (WWII)   D810.S46
Sextants & quadrants   VK583   527.028, 623.894
Shanghai, China   DS796.S2   951.132
Shanghai, China (Ch.-Jpn. Confl.: 1932: invasion)   DS777.51
Shark protection   VK1481.S4
Sharpshooting (infantry: U.S.)   UD333-334
Shells & shrapnel   UF760   623.4513-4518
Shells & shrapnel, Naval   VF490
Shells, bombs, missiles, other delivery units with charges (design)   623.451
                                                                    UF750-755
Shells, Naval artillery   359.82513
Shetland Islands (Scot.)   DA880.S5
Shikoku (Japan)   952.3
Shinto (WWII)   D810.S47

Ship exchanges & canteens (gen.)   VC390   359.341
Ship hulls (naut. engineering)   623.84   VM156
Ship trials (gen.)   VM880
SHIPBUILDING & maintenance appliances & activities (engin.: gen.: SEE TC361 &
                            363 for dry & floating docks)   VM901
Shipbuilding industry   VM298.5-301
Shipbuilding industry (G.B.)   VM298.7.G7
Shipbuilding industry (places besides U.S.)   VM298.7.A-Z
Shipbuilding industry (U.S.)   VM298.6   387.50973
Shipbuilding, Naval (gen. hist.)   VM15
SHIPBUILDING, NAVAL (HIST.: Asia)   VM99-113
Shipbuilding, Naval (hist.: Australia)   VM121-122   623.80994
Shipbuilding, Naval (hist.: Eur.)   VM55-96
Shipbuilding, Naval (hist.: Fr.)   VM71-72   623.80944
Shipbuilding, Naval (hist.: G.B.)   VM57-64   623.80941
Shipbuilding, Naval (hist.: Ger.)   VM73-74   623.80943
Shipbuilding, Naval (hist.: It.)   VM79-80   623.80945
Shipbuilding, Naval (hist.: Japan)   VM105-106 623.80952
Shipbuilding, Naval (hist.: New Z.)   VM122.5
Shipbuilding, Naval (hist.: Rus.)   VM85-86   623.80947
Shipbuilding, Naval (hist.: U.S.)   VM23-25   623.80973
SHIPBUILDING, NAVAL (INSTRUC.: Australia)   VM271
Shipbuilding, Naval (instruc.: Eur.: gen.)   VM205
Shipbuilding, Naval (instruc.: G.B.)   VM207
Shipbuilding, Naval (instruc.: Ger.)   VM223
Shipbuilding, Naval (instruc.: Japan)   VM255
Shipbuilding, Naval (instruc.: U.S.)   VM173
Shipment & packing (naval sci.)   VC537
SHIPS & crews (naval forces)   359.32   V750-895, V750, VA (indiv. ships)
Ships' appliances (engin.)   VM781-861
Ships (Australia. Navy: by name)   VA715.A-Z   359.32520994-.3260994
Ships (Australia. Navy: lists)   VA713.A1-49   359.30994, .320994, .3250994
Ships (Calif. naval reserves: by name)   VA105.A-Z
Ships (design)   623.812   VM297, V765
Ships (Fr. Navy: lists)   VA503.A1-49   359.320944, .3250944
Ships (G.B. Royal Navy: by name)   VA458.A-Z   359.320941, .3252+-.326+
Ships (G.B. Royal Navy: lists)   VA456   359.325+, .320941
Ships (Ger. Navy: by name)   VA515.A-Z   359.320943, .3252+-.326+
Ships (Ger. Navy: lists)   VA513.A1-49   359.320943, .3250943
Ships (Japan. Imper. Navy: by name)   VA655.A-Z   359.320952, .3252+-.326+
Ships (Japan. Imper. Navy: lists)   VA653.A1-49   359.30952, .320952,
                                       .3252+-326+
Ships, Naval   V750 (gen.: SEE here for earlier works on battleships & V815 for
    later works)
Ships (New Z. Navy: lists)   VA723.A1-49   359.309931
Ships, Powered (as units: group op. in squadrons etc., crew duties & life, hist's. of
                    indiv. ships in most cases)   359.325 (SEE ALSO
                    .83 & .835-836 for ships as equip.: PREFER .325+
                    when in doubt)   V750, V765-767, V799-800
Ships' records & accounts (U.S.)   VC503-504
Ships' stores & equipment (except U.S.)   VC275.A-Z
Ships' stores & equipment (U.S.)   VC273-274
Ships (U.S. Navy: by name)   VA65.A-Z   359.32520973-.32560973
Ships (U.S. Navy: lists)   VA61   359.32, .320222

SHIPWRECKS & fires   VK1250-1299 (PREFER D-F 3 #s for specific wars)
Shipwrecks (Asia)   VK1286
Shipwrecks (Australia & Oceania)   VK1289-1294
Shipwrecks (by area)   VK1270-1294
Shipwrecks (by name)   VK1255.A-Z
Shipwrecks (Eur.)   VK1280-1282
Shipwrecks (U.S.)   VK1270-1273
Shipyards & shipbuilding companies (by name)   VM301.A-Z
Shoes & footwear, Naval   VC310
Shoes, footwear, gloves (mil.)   UC490-495
Shooting (marines: inclu. marksmanship, training, etc.)   VE330-335
Shooting (naval seamen: inclu. marksmanship, regs., etc.)   VD330-335
SHORE facilities, yards, stations (navies: gen.)   VC412   359.7, 623.83
Shore patrol (G.B.)   VB925.G7
Shore patrol (gen.)   VB920   359.13323, .34
Shore patrol (Ger.)   VB925.G3
Shore patrol (U.S.)   VB923
Shore service   VF330-335
Shore service (marines)   VE410
Shortwave radio (mil. engineering)   623.7341
Shotguns   UD396
Shrapnel & other antipersonnel devices (design)   623.4514   UF760-765, VF490
Siam (Thailand)   959.3   DS561-589, DS571
Siam (1935-46: time of Rama VIII)   959.3043   DS585
Siam (20th c.)   959.304   DS578
Sian, Ch. (1936: incident)   DS777.514
SIBERIA   DK751-781, DK761   957
Siberia (19th-20th c.)   DK766   957.08
Siberia (Rev., 1917-21)   DK265.8.S5
Siberia & Asiatic Russia (geog. & travel)   915.7   DK755, DK584 (C.Asia)
Siberia (gen.)   DK761
Siberia (gen. hist., exploration, culture, etc.)   DK753   957
Siberia (WWII: gen. particip.)   940.5357 (more likely with Russia at .5347)
                                      D764, D767, DK766
SICILY   945.8   DG869
Sicily (20th c.)   DG869
Sicily (1900-45)   DG869.2
Sicily (geog. & travel)   914.581-582   DG864
Sicily (WWII)   D763.S5
Sicily (WWII: occupied terr.)   D802.S55
Sick & wounded, Care of (mil.: relief societies, etc.: U.S.: gen.)   UH523
Side arms & misc. weapons (design)   623.44   UD380-425
Sidearms, Modern (design)   623.444 (SEE ALSO .441 or .44)   UD420-425,
                                      UD400
Siege artillery   UF460-465
Siege warfare   355.44   UG443-449
Sighting & range apparatus (naval ordnance)   359.826
Sighting apparatus & other ordnance access.   355.826   UF848-856
Sights, Firearm   UF854

SIGNAL corps & troops   UG570-575
Signal corps & troops (U.S.)   UG573
Signal Corps battalions etc. (WWII: U.S.: by #)   D769.363.1st-
Signal Corps (WWII: Ger.: Nachrichten truppen)   D757.65
Signal Corps (WWII: U.S.: gen.)   D769.36
Signal service, Coast (plus coast guard: gen.)   VG50
Signaling, Merchant marine (flags, lights, codes, radio, etc.)   VK381-397
Signaling, Military   UG570-582   358.24, 623.73+, 355.85
Signaling, Military (particular types)   UG582.A-Z
Signaling, Naval (gen.)   V280-285   359.27, .983
Signals, Visual (mil. engineering)   623.731   UG582.V5
Sikorski, Wladyslaw (Pol.: 1918+ biog.)   DK440.5.S55
Sikorski, Wladyslaw (Pol.: 1918-45 period)   DK4420.S5
Silesia (20th c.)   DB660
Silesia Voivodeship (Pol.)   DK4600.S48
Silversides (submarine: WWII)   D783.5.S6
Singapore   DS598.S7   959.52
Singapore (to 1946)   959.5203
Singapore Naval Base (Royal Navy)   VA459.S5   940.5453095952,
                                                            .5453095957 (WWII)
Singapore (WWII)   D767.55   959.5203
Singapore (WWII: gen. particip.)   940.5359527 (SEE .535952 for earlier titles)
                                        D767.5, DS598.S7
Sino-American Cooperative Organization (WWII)   D769.64 (for aerial ops. such
                                                            as Flying Tigers SEE D790)
Sino-Japanese Conflict (1937-45)   DS777.52-533   940.53, 951.042, 952.033
Sino-Japanese Conflict (1937-45: misc. topics)   DS777.533.A-Z
Sino-Japanese War (1894-5: gen.)   DS765
Ski troops   UD470-475   356.164
Ski troops (by country)   UD475.A-Z   356.16409+
Slaughterhouses, Military   UC770
Slavonia & Croatia (1918-)   DB379
Slavonia (Yug.: local Croatia)   DR1633-1636   949.72
Slavs (WWII)   D810.S5
SLOVAKIA (1800-1945)   DB2795-2822+
Slovakia (1918-: in Czech Republic)   DB2805-2822+, DB2806
Slovakia (1918-45)   DB679-679.3 (PREFER DB2000+)
Slovakia (1918-39)   DB2813
Slovakia (1939-45)   DB2815-2822
Slovakia (1939-45: gen.)   DB2816
Slovakia (1944: uprising)   DB2822
Slovakia (1945-68)   DB2826
SLOVENIA   DR381.S6, DR1352-1485+   949.73
Slovenia (1914-18: WWI)   DR1434
Slovenia (1918-45)   DR1435-1443
Slovenia (1918-45: gen.)   DR1436
Slovenia (1941-45: occupation)   DR1443
Slovenia (gen.)   DR1370, 1376
Slovenia (post-WWI territorial ?s)   D651.S53
Slovenia (WWII: occupied terr.)   D802.S67

SMALL ARMS   355.824   UF520-537+
Small arms (19th-20th c.)   U889
Small-arms ammunition (bullets, bazooka rockets, etc.: design)   623.455
                              UF700, UF740-745, UF770, TS538, VF500
Small arms & bayonet training   355.547   UD380-415, U169
Small arms & ordnance (besides U.S.: by place) UF525.A-Z
Small arms & ordnance (gen.)   UF520   355.82
Small arms & ordnance (manufacture: U.S.: gen.)   UF533   338.4762340973
Small-arms & ordnance research (places besides U.S.)   UF526.5.A-Z
Small arms (by region or country)   U897.A-Z
Small arms (gen.)   U884
Small arms (infantry)   UD380-425   355.824+, 623.44
Small arms (infantry: countries besides U.S.)   UD385.A-Z
Small arms (marines)   VE360-390
Small arms (navies)   VD360-390
Small boat service (inclu. armament)   VD400-405   359.3258
Small craft   VM321-349
Small craft (gen.)   VM321
Small craft (naut. engineering)   623.8202   VM320-361, VM321, VM331, VM341
Small craft (naut. handling)   623.8812   VK543, GV811
Smoke screens & tactics   UG447.7
Smolensk, Rus.   DK651.S65
Snipers, bazookamen, machine-gunners, & other special-weapon troops   356.162
                              U167.5.A-Z, UD390+, UF620
Snowshoeing (WWI)   D639.S5
Snowshoes, skis, skates, etc. (mil. transp.)   UC360
SOCIAL aspects (WWII)   D744.6
Social aspects (WWII: by country)   D744.7.A-Z
Social groups (WWI)   940.315   D639.A-Z
Social groups (WWII)   940.5315+
SOCIAL LIFE & politics (Washington, D.C.)   F196
Social life, culture, customs (Berlin, Ger.)   DD866
Social life, culture, customs (London, Eng.)   DA688
Social life, culture, customs (Moscow, Rus.)   DK600
Social life, culture, customs (Paris, Fr.)   DC715
Social life, culture, customs (Pol.)   DK4110
Social sciences   300-399   G-H, J-L, U-V
Social sciences (economics, commerce, sociology, communism)   H   300-319,
                                                                330-389
Social sciences (gen.)   300-309   H1-99
Social services, prisons, & medical services (WWI)   940.47
Social services, prisons, & medical services (WWII)   940.547   D805-809
Social welfare services, Military (U.S. Army)   UH760
Social welfare services, Naval   VG2000-2005
Social work, Military (gen.)   UH750   355.34, .346-347
Social work, Naval (gen.)   VG2000
Social work, recreation, etc. (air forces: U.S.)   UG990
Socialism (WWII)   D810.S6
Societies & associations (WWI)   940.4006   D502, D504 (congresses)
Societies & associations (WWII)   940.54006   D732, D734
Society Islands (inclu. Tahiti, Bora Bora, etc.)   DU870   996.21
Sociological factors of war   355.022 (SEE ALSO 303.66 & 306.2)
Sofia, Bulg.   DR97
Soignes Forest (Bel.)   DH801.S6

Soldiers' & sailors' homes   UB380
Soldiers' & sailors' homes (U.S.: state)   UB384.A-W
Soldiers' handbooks & manuals (gen.)   U110
SOLOMON ISLANDS (inclu. Guadalcanal, New Georgia, Choiseul, Savo, Florida,
        Bougainville, etc.)   DU850   993.5 (works prior to about 1989),
        995.93 (works dated after 1988)
Solomon Islands (geog. & travel)   919.35
Solomon Islands (mil. geog.)   355.47935   UA995.S
Solomon Islands (naval geog.)   359.47935   VA750.S
Solomon Islands (Northern: inclu. Buka, Bougainville, etc.)   995.92
Solomon Islands (pilot & sailing guides)   VK933.S65
Solomon Islands (WWII: by specific is.)   D767.982.A-Z (SEE ALSO D767.99.A-Z
        for alternative #'s)
Solomon Islands (WWII: gen.)   D767.98   940.53935, .5426
Solomons, Battle of the (1942-44)   D774.S45
Somaliland   DT401-420   967.7
Sonar, radio, radar, etc. (naval architec.: places except U.S.)   VM480.5.A-Z
Sound signaling (mil.)   UG582.S68
Sounding apparatus   VK584.S6
SOUTH AFRICA (1909-: Union)   DT779   968.05+
South Africa (1910-61: Union)   968.05   DT779
South Africa (1910-19: Louis Botha)   968.052   DT779.5
South Africa (1914-18: WWI period)   DT779.5
South Africa (1919-39)   DT779.6   968.05-054
South Africa (1939-48: Jan Christiaan Smuts: 2d era)   968.055   DT779.7
South Africa (1939-45: WWII era)   DT779.7   968.055
South Africa & South African military ops. (WWII)   D766.97   940.5368,
        .540968, 968.055
South Africa (mil. status)   UA856   355.00968, .033068
South Africa (naval status)   VA700.S52   359.030968
South Africa (overall)   968   DT751-944, DT766
South Africa (WWII: dipl. hist.)   940.532268 D754.S
South Africa (WWII: Reconstruction)   D829.A33
SOUTH AMERICA   F, F2201-3799+   980-989
South America (1830-)   F2236   980.03
South America (1900-18)   980.032   F2236 (1830-)
South America (1918-49)   980.033   F2236, F2237 (1939-)
South America (1939-)   F2237   980.033+
South America & Latin Am. (gen.)   980   F2201-3799+, F2201-2239, F2231 (GEN.)
South America (gen.)   F2231   980
South America (geog. & travel)   918   F2211, F2223, F2236-2237
South America (mil. geog.)   355.478
South America (mil. status: gen.)   UA612   355.03308, .03328
South America (naval status: gen.)   VA415   359.03098
South America (northern: Brazil, Ven., Peru, etc.)   F2216
South America (southern: Arg., Chile, Uru., etc.)   F2217
South American coasts (gen. & east: pilot & sailing guides)   VK961-968
South & South Atlantic states (1865-1950)   F215   975.04, 976.04
South Atlantic states   975   F206-295, F206-220, F209, F215 (1865-)
South Atlantic states & Florida (geog. & travel)   917.5   F106,
        F207.3 (S.Atl.), F309.3 (Fla.)
South Atlantic states & the South (U.S.: covers south of Mason-Dixon Line)
        F206-220   975-976
South Australia   DU300-330   994.23
South Australia (gen. & descrip.)   DU310-320

South Central states & Gulf Coast   976   F296-475, F296-395 (Gulf),
                                                   F296-301, F396- 475 (Old S.W.), F396
South Dakota (battleship: U.S.: WWII)   D774.S6
South Island (New Z.)   993.15
South Pacific (pilot & sailing guides)   VK925   623.89291646-89291649
South Seas (Oceanica: islands, chains, groups, etc.)   DU520-950
SOUTHEAST ASIA   DS521-689+, DS518 (1904-45: Far E. ?), DS521-605,
                        DS525, DS541   959
Southeast Asia (1900-45)   DS526.6
Southeast Asia (1900-41)   959.051   DS518, DS526.6 (newer titles), DS549
Southeast Asia (1941-45: Japanese occup.)   959.052   DS549, DS526.6
Southeast Asia, Dutch East Indies, Philippines   DS521-689   959
Southeast Asia (gen. histories: older titles have descrip. & travel)   DS525
Southeast Asia (geog. & travel)   915.9   DS508
Southeast Asia (newer titles: gen.)   DS521   959
Southern Africa   DT730-995   968
Southern Anhui (China: Sino-Jpn. Confl.: 1941: incident)   DS777.534
Southern Asia & India   954   DS335-498+
Southern Asia & Indian Ocean Region   DS335-498   954, 958.1, 959.1
Southern California   F867   979.49
Southwest Africa (German Southwest Africa)   DT701-720   967.1, 968.8
Southwest (New: New Mex., Ariz., Utah, Nev.)   F786-850   978.9-979.3, 979
Southwest (Old) & lower Mississippi Valley (Ark., Tenn., Ken., Missouri)   F396-475
                                                   976.7-9, 977, 977.8
Southwestern Asia & Middle East (gen. histories)   DS62
SOVIET Bloc (1945-)   D847
Soviet Central Asia (1920+)   DK859
Soviet prisons & prisoners (WWII: SEE ALSO D805.R9)   D805.S65
Soviet propaganda (1925-53: foreign: gen.)   DK270
Soviet Union & Eur. Russia (geog. & travel)   [SEE ALSO 'Russia' or 'Union of
                                        Soviet ...']   914.7   DK27
Soviet Union (1917-24: Rev. period & Lenin era)   947.0841   DK265 (Rev.),
                                                   DK265-266.5+
Soviet Union (1918-)   DK266   947.084
Soviet Union (1918-: special inclu. espionage, sabotage)   DK266.3
Soviet Union (1918-24: Lenin era)   DK266.5   947.0841
Soviet Union (1924-53: Stalin era)   947.0842 (might ALSO try 948.97032 for
                        Russo-FinnishWar)   DK267-273, DK267 (gen.),
                        DK459.5 (R-F War), DL1095-1105 (R-F War: later works)
Soviet Union (1925-53: Stalin regime)   DK267-273
Soviet Union (1939-45: WWII period)   DK273   947.0842
Soviets (Rus. Rev., 1917-21: councils)   DK265.9.S6
SPAIN   DP1-402+   946
Spain (1868-)   946.08   DP222 (1868-86), DP233 (1886- & 20th c.)
Spain (1886-20th c.: gen.)   DP233   946.08
Spain (1886-1931: gen.)   DP240
Spain (1886-1931: period of Alfonso XIII)   DP234-247
Spain (1914-18: WWI)   DP246

Spain (1918-31)   DP247   946.08
Spain (1931-39: 2d Repub.: inclu. Civil War, 1936-39)   946.081
            DP250-269, DP254 (gen.), DP269 (Civil War)
Spain (1931-36: Alcalá Zamora y Torres era)   DP267
Spain (1936-39: Azaña period)   DP268
Spain (1936-39: Civil War)   DP269-269.9+   946.081
Spain (1939-75: Franco period)   946.082   DP270
Spain (1939-)   DP270   946.0824
Spain (1939-49)   946.0824
Spain & Portugal (geog. & travel)   914.6   DP42, DP525 (Port.)
Spain (mil. status)   UA780-789   355.033046
Spain (naval status)   VA580-589
Spain (WWII: gen. particip.)   940.5346   D754.S7, DP270-271
SPANISH-American War (1898)   E714-735   973.89-898
Spanish Civil War (1936-39)   DP269   946.081
Spanish Civil War (1936-39: foreign particip.: gen.)   DP269.45
Spanish Civil War (1936-39: special topics)   DP269.8.A-Z
Spanish military ops. (Civil War, 1936-39: Insurgents)   DP269.25
Spanish military ops. (Civil War, 1936-39: Loyalists)   DP269.23
Spanish Morocco   DT330   964.2
Spanish West Africa   964.8
Spark-ignition engines (marine engineering)   623.87234
Spaventa, Silvio (It.: 1871-1945 era)   DG556.S6
Specialist forces & warfare (armored land, technical land, & air)   358   UE-UG
Specialist forces, Naval   359.9
Specifications & contracts (naval architec.: gen.)   VM295
Speeches & essays (naval sci.: gen.)   V19
Speeches (Royal Naval Coll., Dart.: by speaker)   V515.F3.A-Z
Speeches (U.S. Naval Acad.: misc.: by speaker)   V415.F5.A-Z
Speeches (U.S. Navy)   VA54
Speer, Albert (Ger.: 1918-48 era)   DD247.S6-7
SPIES, espionage (WWI: by name)   D639.S8.A-Z
Spies, German (by name)   UB271.G32.A-Z
Spies, intelligence (Sino-Jpn. Confl., 1937-45)   DS777.533.S65
Spies (mil. admin.)   UB270   327.12
Spies, Russian (by name)   UB271.R92.A-Z
Spies, secret service, etc. (Rus. Rev., 1917-21)   DK265.9.S4
Spies, United States (by name)   UB271.U62.A-Z
Spies (WWII: by name)   D810.S8.A-Z
Sports in navies   V267-268
Sports, Military (gen.)   U327
Springfield rifle   UD395.S8
Squadrons, fleets, flotillas, etc. (naval units)   359.31   VA, VA63.A-Z (U.S.),
            VB200-205
Sri Lanka (Ceylon: gen.)   DS489.5
SS (Nazi Party: by Ger. locality)   DD253.62.A-Z
SS (Nazi Party: Ger.)   DD253.6-65
SS (Nazi Party: Ger.: by local #)   DD253.1st-
St. Louis public schools (WWI)   D639.E4.S3
St. Louis, Mo.   F474.S2   977.866
St. Petersburg, Rus. (gen.)   DK561
Staff functions (mil. organiz.)   355.33042
Staff positions (naval hier.)   359.33042
Staffs, Army   UB220-225
Staffs, Military (gen.)   UB220

Stalin, Joseph (Rus.: biogs.)   DK268.S8
Stalin, Joseph (Rus.: works by)   DK268.S75
Stalingrad, Battle of (1942-43)   D764.3.S7
Stalingrad, Rus.   DK651.S7   947.4785
Standards, colors, flags (mil.: places besides U.S.)   UC595.A-Z
Standards (naval architec.)   VM293
'Stars and Stripes' (WWII: periodical)   D731.S73
Statesmen (U.S.: collected works: 20th c.)   E742.5.A-Z (SEE E660 for up to 1921)
Statesmen (U.S.: collected works: inclu. some working through 1921)
                              E660.A-Z (SEE E742.5 for rest of 20th c.)
Station drills, Naval (Eur.: gen.: ALSO quarter, watch, etc.)   VD215
Stations, shore facilities, yards (navies: U.S.: by state)   VC415.A-W
Statistics (militray medical: U.S.: unofficial)   UH223.A5
Statistics, Official (military medical: U.S.)   UH223.A4-49
Stavanger (Nor.)   DL576.S8, DL596.S8
Steam engines (marine engineering)   623.8722   VM741-749, TJ735-740
Steamship lines (by co. name)   VM385.A-Z
Steel & iron land defenses   UG408-409
Steerage, Nautical   VM565
Steering gear, Marine (engin.)   VM841-845
Sten machine guns   UF620.S8
Stephenson, William, Sir (WWII: spy)   D810.S8.S85
Stepney, Eng. (WWII: Middlesex)   D760.8.S75
Stimson, Henry (U.S.: 20th c.)   E748.S895
Stockholm, Swe.   DL976
Stockholm, Swe. (area)   948.7   DL976
Stores & supplies, Military (U.S.)   UC263-264
Stores & supplies, Naval (U.S.)   VC263-264   359.80973
Stores, Ordnance (U.S.: gen.)   UF553
Strassburg, Ger.   DD901.S81-89
Strasser, Otto (Ger.: 1918-48 era)   DD247.S8
Strategic Bombing Survey (WWII: U.S.: by industry attacked)   D785.U58.A-Z
Strategic Bombing Survey (WWII: U.S.: gen.)   D785.U57
Strategic lines, bases, etc.   UA930   355.43
STRATEGY, Air force   358.4143   U162-163, UG633-635
Strategy & military ops. (plans, attack, defense, etc.)   355.4   UA11,
                              UA23 (U.S.), U27, U42-43, U102, U161-167
Strategy & naval ops.   359.4 (SEE ALSO .43 for strategic works prior to 1989)
                              V27-55, V101-107, VA, VA10, VA50-750
Strategy (marines)   359.9643   VE21-124 (by place), VE144-146
Strategy (mil. sci.: pubn. 1789-)   U162   355.43
Strategy, Naval   359.43 (PREFER .4 with titles after 1988)   V160-165
Strategy, Naval (gen.: pubn. thru 1800)   V160
Strategy (WWI)   940.401   D521, D530, D550
Strategy (WWI: Allies)   940.4012   D544, D570
Strategy (WWI: Central Powers)   940.4013   D531
Strategy (WWII)   940.5401   D743
Strategy (WWII: Allies)   940.54012
Strategy (WWII: Axis)   940.54013
Stream & river crossing (artillery)   UF320
Street fighting   U167.5.S7
Streets, bridges, etc. (Berlin, Ger.)   DD887
Stresemann, Gustav (Ger.: 1888-1918+ period)   DD231.S83

Structural design (naval architec.: specific materials)   623.818
Structural design (naval architec.: steel)   623.81821   VM146
Structural theory & design (naval architec.)   623.817   VM156-163
Structure & personnel, Air force   358.413   UG770-775, UG1130-1135
Student publications (U.S. Naval Acad.)   V415.J1-7
Sturgeon (submarine: WWII)   D783.5.S8
Stuttgart, Ger.   DD901.S95-97
Subcaliber guns (U.S.: handbooks)   UF563.A8
SUBMARINE & anti-submarine ops (WWII)   D780-784   940.5451
Submarine boats   VM365-367
Submarine boats (gen.)   VM365   359.3257, 623.8257
Submarine cables (mil.)   UG607
Submarine forces & warfare   359.93
Submarine mines, minelaying, minesweeping, etc. (U.S.)   V856.5.U6-7
SUBMARINE OPS. & submarine chasers (WWI)   D590-595   940.451+
Submarine ops. (WWI: Allies)   940.4513   D590
Submarine ops. (WWI: Ger.)   940.4512   D591 (gen.), D592.A-Z (by ship,
                                        battle, etc.)
SUBMARINE OPS. (WWII: G.B.)   940.5451941   D784.G7
Submarine ops. (WWII: Ger.)   940.5451943   D781-782
Submarine ops. (WWII: It.)   940.5451945   D784.I8
Submarine ops. (WWII: Japan)   940.5451952   D784.J3
Submarine ops. (WWII: misc. countries: by place)   D784.A-Z
Submarine ops. (WWII: U.S.)   940.5451973   D783
Submarine warfare (gen.)   V210   359.3257, .42-43
SUBMARINES (besides U.S.)   V859.A-Z
Submarines, Conventionally-powered (navies: as equip.)   359.93832 (SEE .8357 for
                                        works before 1989)
Submarines, Diesel & electric (navies: units)   359.32572
Submarines (gen.)   V857 (SEE ALSO V210-14 for sub warfare & VM365-7 for
                        construc.)   623.8257, .82572, .81257, 359.3257
Submarines (Ger.)   V859.G3   623.82570943
Submarines (Japan)   V859.J3   623.82570952
Submarines, Naval (as equip.)   359.8357 (SEE ALSO .93832 for titles after 1988)
Submarines, Naval (as units)   359.933 (SEE .3257 for titles prior to 1989)
Submarines, Naval (design)   623.81257   V858-859, VM365-367
Submarines, Naval (engineering)   623.8257   VM365-367, V857-859
Submarines (navies: handling)   623.88257   V857-859, V210-214
Submarines (U.S.)   V858   623.82570973, 359.32570973
Submersibles (naut. engineering)   623.8205   VM365-367
Submersibles (naval design)   623.812045
Subsistence & provisions, Naval (inclu. rations, galleys, water, etc.)   VC350-410
Subsistence Dept. (U.S. Army)   UC40-44
Subsistence (mil.: countries besides U.S.)   UC705.A-Z
Subsistence (mil.: gen.)   UC700
Subsistence (mil.: U.S.)   UC703-704
Subversion & sabotage (mil.)   355.3437   UB273-274UB275-277, UB276 (U.S.),
                                        UB277.A-Z (except U.S.)
Subversive activities (in U.S.: propaganda, espionage, 5th column, etc.)   E743.5
Sudan   962.4   DT108 (older works), DT154.1-159
Sudan (1900-1955)   DT156.7
Sudan & Anglo-Egyptian Sudan   DT108, (older works), DT154.1-159   962.4
Sudan (gen.)   DT155.6
Suez Canal (Egypt: inclu. Isthmus)   DT154.S9   962.15
Sultan Muhammad Shah, Sir, Agha Khan (India: 1901+ era)   DS481.S8

Sulu Archipelago (Philip.)   DS688.S9   959.99
Sumatra (Indon.)   959.81   DS646.1-15, DS646.129
Sumatra (Indon.: gen.)   DS646.1   959.81
Sun Yat Sen (China: 1912-49 era: autobiography)   DS777.A3
Sun Yat Sen (China: 1912-49 era: biograpy & criticism)   DS777.A597.A-Z89
Sun Yat Sen (China: 1912-49 era: writings of)   DS777.A2-567
SUPPLIES & equipment (air force: gen.)   UG1100-1105   358.418
Supplies & stores, Military (inclu. procure., storage, specs., surplus, etc.)
                        UC260-267
Supplies & stores, Naval (inclu. stds., procure., storage, etc.)   VC260-268
Supplies & stores, Naval (management methods)   VC266   359.62
Supplies & stores, Naval (misc.)   VC279.A-Z
Supplies, Medical & surgical (mil.)   UH440-445   355.88
Supplies, Medical & surgical (navies)   VG290-295
Supplies, Military (use & disposal)   355.6213
Supplies, Naval (Ger.)   VC180   359.80943
SUPPLY administration (mil.)   355.621   UC260-267
Supply administration (navies)   359.621   VC260-267, VC263 (U.S.)
Supply & administrative services, Military (canteens, post-ex's., messes, etc.)
          355.341 (SEE ALSO 355.6 & .71)   UC, UC750-755, UH80-85
Supply & transport depts. (mil.: G.B.)   UC184
Supply depots, Military   355.75   UC260-269
Supply depots, Naval   359.75   VC260-265
Supply forces & army service forces (WWII: U.S.: gen.)   D769.75
Supply services, Naval (canteens, post exch's, messes, etc.)   359.341
                VC, VC10, VC20-258 (overall by place), VC20-65 (U.S.), VC260-410
Supply ships (naval engineering)   623.8265   V865
Supply transport vehicles (land: mil. design)   623.7474
Supply vessels, transports, service craft, etc. (U.S. Naval Auxiliary Service)
                        VA79
Support & logistics, Military (logistics, camouflage, p.o.w. care, etc.)   355.41
                        U168, UC260-270
Support & logistics, Naval   359.41   V179, VC10
Support ships (naval engineering)   623.826   V865
Support vessels, Naval (units)   359.326   V865
Surgeons, Naval   VG260-265   359.345, 616.98024, 617.99
Surgical & medical handbooks (navies: U.S.)   VG463
Surrender documents (WWII: Ger.)   D814.1
Surrender documents (WWII: It.)   D814.2
Surrender documents (WWII: Jp.)   D814.3
Surveillance, Military   UG475   355.413, 358.45
Surveying, Hydrographic (gen. special)   VK593
Surveying, mapping, & topography (military: gen.)   UG470   623.71
Surveyors, draftsmen, & engineering aids (navies)   VG920-925
Survival (combat: escape & evasion)   U225
Survival after shipwrecks (plus other misc. lifesaving topics)   VK1445-1447
                        623.865

SWEDEN   DL601-991+, DL648   948.5
Sweden (20th c.: 1905-)   948.505   DL860+
Sweden (1905-45)   948.5051   DL860-868
Sweden (1907-50: Gustav V)   DL867-870
Sweden (1914-18: WWI era)   DL868
Sweden (1919-)   DL868.5
Sweden (mil. status)   UA790-799   355.0330485
Sweden (naval status)   VA590-599
Sweden (WWI: dipl. hist.)   D621.S5
Sweden (WWII: dipl. history)   D754.S8
Sweden (WWII: gen. particip.)   940.53485   D754.S8, DL868.5-870
Swiss Guards (Papal Guards)   UA745.5
SWITZERLAND   DQ, DQ54   949.4
Switzerland (20th c.)   DQ201   949.407
Switzerland (1918-45)   949.4072
Switzerland (geog. & travel)   914.94   DQ24
Switzerland (mil. status)   UA800-809   355.0330494
Switzerland (WWII: dipl. hist.)   940.5325494   D754.S9
Switzerland (WWII: gen. particip.)   940.53494   D754.S9, DQ201
Sword exercises (cavalry)   UE420-425
Swords   UD420-425
Sydney (cruiser: WWII)   D775.5.S8
Sydney, Australia   DU178   994.41
Sydney, Australia (area)   994.41   DU178
Sympathizers, Enemy (WWI)   940.3163   D570.8.A6 (U.S.), D636.A-Z (by locale)
Sympathizers, Enemy (WWII)   940.53163   D769.8.A6 (U.S.), D801.A2 (gen.),
                                   D801.A3-Z (by place except U.S.)
SYRIA   DS92-99, DS95.5   956.91
Syria (1516-1920: time of Ottomans)   956.9103   DS97.5-6
Syria (1918-45: French mandate)   DS98   956.9104-91041
Syria (1920-: Mandate & independence)   956.9104   DS98+
Syria (gen.)   DS95
Syria (geog. & travel)   915.691   DS94
Syria (post-WWI territorial ?s)   D651.S9
Syria (WWII)   D766.7.S9-95
Szechwan (China)   DS793.S8
Szechwan Province (China: inclu. Chungking)   951.38   DS793.S8

TABLES, formulae, statistics (marine geonavigation)   623.8920212
Tables, Nautical   VK563-567+   623.8920212
Tables, Nautical navigation (distances etc.)   VK799   623.8920212
Tables, outlines, etc, (WWI)   D522.5
Tables, Tide & current (collections)   VK603
TACTICS, Air force   358.4142   UG700-705
Tactics, Air warfare (bombing, strafing, dog fighting, air mining, etc.)   UG700-705
                                   358.4142, .43
Tactics & maneuvers, Naval   VD157 (PREFER V167-178 & V245)   359.415,
                                   .4152
Tactics & operations, Infantry   356.183

Tailoring (naval clothing)   VC330
Taiwan (1895-1945: gen.)   DS799.7
Taiwan (Formosa: gen. hist., culture, descrip.)   DS799, DS895.F72
Takeoff (aviation)   629.1325212
Tallinn, Rus. (Reval)   DK651.T28
Tanganyika (German East Africa)   DT436-449, DT444   967.82
Tanganyika (to 1960: newer titles)   DT447
Tanganyika (1916-61: Brit. era)   967.8203   DT444, DT447
Tangier Zone, Mor.   DT329.T16   964.2
TANK battalions (WWII: U.S.: by #)   D769.306.1st-
Tank destroyer battalions (WWII: U.S.: by #)   D769.307.1st-
Tank warfare (WWI)   D608   358.18, 940.4+
Tank warfare (WWII)   D793
Tankers (naval architec.)   VM455   623.8245, 387.544
Tanks, armored cars, etc. (attack, defense, & siege: SEE ALSO UE159-302 for
               armored cavalry)   UG446.5   355.422, 357.5, 358.18
Tanks (design)   623.74752   UG446.5
Tarawa (WWII)   D767.99.T3
Target detection & selection (inclu. radar & other methods: engineering)
               623.557 (use .46 for ranging & siting apparatae)
Target practice   UF340-345
Target practice, Naval   VF310-315
Task forces (WWII: U.S.: by #)   D769.53.1st-
Tasmania (Van Diemen's Land)   DU450-480, DU470   994.6
Tatars (in Pol.)   DK4121.5.T3
Teachers (WWII)   940.5315372   D810.E2-5
Technical forces (chem., biol., & radiation warfare: pre-1989 titles may cover
               camouflage construc. & war matériel manufac.)   358.3
Technical forces, Naval (engineering, communic's., etc.)   359.98
Technical intelligence service (WWII: U.S.)   D769.76
Technical troops & artificers (gen.)   UG500   358.2-3
Technical troops & other special corps   UG500-565
Technische Truppen (WWII: Ger.)   D757.855
Technology, medicine, engineering, agriculture, management   600-699
                                       T, R, QA76, S, H
Technology, photography, manufacturing, handicrafts, home economics   T
               600-609, 620-629, 640-650, 660-699, 770-779
Telecommunication (defense)   UA929.95.T4
Telecommunications, Military   UG590-613.5
Telecommunications, Naval   VG70-85   359.415, .85, 623.856, .73
Telegraph, Military (inclu. telegraph troops)   UG600-605
Telegraph, Naval   VG70-75
Telegraph, radar, & radio communications (navies: wireless)   VG76-78
Telegraphy, Wire (mil. engineering)   623.732   UG600-607
Telemark (Nor.)   DL576.T4
Telephone, Military (gen.)   UG610
Telephone, Military (places besides U.S.)   UG610.5.A-Z
Telephone, Naval   VG80-85   623.85645
Telephone, radio, & telegraph (military: gen.)   UG590   623.732-7345
Telephones, Radio (mil. engineering)   623.7345   UG611 (gen.), UG611.3 (U.S.),
               UG611.5.A-Z (other lands), VG76-85
Telephony, Wire (mil. engineering)   623.733   UG610-610.5
Telescopic sights (artillery)   UF855
Television (mil. engineering)   623.735   UG613-613.5
Tempelhof Airfield (Berlin, Ger.)   UG635.G322.T3

Temperance (WWII)   D810.T4
Tents, Military   UC570-585
Terminals, Marine (bunkers, coal supplies, repairs, etc.)   VK358
Territorial questions (post-WWI: by place)   D651.A-Z
Territorial questions (post-WWI: gen.)   D650.T4 (SEE D651 for specific places)
                                    940.31424
Territorial questions (post-WWII: by place)   D821.A-Z
Territorial questions (post-WWII: gen.)   D820.T4 (SEE D821 for specific places)
Territories (U.S.: inclu. Alaska & Hawaii)   F965 (SEE ALSO DU620-629 for Haw.)
Territories (U.S.: island types in gen.)   F970 (SEE ALSO DU647 for Guam &
                                    DU620-629 for Haw.)
Territories (WWII: U.S.: by place)   D769.87.A-Z
Testing (naval armor)   V910-915 (SEE ALSO VF540)
Tests (naval architec.)   623.819
Tests, Ordnance   UF890
Tests, Ordnance & firing (navies)   VF540
Texas   F381-395, F386   976.4
Texas (1846+)   F391 (SEE D570.85.T4-41 for 1914-18 war years & D769.85.T4-41
              for 1939-45)   976.405-406
Texas (1918-45)   976.4062   F391
Texas (geog. & travel)   917.64   F384.3, F391
Texas (WWII: Reconstruction)   D828.T4-41
Thailand (Siam)   DS561-589   959.3
Thailand (19th-20th c.)   DS578   959.303-304
Thailand (1935-46: time of Ananda Mahidol, or Rama VIII)   DS585   959.3043
Thailand (WWII)   D767.47
Thailand (WWII: gen. particip.)   940.53593   DS585
THEATRES, Battle (WWII: Afr. & Mid. E.)   940.5423   D766.8 (Afr.),
                            D766 (Balkans, E. Medit., Near E.)
Theatres, Battle (WWII: Am.)   940.5428   D768 (gen.), D768.18-3 (Latin Am.),
                     D769 (U.S.)
Theatres, Battle (WWII: E. Ind., S.E. Asian, E. Asia)   940.5425 (SEE ALSO
                     951.042 for pre-1941 Sino-Jpn. conflict)
                     D767, D767.6 (India-Burma), D767.35 &
                     D767.45 (Cochin China, Fr. Indoch.)
Theatres, Battle (WWII: Eur.)   940.5421   D743, D756 (W.), D764 (E.)
Theatres, Battle (WWII: misc.)   940.5429
Theatres, Battle (WWII: Pacific)   940.5426   D767 (gen.), D767.9+ (Pac. Is.)
Theory & philosophy (nautical craft)   623.82001   VM156
Theory & philosophy (naval warfare)   359.001
Theory & principles (naval architec.)   VM156-163
Third Reich (Ger.: 1930+-45: contemporary works)   DD253
Third Republic (Fr.: 1871-1940)   DC335
Thompson machine guns   UF620.T5
Tibet   951.5   DS785
Tibet & Central Asia (1951+ pubns.: gen.)   DS786
Tide & current tables   VK600-794, VK602 (gen.), VK610-650 (Atl.: E.), VK628-
           644 (Brit. Isles & Eng. Ch.), VK653-674 (Medit.), VK702-711 (China, Japan,
           Asian coasts), VK715-756 (Pac.), VK727-733 (Australia & Oceania), VK741
           (Am. W. Coast), VK759-792 (Atl. W., U.S., Carib.)   623.8949
Tide & current tables (Atlantic Ocean: all & east: gen.)   VK610   623.894909163
Tide & current tables (by area)   VK607-794
Tide & current tables (Pac. Ocean & islands: gen.)   VK715   623.894909164
Tide & current tables (South Pacific)   VK725
Tientsin, China   DS796.T5

Timber (naval supplies)   VC279.T5
Time periods (WWII)   D755-755.9
Timor   DS646.5   959.86
Tinian (Mariana Is.)   DU648.ST4
Tinian (WWII)   D767.99.T45
Tiso, Jozef (Czech.: 1939-45 era)   DB2821.T57
Tito, Josip Broz (Yug.: 20th c.)   DR359.T5
Tojo, Hideki, Gen., 1884-1948 (Japan: 1926-89 era)   DS890.T64
Tokyo, Japan   DS897.T6 (earlier works), DS896 (later works),
    DS896.64 (1867-1945)   952.135
Tokyo, Japan (1867-1945)   DS896.64   952.13503
Tokyo, Japan (gen.)   DS896.6
Tokyo, Japan (WWII)   D767.25.T5-6   952.135
Tokyo Trials (1946-48)   D804.J32
Toledo, Siege of (Sp. Civil War: 1936: Alcazar)   DP269.2.A4
Toledo, Sp.   DP402.T7-74
Toledo (Sp.: area)   DP302.T51
Tonga Islands   DU880   996.12
Tonnage tables (naval architec.)   VM153
Tools (naval supplies)   VC279.T6
Topography & mapping, Military (places except U.S.)   UG473.A-Z
TORPEDO & mining troops   UG550
Torpedo boat destroyers   V840   623.8254
Torpedo boat service   V837-838
Torpedo boats   V830-838   623.8258, 359.3258
Torpedo boats (Ger.)   V835.G3
Torpedo boats (places besides U.S.)   V835.A-Z
Torpedo boats (U.S.)   V833
Torpedoes (gen.: inclu. propelling or launching devices)   V850   623.4517,
    359.82517
Torpedoes (types or devices: by name)   V855.A-Z
Torres Strait (Queens., Aust.)   DU280.T7
Traffic control systems, Air   629.1366
TRAINING & EDUCATION, Air force   358.415   UG637-639
Training & education, Air force (gen.)   UG637
Training & education, Air force (places besides U.S.)   UG639.A-Z
Training & education, Military   355.5   U400-717, U400 (gen.),
    U403 (modern), U408 (U.S.), U410 (West Pt.), U510-549 (G.B.)
Training & education, Military (modern hist.)   U403
Training & education, Naval   359.5   V400-695 (by place), V411-438 (U.S.),
    V260-265
Training & education, Naval (G.B.: stations, ships, engin. schools, etc.)   V522-525
Training & education, Naval (modern hist.: gen.)   V404
Training & education, Naval (U.S. Coast Guard)   V437   359.9707
Training camps (armor & cavalry: gen.)   UE430
Training camps (armor & cavalry: places besides U.S.)   UE435.A-Z
Training camps, Marine   VE430-435   359.967+
Training (infantry)   356.184   U400-714 (educ.), U320-325
Training (marine navig. & merch. marine)   VK531-537
Training (marines)   359.965   VE430-435, V411-695, VE422 (U.S.)
Training, Military (Ger.: by school location)   U574.A-Z
Training, Naval reserve   359.2232   V400-695

Training, Officer (air forces)   358.4155
Training, Officer (mil. sci.)   355.55   U400-717 (educ.)
Training, Officer (navies)   359.55   V400-695, V411-438 (U.S.: Annapolis etc.),
                VB307-315
Training, Physical (mil. sci.: U.S.)   U323
Training, Physical (navies: countries besides U.S.)   V265.A-Z
Training, Physical (navies: gen.)   V260   359.54
Training planes (design)   623.7462
Training, Reserve   355.2232
Training schools, Naval (misc.)   V425.A-Z
Training ships (U.S. Navy: gen.)   V435
Training (shooting: marines: gen.)   VE330   359.96547
Training, Simulated (navies)   V252
Training stations, Naval (G.B.: by place)   V522.5.A-Z
Training stations, Naval (U.S.: gen.)   V433   359.50973, .70973
Training, Technical (air forces)   358.4156
Training, Technical (mil. sci.)   355.56
Training, Technical (navies)   359.56
Trans-Mississippi & the West (1880-1950)   F595   978.02-033
Trans-Pacific flights   629.130915
Transbaikalia (Sib.)   DK771.T8
Transoceanic flights   629.13091+
Transortation (WWII: inclu. merchant marine)   D810.T8
TRANSPORT & maintenance (mil. sci.: gen. spec.)   UC12
Transport & maneuvers (mil. living conditions)   355.1293
Transport equipment & supplies, Military (vehicles, fuel, trains, etc.)   355.83
                UC270-360, UC270-275, UC340-345, UC260-267, UG615-620
Transport equipment & supplies, Naval (inclu. fuel, vehicles, ships [gen.], etc.)
        359.83   VC530-580, VC270-279, VC276, V750-895, UC320-325
Transport groups (air forces)   358.44   UC330-335, UG633-635, UG1242.T
Transport planes (air force)   UG1242.T7
Transport ships & hospital ships (naval engineering)   623.8264
                UC320-325, VG450 (hosp. ships)
Transport, Medical (mil.: gen.)   UH500
Transport, Military   UC270-360   358.25, .44, 355.27
Transport, Military (besides U.S.: by place)   UC275.A-Z
Transport, Motor (mil. sci.: U.S.)   UC343
Transport, Motor (navies: U.S.)   VC573
Transport, Naval   VC530-580
Transport, Personnel (navies: U.S.)   VC553
Transport, Railroad (mil.: places besides U.S.)   UC315.A-Z
TRANSPORTATION Corps battalions etc. (WWII: U.S.: by #)   D769.733.1st-
Transportation Corps (WWII: U.S.)   D769.73
Transportation (defense)   UA929.95.T7
Transportation, Military (gen.)   UC270   358.25
Transportation, Naval (gen.)   VC530-535   359.83, .27
Transportation service (WWII: U.S.: gen.)   D769.72 (PREFER D810.T8)
Transportation services (mil. engineers)   358.25   UC270-275, UG345 (rail)
Transportation (WWI)   D639.T8
Transylvania (1801-1918) DB740 (SEE DR281.T7 for 1918-)
Transylvania (post-WWI territorial ?s)   D651.T8
Transylvania (post-WWII territorial ?s)   D821.T8
Travel & geography   910-919   G (geog.), D-F (descr. & travel)
Travel routes (mil. sci.: gen.)   UA950
Travel routes (misc.)   UA979

TREATIES (Fin.: 1918)   DK459.3
Treaties (Fin.-Rus.: 1920)   DK459.4
Treaties (Pol., 1921: Riga)   DK440.3
Treaties (Russo-Polish, other Polish conflicts: Riga: 1921)   DK4407.3
TREATIES (WWI: Allies-Central powers)   D643   940.3141
Treaties (WWI: Austria: 10 Sept. 1919)   D643.A8-9
Treaties (WWI: Bulg.: 27 Nov. 1919)   D643.B5
Treaties (WWI: countries other than Ger.)   D643.A8-Z
Treaties (WWI: Ger.: 28 June 1919)   D643.A2-A7
Treaties (WWI: Hungary: 4 June 1920)   D643.H7-9
Treaties (WWI: misc. separate)   D614.A-Z
Treaties (WWI: misc. separate: collections)   D614.A2
Treaties (WWI: results)   940.3142   D511-20
Treaties (WWI: Turkey: S`evres: 10 Aug. 1920)   D643.T8
Treaties (WWI: U.S.-Austria)   D643.A83
Treaties (WWI: U.S.-Ger.)   D643.A68
Treaties (WWI: U.S.-Hung.)   D643.H8
TREATIES (WWII: Allies-Bulg.)   D814.9.B9
Treaties (WWII: Allies-Ger.)   D814.6
Treaties (WWII: Allies-It.)   D814.7
Treaties (WWII: Allies-Japan)   D814.8
Treaties (WWII: Allies-misc. Axis powers: by country)   D814.9.A-Z
Treaties (WWII: Axis powers: collections)   D814.55
Treaties (WWII: results)   940.53142
Treaties (WWII: separate: by name)   D749.5.A-Z
Treaties (WWII: with Axis powers)   D814.55-9
Treatment of prisoners (Geneva & Hague conven.: unofficial)   UH533 (PREFER
                                                    JX5136 &JX5243)

TREATY of Neuilly-sur-Seine (WWI: texts)   D643.B6
Treaty of St. Germain (WWI: texts by date)   D643.A8
Treaty of Trianon (WWI: non-U.S. texts)   D643.H7
TREATY OF VERSAILLES (WWI: 28 June 1919: collected texts)   D643.A2
Treaty of Versailles (WWI: official discussions by date)   D643.A6
Treaty of Versailles (WWI: other official by date)   D643.A65
Treaty of Versailles (WWI: preliminary discussions)   D643.A3-4
Treaty of Versailles (WWI: protocol)   D643.A51
Treaty of Versailles (WWI: reservations by date)   D643.A55
Treaty of Versailles (WWI: texts by date)   D643.A5.1919+
Treaty of Versailles (WWI: unofficial talks)   D643.A7.A-Z
Trench artillery (WWI: U.S.)   D570.327
Trench warfare   UG446   355.44
Trepper, Leopold (WWII: spy)   D810.S8.T65
TRIALS (Leipzig: 1921)   D626.G4
Trials, Ship (by name of vessel)   VM881.A-Z
Trials (WWI: atrocities, war crimes: by country accused)   D626.A-Z
Trials (WWII: atrocities, war crimes: by country accused)   D804.A-Z
Trials (WWII: atrocities, war crimes: Germ.: post-Nuremberg before American Military
Tribunals, 1946-49: by main defendant)   D804.G425.A-Z
Trials (WWII: atrocities, war crimes: Germ.: post-Nuremberg: misc. by defendant)
                                                    D804.G43.A-Z
Trials (WWII: atrocities, war crimes: Jp. except Tokyo: by place or defendant)
                                                    D804.J33.A-Z
Trials (WWII: atrocities, war crimes: Jp.)   D804.J3
Trieste (post-WWI territorial ?s)   D651.T85
Trinidad & Tobago   972.983   F2016 (Windward Is.), F2116 (Tob.), F2121 (Trin.)

Triple Alliance (1882)   D458 (SEE ALSO D397, D443, D511)
Triple Entente (1907)   D459 (SEE ALSO D443, D511)
Tripoli, Libya   DT239.T7
Tripolitania (WWII: occupied terr.)   D802.T7
Trondheim, Nor.   DL596.T8
Trondheim (Nor.: area)   DL576.T9
TROOP support (air forces)   358.41415   UG700-705, UG260
Troop support (communication, supply, medical, p.o.w.'s, etc.)   355.415 (ALSO
          use 355.41 for newer titles on p.o.w. care)   UC260-27, UA940-945
Troop support, Naval   359.415
Troops, Airborne (U.S.)   UD483-484   356.1660973
Troops, Ski & mountain   356.164   UD470-475, U167.5.W5
Troops, Special-purpose   356.16   U167.5.A-Z
Troopships & waterways (mil. transp.: gen.)   UC320
Trophies, Military (WWII: U.S.)   D769.8.T8
Tropical hygiene (mil. sci.)   UH611
Trotsky, Leon (Rus.: 1925-53 era)   DK268.T75
Truk (WWII)   D767.99.T89
Truk Islands (Carolines)   DU568.T7
Truk Islands (pilot & sailing guides)   VK933.T79
Truman, Harry S (U.S.: Pres., 1945-53)   E814
Tsinan, Ch. (N. Exped., 1926-28: incident)   DS777.462
Tsingtao, China   DS796.T7
TUNISIA   DT241-269, DT254   961.1
Tunisia (1881-1957: Fr. Protectorate)   DT264   961.104
Tunisia & Egypt (mil. geog.)   355.4761-4762
Tunisia & Libya (geog. & travel)   916.1
Tunisia (mil. status)   UA867.5   355.0330611
Tunisia (WWII)   D766.99.T7-8   940.53611, 961.104
Tunnels (mil. engineering)   UG340   623.68
Turbines, Marine   VM740   623.87233
TURKEY (20th c.)   DR577   956.102
Turkey (1909-18: Mohammed V)   DR583-588   956.101
Turkey (1914-18: WWI era)   DR588
Turkey (1918-45)   956.102   DR589-590
Turkey (1918-22: Mohammed VI)   DR589
Turkey (1923-60: Republic)   DR590   956.1024
Turkey (1923-38: Kemal Ataturk era)   956.1024   DR590, DR592 (biogs.),
          DR592.K4(Ataturk)
Turkey (1938-50: Ismet Inonu rule)   956.1025   DR590, DR592
Turkey & Albania (primarily Tur.)   DR401-741
Turkey & Asia Minor (lighthouses, beacons, foghorns, etc.)   VK1111-1112
Turkey & Cyprus   956.1   DR401-741, DS47-53, DS54 (Cyp.)
Turkey & Cyprus (geog. & travel)   915.61-66   DR428, DS54 (Cyprus)
Turkey (mil. status)   UA810   355.0330561
Turkey (naval geog.)   359.4756   VA667.T9
Turkey (naval status)   VA667.T9   359.0309561
Turkey (overall)   956.1   DR440
Turkey (post-WWI territorial ?s)   D651.T9
Turkey (WWII)   D766.7.T8
Turkey (WWII: dipl. history)   D754.T8
Turkey (WWII: gen. particip.)   940.53561   D766.7.T8, DR590

Turrets & cupolas, Naval   VF440
Turrets, Revolving (naval sci.: inclu. monitors)   V860
Tuscany & Florence, It.   DG731-760
Tuvalu (Ellice Is.)   996.82   DU590
Tyrol & Vorarlberg (20th c.)   DB780
Tyrol (post-WWI territorial ?s)   D651.T95

U.S.   [SEE ALSO 'United States']
U.S. Army   UA24-39
U.S. Army (gen.)   UA25   355.00973, .30973, .310973
U.S. Army (special troops: by name)   UA34.A-Z
U.S. Coast Guard   VG53   359.970973
U.S. Dept. of Defense   UA23.2-6   353.6-7
U.S. Dept. of Defense (gen. hist.)   UA23.6
U.S. Marine Corps   VE23   359.960973
U.S. Marine Corps (gen.)   VE23.A8-Z
U.S. Marine Corps (official hist's.)   VE23.A3-32
U.S. Marine Corps (official monographs)   VE23.A5
U.S. Marine Corps League   VE23.A13-14
U.S. Military Academy (West Point)   U410.A-R3+   355.0071173
U.S. Military Academy (admin.)   U410.C3-H8
U.S. Military Academy (gen. hist.)   U410.L1
U.S. Military Academy (registers, unoff.)   U410.H5-8
U.S. military education (gen. special)   U408.3
U.S. National Guard (gen.)   UA42.A7-Z
U.S. NAVAL ACADEMY (Annapolis)   V415.A1-R4+   359.0071173
U.S. Naval Academy (Act of incorp.: PREFER KF7353.55)   V415.A1
U.S. Naval Academy (admin.)   V415.C3-H5
U.S. Naval Academy (Cong. docs.: gen.: by date)   V415.E5
U.S. Naval Academy (hist. & descrip.)   V415.L1-P1
U.S. Naval Academy (registers, unoff.)   V415.H5
U.S. NAVY   VA52-79 (SEE ALSO E182)
U.S. Navy (distribution: gen.)   VA62   359.4773, .31
U.S. Navy (gen.)   VA55   359.00973, .30973, .4773
U.S. Navy (gen.: 1881-1970 coverage)   VA58   359.00973
U.S. Navy (misc. units: by name)   VA66.A-Z
U.S. Navy (placement & stations)   VA62-74
U.S. Navy Dept. (official docs.: gen.)   VA52.A1-19
U.S. Strategic Bombing Survey reports (WWII)   D785.U57-63
U.S. Veterans' Administration   UB382-384
U.S. War Dept. (ann. reports)   UA24.A1-149
UKRAINE   DK508-508.9+
Ukraine (1917+: earlier pubns.)   DK508.8
Ukraine (1917-44)   DK508.79-835
Ukraine (1917-44: gen.)   DK508.812
Ukraine (Rev., 1917-21)   DK265.8.U4
Ukraine (1921-44)   DK508.833-835
Ukraine (geog. & travel)   914.771
Ukraine (post-WWI territorial ?s)   D651.U6
Ukrainians (in Arg.)   F3021.U5
Ukrainians (in Pol.)   DK4121.5.U4
Ulithi (Carolines)   DU568.U5

UNCONVENTIONAL WARFARE (air forces: intelligence, propaganda, etc.)
358.41343
Unconventional warfare, Allied (WWI: espionage, intell., infilt., sabotage, etc.)
940.486
Unconventional warfare, Allied (WWII: inclu. espionage, infilt., intelligence,
subversion)   940.5486+
Unconventional warfare, Axis (WWII: inclu. espionage, intelligence, infiltration,
subversion)   940.5487+
Unconventional warfare, Central Power (WWI)   940.487
Unconventional warfare (navies)   359.343   VB230-250
Unconventional warfare (WWI: espionage, intell., infilt., sabotage, etc.)   940.485
D639.S7-8
Unconventional warfare (WWII: inclu. espionage, infilt., intelligence, subversion)
940.5485   D810.S7 (gen.), .S8.A-Z (by spy),
D802 (underground), D802.F8 (Fr. undergr.), UB250-
274, UB273-274 (sabo.), UB251.A-Z (intell., by
country), UB271.A-Z (espion., by country respons.),
VB230-250 (naval intell. & espionage)
Underground movements (Sino-Jpn. Confl., 1937-45)   DS777.533.U53
Underwater demolition teams (navies)   VG86-88
Underwater reconnaissance & demolition (navies: inclu. frogmen)   359.984
VG86-88 (demo.), VG190 (recon.)
UNIFORMS, Air force   358.4114   UG1160-1165
Uniforms, Air force   UG1160-1165   358.4114
Uniforms, Infantry   356.1814
Uniforms, Marine   VE400-405   359.9614
Uniforms, Military (besides U.S.)   UC485.A-Z
Uniforms, Military (gen.)   UC480   355.14
Uniforms, Military (inclu. insignia, etiquette of, etc.)   355.14   UC480-535,
UC483 (U.S.)
Uniforms, Naval (besides U.S.)   VC305.A-Z
Uniforms, Naval (gen.)   VC300   359.14, .81
Union of Soviet Socialist Republics (Russia)   [SEE ALSO 'Russia' or 'Soviet
Union']   947   DK, DK1-275, DK501-973+
United Nations (WWII: Allies: gen. particip.)   940.5332   D743, D748
UNITED STATES   [SEE ALSO 'U.S.']   E-F975+, E151-860+, E178 (gen.)
973-979.9+
United States (1865-1900+)   E660-738   973.8-89
United States (1898: Sp.-Am. War)   973.89 (SEE ALSO 946.08 for Sp.-Am. War,
1898)   E714-735, E715
United States (20th c.)   973.9+   E740-749, E741
United States (20th c.: gen.)   E741   973.9
United States (1913-21: gen.)   E766
United States (1913-21: Woodrow Wilson period)   E765-783, E766,
E780 (WWI era)   973.913
United States (1914-18: WWI era: internal)   E780   973.913

United States (1919-33: inclu. Roaring Twenties)   E784   973.913-916
United States (1921-23: Warren G. Harding era)   973.914   E783-786, E785
United States (1921-23: Warren G. Harding era: gen.)   E785 (SEE JX235 ALSO
                        for arms limitation conference, Pacific possessions
                        treaty, etc.)   973.914
United States (1923-29: Calvin Coolidge)   973.915   E791-796, E791
United States (1923-29: Calvin Coolidge period: gen.)   E791 (SEE ALSO JX1952
                        & JX1987 for Kellogg-Briand Pact of 1928)   973.915
United States (1929-33: Pres. Herbert Hoover: inclu. London & 3-Power naval
                        conferences & treaties)   E796-805, E801 (SEE
                        ALSO JX1974)   973.916
United States (1933-45: gen.)   E806
United States (1933-45: Pres. Franklin D. Roosevelt)   E805-812   973.917
United States (1945-53: gen.)   E813
United States (1945-53: Pres. Harry S Truman)   E813-815   973.918
United States aerial ops. (WWI)   D570.6, D606 (gen.)   940.44973
United States aerial ops. (WWII)   D790   940.544973
United States (air war geog.)   358.414773   UG633
United States & U.S. military ops. (WWII: gen.)   D769.A5-Z (SEE ALSO E806 for
                        internal, general U.S. history, 1939-45)
                        940.5373, .540973, .532273, 973.917
United States automatic machine guns   UF620.U6
United States (biog.: heads of state)   923.173   E176.1 (Presidents: collective)
United States engineering ops. (WWII)   D795.U6
United States (gen. & cultural, serials, societies, etc.)   E151
United States (gen. hist.)   E178   973
United States (geog. & travel: overall)   917.3   E169 (1914-45)
United States (geog. & travel: states, areas, & towns)   917.4-9
United States (lighthouses, beacons, foghorns, etc.)   VK1023-1025
United States (lighthouses, beacons, foghorns, etc.: lists)   VK1243
UNITED STATES (LOCAL), Canada, Newfoundland, Mexico, Central & South America
                        F   974-79+, 971-2, 980-89
United States (local history), Canada, Latin America   F   971-972, 974-989
United States (local: regions, states, towns, etc.)   F1-975+   974-979 (note
                        that Hawaii is placed at 996.9)
United States magazine rifle   UD395.U6
United States (maps & atlases)   912.73   G1200+, G1201
United States medical services (WWI: by overseas locale)   D629.U8.A-Z
United States medical services (WWII)   940.547573   D807.U6-87,
                        .U6 (gen.), .U62.A-Z (by state), .U72-73 (Army
                        hospitals), .U85-87 (Navy hospitals)
United States medical services (WWII: by state)   D807.U62.A-W
United States medical services (WWII: Calif.)   D807.U62.C3

UNITED STATES (MIL. capabil.)   355.033273
United States (mil. geog.)   355.473   UA993
UNITED STATES MILITARY OPS. & U.S. (WWI)   D570-570.9+   940.373,
                                            41273, .40973, 327.73
United States military ops. & U.S. (WWII)   D769-769.99   940.532273,
                                            .5373, .540973, .541273, .5428
United States military ops. (WWI: organiz. units: land, sea, air)   D570.2-.79 (SEE
                                            D570.A4-Z, D545 etc. for overall
                                            participation, battles, etc.)
United States military ops. (WWII: gen. special)   D769.2
United States military ops. (WWII: land,air, & sea)   D769.2-799 (SEE D769.5.A5-Z
                                            for gen. works)   940.541273, .544373, .544973
United States military ops. (WWII: organiz. units: land, sea)   D769.2-779 (SEE
                                            D769.A5-Z, D756.5, D767 etc. for overall
                                            efforts, area campaigns & battles)
United States (mil. policy)   355.033573
United States (mil. status)   355.033073 UA23
United States (mil. status: gen.)   UA23.A2-Z
UNITED STATES (NAVAL geog.)   359.4773   VA49-395, VA50 (gen.)
United States (naval geog.: partic. states)   359.4774-4779   VA90-387
United States (naval hist.)   359.00973   VA49-395, VA50-70, E182, E746 (20th c.)
UNITED STATES NAVAL OPS. & Coast Guard ops. (WWII: fleets, squadrons,
                                bases, etc.)   D769.45-599 (SEE D773-4, D783
                                for overall works, specific ships & engagements,
                                submarines)   940.545973
United States naval ops. (WWI)   D570.4-.5   940.45+, .41273
United States naval ops. (WWI: gen.)   D570.4-5, D589.U5-8 (PREFER)
United States naval ops. (WWII)   D773-774 (SEE ALSO D769.45-599 for
                                specific fleets, squadrons, bases, units)
                                940.545973
United States naval ops. (WWII: by battle, ship, etc.)   D774.A-Z
United States naval ops. (WWII: gen.: inclu. blockade, patrol)   D773   940.545973
United States naval ops. (WWII: special topics: land batteries, defensive areas,
                                Marine Corps except land, etc.)   D769.45
United States (naval policy & status)   359.030973
United States ordnance (gen.)   UF563.A9-Z
United States (pilot guides: gen.)   623.892973   VK993
United States (pilot guides: specific areas)   623.892974-892979   VK947-
                                948 (W. Coast), VK981-982 (E. Coast)
United States propaganda (WWII)   D810.P7.U6
United States submarine ops. (WWII: by battle, ship, etc.)   D783.5.A-Z
United States submarine ops. (WWII: gen.)   D783
United States (WWI: causes, aims, results)   D520.U6-7
United States (WWI: gen.)   D570   940.373
United States (WWI: neutrality & dipl. history)   D619   940.32273, .373
United States (WWI: special topics)   D570.8.A-Z (SEE D639 for outside U.S.)
UNITED STATES (WWII: causes, aims, results)   D742.U5-6
United States (WWII: collections)   D769.A2
United States (WWII: dipl. hist., inclu. neutral years)   D753-753.8
                                940.532573, .532273, 973.917
United States (WWII: gen.)   D769   940.532273, .5373, .540973,
                                .541273, .5428
United States (WWII: gen. particip.: by area or state)   940.5374-5379
                                D769.85.A-Z, D769.87-88, F1-951+
United States (WWII: gen. special)   D769.1

United States (WWII: Reconstruction: by state)   D828.A-W
United States (WWII: Reconstruction: gen.)   D827
United States (WWII: special topics)   D769.8.A-Z (SEE D810.A-Z for outside U.S.)
United States (WWII: states)   D769.85.A-W
Units, Naval air (U.S.: by name: inclu. organizations)   VG94.6.A-Z
Universal service   UB350-355
Universal service & training (mil. resources)   355.225   UB350-355
Ural Mts. region (Rus.)   947.87   DK511.U7
Ural Mts. (Rus.)   DK511.U7   947.87
Ural Mts. (WWII)   D764.6.U82
Urban warfare tactics   355.426   U167.5.S7
URUGUAY   F2701-2799, F2721 (gen.)   989.5
Uruguay (1904-)   F2728   989.5061-5063
Uruguay (1933-51)   989.5063   F2728
Uruguay (gen.)   F2721
Uruguay (mil. status)   UA640-642   355.0330895
Uruguay (naval status)   VA440
Uruguay (WWII: dipl. hist.)   940.5325895 (could ALSO be at .5324895 with Axis)
                                D754.U

V-2 rocket   UG1312.V2
Valencia, Sp.   DP402.V15-25
Valencia (Sp.: area)   DP302.V11-25
Van Diemen's Land (Tasmania: gen. & descrip.)   DU460-470
Vancouver, B.C.   F1089.5.V22   971.134
Vanuatu (New Hebrides)   993.95 (SEE ALSO 993.4 to find works on New
                                Hebrides prior to 1989)   DU760
Vatican City   945.634   DG800
Vatican City (1929-)   DG800
Vatican City (Rome: WWII: gen. particip.)   940.5345634   D763.I82.V or .R,
                                D810.C6, DG800
Vedettes, scout & dispatch boats, other minor craft (gen.)   V880
Vehicles, Military (design: inclu. combat & support v's. & neces. ordnance)
                                623.74   UC270-275+
Vehicles, Motor (air force: ground) UG1400-1405
Vehicles, Motor (mil.: U.S.)   UG618
Venezuela   F2301-2349, F2321   987
Venezuela (1935-)   F2326   987.0632
Venezuela (gen.)   F2321
Venezuela (mil. status)   UA643-645
Venezuelan coast islands (Aruba, Curaçao, Tobago, Trinidad, etc.)   F2016
                                972.98
Venice, It. (city state & modern)   DG670-679
Verdun, Battle of (WWII: 1940)   D756.5.V3
Verdun, Fr.   DC801.V45
Versailles, Fr. (also Trianon)   DC801.V55-57
Vessels (naval architec.: by use)   VM378-466
Vessels, Naval war (modern period)   V765-767   623.80904
VETERANS' benefits   355.115   UB356-405, UB356-358
Veterans' benefits & services   UB356-405   355.115
Veterans' education, employment, etc. (gen.)   UB356   355.1152, .1154
Veterans' homes & hospitals   UB380-385
Veterans' homes & hospitals (besides U.S.)   UB385.A-Z
Veteran's or Armistice Day addresses, services (WWI: U.S.)   D671
Veterans' rehabilitation (places besides U.S.)   UB365.A-Z

Veterinary service (WWII)   D810.V45
Veterinary services (mil.)   UH650-655   355.345
Vichy France (WWII: dipl. hist.)   940.532444 (perhaps ALSO .532544)
                                      D752
Vickers machine guns   UF620.V4
Victoria (Australia)   DU200-230, DU220   994.5
Victoria (Australia: 1851-1950: inclu. descrip.)   DU212
Vienna, Austria   943.613   DB841-860, DB847 (gen.)
Vienna, Austria (20th c.)   DB855
Vienna, Austria (gen. hist. & descr.)   DB847
Vienna, Austria (WWII)   D765.45.V45
Vietnam (Annam)   DS556   959.7
Vietnam (1802-1954)   DS558.8
Vietnam (geog. & travel)   915.97   DS556.36
Vietnam (mil. status)   UA853.V5
Vietnam (WWII: gen.)   D767.35, DS556.36, DS549 (earlier works)
                         940.53597, 959.703
Views (WWI)   D527 (SEE ALSO D522)
Views (WWII)   D746 (SEE ALSO D743.2+)
Virgin Islands (U.S.)   F2136   972.9722
Virginia   F221-235, F226, F231 (1865-1950)   975.5
Visayan Islands (Philip.: inclu. Cebu, Leyte, Negros, etc.)   959.95
                                      DS688.B6 (Bisayas)
Vistula River & Valley (Pol.: Wisla) DK4600.V5
Visual signaling (mil.)   UG582.V5
Vittorio Emanuele III (It.: King, 1900-46: gen. inclu. times)   DG566
Vladivostok, Rus.   DK781.V5
Volga River Valley (Rus.)   DK511.V65
Volgograd, Rus. (also Tsaritsyn or Stalingrad)   947.85   DK651.S7
Voluntary enlistment (navies)   359.22362
Volunteers (Nat. Guard, militia, etc.: Illinois)   UA170-179
Vorarlberg, Austria (WWII)   D765.45.V6
Voss, Nor.   DL596.V6

WACS (Women's Army Corps: U.S.)   UA565.W6
WACS (Women's Army Corps: WWII: U.S.)   D769.39
Waffen SS (WWII: Ger.: Waffenschutzstaffel)   D757.85
Wages & salaries, Air force   358.4164   UG940-945, UC74 (U.S.), UC90+
Wagons & carts, Artillery   UF380-385
Wake Is. (WWII)   D767.99.W35
Wake Island   DU950.W28   996.5
Wales   942.9
Wales (19th & 20th c.)   DA722   942.908+
Wallace, Henry A. (U.S.: 20th c.)   E748.W23
Wallace, Henry A. (U.S.: 20th c.: works)   E742.5.W3

WAR (aftermath: occupation, reconstruc., etc.)   355.028
War & warfare   355.02   U21, U21.2, U102
War (causes)   355.027   U21.2, HB195, JX1952
War correspondents & public relns. (mil.: U.S.)   UH703
War correspondents & public relns. (navies: U.S.)   VG503
War crimes, atrocities, trials (WWI: gen.)   D625   940.405, .472
War crimes, atrocities, trials (WWII: gen.)   D803
War games   U310   355.5
War games, Naval   V250   359.52
Warfare & military forces (types)   356-359   UD-UG, V
Warfare (summary topics)   355.021   U161-162, UA10
Warning systems (defense engineering)   623.37 (SEE .737 for titles after 1988)
Warrant officers (mil.)   UB407-409
Warrant officers (naval: gen.)   VB307   359.332
Warsaw, Pol.   DK651.W2 (earlier works), DK4610-4645
Warsaw, Pol. (1918-)   DK4633
Warsaw, Pol. (area)   943.84   DK651.W2, DK4610-4645
Warsaw, Pol. (gen.)   DK4630
Warsaw, Pol. (WWII)   D765.2.W3
Warship handling (plus other seamanship topics)   VK545   623.8825
WARSHIPS (as equip.: develop., operation, tech. effectiveness)   359.835-836
                                (SEE ALSO .32+ for ships as units or indiv. ships)
Warships (construction, armament, types, etc.)   V750-995+ (SEE VA for status
                                & organiz. of specific navies around the world)
Warships, Fuel-powered (engineering)   623.825   V750, V765, V797-799
Warships, Fuel-powered (handling)   623.8825   VB200-205
Warships (naval architec.)   VM380 (PREFER V750-995+)   623.825, 359.32
Warships (powered: design)   623.8125   V750, V765-767, V799-800
Warships, Sail-driven (engineering)   623.8225   V750-797, V750, V795
Warships (types)   V815-895   623.825-826, 359.83, .325-326
Washington (state)   F886-900, F891   979.7
Washington (state: to 1950)   F891
WASHINGTON, D.C. (1865-1933)   975.303   F198-199
Washington, D.C. (1933-)   975.304   F199+
Washington, D.C. area (1878-1950)   F199   975.303-304
Washington, D.C. (gen.)   F194
Washington, D.C. (streets, bridges, railroads)   F203.7.A-Z
Washington, D.C. (District of Columbia: WWII)   D769.85.D6
Washington, D.C. (WWII: Reconstruction: Virginia)   D828.V8-81
Watch drills, Naval (U.S.: gen.: ALSO quarter, station, other)   VD160
                                359.50973, .1330973, .133220973
Watch duty (merch. duty)   VK233
WATER & sanitation (naut. craft: engineering)   623.854   VM503-505 (water),
                                VM481-483 (san.)
Water, Potable (naut. craft: engineering)   623.8542
Water, Sea (naut. craft: engineering)   623.8543
Water supplies, Military   UC780
Water supplies, Naval (inclu. preservation, purification, etc.)   VC410 (SEE VM503
                                for onboard storage)   623.854
Water supply (mil. engineering)   623.751   UC780, VC410, VM503-505
Water supply (naval architec. & engin.)   VM503-505   623.854

Waterways   UA970-975
Waterways & troopships (mil. transp.)   UC320-325   359.3264
Waterways (Ger.)   UA975.G3
Waterways (outside U.S.)   UA975.A-Z
Waterworks (defense)   UA929.95.W3
Watkin range finder   UF850.W3
Wavell, Archibald Percival Wavell, 1st Earl of (G.B.: 20th c. mil. biog.)   DA69.3.W37
Waves (U.S. naval reserves for women & other non-local U.S. naval res.)   VA390
Wealthy & upper classes (WWII)   940.5315062   D800
Weapons systems (artillery)   UF500-505
Weapons systems, Naval   VF346-348
Weather forecaster, Naval (gen.)   VG610
Weights & measures (mil. metrology)   UG455
Weimar Republic (Ger.: 1918-33)   943.085   DD233-251, DD237 (gen.),
                DD251 (Hindenb. era), DD453 (Prussia)
Weizmann, Chaim (Palestine: 19th-20th c.)   DS125.3.W45
Welding & cutting, Underwater (marine engin.)   VM965
WELFARE & RELIEF SERVICES (WWI)   940.477   D637-638
Welfare & relief services (WWI: by G.B.)   940.477841   D638.G7
Welfare & relief services (WWI: in specific places)   940.4779+   D638.A-Z,
                D657-658 (Reconstruc. in U.S.), D659.A-Z (by place)
Welfare & relief services (WWI: provided by specific countries)   940.4778+
                D638.A-Z
WELFARE & RELIEF SERVICES (WWII)   940.5477   D808-809
Welfare & relief services (WWII: by Australia)   940.5477894   D809.A8
Welfare & relief services (WWII: by G.B.)   940.5477841   D809.G7
Welfare & relief services (WWII: by U.S.)   940.5477873   D809.U5
Welfare & relief services (WWII: in particular countries)   940.547794-547799
                D809.A-Z
Welfare & relief services (WWII: provided by specific countries)
                940.547784-547789   D809.A-Z
Welfare services, Military (U.S.: gen.)   UH755
Welfare services, Naval (U.S.)   VG2003
Wellington, N.Z.   DU428   993.127
Wellington, N.Z. (WWII)   D767.852.W44   993.127
Welsh troops (G.B.)   UA663
WEST Africa   DT471-720   966-967, 968.8
West African islands   DT671.A-Z
West Coast (Am.: plus E. Pac.: pilot & sailing guides)   VK941-956
West Coast (U.S.: Loran tables)   VK561.U57
West Coast (U.S.: pilot & sailing guides)   VK947   623.892916432
West Coast (U.S.: tide & current tables)   VK747   623.8949091643
WEST INDIES   972.9   F1601-2175+, F1608, F1621
West Indies (1898-)   F1623   972.904-905
West Indies (1902-45)   972.9051   F1623
West Indies (gen. hist.)   F1621
West Indies (lighthouses, beacons, foghorns, etc.: lists)   VK1239-1240
West Indies (mil. status)   UA609-611
West Indies (naval geog.)   359.47729   VA409-410
West Indies (pilot & sailing guides: by island[s])   VK973.A-Z
West Point (descrip. & life)   U410.M1.P1
West Point (U.S. Mil. Acad.: official hist's.)   U410.L1.A1-5
West (U.S.) & Trans-Mississippi   F591-705   978

WESTERN Australia   DU350-380   994.1
Western Australia (gen. & descrip.)   DU360-370
Western Europe & Europe (1453+)   940.2   D208, D217
Western Europe (WWII: except Ger., G.B., Fr.)   D763.A-Z
Western Front & Western Europe (WWII)   D756-763   940.5421
Western Front (WWI)   D530-549
Western Hemisphere (gen.) & United States   E   970
Western Samoa (was Ger. Samoa)   DU819.A2   996.14
Western states   978   F591-785, F591-596, F591
Westphalia (Prus.)   DD491.W4-52
White House (Washington, D.C.)   F204.W5
White Russia & Western U.S.S.R. (geog. & travel)   914.76
White Russia (Belorussia)   DK511.W5   947.65
White Russia (Western Russia)   DK507
White Russians (in Pol.)   DK4121.5.W5
Whitehead torpedo   V855.W5
Willkie, Wendell (U.S.: 20th c.)   E748.W7
Wilson, Wilson (U.S.: Pres., 1913-21)   E767
Wilson, Woodrow (U.S.: 1865-1900 era: works)   E660.W7-75
Windward Islands (inclu. Barbados, St. Lucia. etc.)   F2011   972.98
Wings, Aircraft   629.13432
Winter warfare   U167.5.W5
Wireless signals (merch. marine)   VK397
WOMEN (20th c.: collective biography)   D412.5
Women & minorities (navies: gen.)   VB320   359.22
Women & minorities (U.S. Navy: gen.)   VB323
Women & minorities in the armed forces (U.S.: gen.)   UB417
Women & the military (sociology)   U21.75
Women & women's work (WWI)   D639.W7   940.315042
Women & women's work (WWII)   D810.W7
Women (armed forces: U.S.)   UB418.W65
Women (Ger.: 1918-48)   DD245
Women in air forces   358.41348
Women in armed forces   355.0082
Women in naval forces   359.229   VA49-750, VA390.W (U.S. Waves)
Women (Rus. Rev., 1917-21)   DK265.9.W57
Women (U.S. Navy)   VB324.W65
Women's military units   355.348   UA565.W6 (U.S. Wac's)
Women's naval units (gen.)   359.348   VA
Women's reserve, Marine (U.S.)   VE23.4
Women's reserves (U.S.)   UA45
Wooden ships (naval architec.)   VM142-145   623.81
Woodrow Wilson Foundation   E772
WORLD HISTORY (20th c.: collected)   D414-415
World history (20th c.: gen.)   D410-460+, D421-5, D421   909.82
World history (20th c.: several authors)   D414
World history (20th c.: single-author collections)   D415
World history (1919-39)   D720-728
World history, Europe, Africa, Asia, Oceania   D-DX   900-949, 990's
World history (gen.: 1800-)   909.8   D299, D395
World navies (pop. works)   VA41

WORLD WAR I (1914-18)　　　D501-680　　940.3-940.499
World War I (Allies & associates: mil. units & ops.)　940.412+　　D544-550, D569-570
World War I & women　　940.315042　　D639.W7, JX1965
World War I (antisub. ops.)　　940.4516　　D580-589, D590
World War I (Armistice)　　940.439　　D641
World War I (Central Powers: mil. units & ops.)　940.413+　　D531-540, D566
World War I (gen.)　　D521　　940.3, 940.4
WORLD WAR I (GEN. PARTICIP.: Australia)　　940.394　　D547.A8
World War I (gen. particip.: by country: inclu. mobilization)　　940.34-39
World War I (gen. particip.: Can.)　940.371　　D547.C2
World War I (gen. particip.: Fr.)　940.344　　D548, DC387
World War I (gen. particip.: G.B.)　　940.341-342　　D546, DA577
World War I (gen. particip.: Ger.)　　940.343　　D531, DD228.8
World War I (gen. particip.: It.)　940.345　　D569, DG570
World War I (gen. particip.: New Z.)　　940.3931 (SEE ALSO .393 for titles after
　　　　　　　　　　　　　　1988)　　D547.N5
World War I (gen. particip.: Rus.)　940.347　　D550, DK264.8
World War I (gen. particip.: U.S.)　940.373-379　　D570
World War I (medical srvcs.)　940.475　　D628 (gen.), D629.A-Z (by country),
　　　　　　　　　　　　D630.A-Z (biog.)
World War I (mil. units & ops.: gen.)　940.41　　D521
World War I (misc. special)　D639.A-Z (SEE D570.8 for U.S.)
World War I (misc. topics)　940.48
World War I (mobilization)　940.402 (SEE .34-39 for particular countries)
World War I (naval ops.: particular countries)　940.459　　D580-589
World War I (special topics)　D622-639
World War I (submarine ops.)　940.451　　D590-595, D590 (gen.)
WORLD WAR II (1939-45)　　D731-838　　940.53-940.5499
World War II (1939-45: gen.: inclu. overall works on Sino-Japanese War
　　　　　　　　[1937-45])　　940.53　D743
World War II (1940)　　D755.2
World War II (1941)　　D755.3
World War II (1942)　　D755.4
World War II (1943)　　D755.5
World War II (1944)　　D755.6
World War II (1945)　　D755.7
World War II (Allies & United Nations: mil. units & ops.)　　940.5412+
World War II & women　　940.5315042　　D810.W7
World War II (anecdotes)　940.5494　　D743.9
World War II (antisub. ops.)　　940.54516　　D780, D770-784
World War II (Axis Powers: mil. units & ops.)　　940.5413+
World War II (collected works)　　D739
World War II (dipl. hist.)　　940.532　　D748-754, D748 (gen.)
World War II (gen.)　　D743　　940.53, .54

WORLD WAR II (GEN. PARTICIP.: Albania)   940.534965   D766.7.A4,
        DR701.S8-86, DR974 (later works after 1980?)
World War II (gen. particip.: Algeria)   940.5365   D766.99.A4-6, DT295
World War II (gen. particip.: Asia)   940.535
World War II (gen. particip.: Australia)   940.5394   D767.8-82, DU116
World War II (gen. particip.: Austria & Liech.)   940.53436 D765.4 (Austria),
        DB99, D765.45.L (Liech.), DB540.5
World War II (gen. particip.: Belgium)   940.53493   D763.B4-42, DH687
World War II (gen. particip.: Bulg.)   940.534977   D766.7.B8, DR89-90
World War II (gen. particip.: Burma)   940.53591   D767.6, DS485.B89,
        DS530 (later titles post 1970?)
World War II (gen. particip.: by country: inclu. exile govs., undergr. move's., pro- &
        anti-Axis nat. groups, mobilization, etc.)   940.534-539
World War II (gen. particip.: Can.)   940.5371   D768.15, F1034
World War II (gen. particip.: Caroline Is.)   940.53966   DU565-567
World War II (gen. particip.: China)   940.5351   D767.3, DS777.518-533
World War II (gen. particip.: country groups, inclu. nat. groups, pro- & anti-Axis nat.
        groups, mobilization)   940.533
World War II (gen. particip.: Crete)   940.534998   D766.7.C7, DF901. C86
World War II (gen. particip.: Denmark & Fin.)   940.53489 D763.D4-42, DL256 (Den.)
World War II (gen. particip.: Egypt)   940.5362   D766.9, DT107.82
World War II (gen. particip.: Finland)   940.534897 (SEE ALSO .53471 for some
        works before 1980)   D754.F5, D765.3,
        DK459.45+, DL1090-1105+ (works after about 1980),
        DL1090, DL1097
World War II (gen. particip.: Fr. & Monaco)   940.5344   D752, D761, DC397
World War II (gen. particip.: G.B.)   940.5341   D750, D759, DA587
World War II (gen. particip.: Ger.)   940.5343   D751, D757, DD253-256.5
World War II (gen. particip.: Greece)   940.53495   D766.3-32, DF726
World War II (gen. particip.: Guam & the Marianas)   940.53967   D767.G or .M,
        DU647 (Guam), DU645 (Marianas)
World War II (gen. particip.: Hungary)   940.53439   D765.56, DB955
World War II (gen. particip.: India)   940.5354   D767.6, D767.63 (Free India), DS413
World War II (gen. particip.: Iran)   940.5355   D766.7.I55, DS317-318
World War II (gen. particip.: Iraq)   940.53567   D766.7.I57, DS79.53
World War II (gen. particip.: Israel)   940.535694   D766.7.P (Palestine), D766.7.I7
World War II (gen. particip.: It.)   940.5345   D763.I8, DG571-572
World War II (gen. particip.: Japan)   940.5352   D767.2-25, DS888.5-889
World War II (gen. particip.: Libya)   940.53612   D766.93, DT235
World War II (gen. particip.: London, Eng.)   940.53421   D760.8.L7, DA684
World War II (gen. particip.: Luxemb.)   940.534935   D763.L9, DH916
World War II (gen. particip.: Morocco)   940.5364   D766.99.M8, DT324
World War II (gen. particip.: New Guinea)   940.5395   D767.95, DU740-746
World War II (gen. particip.: New Z.)   940.53931 (SEE ALSO .5393 for works after
        1988)   D767.85-852, DU411
World War II (gen. particip.: Nor.)   940.53481   D763.N6-62, DL532
World War II (gen. particip.: Paris, Fr. area)   940.534436   D762.P3, DC737+
World War II (gen. particip.: Philippines)   940.53599   D767.4, DS686.3-4
World War II (gen. particip.: Rumania)   940.53498   D766.4, DR264-267
World War II (gen. particip.: Rus.)   940.5347   D764, D754.R9 or .S65,
        DK267-273, DK273

World War II (gen. particip.: S. Africa)   940.5368   D766.97, DT779.7
World War II (gen. particip.: Singapore)   940.535952 (SEE .535957 for later titles)
                                             D767.5, DS598.S7
World War II (gen. particip.: Solomon Is.)   940.53935   D767.98, DU850
World War II (gen. particip.: Syria)   940.53569   D766.7.S9, DS98
World War II (gen. particip.: Tunisia)   940.53611   D766.99.T8, DT264
World War II (gen. particip.: U.S.)   940.5373   D769, E806-813, E806 (gen.)
World War II (gen. particip.: U.S.: by area or state)   D769.85.A-W,
                                             D769.87-88, F1-951+
World War II (gen. particip.: U.S.: N.Y.)   940.53747   D769.85.N4-5, F124
World War II (gen. particip.: Yug.)   940.53497   D766.6-62, DR366,
                                             DR1289 (later works after 1980?)
World War II (gen. special: deception, strategy, psychological aspects, world
                                             politics, misc.)   D744
World War II (medical srvcs.)   940.5475   D806-807, D806 (gen.)
World War II (mil. units & ops.: gen.)   940.541   D743
World War II (misc. topics)   940.548
World War II (mobilization)   940.5402 (SEE .534-539 for particular countries)
                                             D800, HC, HF, HJ
World War II (naval ops.: particular countries)   940.5459+   D770-784
World War II (Sept. 1939-Dec. 1941)   D755
World War II (Sept. 1939-May 1940)   D755.1
World War II (special topics)   D798-810
World War II (special topics)   D810.A-Z (SEE D769.8.A-Z for U.S.)
World War II (submarine ops.)   940.5451+ (SEE ALSO .542 for ops. by theatre)
                                             D780-784, D780 (gen.), D781-782 (Ger.), D783 (U.S.),
                                             D784.A-Z (other lands)
World War II (VE Day to VJ Day)   D755.8
Wounded, Care of (mil.: inclu. relief societies: gen.)   UH520   361.05, .77, .9,
                                             940.477+
Wrecks, Nautical (research)   623.8885   VK1250+
Writers (WWII)   940.53158   D810.A7
Wroclaw, Breslau, Pol. (WWII)   D765.2.W7
Wyoming (WWII)   D769.85.W8-81

Y.M.C.A., Y.W.C.A. (WWII)   D810.Y7
Yachts (small craft: gen.)   VM331
Yalta, Rus.   DK651.Y25
Yalta, Uk. (Jalta)   DK508.95.I24
Yamamoto, Isoroku, Adm., 1884-1943 (Japan: 1926-89 era)   DS890.Y25
Yamato (battleship: Japan)   VA655.Y25   359.32520952
Yangtze River (China)   DS793.Y25   951.2
Yap (Carolines)   DU568.Y3
Yards & stations, Naval (U.S.: by place)   VA70.A-Z
Yards, Navy (gen.)   V230 (SEE ALSO VA67-750 for particular places)   359.7
Yards, stations, shore facilities (navies: U.S.: gen.)   VC414   359.70973
Yearbooks & almanacs, Nautical (non-American)   VK8
Yearbooks, Naval (official: also lists: by country: SEE ALSO VA #s if dept. reports
                                             involved)   V11.A-Z   359.0025+, .005
Yearbooks, Naval (unofficial)   V10
Yellow Peril   DS519
Yemen   DS247.Y4-48
Yeomen & clerks, Naval   VG900-905
Young Plan (WWI)   D649.G3.A6-7
Youth (WWII)   D810.Y74

YUGOSLAVIA (Serbia)   DR301-396 (earlier pubns.), DR1214-1307+   949.7-71
Yugoslavia (to 1918)   949.701   DR317, DR1274
Yugoslavia (20th c.)   DR357   949.702, .7102
Yugoslavia (20th c. & 1918-)   949.702   DR357, DR1274, DR1282
Yugoslavia (1903-21: Peter I)   DR360-363   949.701-702
Yugoslavia (1914-18: WWI era)   DR363 (earlier pubns.), DR1280   949.7, .701
Yugoslavia (1918-45)   DR1288-1298   949.702
Yugoslavia (1918-45: gen.)   DR366, DR1289   949.702-7022
Yugoslavia (1918-45: inclu. Croatia, Serbia, Slovenia)   DR364-369
                               949.7021-7022, 949.7102 (Serbia)
Yugoslavia (1918-39: Kingdom)   949.7021   DR366, DR1289
Yugoslavia (1918-21: reign of Peter I)   DR1295
Yugoslavia (1921-34: Alexander I)   DR368, DR1296
Yugoslavia (1934-45: Peter II)   DR369, DR1297-98   949.7022
Yugoslavia (1941-45: Axis occup.)   DR1298   949.7022
Yugoslavia (1945-)   DR370
Yugoslavia & Bulgaria   949.7+
Yugoslavia & Yugoslavian military ops. (WWII)   D766.6-62   940.53497, 949.7022
Yugoslavia (central republics: Bosnia, Herzegovina, Montenegro)   949.74
Yugoslavia (gen., descrip., culture, hist.)   DR301-396+ (earlier books),
                               DR1202-1307+, DR1214   949.7
Yugoslavia (gen. hist.)   DR317, DR1245-1246   949.7
Yugoslavia (geog. & travel)   914.971-976   DR309, DR1221 (later books)
Yugoslavia (mil. status)   UA827   355.0330497
Yugoslavia (post-WWI territorial ?s)   D651.Y8-9
Yugoslavia (post-WWII territorial ?s: inclu. Trieste)   D821.Y8
Yugoslavia (WWII: collections)   D766.6.A2
Yugoslavia (WWII: dipl. history)   D754.Y9
Yugoslavian military ops. (WWII)   D766.6
Yugoslavia (1939-45: WWII era)   949.7022   DR369, DR1297-1298)
Yunnan Province (China)   DS793.Y8   951.35

ZAGREB, Yug. (WWII)   D766.62.Z3
Zanzibar (inclu. time as Brit. colony)   DT434.Z3, DT435, DT449.Z2-Z29 (newer titles)
Zanzibar (island & coast)   DT435
Zanzibar (1890-1963)   967.8103   DT435, DT449.Z2-29 (newer works),
                               DT449.Z28
Zionism, Restoration, Judenstaat   DS149-151
Zouaves (WWII: Fr.: infantry)   D761.38
Zurich, Swit.   DQ781-800   949.45

IV. LIBRARY OF CONGRESS SUBJECT & OTHER HEADINGS

The Library of Congress has constructed a controlled vocabulary system of LC subject, biographical, corporate, and other headings and phrases in order to provide consistent and thorough catalog access to its huge collection. Most academic and public libraries in the United States have adopted LC Subject Headings as the standard for catalog indexing, although some smaller public libraries may use the Sears group of headings. These are based on LC and represent a compact version.

As with the classification systems, change is inevitable in the ongoing subject vocabulary shown in this guide. The Library of Congress deliberately but regularly adds, amends, and drops headings and sub-headings in an attempt to keep pace with a changing world and language. Even corporate and other headings change as, for example, government agencies come into existence and then change names or as people's names finally require death dates. Rather than list only the latest approved descriptors, I have opted to include new and old so as to allow for better entrée in modernized or older catalogs. A richer vocabulary should also help with keyword-searching of entire records for buried terms when using online, optical-disk, or other electronic rosters of the future.

In using the LC subject headings, researchers should note that the network is predominately alphabetic and specialized in nature rather than overarching as with some database thesaurus systems. The latter depend heavily upon cross-references within a controlled framework of broader, narrower, and parallel terms and phrases trying to describe their universe. While LC started in the late 1980's to employ scoped cross-references, the prime character remains particularly alphabetic and diverse rather than attached to any classified verbal skeleton.

Some effort is made to incorporate hierarchical concepts within the alphabetic sequence. Hence, under the many headings that begin with 'World War, 1939-1945', LC has placed assorted subheadings and sub-subheadings in alphabetic suborder. Under 'World War, 1939-1945' may be found '—Aerial operations', '—Campaigns', '—Finance', —Great Britain', '—Naval operations', and numerous other subtopics. Under or after ' World War, 1939-1945— Campaigns' may be found many geographical subdivisions such as '—China', '—France', '—Japan', '—Poland', '—Ukraine', '—Western', and others in alphabetical order. Under some topics one can see historical subdivisions in chronological arrangement. Therefore, under the main heading of 'Japan— History' will be seen the subheadings '—20th century', '—1912-1945', '—Taisho period, 1912-1926', '—1926-1945' and '—March and October incidents, 1931' in that sequence.

The use of subdivisions allows for some gathering of similar subject groups within proximate alphabetic sets. Since the system simultaneously allows specialized descriptors and phrases in isolated positions throughout the alphabet, some confusion as to the best search method is natural. A combination of wider terms and subdivisions along with isolated or pinpoint headings is probably best, given the normal LC policy of assigning several terms of subject access to each cataloged title if warranted.

This division of the guide is organized in alphabetic array by LC term or proper-word heading or subject. Thus, mixed together as in many catalogs may be found historical events, tactical concepts, specific weapons, particular ships, airplane types and models, biographical names, government agencies, etc.

Please note that some electronic library catalogs place proper names of people and organizations into a separate file that encompasses these names as both subjects and authors, while many catalogs of whatever format would place such proper names into either subject or author catalogs depending on specific usage of each term. Also valuable to remember is the idea of searching corporate or government-agency authors as a means of quasi-subject searching. One could, for instance, find pertinent materials under 'United States. War Department' as an author that might not be listed under the subject terms considered for a particular search. I have chosen to keep all headings together so that readers need check only one listing and so as to avoid the separation of terms such as 'United States—History' from 'United States. Army'.

Following some of the headings are Library of Congress and/or Dewey Decimal Classification numbers that might be considered for browsing purposes in the stacks or shelflist. When two or more class numbers are given that begin with the same root, certain abbreviated forms may be seen. For example, LC numbers UG630 through UG670 might appear as 'UG630-70'. In the Dewey system, 358.4183 and 358.440973 could be listed as '358.4183, .440973'.

I have tried to include a large sampling of call numbers. Some of them represent typical range areas, but I have also presented a variety of numbers taken from outside the main historical and military spans that otherwise predominate. I did not discover nor devise numbers in every case. Many terms could be placed in a diverse number of classifications depending on individual library needs, and listing class examples would prove somewhat meaningless in these instances. I have attempted, nevertheless, to include at least representative numbers or ranges for the most important topics or topical groups.

Hopefully, the controlled-term section will help researchers to find more materials through knowledge of more headings and of related subdivision patterns and of classification possibilities. As stated in the class introductions, however, a thorough hunt will utilize both call numbers and regulated headings.

LC SUBJECT/BIOGRAPHICAL/CORPORATE HEADINGS: [NOTES]: LC/DEWEY #'S

A-5 rocket
Aachen—Siege, 1944   D757   940.5421
Academy War Film Library
Acheson, Dean Gooderham, 1893-1971 [U.S.: Diplomat]   E748.A15-17, E744,
                              E183.7   973.9180924, 327.73, 353.1
Adachi, Hatazo, 1890-1947   [Japan: Lt. Gen., Commander in New Guinea]
Admirals—Portraits
Adriatic question   D650.T4, D651   940.322497
Aerial gunnery
Aerial reconnaisance   UG760-5   623.72
Aeronautical instruments   TL587   629.135, .15
Aeronautics   TL500-830 (technology)   629.1-13+
   —Biography   TL539-40   926.2913, 629.130922, .1300922
   —History   TL512-32   629.109, .1309, .13009
Aeronautics, Military   UG630-70, JX5124 (int'nal. law), VG90 (naval)
              623.746, 358.4
      —Germany   UC535, UG635   358.410943, .411094
      —Great Britain   UG653   358.4135
      —History   UG623   358.40074
      —Japan   UG625   355.033052
      —Observations   UG630-70   355.413, 358.45
      —Psychology   RC550, UG632   616.85, 623.746
      —Research   UG633   353.63
      —Russia   UG635   358.400947
      —United States   E746, UG633, VG93 (naval), UC333
              355.83, 358.400973, .413320924, .4183, .440973, 629.13
         —History   UG633   358.40973, .4130973
         —Statistics   HE9803   387.74
Aeroplane carriers   V895   359.32
Aeroplanes, Military   [This spelling used mostly before 1980, after which SEE
      'Airplanes...']   TL685-6, UG633-5, VG93-5 (naval)   355.6213, 358.407,
              .4183, 623.740937, .746+, 629.133-134
Afghanistan   DS351-69   915.81+, 958.1+
Africa, North—History—1882-   DT204   916.103, 961.02+
Afro-American seamen
Afro-American soldiers   [For titles before around 1970 SEE 'Negro soldiers—U.S.']
              E185   355.00917496, .330973, 973.0496073
Afro-American veterans
Agents provocateurs—Germany
Agriculture and state   HD1415, HD1773   338.1091724, .13
Air bases
Air bases, American [British, German, etc.]
Air bases, American
Air bases, British
Air bases, German
Air bases, Japanese
Air bases—United States   UG634   358.417058
Air defenses
Air defenses, Military   UF625 (antiaircraft guns), UG630-5 (mil. aeronautics),
              U408   358.13, .39
Air forces—History
Air interdiction   UG700

Air pilots—Correspondence, reminiscences, etc.   TL510, TL540, TL721
                              629.125-126, .1308-1309+, .1325243, .13453, 926.2913
Air pilots, Military   UG626-626.2 (biog.)
—[country]
Air pilots—United States—Biography   TL539-540   358.400922, 629.130924
Air power   JX1391, UG630, VG93   358.41+
—History   UG630   358.4009
—United States   UG633, VG93 (naval)   358.40973, 623.4519
Air raid shelters   TH1097   623.388, 693.8
Air raid warning systems
Air-ships   TL650-68   629.133
Air warfare   UG630-5   358.30904, 358.414, 629.1339
—History   D437, UG625, UG700   358.400904, .414+
—Psychological aspects   UG630   355.23
Airborne troops   UD480   356.166
Aircraft carriers   [SEE ALSO 'Aerocraft carriers' for many works before 1980]
                    V874-5, D770, V895   359.3255+, .83, 623.8255, 940.545
—Aircraft launching and recovery
Aircraft industry   HD9711 (economics), TL724-724.5 (technology)   338.47629+
—Military aspects
—United States   HD9711   382.45629+
Aircraft spotting
Aircraft survival equipment   UG633, VG93, TL697   629.134386
Airdrop
Airlift, Military   UC330-5
Airplane factories
Airplanes   [SEE ALSO 'Aeroplanes' for works before about 1981]   TL670-723,
                                                        TL547   629.133+
—Control systems   TL678
—Design and construction   TL671   629.133-4+
—Ditching   TL711.D5
Airplanes, Military   TL685.3, HD9711, UG633, UG1123, UG1240, UG1245, VG93
                    338.4768, 358.4183, 623.746+, 629.133
—Armament
—Camouflage   UG1245, VG95   358.4183, 940.544943
—History   UG1243-5   358.4183
—Maintenance and repair
—Motors   TL701, VG93   358.4183, .41621, 338.47623746
—Parts
—Registers
—Turrets   UG630-5 (army), VG90-5 (navy)
Airplanes
—Piloting   TL710-13   621.13252, 629.132
—Handbooks, manuals, etc.
—Radar equipment
—Radio equipment   TL693-6
—Recognition   TL670   629.1333
—Registers   HE9769   629.133349
Airports   TL521, TL725   387.736, 629.1363
—Defense measures   TL725   363.35
Aitken, William Maxwell   [SEE 'Beaverbrook, William...']
Akronauplia (Greece: Concentration camp)
al'Alamayn, Battle of, 1942   [SEE 'El Alamein...']
Alam Halfa, Battle of, 1942

Albania
—History   DR701   949.65
—1912-1944
—Politics and government
Albert I, 1875-1934   [Belg.: King]   DH514, DH681-2, D615
        949.3040924, 940.3493, 923.1493, .1403, 929.793
Alexander, Harold Rupert Leofric George, 1st Earl, 1891-1969 [G.B.: Field Marshal]
        DA69.3.A43, .A57, D546.A37, D763.I8   942.0840924, 355.3310924
Alfieri, Dino, n.d. [It.: Fascist gov. official]   D811
Algeria—History—1830-1962   DT284, DT294   965, 965.03
Alliances   JX4005, JX1907   341.2, .72, 327.08
Allied and Associated Powers (1914-1920). Treaties, etc.
.Austria, 1919 Sept. 10   D643.A9
Allied Forces   D756.3
Allied Forces. Southwest Pacific Area. Allied Intelligence Bureau   D810
        940.548673
Allied Forces. Supreme Headquarters. Psychological Warfare Division   D810
        940.54886
Allied Powers (1919-). Reparation Commission   DC59.8.G3, D648-9
Alsace-Lorraine question   DD801   923.544, 944.38308, 320.944383+
Altuzzo, Battle of, 1944
American Cemetery, Manila   D810.D4   940.54655991
American Friends Service Committee
. Foreign Service Section
American Jewish Joint Distribution Committee
American National Red Cross
American Outpost in Great Britain   D731.O
Amery, Leo, 1873-1955   [G.B.: Conservative politician]   DA566.A, D743.9
        940.5304, 923.242
Amiens, Battle of, 1940
Ammunition   TS538, UF543, UF700   355.415, .621, .82, 623.455, 658.57, 688.7
—Transportation   UC323   359.982
Amphibian planes   TL684   629.133348+
Amphibious assault ships   VC263   658.56
Amphibious warfare   U261, U439, D25   359.83, 355.48
Anarchism and anarchists   HX821-970   320.570922, 335.83+, 923.347, 321.07
Anderson, John, Sir, 1882-1958   [G.B.: Cab. member for domestic affairs, inventor
        of Anderson Shelters, Chanc. o/t Excheq.]
Angary, Right of
Anglo-Russian treaty, 1942
Anschluss movement, 1918-1938   DB48, DB97   320.943085, 943.605
Antiairborne warfare
Anti-aircraft artillery
Anti-aircraft guns   UF625   358.13, 623.41
Anti-comintern pact
Anti-Nazi movement   D802.G3, DD256.3   940.534
Antisemitism   BM535, D5145, DS135, DS145, E184   301.451924,
        .452+, 296.387834+, 909.04924081
—Germany   DS135, DS145-146   261.8345+, 301.451924+,
        323.11924043, 956.94001
—History   DS145-147   301.451924, 909.0974+, .04924
—Russia
—United States
Anti-submarine warfare

385

Antitank guns   UF628   358.18, 623.412
Antitank weapons
Antonescu, Ion, 1882-1946   [Rum.: Marshal, Pr. Min.]   DR262.A
                                                                  923.5498
Antwerp, Battle of, 1944
Anzio Beachhead, 1944   D763   940.5421, .5338
Arab countries—History-Arab Revolt, 1916-1918   DS223, DS36-39, DS63,
                              D568.4   953.02, 909.04927, .0974927
Arandora Star (Ship)   D801.G7
Archives—United States   CD3021-3022, CD3065, CD6028   025.171
    —Inventories, calendars, etc.   CD3026-3027, CD3041, HE565, Z6027,
                              Z6366   016.32773, .3312973, .910973,
                              .9405488673, 330.973, 350.0914, 387.2097471
Ardeatine Massacre, 1944   D763   945.091
Ardennes, Battle of the, 1944-1945   D756   940.5421
Argentine Republic
    —History—1852-1933   F2848
    —History—1910-1943   F2848   982..06
Armaments   UA10   355.021, .03300+, .0335, 341.6705
    —Yearbooks
Armed forces   U21, U162, UA10, UA15   355.0330+, .0332
Armed forces
    —Appropriations and expenditures   UA17, JX1977   338.47355
    —History
Armed forces in foreign countries
Armed forces
    —Mobilization   UA910
    —Political activity   U21, UH720, JF1820   322.42, .5091724, 355.123094
    —Prayer-books and devotions   BV4588, BV273, BX2170, BM667
                              242.68, .88, 264.093, 296.4
Armed merchant ships
Armed Services Editions, Inc. [WWII]   Z1039.S6
Armenia—History—1917-1921   DS195   956.62
Armenian massacres, 1915-1923   DS195.5, DS51   361.530924,
                              947.92080924, 956.62, .102
Armenian question   DS194-5, H31   364.15109561, 956.64
Armies   UA10, UA15, UA646   350.895, 355.30944, .3509
    —Equipment   UC460-5   356.186
    —History   U37, UA15   355.0094, .0097
    —Insignia   UC530-5   355.134, .14
    —Officers   UB410-15
    —Organization   UA10, UA15   355.022, 355
    —Staffs   UB220-5   355.33+
Armistices   JX1907   343.31
Armored personnel carriers   UG446.5
Armored trains   UG345
Armored vehicles, Military   UG446   355.83, 623.438, .7475
Armored vessels   V799-800   359.3252, 623.825
Arms and armor   U800-825 (mil.), HD9743 (industry), NK6600-6699 (art)
                              355.82, 623.44, 739.75
Arms and armor, American   U818   355.820973, 623.444
Arms and armor—Bibliography—Catalogs   Z5693 018.1
Army War College (U.S.)   [SEE ALSO 'U.S. Army War College']
Arnaville, Battle of, 1944
Arnhem, Battle of, 1944   D763   940.5421, .54763492

Arnold, Henry Harley ('Hap'), 1886-1950   [U.S.: Gen.]   TL540.A69, D790,
                                     UG633   358.413320924, 940.544973
Arras, Battle of, 1940
Art and war
Art treasures in war   N8750   733.3
Artillery   UF145, UF400, UF560-1   358.109, .12, 623.41, .412
   —Bibliography   Z6724   016.35996
Artillery, Coast   UF450-5
Artillery drill and tactics   UF157-302
Artillery, Field and mountain   UF400-45
Artillery—Great Britain   UF57   358.10942, .120941-120942
Artillery, Self-propelled
Artists for Victory, Inc.   NE508.A
Aschaffenburg—Siege, 1945
Asia—Foreign relations   DS33, DS35, JX1569   327.5+
   —History—20th century   DS35
Asia, Southeastern
   —History   DS511, DS513, DS527, E744   325.5, 915.903, 959.008
Asquith, Herbert Henry, 1852-1928 [G.B.: Prime Min.]   DA566.9.O7
                                     941.0830924, 923.242
Assembly for a Democratic Austrian Republic   [WWII]
Association des Français Libres
Atatürk, Kemal   [SEE 'Kemal Atatürk']
Atlantic Wall
Atlantis (Ship)   [Surface raider]   D772.A74   940.545943
Atomic bomb   D767, D810, HD9698, UF767, QC16, QC773, UG1282
                   355.021708, .2322, .82, 358.39, 539.7, 623.451, 621.483
   —History
   —Moral and religious aspects   BR115, UF767   261.63, 341.672
   —Physiological effect   RA569, RA1231, RC93, U408   614.715,
                                     616.9897, 617.124
Attack and defense (Military science)   UG443-9   355.4
Attlee, Clement, 1883-1967   [G.B.: Pr. Min.]   DA585.A8, DA588, D742.G7
                                     941.08540924, 923.242
Attu Island (Alaska), Battle of, 1943
Auchinleck, Claude, Sir ('The Auk'), 1884-1981   [G.B.: Field Marshal]
                   DA69.3.A8-9, D766.82   940.5423, 923.542
Aung San, U, 1915-1947 [Burma: Gen.]   DS485.B8-9, DS503, DS530, DS530.4
                                     320.959104
Auschwitz (Poland: Concentration camp)   [SEE ALSO 'Oswiecim']
Australia
   . Army
       . A.I.F. 2/19 Battalion   D767   940.541294
       . 36th Infantry Battalion   D767.8   940.541294
       . Royal Australian Regiment. 8th Battalion   DS557   959.704342
   . Australian Army
   . Australian Imperial Force (1914-1921)   D520.A9
       . 28th Battalion
   —Biography   DU116.2, U55   923.594
   —History—20th century   DU110, DU116   994.04
   —History, Military   DU112   355.00994, .310994, 940.5394
   —History, Naval   VB121   359.00994
   . Navy   [SEE ALSO 'Australia. Royal Australian Navy']
       —History   VA713, VB121   359.00994

Australia
—Politics and government—1901-1945   DU112, DU116   320.994042,
994.032
. Royal Australian Air Force   D792.A8, UG635, UG1242   940.544994,
358.400994, .4183
. Royal Australian Army Nursing Corps
. Royal Australian Navy
Australian Comforts Fund
Austria
—Foreign relations—Germany
—History
—1867-1918
—1918-1938   DB96   943.605
—Nazi Putsch, July 1934
—1938-1945   DB97   943.605
—Allied occupation, 1945-1955   D802.A9, DB99   943.605
—Politics and government
—1918-1938   DB96-7   943.605
—1938-1945
Austro-Hungarian Monarchy
Automobiles, Military   UG680-5
Averescu, Alexandru, 1859-1938   [Rum.: Lt. Gen., Prime Min.]   DR217, D565.A2,
D651.R6   949.8

B-17 bomber   [A.k.a. 'Flying Fortress']   D790, TL686   358.42, 623.7463,
940.544973
B-24 bomber   [A.k.a. 'Liberator']   TL685-6, UG1242   358.4183, 623.7463,
940.544973
B-25 bomber   ['Mitchell']
B-26 bomber   ['Martin']
B-29 bomber   ['Superfortress']
Babiy Yar Massacre, 1941   D810   940.5405094771
Badoglio, Pietro, 1871-1956   [It.: Field Marshal]   D754.I8, D763   940.5345
Balfour, Arthur James, 1848-1930   [G.B.: 1st Lord o/t Adm'ty, Sec. of State for
For. Aff.]   DA566.9.B2, D412.6, D570, VA454
942.080924, .0820924, 359.00941, .0942, 920.02, 923.242
Balkan Peninsula
—History
—20th century   DR48, DR36, D562.M32, D562   949.6, 914.9603
—War of 1912-1913   DR46 949.6
—Politics and government   D463, DJK4, DR10   309.1496, 320.9496
Ballistics   UF820   623.51, .50903
Balloons   TL609-39   629.13322
Baltic States—History—German occupation, 1941-1944
Bao Dai, 1913-? [Viet.: Emperor of Assam, King]   DS556.83.B3-36
959.70410924
Baruch, Bernard Mannes, 1870-1965   [U.S.: Fin. adviser and statesman]
E748.B32   973.9130924, 923.273
Battle casualties
Battle cruisers
Battles   D25, D210, D431   355.48
—Europe
—Germany
Battleships   V765-7, V800, VA58, VA454   359.32+, .3252, .32520973,
.83, 623.82530973, .8252

Baum, Herbert, 1912-1942   [Berlin underground participant]   D757.9.B4
Baumbach, Werner, n.d. [Ger.: Head, Luftwaffe Bomber Command]   D787.B3
                                                          940.544943
Bautzen (Germany), Battle of, 1945
Bavaria—Politics and government   DD801.B41
Bayerlein, Fritz [Ger.: Gen.]   D757.55.P35, D757.56.Nr.12, D766.9   940.548
Bazna, Elyesa ('Cicero'), n.d. [Albania: Highly paid Grmn. spy in Tur.]   D810.S8
                                                  940.548643, .5487430924
Beaverbrook, William Maxwell Aitken, Lord, 1879-1964   [G.B.: Min. of Info. (WWI);
        Min. of Aircraft Produc., Min. of Supply, Lord Privy Seal, Lend-
        Lease admin. (WWII); Press empire lord]   DA566.9.B3, .B37,
        .C4 (Churchill), DA577.B35, UG635.G7   942.083-084,
        .0840924, 940.544, 070.50924, 090.50924, 910.544, 923.242
Beck, Ludwig, 1880-1944 [Ger.: Gen., Anti-Nazi conspir.]   DD247.B38,
                        DD256.3, .5, U55.B   943.0860924
Bedell Smith, Walter ('Beatle'), 1895-1961   [U.S.: Gen., Eisenhower's Chief of
                                        Staff]   Z6300.15.S6
Belgian American Educational Foundation
Belgisch Leger der Partizanen. Korps 034   D802.B4
Belgium
    . Armée. Troupes Coloniales   D766.92
    —History—German occupation, 1940-1945
    —Poetry
Belgrade—Siege, 1944
Belvedere, Battle of, 1944
Belzec (Poland: Concentration camp)
Ben-Gurion, David, 1886-1974   [Isr.]   DS125.3.B3-4   956.9404-9405,
                                        923.2569
Benes, Eduard, 1884-1948   [Aust.-Hung.: Politician, Pres.]   DB217.B3-4, .M3,
                DB2191.B45   943.7020924, 923.1437, .2437, 940.3, .53
Beretta submachine gun   UF620.B45
Bergen-Belsen (Germany: Concentration camp)
Beria, Lavrenty, 1899-1954   [A.k.a. 'Beriia, Lavrentii Pavlovich': Rus.: NKVD chief
    (intelligence)]   DK268.B384-45, .S7-8 (Stalin)   947.08420924
Berlin, Battle of, 1945   D757   940.5421
Berlin—History—1918-1945   DD879-880   914.31550385
Bernadotte af Wisborg, Folke, 1895-1948   [Swe.: Humanitarian]   DL870.B47,
                D808.B, DS126.92   956.042, 940.548, 923.2485
Bernard Leopold, 1911-? [Neth.: Prince o/t Neth., Consort of Queen Juliana]
                                DJ289.A3   923.1492
Biak Island (Indonesia), Battle of, 1944
Bible—Prophecies
    —Great Britain
    —Jews
    —Russia
    —U.S.
Biddle, Francis Beverley, 1886-1968   [U.S.: Att. Gen., Nuremberg jurist]
                        K60.B473, KF373   340.0924, 923.473
Biography—20th century   CT119-120, D412   070.924, 364.1524,
                        920.00904, 923.2, 920.02
Bir Hakeim, Battle of, 1942   D766 940.5423
Bismarck (Battleship)   D772.B5, DD72   940.545942, .545943,
                        359.32520943
Bismarck Sea, Battle of, 1943

Black market
—Europe
—United States   HF5415   338.526
Black widow (Fighter planes)   [P-61]
Blackouts in war
Blamey, Thomas, Sir, 1884-1951   [Australia: Gen. (G.O.C., Field Marshal]
                    DU114.B65, DU116.2.B54   355.3310924
Blechhammer E/3 (Blachownia Slaska, Poland: Concentration camp)
Blomberg, Werner von, 1878-1943   [Ger.: Field Marshal]
Blum, Leon, 1872-1950   [Fr.: Socialist intellectual, Pr. Min. (1936-7)]
                    DC373.B5-6, D412.6, D410   944.08150924, 923.244
Boatyards
Battice, Battle of, 1940
Bock, Fedor von, 1885-1945   [Ger.: Field Marshal]   D764.3.M6   940.54210924
Boeing airplanes   TL686   629.133340973, 387.7334
Boeing bombers
Bohlen, Charles Eustis ('Chip'), 1904-?   [U.S.: Ambass. to Rus.]   E748.B5-64
                                327.20924
Bomb reconnaisance   D787   658.47, 940.5412+
Bombardiers   D792.A-Z (by country)
—[country]
Bombardment   JX5117
Bombers   TL685, UG635, UG1242, VG95   358.4183, .420941, 623.7463,
                940.5449+
—Pictorial works   UG635   358.4209+
Bombing, Aerial   UG635   358.409
—Psychological aspects   UG632   363.352
Bombing and gunnery ranges   U300-305
Bombs   TP270, VF373   353.00711, 628.9
Bombsights
Booker T. Washington (Steamship)
Bor-Komorowski, Tadeusz, 1895-1966   [Pol.: Gen., Underground leader]   D802.P6
                                940.53438, .5481
Bordeaux Raid, 1942
Borgo San Dalmazzo (Italy: Concentration camp)
Borneo—History   DS646   919.11, 915.983, 959.83
Boris III, 1894-1943   [Bulg.: King]   DR89
Bormann, Martin, 1900-1945?   [Ger.: Sec. & confidant to the Fuhrer]
                    DD247.B65, .H5 (Hitler)   943.0860924
Bose, Subhas Chandra, 1897-1945   [India: Polit. leader semi-allied with Axis]
                    DS481.B6   954.0350924, 923.254
Bourguébus Ridge, France, Battle of, 1944
Boys anti-tank rifle
Bradley, Omar, 1893-1981   [U.S.: Gen.]   E745.B693, D756.B7   940.54210924
Brain drain—Germany   DD68
Brandt, Willy, 1913-   [Ger.: politician in exile during the war]   DD259.7.B7,
            DD857.B7   943.0870924, 327.430717, 352.043, 940.531
Brauchitsch, Walter von, 1881-1948   [Ger.: Field Marshal]
Braun, Eva, 1912-1945   [Ger.: Hitler's mistress]   DD247.B6-7, .H5 (Hitler)
                                943.0860924
Braun, Werner von   [SEE 'Von Braun, Wernher']
Brazil. Exército. Força Expedicionaria Brasileira, 1944-1945   D768.3, D807.B7
Brazil—History—1930-1954   F2538
Bren machine-gun   UF620.B57

Brereton, Lewis Hyde, 1890-1967 [U.S.: Maj. Gen., aerial commander]
  D790.B67   940.544973
Breslau (Cruiser)
Brest (France)—Siege, 1944
Briand, Aristide, 1862-1932   [Fr.: Prem.]   DC373.B7, DC385, DC387, D548,
  D568.3   944.08, 940.425
Britain, Battle of, 1940   D756, D785-7, DA89   940.5341, .5421, .5442
British Broadcasting Corporation   D799.G7   621.3841930942
British in Asia   DS35   954, 325.342095
British in foreign countries
British Organization in Rome for Assisting Allied Escaped Prisoners of War
  D763.I82.R623   940.547
Brody, Ukraine, Battle of, 1944
Brojce (Poland: Concentration camp)
Brooke, Alan, Sir, 1883-1963   [G.B.: Field Marshal]
Brooke-Popham, Robert, 1878-1953   [G.B.: Air Chief Marshal]
Browning, Frederick ('Boy'), 1896-1966 [G.B.: Lt. Gen. for airborne troops]
Browning automatic rifle
Browning firearms   TS533   683.4
Brzezinka (Poland: Concentration camp)
Buchenwald (Germany: Concentration camp)
Buckner, Simon Bolivar, 1886-1945   [U.S.: Gen.]
Budenny, Semyon, 1883-1973   [U.S.S.R.: Marshal]
Bulganin, Nikolay, 1895-1975 [U.S.S.R.: Polit. Marshal]
Bulgaria
  —History—Boris III, 1918-1943   DR89, DR85-7, DR67   949.77,
    940.534977, 949.7702
  —Politics and government—1878-1944   DR85, JN9609   320.9497703
Bullets
Bullitt, William Christian, 1891-1967   [U.S.: Ambass. to U.S.S.R., Fr.]
  E742.5.R5-6, E183.8.R9, D753   940.5378, 973.90924, 327.47073
Bund Deutscher Offiziere   DD256.5
Burma—History—Japanese occupation, 1942-1945   D802, DS485, DS528-9
    959.1, 940.53591, 959.103-104
Burma-Siam Railroad   D805.J3   940.547252+
Byrnes, James Francis, 1879-1972   [U.S.: Pres. advis., Sec. of State]   E748.B9,
  E813, D814.4, E183.7.B462, D815   940.531,.53220924, 923.273
Bzura River, Battle of, 1939

C-47: SEE Douglas transport planes
Cables, Submarines   TK5661
Caen, Battle of, 1944   D756   940.5421
Caillaux, Joseph, 1863-1944   [Fr.: Deputy]   DC373.C25, DC371, DC387
    944.0810922, .831, 923.244
Calais, Battle of, 1940
California
  —History—1850-1950   F864   979.404
  . National Guard   UA99   355.3510973
California, Southern
    —History—1850-1950   F867-9   979.47-498 917.949035
Cambodia—History   DS554-7   959.6, .704
Cambridge American Cemetery, England   D810.D4   940.5465425
Camouflage (Military science)   UG449, V215 (naval)   358.18, .414
Camp Holmes, P.I. (Concentration camp)   D805.P6   940.547252
Camps (Military)   U180-5, UC400-5, UG635 (camp-making)

391

Canada
  . Army
    . Hastings and Prince Edward Regiment   D768.15
  . Canadian Army. Canadian Expeditonary Force
  —Claims vs. Italy   JX5486.C16
  —Foreign relations—1914-1945   F1034
  —History—1914-1945   F1033-4   971.06, .063
  —Politics and government—1914-1945   F1034 JL197   320.971,
                  923.271, 940.540971
Canadian Broadcasting Corporation   D799.C2
Canaris, Wilhelm, 1887?-1945 [Ger.: Adm., Abwehr chief (mil. intell.), anti-Nazi]
    DD247.C16-35, DD253.6, D810.S7   943.086, 940.548743, 923.543
Canteen (British Navy)   VC395.G7
Canteen (United States Army)   UC753
Canteens (War-time, emergency, etc.)
Capitulations, Military   D815-16   940.54012, .5314
Caporetto, Battle of, 1917   D560-4, D569   940.431
Capture at sea   JX5228
Carlson, Evans Fordyce, 1896-1947   [U.S.: Brig.; formed 'Carlson's Raiders']
                E746.C, DS777.53   923.573
Carol II, 1893-1957   [Rum.: King]   DR266
Caroline Islands   DU563   919.66. 996.6
Carré, Mathilde Bélard ('The Cat'), 1910-?   [Fr.: Double or triple (?) agent]
                D810.S8.C3   940.5486440924
Cartridges   TS538, UF740-5   355.82, 623.455, .4553, 683.406
Cassino (Italy), Battle of, 1944
Catalina (Seaplanes)
Catholic Church
  —Charities   HV530, BX2351 249, 261.83
  —Diplomatic service   JX1801-2
  —History—Modern period, 1500-   BX1330, BX1396, BV601   270-82,
                282.0903
    —20th century   BX1389, BX1746   262.001, 282.0904, .73
Catholic Church in Japan   BX1668   282.52
Catholic Church
  —Political activity
  —Relations (diplomatic)   BX1790-3, BX850-1691 (hist.), BX1908 (legates
        & nuncios), JX1552 (int'nal. law)   261.87, 262.13, 341.33, 261.7
    —Germany   D810.C6, BX1378   262.130924
  —Relations (diplomatic) with Germany   BX1378 262.130924
  —Relations (diplomatic) with Great Britain   BR750, BX1493, BX2470, DA356
                248.894094, 261.7, .87, 282.42
Cavallero, Ugo, 1880-1943   [It.: Marshal, Chief of Gen. Staff]   D766.C3-34
                940.548245, 929.214
Cavalry   UE
  —History   UE15   357.109
Central Europe—History   DR36-48   940.55
Central Utah Relocation Center   [SEE ALSO 'U.S. Relocation Center, Topaz, Utah']
Cephalonia Massacre, 1943
Chamberlain, Neville, 1869-1940   [G.B.: Pr. Min., War Cabinet member]
                DA585.C3-5, DA586.C6-7, DA47.2
        941.0840924, 942.084, 327.42043, 923.242, 940.5312
Changkufeng Incident, 1938   DS784 957.7
Channel Islands (Great Britain)—History   DA670   942.34
Charities—History   HV16 361.0209, .73

Chemical warfare   JX1974-7, JX5135, UG447   341.63, .67, .73, 350.895,
          358.34, 363.352
—History—20th century   UG447
Chengtu Incident, 1936
Chennault, Claire Lee, 1890-1958   [U.S.: Maj. Gen., formed the 'Flying Tigers in
          China']   E745.C35-42, D790, DS777.53.S38-42
          940.544973, 358.41332, 923.573
Cherbourg (France), Battle of, 1944
Cheren, Battle of, 1941
Cherkassy, Battle of, 1944
Chiang Kai-shek, 1887 (1886?)-1975   [Ch.: Generalissimo]   DS778.C4-55,
          DS777.47, .488.C5, .518, DS774, D843
          951.0420924, 320.951042, 923.551
Chiang Kai-shek, Madame, 1898?-   [A.k.a. 'Mei-ling Sung, Mme.': Ch.: Wife & advisor
   to Chiang Kai-shek]   DS778.C55, .A1, D743   951.04, 923.551, 940.5304
China
  . Air Force. American Volunteer Group   923.573
  —Description and travel—1901-1948   DS710   915.103-104
  —Foreign relations   DS740   301.291821051, 327.51
     —Japan   DS740, DS777   327.51052, .52051
     —Russia   DK68, DS740   327.47051, .51047
     —United States   E183, DS740   327.51073, .73051
  —History
     —Republic, 1912-1949   DS773-7   951.04
     —1937-1945   DS777-8, UA837   915.138, 951.042
  —Politics and government—1937-1945   DS740, DS774-7, JQ1502-3
          320.951, 327.51, 951.042-05
Chou En-Lai, 1898-1976   [Ch.: Communist liaison to Chiang Kai-shek]
          DS778.C45-593   951.040924, .050924
Chuikov, Vasili, 1900-   [U.S.S.R.: Gen.]   D764.C48515, D765.C46   940.5421
Church work with military personnel   BV4457   253.5
Churchill, Winston Leonard Spencer, 1874-1965 [G.B.: 1st Lord o/t Adm'ty., Min. of
     Munitions (WWI), Pr. Min. (WWII)]   DA566.9.C4-5, D521, D568, D734,
     D743-4, D750, D753, D842, DA69, DA587   941.0820924, 942.084-
     085, 940.425, .45, .5322, .54012, .540942, 359.3310924, 968.040922
  —Addresses, essays, lectures
  —Anecdotes, facetiae, satire, etc.
  —Bibliography
  —Correspondence
  —Fiction
  —Funeral and memorial services
  —Language   PE1421
  —Oratory
  —Poetry
  —Portarits, caricatures, etc.
  —Quotations
  —Views on international relations
Ciano, Galeazzo, 1903-1944   [It.: Count, For. Min.]   DG575.C516, DG571.A2,
          D769   945.091, .0910924
Ciphers   UB290   652.809
Civil defense   UA926-9, JX1907   355.4307, 363.34-35, 353.007-008
  —Warning systems
Civil supremacy over the military   JF195, JF256, DS919, E835 (U.S. hist.),
     JK558, KF27, U410   353.00895, .032, 355.0213+, 322.50904, .5091724
Clark, Mark, 1896-?   [U.S.: Gen.]   E745.C45   940.548373

Clay, Lucius Dubignon, 1897-1978 [U.S.: Gen.]   E745.C47, DD257
                                            940.531440924, 943.0874
Coast defenses   UG410-48   355.45
Col di Lana, Battle of, 1916   D569.C
Collins, Joseph Lawton ('Lightnin' Joe'), 1896-1963 [U.S.: Lt. Gen.]   E745.C64
                                                                  355.3310924
Colt firearms   TS533-7   683.43, 623.443
Combat patrols
Combat
   —Physiological aspects
   —Psychological aspects
Combat survival
Combatants and noncombatants (International law)
Combined operations (Military science)   U260 (allied nations)
Comité Francais de la Libération Nationale
   . Commissariat `a L'information
   . Commissariat `a L'intérieur
Command and control systems   TK5102   621.38
Command of troops   UB210
Commander Islands (R.S.F.S.R.), Battle of, 1943
Commission to Study the Oragnization of Peace
Commodity Credit Corporation [WWII]   HG2051.U5, HD9035-36
                                       353.00825, .81, 338.13, .173
Communications, Military   UA940-5, U408, UG590   355.6, .85, 358.24
Communism   HX626-795, HX36, HX44, HX56, HX134, DK254, DK274
                  320.91717, 321.642, 335.008, .408-409, .413, .42-43
   —China   DS77, DS711, DS740, DS774-8, HX387-8, JQ1519
                  320.951, 335.430951, .4340951, 355.0951, 951.041-05
   —Germany   HX273   335.40943
   —History   DK254, HC101, HX36-56, HX276, HX312, HX628
                  320.5322, 322.42, 330.904, 335.009, .401, .409, .41-43,
                  .438145, 947.0841
   —Russia   B2430, DK254, DK265-8, DK273-6, HC335, HN523, HX312-14,
                  JN6598   142.7, 301.1520947, 320.53220947, .947084,
                  321.642, 329.947, 330.947, 335.413, .430947, 947.083-085

      —History
      —Sources
Communist International   HX11, HX112, HX237, HX387   329.072, .078,
                             335.0094, .4309597, .44, .441
Concentration camps   HV8963, D256, D804-5   341.4, 365.36, 940.5472
   —[geog. regions or countries]
   —California
   —Germany   D256, D804-5, DD256   131.3169, .3469, 940.547243, 943.086
Concentration camps in literature
Concentration camps
   —Pictorial works   NC139   759.13
   —Poland
   —Psychological aspects   RC451   616.8528, .89
   —United States
Conference for Conclusion and Signature of Treaty of Peace with Japan (1951: San
   Francisco)   D814
Conference for the Reduction and Limitation of Armaments, Geneva, 1932-1934
                         JX1974   341.67, .73
Conference on Jewish Material Claims against Germany   D819.G3

395

d'Aquino, Iva Ikuko Toguri   [SEE 'Tokyo Rose']
Darlan, Jean Francois, 1881-1942 [Fr.: Adm., Fr. Navy Comm. in Chief]
                                              DC373.D35   940.5344
De Gaulle, Charles, 1890-1970   [Sometimes 'Gaulle, Charles de': Fr.: Gen., Free
    French leader]   DC373.G3, DC404, DC412, DC417, DC420, D843.G2813,
         DS127.85   944.080924, .081-082, .0830924, 923.144, 327.44
De Guingand, Francis, 1900-1979 [G.B.: Major Gen.]   U55.D45, D811.D
                                              355.3310924
Defense contracts   UC267, UG633, VC267, HC79   338.091724, 353.00713
    —United States   U393, UC263-7, UG633, VC267 (naval), HC110, HD9743
         338.4735500973, .476234, 343.73013, 346.73023,
                  351.711-712, 355.6210973, .70973, 358.4162110973
Defense information, Classified
Demolition, Military
Denmark
    —Foreign relations—1906-1945
    —History
         —Christian X, 1912-1947   DL148, DL160   948.9
         —German occupation, 1940-1945   D802   940.5421
              —Foreign public opinion
    —Politics and government—1912-1945   JN7013, JN7111, JN7295
                                   301.449209489, 320.09489, .448

Deployment (Strategy)
Depth charges
Desert warfare
Desertion, Military—United States   UB788, KF7618, KF7652   355.1334,
                                   .1330924, .1334
Desertion, Naval—United States
Destroyer escorts
Destroyers (Warships)   V825, VA53, VA454   359.32, .3254+, .6213, 359.83,
                  623.8254
Deterrence (Military strategy)   U162   355.43
Deterrence (Strategy)   U162.6   355.0217, .033+, .033509, .43, .4307
    —Mathematical models   U162   355.03350184
Devastator (Torpedo-bomber)   TL685.3   358.4183
Dieppe Raid, 1942   D756   940.542, .5421
Dietrich, Sepp, 1892-1976   [Ger.: Waffen SS Gen.]   D811.D
Dirksen, Herbert von, n.d.   [Ger.: Diplomat in Tokyo, Moscow, London bet. the
         wars]   DD247.D54, D735   940.53112, 327.43
Diving, Submarine   D784.G3 (Ger.), D780, GV340, GV840, VM965, VM977,
    VM981+   359.98, 387.55, 623.82+, 627.7, .703, .72+, .7209
Doenitz, Karl, 1891-1980 [A.k.a. 'Dönitz': Ger.: Adm., Ger. Navy chief]
                  DD247.D63, D770.D6, D781.D   943.0860924, 940.545943
Dogs, War use of   UH100
Donovan, William Joseph ('Wild Bill'), 1883-1959 [U.S.: Founder of Office of
              Strategic Services (intell.)]   E748.D665, D810.S8, .P7,
              UB271.U52, JK468.I6   940.548673, .5486730924
Doolittle, James, 1896-   [U.S.: Lt. Gen., 1942 Tokyo air raid leader]
              E746.D664, UG626.2.D66, TL540.D62
              629.130924, 926.2913
Doorman, Karel, ?-1941   [Neth.: Rear Adm.]
Douglas airplanes   TL686.D   338.476291
Douglas transport planes   TL686.D65, HE9769   387.7334, 629.1333+
Dowding, Hugh Caswell Tremenheere, Sir ('Stuffy'), 1882-1970   [G.B.: Air Chief
    Marshal]   DA89.6.D6   940.54210924

Drancy (France: Concentration camp)
Dresden (Cruiser)   D582.D8
Drvar, Battle of, 1944
Dry-docks   TC361   627.35
Dukla Pass, Battle of, 1944
Dulles, Allen Welsh, 1893-1969   [U.S.: O.S.S. chief in Switz.]   E748.D87,
                    JK468.I6   973.90922, 327.12
Dummy warships
Dunkerque (France), Battle of, 1940   [SEE ALSO 'Dunkirk...']   D756   940.5421
Dunkirk (France), Battle of, 1940   [SEE ALSO 'Dunkerque...']   D756
                    940.5421, .5756
    —Songs and music

Eaker, Ira Clarence, 1896-1987   [U.S.: Gen. (Air Corps)]   UG626.E24, UG633
                    358.400973
Eastern question (Balkan)
Ebert, Friedrich, 1871-1925   [Ger.: Politician]   DD247.E2, DD221, DD248
Economic assistance   D839, E744, HC59-60, HC101, HC106, HC240,
        HC435, HG136, JX1977, HG4517, KF4668   309.2233,
    338.4730154, .90091724, 343.73+, 353.00722, .00825, 358.00892, 387.1
Economic assistance, American
Eden, Anthony, 1897-1977   [G.B.: For. Sec.]   DA566.9.E28, D750
                    941.0840924, 940.532241, 923.242
Egypt—History—1919-1952   DT107   962.05
Ehrenburg, Ilia Grigorevich, 1891-?   [U.S.S.R.: Novelist, war correspondent,
    propagandist]   PG3476.E5
Eichelberger, Robert Lawrence, 1886-1961 [U.S.: Lt. Gen.]   D767.E37,
                    D769.26.8th   940.54260924
Eichmann, Adolf, 1906-1962   [Ger.: SS col., head of Gestapo's Dept. of Jewish
    Affairs]   DD247.E5, D804.G43, KF211, KF224, E184.J5
                    940.5405, 341.410924, 347.91, 363.234, 923.543, .547
Eisenhower, Dwight David, 1890-1969   [U.S.: Gen., Supreme Allied Commander]
                    D743.E35, D755-6, E745.E35, E835-6, E863, F689,
                    UA23   973.9210924, .920922, 940.5421,
        355.033573, .3310924, 323.40973, 923.173, .573, 978.156
El Alamein, Battle of, Egypt, 1942   [SEE ALSO 'al'Alamayn...']   D766.9
                    940.5423
Elections—United States—History   JK97, JK1965, JK171   324.73,
                    329.0237302-0237303
Electronic intelligence
Ellice Islands
Emergency communication systems
Emergency medical services   RA645.5-7, RA975, RD81   361.5, 362.11,
                    614.875, 940.5475, 344.73041, 362.18
Emergency water supply
Emigration and immigration law—United States   JV6424, JV6507, JV6874,
            JX1977, KF4800, KF4807, KF4819, KF8925   323.60973,
        .6310973, 325.240973, .24580973, 342.73082, 362.8
Émigrés   DC158.1-17   325.244, 942.00441
Enemy property
Enfidaville, Battle of, 1943
Enfield rifle

England   [SEE ALSO 'Great Britain']
—Civilization—20th century   DA566   914.20382-20384
—Social life and customs—20th century   DA566   914.2820385, 941.083,
                                                942.0823
Englandspiel
Enterprise (U.S. aircraft carrier)   D774.E5, VA65   940.545973, 623.8255
Espionage   UB270-1   327.120904, 351.74, 355.343, 364.131, 940.548673
Espionage, American [British, German, etc.]
Espionage, American   UB271   327.120973
Espionage, British
Espionage, German   UB271, D810   327.120943
—United States   D810   940.548743
Espionage, Japanese   UB271   327.120951-120952
Espionage, Russian   DK61, DK266, UB271   327.120947, 355.3432+, 364.13
Estonia
—History—1918-1940   DK511 947.41
—Russian occupation, 1940-1941
—German occupation, 1941-1944
Ethnikon Apeleutherotikon Metopon   D810.S7, DF849
Europe
—Civilization—20th century   CB53, CB417, D102, D429, D1055
                                        910.03924, 914.031-032, 940.2+
—Description and travel—1919-1945   D921, D975, G127 914+
Europe, Eastern
—History   DK440, DR36-8, DR43, DR48   943.804+
    —Autonomy and independence movements   DJK48
Europe
—Economic conditions—1918-1945   HB501, HC41, HC45, HC240, JX1977
                                309.1401, 330.94+, .94009, .94028, .94055, .942
—History
    —20th century   D104, D421, D424, D411   909.82, 940.5
    —1918-1945   D424, D720   909.82, 940.5, .52
—Politics—1918-1945   D413, D443, D720, D727   320.94051,
                                940.50924, .51-2
—Politics and government—1918-1945   D413, D443, D653, D720, D728,
                        D748, JN12   320.9405, 327.11094, .094,
                        .43+, 341.1209+, 940.3142, .509+, .52, .531-2, .5311
—Relations (military) with the United States   D1065   327.4073
European War, 1914-1918   [Newer term for publications after 1981 or so is 'World
                        War, 1914-1918'. Subdivisions may be found under either]
                        D501-680+, D511, D521, D523, D639, D644
                        940.3-940.499, 940.3+, 940.4+
—Aerial operations   D600-607, DA89, TL540, UG633   358.43,
                                623.746, 923.542,940.44,.54
—Armistices   D641-2   940.434, .439
—Atrocities   D541, D626
—Australia   D547.A8   940.394
—Battlefields   D528   940.46
—Belgium   D541-2, DH681-2   940.4313, 949.3040924
—Bibliography   Z674, Z1035, Z6207   016.9403
—Biography   D507, D570   940.30922, .4, .410922, .46
—Blockades   D581, D619   940.452

398

European War, 1914-1918

European War, 1914-1918
—War work   D639-40
—Washington, D.C.   D570+, F199+
—Yugoslavia
European War, 1939-   [Used for books written at the war's beginning. After a
                    time, 'World War, 1939-' was used and, finally after the fact,
                    'World War, 1939-1945']   D739-810, D739-44,
                    D741, D743   940.51-58, .53
—Addresses, sermons, etc.   D739, D743   940.5304
—Aerial operations   D786   940.5449+
—American republics   D752   940.537
—Atrocities   D804   940.54056
—Balkan Peninsula   D766   940.53496
—Belgium   D763   940.542
—Bibliography   Z6207   016.94053
—Campaigns   D743   940.542
    —Africa   D766
    —Belgium   D763
    —Norway   D763
—Canada   D745   940.5371
—Causes   D741-2   940.5311+
—Children   D810   940.53161
—Chronology   D743   940.5302
—Dictionaries   D740   940.53
—Diplomatic history   D750, D735, D741   940.531-2
—Documents, etc., sources
—Drama
—Economic aspects   HG2481, JX1907, HC106   308.2, 330.904, 332.1
    —United States   HC106   330.973, 940.531865
—Fiction
—Finance
    —Great Britain   HJ1023   336.42
    —United States   HJ275, HJ258   336.73
—France   D742, D761, DC397   940.5344, .548144
—Germany   D742, D811, DD94, DD256   940.5343, 943.08
—Great Britain   D742, D760, D811, DA566   940.5341-2, .548142, .5497
    —London   D700, D760   940.5342, 636.88
—Greece   D766   940.53495
—Hospitals, charities, etc.   D807   940.54758
—Humor, caricatures, etc.   D745, NC1479   741+, 827.91
—Iceland   D763   940.53491
—Influence and results   D753, D744   940.5373 (US), .5314
—Jews   D810   940.5315296
—Maps   D743-4   940.5499, .53
—Netherlands   D763   940.584
—Norway   D763   940.53481
—Peace   D815
—Personal narratives   D811   940.5481+
—Personal narratives, American   D811   940.53493, .342, .54771, .548,
                    .5342
—Personal narratives, Dutch   D811   940.5481492
—Personal narratives, English   D811   940.5342, .548142
—Poetry
—Poland   D765, D811   940.544, .5481438
—Prisoners and prisons, French   D805   940.547244

European War, 1939-
    —Propaganda   D753, E744   940.5488, .5488973 (US)
    —Prophecies   D810   940.53
    —Refugees   D809-10   940.53161, .547242
    —Religious aspects   D744   261 940.531
    —Russia   D764   940.542
    —United States   D753, D756, D758   327.73, 940.532, .5373, .5873
    —Women's work   D810   940.5315396
Evacuation of civilians   HV554   355.232
Excess profits tax   HJ4653, KF26-7, KF6471-2   336.243, .274, 343.73052
Executive power—United States   JK501-901, E417, HG2525   328.3456,
                .73, 342.7306+, 347.7326+, 353.008, .0313-0372, 973.61+
Exiles   CT105 (biog.), JX4261 (int'nal. law)
Expatriation   JX4226
Expatriation and repatriation
Explosive ordnance disposal
Explosives, Military   TP268-99

Falaise Gap, Battle of, 1944   D761   940.5421
Falkenhausen, Alexander von, 1878-1966 [Ger.: Gen.]   DH687.F34
Falkenhorst, Nikolaus von, 1885-1968 [Ger.: Col. Gen.]   D804.G4.F3
Farouk, 1920-1965   [Egypt: King]
Fascism   JC481, D443, D842, D726   320.533, .533019, .94, 321.644,
            .94, 335.6, .60904, 909.82
    —Bibliography   Z2361   016.320533
    —Central Europe   D726   320.943
    —Germany   [SEE ALSO 'National Socialism']   DD259, D424, D445, D726,
                    JC481   320.943, .533094, 321.94094
    —Italy   DG571, DG450, DG575   945.091, .091024,
          309.14509+, 320.5330945, .945091, 321.940945, 330.945, 335.60945
    —Posters
    —Spain   DP257   946.081
    —United States   E743, E806   320.5330973, 335.60973
Fascism and architecture
Fascism and culture
Fascism and literature
Fascism and the Catholic Church
Fascism in art
Fascist ethics
Fascists
Fast attack craft
Ferdinand, King of Rumania, 1865-1927   DR217, DR262.A2, DD120.G7
                    949.8020924, 327.430436, 923.1498
Fieseler Fi-156 Storch (Military airplane)
Fighter planes   UG626-626.2
Fighter planes   TL685.3, UG633-5, UG1240, UG1242, VG93
          623.7464+, 629.133, 358.4183+, .43+, .430943 (Ger.),
            .430941-430942 (GB), .430952 (Japan)
    —Piloting   UG633   629.132+
Fighting, Hand-to-hand   U210, GV1111   355.54, 796.8+
Fighting (Psychology)   BF575, BF723   136.727, .7353, 137.33, 158.1, .4245

Finland
   —Foreign relations
      —Germany
      —Russia   DK459, JX1555   327.471047, .470471
   —History—1939-   DK459.45 948.95
 . Maavoimat. 1. Divisioona   D765.32
Fire control (Aerial gunnery)   VG93   623.555
Fire control (Gunnery)   UF848   623.5
Fire control (Naval gunnery)
Firearms   TS535-7 (produc.), UF520, UF800, UF880, UF884, UF897, UD380
          623.44, .4424, .443, 683.4, 355.82+
Firearms, American
Firearms, British
Firearms, German   TS533   683.400943
Firearms
   —History   TS532-5, U818, U884, UD390, UF520   623.4409+,
          355.8209+, 683.4009+
   —Identification   HV8077, VN8077   351.753, 363.33, 364.12+, 683.43012
Firearms industry and trade   HD9743   338.476234, 364.135
    —Great Britain   TS533   338.7683400941
    —United States   TS520, TS535   623.440973, 683.400973
Firearms
   —Maintenance and repair   TS535   683.403
Flame throwers   UG447
Fletcher, Frank ('Black Jack'), 1885-1973   [U.S.: Vice Adm.]
Flight control   TL589.4
Flight crews   TL521   629.1344
Flight engineering   TL671   629.102, .1302, .1325+
Flight—Physiological aspects   RC1075, TL555   616.98, 612.84, 620.13256
Flight training   TL710-12, VG93   623.746, 629.126+, .132+,
          355.622, 358.415
Florida—History—1865-1950   F311, F316   975.906
Focke-Wulf airplanes   TL686.F62   623.7460943
Food relief   HD9000+, HN696, HV696   338.19+, 353.007+, 362.509+, .58, .71
Forced labor   JX1977, HV8900+, HD4800+   331.57, 365.65, 338.09+
   —Germany
   —Russia   HD4875   338.0947, 354.470083
Forrestal, James, 1892-1949 [U.S.: Under Sec. & Sec. o/t Navy]   E748.F68, E813
          973.9170924, .9180924, 353.7, 923.273
Fortification   UG400-409+   355.544
Fortification, Field   UG403
Fortification
   —France
   —Great Britain   DA145   936.22
   —Poland

France
. Armée   DC403, D761, UA700-708   944.01, 940.540944, 355.00944,
              .409033, 320.944, 322.50944
  . 9. Armée   D761.1.9th   940.541244
  . Armée des Alpes—History   D761.1
  . Cavalerie
  . 2. Division Blindée   D761.2.2d
  . Groupement des Commandos de France
  —History   DC46, DC151, UA702   355.00944, 940.540944
  —Infanterie
    —Chasseurs
    —Drill and tactics
  . Légion Étrang`ere   UA703, U55, D810   355.31, .35, .3520944, 940.5405
  —Military life
  . 3. Régiment d'Auto-mitrailleuses [Medical]   D807.F7   940.547544
  . 1. Regiment d'Infanterie   D761.3.1st
  . 3. Régiment de Tirailleurs Algériens   D761.9.A42
—Colonies
. Combattante   D761.9.F7, DC373   940.5344+, .532244, 944.08+
  . Armée. 2. Division Blindée
  . Forces Navales Français Libres
—Foreign relations
  —1870-1940   DC340-2, DC369, DC373, DC385   940.5, 944.081+,
             327.44
  —1914-1940   DC369, DC373, DC389, DC393   327.440+,
             940.5314, 944.081+
  —1940-1945   DC373, DC397   327.440+
  —Germany   DC341   327.44043, .43044
France Forever
France
—History
  —Third Republic, 1870-1940   DC335-7   944.08, .081
  —20th century   DC361, DC389   944.08
  —1914-1940   DC396   944.0816
  —German occupation, 1914-1918   D548
  —German occupation, 1940-1945   DC373, DC397, DC400
             940.5344, 944.0809+, .081, .0816
    —Fiction
    —Italian occupation, 1942-1943
—History, Military   DC46, DC95, DC135   944.04
  —20th century   DC367   355.0330944
—History, Naval   VA503   359.00944
. Marine   D779.F7-8, VA503   359.00944, .3250924
  —History   D779, VA503   940.545944, 359.00944
    —World War, 1914-1918   D583.M33
    —World War, 1939-1945
  —Sea life
—Politics and government
  —1870-1940   DC331, DC340-44, DC354, JN2562, UA700
             320.94408+, 322.50944, 944.081
  —1914-1940   DC373, DC387-9, DC396, JN2863, JN3007
             320.9440816, 944.081
  —1940-1945   DC373, DC397, JN2593 1942
             320.9440816, 944.081
—Relations (general) with Germany   DC59   327.43044, .44043

Franco, Francisco-Bahamonde, 1892-1975 [Sp.: Gen., dictator]   DP254,
    DP264.F7, DP270, DS135.S7   946.0820924, 940.531503924
Franco-German War, 1870-1871   DC285, DC291-3, DC300, DC310, DD219
                                      943.081-082
Franco-Soviet pact, 1935
Frank, Anne, 1929-1945 [Ger.: Jewish victim]   PT5834.F68, DS135.N5, D810.J4
                                      940.531503924, .5315055, .53492
Frank, Hans, 1900-1946   [Ger.: Gov. Gen. of Pol.]
Franklin D. Roosevelt Library, Hyde Park, N.Y.   E742, Z733   016.9739,
                                      027.574733, 026.973917
Fraser, Bruce, Sir, 1888-1981 [G.B.: Adm.]   V64.G72.F73   359.00924
Fraser, Peter, 1884-1950 [New. Z.: Pr. Min.]
Freedom of the seas   JX4423-5 (int'nal. law), JX5203-5268   341.57
Freyberg, Bernard, Sir, 1889-1963 [New Z.: Gen., commander of New Z. troops]
                                      DA69   923.5931
Frick, Wilhelm, 1877-1946   [Ger.: Min. o.t Inter., Reich Protec. of Bohemia &
                                      Moravia]
Friends, Society of. American Friends Service Committee   BX7635, BX7747,
                           JX1953   172.4, 267.1896+, 289.6
Frigates   V767
Fritsch, Werner von, 1880-1939   [Ger.: Gen.]
Fromm, Friedrich, 1888-1945 [Ger.: Gen., Commander o/t Home Army, lukewarm
                           conspirator against Hitler]
Froslevlejren (Froslev, Sonderjyllands amt, Denmark: Concentration camp)
Fuchida, Mitsuo, 1902-?[Japan: Commander, commander of Pearl Harbor attack]
                                      D774.M5   940.545
Fukuoka 14 (Nagasaki-shi, Japan: Concentration camp)
Fuller, John Frederick Charles, 1878-1966   [G.B.: Tank theorist]   U55.F86
                                      355.00924
Funk, Walter, 1890-1960 [Ger.]
Fuses (Ordnance)   UF780   353.00712, 623.4542

Galen, Clemens von, 1878-1946   [Ger.: Archbishop of Münster, Nazi critic]
Galland, Adolf, 1912-   [Ger.: Lt. Gen., Luftwaffe fighter ace & chief]
                  UG626.2.G35, D787   358.4140924, 940.544943
Gamelin, Maurice Gustave, 1872-1958 [Fr.: Gen.]   D761.G, UA702.G 940.5344
Gandhi, Mohandas (Mahatma) Karamchand, 1869-1948   [India: Spiritual leader]
                  DS481.G3, DS423, DS480-1, DS480.45, B133.G4, B5134, DT764,
                  H59.G25, HM278, HN687   954.0350924, .040924, 181.4,
                  301.15, 320.954035, 322.440954, 370.973, 923.254
Garand rifle   UD395   355.82
Garigliano Valley, Battle of, 1944
Gaulle, Charles de   [SEE ' De Gaulle, Charles']
Gela, Battle of, 1943
Gembloux, Battle of, 1940
Genda, Minoru, ?-1989   [Japan: Commander, fighter pilot & tactician]
                                      D767.92.G44
General strike   HD5307   331.892, .89201, .8925
General Strike, Germany, 1920
General Strike, Great Britain, 1926   HD5365-8   331.89250941, .892942

Generals   U51-4 (biog.)
—[Austria, France, etc.]—Biography
—Australia—Biography   DU116.2
—Germany—Biography   DD247   943.0860924
—Great Britain—Biography   DA68-9, DA407, DA426, DA455   355.00924,
                    .3310924, 940.54250924, 941.0660922-0660924, 942.060924
—Russia   DK169   355.3310924
—South Africa—Biography   DT764.5
—United States   E181, E207, E467, E745, U52   973.730120922,
                    .741, .330924, 355.3310924, .3320922-3320924
     —Biography—Correspondence   E207   973.3330924
Genocide   JX5418, JX6731   301.592, 341.4, .77, 364.151
—Germany—History—20th century   D804.G4   940.5405
George II, 1889-1947   [Greece: King]
George V, 1865-1936   [G.B.: King of G.B., Emperor of India]   DA573, D412.6,
                    D546   942.0830924, 920.02, 923.142
George VI, 1895-1952   [G.B.: King]   DA584, DA16, DA28.1, DA112
                    941.0840922, 923.142, 909.0971241082
George C. Marshall Research Foundation
German-Austrian Pact, July 1936
German Library of Information
German reunification question (1949-)   DD257-9   943.087, 320.943, 327.43,
                    943.087, .1087
Germans in Poland
Germans in the Czechoslovak Republic   DB205   327.430437, 943.703
Germany   DD   943, 914.3
—Air defenses, Military
—Armed Forces   D757   940.5443
     —Ordnance and ordnance stores—History   UF525   623.0943
     —Organization   UA710   355.00943
     —Uniforms   UC485.G   355.140943
     —Weapons systems   UG635   355.82
. Auswärtiges Amt. Nazi-Soviet relations, 1939-1941   D754.R9.G42
                    940.532
—Bibliography   Z2249   016.914303
—Biography   DD231, CT1098   920.043, 940.531620924
—Boundaries   D821.A-Z, D821.G4
     —Czechoslovakia
     —France
     —Poland
—Civilization   DD61-7   914.3032, 943.07-08
—Colonies   JV2017-8, JV2027   325.343, .43, 940.5314
     —Africa   DT34   916.6
     —Africa, Southwest   JV2018   325.343068
—Description and travel—1919-1945   DD43   914.3+
—Economic conditions—1918-1945   DD237, DD247, HC286   943.085,
                    330.943, 332.110943, 338.0943, 940.5343
—Economic policy—1933-1945   DD231, HC285-6   940.5343,
                    330.943086, 338.0943
—Emigration and immigration
—Exiles

Germany
—History
  —1871-1918   DD220-1, DD232   943.08
  —William II, 1888-1918   DD228, DD232   943.08-084
  —20th century   DD231-2   943.08-085, .09
  —Revolution, 1918   DD248, DD207, DD234   943.07, .085, 329.943
  —Allied occupation, 1918-1930   D581, D650.M5
  —1918-1933   DD237, DD240, DD256   943.085
  —Kapp Putsch, 1920
  —March uprising, 1921
  —Beer Hall Putsch, 1923   DD247, DD253   943.085, .086, 329.943
  —1933-1945   DD247, DD256   943.086
  —Great Blood Purge, 1934   DD247.R56   943.086
  —Allied occupation, 1945-   DD257-9, D825   943.086-087, 940.5343
  —Bibliography   016.94035693
  —Personal narratives
  —Pictorial works   DD256   943.086
  —Poetry
  —Sources—Bibliography   DD256   016.329943
—History, Military—20th century
—History, Naval—20th century   DD231
—Industries—History   HC285   338.0943
—Intellectual life—20th century   DD67
. Kriegsmarine   VA513, V767, V859, DD231, D639, D770-1   359.00943,
                .3250943, 623.8250943, 940.45120924, .45943, .5451, .545943
  . Oberkommando   D770-1
  —Officers   VB315.G4   359.3320943
  —Registers   V11.G3
  —Sea life   V859.G3, D640   940.450924
  —Uniforms   VC305.G3   359.140943
  —Yearbooks   VA510
. Luftwaffe   D787, UG633, UG1245, TL685   940.544943, .5421,
                358.400943, .410943, .41330943, .430943, 623.7460943,
                356.1660943
  —Biography   D787   940.5449430922 (collected), .5449430924 (indiv.)
  . Fliegerkorps Richthofen   D787   940.544943
  —History—World War, 1939-1945   D771
  —Insignia   UC535   358.41140943
  . Kampfgeschwader 55   D787
  —Medals, badges, decorations, etc.   UB435.G3   355.1340943
  —Pictorial works   UG635.G3   355.3510943, 358.420943
  —Uniforms   UC485   355.140943
—Military policy   DD240, UA710   943.085, 355.033543
—Politics and government
  —1888-1918   DD228
  —20th century   DD232   943.08
  —1918-1933   DD240, DD256   943.084-086, 320.943, 328.943
  —1933-1945   DD247, DD256   943.085-086
. Reichsministerium für Volksaufklärung und Propaganda   D810.P7.G3,
                DD256.5   940.5488743, 301.15230943
. Reichstag—Elections   DD228   329.02343084
—Relations (military)—Great Britain
—Relations (military) with United States
Germany (Territory under Allied occupation, 1943-. Russian Zone)   DD257   943.086
Germany. Wehrmacht   D756   940.5421

Ghormley, Robert Lee, 1883-1958 [U.S.: Vice Adm.]
Giap, Vo Nguyen, 1910-1975 [Viet.: Gen.]
Gibson, Guy, 1918-1944   [G.B.: Wing Commander] D786.G   940.544942
Giffard, George, Sir, 1886-1964
Gilbert Islands   DU615   919.681, 996.81
Giolitti, Giovanni, 1842-1928 [It.: Prime Min.]   DG575.G5, DG555, DG566,
                        DG568.5   945.09, .090924, 327.45
Giraud, Henri, 1879-1949 [Fr.: Gen.] DC373.G5, D766.82.G   940.542,
                        923.544
Glaise von Horstenau, Edmund, 1882-1946 [Austria: Gen.] DB90.G53, D539,
                        D569.V5   943.6040924
Glasgow (Cruiser)   [WWI & II: 2 ships]
Glatz (Grafschaft)—History   DD801.G5   943.14
Gliders (Aeronautics)   TL760-769   629.13333
Glomfjord Raid, 1942
Gneisenau (Battleship)
Goebbels, Joseph, Dr., 1897-1945 [Ger.: Min. of Propaganda]   DD247.G6,
                DD256, DD256.5   943.0860924,
                301.15230943, 923.243
Goering, Hermann, 1893-1946 [Also 'Göring...': Ger.: Luftwaffe chief commander,
    Reichsmarschall]   DD247.G67   943.0860922-0860924, 923.243
Gotha gliders
Government and the press
  —Germany
  —Great Britain   PN4748
  —Russia   PN4748   070.449320947
  —United States   PN4738   070.40973
Government, Resistance to
Graziani, Rodolfo, 1882-1955 [It.: Politician] DG575.G7   355.00924
Great Britain   [SEE ALSO 'England', 'Scotland', 'Ireland'] DA, DA11 941-2
  . Admiralty
  —Air defenses, Military
  . Army
      —Airborne troops   D759   940.544941
      —Eighth Army
      —Biography   DA69.3
      —Black Watch (Royal Highlanders)   UA652.B6   356.110942, 355.31
      —Boys' units   U549.2
      —Coldstream Guards   D760, UA652   940.5421, 356.110942
      —Colonial forces
      —Corps of Royal Engineers. Bomb Disposal Unit   D786
      —East African Rifles   D767.6
      . Field Security Personnel
      —Firearms   UD385   355.82
      —History   UA649, UA853   355.00942, .02130942,
                        .30941, .310941
      . 2d King Edward VII's Own Gurkha Rifles
      . 1st King's Dragoon Guards   D760   940.541242
      . Long range desert group   D766.93
      —Military life   DA68, DA566   923.242

Great Britain
. Army
. Pioneer corps   D760.P5   940.541242
. Princess Louise's (Argyll and Sutherland Highlanders)   D760, UA652
940.541242, .542
. Princess Victoria's Royal Irish Fusiliers   D760, UA652   940.54250924,
356.16
. 7th (Queen's Own) Hussars   D759   940.541242
—Scottish regiments
—Uniforms—History   UC485   355.140941-140942, 356.110942
—Welsh regiments   UA663
—Biography   CB19, CT774-5, CT781-3, DA28, DA566, DA568, DA585
. British Information Services   Z2009
—Civilization—20th century   DA566   914.2, 941.082-083
—Coast defenses   UG429   355.450942
. Colonial Office
—Colonies   D413, DA16, DA563, HC256, JV1009-1018, JV1026-7
320.9171241, 325.342, 326.342, 327.20924,
382.0942, .30942, 909.0971242, 914.203
—Administration
—Documents, sources, etc.
—Africa   DT32   325.34206, .342096
—Africa, Eastern   DT423   916.7
—Asia
—Economic conditions
—Economic policy   HC259   338.9142, 382.0942
—Emigration and immigration   JV1041   325.341-2
—History   DA16-17, DA505, DA566, JV1011   325.34209,
909.0971242, 923.242, 942.08
—Race question
—Tropics
. Combined Operations Command   D760.C63   940.541242, .5421, .548642
—Commerce   HF3503   330.942, 382.0942, .50942, .60942
—Europe   HF3508   382.094204
—History
—Japan   382.0942052
. Committee of Imperial Defence   UA647   355.033542, .0942
. Committee on the Preservation and Restitution of Works of Art, Archives, and
Other Material in Enemy Hands
—Defenses   DA585, DA592, U55, UA647   355.0309171242,
.033041-033042, .033542, .20942, .450942
—Description and travel—1901-1945   DA630   914.2, .20383, .20484
—Diplomatic and consular service   JX1783   327.42
—Economic conditions
—20th century   HC256   330.942
—1918-1945   HC256   330.941083, .942083

Great Britain
   —Public Record Office   CD1048   016.95127
   —Relations (military)—Germany
   . Royal Air Force   UG635, UG1245, D568, D602, D756   358.40942,
                               .420941, .430941-430942, 623.7460941, .74630942,
                                940.44942, .5421
      —Biography   D568.4, D602   940.440924
      . Bomber Command   D786   940.544942
      . Fighter Command   UG635   358.414
      —History   DA585, UG635   940.44942, 358.400941-400942,
                                 .4135, .4183, .430942
      . 617 Squadron
      . 2d Tactical Air Force   D786   940.544942
   . Royal Navy   [SEE ALSO 'Great Britain. Navy']
      —Aviation   VG695.G7
      —Biography   DA70, DA74, DA88.1
      . Coastal forces
      . Fleet Air Arm   VG95.G7
      —History   DA70, VA454   359.3510942
      —Lists of vessels   VA454-6   359.320942
      —Medals, badges, decorations, etc.   VB335, UB435, CJ6113
      —Officers   VB315.G7   355.220942
      —Records and correspondence
      —Registers   V11.G7
      —Sea life   V737
      —Uniforms   VC305.G7
      —Yearbooks   V10
   . Special Operations Executive   D810.S7, D802   940.548641-
                                548642,.5486492
   . Stationery Office   [SEE ALSO 'Great Britain. H.M. Stationery Office']
   . War Office   D546, D759   942.084, 354.42066
      . General Staff   UB225, UA647   355.3310942, .30924
      . Intelligence Division
      —Manuscripts
Greece—History—Occupation, 1941-1944
Greece, Modern
   —History
      —1917-1944
      —1917-1935   DF845
      —Occupation, 1941-1944   D802   940.53495, 949.507
   —Politics and government—1935-   DF701, DF849, DF852   320.9495,
                                 949.507
Gremiashchii (Destroyer)   D779.R9
Grenades   UF765   623.42
Grew, Joseph, 1880-1965   [U.S.: Ambass. to Japan (1932-41)]   E748.G835,
                                 DS849.U6   327.20924
Grey, Edward, Sir, 1862-1933   [G.B.: Sec. of State for For. Aff.]   DA566.9.G8, .A1,
                                 D517, D546   942.0820924, 940.311, .342, 920.042
Grini (Norway: Concentration camp)
Ground support systems (Ordnance rocketry)
Groupe 'Collaboration'   D731.C   940.5344
Grumman Avenger (Bombers)   TL685   623.7463
Guadalcanal Island (Solomon Islands), Battle of, 1942-1943
Guam   DU647   919.67, 996.7

Guderian, Heinz, 1888-1953   [Ger.: Col. Gen., tank commander]   U55.G8,
              D811.G, D793   358.180924, 940.541343
Guernsey Island   DA670   914.2342, 942.342
Guerrilla warfare   U240, U210   355.02184, .425, .425098, 356.15, 335.438+
Guerrillas   D802   355,425+
Guided missiles   D787, UG630-5, UG1310, VF580   358.17, 623.4513, .4519+
Gunboats   V880, V895   359.3262+
Gunnery   UF800, UF150-302 (manuals), VF144-7, VF150-302
Gunpowder   TP268, TP272 (chem.), HD9663 (industry)   662.26-3
Gusen (Concentration camp)   D805.A8

Ha-Histadruth ha-kelalith shel ha-'ovdim be-Eriz-Israel   [WWII]   DS149,
              HD5660   658.3152095694
Haakon VII, 1872-1957   [Norway: King]   DL530
Hacha, Emil, 1872-1945   [Czech.: Pres.]
Haile Selassie, 1891-1976   [Ethiopia: Emperor of Abyssinia]   DT387.7, JQ3760
              963.050924, .0550924, .060924, 923.163, 309.16306, 320.963
Halder, Franz, 1884-1971   [Ger.: Gen.]   DD247.H25-5, UA712   940.5413430924,
              943.086, 355.00943
Half-track vehicles, Military   UG446   355.83
Halhaiin Gol, Battle of, 1939
Halifax, Edward Wood, Earl of, 1881-1959   [G.B.: For. Sec., War Cab. member,
              Ambass. to U.S.] (1941-5)]   DA566.9.H28, D810, DS480.7
              942.080924, 940.548642, 342.54
Halsey, William Frederick ('Bull'), 1882-1959   [U.S.: Vice Adm.]   E746.H3,
              V63   940.54260924, .545, 923.573
Hand-to-hand fighting   GV1111-1141, U167   796.8+, 355.348, .548, .82
Hand-to-hand fighting, Oriental   GV1112-1113   796.815+
Hangö, Battle of, 1941
Hanko (Finland), Battle of, 1941
Harbors—Normandy   D761   940.545
Harriman, William Averell, 1891-1986   [U.S.: Lend-lease negotiator to Rus. (1941),
              jt. allied powers diplomat, Ambass. to Rus. (1943-6)]
              D753   940.532
Hart, Thomas, 1877-1971 [U.S.: Adm.]
Hawaii
    —Civil defense   UA928   353.996900755
    —Description and travel—To 1950   DU623, DU627   919.69044,
              .6931032, 996.902
    —History   DU620-7
Hawaiian Islands
Heads of state
    —Biography   D412   920.02
    —[country]—Biography
Heart Mountain Relocation Center, Wyo.   D753, D769   940.54727309787
Hegra—Siege, 1940
Heinkel 100 (Fighter planes)   TL686   623.7464
Heinkel III (Bomber)   TL685   358.42
Heinkel 162 (Jet fighter planes)   TL686   623.7463
Heinkel 177 (Bombers)   TL686   623.7463
Heinkel aeroplanes   TL686   629.13334
Hel Peninsula (Poland), Battle of, 1939
Helicopters   TL716, TL714, TL723   629.13335+, .1335
Hellcat (Fighter planes)   TL685   623.7464
Hellenike Patriotike Hetaireia   D810.S7, D802.G8

413

Henderson, Nevile, Sir   [G.B.: Ambass. to Ger. (1937-9)]   D750.H4   940.531
Herbicides—War use
Heroes
Hess, Rudolf, 1896-1987   [Ger.: Dep. Führer]   DD247.H37   943.0860924,
        940.548243, 923.243
Hewitt, Kent, 1887-1972   [U.S.: Rear Adm.]
Heydrich, Reinhard, 1904-1942   [Ger.: SS Obergruppenführer, Reich Main
        Security Office chief, Reich Protector of Bohemia-Moravia]   DD247.H42,
        DD253.6, DB215, DB215.3   940.43587, .54050924, 923.543
Himmler, Heinrich, 1900-1945   [Ger.: Reischsführer-SS]   DD247.H46, DD256.5
        943.0860924, 923.243
Hindenburg, Paul von Beneckendorf und von, 1847-1934 [Ger.: Field Marshal, Pres.]
        DD231.H5, DD228, D531.H4813   943.0850924, .085,
        923.143, 940.343, .41430922
Hinzert (Germany: Concentration camp)
Hirohito, 1901-1989 [Japan: Emperor]   DS888.5, DS889.8, D767.2
        952.0330924, 940.5352
History, Modern—20th century   D421, D398, D415, D422-9, D443-5, D643, D720
Hitler, Adolf, 1889-1945   [Ger.: Führer]   DD247.H5, DD240, DD253, DD256,
        D741, D751, D757, D811, DB955   943.0840924,
        .0850924, .0860924, 940.5311, .53187, .5324439,
        .540943, .541343, .5482, 309.143086, 320.533, .943085-
        086, 321.940924, 327.140943, 364.131, 923.143
Ho Chi Minh, 1890-1969   [Viet.: Resistance chief]   DS556.8.H6213, DS557,
        DS559.9   959.7040924
Hobart, Percy, Sir, 1885-1957 [G.B.: Maj. Gen.]   DA69.3.H56
Hokkerup, Battle of, 1940
Holocaust, Jewish (1939-1945)   D810.J4, DS135.E83, DS102, D803
        940.5315, .531503+, .5315296, .5405, .546, 956.9404
    —Hungary
Holocaust, Jewish (1939-1945), in art
Holocaust, Jewish (1939-1945), in literature   PJ5012, PN56   809.88924, .93352
Holocaust, Jewish (1939-1945)
    —Psychological aspects   D810.J4   940.5472
    —Statistics   D810.J4   940.531503924
    —Study and teaching
Homma, Masaharu, 1888-1946   [Japan: Gen.]
Hong Kong—History   DS796   951.25, 915.125
    —Siege, 1941
Hopkins, Harry, 1890-1946   [U.S.: Pres. adviser]   E748.H67, E807.S45,
        HV28.H66   973.9170924, 338.54, 362.50924
Horthy, Miklos, 1868-1957   [Sometimes 'Horthy de Nagybánya, Miklos': Aust.-
        Hung.: Vice Adm., Adm., Regent of Hung.]   DB950.H6,
        DB955, D556, D583   943.9050924, .9105, 940.464436, .5324439
Hospitals, Military   UH460-85   355.345, .92, 353.007+, .008+, 362.11+
Hospitals, Naval and marine   RA975, RA980-93, VG410-50, VG463   616.98024
Hot pursuit (International law)
Houston (Cruiser: CL-81)   D774.H65, VA65   940.5425
Howitzers   UF470-5, UF560-5, VF390-5 (naval)
Hull, Cordell, 1871-1955 [U.S.: Sec. of State]   E748.H93, E183.7, D742.U5
        973.9170924, 940.53112, 923.273
Human experimentation in medicine—Germany—History—20th century
        D804.G4   940.5405

Hungarian Labour Service   D810.J4, D805   940.541243+
Hungary
   —Economic conditions—1918-1945
   —History   DB925   943.9+
      —20th century   DB950   943.91
      —1918-1945   DB955   943.91
      —Revolution, 1918-1919   DB955   943.905, .9105
   —Politics and government—1918-1945   DB955   943.905, .9105
Hurley, Patrick Jay, 1883-1963   [U.S.: Maj. Gen.; Ambass. to New Z., China]
                       E748.H96   327.20924, 923.273
Hürtgen, Battle of, 1944   D756   940.5421
Husum-Schwesing (Germany: Concentration camp)
Hyakutake, Haruyoshi, 1888-1947 [Japan: Lt. Gen.]

I.G. Farben Trial, Nuremberg, 1947-1948
Ibn Sa'ud, 1880-1953 [Saudia Arabia: King]   DS244.53, DA47.9.S4
                       953.8050924
Iceland—History   DL338   949.12
Ickes, Harold Le Claire, 1874-1952   [U.S.: Sec. o/t Inter.]   E748.I28   973.9170924
Ilyushin, Sergei, 1894-1977   [U.S.S.R.: mil. aeronautics engineer]
Imperial War Museum (Great Britain)   N9145.I
Imphal, Battle of, 1944   940.5425
Incendiary bombs
Incendiary weapons   UG447   358.34
Indemnity—Periodicals   D649.G31.A5 (WWI)
India
   —Armed forces
   . Army   D767, UA842   940.540954, 355.00954
    . 7th Division   D767.6
   —History   UA842   355.00954, .352, 356.110954
   —Foreign relations—Japan
   —History
      —1765-1947   DS463-79   954.029-031, .79
      —British occupation, 1765-1947   DS480-1   954.035+
      —1919-1947   DS480-1   954.035+
Indian National Army   D767.63   355.3510954
Indians of North America as seamen
Indians of North America as soldiers
Indochina, French—History   DS550   959.7+
Indochina—History   DS550   959.7+
Indonesia
   —History
      —1798-1942   DS643   959.008
      —Japanese occupation, 1942-1945   DS643.5
   —Politics and government, 1942-1949   DS644   959.8022
Industrial mobilization   UA18 355.26
Industry and state   HD3611-3790   330.08, 338.0186, .091724
Industry
   —Defense measures
   —Germany
   —Russia
   —United States   UA929   363.35+
Infantry   UD
Infantry drill and tactics   UD157-302
Infantry—History   UD15   356.109

Integrated logistic[s] support   UC263   355.621
Intelligence service   UB250   355.3432, 353.0089
    —France
    —Germany
    —Great Britain   D810, JN329   355.34320942, 940.548642
    —Japan
    —Russia
    —Soviet Union
    —United States   D767, UB251, UG633   353.0074, .0081, .00892,
                          940.5426, .548673
Inter-allied Commission on Mandates in Turkey. American Section   D651   956.102
Inter-allied Games, 1919   GV721
Inter-allied Military Mission to Hungary, 1919-1920   DB955   943.905+
Inter-allied Rhineland High Commission   D650.M5
International Labor Office   HD2755, HD7801   341.5, .763, 658.3
International organization   D815   940.5304
International trusteeships   JX1977, JX4021   321.027, 325.21, .31, 341.132, .27
Intrenchments   UG403 (field fortification), UG446 (trench warfare)
Invincible (Cruiser)
Iran—History—1909-1945   DS315-18   955.05+
Ireland
    —History
        —20th century   DA959-60   941.59
        —1910-1921   DA960-65   941.50821, .59
        —1922-1949   DA963   941.5082
    —Neutrality   D754.I6   940.54874309415
    —Politics and government
        —1910-   DA959   941.591
        —1922-1949   DA963   941.59, 320.9415+, 328.415-417
Ironside, Edmund, Sir, 1880-1959   [G.B.: Field Marshal]   DA69.3.I7, D559
                          942.0840924, 940.4147
Islands—Japan
Islands of the Pacific   DU17-28   919, 919.65, 990
    —Description and travel   DU15, DU21-3   919.3, .6
    —History   DU28 990
Ismay, Hastings Lionel ('Pug'), 1887-1965   [G.B.: Baron, Gen., Churchill aide]
                          DA69.3.I8   942.0820924, 940.53
Israel—History—1917-1948   DS126   956.94
Italo-Ethiopian War, 1935-1936   DT387   963.056, .065, 327.44045
    —Causes
    —Diplomatic history
    —Influence
Italy
    . Aeronautica   D792   940.544945
        —History—World War, 1939-1945   D792.I8
    —Boundaries—Yugoslavia   D821.I or .Y8-9
    —Civilization—20th century   DG451   914.50392, 945.092
    —Description and travel—1901-1944   DG428-9, DG601   914.50491
    —Economic conditions—1918-1945   HC305   330.943086, .945091
    . Esercito   [Army]   D763.I8+, UA742   945.08
        . Alpini
        . XIX Brigata Garibaldi   D763.I813
        . Divisione di Fanteria Acqui

Italy
—Foreign relations
    —1914-1945   DG571   327.45
    —1922-1945   DG571   327.45
    —Albania
    —Ethiopia
    —France   327.45044
    —Germany
    —Greece
    —United States
—History
    —20th century   DG555
    —1914-1945   DG568-575
    —1915-1922
    —1919-1945
    —1922-1945   DG571
    —Grand Council, 1943   DG572
    —German occupation, 1943-1945   DG572   940.5421
    —Allied occupation, 1943-1947
        —Posters
. Marina   D775   940.545945
    . 10. Flottiglia Mas   D775   940.545945
. Ministero degli Interni. Squadrad'Azione 'Ettore Muti'
—Politics and government
    —1914-1945   DG568-75   320.945091, 321.940945, 945.091+
    —1922-1945   DG571-7, JN5455   320.445, .945, 330.945, 940.5345,
                            945.091
    —1943-1947   DG572   945.091
Iwo Jima, Battle of, 1945   D767   940.5426

Japan
—Air defenses, Military
—Armed Forces   UA845   355.00952
. Army
    . Artillery
    . Military life
    . Parachute troops
    . Recruiting, enlistment, etc.
—Civilization—20th century
—Commerce—United States   HF3828   382.0952073
—Commercial policy
—Defenses   UA845   355.03252, .033052
—Description and travel—1901-1945   DS810   915.2
—Economic conditions
    —1868-   HC462   330.952
    —1885-1945
    —1918-1945   HC462   330.952, .952032-952033
—Emperors   DS871, JQ1641   320.952, 354.520312, 952.002

417

Japan
  —Foreign economic relations
    —Asia
    —United States   HF1602   338.9152073, 382.095201812
  —Foreign opinion, American
  —Foreign relations
    —1912-1945   DS845, DS885-8, JX1975   327.52, 341.2252, 952.033
    —China   327.52051, .51052
    —Germany   DS849   327.52043
    —Philippine Islands   327.520914
    —Russia   DS849   327.52047
    —United States   E183   327.52073, .73052
  —History
    —1868-   DS881-5   952.03+
    —20th century   DS885   952.03
    —1912-1945   DS888   952.033
    —Taisho period, 1912-1926   DS886   952.032, 309.152032
    —Showa period, 1926-   DS888   952.033
    —1926-1945   DS888.5
    —March and October incidents, 1931   DS888.5
    —May Incident, 1932 (May 15)   DS888.5
    —February Incident, 1936 (February 26)   DS888   952.033
    —Allied occupation, 1945-1952   DS889, E745   940.5338, .5352,
                                                      952.04, 915.2034
  —History, Military—1868-
  —History, Naval—1868-
  —Industries
  . Kaigun   [Navy]   VA653, D777, D777.5.A-Z (by ship)   359.030952,
                                  .052, .3250952, 623.8250952, 940.545952
    —Appropriations and expenditures
    —History   D742, D777, VA653   940.53112, .545952
    . Kamikaze Tokubetsu Kogekitai   D792.J3
    . Kokutai   [Aerial ops.]   VG95   358.4183, 623.74630952
    . Lists of vessels   VA653   359.320952
    . Oka Tokubetsu Kogekitai   D792   940.544952
    . Ordnance and ordnance stores
    . Organization
  —Military policy   UA845, VA50, VA653   355.033552, .33552, 359.030952
  —Politics and government
    —20th century
    —1912-1945   DS845, DS885-9   320.952032-952033, 329.951,
                                                940.5352, 952.033
    —1926-   DS888.2
  —Relations (general) with the East (Far East)
  —Relations (general) with the Philippine Islands   DS849   301.29520599,
                                                                327.520914
  —Relations (general) with the United States   E183   301.2952073, 327.73052
  —Relations (military) with the United States
  . Rikugen   D767, UA845-7   355.30952, 940.541352, 355.00952
    —Armored troops   UG446   358.180952
    . Kokutai   UG635, UG1242   358.4183, 623.74640952
    —Military life   U773   355.00952
    —Parachute troops—History   UD485   356.1660952
  —Social life and customs—1912-1945   DS821   915.20333
  —Territorial expansion

Junkers airplanes   TL686   623.7463
Junkers Ju-88 (Bomber)   TL685   940.544943
Just war doctrine   B105, BT736   261.873

Kaiser, Henry John, 1882-1967   [U.S.: Shipbuilding industrialist]   HC102.5.K3,
          RA413   614.2
Kaiten (Torpedoes)
Kalinin, Battle of, 1941
Kaltenbrunner, Ernst, 1902-1946   [Austria: Austrian SS chief, Reich Main Security
          Office chief]   DD247.K28   943.0860924
Kamenets-Podol´skiy, Battle of, 1944
Kamikaze airplanes   TL685   623.746
Katyn Forest Massacre, 1940   D804   940.5405, .5405094762, .547247
Kawasaki, Japan (Kanagawa Prefecture)—Bombardment, 1945
Keitel, Wilhelm, 1882-1946   [Ger.: Field Marshal, OKW Chief]   DD247.K4
          940.548243
Kelly (Destroyer)   D772.K   940.545942
Kemal Atatürk, 1881-1938   [Tur.: Gen., Pres.]   DR592.K4, DR589, D568.3, .7,
          DK511.C2   956.1, 940.425, .438, 923.1561
Kemal Pasa, Mustafa   [SEE Kemal Atatürk]
Kennedy, John Fitzgerald, 1917-1963   [U.S.: Naval lt., PT commander]
          E840-2+, E748.K375, E169, E183, E185
          973.9220924, .9228, 301.1543973922,
          320.943155087, 327.73+, 338.973, 353.030922, 923.273
Kennedy, Joseph Patrick, 1888-1969   [U.S.: Ambass. to G.B. (1937-41)]
          E748.K376, E747, E807, E843.K43   973.90924
Kennedy, Joseph Patrick, Jr., 1915-1944   [U.S.: Army Air Corps flyer]
          E843.K44   940.54210924
Kenney, George Churchill, 1889-1977   [U.S.: Gen. (Air Corps)]   D767.K4
          940.5426
Kenya, Mount   [Site of British prison]   D805.G7   940.547242
Kepa Oksywska Island, Poland, Battle of, 1939
Kesselring, Albrecht, 1885-1960   [Ger.: Field Marshal]   DD247.K45
          355.3310924
Khanka, Battle of, 1936
Kharkov, Battle of, 1942
Kharkov, Battle of, 1943
Khatyn War Memorial (Byelorussian S.S.R.)
Khrushchev, Nikita Sergeevich, 1894-1973 (1?)   [U.S.S.R.: Polit. Commissar]
          DK275.K5, DK267, DK268.K, DK274, DK276, DD881
          947.084, .0842, .085-0852, 320.947085, 338.1847, 923.247
Kido, Koicho, 1889-1977   [Japan: Marquis, Lord Privy Seal, advisor to the
          Emperor]   DS890.K45   952.0330924
Kiev—Siege, 1941
Kimmel, Husband Edward, 1882-1968   [U.S.: Adm.]   D767.92.K54
          940.54260924
King, Ernest, 1878-1956   [U.S.: Adm.]   V63.K56, D773.A, E182   940.5459730924,
          359.00924
King, William Lyon MacKenzie, 1874-1950   [Can.: Pr. Min.]   F1033.K53, F1034
          971.060924, .06220924, 940.5371, 923.271
Kinkaid, Thomas, 1888-1972   [U.S.: Adm.]   E746.K56
Kites (Military and naval reconnaisance)   UG670
Kleist, Paul Ewald von, 1881-1954   [Ger.: Field Marshal]
Klos (Albania: Concentration camp)
Kluge, Gunther von, 1882-1944   [Ger.: Field Marshal]

Knox, W. Frank, 1874-1944   [U.S.: Sec. o/t Navy]
Kock, Battle of, 1939
Kohima, India (City)—Siege, 1944   D767   940.5425
Kolobrzeg, Battle of, 1945
Kommounistikon Komma tes Hellados   D802.G8, DF849-50   320.949507,
                                                     329.9495
Kommunisticheskaia Partiia Sovetskogo Soiuza   JN6598, JA41, HX314, DK273
                                                     320.0947, 329.947, 947.084
    —Party work
Konev, Ivan, 1897-1973   [U.S.S.R.: Marshal] D755.7.K6+, D764.K   940.5442
Königsberg, Battle of, 1945
Konoye, Fumimaro, 1891-1945   [Japan: Prince] DS885.5.K6   952.0330924
Kornwerderzand, Battle of, 1940
Korsun´-Shevchenkovskiy, Battle of, 1944
Kosovo Polje, Battle of, 1944
Kozara, Battle of, 1942
Kragujevac, Yugoslavia—Massacre, 1941   D766.62.K7   940.5405094971
Krait (Mine vessel)   D772.K7-85   940.545
Kraljevo, Serbia (City)—Massacre, 1941
Kretschmer, Otto, 1912-? [Ger.: Commander]   D782.U15   940.5451
Krueger, Walter, 1881-1967   [U.S.: Lt. Gen.]   D769.26.6th   940.5426
Krupp von Bohlen und Halbach, Alfried, 1907-1967   [Ger.: Industrialist, munitions-
                              maker, chief director & eventual sole owner of Krupp
                              industries, War Economy Leader]   HD9523.9.K7,
                                      UF537.K7   338.7672, 623.4065
Krupp Trial, Nuremberg, 1947-1948
Kuei-lin (China), Battle of, 1944
Kumagaya (Japan)—Bombardment, 1945
Kursk, Battle of, 1943   D764   940.5421
Kutno, Battle of, 1939
Kuznetsov, Vasily, 1894-1964   [U.S.S.R.: Gen.]   D792.R9
Kwajalein Atoll, Battle of, 1944

Lagarde, Battle of, 1940
Lancaster (Bombers)   TL685   623.7463, 940.544942
Landing craft
Landing operations
Langley (Aircraft carrier)   D774.L32
Lanikai (Ship)   D774.L33   940.5425
Last letters before death   D811
Latvia
    —History
        —1918-1940   DK511   947.4384
        —1940-
        —Russian occupation, 1940-1941
Latvian National Foundation
Laval, Pierre, 1883-1945 [Fr.: For. Min., Deputy Head of State during Vichy]
                      DC373.L35, D761   944.0810922, .08160924,
                      940.5344, 923.5344
Le Paradis Massacre, 1940
Leachman, Gerard, 1880-1920   [G.B.: Lt. Col.]   U55.L347
Leadership   UB210 (mil.), VB203 (naval)   355.4, 359.6
Leaflets dropped from aircraft   HE9739

League of Nations   JX1974-5, D442, D642, D644, D650, D727
                                  309.1043, 327.116, .170973 (U.S.), 341.08, .1209,
                                  .22, .26, 963.056
    . Covenant   JX4471   341.58
    —Germany   JX1975   341.2243
    —Great Britain   JX1975   341.12
    —Japan   JX1975   341.2252
    . Permanent Mandates Commission   JX1975.A47
    —Russia   JX1975   341.2247
    —Sanctions   JX1975.6
    —United States   JX1975, E744   341.12973
Leahy, William, 1875-1959   [U.S.: Adm.]   V63.L39, E748   359.00924
Leander (Ship)   D779.N45   940.5459931
Lee-Enfield rifle   UD395   623.442
Legates, Papal   BX1908
Legion des Volontaires Francais Contre le Bolchevisme   D764
Leigh-Mallory, Trafford, Sir, 1892-1944 [G.B.: Air Marshal]   D785.L
Leipzig Trials, 1921
Lemay, Curtis, 1906-1990   [U.S.: Gen. (Air Corps)]   E745.L4, D790.L46
                                  940.544973, 358.413320924
Lend-lease operations (1941-1945)   D753.2   338.9147073, 940.5322, .540944
Lenin, Vladimir Ilich, 1870-1924   [Orig. 'Bronshtein, Lev Davidovich': Rus.: Head
    of the U.S.S.R.]   DK254.L4, DK246, DK262, DK265, DK267-8, D412,
                                  B4249, HF1028, HX40, HX312, JN6598
                          947.08410924, .8410924, 320.53220947, .947084,
                    322.4209, 329.947, 331.880947, 335.43082, .430947, 923.247
Leningrad—Siege, 1941-1944   D764   940.5421
Lenino, Battle of, 1943
Leonberg (Germany: Concentration camp)
Leopold III, 1901-?   [Belg.: King]   DH687   949.30420924
Leros, Battle of, 1943
Letts   [Latvia: post-WWI terr. ?]   DK511.L17, D561.L4
Lewis machine-gun   UF620.L   355.82
Lexington (U.S. aircraft carrier, 1st of the name) D774.L4, D790   940.5426, .545
Liberator pistol   UD413   355.82
Libraries and national socialism
Libya—History   DT224-235   961.2-203
Libyan desert   D766.82
Liddel Hart, Basil, 1895-1970   [G.B.: Capt., mil. theorist & author]   U55.L5, U19
                                  355.008, .00924
Lidvard (Motor ship)   D779.N6   940.5459481
Liechtenstein—History   DB540.5   943.648
Liepaja—Siege, 1941   DB540.5   943.648
Lightning (Fighter planes)   [Also known as 'P-38']   TL685-6, UG1242
                                  623.7464,.74640973, 940.544973
Lightning war   U16.5.L5   355.422
Limited war   UA11   355.0215
Lithuania
    —History
        —1918-1945   DK511   947.5084
        —Russian occupation, 1940-1941   DK511   947.50842
        —German occupation—1941-1944
Little Entente, 1920-1939   D460   341.2

Litvinov, Maxim [Maksim M.], 1876-1952   [U.S.S.R.: Sov. Commissar for For. Aff.,
    Ambass. to U.S. (1941-3), Dep. Comm. for For. Aff.]   DK267.L, DK268.L5,
                                    DS145, E183.8.R9   327.73047
Lloyd George, David, 1863-1945   [G.B.: Prime Min.]   D546.L5, D517, DA566,
                DA577, HN385   941.0830924, .0930924,
        942.0810924, .0830924, 940.341, .40942, 309.142082, 923.242
Lodge, Henry Cabot, 1850-1924   [U.S.: Sen.]   E664.L7, D643, JX1975
                                    973.90924, 328.730924, 923.273
Logistics   U168   355.411, .621, 658.7
Logistics, Naval   V179, VE353   359.41, .621+, 355.41
London
    —Air defenses, Military
    —Bombardment, 1917-1918   D547   940.44943
    —Bombardment, 1940-1941   D760   940.5442
    —Bombardment, 1940
    —History—1800-1950   DA683   914.210373
London. Naval Conference, 1930   JX1974   341.2, .67
London Naval Treaty, 1930   JX1974
London Naval Treaty, 1936   JX1974
Longwy (France), Battle of, 1940
Lorraine American Cemetery, France   D810.D4   940.546544
Los Angeles County, Calif. War Service Corps   D769.85.C21.L89
Los Baños (Los Baños, Laguna, Philippines: Concentration camp)
Luger pistol   TS537   623.443, 683.43
Luxembourg   [SEE ALSO 'Luxemburg']   DH916   949.35
Luxemburg   [SEE ALSO 'Luxembourg']   DH916   949.35

M1 carbine   UD395.M17   623.4425
MacArthur, Douglas, 1880-1964   [U.S.: Gen.]   E745.M28-3, D767, D767.4,
                DS889, DS918,V17.M3   973.910924,
        940.5426, 327.7305, .730924, 355.00924, .0973,
                .3310924, 923.573, 951.9042, 952.04
Macedonia—History—1912-1945   D562.M32
Macedonian question   DR2242, DR381, DR701   320.94976, 949.7
Machine-guns   UF620, VF410 (naval)   355.547, .82+, 623.4424
Madagascar   DT468-9   916.91+, 969.1+
Maginot Line   D756, DC367
Maine—History   F19-20+   974.1+
Maisky, Ivan, 1884-1975   [ALSO 'Maiskii': U.S.S.R.: Ambass. to G.B. (1932-43),
    Dep. Commissar of For. Aff.]   DK268.M3   923.247
Majdanek (Poland: Concentration camp)
Makin, Battle of, 1943
Malaya—History—Japanese occupation, 1942-1945   DS596.6   959.5+
Malenkov, Georgy [Georgil Maksimilianovich], 1902?-?   [U.S.S.R.: Member of
    Comm. for the Defense o/t State, polit. Commissar, Chair o/t Comm. for the
    Restor. o/t Economy]   DK268.M33, DK275.M3   923.247
Malinov, Alexander, 1867-1938   [Bulg.: Min., Pres.]   DR87.7, D20, HD815.S74,
                JN9609.A8   322.440924, 329.94977
Malmedy Massacre, 1944-1945   D804   940.5405094934, .547243
Malta, Battle of, 1940-1943
Malta—History   DG990   945.85
Mandates   D650, JX4021   341.12, .27
    —Cameroons   DT574
    —Palestine   DS126   956.94
Manila (Philippine Islands)

Mannerheim, Carl Gustav Emil von, 1867-1951   [Fin.: Marshal]   DK461.M32,
                DL1067.5.M36   948.97030924, 947.1030922, 923.5471
Mannerheim Cross
Manstein, Erich von, 1887-1973   [Ger.: Field Marshal]   D757.M3213,
                D757.3.M, DD247.M3   940.54013, 355.00924
Mao Tse-tung, 1893-1976 [China: Chairman o/t Chinese Communist Party]
                DS778.M3, DS774-5, DS777, U240   951.040924-
                050924, .90430924, 320.95105, 335.434, 370.951, 923.551
Maps, Military   UA985-97 (mil. geog.), UG470 (topog., surveys), U408, UC30
                526.8, 623.71
   —Symbols   UG470-3
Marauder bomber   [A.k.a. 'B-26']
Marco Polo Bridge Incident, 1937
Mariana Islands   DU645   996.7
Maritime law   JX4408-49 (int'nal. law), JX6311 (private), HE585-7 (shipping laws)
                333.9164+, 341.448, .45-762+, 343.096+, 347.75+
Marne, Battle of the, 1914   D544, D545.M3, D515   940.421
Marne, 2d Battle of the, 1918   D544-5
Marseille, Battle of, 1944
Marshall, George Catlett, 1880-1959   [U.S.: Gen.; Army Chief of Staff] Chair, Jt.
   Chiefs of Staff]   E745.M37, D570.9.M37, E183.7.B462, E183.8.C5,
   E836.A42, U53   973.9170924, 940.48173, 355.3310924, 923.573
Marshall, William, Sir, 1865-1939   [G.B.: Gen.]   D521, D546   940.4
Marshall Islands
Martial law   JX4595 (int'nal. law)
   —United States   JX343-55, KF223, KF5063   342.73062, 344.0973,
                345.730231
Marzabotto Massacre, 1944   D763   940.5421
Masaryk, Jan Garrigue, 1886-1948   [Czech.: For. Min. o/t gov.-in-exile in Eng.]
                DB217.M3, DB2191.M37   923.1437
Masaryk, Tomas [Thomas] Garrigue, 1850-1937   [Aust.-Hung.: Pres. of Czech.]
   DB217.M3, DB215, DB2191.M38, D521.M43, D558, D619, DS141.M33
   943.7020922-7030922, 940.32273, 320.50924, 923.1437
Mass casualties   355.48
Massachusetts—History—1865-1950
Massaua, Eritrea—Harbor
Matapan, Battle of, 1941   D775   940.5421, .545942
Matsuoka, Yosuke, 1880-1946   [Japan: For. Min.]   DS885.5.M3
Mauser rifle   UD395, TS536   623.44231, 683.42
Mathausen (Mathausen, Austria: Concentration camp)
Mechanization, Military—Germany
Medals, Military and naval   UB430-5 (mil.), VB330-5 (naval), UC530, NK6302
                355.134, .134075, .13409, 737.2
Medicine, Military   RC970-1 (med. practice), UH223 (mil. sci.), UH393
Medicine, Naval   RC981-6, VG228   614.864, 616.98024
Mediterranean region—Strategic aspects
Melanesia—History   DU490
Melitopol, Battle of, 1943
Memorials
Menzies, Robert Gordon, Sir, 1894-1978   [Australia: Pr. Min.(1939-41)]
                DU114.M4   994.040924, 940.5342

Merchant marine
—France   D779.F8   940.545944
—Great Britain   HE823, HF3505   382.0941-0942, 387.5142, .70942, .506541
—Japan
—Norway   D779.N6
—Russia   D779.R9
—United States   HD6976, HE741-6, VK23, VK160   343.7309602632,
          353.008775, .82, 387.50973, .5173, .5440973
Merchant seamen   VK221   658.373875
Merchant ships, American   VM7   387.24
Merchant ships—United States
Merrill, Frank, 1903-1950   [U.S.: Brig. Gen. of 'Merrill's Marauders' in Burmese
          jungles]
Mers-el-Kebir, Attack on, 1940   D766   940.5421
Messerschmitt 109 (Fighter planes)   TL686.M44, UG1242   358.43, 623.7464
Messerschmitt 110 (Fighter planes)   TL686.M44, UG1242   623.7464,
          940.544943
Messerschmitt 262 (Fighter planes)   [Jet]   TL686.M   623.7464
Metaxas, John N., 1871-1941 [Greece: Col.: dictator, 1936-41]   DF837-8, DR36,
          DR43, D651.G8   949.506, .6, 940.322495, 327.495
Meteorology, Military
Metz, Battle of, 1944
Meuse, Battle of the, 1940   D756   940.5421
Mexico—History—1910-1946   F1208-34   972.081-082
Michael, 1921-   [ALSO 'Mihal I': Rum.: King]   DR265   923.1498
Michel (Cruiser)
Micronesia—History   DU500   996.5, 919.65
Midget submarines   D784.A-Z, D784.G7 (GB), V857, VM453   940.5451, 623.82
Midshipmen   V415, VB315.G7 (GB)   359.071173 (US)
Midway, Battle of, 1942   D774   940.5426, .5428, .545
Midway Islands
Mihailovi'c, Draza, 1893-1946   [Yug.: Gen.]   DR359.M5, D766.6, D802.Y8
          940.53497, 923.5497
Mikawa, Gunichi, n.d.   [Japan: Adm.]
Mikoyan, Artem, 1905-1970   [U.S.S.R.: Maj. Gen.]
Milch, Erhard, 1892-1972 [Ger.: Field Marshal]   D787   940.544943
Militarism   JX1937-64, U21, UA10   355.01-02, .082, .09
Military administration   UB87, UB145, UA649   355.609+, 355+
Military architecture   NA490-7 (architec.), UG460 (mil. sci.)   725.180902
Military art and science   U, U43, U102-4   355, 355.009+, .02, .109+
—Abbreviations   U26   355.00148
—Dictionaries   U24-6   355.003, 623.03
—History   U27-43, U823, U873, UA702, UG320, V33   355.009,
          .009+, .0209+, .09+, .409+
—Terminology   U26
Military assistance, American   UA12, UA23   355.00715, .0320973,
          343.73019, .73074, 338.473550320973
Military assistance, British
Military attachés   UB260   355.3432
Military attachés, American
Military attachés, British
Military bases, American
Military biography   U51-5, CT220, CT6900   355.00922, .330922,
          .3310922, .3320922, 923.2
Military bridges   UG335   623.6709+

Military calls   M1270, UH40-5
Military ceremonies, honors, and salutes   U350-65, U353 (US), U408 (US),
                            U766 (US)   355.00973 (US), .1709+
Military courts   [For martial law]   341.32
Military departments and divisions—United States
Military dependents   UB400-405
Military discipline   UB790-5, KF7590 (US)   343.73014 (US)
Military education   U400-714   355.0007, .07
    —United States   U408-10, U429   355.0071173, .071173, .11520973,
                       613.7071173
Military engineering   UG
Military ethics   U22
Military field engineering   UG360-90
Military funerals—United States   UG633   355.17
Military geography   UA985-97   355.47
Military geology   UG465
Military government   JF1820, JX5003   322.5, 341.32, .320991
Military helicopters   TL716, UC333, VG93   353.007232, 355.83, 358.4183
Military history   D25, U27-43 (mil. sci.)   904.7, 940.28, 355.0009,
                       .033,.43, .48, 909
    —Bibliography   Z6724, D25, U27-43   016.355009, 355.009, .0009
Military history, Modern   U39-42, D295, D361, D217   904.7, 940.28
    —19th century   D396   355.48, 904, 909.8
    —20th century   D431   909.824
Military intelligence   UB250-70, U220   355.34, .3432, .34320904, .43, 342.73085
Military law   UB461-736   343+
    —United States   KF26-7, KF7204-7210, KF7250, KF7305, KF7606-7609
        343.7301-730184, 355.000973, .133
Military libraries   Z675.M5   026.355, 027.65
Military maneuvers   UD250-5, UD460-5, U250   355.5
Military miniatures   NK494, NK8475, TT154, U311   745.59, .592, .59282,
                       .59282075
Military missions   UA16
Military museums   U13   355.0074013 (US)
Military music   M1270
Military music, American [English, German, etc.]
Military music, American   ML1311, ML3930   784.71973, 785.0671, .130973
Military music, English—History and criticism   ML1331   784.71942
Military music, German
Military music, Russian
Military necessity   JX5135.M5
Military nursing   UH347, UH495   355.345+
Military occupation   JX4093, JX5003, U408   341.32, .63, .66, 355.4
Military occupation damages
Military oceanography   V396-396.5   551.46
Military offenses
    —United States   KF7609   343.7301+
Military paraphernalia
    —Collectors and collecting   U790   355.14075, .8075, .80942
    —Germany   UC465   329.943
    —Prices—Great Britain   U790   355.82
Military planning
    —Germany—History—20th century   U162
    —Soviet Union

Morgenthau, Henry, 1891-1967   [U.S.: Sec. o/t Treasury]
Morocco—History—20th century   DT317, DT324   964.03-04
Mortain (France), Battle of, 1944
Mortars (Ordnance)   UF560-5
Moscow, Battle of, 1941-1942   D764   940.5421
Moscow Trial, 1945
Moscow Trials, 1936-1937   345.470231
Motor-boats   D771, VM341, VM357, VM771   623.8231, .82314-
                       82315, .8723, .88, .8823
Motor-trucks, Military   UG615-20   623.7472
Motor vehicles, Amphibious   TL229.A (technology), V880 (naval sci.)   623.747
Motorization, Military   UC340-5
Moulin, Jean, 1899-1943 [Fr.: Fr. Resistance leader]   D762.C45
Mountain guns   UF440-5
Mountain warfare   U240
Mountbatten, Louis, Lord, 1900-1979   [G.B.: Vice Adm.]   DA89.1.M59,
                       DS480.84   942.0820924, 954.040924
Moving-pictures in propaganda
Mulberry harbors   D761   940.5421
Munich. Universität—Riot, Feb. 18. 1943   DD256   943.086
Munitions   HD9743 (econ.), JX5390 (int'nal. law), UF530-7 (manufacture),
               JX1907, U102, UF520   338.4735582, .476234,
               382.4535582, .453583
   —Germany   UF535   623.0943
   —United States   HD9743, UF533   338.476230973, 343.73025,
                   355.033573, .62110973, 382.456234, 658.80935582
Murphy, Robert Daniel, 1894-1958 [U.S.: Diplomat, F.D.R.'s N. Afr. envoy (1941-3)]
                       E748.M875   327.20924
Music and war
Mussolini, Benito, 1883-1945   [It.: Il Duce]   DG575.M8, DG499, DG571-2,
               DD256   945.0910924, 940.5324, 914.50391, 923.245
Mustang (Fighter plane)   [A.k.a. 'P-51']   TL685.3, TL686, UG1242
                   358.4183, .43, 623.7464, 940.544973
Mutiny
   —Germany   D639   940.45943
Myitkyina (Burma), Battle of, 1944

Nagas   D767.6   940.542
Nagasaki—Bombardment   D767   940.532452, .5426
Nagumo, Chuichi, 1886?-1944 [Japan: Vice Adm.]
Narvik, Battle of, 1940   D763   940.5421
National cemeteries
   —California   353.0086609794
   —United States   E160, E494, UB393-4   343.73025, 353.00866,
                   355.115, .69, 362.8
National characteristics   CB197, CB203, D443   914.03, 940.5, 901.9
National characteristics, American   E169, E173, E784, B1649, BF755
               917.3039+, .303917-303918, 136.4973, 155.8973, 301.3260973
National characteristics, British   DA110   914.2
National characteristics, English   DA118   914.203+
National characteristics, German   DD76, DD256   914.30631, 155.8943,
                   320.943
National characteristics, Japanese   DS821, BF755   915.203+, 136.4952,
                   155.8952, 301.2952
National characteristics, Russian   DK32, DK268, DK276   914.7+

New Britain
New Britain (Island)
New Caledonia   DU720   919.32, .65
New Guinea   DU740   919.5, 995, .3
  —History
New Hebrides   DU760   919.34, 993
New Ireland
New Jersey (Battleship, BB-62)   VA65   359.32520973
New Orleans (Cruiser)   D774.N4   940.545
New York (State)—History—1865-1950   F119-120+   917.4703, 974.7
New York (State) State War Council   [WWII]
New Zealand
  . Army
    . Division, Third. Histories Committee   D767.85.A55
    . 2d New Zealand Divisional Artillery   D767.851.2d
  —History   DU418-427+   919.31, 993.1+, .102, .1022, .10333+
    —1870-
    —1918-1945
Newfoundland—History   F1122-3   971.8
Nicholas II, 1868-1918   [Rus.: Czar]   DK254.A, DK258-9, DK262, D511, D741,
          DD228.7.R8   947.080922, .080924, 940.311, 923.147, 364.131
Night fighter planes   UG1242   358.43
Night fighting (Military science)   U167
Night flying   TL711   629.132+, .1325212
Nijmegen, Netherlands, Battle of, 1944
Nimitz, Chester W., 1885-1966   [U.S.: Adm.]   V63.N55   940.54260924
Nitti, Francesco Saverio, 1868-1953   [It.: Politician, Min. o/t Treasury]   DG555,
          DG570, D643.A7, D651.I6, UA742   945.08-09, 940.3141, 320.94509, 327.45
Nomura, Kochisaburo, 1877-1964   [Japan: Ambass. to U.S. on 7 Dec. 1941]
North Africa American Cemetery, Carthage   D810.D4   940.5465611
North Atlantic region—Strategic aspects
North Carolina—History—1865-1950   F251-8   975.6+
Norway
  —Foreign relations—Germany   DL458   327.481043
  —History   DL449-534+   914.81, 948.1+
    —1905-1940
    —German occupation, 1940-1945   DL532
  —Politics and government—1940-1945   DL458, JN7041, JN7445
Noske, Gustav, 1868-1946 [Ger.: Socialist politician]   DD247.N63, DD85
                                                          920.043
Novorossiisk (Russia), Battle of, 1943
Nuncios, Papal
Nuremberg Medical Trial, 1946-1947
Nuremberg Trial of Major German War Criminals, 1945-1946   D804, JX5437,
          JX6731   341.41, .69, 345.0238, 364.138+

Obstacles (Military science)
Occupation currency   H31   940.53144
Occupation currency, American [British, German, Japanese, etc.]
Oceania   [SEE ALSO 'Oceanica']   DU, DU15-28+   919, 990-999
Oceanica   [SEE ALSO 'Oceania']   DU, DU15-28+   919, 990-999
O'Connor, Richard Nugent, Sir, 1889-?   [G.B.: Gen.]
Oder-Neisse area   DD801.O35   943.805
Oder-Neisse Line (Germany and Poland)

Odessa, Battle of, 1941
Odessa, Battle of, 1944
O'Donnell Camp (Luzon, Philippines: Concentration camp)
Offensive (Military strategy)—History—20th century   U162
Official secrets
   —Great Britain   KD8024   345.420231
   —United States   KF26   342.7305
Oflag II C (Dobiegniew, Poland: Concentration camp)
Oflag VI C (Osnabrück, Germany: Concentration camp)
Oflag XIII B (Hammelberg, Germany: Concentration camp)
Oka (Mine layer)   D779.R9
Okino-daito Island, Battle of, 1945
Oksywie Hill (Poland), Battle of, 1939
Oldendorf, Jesse, 1887-?   [U.S.: Rear Adm.]
Onishi, Takajiro, 1891-1945   [Japan: Vice Adm]
Operation Bolero, 1942
Operation Cerberus, 1942
Operation Citadel
Operation Coronet
Operation Dragoon, 1944
Operation Goodwood
Operation Husky, 1943
Operation Jaywick   940.5426
Operation Jericho
Operation Lila, 1942
Operation Long Jump   D734   940.548743
Operation Menace   D766   940.5423
Operation Mercury, 1941
Operation Mincemeat   D810.S7-8   940.548642
Operation Neptune   D770   940.5421
Operation Overlord
Operation Rimau   D767   940.5426
Operation Sea Lion   D771, D786   940.5342, .5421
Operation Sledgehammer, 1942
Operation Stella Polaris, 1944
Operation Sunrise
Operation Torch   D766   940.5423
Operational rations (Military supplies)
Oppenheimer, J. Robert, 1904-1967   [U.S.: Nuclear physicist, led team that built
   1st atomicbomb]   QC16.O62, .L36, HD9698.U52   530.0924,
                                  323.20973, 353.00183, 358.4182, 364.1310924, 925.3
Oradour-sur-Glane Massacre, 1944   D804   940.5421
Orden Pour Le Merite   D604
Ordnance   UF520-630   355.82+, 356.186+, 623.4
Ordnance, Coast
   —Manufacture   UF530-45   623.4+, .41
Ordnance, Naval   VF15, VF23, VF353   359.82+, 623.4+
Orel, Battle of, 1943
Organisation Gehlen   DD247.G27-37   327.12+
Orion (Auxiliary cruiser)   ['The Black Raider']   D772.O7   940.545943
Orlando, Vittorio Emanuele, 1860-1952 [It.: Pr. Min.]   DG555, DG570, D520.I7,
   D569.I8, .A2, D617, D643.A7   945.09, 940.3141, 327.45

Orphans
Orphans and orphan asylums
Orphans
   —Europe
   —Great Britain   HV1148   362.73
Oslofjorden, Battle of, 1940
Osmeña, Sergio, 1878-1961   [Phil.: Vice Pres., Pres.]
Ossewa-Brandwag (Organization: South Africa)   DT779.8
Oswiecim (Concentration camp) [SEE ALSO 'Auschwitz']   D805.G3, D804.G3
                                            940.547243
Ozawa, Jisaburo, 1896-1966 [Japan: Vice Adm.]

P-38   [SEE 'Lightning (Fighter planes)
P-40 (Fighter planes)   [A.k.a. 'Kittyhawk', 'Tomahawk', 'Warhawk']   TL685-6,
                    UG1242   358.4183, .43, 623.7464, 940.544994
P-47   [SEE 'Thunderbolt (Fighter planes)']
P-51   [SEE 'Mustang (Fighter planes)']
P-61   [SEE 'Black Widow (Fighter planes)']
Pacifism—History   BX7635, BX7748, JX1938, JX1944, JX1961
                    261.873, 289.6, .673 (US), 327.172+
Painlevé, Paul, 1863-1933   [Fr.: Min. of War, Prem.]   DC342.8.P4, DC373.S3,
                    DC385, D548   944.0810922-0810924, 320.944081
Paléologue, Georges Maurice, 1859-1944 [Fr.: Ambass. to Russia]   DC385,
        DK265.P255, D453, D741   944.08, 940.311, .3112, 320.94708
Pankrác (Concentration camp)   D805.G3
Papacy—History—20th century   BX1389   262.130904, 282, 327.45634
Parachute troops   UG630-5, UD480-3   356.166, .6
Parachutes   TL750-8   629.134386
Parachuting   TL750-5, GV770, GV761   629.134386, 797.5609
Paraguay—History—1938-   F2681+   989.2+
Paris
    —History—1940-1944   D762, DC737   940.5421, .534436
    —Posters
    . Peace Conference, 1919   D619, D643-7, D651   940.3141+, .3142,
                           .32273
        . Hungary   D651   940.3142
        . Italy   D651   940.3141
        . Rumania   D651.R6   327.498
        . Russia   D651.R8   940.3141
        . U.S. Territorial Section   D644   940.312
    . Peace Conference, 1919-. Yugoslavia   D651   940.31425
    . Peace Conference (1919-1920)   D647.A2   940.3141
Park, Keith, Sir, 1892-1975   [New Z.: Air Marshal]
Partito nazionale fascista   DG571, JN5657.F3   321.6, .9, 329.945,
                    .940945
Partizanski spomenik (Mostar, Bosnia and Hercegovina)
Pasic, Nikola, 1845-1926 [Serbia: Pr. Min.]   DR359.P283, DR341, DB91, D741,
                DJK4   949.71020924, .7101, .6, 940.311, 943.604
Patch, Alexander McCarrell, 1889-1945   [U.S.: Gen.]
Patton, George, 1885-1945   [U.S.: Gen.]   E745.P293-3, D743, D769,
                D769.26.3d, D805.G3, D811   355.3310924,
                923.573, 940.5421
Paulus, Friedrich, 1890-1957   [Ger.: Field Marshal]   DD247.P38, DD259.4.P3,
                D764.3.S7   355.3310924, 923.543

Peace   JX1901-99 (int'nal. law)   172.4+, 309.2206, 320.94+,
                322.43-44, 327.17+, .172+, 341.1+, 355.027, 940.51
Peace treaties   JX5181
Pearl Harbor, Attack on, 1941   D767, D748   940.5426, .5311, .53112,
                                                .532273, .542, .5426
Pearl Harbor (Hawaii), Attack on, 1941
Peleliu Island (Palau), Battle of, 1944
Pensions, Military   UB370-5 & UB400-5 (army), VB280-5 & VB340-5 (navy),
                E255 (pension rolls)
Pensions, Military and naval—United States
Pensions, Military
    —United States   UB373, UB403, KF26-7   355.115, .11510973,
                                .11560973, 343.73011, 344.73011
        —European War, 1914-1918
        —World War, 1939-1945
Penzberg, Germany—Massacre, 1945
Percival, Arthur, 1887-1966   [G.B.: Lt. Gen.]   D767.5.P
Peron, Juan Domingo, 1895-1975   [Argen.: Pres.]   F2849.P48, F2237, F2843,
                F2848, UA613   982.06, 320.98206, 923.182, 980.03
Perth (Cruiser)   D779.A9   940.545994
Peru—History—1919-1968
Pétain, Henri-Philippe Benoni Omer Joseph, 1856-1951   [Fr.: Gen.]   DC342.8.P4,
                DC280.5.B3, DC397, D507, D530, D756.B46, D761
        944.0810922-0810924, .08160924, 940.410922, .4140922, .5344, .544
Petroleum industry and trade   HD9571.5   338.27282+
    —Military aspects—History—20th century
Philadelphia Experiment, 1943
Philippine Islands
    —History
        —1898-1946   DS685-6   959.903, .9035, 991.4031
            —Japanese occupation, 1941-1945   DS686   915.990335
        —Politics and government—1935-1946   DS685-6   959.9035,
                                320.9599032, 309.1599035
Philippine Sea, Battles of the, 1944   D774   940.5426, .545973
Phillips, Tom, Sir, 1888-1941   [G.B.: Adm.]
Photographic interpretation (Military science)   D810.P4 (WWII), UG476   623.72
Photography, Military
Pietransieri di Roccaraso—Massacre, 1943
Pilsudski, Joseph, 1867-1935 [Pol.: War Min.]   DK440.5.P5, DK439
                943.8040924, 320.9438, 923.1438, .5438
Piombino (Italy)—Battle of, 1943
Pistols   UD410-15 (army), TS537 (manufacture), VD390 (naval),
                GV1175 (shooting)   344.7305330262, 623.44+, .442-3,
                                683.43, 739.74+, 799.202833, .213
Pistols, American   TS537, UD413   623.44, .4430973, 683.43
Pistols, German   TS537   683.43, .430943
Pistols—History
Pius XII, 1867-1958 [Vatican: Pope]   BX1378, BX1753, BX2250, DD256.3
        261.8, 262.130924, .131, 265.5, 364.131, 922.21, 940.531522, .532545634
Plaszow (Poland: Concentraton camp)
Ploesti, Battles of, 1943-1944
Poincaré, Raymond, 1860-1934   [Fr.: Pres.]   DC385, D511, D650.M5, D741
                                944.0810924,940.311
Point 175, Battle of, 1941

Poland
  . Armia   D765+, U773   940.5412438
    . 2. Korpus   D765   940.5412438
    . Polskie Sily Zbrojne. Armia Krajowa   D802.P6 (Underground)
  —Boundaries
      —Germany   D821.P
      —Russia
  —Foreign relations
      —1918-1945   DK4410   940.53438
      —Russia   DK418, DK441, DK4185   327.438047, 943.805
  —History
      —1918-1945   DK440   914.38, 943.8
        —Occupation, 1939-1945   D802   940.5337
  —Military relations—Soviet Union
  —Politics and government—1918-1945   DK440-1   943.8, 320.9438,
                                                      .943804-943805
  . Wojsko Polskie. 22. Pulk Artylerii Lekkiej   D765.13
Police
  —Germany
      —Political activity
Police power—Germany
Polish question   D621.P7
Political atrocities
Political crimes and offenses   HV6254-6321   364.13, .132, .154
Political oratory—Germany
Political parties   JF2011-2111   329.02+
      —Germany—History   JN3933   329.020943
      —Great Britain   JN1111-1129   328.42072, 329.020942, .941-2
      —Japan   JQ1698   329.952
      —Soviet Union
Political poetry, American [British, etc.]
Political posters, German
Political posters, Japanese
Political prisoners
      —Russia   HV8959, HV8964, HV9712-13   365.45, .450947, .60924,
                              940.5472498, 947.080924, .0842+
Political psychology   BF173, JA74-6, JF2051, JN5651   150.1952, 155.2,
                              158.4, 301.592, 320.019, 329.0019
Political purges
      —Germany
      —Japan   940.531440952
      —Russia
Political satire, American [English, German, etc.]
Politics and war
Politics in art—Soviet Union
Polska Partia Robotnicza—History   D802.P62.W26, JN6769   329.9438
Polynesia—History   DU510   996
Popov, Dusko, n.d.   [G.B., Ger.: Double/triple (?) agent]   D810.S8.P6
                                                      940.5486420924
Popov, Markian, 1902-?   [U.S.S.R.: Gen.]
Population transfers
      —Jews
Portal, Charles, Sir, 1893-1971   [G.B.: Air Chief Marshal]

Portugal
—Foreign relations   327.4690+
—History—1910-1974   DP680   946.9042
—Politics and government
   —1910-1974
   —1933-1974   DP680   320.9469042
Postliminy   JX5187 (int'nal. law)
Potsdam Conference (1945)   D734
Pound, Dudley, Sir, 1877-1943   [G.B.: Adm.]
Powder-magazines   UF540-5, VF380 (naval)
Pozna´n, Poland, Battle of, 1945
Prague, Battle of, 1945
Presidents—United States
   —Archives   CD3029   025.171
   —Biography
   —Election
      —1940   E748, E811   329.0237309, 973.917
      —1944   E812   329.023730917
      —Inaugural addresses   J81   353.03, .035
      —Messages   J81, E173   353.035
      —Press conferences   JK518   353.032, 070.11
Press and politics—Germany
Prezan, Constantine, 1861-1943   [Rum.: Lt. Gen.]   D565.A2, DR262.A2
                 949.8020924, 923.1498
Price regulation   HB236   338.52, .526
   —United States   HB236, HC101, HD1761   338.10973, .5260973,
                 339.50973
Prien, Gunther, 1908-1941   [Ger.: Lt., U-boat Commander (U47)]
            V64.G32.P744, V65.P7   940.54510924, 923.543
Prinz Eugen (Cruiser)   359.32530943
Priorities, Industrial   HD3611-16
   —United States   HD3616, HC106   353.00895, 338.973
Prisoners of war   JX5141 (int'nal. law), UB800   341.33, .6509+, 365.6
   —Germany
   —Japan
   —Psychology   RC451   616.89
   —Russia
   —United States   UB774   365.450973
Prisons, Military   UB800+   355.71
Prize law   JX5245-66   341.36
Profiteering
Projectiles   UF750-70 (mil.), VF480-500 (naval)   355.82, 623.42,
             .451109+, .4513
Projectiles, Aerial   UF767
Propaganda   UB275, HM263, JF1525   301.152-154
Propaganda, American   D632, E744   301.1540973, 327.73,
             940.488673
Propaganda, British   D619   940.488642
Propaganda, German   DD255-6   327.43, .140943, 301.15230943,
             .1540943
Propaganda, Russian   DK270, DK278   327.140947, 947.085

Psychiatry, Military   D807.U6, UB323, UH629   616.8, .89, 355.22
Psychological warfare   UB275-7, U22   355.3434, .42-3, 301.1523
Psychology, Military   U22.3, U15, UH629, HQ797   355.0019, .1156,
                          .22, .6133, 301.593, 155.93
Psychology, Naval
PT boats   [SEE 'Torpedo-boats']
Public opinion   D810.P85 (WWII)
   —Germany   DD117, DD228   329.050943
   —United States   D810.P85.U5+   301.1540973
Public shelters
Pyle, Ernest, 1900-1945   [U.S.: War correspondent]   PN4874.P86, D811.5.P
                          070.924, 940.548173, 920.5

Quezon, Manuel, 1878-1944   [Phil.: Pres.]   DS686.3.Q4   959.90350924,
                          991.40350924
Quisling, Vidkun, 1887-1945   [Norway: Head of puppet gov.]   DL529.Q5,
                          DK267   948.1040924, 940.53370924, 947.084

Rab (Concentration camp: Croatia)
Rabaul (New Britain)
Radar   TK6575-80, UG610   621.38+, .3848
Radar defense networks   UG633   629.437, 358.4145
   —Great Britain
Radar in aeronautics   TL695-6, Q180, TL500   621.3848, 629.1355, .1366
Radio in propaganda   JF1525, HE8696   327.1409+, 301.154
Radio, Military   UG610
Raeder, Erich, 1876-1960 [Ger.: Adm.]   DD231.R17   943.080924, 923.543
Railroads
Railroads and state   HE1051-1081, HE2757 (US), HE2801-3600 (other
                          countries)   385+

   —Italy
Railroads
   —Europe   HE3004-8   385.094, .2094
   —Germany
   —Great Britain   HE3015-3020, TF57, TF64   385.0941-0942, .142, 625.18,
                          912.138531
   —History—Europe
   —Russia   HE3135-8   380.50947, 385.0947
Railway artillery   UF490-5   358.12, 623.412
Ramsay, Bertram Home, Sir, 1883-1945   [G.B.: Adm.]
Rapido River, Battle of the, 1944   D763   940.5421
Rationing, Consumer
Ravensbrück (Concentration camp)   D805   940.547243
Rawicz (Leszno, Poland: Concentration camp)
Reconnaisance aircraft
Reconstruction (1914-1939)   D653-9, D638
   —Germany   D659   330.94308
   —Sources   E802   940.531440922
Reconstruction (1939-)   D829.A-Z, D826, HC59   940.53144+, 338.91
Reconstruction (1939-1951)   D825, D816, D840   940.5312, .53144,
                          901.944, 909.82, 327.09044
Red Cross   HV560-83, HV568, UH535-7 (army), VG457 (navy)   361.506, .53
   . Germany. Deutsches Rotes Kreuz   D807.G4
   . U.S. American National Red Cross   UC74.R4, HV576-8, HV640   361.506,
                          .77, 362.7

437

Refugee property
Refugees, Jewish   D810, DS126, HV640, JV8749   940.53159, 956.94,
          909.0492400823, 325.247095694, 361.5309494, 301.451924047
Refugees, Polish
Refugees, Political   JX4292.P6 (int'nal. law), HV640 (relief), D842, JV6477,
          JX1907   325.21, 341.51, 361.53, 940.53159
Reichenau, Walther von, 1884-1942   [Ger.: Field Marshal]   UA712.R4
          940.5497
Reichswald, Battle of,the 1945   D756   940.5421
Relief for Americans in [the] Philippines (New York)   D805.P6   940.5472914
Renunciation of war treaty, Paris, Aug. 27, 1928 [A.k.a. Treaty of Paris (1928)]
          JX1987, E748   341.2, .52, .6, .73, 923.273
Reparations
Repatriation   JX4231
Reprisals   JX4486 341.58
Requisitions, Military   JX5321 (int'nal. law), UC15 (mil. sci.)
Rescue work
Restitution and indemnification claims (1933-)   [for property loss or other injuries]
Retired military personnel—United States
Revolvers   UD410-15 (army), VD390 (navy), TS537 (production), TS535
          623.443, .4434, 683.43
Revolvers, American
Reynaud, Paul, 1878-1966   [Fr.: Pr. Min.]   DC389.R, D761   940.5344
Rhine Valley—History—Separatist movement, 1918-1924
Rhineland (Germany)—History—Separatist Movement, 1918-1924   D650.M5
Ribbentrop, Joachim von, 1893-1946   [Ger.: For. Min.]   DD247.R35
Ridgway, Matthew Bunker, 1895-1987   [U.S.: Gen. (airborne infan.)]   E745.R52
          355.3310924
Rifles   UD390-5 (army), VD370 (navy), TS534-5   355.6212, .82,
          623.442-4425, 683.42
Righteous Gentiles in the Holocaust   DS135.R93
Rio de la Plata, Battle of the, 1939   D772   940.545, .545943
Ritchie, Neil Methuen, 1897-? [G.B.: Gen.]   D766.82   940.5423
Roadblocks (Military science)
Rocket launchers (Ordnance)   UF880, UG633   355.6212, .82
Rocket research—Germany
Rocketry   TL781-2, Q111   629134354, .14353, .4, .409, .42-3, .47509
Rockets (Aeronautics)   TL780-3, UG630, TL732, TL507, QC801   623.451+,
          629.13-14, .133349, .13338, .14353, 629.42
Rockets (Ordnance)   UF767, UF820, UG630-3   623.451, .4519, .54
Röhm, Ernst, 1887-1934   [Ger.: SA chief ('Brown Shirts')]   DD247.R56
          943.086
Rokossovsky, Konstantin, 1896-1968   [U.S.S.R.: Marshal]   D764.R63613,
          D764.3.S7   940.5421
Romania
     . Armata. Divizia Infanterie, 9—History
     —Foreign relations—1914-1944
     —History—1914-1944   DR250, DR266   309.149802, 949.802,
          320.949802
Rome (City)—History—1870-   DG813   945.63209
Rommel, Erwin, 1891-1944   [Ger.: Field Marshal]   DD247.R, U55.R6,
          D756.5.N6, D757, D757.55.A4, D766.32, .82,
          D811.R, D840   940.5421, .5423,
          .54230924, .548142, 923.543
Rooseboom (Ship)   D805.J3 (Jpn. prisoners)   940.548142

Roosevelt, Eleanor, 1884-1962   [U.S.: F.D.R.'s wife, Dir. of Office of Civilian Def.]
          E807.1.R35-572+, E806   973.9170924, 309.175, 362.0924
Roosevelt, Franklin Delano, 1882-1945 [U.S.: Asst. Sec. o/t Navy, Pres.]
          E741-2, E744, E766, E801, E805-7, E811-12, E173, E176.1, E183,
          E183.8, D734.A8, D748, D753, DA566.9.C5 (Churchill)
          973.90924, .9170924, 320.9730917, 327.73+, .7307291,
          329.023730917, .30221, 330.9730917, 338.860973, 353.0313,
          917.303917, 923.173, .573, 940.5320922, .532273
Rosenberg, Alfred, 1893-1946 [Ger.: Nazi philosopher]   DD247.R58, CB425.R74
                                                          320.5330924, 914.30301
Royal Air Force Escaping Society   D805.A2   940.5472
Ruhr Pocket, Battle of, 1945   D756   940.5421
Rundstedt, Gerd von, 1875-1953   [Ger.: Field Marshal]
Russell, Bertrand, 1872-1970 [G.B.: Socialist, pacifist leader]   B1649.R91-4 192.9
Russia [SEE ALSO 'Russia (1923-   U.S.S.R.)' and 'Soviet Union']   DK1-275+
                                                          947, 914.7
—Armed forces   UA646, UA772, DK219, D552   355.00947, .30947,
                              940.4147, 947.080924
. Armiia   UA770, UA772, D550   355.00947, 940.40947
    —Bibliography   Z6725   016.355310947
—Description and travel—1917-   DK267, DK18-28   914.704842,
                                                          .703-7048
—Economic conditions—1918-1945   DK266, HC335   330.947084-5,
                                          336.34350947, 338.947
—Economic policy
    —1938-1942
    —1942-1945
—Exiles
—Foreign economic relations
    —Germany
    —United States
—Foreign relations
    —1917-1945   DK63, DK66, DK265-274   327.09042, .20924,
                              .470+, 341.2247, 940.532247, 947.0841
    —France
    —Germany   327.47043
    —Great Britain   327.47041
    —Japan   DK68.7.J3, DS783, DS849   327.47052
    —United States   E183, JX1555   327.47073, .73047
—History
    —20th century   DK246, DK268, DK275   947.08+, .084-085,
                              914.7038
    —1925-1953   DK267-8   947.0842, 914.703842
    —1939-1945   DK273   947.0842
    —German occupation, 1941-1944   DK273, D802   940.532443,
                                                          .5347, .5337
—History, Military   UA772, DK268, D550   355.00947, 940.40947,
                                          355.4300924
—Politics and government—1936-1953   DK254-268, JN6598
                                          947.0842, .085, 320.9470842
—Relations (military) with Germany
. Voenno-morskoi Flot   VA573, D779.R9   359.00947, .320947, 940.545947

Russia (1923- U.S.S.R.) [SEE ALSO 'Russia' and 'Soviet Union']
. Armiia
  . 5. Armiia D764.5.5th
  . 97. Gvardeiskaia Strelkovaia Diviziia D764.6.G8.97th
. Voenno-Morskoi Flot [Navy] VA570, VA573, D779.R9, UA856
                                359.00947, .030947, .30947, .3250947, 940.545947
  . Chernomorskii Flot [Subs] D784.R9
    . Severnyi Voennyi Flot
. Voenno-vozdushnye Sily [Air force] UG633, UG635.R9
                                358.400947, .40947, 940.544947
Russo-Finnish War, 1939-1940 DK459 947.103, 948.95, 941.103
Russo-German treaty, 1939 D749, D751 940.5312, .532443
Russo-Japanese Border Conflicts, 1932-1941 DS784
Russo-Japanese War, 1904-1905 DS517 952.031, .03185
Rydz-Smigly, Edward, 1886-1943 [Pol.: Marshal, head o/t armed forces]
Rzhev, Battle of, 1942-1943

Sachsenhausen (Germany: Concentration camp)
Saint Malo (France)—Siege, 1944
Saint Nazaire Raid, 1942 D756 940.5421
Saint-Lô (France)—Siege, 1944 D756 940.542
Saint-Valery-en-Caux, Battle of, 1940
Saipan, Battle of, 1944
Saipan Island
Sakai (Osaka Prefecture: Japan)—Bombardment, 1945
Salandra, Antonio, 1853-1931 [It.: Pr. Min.] DG575.S25, DG555, DG568.5,
                                D617, UA742 945.08-09, 327.45, 940.32245, .34502
Salazar, Antonio, 1889-1972 [Port.: Pr. Min.] DP676.S25, DP680
                                946.9040924, 320.9469
Salerno, Battle of, 1943 D763 940.5421
San Pietro, Battle of, 1943
Santa Anita Assembly Center, Calif. D769 940.54779496
Santa Fe, N.M. Relocation Center D769.8.A6
Santo Tomas Internment Center (Manila, Philippines)
Sapping UG510-15
Sardinia—History DG975 945.9
Sauckel, Fritz, 1894-1946 [Ger.: Plenipoten. Gen. f/t Alloc. of Labor]
Saumur, Battle of, 1940
Savez Komunisticke Omladine Jugoslavije HQ799.V8-9[WWII]
Savo Island, Battle of, 1942 D774 940.5426
Scapa Flow D581, V65 940.453094112, .5451
Scapa Flow Scuttling, Scotland, 1919
Schacht, Hjalmar Horace Greeley, Dr., 1877-1970 [Ger.: Reichsbank Pres. (1933-
  9), Min. o/t Econ. (1935-7)] DD247.S33-335 943.085, 332.10924
Scharnhorst (Battleship) [WWI (armoured cruiser) & II (battle cruiser): 2 ships]
                                D771, D772.S35 940.545, .5459, .545941-3
Schellenberg, Walther, 1911?-1952 [Ger.: SS Gen., Combined Secret Srvcs.
  chief] DD247.S338 940.548743
Schirach, Baldur von, 1907-1974 [Ger.: Hitler Youth leader till 1940, Gauleiter of
  Vienna] DD253.S26, DD253.5.S35, DB99 943.605, .086, 329.943
Schleissheim (Displaced persons camp)
Schlieffen Plan
Schmidt, Battle of, 1944
Science and state—Germany—History—20th century D804.G4 940.5405
Scobie, Ronald, 1893-1969 [G.B.: Gen.]

Scotland—History—20th century
Sea control
Sea-power   V25, V17, VA10, VA50, VA513, VA573   359.0309, .409, .43,
                   355.0308, 327.1109, 325.308
Seamanship—History   VK541   623.809
Seamen   G225, G545   359.109
Seamen
   —[country]—Biography
   —Great Britain—Biography
   —United States—Biography   E207, V63   359.3380924, 973.350924
Seaplanes   TL684   629.13334709, 387.733470904
Search and rescue operations   TL553.8, VG55   353.0075, 359.9709
Search, Right of   JX5268   323.4
Security classification (Government documents)
   —United States   JK468, KF26-7, KF4774, KF7695
                   342.7304, .73068, .73085, 343.73013, .730531,
                   353.00714, 355.61, 364.131, 328.7305-07
Seizure of vessels and cargoes   HJ6645   353.0074
Self-determination, National   JX4054   320.13, .158, 323.1, 341.26, .52
Serbia   DR317, DR360   949.71
   —Foreign relations
      —Europe
      —Russia   DR327   327.4704971
Sevastopol, Battle of, 1944
Sevastopol—Siege, 1942
Seyss-Inquart, Artur von, 1892-1946   [Austria: Reich Commissioner o/t Neth.]
Shawcross, Hartley, Sir, 1902?-   [G.B.: Brit. Chief Prosecutor at Nuremberg trials]
Sherman tank   UG446.5
Ship-building   VM, VM15, VM144-6, VM298   623.8, .823, .809, 387.209
   —United States—History   VM23, VM140, VM299   623.8203,
                   387.50973, 359.830973, 338.4762382
Ship-building workers
Ships—History   VM15-23, VM121, VM307, VK20   387.209, .2074013,
                   .20977, .09687, 623.82009, .821
Ships' stores and Navy exchanges (United States Navy)   VC393   646.024359
Shipwrecks   JX4436 (int'nal. law), G525-30 (narratives), VK1250-99 (reports)
                   910.091636, .45, .453, .45308, 904.5
Shipyards   VM12-124   623.809, .8309+, .830973 (US), 338.476238309
Shooting, Military   UD330-5, UD383   356.162, 623.442, .5, 683.409+
Siberia (R.S.F.S.R.)
   —History   D558
      —Revolution, 1917-1921   DK265   957.084
Sicily—History—1870-1945   945.7
Sidra, Gulf of, Battle of, 1942   D775   940.5423
Sieges   JX5117 (int'nal. law)
Signals and signaling   UG570-82 (mil.), V280-5 (naval), VK385   359.983, 384.9
Signals and signaling, Submarine   VK388
Siiranmäki (Finland), Battle of, 1944
Sikorski, Wladyslaw, 1881-1943   [Pol.: Gen., Free Polish Forces commander]
                   DK440.5.S55, D821.P7   943.8050924, 940.53438
Sikorsky helicopters   TL540, TL714-16   629.13, .133, .13335,
                   380.14562913335
Silesia, Upper (Poland and Czechoslovakia)—History—Partition, 1919-1922
Simovi´c, Dusan, 1882-1962   [Yug.: Gen., Prem. o/t gov.-in-exile]
Singapore—History   DS598   959.5, .52, 915.952

Sino-American Cooperative Organization   D769.64   940.548673, .545
Sino-Japanese Conflict, 1937-1945   DS777-8   940.5312, 951.042, 952.031-033
    —Aerial operations
    —Aerial operations, American
    —Aerial operations, Japanese
    —Anniversaries, etc.
    —Atrocities   DS777   940.540509520951
    —Blockades
    —Campaigns
        —China   DS777   951.042
    —Causes
    —Children
    —Civilian relief
    —Collaborationists   DS777   952.033
    —Destruction and pillage
    —Diplomatic history   DS777   952.033
    —Economic aspects   HC427   330.95143042
    —Education and the conflict
    —Humor, caricatures, etc.
    —Naval operations
    —Naval operations, Japanese
    —Personal narratives, American   DS777   940.53, 951.042
    —Personal narratives, Australian   DS777   951.042
    —Personal narratives, Chinese
    —Regimental histories
    —Underground movements   DS777   951.042
Sirvintà, Battle of, 1941
Sittang River, Battle of the, 1945
Ski troops   UD470
Skorzeny, Otto, 1908?-1975   [Ger.: Lt. Col. (special missions)]   DD247.S54, D756
                            940.54870924, .548743, .548748
Slapton Sands (England), Battle of, 1944   D756.5.S57
Slave labor
    —Germany
    —Soviet Union
Slavic countries—History
Slavs—History   D147   930.04918
Slim, William, 1891-1970   [G.B.: 1st Viscount, Gen.]   DA69.3.S55, D767.6.S55,
                            U55.S54   940.54250924, 355.3310924
Smederevska Palanka (Smederevska Palanka, Serbia: Concentration camp)
Smith, Holland McTyeire ('Howlin' Mad'), 1882-1967   [U.S.: Gen. (Marines)]
                            D769.369.S58   940.541273
Smith, Ian, 1919-   [Rhodesia: Fighter pilot, Pr. Min. of Rhod. after war]
                            DT962   968.91040924
Smith and Wesson firearms   TS537   623.443, .4434, 683.43
Smoke screens   UG447.7
Smolensk, Russia (City), Battle of, 1941
Smolensk, Russia (City), Battle of, 1943
Smuts, Jan Christiaan, 1870-1950 [S.Afr.: Gen., Brit. War Cabinet member (WWI);
    Pr. Min. (WWII)]   DT779.8.S6, D517   968.050924, 923.568, 940.304
Sobibor (Poland: Concentration camp)
Socialist International
Société Nationale des Chemins de Fer Français   D810.T8, TJ603   385.3610944
Society for the Prevention of World War III   D731.P   940.531405
Sociology, Military   U21, UA25   355.009, .022, .1209, .3, .61, 301.593

Sokolovsky, Vasiliy, 1897-1968   [U.S.S.R.: Marshal]   U162.S, UA770
Soldiers   U1-145, U750-73   355.009, .12, .33809
Soldiers as authors
Soldiers
—Attitudes
—Billeting   UC410
Soldiers' bodies, Disposition of   UC34, D810.D4 (WWII)   355.69
Soldiers
—Conduct of life   U408   174.9355
—Family relationships   U21   355.135
Soldiers' homes—United States
Soldiers in art   N8260, NX549   704.949355
Soldiers in literature
Soldiers
—Japan   U43   355.00952, .133
—Language (New words, slang, etc.)
Soldiers' libraries
Soldiers' monuments   NA9325-55
Soldiers
—Recreation
—Religious life   UH23, BV4457, BV4588   355.34, 248.8
—Sexual behavior
—Suffrage   JX1876-8 (US)
—United States   U22, U766, E607   355.100973
—United States
—Attitudes
—Biography   E181, E263   355.3380924, 973.330924
Soldiers' writings, English [French, German, etc.]
Solomon Islands   DU350, DU850   993.5, 919.35
Somerville, James, Sir, 1882-1949 [G.B.: Adm.]
Sonar   VK388, VK560 (navig.), V214, VM480, Q180   621.38953,
            623.73, 359.85
Sorge, Richard, 1895-1944   [U.S.S.R.: Spy in China & Japan]   D810.S8,
        UB271.R92   351.74, 355.34320924, 364.13, 923.547, 952.033
South Africa
. Air Force. 24 Squadron   D792.S6
. Army. 6th Mounted Regiment   D766.97
. Police Brigade   D766.97
South America—History—20th century   F2237   980.03
Soviet Union   [SEE ALSO 'Russia']
. Armiia
—Biography
—History   UA772, DK264
—Foreign relations
—History
—Nicholas, 1894-1917
—Revolution, 1917-1921
. Sovetskaia Armiia. Chekhoslovatskii Korpus, 1
. Voenno-Morskoi Flot
. Baltiiskii Flot
Sozialdemokratische Partei Deutschlands   D810.G6, DD231, HX274-6,
    JN3946, JN3970-1   320.530943, .943084, 335.00943, 341.242, 943.07
Spaak, Paul Henri, 1899-1972 [Belg.: For. Min.]   DH689.S6   327.493, 923.2493
Spaatz, Carl ('Tooey'), 1891-1974   [U.S.: Gen.]   UG633   358.400973

Spain
—Foreign relations
—1931-1939
—1939-1975   DP270, JX1977   946.082, 341.13946, 327.460+
—Germany
—Russia
—History
—Revolution, 1931
—Republic, 1931-1939   DP254, DP257   946.081
—Civil War, 1936-1939   DP269   946.08-081
—Causes   DP257   946.081
—Foreign participation   DP269   946.08-081
—Foreign participation, German [American, Italian, Russian, etc.]
—Foreign public opinion
—Personal narratives
—1939-1975   DP270-1   946.082
—Politics and government
—1931-1939   DP257   320.94608-081, .446081, 329.946, 946.081
—1939-1975   DP270, JN8221   320.946082, 946.081-082
Special operations (Military science)   VE153   359.9609+
Speer, Albert, 1905-1981 [Ger.: Architect, Min. of Armaments (1942-5)]
          DD247.S63, HC286   943.0860924, 338.0943
Speidel, Hans, 1897-?   [Ger.: Gen., anti-Hitler supporter]
Sperrle, Hugo, 1885-1953 [Ger.: Field Marshal (Luftwaffe)]
Spies   JX5121 (int'nal. law), UB270 (mil.), VB250 (naval), UB271-5
          355.34, .342-343, .34309, .3432, 940.5487+, 327.12, .1208,
          .120922, 335.343, 351.74, 364.13
Spitfire (Fighter planes)   TL685   358.43, 940.544
Springfield rifle   UD395   623.4421
Spruance, Raymond, 1886-1969 [U.S.: Vice Adm.]   V63.S68, D767
          940.54260924, .5450924
Spy films—Catalogs   PN1998   016.79143
Spy stories [fiction]
Stalag IV B (Mühlberg, Bad Liebenwerda, Germany: Concentration camp)
Stalag 12 D (Trier, Germany: Concentration camp)
Stalag 344 (Lambinowice, Poland: Concentration camp)
Stalag 367 (Concentration camp: Czestochowa, Poland)
Stalag Luft I (Germany: Concentration camp)
Stalag Luft 3 (Zagan, Poland: Concentration camp)
Stalin, Joseph [Iosif] ('Uncle Joe'), 1879-1953   [U.S.S.R.: Dictator, Comm. in Chief
          o/t Armed Forces]   DK268.S8, DK267, DK274, D764, D16,
          DS740, HX40   947.080924,
          .08420924, .085, 940.540947, 320.9470842,
          335.4, 355.4300924, 923.247, 951.042
Stalingrad, Battle of, 1942-1943   D764, DD247   940.542, .5421, .548243,
          355.3310924
—Poetry
Stamboliski, Alexander, 1879-1923   [Bulg.: Politician]   DR88.S77, D643.B6,
          HD815.S74, JN9609.A8   320.94977, 322.440924, 329.94977
Stangl, Franz, 1908?-1971   [Ger.: Treblinka concen. camp commander]
          D805.G3   940.54050924, .54724304355
Stark, Harold ('Betty'), 1880-1972 [U.S.: Adm., Chief of Naval Ops. (1939-42),
          Commander of U.S. naval forces in Eur. (1942-5)]
Stauffenberg, Claus von, 1907-1944   [Ger.: Col., planted bomb in attempt on
          Hitler's life]

444

Sten machine carbine   UF620.S8
Stettinius, Edward Reilly, 1900-1949   [U.S.: War produc. advisor, Lend Lease
                           admin., Under Sec. (1943-4) & Sec. of State (1944-5)]
                           E748, E183.7   973.9170924
Stilwell, Joseph Warren ('Vinegar Joe'), 1883-1946   [U.S.: Gen., Nat. Chinese Chief
                           of Staff (1942-4)]   E745.S68, D767.S76,
                           D767.6.S74, D769   940.54250924, 951.0420924
Stimson, Henry Lewis, 1867-1950 [U.S.: Sec. of War]   E748.S883, E183.7,
         E183.8.J3   973.90924, .910924, .917, 327.73052, 923.273
Stirling, David, 1915-?   [G.B.: Lt. Col., desert commando leader]   D766.82
                           940.542, .548642
Stopford, Montagu, Sir, 1892-1971 [G.B.: Gen.]
Storm (Submarine)   D784.G7   940.5451
Strategic materials
    —United States   HC110, UA23   333.80973, 355.240973, .6213, .75
Strategy   U161-3 (mil.), V160-5 (naval), UA11   355.021, .0217, .03, .4,
         .43, .4301-07, 359.43
Stream-crossing, Military   U205, UG335   623.65
Street fighting (Military science)   U167   355.426
Streicher, Julius, 1885-1946   [Ger.: Newspaper ed., Gauleiter of Franconia (till
                           1940), rabid anti-Semite]   DD247.S834,
                           DS146.G4   943.0850924, 305.8924043
Stresemann, Gustav, 1878-1929   [Ger.: Politician]   DD231.S83, DD901
                           943.085, 320.94382, 940.3141, .32443
Stuart (Destroyer)   [Australia]   D779.A9
Student, Kurt, 1890?-1978   [Ger.: Gen. (airborne infan., regular army)]
                           D757.63, UG635   940.541343, .544943
Studzianki, Poland (Kozienice), Battle of, 1944
Stuka (Bombers)   TL685-6   623.7463
Stülpnagel, Karl von, 1886-1944   [Ger.: Gen., Mil. Gov. of Fr., anti-Hitler conspir.]
Submachine guns   UF620.A2   355.82, 623.4424
Submarine boats   V858-9 (by country), VM365 (construc.), V210 (war use), V857
                           359.3257+, .325709, .92, 355.03+, 623.82, .825, .8257,
                           .82572+, .825720943 (Ger.), 940.5451
    —Bibliography   Z6834, V857-9   016.623825
    —History   V857-9, V210, VM365   359.325709, .3257209+, .83, 387.257
Submarine chasers   D590 (WWI)
Submarine disasters   VK1265   613.69
Submarine warfare   V210, VB230, JX1295   359.32, .3257, .4, .83,
                           623.825, .8257, 940.451
Sugiyama, Hajime, 1880-1945 [Japan: Gen.]
Sukarno, Achmed, Dr., 1901-1970 [Indon.: Head of Indon. Nat. Party, worked with
                           Japan most o/t war]   DS644.1.S8, DS643
                           959.8030924, 320.9598022, 991.030924
Sunda Strait, Battle of, 1942   D779   940.545994
Sunderland (Seaplanes)
Suomen Vastarintaliike   [Finn. Underground]   D802.F5
Surgery, Military   RD151-498   617.02, .99
Surgery, Naval   RD151-498
Surplus military property   UC260-5
Surplus military property, American   KF26-7   353.00713, 355.6213
Survival (after airplane accidents, shipwrecks, etc.) TL553.7, U408, VK1259,
         VK1447, G525-40   613.69, 623.865, 629.13443, 910.091641, .09165, .453
Sutjeska River, Battle of the, 1943
Suzuki, Kantaro, 1867-1948   [Japan: Pr. Min., 5 Apr-Aug 1945]

Sveti Nikola (Concentration camp: Bulgaria)
Sweden
    —Foreign relations—1905-1950   DL658   327.485
    —History
        —1905-   DL658+
        —Gustavus V, 1907-1950
    —Politics and government—1905-1950
Switzerland
    —History—20th century
    —Politics and government—20th century

Tacloban (Leyte Island, Philippines: Concentration camp)
Tactics   U133, U164-5   355.402, .42
    —Bibliography   Z6724   016.35542
Taiwan—History—1895-1945   DS799   951.24904, 320.95124904, 915.124904
Tallinn, Battle of, 1941
Tanaka, Raizo, n.d.   [Japan: Rear Adm.]
Tank gunnery
Tank warfare   UG446, U55, D608   358.1809, .180904, 355.331+,
                                623.438, 940.412
Tanks (Military science)   UG446.5, UF537   358.18, .1809+, .180941 (GB),
            .180943 (Ger.), .180973 (US), 623.7475+, 355.621, .8209, .83, 356.5
    —Pictorial works
Taranto, Battle of, 1940   D786   940.5421
Tarawa, Battle of, 1943   D767   940.542, .5426
Taylor, Maxwell, 1901-1987   [U.S.: Gen. (airborne)]   E745.T317   355.3310924
Tedder, Arthur, Sir, 1890-1967   [G.B.: Air Marshal, Dep. Supr. Comm. of
                                Operation Overlord]   D785.T4   940.544
Telephone—Defense measures
Telescopic sights
Terauchi, Hisaichi, 1879-1945 [Japan: Field Marshal]
Terezin (Czechoslovakia: Concentration camp)
Ternopol (City)—Siege, 1944   D764.7.T43
Terrain study (Military science)
Texas (Battleship)   VA65   623.82520973
Theater in propaganda
Theater of war
Thompson submachine gun   UF620   623.4424, 683.4
Thunderbolt (Fighter planes)   [A.k.a. P-47]   TL686.R42 (Republic Co.), UG1242
                                623.7464, 358.43
Tibbets, Paul, 1915-   [U.S.: Col. (Air Corps), trained atom bomb pilots & flew
                        'Enola Gay' on 6 Aug. 1945 over Hiroshima]
                        UG626.2.T5   940.5449730924
Tiger (Tank)
Tikhvin, Battles of, 1941
Timoshenko, Semyon, 1895-1970 [U.S.S.R.: Marshal]   DK268.T5   923.547
Tinian Island
Tirpitz (Battleship)   D772.T5   940.5421, .544942, .545
Tiso, Joseph, 1887-1946 [Slovakia: Pres.]   DB2821.T57
Tito, Josip Broz, 1892-1980   [Yug.: Marshal]   DR359.T5, DR367.R9, DR370,
                DR1300, D754, D766.6, D802.Y8   949.7020924,
                940.53497, .542, 327.4970947, 923.1497, .5497
Tizard, Henry Thomas, Sir, 1885-1959   [G.B.: Radar scientist, tech. advisor]
                Q143.T5, Q127, Q127.G4   506.9, 925
Tobruk, Battles of, 1941-1942   D766-7   940.5423

Togo, Shigenori, 1882-1950   [Japan: For. Min.]   DS886, D742.J3   952.033,
                                                 940.5352
Tojo, Hideki, 1884-1948   [Japan: Pr. Min. (1941-4)]   DS888.5.T5995,
        DS890.T57, DS890, D804.J   952.030924, .0330924, 940.53452
Tokushima (Japan)—Bombardment, 1945
Tokyo
    —Bombardment, 1942   D790   940.5441-2
    —History   DS896-7   952.135
Tokyo Rose, 1916-   [Also 'Iva Ikuko Toguri d'Aquino': Japan, U.S.: Radio
    propagandist]   CT275.T717   940.54889520924
Torpedo-boat destroyers
Torpedo-boats   V830-8   359.32, .3254, 359.83, 940.5459+
Torpedo bombers
Torpedoes   V850-5   359.4, .82
Totalitarianism   JC481, JC233   320.53-533, 321.6-6082, .64, .9, 335.4-6
Tovey, John, Sir, 1885-1971   [G.B.: Adm.]
Toyoda, Soemu, 1885-1957   [Japan: Adm., Combined Navy Chief (1943-5)]
                                                 DS885.5.T62
Trading with the enemy   JX5270-1   341.3, 343.73087
    —History—20th century
Transportation and state   HE148-51, HE193   350.87, 380.5, 388.109+
Transportation, Military   UC270-360, UH500-505 (med.), VC550-5   355.27,
                                 .341, .8309+, 623.746
    —Cold weather conditions
Treason   HV6275, JC328 (polit. theory)   364.13
    —France
    —Germany
    —Great Britain   343.41
    —South Africa
    —United States   KF9392, E179   343.3, 345.73023108, 351.74, 364.131
Treaties   JX4161-71, JX120-191 (collections), JX235-6, JX351-1195, JA40
                341.026, .2, .273, .2016
    —Catalogs
    —Collections
Treaty of Trianon (1920)   D643.H9
Trench mortars
Trenchard, Hugh Montague, 1873-1956 [G.B.: Air Marshal, R.A.F. founder before
    WWII]   DA89.6.T7   923.542
Trepper, Leopold, 1904-? [Pol.: Soviet spy in Belg.]
                                 D810.S8   940.54860924, .548647
Trials (Crimes against humanity)
Trials (Genocide)
Trials (Military offenses)   355.1332+
Trials (Naval offenses)
Trials (Political crimes and offenses)   KF221 (US)   345.730231 (US),
                                         .47023 (Russia), .023
Trianon, Treaty of, June 4, 1920
Trianon, Treaty of, June 4, 1920 (Hungary)   D651.H7, D643   940.3141-3142
Trieste
    —History   DB321   943.68
    —Politics and government   DB321, DG975   320.945393, 327.450497
Trigger (Submarine)   D783.5.T5-7   940.5451
Troina, Sicily, Battle of, 1943
Trophies, Military

447

Trotsky, Leon, 1879-1940   [A.k.a. 'Trotskii, Lev': Rus.: Politician]
    DK254.T6, DK265, HC335, HX312   947.083, .0840924, 327.47,
    330.947084, 335.433, 345.470231, 347.9947, 349.4704, 923.247
Trowbridge, Ernest Charles Thomas, 1862-1926   [G.B.: Adm.]   DA565.T7, D580
Truk Island
Truman, Harry S, 1884-1972   [U.S.: Pres.]   E813-15, E176.1, E742.5.T6, E806,
                    HD7293, HD8072, JC599, JK558   973.9180924,
                    301.540973, 323.40973, 329.023, 917.3039, 923.173, .573
Tula, Russia—Siege, 1941
Tule Lake Relocation Center (Calif.)
Tunisia—History—French occupation, 1881-1956   DT264   961.1
Tupolev, Andrey, 1888-1972   [U.S.S.R.: Gen., aircraft engineer]
Turkey
    —Foreign relations
        —Europe
        —Germany
        —Great Britain   DR562   327.4961042
    —History—1918-1960   DR590-2   956.102, 915.61033
    —Politics and government
        —1918-1960   DR590   320.956103
Turner, Richmond Kelly, 1885-1961   [U.S.: Adm.]
Turret ships   V860
Twentieth century   CB425-7 (civiliz.), D401-725 (hist.), D421, D840
                940.5, 914.035, 901.904, .94, .946, 909.82, 301.24
Twentieth Century Fund. Labor Committee   HD8072   331.0973

U-505 (Submarine)   D782.U12   940.5451
U-977 (Submarine)   D782.U2   940.54512
Udet, Ernst, 1896-1941   [Ger.: Lt. Gen., Luftwaffe tech. chief]   TL540.U3
                                    940.449430924

Ukraine
    —History   DK508   947.7, .71
        —German occupation, 1941-1944   D764   947.7
Ukrainska Nationlna Armiia   D764.7.U5
Ukraïnska Povstanska Armiia   D802.U4   940.534771
Ulithi, Caroline Islands   DU568.U5   996.6, 919.66
Ultrasonic waves—Military applications
Umezu, Yoshijiro, 1880-1949   [Japan: Gen.]
Underwater demolition teams
Unified operations (Military science)   U260 (jt. ops. of one nation's service branches)
Uniforms, Military   UC480-5, UA712, UE445, VC300   355.14, .1409+,
                .14094, .81, 357.1, 359.14094
Union des Femmes Françcais   D802.F8
United Nations—History   JX1976-7   341.1309, .23, .2309+

450

United States
. Army
. Cavalry   UA30, UE23   357.10973
. 1st Cavalry Division   D769.335.1st   940.541273
. 113th Cavalry Group   UA31.113th   940.541273
. Chaplain Corps   UH23   355.34, .3470973
. Chemical Corps   D769   358.340973
. Coast Artillery   UF453, UF625
. 442d Combat Team   D769.31.442d
. 5307th Composite Unit (Provisional)   D767.6   940.5425
. Corps of Engineers   UG23   355.6213, 356.94, 358.20973
. Corps of Military Police
. Demobilization
. 24th Division   D769.3.24th
. 36th Division   D769   940.5421
. 42d Division   [Rainbow Division]
. Division, 82d   D811   940.548173
. 101st Division
—Drill manuals
. 276th Engineer Combat Battalion   D769   940.54210924
. European Theater of Operations
—Examinations   U408, UG610   355.07, .338076, 623.7348
. Field Artillery   UF403   358.12
—Finance   UC23
—Firearms   UD383-4, UD395 (rifles)   355.62120973, .82,
        623.440973, .4420973, .4425
. Forces in the Far East
. Forces in the Pacific
—Foreign Service
. 1st Gas Regiment. Company E
—Guard duty   U193
—Handbooks, manuals, etc.   U113, U133, U408, UB413
        355.00911, .0973, .4209597
—History   UA23-5, E181   355.00973, .033573, .30973, .3510973,
        .1150973
    —Bibliography   Z1249   106.355
    —Sources—Bibliography   Z6725, CD3033   106.97389
    —World War, 1939-1945
—Indian troops   E99   970.3
. Infantry   UA28-9, UD23   356.110973, 959.7043373, .70434
. Infantry, 339th—History [Exped. force in N. Russia, 1918-19]
                                D570.33.339th
. Infantry
    —Drill and tactics   UD160, U15   355.54, 356.10973, .18
    —History   UA28, D769   940.541273
. Judge Advocate General
—Maneuvers   U253
—Medals, badges, decorations, etc.   UC533, CR4509
. Army Medical Department   UH223   355.3450973
. Army Medical Service
. Army
—Military construction operations
—Military life   U766, UA25, D570, E745   355.00973, .10973,
        .12920924, .3380973, .54097
. Military Railway Service   UG523   356.95, 358.2

United States
. Army
    —Mobilization   UA913   355.280973
    —Negro troops   [SEE ALSO '...Afro-Am. troops']   D639, E185, U21
                        940.403, 917.80696, 355.00917496, .30978,
                         .330973, .61330973, 356.110973
    —Non-commissioned officers   UB210   355.547
    —Officers   UB412-14, UB210   355.0023, .33, .332019,
                      301.1543355332
    —Officers' handbooks   U133   355.02, 356.3
    —Ordnance and ordnance stores   UF523-63, UF753, U897
                  355.830973, .820973, 343.73025, 623.40973, .440973
    —Organization   UA23-33   355.00973, .3
    —Parachute troops   D769.347, UD483   356.1660973
    —Pay, allowances, etc.   UC70-5, UB403   355.135, .640973
    —Physical training   U323, U408
    —Pictorial works
    —Political activity
    —Postal service
    —Prisons   KF7675   355.71
    —Procurement   UC263-7, UF780   355.62120973, .82, 358.18,
                  .4183, 338.43641371, 343.73013
    —Promotions   UB412-14
. 1st Ranger Battalion   D769   940.541273
. Ranger Battalion, 4th
    —Records and correspondence   UB163   355.61
    —Recruiting, enlistment, etc.   UB323, UB343, UB147, U15   355.220973
       —European War, 1914-1918
       —World War, 1939-1945   UB323   355.22
. Regimental Combat Team, 442nd   [Jpns.-Am's.]
    —Registers   U11   940.41273
    —Registers of dead   E181
    —Regulations   UB501-2, KF7305   355.1
. Reserve Officers' Training Corps   U428   355.2232, .37
    —Sanitary affairs   UH223
    —Security measures
    —Service clubs
United States Army Service Forces
        . Special Service Division
United States Army Service Schools, Fort Leavenworth, Kan. Dept. of
        Military Art   [WWII]
United States
. Army
    . Signal Corps   UG573   358.240973
    —Signaling   UG573
    —Ski troops
    —Social services   UH755
    —Songs and music   M1629-30
    —Sports
    —Staffs   UB223   355.330973
    —Statistics   UA23-4, D797.U
    —Supplies and stores   UC263-7   355.3410973, .6210973,
                  .6212, .80973, 658.78
    . Surgeon General's Office
    —Surgeons   UH223

United States
  . Army
    . 761st Tank Battalion   D769.306.761st
    —Target practice   UD333
    —Test shooting [Gunnery]   UF810
    —Transport service   UC273   353.62
    —Transportation   UC273, UC333   355.83
    . Transportation Corps   UC323, D769.U   358.250973, 940.541273
    —Uniforms   UC483, UC493   355.14094, .140973
        —Catalogs
        —History   UC483, UC523   355.140973, .140977656, .310973
United States Army War College, Washington, D.C.
      [SEE `ALSO 'Army War College (U.S.)']
United States
  . Army
    . Western Defense Command and Fourth Army   D769.8   940.547273
    . Women's Army Corps   UA565.W6, D759.U, D769   355.348,
          940.548173
  —Bibliography   Z1215, Z1236-7   016.917303, .973
  —Bio-bibliography   Z1224
  —Biography   E176, E178, E184, E187, E747, CT215-20   920.073,
          973.0922, 320.0922
    —Bibliography   Z5305   016.920073
    —Dictionaries   E176   920.073
    —Indexes
    —Portraits   E813, N7593, ND1337   920.073, 759.13, 704.9420973
  . Bureau of Aeronautics (Navy Dept.)
  . Bureau of Construction and Repair   [Navy]
  . Bureau of Insular Affairs
  . Bureau of Labor Statistics
  . Bureau of Manpower Utilization
  . Bureau of Naval Personnel
  . Bureau of Naval Weapons
  . Bureau of Ships   [Navy]
  . Bureau of Veterans' Reemployment Rights
  . Bureau of War Risk Insurance
  . Bureau of War Risk Litigation
  . Bureau of Yards and Docks   [Navy]
  . Cadet Nurse Corps
  . Central Intelligence Agency—Officials and employees—Biography
  . Chemical Warfare Service
  —Civil defense   UA927-9   355.232, 353.007232, 363.340973, .350973
  —Civilization
      —1865-1918   E168-9   917.3037-3039, .303911, 301.2973,
          309.173089
      —1918-1945   E169, E806   973.91, .916, 917.30316, .30391+,
          .303916-303917, 309.173
  —Claims   JX238 (int'nal.)   342.73088, 347.7328
  —Claims against Germany   JX238.G
  —Claims against Great Britain
  . Claims Board (War Dept.)
  —Claims vs. Yugoslavia

United States
  —Coast defenses   UG410-12   355.45
  . Coast Guard   VG53, D773   359.970973, 343.7301997, 344.73053,
                              614.864, 940.545973
  . Coast Guard Reserve. Women's Reserve   ['SPARS']
  . Command and General Staff School, Fort Leavenworth
  —Commerce
      —France
      —Germany
      —Great Britain
      —History   HF3021-3031, HF3003-7, HF3155   330.973,
                              338.0973, .9141073, 380.10973, 381.0973
      —Japan   HF3127   382.0973052, .0952073
  —Commercial policy   HF1455-6, HF1731, HF1756, HF3008, HF3025
                              337.9173, 338.973, 343.7308, 380.130973,
                                381.0973, 382.06373, .0973+, .30973, .3973
  —Commercial treaties   HF1731-2   337.9173, 341.57
  . Commission to Investigate and Report the Facts Relating to the Attack Made by
      the Japanese Armed Forces upon Pearl Harbor in the Territory of Hawaii on
      December 7, 1941
  . Committee on Public Information   D632   940.488673
  . Congress   JK516, JK570, JK1021   320.97309+, 328.7309, 353.032
      . House   JK1316, JK1323 yr.   328.730+
          . Committee on Military Affairs
          . Committee on Naval Affairs
          . Select Committee Investigating National Defense Migration
          . Special Committee on Un-American Activities
      . Joint Committee on the Investigation of the Pearl Harbor Attack   D767.92
      . Senate   JK1158-70+   327.730+, 328.3690973, .730+, .739
          . Committee on Military Affairs
          . Special Committee Investigating the National Defense Program
                      [The Truman Committee]   UA23   328.345
          . Special Committee to Investigate the Munitions Industry   328.345
  . Consulate. Paris
  . Council of National Defense
      . Advisory Comission
      . Committee on Women's Defense Work
      . Dept. of Food Production and Home Economics
      . Field Division. Child Conservation Section
      . General Munitions Board
      . Munitions Standards Board
  —Curiosa   E179   917.30302
  —Defenses   UA23   355.02130973, .033273, .033573, .6220973,
                      358.4030973, 327.730599, 353.00895, .60924
  . Department of State   JK851, JX1293, JX1417, JX1428, JX1705-6
                      327.072073, .6073, .73, 353.00712, .007232
      . Historical Office
      —History
      . Office of Public Affairs
      —Records and correspondence
  . Department of the Army
      . General Staff—History   UB200   355.3310973
      . Office of Military History   D570   940.41273

United States
—Diplomatic and consular service   JX1705-6, JK851   327.20973,
                                     341.70973, 353.00892, 355.033573
—Germany
—Great Britain
—Italy
—Japan
—Russia
—Economic conditions
——1865-1918   E661, HC105-6, HD8051   917.3038, 330.97308,
                .9730913, 309.17308, 333.70973, 339.20973
——1918-1945   HC106.3-4, HC101, E801   330.973091,
                339.20973, 309.1730917
—Economic policy—1933-1945   HC106, HG538   330.9730917,
                332.4973, 338.973, 309.1730917, 973.917
. Embassy
. Germany
. Great Britain
. Japan
. Russia
. Soviet Union
—Emigration and immigration   JV6403-7127, E158, E184   325.7309,
                301.3230973, .32845073, .32847073, .4534073,
                331.880973, 917.30356, .309749162
. Employment Service   HC101, HD5873-5   330.973,
                331.1106173, .110973, .13770973, 353.008485
—Executive departments   JK631-821   328.7307+, 342.730602+,
                .73064, 353.0002-0003, .00722, .008236, .01-09
—Records and correspondence   CD3030-3041, KF5101
                342.73066, 353.0372
. Federal Bureau of Investigation   E743, HV6791, HV7914, HV8138-47
                344.730523, 345.730231, 353.0074,
                364.1206173, .120924, .120973, .1320973, .973
. Food Administration   D637   940.477873
. Foreign Claims Settlement Commission   [WWII]   KF27   341.55,
                353.00892
—Foreign economic relations   HF1455-6, HF73, HC106   330.973,
                337.9173, 338.9173, .973, 343.73+,
                353.008, 382.0973, .10973
—Germany   HF1456   338.9173043, 382.0973043
—Great Britain   382.0973042
—Japan   HF1456   338.9173052, 382.0973052
—Russia
—Foreign relations   JX1405-28, JX1971, JX1987, E183, E713   320.973,
                341.2373, 343.73+, 909.82
—20th century   JX1416-17, JX1916, D413, D570, E173, E744-8, E840
                327.062073, .20973, .730+, 330.973, 973.92+
——1933-1945   1416, E173, E742-8, E806-7, E813   327.20924,
                309.173092, 940.532273, 973.90924, .917
—Germany   E183, E748   327.73043, .43073, .9613, 943.086,
                973.917+
—Great Britain   E183, E664   327.73041-2, .42073
—Italy   327.73045
—Japan   E183, DS518, JX233   327.73052, .52073, .5073,
                301.15439152, 940.5312

455

United States
—Foreign relations
    —Law and legislation   KF4650-1   328.730765, 342.7306-73064,
            353.00892
    —Russia   E173, E183, E744, E748, JX1974-81, D651, DK69
            327.73047, .47073
    —Speeches in Congress   E173 (collections)
    —Treaties   JX570-3, JX235-6 (texts), JX1407   341.273,
            .762026, .7304, 328.7307+
. General Staff
—Government publications   Z1223 (bibliog.), Z208, Z695, Z7164   015.73,
            016320973, .01573, .309173, .320973, .32873
—Historical geography—Maps
—History   E, F1-975+ (local), E178   973+, 974-9 (local)
    —20th century   E740-2, E173   973.9, .9082, .91, .916
    —1901-1953   E740-1, E766   973.9, .91, .913
    —1913-1921   E766, E780   973.91, .913
    —1919-1963   E784   973.913
    —1919-1933   E741, E784-91, E806   973.91, .914-15, .917,
            .9108, 917.303915, 309.173091
      —Sources   E743, E784-5, E791   973.9108, .914-17
    —1933-1945   E741, E806, E173   973.91, .917,
            917.30391708, .30392, 309.1730917
      —Miscellanea   E806   973.91708
      —Pictorial works   NE1336   769.924
      —Sources   E806, J82   973.91708, 353.035, 320.973,309.173
    —Addresses, essays, lectures
    —Anecdotes, facetiae, satire, etc.   E178-9   973.08, 917.30308
    —Bibliography   Z1215, Z1236, Z8462   016.9173, .917303
      —Catalogs
    —Chronology   E174.5   973.0202, .03
—History, Comic, satirical, etc.   E178.4, NC1427   973.0207, 741.5973
—History
    —Dictionaries   E174, E18   973.03, 917.30303
    —Fiction
    —Historiography   E175   973.07
—History, Local   E175, E180, F1-970   974-9, 917.303
—History, Military   E181, E183, U133   355.420973, 357.10924, 923.573
    —20th century   E745, E840   901.9
    —Bibliography   Z1249   016.355
    —Chronology   E181   355.00973
—History, Naval   E182, E746, VA58-63   359.00973, .0973, .310973,
            .325, 387.20973
    —20th century   E746-8, E182   359.009, .3310924
    —Bibliography   Z6835   016.35900973, .35930973
    —Sources   E182   359.332+
      —Bibliography—Catalogs   Z1249, Z6616, Z6835
            016.3593310924, .359, .35900973
—History
    —Philosophy   E175.9, E179   973.01, .04, .072, 917.303013
    —Sources   E173, E178, E183   973.08, .082, .908, 917.303,
            .30308, 320.973
      —Bibliography   Z1236, Z6616, CD3027, CD3049   016.9739,
            .917303, .301450973
      —Directories   E175   973.02573

United States
  . International Claims Commission [WWII]
  . Joint Army-Navy Assessment Committee
  . Mare Island Naval Shipyard, Vallejo, Calif.   VA70.M3
  . Marine Corps   UB210, UG632, VE23, VE422, D570, D767, D769, D821,
                  TL685   359.96, .9609, .960973, 629.1339,
                        940.45973, .5412730952, .5426, .544973, .545
    . Attack Squadron 223—History   D790
    . Aviation—History   VG93, UG633   358.41830973
    —Biography   E182   359.960973, 923.573
    . 1st Division   D767, DS918, DS557   940.541273, 951.9042, 959.704
    . 3d Division   D769.37.3d
    . Division, 4th
    —History   VE23, VE21-3, E746, D767   359.960973, 940.5426
        —Anecdotes   VE500   359.960973
        —World War, 1914-1918
        —World War, 1939-1945   D769   940.541273
    . History and Museums Division
    —Insignia   VE403
    —Medals, badges, decorations, etc.   VE23
    —Military life   VE23   359.96
    . 3d Regiment   D767.98, VE23.25.4th   940.542, 359.96
United States Marine Corps Reserve   VE23.3   359.960973
United States
  . Marine Corps
    —Target-practice   VE333
    —Uniforms   VE403, UC483   359.960973, 355.14, 646.47
    —Women
United States Marine Corps Women's Reserve   UA565.W6   940.541273
United States Marine Fighter Squadron 214 ['Black Sheep']   D790
United States Military Academy, West Point   U408-10
    —Biography   U410   355.0071174731
    —History   U410, U408   355.0071173, .0071174731, .02130973
    . Library
    —Registers
    —Songs and music
United States Military Mission to Russia
United States
    —Military policy   UA23, UA25, UA646, V63, VE23   355.033073,
                .0330973, .0335182, .033573, .0973, .430973, .820973,
          .02130973, 358.4030973, 359.960973, 327.1740973, .10973
    —Bibliography   Z1215, KF7201   016.3550330973
    —Case studies   UA23   355.033573
    —History   UA23, UA25   355.00973, .033573
  —Militia   UA42   355.35
  . National Archives   CD3028, E179   016.6314, .911777, .91273, 344.73092
  —National Guard   UA42-3, U230   355.3510973, .370973, .4260973, .54,
                343.73013
  —National security   UA23, JK1051   355.033073, .033573, 328.7307412
  . National War College   355.622, .0711753
  . National War Labor Board   [1942-5]

United States Naval Academy, Annapolis   V415
United States Naval Academy (Annapolis)
    . Alumni Association
    —Buildings
    . Dept. of Engineering and Aeronautics
    . Dept. of Seamanship and Navigation
    —Examinations   V415   359.071175256, 355.071173
    —History   V415, U408
    . Library
    . Museum
    —Registers
    —Songs and music
    .Trident Society
United States Naval Air Station, Pensacola, Fla.   VA70.P44
United States
    . Naval Flying Corps—History   VG93   358.400973
    . Naval History Division. Operational Archives   CD3034   016.940545973
United States Naval Hospital, Norfolk, Va.   VG425.N6
United States Naval Institute, Annapolis
United States Naval Medical Research Institute, Bethesda, Md.
United States Naval Medical School, Bethesda, Md.
United States—Naval militia   VA80
United States Naval Observatory   QB82, Z5156   353.00855
United States Naval Photographic Interpretation Center
United States Naval Postgraduate School, Monterey, Calif.
United States Naval Research Laboratory, Washington, D.C.
United States Naval Reserve   VA80   359.370973
    —Registers
    . Women's Reserve   UA565.W6   355.34
United States Naval Training Station, San Diego, Calif.
United States
    . Navy   V25, V133, V399, V736, V825, V858, V874-80, VA49-58, VB23,
            VM470   359, 359.00973, .030973, .12920973,
            .32520973, .32540973, .32620973, .830973, 623.8250973, .8257,
                .8433, 940.545973
        —Accounting   VC503   359.6223
        —Afro-Americans   [SEE ALSO '...—Negroes']   VB853   359.1332
        —Airmen
        . 7th Amphibious Force   D769.52.7th   940.5426
        —Anecdotes, facetiae, satire, etc.   E182, V736   359.00973, .10973
        —Appropriations and expenditures   VA53, V858   359.83, 343.73013
        —Artificers' handbooks   VG603   535.33
        . Asiatic Fleet   VA63.A78   359.310973
        . Atlantic Fleet   D770, VA63   940.545973, 359.310973
        —Aviation   VG93, TL685, TL721   358.400973, .41, .4183,
                .4140973, 623.4519, .74607, .7460973, .74640973, 629.130911
          —Job descriptions
        —Aviation electricians   VG93   629.143, .1354
        —Aviation machinists   VG93   623.746, 629.134352
        —Aviation supplies and stores   VG93   355.62120973,
                358.41621, 359.62120973, 623.746, 629.13443
        —Barracks and quarters   VC423

United States
. Navy
    —Bibliography   Z6835, E182   016.35930973, .35900973
    —Biography   E182, V23, V62-3   359.310922, .3310922,
                                      .3320922, 923.573
        —Dictionaries
    —Boats   V880
    —Boatswains   VG953   623.825
    —Boatswain's mates
. Bombing squadron 109   D790   940.544
. Chaplain Corps   VG23
. Civil Engineer Corps
    —Communication systems   VG77, V283   359.983, 623.8560973
    —Congresses
. Construction battalions [Seabees]   VG597, D769.55   359.982
        —Handbooks, manuals, etc.   VG597
    —Demobilization
. Navy Department
        —Appropriations and expenditures
          . Board on Regular and Reserve Aviation Personnel of the Navy and
                Marine Corps
        . Board on Submarine, Destroyer, Mine, and Naval Air Bases
        —History   VB23
        . Office of Industrial Relations
        . Office of Public Relations
        —Officials and employees   VB183
        —Personnel management
. Navy
    . Destroyer Forces   D773   940.545973
    . Destroyer Squadron 23   D769   940.545973
    —Drill manuals   VD160 (seamen), VE160 (Marines), VF160 (ordnance)
    —Engineering aids   VG923   526.9024359
    . Escort Carrier Force   D769.52.E7
    —Examinations   V411, VB273   359.0076, .338076, 371.2640715
    —Facilities
    —Fast Carrier Task Force   V874   359.32550973
    —Fiction
    —Field Service   V175
    —Finance   VA60   359.620973
    —Firearms   VF23 (ordnance), VF353-420, VD363-90 (small arms)
               623.440973, .442
    —Firing regulations   VD333
    —Flags
    . 3d Fleet   D767   940.545973
    . 7th Fleet   V179   359.6210973
    . 10th Fleet
    —Flight officers
    —Fuel   VC276.A47   338.82, 359.83
    —Gunners
    —Gunner's mates
    —Handbooks, manuals, etc.   V113, V123, V133, V143 (officers,
               seamen, etc.), V310 (ceremonies), VA55, VB200, VM605
               359.00202, 623.872

United States
  . Navy
    —History   E182, V767, V833, V874, VA55-8, VB23, D773, E746
                      359.30973, .310973, .32550973, .3320924, .370973,
                      .621, 623.82530973, 940.542, .545973, 973.75
      —Addresses, essays, lectures   VA58   359.070973
      —Bibliography   Z6835   016.35900973
      —World War, 1914-1918
      —World War, 1939-1945
    . Hospital Corps   VG320   359.3450973
    —Hospital Corps—Drill regulations   VG320   359.34, 610.2
    —Illustrations   VA59   359.3250973
    —Indians
    —Insignia   VC345, UC530-3
    —Job descriptions   VB258
    . Judge Advocate General's Corps   KF26   332.6323
    —Lawyers
    —Lists of vessels   VA61   359.32, .320973, .3250973
    —Management   VB203, VG593, VK1474, VM147   359.31, .621,
                      .9820973
    —Maneuvers   V245, V169, VK597   359.5
    —Medals, badges, decorations, etc.   VB333 (medals, decorations),
          VC345 (badges, insignia), UB433, UC533-5, CR4651   355.134
    . Medical Corps   VG425
    . Medical Dept.   VG123, R847, D807.U6   359.3450973, 610.71073
    —Messes   VC383
    —Military construction operations   VA68   341.725
    . Mobile base hospital no. 3   D807.U6-8+   940.547673
    . Motor Torpedo Boat Squadrons   D773, V833   940.545, 359.83
    —Negroes   [SEE ALSO '...—Afro-Americans']   E185, D810
                      325.260973, 940.54516
    —Officers   VB313-14, VB203, UA23   359.3320973, 353.00895,
                      343.73019
      —Classification   VB313   359.332
      —Correspondence, reminiscences, etc.
    —Officers' handbooks   V133, VM600   359.00973, .02, .31, .33, 623.87
    —Ordnance and ordnance stores   VF353-420, VF580, VF160, VF850
                      359.82, .820973, 353.00711, 623.4519
    —Ordnance facilities   VF383
    —Organization
    —Pacific cruise, 1907-1909
    . Pacific Fleet
    . Pacific Fleet and Pacific Ocean areas
    . Pacific Fleet. Submarine Force. U.S. submarine losses, World War II
                      D783.U
    —Painting of vessels   V980
    —Pay, allowances, etc.   VC50-65, UC74   355.135, .64, 353.007232,
                      343.73013
    —Periodicals
    —Personnel management   VB258, VB313   359.341, .61330973
    —Petty officers   V398, VD430, VM147   359.002854, .3380973
    —Petty officers' handbooks   V123   359.00973, .30973, .3380973
    —Physical training   V263   355.12, 358.407, 371.74, 796.4
    —Pictorial works   VA59   359.3250973
    —Postal service   VG63   359.6133

United States
. War Ballot Commission
. War Claims Commission   [WWII]
. War Department   UB23   353.62
—Appropriations and expenditures
. Army Pearl Harbor Board   D767.92   940.542
—Biography
. Board on Officer-enlisted Man Relationships
. Bureau of Public Relations
. Committee on Education and Special Training
. Conference of Industry, Labor, and Newspaper Leaders,
      Washington, D.C. Sept. 27-28, 1943
. Division of Insular Affairs
. Division of Military Aeronautics   UG633
. General Staff
—History   UB251   355.34320973
—History   UB23, UB223   353.6
—Manuscripts   CD3026   016.9733
. Military Dictionary Project   U25
—Records and correspondence   UB163   651.5336
. War Food Administration
. War Industries Board   HC106.2   338.0973
. Price Fixing Committee   HB236.U
. War Manpower Commission   HD7801   331.152
. Bureau of Training
. Employment Service
. War Policies Commission   HB195   355.210973, 353.0089
. War Production Board   HC106.4, UA23   338.0973, 353.0912, .26,
      .2606173, .260973
. Steel Division   HD9514
. War Refugee Board   D808.U55-66   940.53159
. War Relocation Authority   D769.8.A6   940.547273
. War Relocation Center, Manzanar, Calif.   E184.J3   940.547273
. War Shipping Administration
. Wartime Civil Control Administration   D769.1
. Women's Bureau   HD6093.U   331.406173, 353.008
. Work Projects Administration
Uruguay—History—1904-1973   F2728   989.506, 918.95036
U.S.S. Arizona Memorial (Hawaii)

V-1 bomb   D785   940.544943
V-2 rocket   D787, UF767, UG635   940.544943, 358.3, 623.451, 926.23
Vågsøy, Battle of, 1941   D756   940.5421
Vandegrift, Alexander Archer, 1887-1972   [U.S.: Lt. Gen.]   E746.V3,
                VE25.V, D767   355.3320924, 923.573
Vandenberg, Arthur Hendrick, 1884-1951   [U.S.: Sen., isolationist then
      internat'ist.]   E748.V18, E742   973.910924, .9150924, .9170924
Vargas, Getulio Dornelles, 1883-1954   [Brazil: Pres.]   F2538.V33, F2237
                981.060924, 980.03, 320.98106
Vasilievsky, Alexander, 1895-1977   [U.S.S.R.: Marshal]
Vatutin, Nikolay, 1901-1944   [U.S.S.R.: Gen.]
Vehicles, Military   UC340-3, UG615-18, UG680-5   355.621, .6211,
      .82-3, .830942 (GB), .830943 (Ger.), 623.74, .747, .7409+, .7472
Veluwe (Netherlands), Battle of, 1945

Walther pistols   UD415   623.443
War   U (mil. sci.), V (naval sci.), U21, U102-5, U750, JX1930-64, JX1291
     355, 359 (naval), 355.02+, 327.17+, 341.5-6
War and civilization   CB481   901.9
War and crime   HV6189
War and education
War and emergency legislation—United States   KF26-7, KF5900   342.73062,
     343.7301, .7307
War and emergency powers—United States   JK558-60, JK339, KF26-7,
     KF5060   328.730746, 353.032, .039, 343.73078, .7304, 342.7304
War and literature   PN3448.W3 (fiction: hist. & crit.: gen.), PN56.W3 (lit.: h. & c.)
War and morals   U21-2, JX4521   172.4
War and religion   BL65.W2, BR115.W2 (Christianity), JX1949-52   241.697,
     261.63-7, .87308, 301.635
War and society   CB401, HM36   301.23, .63, 172.4, 355.02
War—Casualties (Statistics, etc.)   D25.5 (mil. hist.), UH215 (mil. med. srvc.), D445
     301.322
War correspondents   PN4823, PN4871   070.40922, .41, .43, .44990+, .9
War correspondents, American   PN4871, PN4874, VG503   070.40922, .9,
     359.960973
War, Cost of   UA17, HB195   355.023
War crime trials
     —Czestochowa, Poland, 1945-1950
     —Dachau, 1946
     —Dachau—Buchenwald Case, 1947
     —Germany   D804   364.1380943
     —Krasnodar, 1943
     —Leipzig, 1921   D626   341.69
     —Manila, 1946   D804   341.69
     —Nuremberg, 1946-1949   341.41
     —Nuremberg
         —Einsatzgruppen case, 1947-1948
         —Flick case, 1947-1949
         —High Command case, 1948-1949
         —Hostage case, 1947-1949
         —Justice case, 1947
         —Milch case, 1946-1947   341.69
         —Ministeries case, 1948-1949
     —Shanghai, 1946
     —Tokyo, 1946-1948   JX1907, JX6731, DS801   341.3, .4, .69
         —Indexes   DS801   016.34141
     —Yokohama, 1945-1949
War crimes   JX6731   364.138, 341.3-4, .69
War criminals   D804   364.120924
     —Germany   D804, DD244, DD247   940.547243, 943.086, .0860924,
     923.243, 364.1380924
War damage compensation   [indemnification to property owners by their gov. for
     damage suffered from attacks]   341.3
War damage, Industrial   UA929.5-9, HD28   355.26, 658.28, .401
War
     —Economic aspects   HB195, HC110   330.9, .973092, 338.9, 355.02,
     .0273 (US), .027309034, .26, .03, 940.531
     —Film catalogs   U21   016.35502
War films—History and criticism   PN1995   791.4309093, .437

War games U310, UA673, V250, V253 355.02, .08, .4, .48, .48094, .5, .54,
  356.11+, 904.7, 940.541241
War games, Naval V250 793.9
War in art N330, N8260, NC968, NX650 704.949399, .9499047,
  741.65, 769.973
War in literature
War (International law) JX68, JX1907, JX1916, JX4505, JX4508, JX4511,
  JX4521, JX5001 341.3, .31, .5, .6026, .65-67, .30902
War libraries Z675.W2
War, Maritime (International law) JX5203-5268
War—Medical aspects
War memorials NA9325
  —Europe—Guide-books D663 914.0455
War neuroses RC550 616.85, .852109
War (Philosophy)
War poetry PN6110.W28 (gen.), PR1195.H5 (Eng.), PS595.H5 (Am.)
  808.8193, 821.00803 (Eng.)
War poetry, American
War poetry, English [British]
War Poetry, French
War —Protection of civilians JX5144 (int'nal' law) 341.481
  —Psychological aspects U22 355.02019, 150.194, 155.935, 172.4, 301.2
  —Quotations, maxims, etc. PN6084 808.882
War relief—Case studies HV639 361.53
War—Relief of sick and wounded UH201-551
War-songs
War-songs, American M1628 784.71973, .68973
War-songs, English
War-songs, French
War-songs, German
War stories
War stories, American
War stories, English
War stories, French
War stories, German
War victims
  —Law and legislation
War wounds RD156 617.1
War—Women's work
Warfare, Conventional
Warlimont, Walther, 1894-? [Ger.: Gen.] D757.W38+ 940.54013
Warsaw, Battle of, 1945
Warsaw
  —History
    —Uprising of 1943 D765 940.534384, .5405094384, 943.84
      —Pictorial works N6999 741.9438
    —Uprising of 1944 D765 940.534384, .5486438, 943.805
Warsaw (Poland)—History—Uprising of 1943
Warsaw—Siege, 1939 D765 940.54763438

War-ships   V800   623.825
Warships   V750-980 (construc.), VA (naval organiz.), V750-800, VA40-61,
                   VA454-6,VA503, VA513, VA653, VA700   359.325+, .32, .83+,
                   623.825+, .8252, .82509+, 940.5459+
  —Camouflage   V215
  —Costs
  —Handling   VK545   623.88, .8825
  —History   V750, V765, VA456, VA513   359.325+, .32509+,
                                .3250942 (GB), .3254+, .83, 623.82509, .8250904
     —Collected works
Warships, Internment of
Warships
  —Models   VM298   623.82015
  —Recognition   V767   623.825, 359.3250222
War ships, Scuttling of
Warships, Scuttling of
Warships
  —Turrets   VF440
  —Visits to foreign ports
Warspite (Battleship) [WWI & II]
Washington, D.C.—History   F191-205   917.53, .5303, .303, 975.3
Washington naval treaty (1922)
Wasp (Aircraft carrier)
Watson-Watt, Robert Alexander, Sir, 1892-1974 [G.B.: Radar scientist]
                                UG610.W3, TK6545   358.04, 926.2138
Wavell, Archibald Percival, 1883-1950   [G.B.: 1st Earl, Field Marshal]
    DA69.3.W37, DS481.W35   940.54250924, 325.3420954, 923.542
Wedemeyer, Albert, 1897-?   [U.S.: Major Gen., Chief of Staff to Chiang Kai-shek
    (1944-5)]   E183.8.C5   327.73051
Weisse Rose (Resistance group) [German]   DD256.3, D802.G3
Weizmann, Chaim, Dr., 1874-1952 [G.B., Israel: Zionist leader, scientist, chem.
    advisor to G.B., 1st Pres. of Israel (1948)]   DS125.3.W45, DS151.W4,
    DS126, DS149   956.94050924, 922.96, 923.15694
Wellington (Bomber)   TL685   358.42
Wemyss, Rosslyn Erskine, 1864-1933 [G.B.: Baron, Adm.]   DA89.1.W4, D568.3,
                                D580, VA454   359.00941, 923.542
Westerbork (Concentration camp)   D805.N3   940.5472430924
Westerplatte Peninsula, Poland, Battle of, 1939   D765.2.W45
Weygand, Maxime, 1867-1965   [Fr.: Gen. (WWI & II), Supr. Allied Comm. (1940)]
                                U55.W45, .F6, D530.F, D761.W, D811.W443, DC342.8.F6
                                944.0810924, 940.5344, 928.544
Wielkopolska (Poland)—History—Uprising, 1918-1919   D651.P7
Wilhelm II, 1859-1941   [Ger.: Kaiser, Emperor-King]   DD218, DD228.5,
                                DD229, D531   943.0840924, 923.143
Wilhelmina, 1880-1962   [Neth.: Queen]   DH620   949.3
William and Mary College, Williamsburg, Va. Hampton Roads-Peninsular War Studies
    Committee   HC107.V82.H48   309.1755
Willkie, Wendell Lewis, 1892-1944   [U.S.: Internationalist, Pres. candidate, F.D.R.
    world envoy]   E748.W7, .R69, E811.W   973.9170924,
                                329.023730917, 923.273, .373

Wills, Military

Wilson, Henry Maitland, Sir, ('Jumbo'), 1881-1964 [G.B.: Field Marshal]   D766.W,
                                                                   D811.W
Wilson, Woodrow, 1856-1924   [U.S.: Pres.]   E765-768, E780, D570, D611,
                                   D619, D644, D651, E780   973.0992, .80924,
                                   .912-913, .9130924, 940.3141, .32273, .373, .45,
                                   327.7304+, 378.74967, 923.173
Winant, John, 1888-1947 [U.S.: Ambass. to G.B. (1941-5)]   E183.8.G7
Wingate, Orde Charles, 1903-1944   [G.B.: Maj. Gen., commanded special forces
    ('Chindits') in Burma]   DA585.W6, D767.6   942.082, 940.5426, 923.542
Winter warfare   U167.5.W5   355.423
Wisconsin War Fund, The   D769.85.W75
Witzelben, Erwin von, 1881-1944   [Ger.: Field Marshal]
Wizna (Poland), Battle of, 1939
Wolff, Karl, 1900-?   [Ger.: SS Gen.]
Wood, Kingsley, Sir, 1881-1943   [G.B.: Sec. of State for Air (1938-40), Chanc. o/t
                                   Excheq. (1940-43), econ. innovator]
World politics   D, J, D21, D105, D363, D397, D413, D421, D443, D455, D720,
                         D727,JC251-2, JX1315, JX1395, UA11, UA646   940.28,
                         .51, .55, 301.1523, 327.0904, 341.09, .1818+, 901.9, 909.82
  —19th century   D363, D397   327.09034, 320.94028, 335.4, 909.81
  —20th century   D440-72, D419, JC252   320.904, 327.0904, 330.15,
                         909.82
  —1900-1945   D413, D443, D450   940.531, 901.94, 327.14
  —1900-1918   940.312
  —1919-1932   D727, DA565, JX1975   940.5311, 327.209+, 341.12,
                         .22+, 309.1
  —1933-
  —1933-1945   D442-3, D445, JX1395, JX1937, HN17   940.5,
                         .53144, 327.09+, .09043, 341.1, 309.1043
World War II Recorded History Collection   [Gathered by Library of Congress]
World War III   U21.2, U263 (Australia), U313, UA23, D359.7 (world politics:
                         20th C.), D849.5 (world politics: 1975-85)
World War, 1914-1918   [For older books prior to around 1982, SEE 'European
                        War, 1914-1918'. Subdivisions listed in either area may be
                        found under either heading]   D501-680, D511, D521-3,
                        D639, D644, JX1952-3   940.3-940.499, 940.3+, 940.4+
  —Addresses, sermons, etc.   B945, D443, PS2120   301.593, .953,
                              940.308, .34208
  —Aerial operations   D600-607, D788, DA89, TL515, TL540, UG633   358.43,
                         623.746, 923.542, 940.44, .54
  —Aerial operations, American   UG633, D606
  —Aerial operations, British   UG635.G7, D786, D602, D545   940.48142,
                         .447
  —Aerial operations, German   D546, D604, UG635.G3-4   940.44943
  —Africa   D651.A4, DT31-4
  —Africa, North   DT204, HC56.C38
  —Afro-Americans   D639.N4, D570.33.369th   940.403, .41273
  —Arab countries   DA47.9.S4
  —Argentina   D621.A8, F2846-8
  —Armenia   DS195.5, D651.A7, D638.A7, DS195.3.A65   947.92
  —Armistices   D641, D509   940.452, .43, .439
  —Atrocities   D625-6, JX1906, DS195.5, DH682, D626.G3 (Ger.),
                    D520.T8 (Turkish), D638.A7 (Armenians)   940.488
  —Australia   D520.A9, D568.2-7, DU116, DU212, DU161, D547.A8,
                    D568.A2, DU110, D609.A8   919.4034, 940.41294, .394

World War, 1914-1918
- —Balkan Peninsula   D562.M32, D560-1   940.3496
- —Baltic States   DK511, DK511.L17, D633
- —Battlefields   D521, D527-8, D542-5, D542.Y7 (Ypres), DC16,
                           DH416, DR416.E45-49t (Gallipoli)
  - —Guide-books
- —Belgium   D526.2, D626.B4 or .G3, D651, D541, DH681-82, DH401,
                    DH523, D623.B4   923.1493, 940.3493, .4313
- —Bibliography   Z6207.E8, D613, D570.1, D509   016.9403
- —Blockades   D580-1, JX5225   940.322, .3481, .452
- —Brazil   D621.B8, F2537, VA422
- —Bulgaria   D621.B9, D643.B6, DR72   940.31412
- —California   D570.85.C2
- —Campaigns   D529-78, D511, D521-3, U738, U162   940.4+, .413-414+
  - —Africa   D573-6
  - —Africa, East   D576, D576.G3
  - —Africa, North   D766.82
  - —Arab countries   D568.4, U55.L347
  - —Balkan Peninsula   D569.2, D560-3   940.41496
  - —Belgium   D541-2   940.481
  - —Bibliography   Z6207.E8
  - —Bulgaria   D640.M3648
  - —Czechoslovakia
  - —Eastern   D550-569.5, D539.5   940.4147
  - —Egypt   D629.E3, D568.2, D566
  - —Far East   D520.O8, D574
  - —France   D544-5, D548-9, D570.9, D629.F8, D640, D541, U53.P4,
                    DC342.8.F6   940.4144, .48144, .457
  - —Greece
  - —Iran   D568.8
  - —Iraq   D568.5
  - —Italy   D569
  - —Lithuania
  - —Macedonia   D562.M32
  - —Maps   G1037
  - —Near East   DS125.5, D566, D640, D568.4
  - —New Guinea (Territory)   D578.N4
  - —North Sea   D581
  - —Poland   D550-2
  - —Romania   D565
  - —Soviet Union   D550
  - —Syria   D568.6
  - —Turkey and the Near East   D568+, DR448, DS315, D566, D651+
                                     940.415
  - —Ukraine   D550-7
  - —Western   D530-549.5, D663, D640, D570   940.34, .343, .344, .4
  - —Yugoslavia   D560-4
- —Canada   D520.C2, D547.C2, D640, F1027   971.4, 940.31412
  - —Addresses, essays, lectures   D547.C2   309.1705
- —Caricatures and cartoons   D526, D526.2, D526.5
- —Casualties (Statistics, etc.)   HB871.H47, HB881, HB3607, D635, D609,
                                        UG447   940.37305, .34705, 312.0947
- —Catholic Church   D622

World War, 1914-1918
—Food question   HD9000-9049, D637   940.477873
    —Europe   HD1917
—Food supply   D570.1
—France   D516, D548, D520.F8, DC387-9, DC367, DC373   940.405,
              .431, .344, 320.944081, 944.0815
—German East Africa   D576.G3
—Germany   D515, D531, D609-13, DD231-232.5, DD221.5, DD228.6-8,
              DD229.8, U738, UA647, UA712   940.53112, .4886,
              .32443, .343, 327.43+
—Great Britain   D546, D544-7, D517, D521, D547.8, D611, D645,
              DA68.32, DA566.9.A-Z, DA577   942.083, 940.342,
              .31, .41241-41242, .34207, 923.542
—Greece   DF838, D616, D610, DF833-8
—Historiography   D515, D522.42, D743.42, DB36.8, DD86, U21
—Hospitals   D629.G7
—Hospitals, charities, etc.   D638, D541, D629, D640, D809   360.6273,
                   940.47709+, .4771, .34207, 352.047
—Humor   D526.2, .2-7
—Hungary   D643.H9, D539-40, D651.H7, DB947-55
World War, 1914-1918, in art   N6888, ND623
World War, 1914-1918, in literature   PR605.W3
World War, 1914-1918, in motion pictures   PN1993.5.U6, D522.33
World War, 1914-1918
—India   D520.I6, D547.I5
—Influence and results   D443, D511, D523, D639.D45, D643.A7, D653,
              D741, CB155   940.5, .51, .314, .3149+, 909.82
—Iran   D640, DS315
—Iraq   D566
—Ireland   DA952-62
—Italy   DG568.5, DG570, DG799, D520.I7, D526.7.I8, D569.A2, D617,
        D621, D640, D651.I6, DB879   940.32245, .345, .34502, .4145
—Japan   D520.O8, DS518, DS845
—Jews   DS135.G33, DS135, D609.G3, D639.J4   940.315296
—Juvenile fiction
—Language (New words, slang, etc.)   D526.2, PE3727.S6, PC1977.S6,
                   PC3747.S6   427.09, 821.04
—Latin America   D520.S8
—Law and legislation   JX5003   341.3
—Libraries (in camps, etc.)   Z675.W2   027.652, .777829
—Literature and the war   PN56.W1, PN3448, PN3503, PR106, PR478.E8,
           PR605.W3+ (Brit. poetry), PR610, PR888.E9, PR2976.H385,
              PS228.W37 (US), PT405, PT553 (Grmn. poetry), PT772,
              PQ307.W3 (Fr.)   810.9005, 809.33
—Lithuania   DK511.L2
—Macedonia   D629.G8
—Maps   G1037, D521, D540   912.4
—Medical and sanitary affairs   D628-30   940.5476+, .475+
—Mexico   F1234, E183.8.M5
—Monuments   D663
—Moral and ethical aspects   D523-4
—Museums

World War, 1914-1918

World War, 1914-1918
—Psychological aspects   D523, D525
—Public opinion   D639.P88, .R4, D509, D523, D570.1, D619, D639
                         940.3152, .37+, .4886-4887+
—Quotations, maxims, etc.   PN6084.W35
—Refugees   D637-8   940.3159+
—Regimental histories   D547.A-Z   940.409+, .412+
    —Australia   D547.A8, D568.A2   940.41294
    —Canada   D547.C2   940.40971
    —France
    —Germany   D609.G3, D534.3
    —Great Britain   D547.B74, .G7, D546   940.41242
    —India   D547.I5
    —Ireland   D547.I6
    —Italy   D569.A2
    —New Zealand   D547.N5
    —Russia   UA774, D552
    —United States   D570.3-33. D570-570.9   940.41273
—Registers, lists, etc.   D639.E4, D547, D570.85
—Registers of dead   D609, D639.E
—Religious aspects   D639.R4   940.3152, .3182
—Reparations   D648-9, D644, DC59.8.G3, HG186.F8, HG1997.I6,
                           HG3949, HJ8654, HJ8751, JX1908   940.31422,
                           330.904, 336.309, .30943, .497
—Romania   D520.R8, DR205, D651.R6   940.3498, .482+, 949.8
—Russia   DK265, DK254, D646, D514, D550, D585   940.347, .34705,
                .4147, 947.08
—Russia, Asiatic   D567.A2
—Science
—Secret service   D639.S7-8, .C75, D619.3, UB250, UB271
                        940.486-487+
    —Germany   D639.S7-8, D619.3   940.48743
    —Great Britain   D639.S7, D616   940.48642
    —Jews   DS125.5
    —United States   D639.S7, D619.3   940.48673
—Siberia   DK265, D558, DB215   940.482
—Social aspects
—Societies
—Songs and music   D526.2, M1646   427.09, 821.04
—Sources   D505-9   940.31412, .4, 943.084 (Ger.)
—South Africa
—Soviet Union   DK254-65, D639.S9, D521
—Spain   D621.S73
—Statistics   D521, D550, D570.1.U
—Study and teaching
—Sweden   D621.S5, DL658
—Switzerland   D621.S8, DQ48, DQ69   940.3494
—Syria   DS98
—Tank warfare   UG446.5

World War, 1914-1918
—Territorial questions   D650.T4, D651.A-Z, D645, D443, JV2018, JX1975
                          940.314+, .3141, .31424, 943.91, 321.07, 325.343, 341.1
  —Africa   D651.A4, DT32.5   309.16, 333.096
  —Austria   D645, D651.A95   940.31424
  —Baltic Provinces   DK511.L17, D651.L4
  —Belgium
  —Bibliography   Z6207.E8   016.321027
  —Bulgaria   D651.B8   323.1497
  —China   DS793, DS793.S4
  —Czechoslovakia   D651.C9, DB205.8, DB215
  —Czechs
  —Egypt   D651.E3
  —Estonia
  —Finland   DK451, DK459.3
  —Fiume   D651.I6
  —Galicia (Poland and Ukraine)   D520.U35, D651.G18, .P7
  —Georgia (Transcaucasia)   DK511.G3
  —Germany   D651.G3, D643-4 940.31424
  —Greece   DF701
  —Hungary   D651.H7, D643.H9, DB215, DB917, DB955
                       940.31412, 943.91
  —Istria   D651.I5
  —Italy   D520.I7, D651.I6-7, D617   940.5082, .31424, .32245,
                       34502, 949.6
  —Latvia   D651.L3-4
  —Lebanon   D651.S9
  —Lithuania   DK511.L26-273, D651.L5-7, .V4, .P7   940.31424
  —Macedonia   D651.M3, DR701.M4
  —Mesopotamia
  —Palestine
  —Poland   D651.P7, .L5, DD901.D25, .D28, DA578, DB215, DK440,
                       DK511.L273, JX1907   940.31424, 943.12, .8, 341.6082
  —Prussia, East   D651.P7+, DD247.W5-7   940.31424, 943.8
  —Rhine River Valley   D650.M5, DD801.R75
  —Romania   DB48
  —Saar River Valley (France and Germany)   DD801.S13, D651.S13
                       943.42
  —Saudi Arabia   D651.S32
  —Schleswig   DD491.S622
  —Silesia, Upper (Poland and Czechoslovakia)   D651.S5
  —Syria   D651.S9, DS98
  —Transylvania   D643.H9, D651.T8, DB730.7, DR281.T7   943.91-2,
                       323.1094392
  —Trieste   D651.T85
  —Turkey   DR477, DR584, D651.T9, D610, DF833, DS63   949.6,
                       956.101
  —Tyrol   DB779, D651.T95   943.64
  —Ukraine   D651.U6, DK508.8
  —Yugoslavia   D651.Y8-9, D465, D561, DR317   940.322497
—Transportation   D568.5, D639.T8   940.41242, .453
—Treaties   D650.T4, D450, D644, JX846   940.31424
—Trench warfare   D523, D530
—Turkey   D520.T8, D568.4, D587, DR448, DR584-92   940.4153,
                       949.6, 956.101, 327.430561

475

World War, 1914-1918
—Ukraine   D520.U35, D614.B5, DK188, DK265.8.U3-4, DK508
—Underground movements   DC611
—United States   D570-570.7, D619, D632, D639, E664, E743-5, E766-7,
     E780, E784, E802, JK464   940.373, .5373, .32273,
     .3141, .488673, .48743, 973.913, 355.0973
—War work   D570.85, U766
—Washington, D.C.   F199
—Women   D639.W7
—Yugoslavia   DR363, DB215, D651.Y8
World War, 1918-1945
World War, 1930-
World War, 1930-1945
—Campaigns—Guadalcanal Island
—Fiction
—Humor, caricatures, etc.
—Personal narratives, American
—Regimental histories—U.S.—Marine Corps. 1st Division
—Underground movements—France
World War, 1935-1945
World War, 1936-1945
World War, 1939-   [Used for some books written and cataloged before the
     end of hostilities. SEE 'World War, 1939-1945' for titles penned
     post-war. Subdivisions listed here under the latter may
     sometimes be found under the former.]
—China
—East (Far East)
—Mediterranean Sea
—Naval operations
—U.S.
World War, 1939-1943
World War, 1939-1945   [For contemporary works early in the period SEE
     'European War, 1939-' and 'World War, 1939-'. Some titles
     may ALSO be found under 'World War, 1930-1945',
     '...1935-1945', '...1936-1945', '...1930-', etc.]
     D731-838, D741 (overall works), D743-4, D755, D757
     940.53-5499, .53, .54
—Addresses, essays, lectures   D742-3, D743.9   940.53, .5304, .54
—Addresses, sermons, etc.   D742-3, D764   940.53, .5304, .531,
     .534-5, .5804
—Aerial operations   [SEE ALSO 'Bombardment' under names of cities]
     D785-7, D767, D790, D811, TL685.7, UG630   623.746,
     940.544, .5449+, 358.4+
—Aerial operations, American [British, German, etc.]
—Aerial operations, American   D785+, D790, D757.9.A-Z, D767+, D769+,
     UG633   940.5423-26, .5440973 (US), .544973,
     923.573, 358.4140973, 338.4762913
     —Chronology
     —Periodicals   D790
     —Sources   D785.U
       —Bibliography—Catalogs
—Aerial operations, Australian   D792.A8   940.544994
—Aerial operations
     —Bibliography   Z6207.W8
     —Brazilian   D768.3, D792.B7

World War, 1939-1945
—Aerial operations, British   D785-6, D757.9.A-Z, DA69   940.5421,
                               .544941-544942, .54942, 923.2913, 926.2913,
                               623.7464
—Aerial operations, Canadian   D792.C2   940.544971
—Aerial operations, Chinese   DS777.53   358.413320924, 923.573
—Aerial operations—Chronology   D785
—Aerial operations, Czech   D792   940.544
—Aerial operations—Dictionaries   D743
—Aerial operations, Dutch   D792.N38
—Aerial operations, East Indian   D792.I4
—Aerial operations, English
—Aerial operations, Finnish   D792.F5, DK459.45-5
—Aerial operations, French   D788, D761.9   940.544944
—Aerial operations, German   D787, D757+, D757.63, D811, TL540.A-Z,
                               UD485, UG633, UG635.G3   940.541343,
                               .544943, .544947
        —History   UG630   358.400904
        —Pictorial works
—Aerial operations, Indian   UG635.I3
—Aerial operations, Italian   D792.I8   940.544945
        —Pictorial works
—Aerial operations, Japanese   D792.J3, D767+, D767.2, TL515, UD485,
                               VA653, VG95.J3   940.5425, .544952,
                               356.1660952
        —Periodicals
—Aerial operations—Personal narratives   940.5441
—Aerial operations, Polish   D792.P6, D765.2.W3, D770, D811
        —Fiction
—Aerial operations, Russian   D792.R9, .S65, D764, UD485.S65, UG633, AS36
                               940.544947, .5441
—Aerial operations, South African   D792.S6
—Aerial operations, Yugoslav   D792.Y9
—Aeroplane carrier operations, American   D774   940.545973
—Africa   D739, D753-4, D761, D766, D802, D811   940.548173,
                               .542, .536, 960.4, 355.49
—Africa, Eastern   DT736
—Africa, French Equatorial   DT766.96
—Africa, French-speaking Equatorial   DT766.98
—Africa, French-speaking West   DT766.98
        —Dakar
—Africa, Italian East   D802.A2   940.53635
—Africa, North   D756.3, D766.82, .99.A-Z, D811   940.5322+,
                               .5361, .542, .5423, .54753
        —Fiction
—Africa, Northwest   D753.2.F8
—Africa, South   [SEE ALSO 'World War, 1939-1945—South Africa']
                               D766+   940.5368
—Africa, West   DT494, DT553, D761   916.6
        —Dakar   DT553.D3
—Afro-American troops
—Afro-Americans   D810.N4   940.53150396073, .541273, .5403
        —Sources
—Alabama   F326   917.61
—Alaska   D769.87.A4, DR701, F909   940.5403, .53798, 917.98

World War, 1939-1945
—Albania   D76.7.A4   940.548142
    —Biography   CT1399.8
    —Maps   G2006.S7
—Aleutian Islands   D769.87.A4, F951   940.542, .53798, 917.98
—Algeria   D766.82, .99.A3, DT295   940.5423
    —Algiers (City)
    —Mers-el-Kebir   D766.99.A3, D779.F8
—Alsace-Lorraine   D762.A4, D802.A45, DD801.A35   940.5344, .5404,
                944.38
—America   D769, E18.85, F1418   355.097
—American republics   D752.8, D742.A5, F1203, F1405-18   940.537-38,
                972.0082
—Amphibious operations   D744, D756, D761, D767-70, D767.917, D769,
                D773   940.5421, .5426, .545
—Andorra   D811
—Anecdotes   D743-5, D743.9, D839   940.53082, .542, .548, .5494, 920.5
—Anecdotes, facetiae, satire, etc.
—Anniversaries, etc.
—Anti-aircraft artillery operations
—Arabia   DS63
—Archives
—Arctic Ocean   D771   940.5450916611
—Arctic Regions   D763.5, D771
—Argentina   F2848
—Argentine Republic   D754.A7, F2846-9   940.532582, 982+
—Armenia   D764.7.A7, D779.R9
—Armistices   D812-14, D752, D802   940.5322+, .5314
    —Sources
—Art and the war   D810.A7, N6492.2, N6512, N6918, N6921.F6, N7445,
                N9145, N9165.F8, NC1070   940.53187, .5497,
                704.91, 709.22, 741.9
    —Exhibitions
—Artillery operations
—Artillery operations, American
—Artillery operations, British
—Artillery operations, Japanese
—Asia   DS518
—Asia, Southeastern   D767+, D767.45, .6, D792   940.5359, .548644
—Atlantic Ocean   D770-1, D781, VM395   940.5429, .5459
—Atrocities   D803-5, D804.G3, D805.G3, D810.J4, DD247.E34,
                DD253, DD253.6, DS135.P63   940.54056, .547243,
                .5472475, .54724972, .5405+, 943.086
    —Bibliography   Z6207.W8
    —Fiction
—Atrocities, German
—Atrocities
    —Pictorial works
    —Poetry
    —Psychological aspects   R852.H8
    —Public opinion
    —Sources   D804   940.5405094771
—Audio-visual aids—Catalogs   D743.22.U5

World War, 1939-1945
—Australia   D754.A, D742.A8, D767, D767.8-95, D767.95.A8, D779.A9,
                 DU107-110, DU116-17   940.5394, .5304, 330.994
    —Cowra (N.S.W.)   D805.A8
    —Darwin   D767.82.D2   940.5426
    —Darwin (N.T.)
    —New South Wales
    —Sources   D754.A8
    —Sydney (N.S.W.)   D783.7
—Austria   D731, D765.4, D809.G7, D839.3, DB34.5   940.53436
    —Periodicals   DB99.A1
    —Tyrol   DB879.I6
—Austria, Upper   DB169
—Austria
    —Vienna   DB855, D765.45.V
    —Wiener Neustadt   D765.45.W63
—Autographs
—Azerbaijan   D764.7.A93
—Azerbaijan S.S.R.
—Azores   D754.P8
    —Flores Island
—Balkan Peninsula   D750, D754.B3, .R9, DR48, DR2242
                        940.532449+, .5337, 949.6
—Balloons
    —Great Britain
—Baltic Sea   D772.3, D779.R9
—Baltic States   D742.B2, D754.B3, D802.B3, DK511.B3   947.4, 327.474
—Baptists
—Barents Sea   D771, D784.R9   940.545
—Battlefields
    —Guide-books   D747
—Battles, sieges, etc.   [SEE 'World War, 1939-1945—Aerial operations ',
                          '...—Campaigns—{Geog. subdiv.}',
                          '...—Naval operations' and specific battles]
—Bavaria   D757.9.B3   940.5401
—Belgium   D742.B4, D763.B4+, .B42.A-Z (places), D802.B4, DH401,
                   UA680   940.542, .53493, .5404, 949.3
    —Brussels
    —Eupen and Malmédy   D802.A45   940.5404
    —Flanders
    —Gilly   D763.B42.G54
    —Louvain
    —Periodicals
    —Renaix
    —Spa   D763.B42   940.53493
—Berlin   DD256.3
—Berlin (Germany)   D757.9.B4
—Besserabia   DS135.R93
—Bibliography   Z6207.W8, Z6725, D731-838, D734, D746
                   016.94053-94054, .36, 940.52-4
—Biography   D736-7, D769, D797, D507   940.5412, .5413, .5464,
                   .540922, .5481+, .5373, 923.573
    —Bibliography—Catalogs
    —Congresses
    —Dictionaries

World War, 1939-1945
—Biological warfare
—Black Sea   D779.R9
—Blacks   [SEE ALSO '...—Negroes']   D810.N4   940.5403, .541273,
                                                                .54516
—Blockades   D770-84, D771   940.5452, .5082
—Bolivia   F3325
—Bomb reconnaisance   D810.B66
—Borneo   D767.99.B6, D805.J3   940.5426
—Book reviews   Z6207   808.8393
—Bosnia and Herzegovina   DB250, DB539
—Brazil   D754.B8+, D768.3, F2523   940.5381
    —Fernando de Noronha Island
—Brittany   DC611.B85
—Buddhism [Islam, etc.]
—Buddhism
—Bulgaria   D766.7.B8, D754.B9, D802.B8, D814.9.B8, DR327.B9,
            DR73, DR89-90, E183.8.B8 (U.S. for. rel'ns.)   940.53141
    —Sources   D766.7.B8
—Burma   D767.6, D807.B8, D811-811.5, D742.B9   940.548142,
                            .53591, .542, .5486, 959.1
    —Personal narratives
    —Shan states
—Burman
—Byelorussian S.S.R.   D804.B93
—California   UA928.C21, D769.85.C21
    —Los Angeles County
    —San Francisco
    —Santa Barbara
—Camouflage   D810.C2
—Campaigns   D743-4, D755-7, DA69, E836   940.53-4, .5401,
                            .5408-5409, .541-2,   923.542
    —Addresses, essays, lectures
    —Admiralty Islands   D767.99.A23   940.542
    —Africa   D766-766.82   940.542
    —Africa, East   D766, D766.84   940.5421, .5423
    —Africa, French-speaking West
    —Africa, North   D766.82-9+, D736, D766, D769, U740   940.5423,
                            .548642, .542
        —Literary collections
    —Alaska
    —Albania
    —Aleutian Islands   D769.87.A4   940.5428
    —Algeria   D766.99.A3-4
        —Morocco
    —Alps, Western   D763.I72-82
    —Alsace   D761
    —American armies   D769.U
    —Angaur (Island)
    —Arctic regions   D763.5, D772   940.542, .54520916
    —Asia
    —Asia, Southeastern   D767   940.5425
    —Atlantic Ocean
    —Balkan Peninsula   D766, D731   940.5421
    —Baltic States   D764.7.B3

World War, 1939-1945
—Campaigns
  —Belgium   D763.B4, D757.54, D755.2   940.54, .542
    —Scheldt   D763.N4
  —Bulgaria   D766.7.B8
  —Burma   D767.6, D769, DS767, UG633   940.5423, .5425,
                    .544, .548673
  —Byelorussian S.S.R.
  —Caucasus   D764.3.C3
  —China   D767.3
    —Manchuria   D767.2
    —Sources—Bibliography—Catalogs   Z6614.C48
  —Courland
  —Crete   D766.7.C7, D766.3   940.5421, .5423
  —Czechoslovak Republic   D765.5, .55
    —Ostrava region   D765.55.O8
  —Czechoslovakia
  —Denmark   D763.D4, D757, D802.D4   940.5342
  —Dnieper River   D764
  —East Asia   D767
    —Sources
  —East (Far East)   D767, D767.8, D769   940.5412, .542
  —Eastern   D755.1, D757+, D764, D764.6, D765.13, D787-8, DK4185,
                    UG633   940.541244, .5421, .54210924
    —Public opinion   D764
  —Egypt
  —England
  —English Channel
  —Estonia
  —Ethiopia   D766.92   940.542
  —Europe   [SEE ALSO 'World War, 1939-1945—Campaigns—Eastern'
             and '...—Campaigns—Western']   D756.5, D769,
             D769.31, DD256.5
    —Chronology   D757
  —Europe, Eastern   D764
  —Europe—Sources   D757
  —Finland   D765.3, .32, .35.A-Z
    —Lapin laeaeni   D765.35.L35
  —France   D743, D755.2, D756, D761-2   940.540944, .5421
  —France (1944-1945)   D755.6, D761, E745   940.5421, 944.081
  —France
    —Alps, French   D761.1
    —Moselle   D762.M57
    —Normandy   D756.5.N6   940.5421
      —Chronology
    —Pictorial works
    —Provence
    —Riviera   D762.R5
  —France, Southern   D762 940.5421

World War, 1939-1945
—Campaigns
—Germany   D755.7, D757, .9, D769.U   940.5401, .542
   —Addresses. essays, lectures   D755   940.5421
—Germany (East)
—Germany
   —Pictorial works
—Germany (West)
     —Ruhr River Valley   D757.9.R5
—Gilbert Islands   D767.917, D769.U   940.5426
—Great Britain
—Greece   D766.3, .32   940.5421
   —Crete   D766.7.C7
—Guadalcanal Island   D755, D767.98, D769.A or U (U.S. Army: official)
           940.541, .5426, 355.3320924
—Hawaii
—Hong Kong   D767.3
—Hungary   D765.56
—India
—Indochina   D767, D767.45
—Indonesia   D767.7
   —Java
—Iran   D767.6   940.5423
—Iraq   D766.7.I75, D767.6   940.5423
—Italy   D763.I8+, D768.15-3, D769.A or U (U.S. Army)
           940.5421, .548173
   —Literary collections   PR1195.W6
   —Pictorial works
   —Sicily   D763.S5, D810.S7   940.5421
—Japan   D757
   —Okinawa Island   [SEE ALSO '...Campaigns—Okinawa Island']
           D767.99.O45
—Karelia   D757.85
—Kiribati   D767.917
—Levant   D766+, D767.8
—Libya   D766.93, D767.8   940.542
   —Fezzan
—Lusatia   D765
—Luxembourg
—Malay Peninsula   D767.5, .55   940.5425, .547252
—Malaya
—Malta   D763.M3
—Mariana Islands   D767.99.M27, D769.A or U   940.5426
—Marshall Islands   D767.99.M3, D769.A or U   940.542
—Mediterranean region
   —Bibliography
   —Historical geography—Maps   G1038
—Mindoro   D767.4
—Near East   D766
—Netherlands   D763.N4, D755.2
   —Limburg   D763.N42.L53
   —Walcheren   D763.N42.W

World War, 1939-1945
—Campaigns
—New Britain (Island)   D767.99.N4   940.542
—New Guinea   D767.94-5, D767.8, D769.A or U, DU740
                 940.5426
—New Guinea (Territory)   U165
—Normandy   D755-6, D756.5.N6, D762, D765   940.5421, .5485
    —Congresses
—North Pacific Ocean
—Norway   D763.N6, D779.N6, D757, D802.N   940.5421
—Okinawa Island   [SEE ALSO '...Campaigns—Japan—Okinawa Island']
                 D767.99.O45, D769.A or U (official U.S. Army)   940.5426
—Pacific area   D767   940.5426
—Pacific Ocean   D767+, .9, .98, .99.A-Z (by place: island group etc.),
                 D773-4   940.5425-5426
—Palau—Peleliu Island   D767.99.P4
—Papua New Guinea   D767.95-8
    —Guadalcanal Island   D767.98   940.5426
—Pelew Islands   D767.99.P4, D769   940.5426
—Philippine Islands   D767.4, D805.P6   940.5426
    —Bataan
    —Biscayas   D767.4
    —Leyte   D767, D769.A or U   940.5426
    —Luzon   D767.4   940.5426, .547252
    —Mindanao
    —Palawan Island
    —Zamboanga (Province)
—Philippines   D767.4, D769.A or U, D805.J3 or P6, DS688
                 940.5426, .547252
    —Anniversaries, etc.
    —Bataan (Luzon)
    —Bataan (Province)
    —Corregidor Island
    —Luzon
—Poland   D765, D765.13, D765.2, D764.7, UA772, UA829.P7
                 940.542, .5421, .544, 943.804
—Poland (1944-1945)
—Poland
    —Bialystok (Voivodeship)   D765.2.B47
    —Katowice (Voivodeship)
    —Lublin region   D765.2.L8
    —Vistula River   D765.2.V57
—Pomerania   D765.2.P6
—Portuguese Timor   D767.7
—Prussia, East   D765.2.E2
—Prussia, East (Poland and R.S.F.S.R.)   D765.2.P68
—Rhine River Valley   D757.9.R5
—Romania
—Russia   D764, D757.32, .85, D764+, DK266-8, UA770
                 940.5421, .5481438
—Russia, Northwestern   UG446.5
—Russia—Pictorial works
—Russian S.F.S.R.—Karelian Isthmus
—Saipan   D767, D769.1.A   940.5426
—Scandinavia   D763.S3

World War, 1939-1945
  —Campaigns
    —Scheldt   D763.S   940.542
    —Senegal
    —Sicily   D763.S5, D769.A or U (U.S. Army)   940.5421
    —Singapore   D767.55, .813
    —Solomon Islands   D767.98   940.5426
    —Sources   D735
    —South-West Pacific   DU740
    —Southern France   D762.P9   940.5421
    —Soviet Union   D757, D764+, DK268   947.0842
    —Sudan
    —Sweden
    —Syria   D766.7.S9, D766.7.I75, D767.6   940.5423
    —Tarawa   D767   940.5426
    —Tinian   D767.99.T5
    —Truk Islands   D767.99.T7
    —Tunis   D766.99.T8
    —Tunisia   D766.99.T8   940.5422-5423
      —Tunis
    —Ukraine   D764.7.U5, D764
    —West   D756   940.53
    —Western   D756-763, D756, D756.3, D743, D768-9+, E836
                     940.53-5421, .549
      —Maps   G1038
    —White Russia   D764.7.W5
    —Yugoslavia
  —Canada   D742.C2, D754.C2, D768.15, D769.2, F1034, F1008,
                     UG635.C2   940.532, .5371, .541271
    —Bibliography   Z1361.D4
  —Caribbean Sea   D768.18
  —Caricatures
  —Caricatures and cartoons   D745.2-3
  —Carinthia   DB296, D805.A9   943.66
  —Cartography
  —Casualties (Statistics, etc.)   D797, D797.U (US), D820.P72
                     940.5467, .546773 (US)
  —Catholic Church   D810.C3-6, .J4 (Jews), D807.I8, BX1378, BX1536,
                     BX1566   940.531522, .53152208, .5478,
                     .54824563, 327.45634
  —Caucasus   D764.7.C3, D802.N3
  —Causes   D727, D741-2, D748, D753, D816.5, E806   940.5311+,
             .53112, .53114, .5312, .532244, .532443, .5352, .5373, .5375,
             943.086, 973.917, 327.4104, .43073
    —Addresses, essays, lectures
    —Collected works   D727
    —Congresses
    —Historiography
    —Sources
  —Cavalry operations   D794

World War, 1939-1945
  —Censorship   D798-9+   940.5405
     —Australia   D810.P7.A84
     —Belgium   D799.B4
     —France   D799.F7
     —Great Britain   D799.G7, Z657
     —Sweden
     —Switzerland   D799.S9
     —United States   D799.U5-6   940.5405
  —Central Europe   D764
  —Cephalonia   D766.32.C3
  —Channel Islands
     —Jersey   UG430.J47
  —Chaplains
  —Chemical warfare   [SEE ALSO '...—Chemistry']
  —Chemistry   [SEE ALSO '...—Chemical warfare']   D769.U, D810.S2
                        358.34, .340973, 940.53185
  —Children   D810.C4, .J4 (Jewish), D811.5, HQ784.W3, HQ792, HV741,
                      LC4069.W3   940.53161, 943.8405+, 362.7061+,
                      .71063+, .74, 371.9
     —Austria
     —Canada
     —Fiction
     —Germany
     —Great Britain
     —Poland
     —Yugoslavia
  —Chile   F3095 983
  —China   D742.C6, D410, D651.C4, D767, D769.A or U (U.S. Army),
             DS710, DS774, DS777.47-53, E183.8.C4, E745.S857 (Stilwell)
             940.5351, .5425, .544973, .548173, .548673, 951.042, .0425,
             915.1, 329.006273, 341.05
     —Periodicals
     —Shanghai   DS796.S2   940.5351
     —Sources   D767   940.54250924
  —Chios (Island)   D766.32.C45   940.53499
  —Chronology   D743.5, D743   940.53, .5302, .5373, .540202,
                      .542, .545973 (U.S. Navy)
  —Church of the Brethren   UB342.U5   355.22
  —Churches   [SEE specific denominations or religions as subheads under
                 'World War, 1939-1945' and 'World War, 1939-1945—War work']

World War, 1939-1945
  —Civilian relief   D808-9, BX7747-9, BX7827, E744, JX1543, JX1977
              940.477873, .53144, .53159, .5342, .54771, .54778494, 266.65
      —Bibliography   Z6207.W8
      —Belgium   D809   940.53159493
      —China   D809.C5, HC101   940.5314451
      —Europe   D809.E, .U5 (by U.S.), HC101   940.53183381, .53144
      —Finland   D809.F5   940.54779471
      —France   D809.F
      —Germany   D809.G3   940.5477943
      —Great Britain
      —Hungary

      —Norway   D809.N6   940.53144481
      —Societies, etc.   D809.U5   940.477873
      —Sources—Bibliography—Catalogs
      —United States   D809.U5   940.5477873
  —Claims   [SEE ALSO names of claimants, vessels, etc.]   JX5326,
          JX5486, KF26-7   341.52, .67, 343.7301, .7303153, 940.53144914
      —Periodicals
  —Collaboration—France
  —Collaborationists   D802.A2+   940.53163
      —Denmark
      —France   D802.F8, D761, D829.F8, DC397   320.944
        —Ariege   D802.F82.A765
      —Germany
      —Netherlands   D802.N4
      —Norway   D763.N6, D802.N, DL529.Q5 (Quisling)   940.53481
        —Drama
      —Philippine Islands   D802.P5   991.4035
      —Philippines   DS686.4
      —Psychological aspects D802.A2
      —South Africa
      —Yugoslavia
      —United States   D804   940.5487
  —Collected works
  —Collectibles
  —Collections   D731, D739   940.53, .53082, 943.53082
  —Colombia
  —Commando operations   D794.5
      —Asia, Southeastern   D767
      —Europe
      —France   D802.F8
      —Great Britain
      —United States
  —Communications   D810.C7   940.5412

World War, 1939-1945
—Concentration camps   [SEE ALSO names of specific camps]
              D804 (atrocities), D805.A-Z, D809, D810.J4 (Jews)
  —Albania
  —Australia   D809.A8
  —Austria
  —Bibliography
  —California
  —Canada   D805.C2, D627.C2
  —Czechoslovakia
  —Denmark
  —France
    —Natzwiller
  —Germany   D804.G4, D805.G3
  —Germany (East)
  —Germany
    —Public opinion
  —Germany (West)
      —Baden-Wuerttemberg
  —Greece
  —History
  —Italy
  —Japan
  —Netherlands
  —Norway
  —Philippines   D805.P6
  —Pictorial works
  —Poland
    —Pustkow
  —Spain
  —United States
  —Yugoslavoa
—Confiscations and contributions   D810.C8
  —Argentine Republic   JX5313.A7
  —Germany   D810.C8, HC286.4   330.943
  —Jews   D810.J4
  —Poland
  —United States   JX5313.U5
—Congo, Belgian   D766.92   940.542
—Congo (Democratic Republic)   D766.95
—Congresses   D734
—Congresses, conferences, etc.   D734, D504, E807   940.5314,
                                        .532, .5306373, 973.917
—Conscientious objectors   UB342.C2
  —Great Britain   UB342.G7
  —United States—Finances

487

World War, 1939-1945
—Conscript—Burma
—Conscript labor   D811
      —Europe, Eastern   D810.J4
      —France—Mayenne (Dept.)   HD4875.F8
      —Germany   D805.G3, D810.J4, DK402, HD8450
      —Hungary   D805.H8, D810.J4, DS135.H9   940.541243
      —Japan   D801.J3
      —Netherlands   D763.N42
      —Poland   D765, D805.P7, DK402
        —Lublin (District)
        —Sources   DK402
      —Russia   D811.5   940.548243
—Corfu   D766.32.C3-4
—Corsica   DC611.C835
—Correspondence
—Cossacks
—Costa Rica   F1547   972.86
—Counterfeit money   D810.C8, HG339, HG339.G3 (Ger.)   940.5488
—Crete   D766.7.C7   940.534998
—Croatia   D804, D411, DB372.P2, DB379   949.7202
    —Baranja   D802.Y82.B37
    —Sources   DR1591
—Cryptography   D810.C88-95, D756.5.N6   940.548641, .5486701
    —Indexes
—Cuba   D742.C9, D754.C92, F1787   940.537291, 972.91
—Czechoslovak Republic   DB215, D765, D802   940.53487, .53437
    —Lidice   D804   940.542
—Czechoslovakia   DB215-17, DB215.3, D754.C95, D802.C95, D804.C9,
                         DD101, DD247.F68   943.7, 940.53437
    —Jihomoravsky kraz
    —Periodicals
    —Prague   D765.55.P7
    —Severocesky kraj   D765.55.S48
    —Slovak Socialist Republic   DB2818-2822
    —Slovakia   DB2822
—Czestochowa, Poland   D804.G4
—Dalmatia   D766.62.D3
—Denmark   D763.D4, D799.D4, D802.D4, D731, DD491, DS135.D4 (Jews)
              940.53489, .54886, 327.4890943
    —Copenhagen—Fiction
    —Gilleleje   DL291.G46

World War, 1939-1945
  —Deportations from Belgium   D810.D5
  —Deportations from Bulgaria   D810.J4
  —Deportations from Czechoslovakia   DB2742
  —Deportations from France   D810.D5, D810.J4 (Jews), D805.G3,
                                     D802.F82, DS135.F8-83 (Jews)   940.5315, .5405
  —Registers
  —Sources   DS135.F8
  —Deportations from Hungary   JX5141
  —Deportations from Italy   D810.D5, D805.G3
  —Deportations from Java (Indonesia)   D805.I55
  —Deportations from Latvia   D810.D5
  —Deportations from Peru   D769.8.A6
  —Deportations from Poland   D810.D5, D805.G3, D805.P7, D802.P62
  —Sources
  —Deportations from Seine-Maritime (France)   DS135.F85.S442
  —Deportations from the Baltic States   D810.D5
  —Deportations from Channel Islands
  —Deportations from Yugoslavia
  —Desertions
  —Destruction and pillage   D810.D6, .A7 (art), .C8 (carillons),
                                     D785.U (bombing), N6492.2-3   940.53187
    —Bavaria
    —Belgium—Louvain   D804.G3   027.7493
    —Czechoslovakia—Lidice   D765.55.L43
    —Dresden   D757.9.D7
    —East Asia
    —East (Far East)   D810.D6
    —Europe   D785, D810.D6, N6492.2   940.53187
    —France   D810.D6, D819.F7   940.53187, .5405
      —Rouen   D762.R6   940.5405
    —Germany   D810.D6, D785-6, Z801 (libraries)   940.5442
      —Cologne   D757.9.C6
      —Darmstadt   D757.9.D3   940.5421
      —Dresden   DD901.D78
    —Germany (West)
      —Hamburg   D757.9.H3
      —Wuerzburg   D757.9.W8
      —Würzburg   D757.9.W8
    —Great Britain—London
    —Greece
    —Hungary
    —Italy
      —Florence   D763.I82.F6, N6921.F6   708.5
    —Japan   D785.U   940.544, 621.312
      —Nagoya
    —Periodicals
    —Poland   D810.D6, .D6.P73, D804.G3, NC268.P6
                     940.5405, .53438
      —Warsaw
    —Russia   D829.R8
    —Yugoslavia   DS10   940.5318910453
  —Dictionaries   D740, D744   940.53, .5303, 411.5
    —Dutch
    —Polish

489

World War, 1939-1945
—Diplomatic history   D748-754, D748, D754, D735, DB955, DD256+,
                           DD523, DK268, E744, E183.8.A-Z (U.S.-other places)
                           940.430+, .520+, .5314, .5322, .5324, .5332, .5373, .542,
                           .582, 327.73081
—Addresses, essays, lectures
—Congresses
—Sources
—Yugoslavia   D754.Y9
—Discography   ML156.2   789.913
—Displaced persons [SEE ALSO '...—Refugees']   D808-9, DS135, D810.J4,
                           D820.P72, JV6416, JV6424, JV9125   940.53159,
                           378.12, 301.452309+
    —Case studies   HV43   361.53
    —Registers, lists, etc.
—District of Columbia
—Documents and sources   D734-5
—Documents, etc., sources   D735, DD253   327.43
    —Bibliography
—Documents, sources, etc.   D735   940.53082, .5322, .5332, .52
—Dogs   D810.D   940.541273
—Draft resisters
    —United States
—Drama   PN6120.R2   792+
—Dutch East Indies   DS644, DS889.3.D9, D767.7, D805.J3 (prisons),
                           D811.5   940.5391, .547252
—East Asia   D742.J3, D753, D767
    —Bibliography
—East Cameroon   D766.98
—East (Far East)   D767+, D802.A2+, D805.J3, D811.5, DS518,
                           E745.C42 (Chennault)   940.5425-5426, .548173,
                           .54867+, 915.2, 950+
—Economic appeals
—Economic aspects   D800, HB195, HC58, HC101, HC286.4, D785.U
                           940.5485, .53144, .531833, 330.19355, .5452, .904
    —American republics   HF3080
    —Argentina
    —Argentine Republic
    —Asia   HC412   330.95
    —Australia   HC605, HD7957, D767.8.A, D829.A2   331.154, 338.0994
    —Belgium   HC315, DH687
    —Bibliography   Z6207, Z6464.Z9, Z7164.L1, HD6961, JS303
                           016.33019355, .331
    —Brazil   HC187
    —California   HC106.4
    —Canada   HC115   330.971, .19355
    —Case studies
    —China   HC427.8, HD3224   334.64
    —Colombia   HC197

World War, 1939-1945
—Economic aspects
    —East (Far East)   HC462
    —Europe   D815   940.531444
    —Finland   HE848.3, HF5415.12.F5
    —France   HB236.F8, HC276, HF5349.F8, HG8055, D742.F7-8, D800
                   330.944, 338.50944, 355.23, 940.531833
    —Germany   HC286.4, .5, HD3616.G32-35, HD8450-58, HD9743.G3-
                   48, D785.U5-6 (U.S. bombing), D800   330.943,
                   331.50943, 338.47621822, .476655, .943, 354.430082+,
                   358.30943, 940.5343+, .5310943, .531833
    —Gold Coast   HF5349.G5
    —Great Britain   HA1125 (statistics), HB195, HB236.G7, HC256.4,
                 HD1925 (agric.), HD4145, HD6664 & 8390 (unions &labor),
                 HD7801, HD9551.5,HD9743.G6-7 (munitions), HJ1023 (public
                 finance), D800   330.19355, .942, 331.0942, .1082,
                 .137082, .880942, 336.42, 338.942, 355.26, 658.3152,
                 690.942, 940.534205
    —Iceland   HC357.I3   330.9491
    —India   HC435, HD7801.I6+   330.954
    —Italy   HC305
    —Jamaica
    —Japan   HC462, D785.U5-6 (U.S. bombing)   330.952,
                 338.952, 355.26
    —Latin America   HC163, E744.A2   330.98
    —Maritime provinces, Canada   HC117.M35   330.971
    —Mauritius   HC507.M44, HC517.M5   338.96982
    —Mexico   HC131-5, HF3236   338.526
    —Michigan   HC107.M58
    —Near East   HC410.7   338.956
    —Netherlands   HB236.N4, HD4905.5
    —New Zealand   HB236.N4, HC622   330.9931, 338.526
    —Norway   HC365
    —Periodicals
    —Poland   HC337.P7, HD8538
    —Russia   HC335-335.6, HD6732 (unions), HD8526 (labor),
                 HD9735.R92 (manufacturing)   330.947
      —Bibliography   Z7165.R9
      —Maritime Province
      —Siberia   HC487.S5, HD8749.S5
    —South Africa   HC517.S7
    —Soviet Union   HC335.6
    —Spanish America   HC163   330.98+
    —Sweden   HC371-5
    —Switzerland   HF3706

World War, 1939-1945
   —Economic aspects
     —United States   HB236.U5 (prices), HC101, HC106.3-6, HD3616
                 (industry & state), HD5660.U5, HD6058 (women),
                 HD6961 (indus. relns.), HD6983 (costs, wages, profits),
                 HD7293 (housing), HD7801 (union-mgt. coop.), HD7833 (labor
                 laws), HD8051.A or U (cost of living), HD8072 (labor), HD9105
                 (sugar), HG538 (inflation), E173, TX326 (consumers)
                 330.973, 331.0973, .8310973, .880973, 332.414, 337.0973,
                 338.0973, .476641, .50973, .91, 339.4973, 355.260973,
                 940.5315396
        —Bibliography   Z5074.E3 (agric.)   016.6311
        —History   HD5325.A8 (strikes-auto)
     —West (U.S.)
   —Education and the war   D810.E3-5, LC4069.W3   940.531537,
                 .531837, .5345, 370.973, .61764, .9752, 371.206273,
                 .80631, .9, 378.764
     —Congresses
   —Egypt   D742, DT70, DT107.82   940.5362, 916.2
   —Electronic intelligence—United States   D810.C88
   —Emilia-Romagna   D763.I82
   —Engineering and construction   D769, D792, D795   940.541273 (U.S.),
                 .542, .5459, 359.982
   —England
     —Channel Islands   D760.8.C5   940.534234
     —Fiction
     —London
     —Watford—Pictorial works   D760   942.5892084+
     —Westminster
   —Equipment and supplies   UC480-5, UG446.5
   —Eritrea   D766.84   940.548142
   —Estonia   DK511.E45-6, D764.7.E8   947.4
   —Ethiopia   D766.92
   —Europe   D755-7, D802.A2, D785.U (bombing), D922   940.5337, .544,
                 .5308
     —Biography
   —Europe, Eastern   D802.E92, DJK49
   —Evacuation of civilians   D753.8.U, D768.15 (Jpns. reloc. in Can.),
                 D769.8.A6 (Jpns. reloc. in. U.S.), E184.J3 (Jpns.-Am's.),
                 D810.C4 (children), HC101   940.53161-
                 53163, .5472+, .547273 (U.S.), 330.973
     —Bibliography   Z1361.J2, Z6207.W8
     —Canada   D768.15
     —Great Britain   D801.G7, D809.G7
     —Netherlands
     —Pictorial works   F857
     —Prussia, East (Poland and R.S.F.S.R.)
     —Prussia (Germany)   D809.G3
     —United States—Periodicals   D769.8.A6
   —Evangelical and Reformed Church   D810.C64   284.173
   —Exhibitions   D733
   —Fiction   [Usually classified with individual author within
                 nationality/language groups]
     —Collections
     —History and criticism

World War, 1939-1945
—Fiji Islands   D767.99.F5   940.5412961
—Film catalogs   D743.22
—Finance   D800, HC57, HJ8011   336, 336.34
    —Australia   HJ1703   336.94
    —Belgium
    —Canada   HC115, HJ793-6   330.971, 336.71
    —China   HJ1414   336.51
    —France   HJ1091   336.44
    —Germany   HF3099   336.43
    —Great Britain   HC256.4, HJ1023, HJ8627   332.0942, 336.343,
                       .42, 355.21, .26
    —India   HJ1312   336.54
    —Indiana
    —Netherlands   D800, HG1064   332.49492
    —South Africa
    —Spanish America   HJ8085
    —United States   HC106.4, HF3099, HG4063, HJ275, HJ257-8, HJ8119
                       & 8627 (public debts), D753   332.414 (inflation), .45,
                       336.343, .73, 658.1480973
—Finland   D754.F5, .S29, D765.3, D804.F5, DD120.F49, DK451-61, DK461,
            DK511   947.103, 327.430471, .471+
    —Anecdotes   D765.3
    —Fiction
    —Lapin laeaeni
    —Public opinion
    —Religious aspects   UH25.F5
    —Tornio   DK465.T63
—Food question   [SEE ALSO '...—Food supply']   HC101,
                   HD1761 (agric.), HD9000.1, .5, .62, HD9015, HF5415
                   (rationing), TX357, TX551, D410, D808   306.273, 338.1,
                   .10611, .10631-10637+, .18355, 612.39082, 940.53144,
                   .5318338, .53405
    —Belgium   D802.B4   940.53493
    —California
    —Congresses
    —Europe   HD9000.1, HD9013.6, HD9015   338.1094, 940.53183381
    —Germany   HD9013.5-6   338.10943, 940.53183381
    —Great Britain   HD1925-7 (agric.), HD9000.1, HD9011.5   330.82,
                       338.10942, 940.53186132
    —India   HD9016.I4
    —Japan   HD9016.J2   338.10952
    —Near East   HD9016.A7   338.15
    —Netherlands   HD9015.N38
    —Russia   HD915.R9-92, HD1491.R9
    —Switzerland   HD9015.S9
    —United States   HD1751 (meat, agric.), HD9001, HD9005-9006,
                       HG2051.U5, TX555   338.10973, .176, .18355
—Food supply   [SEE ALSO '...—Food question']
    —Europe
    —Germany
    —United States   HD9001
—Forced repatriation   D805.A2   940.5314, .5473

World War, 1939-1945
—France   D742.F8, D752, D761, D802.F8+ (underground occupied terr.),
                   D811, D819.F, DC340, DC373, DC389, DC396-7
                   940.5344, .540944, .5421, .548144, .5486, .5311, .532244,
                   944.081, 923.544
    —Abbeville   D762.A2
    —Aerial operations   D761.9
    —Allier (Dept.)   D762.A38
    —Alsace   D802.F82.A45 (occup. terr.)
    —Ard`eche (Dept.)   D762.A67, DC611.A67
    —Ariege   D802.F82.A765
    —Arles   D762.A7
    —Arras   DC801.A79   944.27
    —Auvergne   D802.F82.A
    —Beauvais—Pictorial works   D762.B42
    —Biography   DC373
    —Boulogne-sur-Mer   D762.B63
    —Brest
    —Brittany   D802.F82.B745 (underground)
    —Caen   D802.F82.C343
    —Calais   D762.C34
    —Cerizay   DC801.C295
    —Chambon-sur-Lignon (Le)
    —Chartres   D762.C45
    —Children's literature   D743.7
    —Chronology   D761
    —Clermont-Ferrand   D802.F82.C627
    —Cleurie River Valley   DC611.C655
    —Collected works   D761
    —Colonies   D761.9.A1
    —Congresses D744.4, D765, D802.F8
    —Cote D'Or   D762.C76
    —Cotentin   D756.5.N6   940.5421
    —Eure-et-Loir D802.F82.E878
    —Finisterre D802.D82.F567
    —Franche-Comte   D802.F82.F77
    —Granville
    —Guenrouet   D802.F82.G833
    —Haute Savoie
    —Hautes-Pyrenees
    —Havre   D762.H2
    —Juvenile literature
    —La Vallette-du-Var
    —Laon
    —Le-Chambon-sur-Lignon   DS135.F85.L434 (Jews)
    —Literary collections   D745.2
    —Literary questions
    —Loir-et-Cher—Battles, sieges, etc.
    —Lyons region   D762.L93
    —Maillé
    —Manche   D802.F82.M364
    —Marseille   D762.M3
    —Metz   D802.F82.M4378 (occup. terr.)
    —Meurthe-et-Moselle (Dept.)   D762.M4   940.541244
    —Morbihan   D762.M55

World War, 1939-1945
   —France
      —Moselle   D802.F82.M
      —Mulhouse   D802.F82.M857
      —Nantes   D802.F82.N362
      —Naval operations—Sources   Z6834.H5
      —Nord (Dept.)   D762.N57
      —Normandy
      —Oleron, Ile d'   D762.O42
      —Oradour-sur-Glane   D804.G3-4 (atrocities)   940.54056
      —Oullins   D762.O94
      —Pamphlets
      —Paris   D762.P2-3, D802.F82.P375-376 (underground),
                      D809.F8 (evac. of civilians)   940.5344, .534436
      —Pas-de-Calais (Dept.)   D762.N57
      —Periodicals   D731
      —Poetry
      —Provence   D762.P9
      —Saint Nazaire
      —Saint-Etienne Region (Loire)   D802.F82.S224
      —Saint-Lô
      —Sainte-Mere-Eglise   D762.S25
      —Sarreguemines   D762.S29
      —Saumur   D762.S2
      —Strasbourg   D802.F82.S777
      —Tarentaise   D762.T29
      —Toul   D762.T57   940.540944382
      —Toulon   D779.F8
      —Toulouse   D762.T583
      —Tournissan   D762.T6
      —Tours   D762.T6
      —Tulle
      —Vercors   D762.V4
      —Vienne (Dept.)   D762.V5
      —Vincennes
   —Free and resistance movements, Jewish
   —Free India   D767.63   940.5354, 954035
   —Friends, Society of   D827, BX7635   940.53144
   —Friesland (Netherlands)   D785, D802.F85
   —Fuel supplies   D810.F83   940.53
   —Gascony   D802.F8   940.5344
   —Georgians (Transcaucasians)

World War, 1939-1945
—German Americans
—German occupation—Netherlands   940.53492
—Germany   D735-7, D741, D742.G3, D751, D757+, D764,
    D781 (naval ops.), D785.U5-6 (bombing of), D804.G3 (atrocities),
    D809.G3 (refugees), D811, D819.G3, D821, DD94, DD232, DD247,
    DD247.H5 (Hitler), DD253, DD256+   940.5314, .5343,
    .54013, .540943, .541343, .5421, .5440943, .5482, .548743,
    943.086, .1087, 355.331, 623.194
—Addresses, essays, lectures
—Addresses, sermons, etc.
—Aerial operations   D787
—Augsburg
—Berlin   D757.9.B4, DD256.3, DD880-81
—Bibliography   Z6207.W8
—Biography   DD243.A-z, DS135 (Jews)
—Bremen   D757.9.B67
—Campaigns   UA713   940.541343
—Cologne   D757.9.C6
—Constance, Lake of   D757.9.C76
—Dresden   D757.9.D7
—Germany, East
    —Dresden   D757.9.D7
    —Greifswald
    —Halle (Bezirk)
    —Harz Mountains Region   D757.9.H35
    —Magdeburg (Bezirk)
    —Peenemunde   D757.9.P37 (bombing)
—Germany
    —Fiction
    —Frankfurt am Main   D757.9.F7   940.5343
    —Hamburg   DD901.H28
    —Hanover (City)   D785.U5-6 (U.S. bombing)
    —Heilbronn   D757.9.H36
    —Juvenile literature
    —Kolberg   D757.9.K83
    —Münsterland   D757.9.M78
    —Nuremberg   DD901.N94
    —Oldesloe
    —Periodicals   D731
    —Pictorial works   NC251   741.5943
    —Propaganda
    —Religious aspects
    —Reutlingen (Landkreis)   D757.9.R47
    —Sources   D757, DD247
    —Stralsund   DD901.S8
    —Transportation—History

World War, 1939-1945
—Germany, West
    —Augsburg   DD901.A93
    —Bavaria   D757.9.B3
    —Bremen   D757.9.B67
    —Bremerhaven   D757.9.B68
    —Cologne
    —Hamburg   DD901.H28, D757.9.H3
    —Hesse   DD801.H64
    —Koblenz   D757.9.K58
    —Marburg
    —Muensterland   D757.9.M78
    —Nuremberg   D757.9.N8
—Gibraltar   D754.S7
—Gift-books
—Gipsies   [SEE ALSO '...—Gypsies']   D810.G5   940.5485
—Governments in exile   D810.G6
—Graffiti
—Great Britain   D742.G7, D743, D750, D755, D759, D786, D810-811.5,
        DA566, DA566.9.C4 (Churchill), DA586-7   940.342,
        .5304, .532, .532241, .5341-5342, .540942, .542, .5421, .544,
        .548142, .548173, .548642, .5842, 941.084, 942.084, .0840922,
        923.242 (biog.), 320.942, 327.420+ (for. rel'ns.), .42043 (for. rel'ns.
        w. Ger.), .42073 (w. U.S.), 355.480942 (generals)
    —Addresses, essays, lectures   D742, D759   940.5342, .54012
    —Bibliography
    —Biography
    —Cambridge   D810.C4 (children)   940.53161
    —Channel Islands   D760.8.C5   940.534234
    —Colonies   D760   940.5342, .542
    —Dover
    —Exeter   D760.8.E88
    —Fiction
    —Film catalogs   D743.22
    —Kent
    —Liverpool
    —London   D760.8.L7, D811.5   940.534203, .53421, .54422
    —Periodicals   D731
    —Secret service
    —Sources   D750-754
    —West Ham   DA690.W5025
—Greece   D766.3+, D802.G8 (underground), D805.G8 (prisons), DF836,
        DF849, HV8959.G7 (polit. prisoners)   940.53495,
        949.507, 914.95
    —Athens   D766.32.A8
    —Crete   D766.7.C7
—Greenland   D763.5   940.542
—Guam   D767.99.G9, D811.T9 (Am. fugitive), .Y55+ (Jpns.
        soldier's 28-yr. fight)   940.5426, .548252
—Guernsey   D760.8.G8
—Guerrillas   [SEE '...—Underground movements']
—Gypsies   [SEE ALSO '...—Gipsies']   D810.G9   940.5485
    —Austria
    —France
    —Germany   D810.G9, DX229

World War, 1939-1945
—Hawaii   D767.92, DU623, DU624.7, HC687.H3   940.53969, .5426
—Hawaiian Islands   D767, D810   940.53969, .5477
    —Pearl Harbor   D767   940.53969
—Health
—Health aspects   D805, D807
—Himalaya Mountains   D790   940.5425
—Historiography   D742, D743.42, D748, U21   940.53072, .541273
    —Congresses   D743.42, D764
—History   —Fiction
—Hongkong   D802.H6, DS796.H75-757   940.5351
—Horses
—Hospitals
—Hospitals, charities, etc.   [SEE ALSO '...—Medical and sanitary affairs.]
—Humor   D745.2-7
—Humor, caricatures, etc.   D745.2 (Am. & Eng.), D745.2.P8 ('Punch'),
        D745.3 (Fr.), .5 (Ger.), .7.A-Z (other places), .7.F48 (Finnish),
        D811.Y16-3 ('Yank'), NC1428, NC1429.N ('New Yorker'), NC1479
        940.548141, .548173 (US), .5496-5497, 741.5973, 358.400973
—Hungary   D742.H9, D754.H9, D765.56, D802.H89, DB950-56,
        DS135.H9 (Jews)   940.534391, .5482439, 943.9105
    —Balatonszarszo   D765.562.B32
    —Budapest   D764, DL870
    —Ujpost   DB999.U54
—Iceland   D763.I2   940.53491
World War, 1939-1945 in art   ND1442.G76 (G.B.)
World War, 1939-1945 in literature   [SEE ALSO '...—Literature and the war']
        PR605.W3 (Eng. poetry for WWI & II), PG3026.W3 (Russ. poetry)
World War, 1939-1945 in pictures   D743.23, PN1997   940.5300222, 791.437
World War, 1939-1945
—India   D742.I4, D754.I4, D767.6+, D811.5, DS480.82-3, DS481
        940.548142, .5354, 923.254 (Gandhi)
    —Bengal
    —Bombay
—Indian Ocean   D767.6
—Indians   D810.I5, .C95 (cryptography: Navajos)
—Indochina   DS549
—Indo-China, French   D767.45, DS549-550   940.5359, .53597, .5425
    —Laos
—Indonesia   D767.7, DS643.5-644 991
    —Java
    —Sumatra   D805.J3
    —Timor Timor   DS646.5
—Influence   D727, D741, D744, D749, D753.2
—Influence and results   D511, D741, D744, D753, CB203, E744, HC58
        940.53, .531, .5314, .531815, .5373, 330.904
—Influence—Sources
—Intelligence service
    —France
    —Great Britain
—International law   JX5144
—Iran   D766.7.I7, D769, DS318   940.5355
—Iraq
—Ireland   D754.I5-6, DA963   941.591
—Islam

World War, 1939-1945
  —Islands of the Aegean   D766   940.5421
  —Islands of the Baltic   D764.7.B3
  —Islands of the Pacific
  —Italy   D742.I7, D754.I8, D763.I8, D802.I8 (underground), D813.I8,
        D829.I8, DG498, DG571-2, DG575   940.5320924, .5345,
        .5421, 945.091
  —Addresses, essays, lectures
  —Bari (City)   D763.I82.B2-374   940.548673
  —Bibliography
  —Bologna
  —Congresses   DG572
  —Costrignano
  —Emilia Romagna—Periodicals   DG975.E53
  —Exhibitions   D763.I8
  —Finance
  —Florence   D763.I82.F6   940.534551
  —Frascati   D763.I82.F8
  —Gorizia (Province) D802.I82.G (occup. terr.)
  —Milan   D763.I82.M52
  —Monchio   D763.I82.M65
  —Naples   D763.I82.N36   940.5441
  —Orcia River Valley   D763.I82.O746
  —Ossola Valley   D802.I82.O82
  —Po River and valley
  —Posters   DG571
  —Propaganda   DG571
  —Rome
  —Rome (City)   D763.I82.R6-68   940.5421, .5485 (secret srvc.)
  —Rome—Fiction
  —San Martino Valle Caudina   D763.I82.S267
  —Sicily   DG869-869.2
  —Study and teaching—Congresses
  —Trials
  —Trieste
  —Tuscany
—Japan   D742.J3, .U5, D754.J3, D767+, D767.2+, D804.J3 (atrocities),
      D810.P7.J352 (propaganda), D814.8 (peace), D821J3, DS503,
      DS530, DS806, DS830, DS843, DS885-90   940.5314+,
      .53452, .5352, .540952, .5412730952, .541352, .542, .5425,
      .5441, .548173, .5488752, 952.03, .033, 915.2
  —Hiroshima   D767.25.H6, D790, UF767.U5-6   940.5425,
      .544, 623.45
  —Hiroshima-shi
  —Nagasaki   D767.25.N3, UF767.U5-6 (atom bomb)   623.45
  —Periodicals
  —Japan, Sea of   D780
  —Supplies   UD446.5, UD485.J3   356.1660952, 358.180952
  —Tokyo   D790
—Japanese-Americans   D753.8, D769.8.A6 (evacuation)
—Java   D767.7, D802.J32-38, D805.J3 (prisons), DS646.27
      940.53922, .5337, 992.2
—Jersey   D760.8.J4, D802.J4   940.5342, .534234

World War, 1939-1945
—Jews   D810.J4, DS135.A-Z, DS135.E8+ (Europe), .P (Poland),
              .R (Russia), D802.P62, D804.G3, D805.G3, D816.J4, DD253.6,
              PJ5129 (lit.)   940.5315296, .53159, .5344, .53492,
              .5404-5405, .54056, 949.2, 296
   —Australia
   —Bibliography   Z6207.W8, Z6373   016.914306924, .940535693,
                     940.5315296, .5404+
   —Collected works
   —Fiction
   —France
—Jews in Denmark
—Jews
   —Poetry
   —Poland   D802.P62, D804.G4, D816.J4, DS135.P
   —Rescue   D805.S9 (Switzerland), D810.J4, DS135, JV8749.P3
              940.5315, .531529+, .53438, .5405
      —Berlin (Germany)   DS135.G4.B45
      —Bulgaria   DS135.B8
      —Congresses   D810.J4
      —Denmark   D810.J4, DS135.D   940.531529609489
      —France   D810.J4, DS135.F9   940.531503924
         —Le Chambon-sur-Lignon
      —Hungary   D810.J4, DS135.H9   940.531503924
        —Budapest   DS135.H92.B838
      —Italy—Assisi
      —Japan   DS135.C5
      —Poland   DS135.P6
        —Warsaw
      —Ukraine—Rovno (Rovenskaia Oblast')
      —United States
      —Yugoslavia
  —Societies, etc.   D810.J4
   —Statistics
   —Yugoslavia
—Journalism, Military   D798-9
—Journalists   D799.A-Z, D799.A (American), C2 (Canadian),
              .R9 (Russian), D756.3, PN4784.F6
   —Biography
—Julian March   D763.I82
—Jungle warfare
   —Malaya   D767.813
—Juvenile fiction
—Juvenile literature   D743, D756   940.53-4, 355.23, .8
—Juvenile participants   [SEE ALSO '...—Participation, Juvenile']
—Kansas
—Karelia   D764.7.K28
—Kazakhstan   D764.7.K3
—Kongo, Belgian   D766.92   940.542
—Korea   D829.K8, DS916
—Kurile Islands   D767   940.544973
—Language (New words, slangs, etc.)   PE1693, PE3727.S7,
              PF5997.S6-7 (Grmn.)   940.53014, 427.09
—Lapland   D765.35.L36
—Latin America   D754.L29, D742.U

World War, 1939-1945
    —Latvia   D742.L3, D802.L3   940.53474, 947.4
        —Courland
        —Riga   D802.L32.R4 (occupied terr.)
    —Law and legislation   JX4511 (int'nal. law), JX5270 341.3
        —Africa, North
        —Bombay (State)
        —Canada   KE6818
        —Europe
        —France   D802.F8 (Grmn. occup.), D829.F8 (collaborationists),
                           K25.F84, K50.F8
        —Germany   D802.A2.G7 & JX4514 (occupied terr.),
                           D810.C8 (confiscations)   940.5337
        —Great Britain
        —India   D767.6
            —Bombay (State)
        —Ireland   K25.I68
        —Italy   K25.I8
        —Peru
        —Poland
        —Silesia, Upper (Poland and Czechoslovakia)   DK4600
        —Silesia, Upper (Province)
        —United States   HD3622.U5, J82, JK560, JX5270, UB773 (srvcmen.)
                           353.03, 355.134
            —States   JK2430, KF165
        —Uruguay
        —Virginia   JK3916
    —Lebanon   D750
    —Levant   D739, D754.L4, D766, D810.J4,(Jews), DS49, DS126.3
                       940.5356, .536, 956+, 915.6
    —Libraries   Z665, Z672, Z675.W2   021.93, 027.652, 940.531802
    —Libya   DT227   961.2
    —Literary collections   PN6071.W75
    —Literature and the war   D810.A7, .P7, PN131, PG3026.W3 (Russian),
                       PG3096.W67, PQ307.W3 (French), PR605.W3 (Br. poetry),
            PS228.W37 (Am.)   940.54886+, 029.60621, 808.0668, 810.904
        —Bibliography   Z6519
    —Lithuania   D742.L8, D754.L77, D802.L5, DK511.L2-27
                       940.53475, 947.508
    —Logistics
    —Lutheran Church
    —Luxemburg   [SEE ALSO '...—Luxembourg']   D763, D802.A45
                                               940.53493, .5404
    —Macedonia   D766.62.M2, D766.6
        —Poetry   PG1189.M289-3, D745.7.M3
    —Madagascar   D766.99.M3
    —Mainly Peninsula   D767   940.53595
    —Malacca, Strait of   D767
    —Malay Peninsula   D767.5, D802.M2 (occup. terr.), DS595-8+,
                   DS598.P38 (Penang)   940.53595, .542, .547594, 915.95
    —Malaya   D767.5, DS595+   940.5425, 959.5+, 915.95
    —Malaysia
        —Malaya   D767.5
    —Malta   D763.M3, D768, D784.G7   940.5453, .5442, .5421
    —Manchuria   D767.2

World War, 1939-1945
—Manpower   [mil. & econ. discussions]   HD6961, HD8051
                                            331.061+, .137
    —Belgium   HC315
    —Bibliography   Z6207.W8, HD6961
    —Canada
    —Columbus, Ohio   HD5726.C7
    —Finland   HD8533
    —Germany   HD4813, HD5701, HD7801   331.137082, .57
    —Great Britain   HD5767, HD5917   331.1120942, 355.220941
    —Los Angeles   HD5726.L7-77
    —The West
    —United States   HD5723-5724, HD5873, HD6511 (unions), HD6961,
            HD8072, HB1765.A5.1940, UB343, D769   331+,
            331.06173, .071174967, .112, .152, .880973, 306.27471,
            312.0973, 330.973, 355.220973, .260973
        —History   HD5724
—Manuscripts—Catalogs   Z6611.H5
—Maps   D427, D731, D743, D743.3, D767.4, D820.T4, E744, G1038
            940.53-4, ,5314, .5499, .58
    —Bibliography   Z6207.W8
—Medals
—Medical and sanitary affairs   D806-7, D807.A-Z (by place or by country
            responsible), D807.B8 (Burma), .U5-6+ (U.S. medical work), D629,
            D769, .A or U, D785.U5-6+ (U.S. bombing), D805, D811, R722,
            RA776, RA790, RC971   940.5475+, .54752, .547542 (GB),
            .547547 (Rus.), .547573 (US), .547643 (Ger. hospitals),
            .5476732 (U.S. hospitals)
—Medical aspects
—Medical care   D807
    —Australia   D807.A8, UH321
    —Brazil   D807.B7
    —Netherlands
—Mediterranean region   D731, D766+, D766.82
—Mediterranean Sea   D766, D766.82, D770, D779.A-Z (naval ops.: by
            country: not limited to Med.), D779.A9 (Australian),
                        D843, D973   940.542, .5421, .545
    —Congresses
—Mennonites   D810.C665
—Mexico   D754.M6, D769.2, F1203, F1234, F1392.G4 (Grmn. refugees—
            anti-Nazi)   940.5372, 972.0082, .08, .082, 327.72
—Micronesia (Federated States)—Ponape Island   DU568.P7
—Midway Islands   D767   940.545
—Military currency   HG353.5   769.55+, .550216
—Military intelligence
    —Germany   D810.S7
—Mindanao   D767.4.M17-25   940.5426
—Miscellanea   940.504
—Missing in action
—Missouri
—Missouri (Battleship)—Normandy   D769   940.53778
—Moldavia   D764.7.M55
—Montenegro   D766.62.M6

World War, 1939-1945
—Monuments
 —Hawaii
 —Yugoslavia
—Moral and ethical aspects   D744.4, D790 (bombing), UA26
—Moral aspects   D744.4, D810   940.53181781, .5304, .548, 901.9
—Moravia   D765.55.M6
—Moton pictures and the war   D743.23, D810.E8, .P7 (propaganda),
                                PN1995.2.H5
—Mukyokaishugi Shukai
—Museums
—Music and the war   D810.E8
—Muslims   D810.M6
—Naval operations   [SEE ALSO names of individual ships,
                e.g. 'Hotspur (Destroyer)]   D770-784, D767, D769,
        D770, D773, D779, D786, D811, UG1240+ (aviation),
        V767, VA58   940.542, .545+, 359+, 359.32, .3252, .3255+
—Naval operations, American   D773-4, D767, D769, D783+, V833, VA63-5+
                        940.5426, .544973, .545, .5451373 (subs),
                        .545973, .548173, .548673, .54973,387.54

 —Fiction
 —History—Sources—Bibliography—Catalogs   Z6835.U5
 —Pacific   D767   940.545973
—Naval operations, Australian   D779.A9, D767.8.A938, VA715
                        940.545994
—Naval operations
 —Baltic Sea   D764
 —Bibliography   Z6207.W8
 —Brazilian   D768.3
—Naval operations, British   D771, D772.A-Z (ships), D780, D784.G7 (subs),
                        DA89.1.A-Z (biog.), V835, VA454
                        940.545941-545942, .548642, 359.3320922-24
 —Fiction
—Naval operations, Canadian   D779.C2, D770-2, D756.5.D5 (Dieppe Raid)
                        940.545971
—Naval operations
 —Chronology   D770   940.545
 —Congresses   D775
—Naval operations, Dutch   D779.N4   940.5459492
—Naval operations, Finnish
—Naval operations, French   D779.F7-8, D784.F7, D788, DS553.1
                        940.545944
—Naval operations, German   D779.G3, D768.18, D771-3, D772.3,
                        D781 (subs), D781.A-Z, .D6+ (Dönitz), D784.G3,
                        DD770, VA513, VD74   940.545, .545943
—Naval operations, Greek   D779.G, DF775
—Naval operations, Indian   D779.I4
—Naval operations, Italian   D775, D780   940.545945
—Naval operations, Japanese   D777, D777.5.A-Z (by ship), .Y33 (Yamato),
                        D784, D792.J3 (aerial ops.), DS890.A-Z (biog.),
                        .Y25 (Yamamoto), VA653   940.5451, .545952,
                        359.320952
—Naval operations, Mexican   D779.M, D754.M6
—Naval operations, New Zealand   D779.N45   940.5459931

World War, 1939-1945
   —Naval operations, Norwegian   D779.N6, D763.N6, D763.5, D802.N8
                                                           940.5459481
   —Naval operations, Polish   D779.P6, D765.2.G37, D770
   —Naval operations, Portuguese   D779.P8
   —Naval operations, Russian   D779.R9 or S65 (Soviet Un.),
                                         D784.R9 (subs), VA573   940.545947
   —Naval operations, Submarine   D780-4, D782 (Ger.), D782.U15 (U-99),
                                       D783 (US), D783.5.A-Z (names etc.), D784.A-Z (misc.
                                       countries), .F7 (Fr.), .G7 (GB), D771-3, V859.A-Z,
                                       .G3 (Ger.)   940.5451, .54513+, .5451342 (GB),
                                       .5451373 (US), .54516, .545943 (Ger.), .5465756
     —Fiction
   —Near East   D766, D731, D754, D769.U or A, DS63.2.A-Z   940.542
   —Negroes   [SEE ALSO '...—Blacks']   D810.N   940.5403, .541273, .54516
   —Netherlands   D754.N4, D763.N4, D793, D802.N4 (occup.), D811+,
                   D829.N2 (reconstruc.), DJ287, DS643
                   940.53144492, .53492, .5481492, 949.2+
     —Arnhem   D763.N42.A75   940.53492
     —Delft   D797.N4
     —Goes   D763.N4.G55-56
     —Gorinchem   DJ411   914.92
     —Heusden   D763.N42.H45-48
     —Leeuwarden   D763.N42.L51
     —Overijssel   D763.N42.O
     —Periodicals
     —Rotterdam   D763.N42.R74
     —'s-Hertogenbosch   D763.N42.H4
     —Twente   D763.N42.T86
     —Walcheren   D763.N42.W3
     —Wisch
   —New Britain (Island)   D767.99.N4, D805.J3 (prison)   940.5497, .548173
   —New Guinea   D767.95, D792.A8 (Australian air force), D811.5
                   950.542, .544994
   —New Ireland (Island)   D767.99.N45   940.5426
   —New Jersey
World War, 1939-1945 (New words, slang, etc.)
World War, 1939-1945
   —New York
   —New York (City)
   —New York (N.Y.)
   —New York—Oswego
   —New York (State)   D769.85.N4
     —New York
   —New Zealand   D742.N4-45, D743.9, D754.N45, D767.85
                   940.53931, .542
     —Chronology
   —Nigeria   DT296, DT515.75   966.903
   —North Carolina
   —North Sea   D771, D802.N8

World War, 1939-1945
—Norway   D742.N6, D754.N6, D755.2, D763.N6, D735.G3,
               D802.N7 (underground), DL529, DL532
               940.5082, .532, .53481, .541481, .5459481, 948.1,
               327.7309481 (U.S. dipl. relns.), 387.509481
   —Bergen   D763.N62.B43
   —Bibliography Z6207.W8
   —Dombas   D763.N62.D
   —Drama
   —Lesja   D763.N62.L475
   —Rjukan   D802.N72.R583
   —Svalbard   D763.N62.S923
—Occupied territories   [collective works: for occupation of single countries,
               SEE '{Name of country}—History—German {Japanese, etc.}
               occupation, {date span}']   D802.A-Z, .A2, D769.A or U (U.S.
               Army)   940.5337-5338, .53144, .54056, 355.4909
   —Congresses   D757, DD257
   —Periodicals
   —Sources
—Oceania   D767+, D767.9
   —Bibliography—Catalogs   Z6207.W8
—Oceanica   D767-9+, D767.9, D810.S7 (coastwatchers), DU29, E847
               940.54099, .5426, .545, .548694 (coastwatchers)
—Oceanics
—Orthodox Eastern Church, Serbian
—Outlines, syllabi, etc.   D427, D743.5, D745   940.5302, .53076, .5373, .54
—Pacific area   D767+, D767.9, D769   940.5425-5426, .544-545
—Pacific Coast   D769.1   940.5428
—Pacific Ocean   D767+, D769+, D769.A or U, D773-4, D777 (Jpns. navy),
               D783 (subs), D790 (air warfare), DS518, DU29, E745,
               E842, VA63.A-Z, VE500   940.5425-5426,
               .5352 (Japan), .542, .54260924 (biog.), .543-545,
               .545973 (U.S. Navy), 923.573 (biog.), 359.960973 (U.S. Navy)
   —Campaigns—Pictorial works
   —Pictorials
   —Sources
—Palestine   DS126.3, DS149, D810.J4 (Jews)   956.9
   —Biography
—Pamphlets
—Papua New Guinea   D767.95
   —Trobriand Islands   D767.99.T76   940.548194
—Participation, Afro-American   D810.N   940.541273
—Participation, Female   D810.W7
—Participation, Jewish
—Participation, Juvenile   [SEE ALSO '...—Juvenile participants']
—Peace   D734, D754.V (Vatican), D814-16+, D821, D825, D829.A-Z,
               DD259.4, E813, JX77, JX1392.5, JX1577, JX1952
               940..5304, .531, .5314, .53141.53144+, .532273,
               .5352 (Japan), .537, .54012, 909.82
   —Bibliography   Z6207.W8   016.940531
   —Collected works   D815.A
   —Periodicals
   —Societies, etc.
   —Sources   D814   940.5312, .5314
—Pechenga region   D765.3   947.103

World War, 1939-1945
—Pennsylvania 940.53748
—Periodicals D731.A-Z (by title), D732, D735
—Persia DS318
—Personal narratives [SEE ALSO call number ranges for particular areas,
        campaigns, topics, etc.] D811, D811.5, D743,
        D765, D802 (underground & occupied areas), D810,
        D810.J4 (Jews) 940.5481-5482, .5449+ (aerial
        ops.), .542 (battles etc. by theatre), .5315 (social groups)
—Personal narratives, Albanian
—Personal narratives, Alsatian
—Personal narratives, American D811, D811.5, D761 (Fr.), D763.I8 (Italy),
        D767 (Pacific), D767.99.I9 (Iwo Jima), .W3 (Wake Is.), D790 (aerial
        ops.), D805.P6 (Phil. prisons), D811.A2 (group) 940.548173,
        .44973 (Army air forces), .541273, .544, .545 (Navy), .547243
        (Ger. prisons), .547252 (Jpns. prisons), .54771, .548673, .5496
—Personal narratives, Australian D811, D811.5, D766.82 (N. Africa),
        D767.82.D2 (Darwin), D805.J3 (Jpns. prisons)
        940.548194, .548394
—Personal narratives, Austrian D811, D802.A9 (underground),
        D805.R9 (Rus. prisons) 940.5481436,
        .5482436, .53159, .5344
—Personal narratives, Belgian D811, D811.5 940.53493
—Personal narratives, Brazilian D811, D763.I8 (in Italy), D768.3, D807.B7
—Personal narratives, British [SEE ALSO '...—Personal narratives, English']
        D811 & 811.5, D811.A2 (group)
        940.544942, .548142
—Personal narratives, Bulgarian D811 940.53496
—Personal narratives, Byelorussian
—Personal narratives, Canadian D811 940.540971, .544-545, .548171, .594
—Personal narratives, Chinese
—Personal narratives, Collections D811 940.5481
—Personal narratives, Croatian D811, D802.Y8
—Personal narratives, Czech D811, D805.G3 (Ger. prisons), DB215-17
        940.5482437, .547243
—Personal narratives, Danish D811, D802.D4 940.5481489
—Personal narratives, Dutch D811, D802.I52 (Indonesian underground),
        .N4, D805.J3 (Jpns. prisons) 940.5472492,
        .5481492
—Personal narratives, East Indian D767.63, D799.I4 (journalists)
        940.5354, 355.3510954
—Personal narratives, Ecuadorian
—Personal narratives, English [SEE ALSO '...—Personal narratives,
        British'] D811 & 811.5, D756 (Western), D763,
        D766-767, D766.82 (N. Africa), D767.6 (Burma),
        D786 (aerial), D805.G3 (Ger. prisons), .J3 (Jpns.
        prisons) 940.548142, .5342, .5421,
        .544942, .547243, .548642
—Personal narratives, Estonian
—Personal narratives, Faroese
—Personal narratives, Filipino D811+, D767.4, DS686.4
        940.5481914, .5409599, .5426
—Personal narratives, Finnish D765.3

World War, 1939-1945
—Personal narratives, French   D811+, D761-3, D766+, D766.82 (N. Africa),
    D788 (aerial), D802.F8 (underground), D805.G3
    940.548144, .5344, .5348144 (underground), .544,
    .544944, .547243 (Ger. prisons), 944.0810924
—Personal narratives, German   D811 & 811.5, D757, D763.N6 (Norway),
    D764 (Rus.), D787, D805.F8 (Fr. prisons), .R9 (Rus. prisons),
    .U5 (U.S. prisons), D810.S8 (secret srvc.), DD256, DD259.7
    940.548243, .542, .544943 (aerial), .547244 (Fr. prisons),
    .547273 (Am. prisons), 943.086
—Personal narratives, Greek   D811 & 811.5, D766.3-7,
    D802.G8 (underground)   940.5482495, 949.507
—Personal narratives, Hungarian   D811 & 811.5, D765.56, D805.P7
    940.54814391, .534391, .54814391,
    .547243 (Ger. prisons) & concen. camps)
—Personal narratives, Icelandic
—Personal narratives, Italian   D811+, D754.I8, D763.I8,
    D802.I8 (underground), D805.F8 (Fr. prisons),
    .G7 (Brit. prisons), D807.I8 (medical)
    940.53161, .5345, .547242, .548245
—Personal narratives, Japanese   D811 & 811.5, D767+, D767.25.H6
    (Hiroshima), D767.4 (Philippines), D767.5 (Malay
    Penin.), D767.92 (Pearl Harbor), D767.99.A-Z,
    D767.99.I9 (Iwo Jima), D777 (navy), DS890
    940.548252, .5426+, .547242 (Brit. prisons)
—Personal narratives, Jewish   D811+, D765.2.W3 (Warsaw), D804.G4,
    D810.J4, DS125.5-135, DS135.A-Z, .L5 (Lithuania),
    .R9 (Russia)   940.5315+, .531503, .531503924,
    .53150693, .5315296, .53156, .53159, .53161, .534380924,
    .53492, .535694, .5404-5405, .547243 (Ger. concentration
    camps), .5478, .5481+, .548143, .5481438, 943.805, .8405+
—Personal narratives, Latvian   D811+   940.54814743
—Personal narratives, Lettish
—Personal narratives, Lithuanian   D805.R9 (Rus. prisons)
—Personal narratives, Mexican   D811.5
—Personal narratives, Montenegrin   D811.A2
—Personal narratives, New Zealand   D811 & 811.5, D805.G3 (Ger. prisons),
    .J3 (Jpns. prisons)   940.5481931, .548194, .542
—Personal narratives, Northern Ireland   D770
—Personal narratives, Norwegian   D811+, D779.N6, D802.N8
    (underground), D805.G3 (Ger. prisons), D809.N8
    940.5481481, .547243 (Ger. prisons)
—Personal narratives, Palestinian   D811, D805.G3, D810.J4 (Jews), DS126.3
—Personal narratives, Philippine   D767.2-4
—Personal narratives, Polish   D811+ D811.5, D765-765.2, D792,
    D799.P7 (underground lit.), D802.P6 (underground),
    D804.R9 (Rus. atrocities), D805.G3, .P7, D809.P6
    940.5481438, .547243, .547247 (Rus. prisons)
—Personal narratives, Portuguese   D811.5, D767.7
—Personal narratives, Romanian
—Personal narratives, Rumanian   D811+   940.5481498
—Personal narratives, Russian   D811+, D764+, D792.R9 (aerial ops.),
    D802.U4 (Ukrainian underground), D805.G3
    (Ger. prisons), DK265.7
    940.548147, .540947, .542

World War, 1939-1945
—Personal narratives, Scottish
—Personal narratives, Serbian   D811, D766.62.A-Z, D802.Y8 (underground)
—Personal narratives, Serbo-Croatian
—Personal narratives, Serbocroatian
—Personal narratives, Slovenian   D811 & 811.5, D766.62.S45, D802.S63,
          D810.S7   940.53161
—Personal narratives, South African   D811, D766.97, D792.S6, D805.A4
          940.5368, .548168
—Personal narratives, Spanish   D811, D764, D805 (prisons), DP269.9
—Personal narratives, Swedish   D811+, D808   940.548
—Personal narratives, Swiss   D811.5, D754.S9   940.5481494
—Personal narratives, Ukrainian   D811 & 811.5   940.54814771
—Personal narratives, Uruguayan
—Personal narratives, Wendic
—Personal narratives, Yugoslav   D811+, D754.Y9 (diplomats), D766.62,
          D802.Y8 (underground)
—Peru   D769.8.A6
—Philippine Islands   D767.4, D811, E806   940.5425-5426, .5481914,
          973.917
  —Bataan (Luzon)   D767   940.5426, .547673
—Philippines   D767.4, D773, D805.J3 (Jpns. prisons), .P6, DS685,
          DS686.3-4, E806   940.542, .547252, 991.4,
          919.40335+, 923.1914, 973.917
  —Bataan (Province)
  —Bibliography   DS503
  —Lubang Island
—Photography   D810.P4   940.5441, .5486, .548173
—Pictorial works   [SEE ALSO numbers for various specific areas,
          campaigns, etc.]   D731, D743.2, D746, D762, D767 (Pac. &
          Asia), D785 (aerial ops.), UG446, N6512, NC1200, ND1240,
          ND1839, NE2210   940.530222, .53084, .531867+, .5347,
          .540022, .5421, .548173, .5497, 741.91, 743.973, 756, 759.13
  —Catalogs   D743.22
—Pigeons
—Poetry   D745+, D745.2, .3, PG3026.W3 (Rus.), PG3488.S692
          (Solzhenitsyn), PQ307.W3 (Fr.), PR1149, PR1195.W66 (Eng.:
          overall), PR1225   820.800912, 821.91082,
          841.91082, 891.7177
—Poland   D731, D742, D754.P7, D765-765.2, D802.P6 (underground),
          D804.P6 (atrocities), D809.P6 (refugees), D810.G6 (exile gov.),
          DK268, DK440-1, DK4419, DK4600, JK1555.7 (occup.), U773
          940.481438, .5322438, .53438, .5405, .54056, .542, .544, 943.8,
          327.4380943 (for. relns. w. Ger.), .4380947 (w. Rus.),
          .4709438 (Rus. for. relns. w. Pol.)
  —Bialystok (Region)   D765.2.B47
  —Bibliography   Z6207.W8
  —Bydgoszcz region   D802.P62.B98 (underground)
  —Bydgoszcz (Voivodeship)
  —Collected works
  —Czestochowa   D765.2.C9, DS135.P62.C99 (Jews)
  —Drama
  —Fiction
  —Gda´nsk region   D765.2.G37, D802.P62.G375
  —Jaslo (District)   D802.P62.J378, D805.P7.J28-32

World War, 1939-1945
—Poland
   —Kraków   D802.P62.K767-85
   —Lemberg
   —Lód´z
   —Opole region   D765.2.O6
   —Periodicals   D731, DK401.P7+
   —Pictorial works   D765
   —Podlasie   D802.P62.P5886
   —Pomerania   D765.2.P6
   —Pozna´n
   —Rzeszów, Poland (Voivodeship)   D802.P62.R939
   —Siedlce   DS135.P62.S55 (Jews)
   —Sosnowiec   D765.2.S6
   —Sources   DK402
   —Warsaw   D765.2.W3, D765, D799.P7 (underground lit.),
                           D802.P62.W26-32 (underground), D810.J4, DK4633,
                           DS135.P62.W2-3 (Jews)   940.53438, .542,
                           .5481438 (personal narratives)
      —Pictorial works   D802.P62.W33
   —Warsaw region   D802.P62.W3726
      —Sources
   —Wielkopolska   D765.2.W5, D810.D5
   —Zakopane   D804.G4 (atrocities)
   —Zamo´s´c (Region)   D802.P62.Z385
—Pomerania   D802.P62.P62, DD491.P78, DK4410
—Pomerania (Poland and Germany)   DK4410
—Portraits
—Portugal   D754.P8, DP556, DP680   327.469
—Postal service   D800
—Posters   D743+, D743.25, D522.25   769.4994053
   —Catalogs   D522.25 (WWI & II)
   —Exhibitions   D743.25, D527.5 (WWI & II)
—Pribilof Islands   D769   940.542
—Price regulation   [SEE 'Price regulation']
—Prisoners and prisons   D763, D804 (war crimes & atrocities), D805.A2,
                    D806 (Red Cross etc.), D811+ (personal narratives)
                    940.5472+, .547252 (Jpns.), .547243 (Ger.), .5315
—Prisoners and prisons, American [British, German, etc.: prisoners held in
                    {U.S., Brit., Ger., etc.} prisons as well as
                    prisons run by {U.S., G.B., etc.}]
—Prisoners and prisons, American   D769.8.A, D805.U5,
                    DD247.G67 (Goering)   940.547273, .548243
   —Bibliography
—Prisoners and prisons, Australian   D805.A77-8
—Prisoners and prisons, Belgian   D805.B4
—Prisoners and prisons, British   D805.B9, .G7 (GB), D811, DA89
                    940.547242-547243, .5488941
—Prisoners and prisons, Bulgarian
—Prisoners and prisons, Canadian   D805.C2
—Prisoners and prisons—Fiction
—Prisoners and prisons, French   D805.F8, .M8 (Morocco), DC397
                    940.547244

World War, 1939-1945
—Prisoners and prisons, German   D805.G3, .A9 (Austria), .F8 (Fr.),
                                      .P7 (Poland), D802 (underground), D802.A2,
                                      D804.G3-4 (concentration camps), D810.J4 (Jews),
                                      D811-811.5   940.547243, .5405, .541243+,
                                      .5481+, .54814, .548642
        —Anniversaries
        —Bibliography   Z6207.W8
        —Fiction
        —Pictorial works   D805.A2, .G3
—Prisoners and prisons, Greek
—Prisoners and prisons, Hungarian   D805.H8   940.54724391
—Prisoners and prisons, Italian   D805.I8   940.547245
—Prisoners and prisons, Japanese   D805.J3, .I55 (Indonesia), .J4 (Java),
                                      .P6 (Philippines), .S5 (Singapore), .T5 (Thailand),
                                      D767+, D811+, DS485 (Burma), DS644 (Bali), DS796
                                      940.547252, .547259, .548142, .548194, 951.05
        —Exhibitions
        —War crime trials—Tokyo, 1946-1948   D804   940.547252
—Prisoners and prisons—Kenya—History—Sources   DT387.92
—Prisoners and prisons, New Zealand   D805.N, .A77 (Australian)
—Prisoners and prisons—Periodicals   D805.A1
—Prisoners and prisons, Polish   D805.P, .G3 (Ger.), D804.G
—Prisoners and prisons, Rumanian   [ALSO '..., Romanian']   D805
                                                                    940.5472498
—Prisoners and prisons, Russian   D805.R9, .S65, D810.J4 (Jews), D811+
                                      940.547247, .547243 (Ger.), .5405094762
—Prisoners and prisons, Soviet
—Prisoners and prisons, Spanish   D805.S7
—Prisoners and prisons—Statistics
—Prisoners and prisons, Swiss   D805.S9
—Prisoners and prisons, Yugoslavian   D805.Y8
—Prizes, etc.
—Propaganda   D639.P7 (WWI & II), D810.P6-7, D810.P7.A-Z (by origin),
                  .P7.F73 (Fr.), .P7.G3+ (Ger.), .P7.G7 (Brit.), .P7.J3 (Jpns.),
                  .P7.U39-5 (US), DD256.5 (Ger.)   940.4886+, .4889+, .534886+,
                  .5486+, .5488, .54886+, .5488642 (Brit.), .5488673 (US), .54887+,
                  .5488743 (Ger.), .5488752 (Jpns.), .54889+, .5488973
        —Bibliography   Z6207.W8
        —Catalogs
        —German   D810.P7.G3
—Prophecies   D810.P75, DK254.R3 (Rasputin), BF1815 (Nostradamus)
                  940.53181333, .53182201, .53181599613, 159.9613, 133.3
—Protest movements
—Protestant churches   D810.C5
—Prussia, East (Poland and R.S.F.S.R.)
—Prussia, East (Province)   DD491.O66   940.53159
—Psychological aspects   D810.P6-7, .P7 (propaganda), BF698, HM263,
                  HM291, RC602   940.53019, .54886+ (propaganda),
                  .5488642 (GB), 301.1522+, 355.115, 616.8
        —Bibliography—Catalogs   Z6207.W8

World War, 1939-1945
—Public opinion   D810.P85, .P7+, HM261   940.5342
—Canada
—France   D810.P85.F72-8
—Germany   D810.P85.G3
—Great Britain   D810.P85.G7
—Congresses
—Switzerland   D810.P85.S95
—United States   D810.P85.U5-56   940.5373
—Quebec (Province)   D754.C2, D768.15
—Quotations, maxims, etc.
—Radar   D810.R33   940.5421
—Radio, radar, etc.   D810   940.5318621384, .545942
—Railroads   [SEE '...—Transportation']
—Rationing   [SEE 'Priorities, Industrial' or 'Rationing, Consumer']
—Reconnaisance, American
—Reconnaisance, Japanese
—Reconnaisance operations   D785
—Reconnaisance operations, American [German, etc.]
—Reconstruction   [SEE 'Reconstruction (1939-1951']
—Red Cross   HV579
—Refugees   [SEE ALSO '...—Displaced persons']   D809.A-Z (by place),
        .C2 (Canada), .E8+ (Europe), .F7 (Fr.), .G3 (Ger.), .S65 (Sov. Un.),
        .S9 (in Switz.), D806, D808, D810.J4 (Jews), D820.P72.A-Z (pop.
        transfers by country), JV6601   940.53159+, .5315943 (Ger.),
        .5315944 (Fr.), .5344, .5486+, .548673, 301.3284
—Archival resources   Z6207.W8
—Bibliography   Z6207.W8
—Pictorial works
—Regi-Esercito. Divisione di fanteria Acqui   D766.32.C3
—Regimental histories   [Subdivided by country, regiment, division, etc.: SEE
                ALSO names of individual units by country, branch,
                then specific unit name as alternative entries]
—Africa, South—Engineer Corps   D766.97
—Australia   D767+, D767.8, .813, .99   940.541294
—2/7th Cavalry Regt.   D767.813
—14th Infantry Battalion
—2/28th Infantry Battalion
—36th Infantry Battalion   D767.8   940.541294
—Belgium—Troupes coloniales   D766.92
—Brazil   D768.3
—Batalhão Carlos Camisão
—Força Expedicionaria Brasileira   D768.3
—Força Expedicionaria Brasileira, 1944-1945
—11. Regimento de Infantaria
—Canada   D768.15
—West Nova Scotia Regiment   D768.15
—Croatia
—Czechoslovakia   D765.53
—1. cs partyzanská brigáda Jana Zizky
—Finland   D765.32
—Raateen pataljoona
—Sissipataljoona 3.
—Forca Expedicionaria Brasileira, 1944-1945   D768.3

511

World War, 1939-1945
—Regimental histories
—France   D761-761.9   940.541244
  —7. armée
  —9. armée   D761.1.9th
  —Bataillon des volontaires du Pacifique   D761.9.F7
—France combattante
    —2. division blindée   D761.9.F7
—France
    —Corps expéditionnaire français   D761.15
    —4e division cuirassée   D761.2.4th
  —3. division d'infanterie algérienne   D761.9.A4
  —3. Groupement de choc   D761.9.G7
  —6. régiment d'infanterie   D761.3
—Germany   D757-757.85+, D757.55, .57, .85, D764, D766+
                 940.541343, .5423
  —12. Armee
  —12. Armee (1945)
  —28. Freiwilligen-Panzer-Grenadier-Division 'Wallonien'   D757.85
  —Geheime Feldpolizei
  —Grenadier Regiment 67   D757.57.67th
  —Heer.1.Panzerarmee   D757.56.Nr.1
  —Heeresgruppe Afrika
  —Heeresgruppe Süd   D757.1
  —12. Infanteriedivision (1935/36-1944)   D757.33.12th
  —Infanterie-Regiment 67   D757.57.67th
  —97. Jäger Division   D757.32.J3
  —Nationalsozialistische Deutsches Arbiter-Partei. Waffenschutz-
      staffel. III. (Germanisches) SS-Panzer-Korps   D757.55.G31
  —Oberkommando. Abteilung Fremde Heere Ost
  —Panzerarmee, 3
  —Panzerarmeekorps Afrika   D757.55.A4, .G4
  —Panzerdivision 'Grossdeutschland'
  —Panzer-Division Hitlerjugend
  —Panzer-division nr. 11   D757.55.11th
  —17. Panzergrenadier-Division. Aufklärungsabteilung
  —Panzer-Grenadier-Regiment 67   D757.57.67th
  —Panzergruppe 3   D757.54
  —XIV. Panzerkorps
  —LVII. Panzerkorps   D757.56.57th
  —Panzerlehrdivision   D757.55.P19
  —Panzertruppen   D757.54
  —SS-Gebirgs-Division Nord
  —Sturmartillerie
  —Technische Truppen   D757.855
  —Waffenschutzstaffel
  —Waffenschutzstaffel. 33. Grenadier-Division 'Charlemagne'
  —Waffenschutzstaffel. 3. SS-Panzer-Division Totenkopf   D757.85

World War, 1939-1945
—Regimental histories
    —South Africa   D766.97   940.5449
        —Police Brigade
        —6th Division
        —6th Mounted Regiment
    —Soviet Union   D764.6, D765.32
        —Chekhoslovatskaia Brigada, 1
    —United States [Numerical entries may be filed or listed in some catalogs
                such that Arabic numbers precede spelled-out versions
                {e.g. '3d Cavalry', '5th Army', 'Second Army'}. The present
                guide—for simplicity—tries instead to place entries in
                alphabetical order by army, division, or other unit type
                regardless of the preceding specific unit number except in the
                case of units with distinctive, non-numerical names. Note that
                histories of units may ALSO be classified or have subject
                headings assigned pertaining to particular or general
                campaigns or geographical areas.]
    —535th Anti-Aircraft Artillery Battalion   D769.343.535th
                                    940.544973
    —3d Armored Division   D769.305.3d
    —6th Armored Division
    —67th armored regiment   D769.3055.67th
    —Third Army   D769.26.3d   940.5421
    —Sixth Army
    —Seventh army
    —8th Army   D769.26.8th
    —Eighth Army
    —113th Cavalry
    —1st cavalry division
    —79th Cavalry Reconnaisance Troop
    —5307th Composite Unit (Provisional)
    —102d Construction Battalion
    —IV corps   D769.27.4th
    —VII Corps
    —Corps of Engineers   D769.U5+ or A5+
    —1st Division
    —10th Division
    —78th Division
    —102d Division   D769.3.102d
    —104th Division
    —2d Engineer Special Brigade
    —141st Field Artillery
    —36th Infantry
    —305th Infantry
    —550th Infantry Airborne Battalion
    —329th Infantry Regiment   D769.31.329th
    —Marine Corps   D767+, D769+   940.541273, .5426
        . 3d Division
        . 6th Division
        . 9th Regiment
    —Mars Task Force
    —Quartermaster Corps

World War, 1939-1945
   —Regimental histories
      —United States
         —727th Railway Operating Battalion
         —3d Ranger Battalion
         —Ranger Battalions   D769   940.541273
         —Signal Corps
         —19th Tank Battalion
         —771st Tank Battalion   D769.306.761st
         —Transportation Corps
      —Yugoslavia   D766.613.A-Z
         —Druga prekomorska brigada   D766.613.D
         —Gubceva brigada   D766.613.G8
         —Presermova brigada   D766.613.P75
   —Registers
   —Registers, lists, etc.   D797.A-Z (by place), D810.J4 (Jews)
                          940.5467+, .546773 (US), .5404, .541273
   —Registers of dead   [SEE ALSO 'Registers of dead' as subdiv. of military
               branches {e.g. 'U.S. Army—Registers of dead'}]   D797.A-Z
      —Germany
      —Netherlands
      —Poland
         —Krakow (Voivodeship)   D797.P72.K76
         —Warsaw   D797.P62.W2
      —Soviet Union   D810.D4
      —United States   D797.U6
   —Religious aspects   D744.4, D810.C35-36 (chaplains), D816, BR479
                    940.5304, .531+, .53152+, .53182, .5478, 248+, 264.1
   —Reparations   [In general, SEE ALSO 'War damage compensation' and
             'Restitution and indemnification...']   D818-19, D819.A-Z (by place),
             .G3 (Ger.), .J3 (Japan), D821, HC337   940.531422, .53144,
                    .5315296 (Jews), 330.9471, 338.943
   —Resistance movements   [SEE 'World War, 1939-1945—Underground
             movements']
   —Rhine River Valley
   —Rhine Valley
   —Rhodesia, Southern   D766.99.R346   940.536891
   —Riverine operations
   —Riverine operations, American [British, etc.]
   —Romania   D766.4, DR264
      —Ploesti
      —Transylvania   DR280.7
   —Rome   D763.I82.R6
   —Rumania   D766.4, .6, DR262-6   940.53497-53498
      —Ploesti

World War, 1939-1945
    —Russia   [SEE ALSO '...—Soviet Union']   D735.R9, D736,
                    D742.R9,D753.2.R9, D764+, DK265-8, DK273, UA772+
                    940.5347, .540947, .548147, .532, .5322, .5421+, 947.084,
                    327.47+ (for. relns.), 330.947 (econ. conditions)
        —Addresses, sermons, etc.   D742.R9
        —Bibliography
        —Caucasus
        —Congresses   D764
        —Crimea   D764.7.C
        —Donets Basin   D764.7.D65
        —Fiction
        —Kerch Peninsula   D764.7.K35
        —Kiev   D764.7.K43
        —Kiev (Province)
        —Leningrad   D764.7.L54, D764.3.L4
        —Liudinovo   D764.7.L7
        —Moscow   D764.7.M6, DK601   940.5347, .542
    —Russia, Northern   D764.N6
    —Russia, Northwestern
    —Russia
        —Odessa   D764.7.O38
        —Pictorial works
        —Sevastopol
        —Societies, etc.
        —Stavropolskii   D764.3.S78
        —Ternopol (City)   D764.7.T43
        —Vitebsk   D552.V83
        —Yasnaya Polyana   DK651.Y3
    —Russian S.F.S.R.
        —Leningrad   D764.3.L4
        —Murmansk   D771
    —Saipan   D767.99.S3   940.542
    —Scandinavia   D742.S29, .B2 (Baltic States), D754.S29, DL83
    —Science   D810.S2   940.53156, .53185, .541242
    —Search and rescue operations
        —United States
    —Secret service   D810.S7-8, .S7 (gen.), .S8.A-Z (by biog. name),
                    D810.C88(cryptography), D802.A-Z (underground),
                    DD247 (Ger.), E748.D665 (Donovan, Wm.), UB250
                    940.5485-5487+, .548642 (Brit. spies), .548644 (Fr.),
                    .548647 (Rus.), .548673 (US), 940.548743 (Ger.),
                    .548752 (Jpns.), .485, 327.120924 (biog.), 351.742, 355.34
        —Africa, North   D766.82
        —Asia   DS10 351.74
        —Australia   D810   940.5485, .548694
        —Bibliography   Z6724.I7
        —Brazil
        —Burma
        —Czechoslovakia
        —Egypt
        —Europe
        —France   D810.S7, .S8.A-Z

World War, 1939-1945
—Songs and music, German
—Songs and music—History and criticism
—Songs and music, Russian
—Sounds
—Sources   [SEE ALSO numbers for countries or other topics]   D734,
                D735, D735.A (official), D814 (peace)   940.52, .5308+,
                .5314+ (peace), .5322, 940.54012-54013, .5408
—Bibliography   D734, Z1361, CD1043   942.084, 016.94054+
—Congresses   CD3028.A-Z (by country), .G3 (Ger. sources)
—Directories
—South Africa   D742.A4, D766+, D766.84, .97 (regiments), DT763,
                DT779.6-8   968
—Sources   D547.A4 (WWI & II)
—South America D752.8, F2208   940.538
—South Asia   DT736
—Soviet Central Asia   D802.R8
—Soviet Union   [SEE ALSO '...—Russia']   D764, D754.S65 (diplomacy),
                D804.G3.R9 (atrocities by Ger.), DB2207, DK68.7.A-Z (for. relns.
                by place), DK268, DK273, DK651, UA772 (Red Army)
—Bibliography   Z6207.W8
—Microform catalogs   DK266.A3
—Fiction
—Soviet Union, Northwestern
—Soviet Union
—Personal narratives, German   DK268.3
—Societies, etc.   DK273
—Sources   D754.S65
—Vitebsk
—Spain   D763.S7, D754.S7 (diplomacy), DP269-70
                940.5346, 946.08
—Straits settlements
—Study and teaching   D743
—Russia
—Soviet Union
—Sudan
—Sudan, Egyptian   D766.99.S8   940.53624
—Sumatra   D805.J3 (Jpns. prisons)
—Supplies   D753-4, D756, D769.A or U, D769.75.A or U, D810.T8, UD385,
                UF520-35, UG145, VC263   940.53+, .5318385,
                .5373 (US), .5412+, 355.8+, 623.44
—Bibliography   CD3027.S8   016.94053+, .973917
—Susano (Modena)   D763.I82.M65
—Sweden   D754.S8, D829.S9, DL641, DL658-658.8, DL868.5, DL870,
                UA790   940.53485, 948.5
—Switzerland   D745.S9, D754.S9 (diplomacy), DQ59, DQ70 (for. relns.),
                DQ203-5, DQ207.A-Z   940.53491, .54814
—Syria   D766.7.S9, D750   940.535691
—Tahiti   DU870   919.82
—Tangier (Zone)   DT329.T15
—Tank warfare   D793, D764.6, D767.6   940.5412, .542
—Technology   D787, DD68 (Ger.), T26.G3 (Ger.)

518

World War, 1939-1945
 —U.S.   [SEE ALSO '...United States']
 —Ukraine   D764.7.U5, D802.U4 (underground), DK508.8
                     940.534771
  —Kiev   D764.7.K43
  —Krasnodon
  —Starobelsk   D804.S65
 —Underground
  —Cuneo, Italy
  —Underground literature   D798, D799.A-Z (by place), D799.D4 (Denmark),
                     .F7 (Fr.), .I8 (It.), D731 (periodicals), D802.A-Z
       —Bibliography   Z6514.U5, Z6941.P41 or U5, Z6207.W8
         —Catalogs
         —Union lists
       —Byelorussian S.S.R.   D799.R9
       —Czechoslovakia   D799.C95
       —Denmark   D802.D4
       —France   D799.F7
       —Italy   D799.I8
         —Venice
       —Poland   D799.P7
         —Kielce (Region)
  —Underground movements   D802, D802.A2 (gen.), .A3-Z (by place),
                     D756, D810.S7-8 (secret service)
                     940.5315, .5337, .534, .5485, .548743

   —Albania
   —Africa, West   D761.9.F7
   —Alessandria, Italy (Province)   D802.I8   940.5345
   —Alps, French   D802.A43
   —Alsace   DD801.A58, DC610.A58   944.383
   —Austria   D802.A9, DB97-9   943.6, .605
     —Bibliography
     —Biography
     —Carinthia   D802.A92
   —Auvergne   D802.F82.A953   940.534459
   —Balkan Peninsula   D802.B29, D766   940.53496
   —Belgium   D802.B4   940.5486493
     —Biography
     —Hainaut
   —Belgrad   D766.62.B4
   —Berlin
   —Berlin (Germany)   D757.9.B4
   —Bialystok, Poland (Voivodeship)   D802.P62.B47
   —Bibliography   Z2241.A53 (anti-Nazis), Z6374.H6 (Holocaust),
                     Z6724.I7 (intelligence)
   —Bohemia   D802.B6
   —Bologna   DG975.B64   940.534541
   —Borneo   D802.B65
   —Bosnia and Herzegovina   D802.Y82.B665, D766.62.B6
   —Bouches-du-Rhône   D802.F8
   —Brescia (Province)   D802.I82.B75
   —Bryansk, Russia (Province)   D802.R82.B71
   —Bulgaria   D802.B77-78

World War, 1939-1945
   —Underground movements
      —Burma   D802.B92
      —Byelorussian S.S.R.   D802.S752.B948
         —Minskaia Oblast
      —Camonica Valley   DG975.C167
      —China   D802.C, D769.64   940.548673, 951.04258
      —Congresses   D802.A2, D734
      —Crete   D802.C6
      —Crimea
      —Croatia   D802.C7, .Y82.C77
         —Nova Gradiska   D802.Y82.N682
         —Okucani
         —Periodicals
      —Czechoslovakia   D802.C95, D799.C95, D765.5
         —Karlovy Vary region   D802.C952.K374
         —Moravia   D802.C952.M67
         —Slovak Socialist Republic   D802.C952.S676
           —Poetry   D745.S7.S5
         —Sources   DB2822
      —Denmark   D802.D4   940.534, .53489
         —Fiction
      —Emilia-Romagna, Italy   D802.I82.E447
      —Estonia   D802.E6
      —Europe   D802.E9, .A2, D805.A2   940.534
         —Addresses, essays, lectures   D802.A2   940.534
         —Sources—Bibliography—Catalogs   Z6207.W8
      —Fiesole—Drama
      —Finland   D802.F5
      —Flanders   D802.F
      —Florence
      —France   D802.F8, .A2, D761, D811, DC373.A-Z (by person),
                      DC397, DS135.F83 (Jews)   940.5344, .5485,
                      .548644, 944.081

         —Artois
         —Aude   D802.F82.A92
         —Auvergne   D802.F82.A953-956
         —Bibliography
         —Bigorre   D802.F82.B536
         —Biography   D802.F8, DC373.A-Z
         —Calais   D802.F82.C253
         —Calvados   D802.F82.C343
         —Charente   D802.F82.C52
         —Congresses   D802.F8, D765
         —Cote d'Or   D762.C76
         —Dabo
         —Dauphine   D802.F82.D388
         —Eure-et-Loire   D802.F82.E878
         —Finistere   D802.F82.F566
         —Franche-Comte
         —Is`ere (Dept.)   D802.F82.I838
         —Jura   D802.F82.J87
         —Lorraine
         —Lot (Dept.)—Biography   D802.F82.L676
         —Lyon   D802.F82.L9477-948

World War, 1939-1945
—Underground movements
—France
—Medoc   D802.F82.M433
—Morvan   D802.F82.M67
—Moselle (Dept.)   D802.F82.M676
—Ni`evre   D802.F82.N535-36
—Nievre (Dept.)
—Paris   D802.F82.P373-3753
—Periodicals
—Picardy
—Poetry
—Quercy   D802.F82.Q475
—Riviera   D802.F82.R584
—Saint-Clair   D802.F82.S34
—Sarrebourg   D802.F82.S273
—Vercors   D802.F82.V472, D762.V4
—Vosges   D802.F82.V672
—Friesland   D802.N4
—Friuli   D763.I82.F9
—Friuli-Venezia Giulia
—Genoa   DG639
—Germany   [SEE ALSO 'Anti-Nazi movement']
                        D802.G3, DD256.3   940.548643
—Germany (West)
—Munich
—Trier Region   D802.G32.T753
—Goes   D763.N4.G55
—Gorski Kotar
—Greece   D802.G8, D750, D766.3, D810.S7, DF765, DF849
                        940.53495, .5486, .5486495
—Biography
—Crete   D802.G82.C748
—Greece, Modern
—Greece
—Pictorial works
—Thessaly   D802.G82.T34
—Velvendos
—Haute Savole   D762.H15
—Hrvatsko primorje   D766.62.H7
—Hungary   D802.H89, DB955
—Indonesia   D802.I5
—Doberai Peninsula   D802.I52.D634
—Istria   D766.62.H7

World War, 1939-1945
  —Underground movements
    —Italy   D802.I8, D799.I8, DG571-5, DS135.I8 (Jews)
                    940.5345, .548142, .548745
      —Bibliography   Z2361.U56
      —Biella Region   D802.I82.B532
      —Bologna   D802.I82.B63
      —Bologna (Province)—Pictorial works
      —Brescia (Province)   D802.I82.B746
      —Campania   DG975.C173
      —Cavriago   DG975.C316
      —Cingoli   D802.I82.C563
      —Collected works
      —Congresses
      —Emilia-Romagna—Periodicals   DG975.E53
      —Exhibitons   D763.I8
      —Fiction
      —Forli   D802.I82.F654
      —Forli (Province)
      —Friuli-Venezia Giulia   DG975.F85
      —Liguria   D802.I82.L5317
      —Lombardy   D802.I82.L657
      —Marche—Bibliography   D802.I82.Z994, .I82.M344
      —Milan (Province)   D802.I82.M545
         —Chronology
      —Milan—Sources   D802.I82.M532
      —Ossola Valley   D802.I82.O85
      —Padua (Province)   D802.I82.P334
      —Periodicals
      —Piemonte   D802.I82.P534
      —Po River Valley   D802.I82.P626
      —Ravenna   DG975.R25
      —Reggio Emilia (Province)—Biography   D802.I82.R42
      —Rome   D802.I82.R625
      —Ronchi   D802.I82.R67
      —Savona   D802.I82.S295
      —Sesto Fiorentino   D802.I82.S526
      —Trentino-Alto Adige
      —Trieste
      —Tuscany   D802.I82.T87-929
        —Biography
      —Veneto—Congresses   DG975.V38
  —Jastrebac Mountains, Serbia   D802.Y82.J32

World War, 1939-1945
—Underground movements, Jewish   D810.J4, DS135.A-Z (by country),
             .G33 (Ger.)
      —Algeria   DS135.A3
      —Bibliography   Z6374.H6
      —Byelorussian S.S.R.—Nesvizh   DS135.R93.N453
      —Congresses   D810.J4
      —France   DS135.F83
      —Greece   DS135.G7
      —Hungary
      —Lithuania
      —Poland   D805.P7
      —Sobibor
—Underground movements
    —Jews   D810.J4, DS135.A-Z (by place)   940.531503924, .534,
             .5405, .5485
      —Congresses
    —Karelia   D802.K36
    —Kaunas
    —Kosovo-Metohija (Albania)
    —Krakow
    —Leningrad (Province)   D802.R8, .L4
    —Lithuania   D802.L5, .S752.L573   940.53475
      —Vilnius
    —Ljubljana   D802.Y82.L7, .S63-67.L46-762
    —Loiret   D802.F82.L
    —Lower Styria   D766.613.S7
    —Luxembourg   D802.L9
    —Lyons
    —Macedonia   D802.M15, D766.62.M2-3
    —Macedonia (Modern Greece)
    —Malay Peninsula
    —Malaya   D802.M2
    —Malopolska   D802.P62.M3822
    —Masovia
    —Milan (Province)   D802.I82.M545
      —Chronology
    —Minsk (Province)   D802.M5, .R82.M66
    —Montenegro   D766.62.M6
    —Moravia   D802.C952.M67
    —Moscow (Province)   D802.R8.M6-85
    —Museums   D733
    —Naples   D763.I82.N36
    —Negros Occidental, Philippines (Province)   D802.P5
    —Negros Oriental, Philippines (Province)
    —Netherlands   D802.N4, D799.N4   940.5486492
    —New Britain (Island)   D767   940.5395
    —Norway   D802.N7-8, D809.N8, DL532   940.5481481,
             .54860481, .5486481
      —Biography
      —Finnmark Fylke—Fiction
    —Nova Gradiska, Croatia   D802.Y82.N682
    —Oder-Neisse area   DK4600.O33
    —Okucani, Croatia
    —Ossola Valley   D802.I82.O82

World War, 1939-1945
—Underground movements
  —Panay (Island)   D802.P5   940.5486914
  —Parczew Forest, Poland   D802.P62.P377
  —Pavlograd, Ukraine (Dnepropetrovsk Province)   D802.U4
  —Periodicals—Indexes   D731
  —Philippine Islands   D802.P5   940.53599, .53914,
                          .5483914, .5486914
  —Philippines   D767.4.U
    —Negros Island
  —Piacenza
  —Piedmont   D802.I82.P2
  —Poland   D802.P6, D805.P7 (prisons, concentration camps)
                 940.53438, .547247, .5481438
    —Bialystok region   D802.P62.B4838
    —Bibliography
    —Biography   DK4419-20
    —Congresses
    —Fiction
    —Katowice (Voivodeship)   D802.P62.K37
    —Krakow   DS135.P62.K8 (Jews)
    —Krakow (Voivodeship)   D802.P62.K75-8
    —Lodz (Voivodeship)   D802.P62.L624
    —Masovia   D802.P62.M365
    —Opatow (Powiat)   D802.P62.O635
    —Parczew Forest   D802.P62.P377
    —Podhale   D802.P62.P582
    —Podlasie
    —Radomsko (Powiat)   D802.P62.R336
    —Sandomierz (Powiat)
    —Siedlce region   D802.P62.S546
    —Sources   DK4400-4410
    —Warsaw   D802.P62.W26-3736
      —Biography   D802.P62.W26
    —Warsaw (Voivodeship)
    —Western and Northern Territories   DK4600.O33
    —Zawiercie (Powiat)   D802.P62.Z3
  —Polish
  —Pyrenees (France and Spain)   D802.F82.P973
  —Rablow, Poland
  —Radomsko (Powiat), Poland   D802.P62.R336
  —Rizal, Philippines (Province)
  —Rome   D802.I82.R6+, D763.I82   940.5345
  —Ronchi, Italy   D802.I82.R67
  —Russia   D802.R8, D764, JN6598.K785   940.5347, .548647
  —Rzeszow region   D802.P62.R938
  —Savoie, Haute   D802.F8
  —Serbia   D802.S47, D766.62.S4, DR369.5
  —Siam   D802.S5   940.53593
  —Skopje, Yugoslavia   D802.Y82.S525
  —Slavonia   D766.62.S43-45
  —Slovakia   D802.C952.S6535-675, D745.7.S5
  —Slovenia   D802.S63-67, D766.62.S45, D802.Y82.S5826
  —Slovensko Primorje
  —South Africa

World War, 1939-1945
  —Underground movements
    —Soviet Union   D802.R8, .S6+
    —Srem (Region)   D766.62.S7
    —Thailand   D802.T32
    —Trento (Province)   DG975.T72
    —Turin
    —Tuscany   D802.I82.T87-922
    —Ukraine   D802.U4
      —Personal narratives
      —Volhynia   D802.R82.V642
    —Vercors, France   D762.V4
    —Vilna
    —Volhynia   D802.R82.V642, .U4
    —Warsaw   D802.P62.W26+
    —Warsaw (Voivodeship)
    —White Russia   D802.R8, .W5
    —Yugoslavia   D802.Y8, D766.6, DR367.A-Z, DR369.5
                  940.5342, .53497, .54864209497

      —Biography
      —Bosnia and Herzegovina   D802.Y82.B665
      —Croatia   D802.Y82.C76946, D766.62.C7
      —Ljubljana   D802.S63.L762
      —Ljubljana (Slovenia)   D802.Y82.L7
      —Montenegro
      —Periodicals   DR367
      —Serbia   D802.Y82.S466, DR369.5
      —Slovenia   D766.62.S45
      —Tuzla (Bosnia and Hercegovina)   D802.Y82.T887
    —Zagreb   D766.62.Z3
    —Zamosc, Poland (Region)   D802.P62.Z15
  —Underground printing plants
    —Belgrad   D799.Y8
    —France
  —United States [SEE ALSO '...—U.S.]   D769+, D731, D742-3, D742.U5,
                  D753+ (diplomacy), D749, D761, D767, E173, E744,
                  E806-7   940.5312, .532, .532273, .5373, .53973,
                  .540973, .541273, 973.917, .92, 327.73 (for. relns.)
    —Addresses, essays, lectures   D753   940.532273, .5373
    —Bibliography   Z6207.W8   016.3552, .94053
    —Biography
    —Collected works   D753   940.5373
    —Economic aspects
    —Periodicals   D731, D790
    —Societies, etc.   D570.A (WWI or II)
    —Sources   D769, D769.1   940.5373
      —Bibliography—Catalogs   CD3031 (Dept. of State archives)
  —Unknown military personnel
  —Unknown military personnel, American [British, etc.]
  —Uruguay   D754.U8, F2726
  —Vatican City   D754.V4
  —Veterinary service   D810.V45
  —Vienna   D811.5.P7495.A3
  —Virginia   D769.85.V8   940.53755
    —Hampton Roads   D810.T8, HC107.V82.H48 359.7

World War, 1939-1945
 —Vis Island   D766 940.547642
 —Wake Island
 —War work [Civilian participation] D769.85.A-Z (U.S.: by state),
      D807-810, BX7749 (Am. Friends) 940.5477-5478,
      .5477873 (US), .5481497
  —American Legion D769.8.A
  —Boy Scouts D810.B7
  —Catholic Church D810.C6
  —Christian Science D810.C45 940.53152895
  —Churches D810.C6
  —Elks D810.E 940.54777
  —England—London
  —Friends, Society of BX7747-49
  —Girl Scouts
  —Great Britain
  —Jeunesse ouvri`ere chrétienne D802.F8 940.531522
  —London
  —Methodist Church D810.M
  —Presbyterian Church
  —Red Cross D806-7, D805.G3, UH535 940.54771,
      .54824563, 361.53
  —Russia
  —Salvation Army D810.S15
  —Schools D810.E3+ 940.531537, 355.071173
  —Seventh-Day Adventists D810.S 940.53152867
  —Society of Friends BX7747
  —Soviet Union DK273
  —Unitarian churches
  —Y.M.C.A. D810.Y7 940.54774
  —Y.W.C.A. D810.Y7+ 940.54774
  —Young Men's Christian associations
  —Young Women's Christian Association D810.Y7
 —Washington, D.C. F199 917.53034
 —Weapons [SEE '...—Supplies', names of classes of weapons, and names of
      particular ones as well]
 —West Indies, French D754.W4 940.537297
 —White Russia D764.7.W5
 —Wisconsin D769.85.W6
 —Women D810.W7, DK4419 (underground: Poland), HQ1420,
      HQ1623 940.53161, .5485
  —Bibliography
  —Congresses
  —France D802.F8
  —United States HQ1420
 —Women's work D810.W7, D769, HD6093-5 940.5315396,
      .5318396, .541273, 306.27471, 331.112, .406173 (US), .48219
  —Great Britain
  —United States HD6093.U 331.406173
 —Wyoming

World War, 1939-1945
—Yugoslavia   D735, D754, D766.6+, D802.Y8+ (underground),
                     DR327.A-Z (for. relns.: by country), .B9 (with Bulgaria),
                     DR359.A-Z (biog.: by person), .M5 (Mihailovic), DR366-70,
                     DR1294.A-Z (biog.: by person)   940.5349, .53497,
                     .54056, .5409497, 949.7, .702, 914.97, 923.5497
—Addresses, essays, lectures
—Belgrade   D766.62.B4
—Bibliography   Z6207.W8
—Bihac   D766.62.B6
—Cacak   D766.62.C3
—Collected works
—Crepaja   D766.62.C67
—Crna Trava   D766.62.C68
—Croatia   D802.Y82.C76958 (underground)
—Drugovac   D766.62.D75
—Dubrovnik   D766.62.D8
—Fiction
—Karlovac region   D766.62.K28
—Kokevski Rog Mountain region   D766.62.K56
—Kozara Mountains   D766.62.K65
—Leskovac   D766.62.L4
—Lower Styria
—Luznica   DR381.L8
—Maps   G2011.S54
—Maribor   D766.62.M35
—Montenegro   D802.Y82.M656 (underground)
—Paracin, Serbia   DR396.P24-33
—Prekmurje   D797.Y82.P7-92
—Salek Valley   D766.62.S3   940.53497
—Serbia   D802.Y82.S435 (underground), DR2038.5
—Slavonia (Croatia) D766.62.S43
—Sources
—Slovenia   D802.Y82.S5824, DR361   940.534973
—Smartno ob Paki   D766.62.S
—Sources   D766.6.A, D802.Y8 (underground), DR1298
—Spodnje Gorje   D766.62.S63
—Srem (Region)   D766.62.S7
—Styria, Lower (Slovenia)
—Sutjeska   D766.62.S9
—Urosevac   D766.62.U7
—Valjevo, Serbia   DR396.V28
—Veliki Kupci   D766.62.V4
—Vipava Valley   D766.62.V48
—Voivodina (Serbia)   D766.62.V6
—Zgornje Gorje   D766.62.S63
—Zaire
Wormhout (France), Battle of, 1940
Wronki (Pila, Poland: Concentration camp)
Wuhlheide (Berlin, Germany: Concentration camp)

Yamamoto, Isoroku, 1884-1943   [Japan: Adm., Min. of Navy, Comm. in Chief o/t
    1st Fleet]   DS890.Y25   940.5459520924, .5426
Yamashita, Tomoyuki ('Tiger of Malaya'), 1885-1946   [Japan: Lt. Gen.]DS890.Y3,
            D804.J33, JX5441.M3   940.54260924, .54056, 341.4, .69
Yeo-Thomas, Forest Frederick Edward ('White Rabbit'), 1902-1964 [G.B.: Wing
    Commander, Underground agent in Fr., advisor to Free French Resistance]
                                    D802.F8   944.081, 940.5344
Yeremenko, Andrey, 1892-1970   [U.S.S.R.: Marshal]
Young Men's Christian Associations   BV1030, BV1090, BV1172, BV1185
                                        267.3063771, .341082, .369, .3973
Young Women's Christian Associations   BV1340, BV1375, BV1392 267.5, .5973
Yugoslavia
    . Armija
        . XIV Divizija (Seirinajst)   D766.613.S7
        . Prva Prekomorska Brigada   D766.613.P7
    —Boundaries
        —Italy   D821.Y8-9 or I
    —Foreign relations
        —1918-1945   DR366   949.702
    —History
        —1918-1941   DR366-9   949.702
        —Coup d'état, 1941   DR369   949.702
        —Axis occupation, 1941-1945   D802.Y8, DR369   949.702
    —Politics and government—1918-1945
    . State Commission for the Investigation of War Crimes   D804.I8.Y83+

Zakroczym, Poland—Siege, 1939
Zeitzler, Kurt, 1895-1958 [Ger.: Gen.]
Zero (Fighter planes)   TL685 358.4183
Zhdanov, Andrey, 1896-1948 [U.S.S.R.: Polit. Gen.]   DK267
Zhukov, Georgii Konstantinovich, 1896-1974   [U.S.S.R.: Marshal, Dep. Supr.
    Commander]   DK268.252, D764.Z487   940.54210924, 355.3320924

ABOUT THE AUTHOR

BUCKLEY BARRETT earned his M.S. in Library Science at the University of Southern California in 1973, and began his career as a librarian in the same year. He has served in a number of faculty positions at California State University, San Bernardino since joining the staff in 1982. He was Head of Technical Services from 1987 to 1994, and now serves as Head of Automation Services. Prior to his term at CSUSB, Barrett worked as Library Director at Marymount College in Rancho Palos Verdes, while providing part-time reference services at CSU Dominguez Hills and CSU Fullerton. Earlier, he held professional posts at the California State Library and the South Dakota State Library.

With Mary Bloomberg, Barrett co-authored *Stalin: An Annotated Guide to Books in English* (Borgo Press, 1993) and *The Jewish Holocaust: An Annotated Guide to Books in English* (Borgo Press, 1995). On his own, he wrote *World War I: A Cataloging Reference Guide* (Borgo Press, 1995) and *The Barstow Printer: A Personal Name and Subject Index to the Years 1910-1920* (Borgo Press, 1985). Forthcoming are annotated bibliographies on Sir Winston Churchill and Adolf Hitler.

The author has two children, and lives in San Bernardino with his long-suffering and patient wife, Nette Bricker-Barrett, also a librarian.

www.ingramcontent.com/pod-product-compliance
Lightning Source LLC
Chambersburg PA
CBHW031227090426

42742CB00007B/108